FREDERICK ASHTON

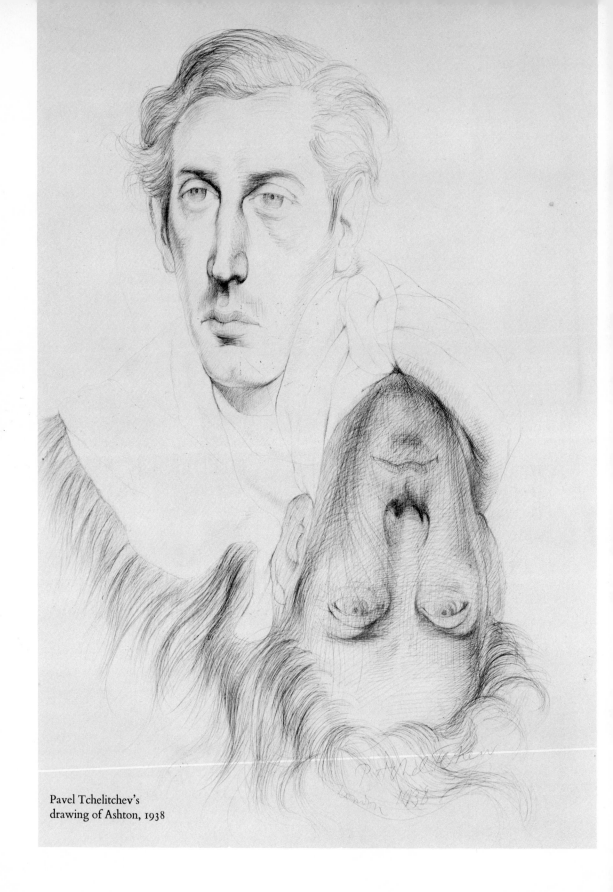

Pavel Tchelitchev's
drawing of Ashton, 1938

FREDERICK ASHTON
and his ballets

DAVID VAUGHAN

Adam and Charles Black · London

792-82
VAU

First published 1977
A & C Black Ltd.
35 Bedford Row London WC1R 4JH

ISBN 0 7136 1689 X

© *1977 A & C Black Ltd.*

Vaughan, David, b. 1924
Frederick Ashton.
Bibl. – Index.
ISBN 0-7136-1689 X
792.8'092'4   GV1785.A8
Ashton, *Sir* Frederick

Printed in the United States of America

CONTENTS

ILLUSTRATIONS

Illustrations

Illustrations

Endpapers: Newspaper cuttings and other pictures mounted on folding screens by Frederick Ashton in the 1920s and 1930s
Collection : Alexander Grant

† These pictures from the Victoria and Albert Museum are Crown Copyright.

ACKNOWLEDGMENTS

To Sir Frederick Ashton above all my thanks are due for his patience in submitting to my questioning: unless otherwise specified, all quotations from him are from personal interviews conducted over the past three years. This book could not have been written without his help and that of Dame Marie Rambert, who gave me much of the information contained in the earlier chapters and allowed me to use many of the rare photographs in her collection.

Grateful acknowledgment is also due to all those whose words are quoted, whether from personal conversation or correspondence, or from printed sources. Their names will be found in the text or in the Notes at the end. Others who generously gave of their time to talk to me or answer my written enquiries include the following: Gordon Anthony, Dennis Arundell, Reinhard Beuth, Petrus Bosman, Peter Brinson, Louise Browne, Philip Chatfield, Jacques d'Amboise, Alexandra Danilova, Helen Dawson, Mrs E G Derrington (Mona Inglesby), Dr G P Dienes, Anton Dolin, Leslie Edwards, Richard Ellis, Domari Espósito, Royes Fernandez, Barbara Fewster, Dame Margot Fonteyn de Arias, the late Hilda Gaunt, Mrs Howard Gee (Anna Ludmila), Noël Goodwin, Walter Gore, Jill Gregory, Arthur Hammond, Sir Robert Helpmann, Spike Hughes, Mr and Mrs Ronald Hynd, Dr Gordon Jacob, Virginia Kelly, Frances James Klin, Svend Kragh-Jacobsen, Hugh Laing, the late Tilly Losch, Donald Mahler, Inés Malinow, Keith Martin, Léonide Massine, Geyvan-Yilmaz Orencik McMillen, James Monahan, Charles Murland, Marilyn Burr Nagy, Michael Pink, Freda Pitt, Tom Schoff, Mary Skeaping, Michael Somes, Muriel Stuart, Arthur Todd and Mrs Eric Toye (Doris Sonne).

I am especially grateful to Mrs L F Haddakin for permission to quote at length from the writings of her late husband, A V Coton, to Edwin Denby for permission to quote from *Looking at the Dance* and *Dancers Buildings and People in the Streets* (copyright © 1939 by the League of Composers Inc.; copyright renewed 1966 by the League of Composers Inc./International Society for Contemporary Music, U.S. Section), to Random House Inc. for permission to reprint the brief excerpts from *Everybody's Autobiography* by Gertrude Stein (copyright 1937 and renewed 1965 by Alice B Toklas) and to Walter Terry for permission to quote from his interview with Sir Frederick. Portions of this book have previously appeared, in somewhat different form, in Ballet Review and the Dancing Times.

For permission to reproduce the illustrations, I have to thank the photographers, owners and copyright holders whose names appear in the List of Illustrations on page vii.

For their help in making easier the task of research I must thank Raymond Mander and Joe Mitchenson; Anthony Latham and the staff of the Gabrielle

Enthoven Collection, Victoria and Albert Museum; Terry Benton, Boris Skidelsky and Margaret Nicholson of the Royal Opera House Archives; Genevieve Oswald, Curator, and the staff of the Dance Collection of the Library and Museum of the Performing Arts, New York; Helen Willard, former curator of the Harvard Theatre Collection and her successor, Jeanne T Newlin; Martine Kahane of the Bibliothèque de l'Opéra, Paris; the staff of the Museo Teatrale e Biblioteca Livia Simoni della Scala, Milan; Bengt Häger, intendent, Dansmuseet, Stockholm. Also the Hon Kensington Davison, Organising Secretary of the Friends of Covent Garden; Iris Law, of the Royal Ballet Administration; Richard Jarman, Assistant to the Administrative Director, the London Coliseum/English National Opera; Miriam Rapp, British Broadcasting Corporation; D R Cope, Headmaster, Dover College, and his secretary Miss E B Dudley; Jeremy Boulton, Films Viewing Supervisor, National Film Archive; John Lazzarini, President, the Pavlova Society; David Johnson of the Mansell Collection; and Alan Gray of the British Museum (who attended many performances of the Sadler's Wells Ballet with me when we were both at Raynes Park County School).

I must also acknowledge the cooperation and assistance of the administrative and public relations officers of various ballet companies, as follows: the Royal Ballet, Ballet Rambert, Ballet for All, London Festival Ballet, Royal Danish Ballet, Norwegian National Ballet, Ballet van Vlaanderen, New York City Ballet, American Ballet Theatre, City Center Joffrey Ballet, Pennsylvania Ballet, Chicago Ballet, Minnesota Dance Theatre, Royal Winnipeg Ballet, Associação de Ballet do Rio de Janeiro, the Australian Ballet, the New Zealand Ballet, CAPAB Ballet Company, PACT Ballet.

Finally, I must express my gratitude to the Ingram Merrill Foundation for a generous award that enabled me to complete the research for this book, and to the many friends whose help and encouragement have taken many forms: in particular, Lindsay Anderson, for his hospitality during several lengthy stays in London, Mary Clarke, the book's fairy godmother, Robert Cornfield, Arlene Croce, Parmenia Migel Ekstrom, Francis Francis, William Gaskill, Maxine Groffsky, David Leonard, Sylvia Lockwood, Barbara Newman and Patrick O'Connor. P W Manchester and Dale Harris read the manuscript and made valuable suggestions: to them, and to my publishers, my thanks. Needless to say, responsibility for the book's final form, and for its shortcomings, is entirely my own.

David Vaughan
London – New York
1973–1976

FOREWORD

This book is not intended to be a biography of Sir Frederick Ashton in the usual sense of the term. He is, as one very quickly learns, a very private person, not given to intimate revelation. For this reason, and because I believe that a desire for privacy should be respected, those who look for gossip or possibly scandalous speculation will not find it here. Of Ashton, as of many artists, it is true to say that his life *is* his work. Some years ago, in answer to an interviewer's request that he define choreography, he replied: 'Choreography is my whole being, my whole life, my reason for living. I pour into it all my love, my frustrations, and sometimes autobiographical details. To me, in many ways, it has more reality than the life which I live, and I couldn't conceive of existing unless I could do choreography'.[1]

This book, then, is an attempt to write a biography of Ashton *through* his work, in preparation for which I have tried to collect as much information as possible on his ballets and his choreographic methods. In doing so it has become my conviction that the creative process is nowhere more mysterious than it is with Ashton. It may be that the kind of information I have been able to find – even his own notes and other documentary material – is finally peripheral to this central mystery, but I hope that at least some light will be cast on his way of working.

At the time that Ashton became a choreographer – some fifty years ago – it was not a profession that many British dancers aspired to. There were a few who arranged dances for themselves, fellow dancers or pupils, but the possibility that any might become a choreographer of the calibre of Michel Fokine or Léonide Massine, mounting full-scale ballets for a company like Diaghilev's Ballet Russe, simply did not exist, least of all for a native ballet company, for there was none. Even now most choreographers have to learn their art and craft by practising it – Ashton was lucky at the beginning to have the help and encouragement of his chief teacher and mentor, Marie Rambert, and a little later the example of choreographers he worked with as a dancer, like Massine and especially Bronislava Nijinska.

Inevitably, this book is also to some extent an account of the history of British ballet, in the development of which Ashton has played such an important part. Principally, however, it is a kind of extended *catalogue raisonné* of his works, the extraordinary number and variety of which show that no other choreographer of his time has been so prolific, with the single exception of his exact contemporary, George Balanchine. Both men have pursued unremittingly the profession, the *métier*, of choreography. While the nature of their gifts may ultimately be as mysterious to them as it must be to us, they are both craftsmen, and proud of the fact. As Balanchine once said, in a rare tribute to another choreographer, 'Mr Ashton and I may make bad ballets, but we never make incompetent ballets.'

Choreographers fall into two main categories, as far as methods are concerned: those like Fokine, Nijinska and de Valois whose habit is to come into rehearsal with everything figured out in advance, and those like Ashton and Balanchine who come in with some general idea of what they are going to do, but which does not begin to assume a specific shape until they actually have the dancers before them. The degree of advance preparation in the latter kind varies but usually would include some idea of the structure of the plot, if any, in relation to the score, or in the case of a plotless ballet a certain degree of familiarity with the music and perhaps a fairly clear idea of the general lay-out. The amount of musical preparation obviously depends on the extent of the choreographer's technical knowledge of music, his ability to read a score, and so forth. Balanchine, for instance, is a thoroughly trained musician who has been known to prepare a piano reduction of a score when none existed for rehearsal purposes and, on occasion, to conduct the orchestra in performance. Further, choreographers who fall into this second category may be sub-divided into those who may not have the steps worked out in advance but do actually demonstrate them to the dancers when they begin to compose, and those who do not.

Ashton, unlike Balanchine, does not read a score nor play an instrument, but he does familiarise himself thoroughly with the music and then relies on the collaboration of the arranger and/or rehearsal pianist to help him with such technical analysis as may be necessary, such as breaking the music down into counts for the dancers. In the case of a dramatic ballet, he knows when the various incidents and dances occur in relation to the music; he calls this the 'scaffolding'. When the score is being composed or arranged for him, Ashton usually prepares a 'minutage' for the composer's guidance, giving the exact length of time each number should last.

It is not Ashton's habit to demonstrate the actual steps and movements in any detail – and here we come to the most elusive part of the mystery of how he composes. Very often Ashton asks the dancers to show *him* something: for solo variations, for instance, designed to display individual dancers, he will ask them to show him the kind of step they would like to do. Or he will give the dancers some indication of the idea behind a dance and ask them to improvise on that idea – it may be vaguely expressed ('like a fountain') or more specific, but in either case is likely to be in terms of a physical or natural image.

This procedure sometimes leads the dancers to suppose that they have 'done it all themselves'. But in fact what seems to take place is a kind of joint creative act whose success depends very much on the existence of a deep rapport between Ashton and his dancers – as one of them said to me, 'You seem to know what he wants'.[2] Many dancers have spoken of the way in which Ashton 'draws' the movement out of them – to which Ashton himself adds, 'and out of the music'. An essential part of the process is Ashton's shaping of the raw material the dancers supply him with, beginning with selection – keep this, discard that, explore that further – and going on to edit and refine what he selects, changing a *port de bras* or *épaulement*, often literally moulding the movement on the dancers' bodies with his hands, like a sculptor. Over the years Ashton has learned the importance of eliminating whatever is inessential, of making his effects by the simplest means: as he once said, 'It's not what you put into a ballet, it's what you take out'.[3] What results is unmistakably Ashton's, but the quality of the choreography depends not simply on the nature of the material the dancers give him but on their ability to enter into this symbiotic relationship with him, and to share his intuitive response to the music.

Very often, the fitting of the dance to the musical phrase is done afterwards, by further adjustment, and for this reason the relation between the two is something that has to be felt by the dancers rather than analysed. When I asked the dancer quoted above how Ashton fits the movements to the music, he said, 'If I knew that, we could all be choreographers'.[4] Naturally the subtlety of the relation of music and dance is often lost in the course of time, through that familiar process by which dancers tend to 'iron everything out', in Michael Somes's phrase, and revert to a more conventional way of doing a given step.

I think it will be clear from a reading of this book that increasingly throughout his career Ashton has regarded dance itself as the subject matter of ballet†; his belief in dance, and in particular the classic dance, as a means of expression, has grown with his own ability to handle that means. Not that he has not frequently told stories, but his attitude towards narrative ballets is probably similar to that of E M Forster towards the novel: 'Yes – oh dear yes – the novel tells a story'.[5] In point of fact, Ashton has grown to be an expert at telling a story and, especially, revealing character through dancing, but narrative for its own sake probably does not interest him any more than it did in earlier years when, as de Valois has said, she often had to force Ashton to 'get on with' a new ballet and bring it to a proper, logical conclusion.

I have tried to give some kind of description of most of Ashton's works, whether dramatic or 'abstract', to use an inexact but useful word. It will be obvious that I cannot have seen all of them myself, but in cases where I have no direct knowledge of a ballet, the description is based on Ashton's own recollections or those of people who danced in or saw the work concerned, or contemporary accounts (or a combination of these). I am aware that to describe dancing is often a fruitless exercise, but feel that the attempt must nevertheless be made. For the sake

† See Appendix A.

of precision, I have decided to use technical terms where necessary; readers whose knowledge of such matters is limited are referred to Leo Kersley and Janet Sinclair's admirable *A Dictionary of Ballet Terms*. For those who wish to read a more elaborate analysis of the technique involved, I would recommend Muriel Stuart's *The Classic Ballet*.

A certain amount of biographical information is necessarily included: it is obviously helpful to the reader to know something of Ashton's background and earlier years, even if no startling new revelations are to be made. I have gone into his early experiences as a dancer in rather more detail. But especially in the later part of the book my concern has been almost exclusively with his work. Most of Ashton's closest relationships have been with professional colleagues, artistic collaborators such as Sophie Fedorovitch and Constant Lambert, his most important teacher, Marie Rambert, fellow-dancers like William Chappell, Walter Gore and Birger Bartholin, and later those who were his chief interpreters, such as Margot Fonteyn, Robert Helpmann, Michael Somes, Alexander Grant and Brian Shaw. There have of course been others, friends from all walks of life like Alice Astor (the late Mrs David Pleydell-Bouverie), W B Yeats, the Sitwells and, by no means least, his devoted housekeepers, Mrs Dade and the late Mrs Lloyd.

It perhaps need hardly be said that writing this book has been a labour of love on my own part. As my brother, Paul Vaughan, said when I first told him I was going to write it, it's the book I have been preparing to write all my life. And no greater reward could come to me than the opportunity it has given me to know its subject personally, and to count him as a generous, lovable, witty, sometimes exasperating, always utterly human friend.

For James Waring
Choreographer
1922–1975

If there is an important thing, might it not be joy?
Joy is the sharing of love and delight, and in order
to share, again you have to measure and divide:
some for me, some for you.   J.W.

Chapter One

1904–1926

FREDERICK WILLIAM MALLANDAINE ASHTON was born in Guayaquil, Ecuador, on 17 September 1904. There was nothing in his background to suggest that he was to become one of the greatest choreographers of his time and one of the most important figures in the history of British ballet. At that time, indeed, British ballet did not exist, and dancing was not a respectable profession, particularly not for a man. Ashton has described his family as 'middle-class', but the description is, characteristically, modest. His father, George Ashton, was a minor diplomat, 'a sort of honorary consul' and, Ashton believes, 'worked for a cable company as well',[1] having settled in South America in the 1890s; his mother, Georgiana (née Fulcher), had left home in 1895 to marry him, but also because she wanted 'to get away from Suffolk'[2] where her family lived (and where Ashton now has a country house). Ashton was the youngest of their four sons; about eight years after he was born, there was a fifth child, his only sister Edith. There was also a step-brother. When Ashton was two years old he was taken to Britain by his parents, and he remembers seeing King Edward VII and Queen Alexandra riding in the royal coach in the Lord Mayor's procession. Soon after their return to South America the family moved to Lima, Peru, where Ashton spent most of his childhood.

He was educated at the Dominican school in Lima, but says that all he can remember learning there was 'how to pray'.[3] His family was not Catholic and his mother refused to let him take Communion, but he still used to assist at Mass in the Cathedral and was the Archbishop's favourite acolyte because of his fair complexion. 'I liked doing these ceremonies,' he once wrote, 'and I learnt to time things rightly and to make effects at leisure, and the proper times for climaxes and the whole rightful measure of things and the ecstasy of ritual'.[4] It was in Peru too that Ashton learned to love the sea, a passion that has also had a profound effect on his work: he remembers his childhood as 'years of sunshine and beautiful bathing, sometimes in and out of the water from morn to moonrise, having our last dip as the huge moon rose in the black sky'.[5]

His mother took seriously her role as a diplomatic hostess and held receptions at which 'elegant ladies rather plump in slit skirts, enormous hats and tango shoes

Ashton's father and mother, George and Georgiana Ashton

would all pour into our house [and later found their way into some of Ashton's ballets], and the Chinese Minister would arrive with a Japanese wife and gradually empty the rooms because no one could stand his poppy scent; the waisted bejewelled men and the Kaiser's ex-mistress in coffee lace, who came back from Europe with blonde hair and wonderful gestures and photogenic attitudes'.[6]

Although all this fascinated Ashton his family life seems not to have been very happy: his mother and father had little to do with each other and even less with their children. Ashton was terrified of his father, who was very strict, though at times generous to a fault; his mother was busy with her social life. It appears that Ashton had little in common with his older brothers and played mostly with Peruvian children – he spoke as much Spanish as English, and still speaks it fluently when occasion demands. Since the Dominican fathers conducted school lessons in French, he was in fact tri-lingual from an early age.

But even though he was left largely to his own devices as a child, it was taken for granted that he, like his brothers, would conform to convention as he grew older; it was intended that he would attend public school in England and perhaps a university, and then choose a suitable career such as the diplomatic service or business of a respectable kind.

In 1917, when Ashton was in his thirteenth year, Anna Pavlova came to Lima on her South American tour: Ashton was then living with a family called Watson,

Anna Pavlova and
Nicholas Legat in
a Fille mal gardée, 1912

in Miraflores, a suburb of Lima, his father's business having taken him back to Ecuador, and he went with them to see her company dance, at the Teatro Munici-pal. In a state of great excitement, he kept asking, 'Is that her?' but when she finally came on he was disappointed by the way she looked, for she seemed old and ugly to him – until she started to dance and then he thought she was 'quite, quite beautiful. Seeing her at that stage was the end of me. She injected me with her poison and from the end of that evening I wanted to dance'.[7] He remembers that she danced in *Fairy Doll* that night and also in an excerpt from *Raymonda*, about which he can recall nothing except her first entrance, travelling in *pas de bourrée* along a diagonal path marked out by roses; then there was all the 'carry-on' with her eyes and hands as she sat on a throne. After the performance he saw her getting into a cab, walking, he said years later, 'like a bird'.[8]

Several years were to pass before Ashton could take steps towards the fulfilment of the ambition that Pavlova had inspired in him – to become 'the greatest dancer in the world'. Pavlova saw Ashton's oldest brother, who was a marvellous ball-room dancer, at a *thé dansant* and invited him to join her company. 'He was,' Ashton has said, 'horrified and absolutely shocked and refused point blank'.[9] As for Ashton himself, in due course the time came when he had to acquire some proper education. Once the First World War was over, he was sent back to Eng-land with the Watsons, in the autumn of 1919, to attend Dover College, a small public school in Kent. Guy Watson, who was about Ashton's age, went there at the same time and had no trouble fitting in, but for Ashton it was 'quite hopeless'.[10] His years at school in Lima had left him totally unequipped for any more formal education, and he was no good at any sport except swimming. The chilly, damp English climate made him miserable and the other boys made fun of his Spanish accent. He could expect no sympathy from his family in this situation – all he could do was 'accept the jungle law'[11] and get through somehow.

During the three years he was at Dover College he did make a few friends, and there was one sympathetic master who shared, wrote Beryl de Zoete, 'his taste for Edwardian beauties'[12] and awakened his interest in poetry – Ashton is of course a very cultivated man, but he insists that he is chiefly self-educated because of the wide reading he has done in preparation for various of his ballets. At Dover, Ashton began to act in school plays, and played Charlotte Verrinder in Pinero's *The Magistrate*; he was to have appeared as Lydia Languish in *The Rivals*, but for some reason that production was cancelled.

Otherwise, the only oases in what he has called 'an absolute desert'[13] were the holidays, when he stayed with a friend of his mother's in Chelsea and went to the theatre as often as he could. In April 1921 Isadora Duncan appeared at the Prince of Wales Theatre, and Ashton saw her dance, an experience that had almost as profound an effect on him as seeing Pavlova four years before. Many years later, he said, 'I didn't think I'd like it, but I was completely captivated. I suppose she was rather blowsy about that time – I remember she had red hair – and the first impact of her gave me a bit of a shock, but that soon passed. I find that people . . .

now stress her life, this appalling life that she led, and the sexual side – but I didn't get that impression at all, I got an impression of enormous grace, and enormous power in her dancing, I can remember the Brahms waltzes that she used to do being absolutely exquisite. She had also the most extraordinary quality of repose, she would stand for what seemed quite a long time doing nothing, and then make a very small gesture that seemed full of meaning. She also covered the stage in a most remarkable way, she had a wonderful way of running, in which she what I call left herself behind, and you felt the breeze was running through her hair and everything else. And she had the most beautiful square feet, I remember, and the most impressive hands, and she wasn't really the old camp that everyone makes her out now, she was very serious, and an immensely strong personality that came right across the footlights and held the audience and compelled them completely; she was very considerable I think, as an artist and as a dancer'.[14]

Later in 1921, Ashton saw a company that Loïe Fuller brought to the Coliseum and the Diaghilev production of *The Sleeping Beauty* at the Alhambra; and in 1922 the Ballets Suédois. Whenever he could get to London, Ashton went to as many theatres and concerts as possible, sometimes two in a day, as well as museums and galleries – and he also found his way to Cyril Beaumont's bookshop in the Charing Cross Road, where ballet-lovers could browse among the dance books and converse with the proprietor when he emerged from his tiny office at the back.

Because of his total inability to pass any kind of academic examination, a diplomatic career was out of the question when he left school in 1922, much less the university. Soon afterwards, his father was dead, a suicide, and Ashton had to earn his living somehow. A job was found for him with a firm of import-export merchants in the City, and he lived at first with his mother's friend Maud Lawson, then later with a Mr and Mrs Paley in Croydon, travelling up by train every day to the City. His guardian's brother was a partner in the business and, in due course, Ashton was promoted from being office boy to junior foreign correspondent, translating letters and orders not only in French and Spanish but in languages of which he knew nothing. His father had left very little money and his mother had soon to return to England: at first she and Ashton lived in a succession of private hotels in Kensington, then in a small flat in West Bolton Gardens.

In the meantime Ashton had decided that if he were to fulfil his ambition of becoming a dancer, he must do something about it: he was already eighteen years old. At that time, Léonide Massine, having broken with Diaghilev early in 1921, had briefly settled in London and opened a small studio off Oxford Street. A friend of Ashton's showed him Massine's advertisement in the paper and Ashton wrote asking for a trial lesson, for which he appeared in cricket flannels and a shirt (Massine's suggestion of pyjamas seemed to him inappropriate). Because of his job, Ashton could take lessons only on Saturday afternoons: his wages were thirty shillings a week, of which one guinea was spent on the lesson (he still received a small allowance from his family, which paid for his board and lodgings, but there was very little left over for extras).

Frederick Ashton, 1922

At first Ashton could not understand why Massine made him repeat the same exercises over and over, and finally asked when he was going to learn a dance: Massine replied, 'In three years' time'.[15] Penelope Spencer, a pupil of Margaret Morris (the originator of a 'free' style of dancing), who was beginning to have some success as a solo recitalist, remembers that Ashton came to see her about that time, seeking advice. He was, she says, very amusing even then and impressed her with his single-minded determination to become a dancer. For her part, she thought that at his age, with only one lesson a week, 'it was pretty hopeless'.[16]

His mother could not understand why he had no money, and finally Ashton had to confess that he was studying ballet. She was horrified and told him he must stop. He became more and more unhappy and frustrated; his job became unbearable, particularly after he caused his firm to lose £1000 through misquoting the exchange rates. Finally, he says, he 'staged' a nervous breakdown, took to his bed and refused to get up. A family doctor was called in, an elderly Scot who, Ashton says, 'must have been a very wise old bird', for he told Ashton there was nothing wrong with him, but asked what was really the matter. Ashton told him and the doctor said to his mother that the boy must be allowed to dance, or he really would go mad. So he was allowed to leave his job and study every day – one of his brothers paid his tuition as long as he promised not to become a chorus-boy.

From Massine, Ashton says, he learned 'about style and about the beauty of *port de bras'* – nothing about choreography, though the influence of Massine was strongly apparent in some of his early work, particularly his choreography for himself. When Massine had to go over to Paris he sent Ashton to Marie Rambert, who then shared a studio with a woman sculptor in Bedford Gardens. Rambert, a Polish pupil of Dalcroze, had been engaged by Diaghilev in 1913 to help Nijinsky to overcome the musical difficulties of Stravinsky's score for *Le Sacre du printemps.* (Her real name was Miriam Ramberg, whence comes her nickname, Mim.) As a

Ashton with Marie Rambert, left, and Frances James, right, in pose from *Les Sylphides*; taken in the street near Rambert's Studio, probably in the summer of 1925

result of her exposure to the Ballet Russe – the brilliant productions, the artistry of dancers like Nijinsky and Karsavina, and the rigorous classes taught by Cecchetti – Rambert became a convert to ballet, and although she began her training in the classic technique too late to become a very accomplished dancer herself, she absorbed enough to become a committed and inspiring teacher. Perhaps her most remarkable gift was her ability to bring out hitherto unsuspected talents in her pupils. Without Rambert, it is possible that Ashton and Antony Tudor, or for that matter Andrée Howard, Frank Staff and Walter Gore, would never have discovered and developed their talent for choreography. The Ballet Rambert, in its original form, was the cradle of British ballet.

Though Ashton also studied with Astafieva, Legat and Margaret Craske, and later at Ninette de Valois's Academy of Choreographic Art (which opened in 1926), he kept going back to Rambert if only because she allowed him to study for nothing. When Massine left London for good early in 1925, to go back to Diaghilev, Ashton became one of her regular pupils.

By this time the family business had failed completely and Ashton and his mother were without funds. They lived in a series of furnished rooms, each cheaper than the last; Ashton slept in the kitchen and his mother in the living room. As he says, it was worse for her because she had been used to comparative luxury, but she faced poverty with unfailing bravery and cheerfulness. He tells of coming home one day in the summer and finding the furniture all rearranged; his mother said, 'We're at the seaside.' She sold what jewellery she had left, and her sister let her have a little money, but it was, Ashton says, 'a hard life'.

Because of her connection with Diaghilev, Rambert was able to take her pupils to his company's performances free of charge, and so Ashton was able to continue his ballet-going during the last years of the Diaghilev era, seeing the works of Massine, Balanchine and especially Nijinska which were to influence his own early ballets. Their new productions often seemed shocking to older critics who remembered the pre-war ballets with their barbaric, exotic splendours or delicate romanticism, and the performances of such artists as Karsavina, Nijinsky and Bolm. But the new ballets were exciting to Ashton as to other young people because they were an expression of the age they were living in: '*Le Train bleu* was wonderful, I thought. I remember going expecting to see someone wearing a dress with a long blue train, I had no idea what the title meant, but it was extraordinary the way Nijinska brought the modern world on to the stage. She herself was a sort of Suzanne Lenglen figure, and Dolin was marvellous in it. There was a moment when an aeroplane flew over and dropped leaflets, and the dancers all went into slow motion.'

But however impressive these ballets were to him, he did not lose his respect for the more traditional values in ballet, especially as personified by his beloved Pavlova, who also came frequently to London during the 20s. It was, Ashton has said, 'my memories of her which kept me going when I couldn't find work as a dancer and at school, when I was young, and when my mother and I had no money'.[17] He saw her dance whenever he could and from being a magical being who had changed his life as a boy of thirteen, she became an ever-present influence in his work (Robert Helpmann has said that every role Ashton has ever created for a ballerina could ideally be for her). Indeed, Ashton later formed the habit of including somewhere in almost every ballet a 'signature step' referred to by his dancers as the 'Fred step', which is actually from her famous duet, the *Gavotte Pavlova*, which, like many of her numbers, was arranged to music of the most banal kind (*The Glow-worm* by Lincke), but whose 'sheer glory,' Ashton says, 'was indescribable'.†

In September 1925 Pavlova danced at Covent Garden, and during the season Ashton plucked up courage to ask for an audition. He went to the theatre and watched a rehearsal of *Giselle* first: 'She was doing the scene with the sword in the first act,' he says, 'and it wouldn't go right; she got angry with her partner, Novikoff, and finally stopped the rehearsal and sent for her cabin trunk. When it was brought she pulled out several dresses and went off to her dressing-room. Then I did my audition for Pianovsky, the ballet master – it was dreadful.'

Even so, Ashton was beginning to dance in public, ready or not. His début took place on the Palace Pier at Brighton on Good Friday, 10 April 1925, in one of H Bernhardt's Popular Concerts. Item 4 was a *Fandango* by the 'Duenna Dancers', consisting of Doris Sonne, Eleanor Shan, Mary Davies and Ashton. Miss Sonne had been dancing in Nigel Playfair's production of Sheridan's *The Duenna* at the Lyric Theatre, Hammersmith, with choreography by Rupert Doone. The other dancers included Doone himself, Joyce Berry, Aubrey Hitchins and Keith Lester but, according to Miss Sonne, they were 'too grand' to accept this engagement at Brighton, so she had to get a group together herself, for which she staged the *Fandango* to a piece called *Santiago* by one A Corbin.

That same summer he began to appear in danced 'prologues' to films at the Shepherd's Bush Pavilion, where the company also included Betty Scorer, now better known as Elizabeth Frank, the journalist. 'They started in the summer of 1925,' she says, 'and went on until the spring of the following year; we did a different show every week, though not all of us were in every one. I remember doing *Sally in Our Alley*, and *Treasure Island*, and *Peter Pan* – I think Fred was Captain Hook.* There was myself and Topsy Harries and Muriel Baddeley, Angela and Hermione's sister; Fred and Harry Webster, known as 'Webbles', were the only boys. The prologues were designed and produced by Hugh Gee, Muriel's husband, who was very brilliant, and the choreography was either by Flora Fairbairn or Daphne Jay. The musical director was Louis Levy, who went to Gaumont-British later on.

'We got £3.10 shillings a week for doing two or three shows a day. I remember

---

†In technical terms, the *enchaînement* is as follows – *posé en arabesque, coupé dessous,* small *développé à la seconde, pas de bourrée dessous, pas de chat.*

*This may have been in conjunction with the silent film of Barrie's story, starring Betty Bronson, made in 1924.

one show where poor Fred had to lead on a donkey – there were always lots of animals, in *Peter Pan* there were real ducks – and I remember doing a Trepak that was *very* impassioned. In *Treasure Island* there was lots of real smoke – this was before the days of dry ice – which made everyone cough a lot'.[18] Ashton remembers doing a 'nymphs and satyrs' number there with Muriel Baddeley, and a Hungarian dance that they did 'in front of *The Eagle*', with Rudolph Valentino.

Flora M Fairbairn had a school, the Mayfair School of Dancing, in Westbourne Grove, and sometimes her students performed under the name of the Mayfair Dancers. Early in 1926 they formed the nucleus of a little company, the Cremorne Company, named after the famous 18th-century pleasure gardens. Miss Fairbairn was the General Director, and the Artistic Director was Cyril Beaumont. Mr Beaumont had made previous attempts to form a company, first with Ninette de Valois, then with Margaret Craske (the Beaucraske Dancers), but neither of these projects got off the ground. However, in the March 1926 issue of the Dancing Times it was announced that the first performance of the Cremorne Company, a matinée, would take place at the Scala Theatre in Charlotte Street on the 11th of that month.

The programme was to consist of three ballets devised by Mr Beaumont himself, *The Christmas Tree*, a fantastic ballet in one act after Hans Christian Andersen's story 'The Little Match Girl'; *Circus*, a burlesque ballet in three scenes, set on Hampstead Heath in the 1890s; and *Bal Mabille*, which appears to have foreshadowed, in a small way, Massine's *Gaieté parisienne*. The choreography of these was jointly credited to Miss Fairbairn and Mr Beaumont. Other numbers included Penelope Spencer's *Funeral March for the Death of a Rich Aunt*, to music of Lord Berners, and several dances staged by Flora Fairbairn and Daphne Jay, some of which may have originated at the Shepherd's Bush Pavilion: *Russian Finale*, to music of Brahms and Tscherniawsky, in which Ashton danced, may well have been the 'Hungarian' dance he remembers doing before *The Eagle*.

In *The Christmas Tree* Ashton (billed as Fred Ashton) appeared as both A Cruel Old Man and one of two Young Men; in *Circus* he was a Dervish Dancer (though not as warlike, Mr Beaumont said, as he had wanted him to be); and in *Bal Mabille* there were again Two Young Men, Ashton and Stanley Judson. Ashton was also in a 'Song Scena', *The Song of the Archer Prince*, for which no choreographer was named: he was the Son of the Khan, and Aileen Harries was the Love of the Son of the Khan. The advance announcement in the Dancing Times had stated that 'the entire personnel is British in composition, but we wish it to be clearly understood that we make no claim to the formation of a national ballet'. The disclaimer proved to be a prudent one, for the performance was poorly received, and described in the following month's Dancing Times as being on the level of a teacher's display. There was no mention of Ashton. There were no further performances by the Cremorne Company, but Mr Beaumont recalled that at about that time Ashton suggested to him that they should collaborate on a revival of *La Sylphide*.

Sophie Fedorovitch,
about the time Ashton
first met her, early
summer, 1925

One of Rambert's pupils, Frances James, who was the sister of the fashion designer Charles James and married Ninette de Valois's brother Gordon Anthony, the photographer, had begun to arrange ballets for her fellow-students. On 16 July 1925 she and Rambert presented a matinée, also at the Scala, whose programme included a ballet called *Les Nénuphars*. The costumes were designed by a young artist named Sophie Fedorovitch, who was born in Minsk (then part of Poland) in 1893 and had come to London after the Russian Revolution via Moscow, Leningrad and Paris. Rambert had met her during the run of Diaghilev's *Sleeping Princess* in 1921, when she used to go to Cecchetti's class to sketch. To give her ideas for *Nénuphars* Rambert had shown her a volume of the *Monumenta Scenica*, a collection of stage designs by Burnacini and others, from the Albertina Museum in Vienna, that Rambert had given to her husband, Ashley Dukes, for his fortieth birthday in May 1925. From one of the plates in this volume Fedorovitch took the kind of accordion pleating that she first used in Frances James's ballet and that became one of her trademarks as a designer.[19]

A Tragedy of Fashion: Left to right, Elizabeth Vincent as Désir du Cygne, Ashton, Rambert, Esme Biddle as the Viscountess Viscosa, W Earle Grey as the Viscount Viscosa, Frances James as Rose d'Ispahan

Ashton did not dance in *Les Nénuphars,* though just before Christmas, on 20 December, he probably appeared in some other ballets by Frances James at the Century Theatre, including *L'Espoir manqué, Fidèle infidélité* (to waltzes by Brahms), and another to music by Schumann that she remembers as being a 'Harlequinade'.

But through Rambert, Ashton met Fedorovitch: 'I was fascinated,' he says, 'by her appearance – she was the first woman I had seen who wore her hair cut very short, and she dressed in a very singular way – she was a *garçonne* type, with a marvellously beautiful choirboy's face.' They went to Rambert's house for lunch after class, and as they were still hungry went afterwards to the Express Dairy in Notting Hill Gate, the kind of place where poverty-stricken dancers could sit for hours over a cup of tea and a bun. They became firm friends from that time on, and in the following year Fedorovitch designed the décor and costumes for Ashton's first ballet.

Chapter Two

1926–1930

In the summer of 1925 Marie Rambert and Ashley Dukes spent their holiday in the South of France. He was reading a volume of the letters of Madame de Sévigné, and one day at dinner quoted the story she told of the great chef Vatel, who was preparing a banquet for Louis XIV; the fish arrived too late and Vatel, feeling that his professional pride was dishonoured by this failure, committed suicide. Dukes turned to Rambert and said, 'By the way, that would make a very good subject for a ballet.' They discussed it further: Rambert felt that if the central character were a chef the ballet would end up looking like the dinner scene in Massine's *Les Femmes de bonne humeur*, so she said that he should be a couturier instead. She decided to produce the ballet with some of her pupils, and to entrust the choreography to Frances James. Ashton was at that time her only regular male pupil, so the role of the couturier, Monsieur Duchic, fell to him. The day after Rambert told him about it, he came into the studio and showed her some movements he had thought of, and Rambert thereupon decided that he should undertake the choreography. One of the gestures was that of racking his brains for new ideas, shaking his head with clenched fists pressed to his temples, a characteristic personal gesture of Ashton's that he later used in his Ugly Sister's dance in *Cinderella*, when she forgets her steps. He was at first unwilling to accept responsibility for the entire ballet, but Rambert pushed him into it (thus establishing a pattern for their collaboration over the next decade).

His ideas were grandiose – with such Diaghilev ballets as *Le Train bleu* and *Les Biches* in mind, he wanted music to be commissioned from Auric or Poulenc, and costumes from Chanel. Rambert told him that there was no money for that kind of thing, and in any case for his first effort he would be wiser to use existing music. She brought in several pieces she thought suitable, none of which he liked, and finally produced Eugene Goossens's *Kaleidoscope*. Again this did not appeal to him, and in desperation Rambert herself arranged a solo to a number from the suite and showed it to him: Ashton immediately started making suggestions and altered the movements in a way that made them look quite new, and this fired his imagination. He accepted the music, *faute de mieux*, and began work.

A Tragedy of Fashion:
LEFT Ashton with
Marie Rambert as
Orchidée;
BELOW Ashton as
Monsieur Duchic;
BOTTOM LEFT Diana
Gould in the
Mannequin Dance

As for the costumes, Rambert felt that Diaghilev's choice of Chanel to design the clothes for *Le Train bleu* had been an artistic error: the obvious choice of designer was Fedorovitch, who was always at the studio. Ashton worked on the ballet with Rambert and Frances James, with no thought at first of producing it anywhere. Nigel Playfair, however, was looking for a novelty to add to his revue *Riverside Nights*, which had opened at the Lyric, Hammersmith, in April 1926, then moved into the West End at the time of the General Strike; now he was planning to reopen it at the Lyric and needed an excuse to invite the critics again. He heard about the ballet and invited Rambert to present it as part of his show. To Ashley Dukes's title *A Tragedy of Fashion*, A P Herbert added the subtitle, *The Scarlet Scissors*.†

The idea of the dressmaker's using his shears as the instrument of his suicide was Ashton's – he clearly could not hang himself, for instance, on stage. Even so, the ending would have been a little gruesome, so Ashton had the idea of bringing the mannequins on again for a funeral dance. At Playfair's insistence the cartwheels and other tricks for which Rambert was famous were introduced into the ballet, but she said she would have to have a suitable costume, so the model she displayed had a kilt-like skirt and was called Le Sporran.

Although both Ninette de Valois and Margaret Craske came backstage to congratulate Ashton and Rambert, the reviews were only mildly enthusiastic, using words like 'elegant' and 'tasteful'. One critic said that the ballet was 'rather amateurish' but nevertheless showed 'traces of real imagination'. Another said that Ashton's convulsions as he expired, to a dirge in 5/4 time, were 'most realistic' but amused the audience. The Dancing Times thought that the choreography was modelled on that of Massine, and that Penelope Spencer's work in the revue (she again did her *Funeral March for the Death of a Rich Aunt*) was 'far cleverer'.

Goossens had conducted for Diaghilev, and brought him to see the ballet; Diaghilev was polite to Ashton, but clearly more interested in Elsa Lanchester, who had a very strange physical appearance and performing quality. At all events, Ashton received no invitation to work for the Russian Ballet, nor did any other offers come his way, and after about six weeks Playfair dropped the ballet from the revue, since the four dancers were being paid just for that – Ashton's salary was £15 a week, unprecedented wealth for him at that time. (The roles of the customers were performed by actors who were in the rest of the revue.)

However, two dances from *A Tragedy of Fashion* survived. In a 'Programme of Danse-Divertissements' given at the Royal Academy of Music by the Mayfair Company of English Dancers on 29 November 1926, 'supported by Frederick Ashton, Harry Webster and members of the Cremorne Company', Ashton danced a solo called *Youth* – '*The Swaggerer*', which was from the ballet, although since his costume was unavailable he wore white tennis clothes, with red shoes, a red scarf and red beret. Frances James's solo had a longer life: it was performed by

†For Ashley Dukes's synopsis, see Appendix B.

Diana Gould under the title *Mannequin Dance* at the Arts Theatre Club on 9 March 1928 and on several other occasions. In this guise the dance always had a great success: Diana Gould remembers seeing a film of mannequins at a cinema in the King's Road and thinking the dance could be more amusing if performed with their 'snooty, deadpan' air. Also she looked gorgeous in the costume Fedorovitch had designed, in pink satin with low-cut back, a large bow at the base of the spine, and pearls. The Dancing Times wrote after she had danced it at a reception in Rambert's studio that it was 'one of the wittiest arrangements of simple movements *sur les pointes*', and reported that at the Lyric Theatre in February 1930 she 'had to repeat her cleverly arranged *Mannequin Dance* for which she is so admirably suited'.

Although Ashton now says that *A Tragedy of Fashion* was shamelessly derivative from *Les Biches* and other Diaghilev ballets, the fragment of her solo that was shown to me by Diana Gould is not without individuality: she enters in a *pas de bourrée* across the stage with back to the audience, turns to face them and *bourrées* across the other way, one hand at her shoulder and the other straight down at her side (changing hands as she turns); then a series of *chassés* into 4th position *effacée*, followed by *relevés* in *arabesque* with exaggerated *épaulement*, arms thrust down with palms flat; the final gesture and pose, with right arm crossing the body ending with the hand at the left shoulder, left arm again straight down, while certainly reminiscent of the style of *Les Biches*, show that Ashton had learned to use a few basic gestures and vary them to create an appropriate style – or did so instinctively.†

On the evening preceding the first performance of *A Tragedy of Fashion*, Rambert and Ashton had gone to the opening of the Diaghilev season at His Majesty's Theatre, when the programme included the London première of Nijinska's *Les Noces* (which he invited her to revive for the Royal Ballet forty years later). Later in the year Diaghilev had a winter season at the Lyceum, and it was probably then that Ashton went one day to audition for the company – but he was unable to summon up the courage actually to enter the theatre. Miserably, he went home and made up a story to explain his failure to his mother, who still thought of his desire to dance as a kind of madness. After this failure on Ashton's part, and the elimination of *A Tragedy of Fashion* from *Riverside Nights*, the financial situation for him and his mother was again desperate, and she told him he must give up the idea of dancing and go back to work in an office. Fedorovitch came to the rescue with the offer to give him a pound a week so that he could go on studying.

During the following months, Ashton, like any young dancer, continued to perform wherever he could. He rehearsed some cabaret numbers with Molly

†Interestingly, this fragment in some ways resembles Ninette de Valois's 1930 solo *Pride* (included in Ballet for All's programme The Birth of the Royal Ballet, 1972) – at that time she also was very much under the influence of Nijinska, who had choreographed her own solo as the Hostess in *Les Biches* on de Valois. (De Valois conversation)

Lake and Elsa D'Arcy, both of whom had danced in Pavlova's company, but these do not seem ever to have been performed. There were performances with Flora Fairbairn's Mayfair Dancers at places like Bournemouth and Littlehampton (the latter in a tent), and, as previously mentioned, at the Royal Academy of Music on 10 November 1926. These programmes included his '*Swaggerer*' solo and a *Pas de deux* that Ashton arranged to Chopin's *17th Prelude* for himself and Phyllis Stickland. All that he can remember of this dance is that she wore a mauve tutu with a purple bodice, decorated with large purple flowers, and he a tunic like the one worn by the man in *Les Sylphides*, also in purple. (At the Royal Academy Ashton, Stickland and Harry Webster performed another dance to music of Chopin, *Les Sylphes*, with choreography by Miss Fairbairn herself.)

It was probably at this time, too, that he danced in opera-ballets with the Carl Rosa Opera Company, of which Ailne Phillips was *première danseuse* and Margaret Craske ballet-mistress. The company was run by Miss Phillips's mother, who felt that a man was needed in the ballets when the company played large towns, and accordingly Ashton was engaged for seasons at the King's Theatre in Hammersmith and cities like Glasgow. Before that, Miss Phillips had been partnered, even at the Lyceum Theatre in London in June 1925, by another girl *en travesti*. The ballet in *Faust* was arranged by Lydia Kyasht, and that for *Romeo and Juliet* by Miss Craske; in *Carmen* it was decided to use the 'Humming Chorus', usually cut, in the Tavern Scene and Ailne Phillips and Ashton arranged and danced it together (the other dances in the opera were choreographed by Elsa Brunelleschi). For this, Ashton found a blue velvet and silver bolero jacket in the Carl Rosa wardrobe and took the opportunity to have a pair of trousers made like those Massine wore in *Le Tricorne*.[1] In addition, one-act ballets were sometimes given with short operas like *Hansel and Gretel*; one such was *On the Beach* by Margaret Craske, to music by Bach, in which Ashton appeared as a Balloon Man (other characters included A Lady from Clapham and Three Flappers).

He continued to study at Rambert's studio, where there was a group of students who were to form the nucleus of her company soon afterwards, including Andrée Howard (who sometimes danced under the name of Louise Barton), Maude Lloyd from South Africa, Diana Gould, Pearl Argyle (who at that time appeared variously as Pearl Wellman or Williams), Harold Turner, William Chappell and, a little later, Walter Gore who like Ashton had begun his studies with Massine, and Antony Tudor. Ashton was notoriously lazy about going to class and well aware of it, and used to make either Sophie Fedorovitch or Maude Lloyd come to collect him (and if necessary get him out of bed) on the way to the studio. But once there he used to stay after class and experiment with steps and make dances for his fellow-students.

Occasionally, these were done for a specific performance. In June 1927 the Purcell Opera Society and the Cambridge Amateur Dramatic Society joined forces to present a production of Henry Purcell's opera *The Fairy Queen* at the Rudolf Steiner Hall in Park Road at the north end of Baker Street. Cambridge had been

The Fairy Queen:
Three Swans: left to
right in first picture,
Maude Lloyd, Pearl
Argyle, Violet
Reynolds

the centre of a minor Purcell revival during the 1920s, and an earlier production of *The Fairy Queen* at the New Theatre there, on 10 February 1920, had in fact been the first stage revival since 1692, the year of its composition. Dennis Arundell had been associated with that production as assistant to the producer, Clive Carey, who arranged the dances himself. Arundell was producer of the rather more ambitious revival seven years later, which used the complete spoken text from the original version; he decided to enlist the aid of Marie Rambert and her students and again she entrusted the choreography of the most important dances to Ashton. The others she did herself, using the untrained undergraduates as dancers. Although the production was intended to be musically as authentic as possible, Ashton did not attempt a reconstruction of 17th-century dance style.

His most important contributions were the Echo Dance and the dances for the Followers of Night and the Three Swans. In the programme only Diana Gould is

The Fairy Queen: Maude Lloyd and Pearl Argyle as Attendants on Spring

Les Petits riens: Rambert and Ashton in the Gavotte sentimentale

listed for the Echo Dance, but it seems certain that she did it as a duet with Maude Lloyd; Gould at that time was the shorter of the two, though she grew to be unusually tall for a dancer, and in the dance she 'echoed' Lloyd's movements farther upstage, giving the illusion of a greater distance than in fact existed. The small photographs of the Swans' dance show that Ashton created very beautiful groupings for them, the arrangement of the arms being especially exquisite. According to Rambert, the dances were 'full of invention . . . translating well both the gravity and gaiety of Purcell's music'.[2]

Exactly a month later Rambert presented three small works by Ashton as her contribution to the rather grandly-named Imperial Society of Teachers of Dancing Annual Dance Festival (a matinée performance at the New Scala Theatre): a *Pas de deux* to music of Kreisler, an *Argentine Dance* to music by Artello – both of these danced by himself and Eleanora Marra – and a *Suite de danses* to music from Mozart's *Les Petits riens*, which he danced with Rambert. The two duets with Marra (whom Ashton had probably met at Massine's studio) were also performed by them in cabaret at Murray's Club in Beak Street at about this time, together with a solo for Marra that Massine had arranged. Matilda Etches writes of making costumes for the duets, from designs by Fedorovitch, in the commemorative volume *Sophie Fedorovitch: Tributes and Attributes*. In the ISTD programme, however, Ashton was not credited with the choreography, nor Fedorovitch with the design.

20

Ashton had started work on the Mozart dances before those for *The Fairy Queen*, after going to see Yvonne Printemps in the musical play *Mozart* (the music of which is in fact by Reynaldo Hahn) at the Gaiety Theatre. Mary Clarke writes (in *Dancers of Mercury*) that 'he wanted to express the tender grace, the wit and gaiety of Mozart's music rather than the stilted elegance of the 18th century'. His *Suite de danses* is given the title *Galanteries* in the Dancing Times review of the performance, though not in the programme, and described as a collaboration between Ashton and Rambert. A more extended version of the ballet was given in the following year, under the title *Nymphs and Shepherds*, in a 'Ballet-Divertissement' by Pupils of Marie Rambert at the Arts Theatre Club on 9 March 1928, repeated at her studio in Ladbroke Road the following day. Years later, in the late 60s, Ashton again considered making a ballet to Mozart's score, originally composed for Noverre, but the project came to nothing.

In between making the first two versions of *Les Petits riens*, Ashton danced with the Nemchinova-Dolin Ballet at the London Coliseum. At that time ballets were still given there as one part of a twice-nightly music-hall bill, sharing the programme with such acts as G H Elliott ('The Original Chocolate-Coloured Coon') and Norman Long ('A Song, a Smile and a Piano'). In this engagement, which extended intermittently over a period of three months, beginning on 5 September 1927, Ashton danced as one of the guests in Dolin's ballet *The Nightingale and the Rose* (from the story by Oscar Wilde), partnering Doris Sonne. Nemchinova was the Nightingale, Dolin the Student, Margaret Craske the Maiden and Rupert Doone the Rival. At one point during rehearsals, Miss Sonne recalls that Ashton was sent offstage to fetch her, making his exit by jumping off through a window in the set, whereupon Dolin told him that if anyone was going to do any jumping through windows in the ballet, it would be himself. In the final week of Ashton's engagement he and Rambert danced their *Gavotte sentimentale* in a divertissement.

In the early summer of 1928, Ashton got a job as a dancer in the Royal Opera season at Covent Garden, where Ninette de Valois was ballerina. He was in the ballets in Gluck's *Armide* (1 May) and *Tannhäuser* (7 May), and appeared as a page in *Die Meistersinger von Nürnberg* (10 May). The choreographer was François Ambroisiny, from Brussels. Although this was the usual prestigious international opera season with such singers as Lotte Lehmann, Frida Leider, Herbert Janssen and Lauritz Melchior, conducted by Bruno Walter and others, the ballets were not considered to be very important, and the dancers were correspondingly ill-paid. However, male dancers were in short supply, and Ashton was delegated to discuss salary with the management. His demand for £5 was at first refused, but he stuck to it, and finally won. 'Of course,' he now says, 'I was talking about £5 a *week*, but they thought I meant £5 a performance, and when we got our pay-packets at the end of the first week and found we had got £15 or £20, we absolutely reeled.'

Ambroisiny's methods, Ashton remembers, were 'fairly haphazard'. He would come to each group, when arranging the Venusberg ballet in *Tannhäuser*, and ask, 'Qu'est-ce que vous allez faire ici?' and when Ashton sketched a movement he would say, 'Bien!' and go on to the next. 'There were moments when we all came together and did something that he'd fixed, but in between times we just literally improvised, it was as loose as that. But somehow, he knew what he was doing, all the same – he knew that it didn't matter, because people were singing, and lying around, being bacchanalian. And in *Armide* it was the same, we were the underworld – and we used to make up in the most incredible way. I remember taking my stick of black and making my face like a corkscrew, then another time a long stream of tears – nobody objected at all.' In those days chorus singers used to wear their costumes over their street-clothes and, standards of hygiene being what they were, the smell under the hot stage-lights became fairly overpowering; Ashton remembers that in the Hall of Song scene in *Tannhäuser* the chorus used to sit in tiers, with the dancers at the back after they had done their 'little bit', and one dancer would give the word, 'Now, move!' and they would all move up one rung together – 'Nobody noticed, and then we'd say, "Now!" and go up to the next one, until we ended up on the top tier with a great gap between us and the singers, to get away from the smell!'

Ashley Dukes, in the spring of 1928, was preparing a stage adaptation of Lion Feuchtwanger's novel *Jew Süss*. 'There was a scene,' Rambert recalls, 'in which Süss was giving a banquet and as part of the entertainment there was to be a short opera, but then Ashley said, "I don't know anything about opera, let's have a ballet instead." My first idea was to do *Leda and the Swan* but then the play was postponed.' However, she and Ashton worked on the ballet together, using some of the ballet music from Gluck's *Orpheus*, and it was given, under the title *Leda*, at a reception in Rambert's new studio in Ladbroke Road, in June, then again at the annual matinée organised by the Dancing Times in aid of the Sunshine Homes for Blind Babies, at the Apollo Theatre, 10 July 1928, and also at a midnight matinée arranged by Grace Lovat Fraser at the Savoy Hotel. The performance at the Apollo was conducted by Constant Lambert.

After the afternoon reception in June, Rambert went to the Diaghilev ballet, which was again appearing at His Majesty's Theatre. She spoke to Diaghilev, who had heard about Diana Gould and wanted to see her dance, so she invited him to come and watch a class. He did so, with his secretary Boris Kochno, and after the class Gould and Ashton danced the *pas de deux* from *Leda* for him. Although he apparently liked this choreography better than *A Tragedy of Fashion*, he again did not offer Ashton a job, but he invited Gould to join his company. Because of her youth, it was agreed that she should wait a year – by which time Diaghilev was dead.

Les Petits riens: Ashton as L'Indifférent ▷

Leda and the Swan: Diana Gould as Leda, Ashton as Zeus

A revised version, *Leda and the Swan*, was presented at the Lyric, Hammersmith, on 25 February 1930. As before, Ashton and Diana Gould danced the leading roles, but this time the choreography was entirely his work. That his feeling for line and gift for grouping were already asserting themselves is evident from the photographs. The ballet was described in the programme as being 'Botticellian in its spirit and line', and indeed like many early ballets by Ashton and others it took its inspiration from pictorial sources.

Arnold Haskell wrote at the time of Ashton's unusual conception of his own role as the god disguised as a swan, 'without any of the customary trappings'. He was carried in by two male Zephyrs (Turner and Chappell) in a swan-like pose, and the ballet, said one reviewer, 'gathered dramatic force as it went on from various movements off the ground that kept the whole ballet in the same key'. The critic of Punch said 'this pretty pastoral had the air of an orchestral piece adapted to

Leda and the Swan: Rehearsal at the Ballet Club, 1930: Diana Gould and Ashton, centre, with, left to right, Pearl Argyle, Harold Turner, Andrée Howard, Prudence Hyman, William Chappell, Joan Benthall

Leda and the Swan: Diana Gould and Ashton, centre, with, left to right, Harold Turner, Andrée Howard, Elisabeth Schooling, Pearl Argyle, Doodie Millar, Doola Baker, Prudence Hyman, William Chappell

the harpsichord. The graceful mazes of the nymphs ere Jupiter descended from the Empyrean to scatter them and make his choice, his brief but tender dalliance with Leda, the feigned consummation indicated by the fluttering hands of the nymphs who screened these rites, and Jupiter's swan-like return in triumph to Olympus, were admirably designed to display the arts and aims of these young dancers'.[3] Ashton's feathered helmet was a hat belonging to the Princess Galitzine, a White Russian who was, he says, the Ballet Club's Fairy Godmother.

Shortly before the first production of *Leda*, Ashton had taken a step that was a decisive one in his development as a dancer and choreographer. Borrowing £5 from Sophie Fedorovitch, he went over to Paris to audition for Bronislava Nijinska. She was assembling a company for the wealthy dilettante Ida Rubinstein, who had created a sensation in the early seasons of the Diaghilev ballet by her appearances as Cleopatra and as Zobeida in *Schéhérazade*. Diaghilev, however, had realised that she must be confined to roles that made full use of her great physical beauty and somewhat smaller acting talent, and no demands to speak of on her severely limited technique as a dancer. But in a company that was being financed, and generously, by her lover, Rubinstein could insist on dancing leading roles in ballets made for her by some of the most distinguished artists of the time: the repertory was to be choreographed by Nijinska and Massine, with scores commissioned from Stravinsky, Ravel and Auric, and with décors by Alexandre Benois.

Nijinska accepted Ashton and he began rehearsals on 1 August 1928, at a salary of 1000F a month (it was to go up to 1300F when performances began) – then worth about £20. (Fedorovitch had told him, 'You won't be able to have a bath every day on that salary,' at which he burst into tears.) Working for Rubinstein had its bizarre aspects. She took class and rehearsed separately from the company for the most part, but when it was necessary to piece things together and for her to appear at a full rehearsal, a red carpet would be laid from her car to the door of the rehearsal hall, and the male dancers were instructed to wear clean shirts and issued with eau de cologne. Rehearsals went on for the better part of four months on a repertory of seven ballets by Nijinska and two by Massine, with a gruelling daily schedule: class from 9 to 10 am, followed by rehearsal until 1 pm. After a two-hour break for lunch, rehearsal resumed until 6. Then there was a two-hour dinner break, followed by another three-hour rehearsal (the evening rehearsals were with Massine), finishing at 11 pm. The company was known among the dancers as 'La Compagnie des répétitions de Madame Ida Rubinstein'. Not surprisingly, this régime almost crippled Ashton at first, and he even asked Nijinska if he could be excused from rehearsals for a while to recuperate. She naturally refused and told him that he would get used to it.

Anatole Vilzak was the *premier danseur*, with his wife Ludmilla Schollar as second ballerina; the company also included Nadejda Nicolaeva (Legat), Nina

Verchinina, David Lichtenstein (Lichine), Alexis Dolinoff, Roman Jasinski, Yurek Shabelevsky, and three compatriots of Ashton's, Joyce Berry, Rupert Doone and William Chappell. Chappell joined the company a little later than Ashton, after rehearsals had started – passing through Paris on his way home from a holiday, he auditioned for Nijinska at Ashton's insistence, and was surprised when she took him, which she may have done partly because she felt sorry for Ashton, who had nobody to talk to. Another dancer, who was to become one of Ashton's closest friends, was the Dane, Birger Bartholin. There was also a promising young American dancer, Anna Ludmila, whose name was Russianised to Ludmilova to avoid confusion with Schollar.

In later years, Ashton has often said that, unlike many dancers, he always enjoyed dancing in the corps de ballet. But Nijinska also used him sometimes in a male quartet of which the other members were Lichine, Jasinsky and Shabelevsky, which gives an indication of how much his dancing must have improved – in his favour was his ability to do small *batterie*, although he was less good at *pirouettes*, and *tours en l'air*, he says, were 'problematical'. He remembers that once Nijinska had set a step and then made each of the men do it separately. 'When it came to my turn I was absolutely terrified, but she said I was the only one who got it right, and put me at the front, before Lichine and Shabelevsky and all the others.' Ashton was popular with the other dancers because of his ability (which he has not lost) wickedly to mimic Rubinstein and Nijinska.

All the same, Ashton worshipped Nijinska. She told him years later that she was very touched at the time by his request to be allowed to watch her rehearsals even when he was not called – he would sit for hours in this way, learning his craft.

Unfortunately, although the company had excellent dancers who were rehearsed to a pitch of perfection, and in spite of the distinction of the artistic collaborators, the ballets all had to be made around Rubinstein herself. She was then in her early forties and unusually tall but, 'She insisted,' Ashton said in an interview with Don McDonagh, 'on going up on point, hauling herself up', and when she came on, after the other dancers had built everything up towards her entrance, the ballet 'would sag right down',[4] a situation not improved by the fact that when she went out on stage the *grande dame* became a frightened girl. Not that there were many performances – only about a dozen, apparently, in all the time Ashton was with the company, beginning with a short season at the Paris Opéra, which opened on 22 November 1928, followed by a European tour.

In the opening programme Ashton danced as one of the four winds and as a faun in *Les Noces de Psyché et de l'Amour* (Bach/Honegger), in the Carnival scene in *La Bien-aimée* (Schubert-Liszt/Milhaud), and as one of the group of men supporting Rubinstein in Ravel's *Bolero*. Later he danced in *Le Baiser de la fée* (Stravinsky), in which he had one brief entrance with Schollar, who was the Fiancée, *Nocturne* (Borodin/Tcherepnin), *La Princesse Cygne* (from *Tsar Saltan* by Rimsky-Korsakov) and *La Valse* (Ravel) – all of the ballets so far mentioned were by

27

Nijinska – and in the two by Massine, *David* (Henri Sauguet) and *Les Enchante-ments de la fée Alcine* (Georges Auric). Even allowing for Diaghilev's bitterness towards his former collaborators who had, in his view, sold themselves to work for Rubinstein, his assessment of the first night (in a letter to Lifar, quoted in the latter's *Serge Diaghilev*) as 'astonishingly provincial, boring and long-drawn-out' was probably not far from the truth.

Ashton, young and inexperienced as he was, had no illusions about this aspect of what he was doing, and was indeed shocked that people like Stravinsky and Ravel, who must have known better, would come backstage to praise Rubin-stein's performance – usually talking vaguely about the beauty of her gesture, which was all they could find to say, while Rubinstein would murmur, 'Vous trouvez?' Even Nijinska said to the dancers one day, 'Madame Rubinstein peut faire tout sauf la virtuosité'.

But still, the experience, Ashton now says, turned him from an amateur into a professional. Even in such a situation of compromise, the contact with so many creative spirits was exciting, and in particular the exposure to the Gallic sensibility in art was to have a profound influence on Ashton throughout his career. From the point of view of choreography, what impressed him most about Nijinska was not her actual method of composition – she used to analyse the music in great detail in advance and begin by giving the dancers their counts, a procedure for which he

On tour with the Rubinstein company: Bronislava Nijinska is at centre, with Ashton on her left

Ashton as he appeared
in Massine's *Les
Enchantements de la fée
Alcine,* with Ida
Rubinstein's company

possesses neither the inclination nor the musical training – but her theory of movement, the way she used the torso: the simplest movements in class, *battements
tendus* or *changements de pieds*, all were done with adjustments of *épaulement* or with
the body bending from side to side. 'She gave class every morning at which
attendance was compulsory because often she would work out choreography in
class. And always with wonderful music – one day all Bach, then another day

29

Chopin, or tangos. . . . Working with her I became saturated with movement, which is very important when you are young.'

The European tour took the company only to major opera houses, in Monte Carlo, Venice, Milan, Naples, Rome, Vienna and Brussels, but engagements were frequently cancelled or curtailed and the dancers left stranded. Even so, the tour itself was an important experience for Ashton, who 'fed passionately', wrote Beryl de Zoete, 'on the artistic treasures of Italy'. In an article on Ashton, she quotes an account of the tour from a letter by William Chappell: 'He had, the whole year we were away, a kind of unconsciously crusading spirit, as though he knew he was building up the foundations of the career that flowered so beautifully later . . . He imbibed so much from the teaching of Nijinska and Massine, being affected by them not in a purely derivative way but only receiving the things that pupils of genius take from their early masters. He has always seemed to me to have an extraordinary capacity for being influenced by the great choreographers and then carrying that influence much further than the original had ever been able to do . . . You can imagine how on top of all the heat and revolutions and mysticism and tropic quality of his Peruvian childhood (all came out in *Rio Grande* and the Brazilian in *Façade*) this crazy, half-starved tour of the great opera houses made a deep and lasting impression on him: rehearsing in one of the lounges in the Scala, seeing Vienna in the snow, Naples in the spring, dancing in that haunted Paris Opera House, and rehearsing in the same rooms in Monte Carlo which had seen the creation of so many of the Diaghilev ballets'.[5]

Although there were further performances in Paris in May 1929, Ashton decided not to renew his contract, especially since Nijinska had resigned. Rambert had come over to Paris to persuade him to return to London, where the plans to produce her husband's dramatisation of *Jew Süss* were going forward again. It was necessary to do another ballet to take the place of *Leda*, since that had been produced elsewhere, and Ashton agreed to come back to choreograph it.

Jew Süss opened at the Opera House, Blackpool, on 29 July 1929, and at the Duke of York's Theatre in London on 19 September. The subject Rambert had decided on for the new ballet was *Mars and Venus*; she had chosen music from Domenico Scarlatti's Sonatas, which were orchestrated by Constant Lambert. The action she devised took place in three episodes: the toilet of Venus, the entrance of Mars, and his disarming and seduction by Venus. Pearl Argyle's beauty made her the obvious choice for Venus, and Turner was a handsome, virile Mars. In the third part Ashton originally wanted Venus and her two attendant nymphs to ensnare Mars with garlands of roses, but they kept getting tangled, so silver ropes were used instead. The pattern made by these ropes played an important part in the choreography. A film exists of the ballet in a later revival, from which one can see that the choreography was very stylish, evidence of Ashton's increasing assurance in the use of the classic vocabulary (one brief section uses a great variety of *sissonnes*).

The Ballet of Mars and Venus as it was staged in *Jew Süss*. On the inner stage, Pearl Argyle as Venus, Harold Turner as Mars, with Andrée Howard and Anna Brunton as Nymphs

Some of the figures are quite Balanchinean, and there is a very elegant *pas de deux*.

As given in *Jew Süss*, the ballet was danced on a stage within a stage. Although the play was a success and ran for several months (it was even serialised in the Evening Standard), then went on tour, the ballet did not meet with much approval from the critics, one of whom went so far as to remark, as Dame Marie is fond of quoting, 'what a pity dramatic authors have wives, and those wives meddle in ballet.' However, in its revised form, as presented in 1930 by the Marie Rambert Dancers and in 1931 by the Camargo Society, it was more favourably noticed. The critic of Punch said, 'The pattern is intricate and lovely, the argument is clear, and the beautiful stylised movements in particular of Miss Pearl Argyle tempt me to extravagant words of praise . . . This little gem could have been presented on any of the great evenings we have known and have had no reason to blush for itself'.[6]

Mars and Venus: Harold Turner as Mars

Since Ashton did not dance in *Mars and Venus* himself, he was free to accept other engagements – and no doubt needed to do so to keep himself and his mother alive. In September, therefore, he was once again dancing with Anton Dolin's company at the Coliseum. Anna Ludmila had replaced Nemchinova as Dolin's partner, dancing with him in a *pas de deux*, *Jack and Jill*, choreographed for them by Balanchine and in revivals of Dolin's *Rhapsody in Blue* and *Revolution* (to music of Chopin), both of which dated from the previous year. The Gershwin ballet was given in the week of 9 September, with Ashton in the role of the Barman, now called the Cocktail Shaker, formerly danced by Nicholas Zverev. It appears that Dolin paid little attention to setting this role, and Ashton was left more or less to his own devices. He gave himself some fairly spectacular choreography, jumping up on top of the bar and in general making himself conspicuous, until a friend of Dolin's came backstage and asked him who the barman was, whereupon Ashton was told to modify his antics. A picture of a grouping from the ballet shows a young man wielding a trombone – unmistakably Ashton, from the dark hair slicked down across his forehead.

The following week *Revolution* went on, with Ashton in the corps – again he behaved rather naughtily, changing choreography on the spur of the moment when he felt like it, and visiting other members of the company such as Joan Lawson and Mary Skeaping in their dressing-rooms during waits to entertain them with imitations of Queen Victoria, Pavlova, Rubinstein and others. Joan Lawson says that he used to do an act lasting twenty minutes as Queen Victoria, called Fifty Years a Queen, wearing a black kimono, with a powder puff on top of his head – 'and all of it absolutely correct historically!' Or he would put on

Ashton as Queen Victoria in
a bathchair

'Jeunes filles en fleur and male fledglings': the Marie Rambert Dancers in rehearsal, 1930; left to right, Andrée Howard and Harold Turner, Diana Gould and Robert Stuart, Pearl Argyle and Ashton, Prudence Hyman and William Chappell

one of their *Sylphides* costumes and do Ida Rubinstein taking an *arabesque* and dropping her false teeth. This was the week that *Jew Süss* opened across the street at the Duke of York's, but as before the Dolin ballet was just one item in a twice-nightly music-hall bill, so that Ashton was able to keep an eye on his own piece, as well as watching the great American female impersonator and trapeze artist, Barbette, also on the bill at the Coliseum, from the wings.

It was probably at the conclusion of this engagement that Ashton went on a provincial tour with Dolin and his company. He danced among other things a *Chinese Dance* to music by Ramel – a *pas de trois* with Christine Rosyln and Mary Skeaping, which he remembers being taught them by Mr Mitchell, Dolin's manager, who assured the unbelieving dancers that it would stop the show. Much to their surprise, it did just that.

Early in 1930 Ashton proposed to Rambert that she should present her pupils in a public matinée – '*jeunes filles en fleur* and male fledglings', as he later described them. Her first reaction was to say no, she could not bear dancing-school displays, but he felt they now had enough things to show and talked her into it. She persuaded Nigel Playfair to let them use the little Lyric Theatre, Hammersmith, and the performance took place on 25 February. The programme included the revised *Leda and the Swan* and *Mars and Venus*, and among the divertissements dances from *A Tragedy of Fashion*, *The Fairy Queen* and *Les Petits riens*; there were also two new ballets, *Our Lady's Juggler* by Susan Salaman, in which Ashton danced the role of the Minstrel, and *Capriol Suite* by Ashton. The performance was an immense success: Ashton's faith in the material they had to offer was justified in The Times review the next day, which said that 'it was not . . . a pupils' demonstration, but the first production of a company directed by Madame Rambert and Mr Frederick Ashton'.

Reviews of Ashton's early ballets often commented on the fact that they were strongly influenced by the style of the late Diaghilev ballets – *A Tragedy of Fashion* by *Les Biches, Mars and Venus* by *Zéphyre et Flore,* and so on. But with *Capriol Suite* Ashton took a step forward and began to assert his own individuality and his essential Englishness. (Looking back, he says that he is surprised that the ballet was not more influenced by Nijinska.) The music is based on themes from the 16th-century French treatise by Thoinot Arbeau, pseudonym of Jehan Tabourot: the book contains not only the music for but also descriptions of such dances as the Pavane and the Galliard. Ashton heard Peter Warlock's suite (named for Arbeau's interlocutor in *Orchésographie*), and asked him for permission to use it for a ballet.

Ashton in the late 20s

He based some of the movements on the pictures in *Orchésographie*, and also took some things, such as the use of handkerchiefs, from a display of English folk dancing that he saw at the Albert Hall. He had also looked at Elizabethan paintings, such as the famous one of 'Queen Elizabeth being lifted with her feet dangling in the air' (in La Volta), but *Capriol Suite* was essentially an imaginative re-creation of old dances rather than an attempt at any kind of authentic reconstruction. Basically, their technique is classic, with an added period flavour, whether courtly or bucolic – the women, for instance, were not on point.

The earlier ballets had been done, to a greater or lesser extent, with Rambert's help. But *Capriol Suite* was entirely Ashton's own idea: when she suggested that at the reprise of a musical theme in the last movement he should repeat the earlier steps, he disagreed, and she had to admit to herself that he was right. All the same, the ballet certainly benefited from all the lessons he had learned from Rambert, and not only in terms of arranging steps and making them fit the music – she was a cultivated woman with a tremendous knowledge of poetry which she could recite at length, and she made her students read poetry too. Ashton was already familiar with Shakespeare's sonnets and other Elizabethan lyrics, which undoubtedly helped him to capture the flavour of the period.

A programme note said that 'the *Capriol Suite* of Peter Warlock contains themes from old French dances . . . and these are amusingly modernised in Frederick Ashton's choreography', but there is a robust boisterousness in some of the dances, as in the men's quartet Mattachins, in which alternate pairs of them do *entrechats* with flexed feet and roll across each other's backs. This was a new quality in his work, which previously had tended to be 'amusing' in the rather precious way that the word usually indicated at that time. In any case, the ballet was an instantaneous success with the audience and several numbers had to be repeated. After the performance at the Camargo Society a year later, the Dancing Times wrote that it was 'surely destined to become a classic', and so it proved. In the December 1940 issue of the same magazine Rambert wrote, 'The perfection of pattern, the freshness of steps and the complete correspondence to music make it a small masterpiece, whose vitality is unimpaired now after ten years of performances on stages ranging from the Mercury to the enormous Opera House at Manchester.'

The ballet was mounted with the economy that was by now characteristic of Rambert's productions: for the costumes she and Chappell bought beige linen at sixpence a yard and pink linen at two shillings and sixpence a yard at John Barker's basement in Kensington High Street, and he decorated them with black tape. Originally Diana Gould, Ashton and Turner changed costumes for the Pavane, in which a woman is courted by two suitors, one with a poem on a scroll and one with a rose, but Ashton later decided that he would prefer it if the whole cast wore the same costumes throughout the ballet – much to the sorrow of Diana

Ashton as he appeared in *Capriol Suite* ▷

Gould, who lost her beautiful red velvet dress. The total cost of the production was £5.

Capriol Suite was also given by the Rambert Dancers at that year's Sunshine Matinée at the Scala, on 8 July, where it was seen by Pavlova. She was sitting behind Arnold Haskell, and asked him about Ashton, whose work impressed her. Hearing this, Ashton wrote to her the next day and said he would like to hear her opinion, and in reply got an invitation to tea from her husband, Victor Dandré. 'When I arrived at Ivy House I was shown in and I sat and talked to her husband for a bit, and I remember there was a sort of double door with glass panels and a curtain that only went up to a certain height, and I remember Pavlova coming in very slowly and looking at me before she came in, and then when she did she said, "Ah, so young!" – those were her first words. And then somehow we seemed to get on frightfully well. I remember that when the tea was brought she had hundreds of little pots of jam, in the Russian way, and she helped herself to different jams which she put into her tea, and I'd never seen that done, it was very fascinating. And I'd always thought she had the most marvellous and beautiful hands, because on the stage the use of the hands was so extraordinary, and she gave the impression of having the most wonderful tapered fingers, but I was surprised to see that they really weren't at all – I mean they were nice hands, but they weren't exquisite – she seemed to have a lump on one knuckle, and she had a marquise ring with a huge opal, whether that was to hide that joint I don't know. But even then when she was talking she used her hands a lot – it was fascinating to me to see it.

'I was terribly young and cheeky, and I remember saying I have other things that you could see, could you come to the Rambert studio? And she said, Oh, but I'm going on tour right away. And I said, Well, what time's your train? And she laughed, and I said, You could come on the way to the train. She thought that was terribly funny, anyway she did come to the Rambert studio and we did *Leda and the Swan* for her. She was very sweet, and I went to see Dandré again, and he said, It's a question of engaging you or Paul Haakon – he was quite honest, he said, What we need is someone who can do all those numbers in the divertissement. So I said, He's a much better dancer than I am, you should take him. But he said, When we come back from this tour Madame Pavlova's going to reorganise the company and then she'll take you, and you will arrange ballets for some of the people and if she likes them she'll take them on. And then of course she went away and that was the end – she died.

'I saw her once again when I went to the last matinée she gave at Golders Green [13 December 1930]. I went to the stagedoor and said I'd like to see her, but the man said, She never sees anyone after the matinée. So I said, Well, can I see Mr Hitchins? and instead of going to see him I went straight down and knocked at her door, and Dandré opened it and I said, Can I see Madame? and he said, I think she will see you. So I went in and she took my hand and was very sweet, and I was saying to myself, Now look at her make-up and everything about her. But she

Capriol Suite: Diana Gould,
Ashton and William Chappell
in the Pavane

had a hole in her chest, where she'd apparently stabbed herself once in *Bayadère*,
and instead of looking at her make-up I was riveted by this hole in her chest.
And then she gave me a kind of blessing – she said to me, You will have a great
future; it will come slowly, but it will come. And that was it – I remember she
was in the costume for that Russian thing she used to do, with the great headdress.'

Among Ashton's papers there is a contract, or Memorandum of Agreement, with
an organisation called The Diaghileff Russian Ballet (1930) Ltd, for him 'to enter
the Ballet Troupe of the Company for the purpose of taking part in Ballet, Opera,
and dramatic performances', at a salary of 500F, or £8, a week, for the period
5 May 1930 to 31 July 1931, with the option of renewal for another year. It seems
likely that this was the company organised by Grigoriev to perform in the opera-
ballets at Monte Carlo, in which Markova danced, as well as Danilova, Tchernicheva, Schollar and Vilzak, that is referred to in *Alicia Markova, Her Life and Art*,
by Anton Dolin. Ashton has no recollection of any dealings with this company;
in any case he obviously decided not to accept the engagement, since the contract
is signed by neither party. Ashton thinks now that, whatever it was, he probably

39

turned it down on Rambert's advice – a wise decision in view of future developments in Britain, and of the fact that the company folded after a couple of months.

Nigel Playfair was sufficiently impressed by the success of the February matinée to suggest that Rambert give a short season at the Lyric in the following June. No doubt Rambert felt that what she could provide was a poor substitute for the summer seasons of the Diaghilev ballet, the last of which had taken place the previous year, but Playfair persisted: success would be assured, he said, if Karsavina would come in as guest artist. She agreed to do so, and danced in solos of her own and in *Les Sylphides* with Harold Turner. During the two weeks no new ballets were presented, but Ashton had choreographed two short numbers that were given as divertissements: *Saudade do Brésil*, a solo for himself, and *Mazurka des Hussars*, danced by himself and Rambert.

A Punch caricature of Ashton in his solo
Saudade do Brésil

The solo was described in The Daily Telegraph as being 'somewhat in the Massine manner' – presumably both this and the earlier *Argentine Dance* that he did with Eleanora Marra drew upon his reminiscences of life in South America. Ashton felt that it displayed his talents sufficiently well to perform it for Pavlova on the occasion when she visited the studio. The *Mazurka* remained in the repertory during the first season of the Ballet Club the following year, when Rambert was partnered by Walter Gore, who struck C W Beaumont, reviewing it in the Dance Journal, 'as a young man of promise'. Beaumont also noted that the costumes were 'based on those for the once-famous *Pas des Patineurs*',[7] presumably as depicted in the Brandard lithograph of Rosati and Charles in the ballet of that name (also known as *Les Plaisirs de l'hiver*) from Meyerbeer's *Le Prophète*.

Marriage à la Mode: Markova and
Ashton in the *pas de deux*

Again, the season was a success, as Playfair predicted, thanks to Karsavina, who besides giving the young dancers the cachet of her presence also gave them inspiration by her artistry and sweetness – and paid them the compliment, says Elisabeth Schooling, of treating them as professionals like herself. As Ashton wrote years later, 'Karsavina [danced] with us, inspiring and encouraging us with the full generosity of her beautiful nature; giving us her advice and putting her vast international experience at our disposal. When she danced with us we watched her every movement, admired her discipline, her exquisite manners, her humanity and her approach to the public; we loved and respected her as she moved among us an exiled queen from a bigger and more glorious world... She blessed us and we flourished, and we must be for ever grateful for the privilege of touching the fringe of her glory'.[8]

In October 1930 Ashton was again performing at the Lyric, this time in Nigel Playfair's production of Dryden's comedy *Marriage à la Mode*, in which he partnered Alicia Markova. Ashton was asked to stage the incidental dances and a brief ballet at the end, and first thought of asking the English dancer Vera Savina (Clark), a former member of Diaghilev's company who was Massine's wife at the time Ashton studied with him, to dance in it, but finally decided to ask Mar-

Group from *Marriage à la Mode*: Alicia Markova and Ashton, kneeling at left and right of centre couple, with Marie Nielson, Anna Brunton, Hedley Briggs and Walter Gore seated on floor

kova instead. Markova was without work, and was therefore delighted to accept his offer. When she asked him why he wanted to work with her, he replied, according to Anton Dolin, that he had seen her many times in the Diaghilev company, and that she reminded him of Pavlova.[9] Reviewing the dances in the *Dancing Times*, Haskell wrote, 'Like all true artists, Markova and Ashton have not sought to shine at the expense of the ensemble. Their work fits in and rounds off an entirely artistic production.'

The music was played by a quartet of ladies who used to 'collapse', Ashton says, from time to time, but Athene Seyler, who was in the cast and was the wife of the composer Sterndale-Bennett, used to save the situation by 'humming and banging the tune out to keep us going until they had recovered themselves'.

Markova wore a large dress of Charles II's period and was in fact, she says, got up to look like Nell Gwynn, 'with a huge red wig that Fred had off me as quickly as possible – he said, it makes your head look big, and I said, yes, Diaghilev always said one's head must look small, so after a couple of performances I unloaded the wig and had my little black curls to look in the period.' She also shortened her skirt, but still the costume was fairly cumbersome, with big sleeves, and there was the problem of 'coping with all that in this little space, and that was when I first realised that Fred was someone who had the ingenuity to deal with all of that.' Again, he had not attempted an authentic period reconstruction – Markova, in fact, was in point shoes.

The dances from *Marriage à la Mode* were announced for the repertory of the Ballet Club but never actually given there, presumably because it was felt that they were essentially incidental to the play, but they served the useful purpose of giving the dancers employment for a while and the important one of initiating Ashton's collaboration with Markova.

Chapter Three
1930-1931

In the meantime, Ashton was making a major contribution to a project that was to play a significant role in the development of British ballet. The Camargo Society had been formed as a result of a conversation between Haskell and P J S Richardson, editor of the Dancing Times, over lunch one day at a restaurant called Chez Taglioni, in October 1929. They agreed that a society should be formed 'for the production of ballet'; in part they wished to make some attempt to fill the gap left by the death of Diaghilev and the disbanding of his company, in part to further the growth of a native, British ballet by the encouragement of British choreographers and dancers. There were a few informal dinners at which the matter was discussed further with such people as Ninette de Valois, Grace Lovat Fraser and Edwin Evans, committees were elected and a name decided on. A formal inaugural dinner was held on Sunday 16 February 1930, with Adeline Genée in the chair. Lydia Lopokova was named Choreographic Director, Haskell Art Director and Edwin Evans Musical Director, each of whom headed a sub-committee dealing with one of the component arts of ballet. Ashton (who, noted the Daily Sketch, reporting on the dinner, 'is said to be Nijinsky's successor') was on the committee on Dancing, together with Rambert and de Valois, Karsavina and Astafieva, Margaret Craske, Dolin and Anna Ludmila. George Balanchine, who was working in London at the time, was at the dinner, and so was Boris Kochno.

Subscribers were to pay from one to four guineas a year, for which they would see four performances. The list of subscribers was an imposing one, including not only many dancers but also many people from fashionable and intellectual society, such as Anthony Asquith, Lord Berners, Kenneth Clark, Samuel Courtauld, Lady Cunard, Lady Juliet Duff, A P Herbert, Augustus John, Edward Marsh, Lady Ottoline Morrell, the Countess of Oxford and Asquith, Anthony Powell, Vita Sackville-West, Siegfried Sassoon, Osbert Sitwell, Lytton Strachey, H G Wells, Rebecca West, and Leonard and Virginia Woolf. There was an important connection between the ballet world and that of Bloomsbury – most notably, Lopokova was the wife of the economist John Maynard Keynes, who became the Society's treasurer, and with the secretary, M Montagu-Nathan, its chief support.

At the inaugural dinner Mme Genée had proposed that a silent tribute be paid to the memory of Diaghilev, and although it was realised that the Camargo Society could not alone take the place of his company, a conscious effort was made to continue its traditions in such matters as the quality of artistic collaboration. Décors were commissioned from important painters, as well as drop-curtains to be displayed during the playing of musical interludes, also a Diaghilev practice. For example, the American-born poster artist E McKnight Kauffer, who later designed *Checkmate* for de Valois, did one for William Walton's 'Portsmouth Point' overture, and William Roberts painted a curtain called *The Rehearsal* for the suite from Constant Lambert's ballet *Romeo and Juliet* (which had been produced by Diaghilev).

The first performance of the Camargo Society took place ten days after the opening of *Marriage à la Mode*, on a Sunday evening, 19 October 1930, and included, as was also proposed in the Society's policy, a 'period revival' (the ballet scene from Meyerbeer's *Robert le Diable*) as well as new dance works: a comedy number by Penelope Spencer called *A Toothsome Morsel* (Scenes from a Dentist's Waiting-Room), Ninette de Valois's choreography for Debussy's *Danses sacrée et profane*, a *Dance-Suite* by Amy Boalth, a *Finale: Variations and Coda* arranged by Nicholas Legat to music by Glinka, danced by de Valois, Dolin and company, and a new ballet commissioned from Ashton, *Pomona*.

The score of *Pomona*, originally in the form of a Divertimento in seven movements, had been composed by Constant Lambert in 1926 (the same year as *Romeo and Juliet*). For the ballet a Passacaglia from *Adam and Eve*, an earlier ballet score, was added, and the first movement, Intrata, was a piece called *Champêtre* (itself an orchestration of Lambert's *Pastorale* for piano). Its first presentation as a ballet was at the Teatro Colón, Buenos Aires, on 9 September 1927, with choreography by Nijinska; it was also announced for inclusion in Dolin's season at the Théâtre des Champs-Elysées in Paris, which opened on 31 March 1928, but was apparently not given at that time (no choreographer was named).

The story of the ballet, by Thomas McGreevy, told of the courtship of Pomona, Goddess of Fruits (Anna Ludmila), by Vertumnus (Anton Dolin), a theme that afforded the pretext not only for dances in the neo-classical mode, but for some fairly broad comedy as well, when Dolin at one point appeared *en travesti*.†

There is no doubt that the success of the first Camargo Society performance was almost entirely due to *Pomona*. During the evening Lydia Lopokova made a speech in which she informed the audience that they were assisting at the birth of British ballet, a statement that ignored all the previous manifestations that could be said to represent at least the labour-pangs of such an event, some of which have been mentioned in these pages. All the same, the Camargo performance gave further confirmation that Ashton had now to be taken seriously. As 'Sitter-Out'

† For a detailed synopsis, see Appendix B.

wrote in the Dancing Times – the sobriquet disguised the identity of the editor, P J S Richardson – 'that hitherto mythical personage, a British choreographist of the first rank, is amongst us', an accolade qualified by the criticism that 'he introduces movements and poses very reminiscent of some of the bizarre postures of the late Diaghilev productions'. Nevertheless, the review continued by saying that his choreography 'with its strong sense of design in his groupings, and its brilliant *pas de deux*, . . . truly interprets the score. . . I was particularly delighted with some contrapuntal effects towards the close when the corps de ballet at the back moved to a slower rhythm than . . . the soloists in front'.[1] (Some years later, when *Pomona* was performed in Paris by the Vic-Wells Ballet, Ashton was sitting in a box with Kchessinska, who said to him, 'Comme je voudrais être jeune pour danser ce pas de deux.')

His achievement was even more enthusiastically endorsed by Arnold Haskell, who called *Pomona* 'glorious'. It was, he said, 'a modern conception of a classical subject, without any sacrifice of classical feeling. Ashton has discovered new movements for the human body, without ever resorting to "*truquage*" or distortion. Unlike many modern inventions in ballet Pomona is a role of deep emotional significance. Pomona's human couch and the final triumphal path are not the least of his discoveries here'.[2] (As Ashton says, 'In those days we were all doing human couches and boats and things.')

Haskell's reviews of the ballet in the December 1930 and April 1931 Dancing Times make it clear that in *Pomona* Ashton already gave evidence of another gift

Group from *Pomona*:
Anton Dolin and
Anna Ludmila at rig

that was to become a very important factor in his later works, an ability to discern the special talents and qualities of his dancers, especially the women, and to bring them out and enhance them. Ashton had had the opportunity to observe Anna Ludmila's work both in the Ida Rubinstein company and with Dolin at the Coliseum, and now this observation bore fruit. While at the Coliseum, Ludmila had torn her Achilles tendon, and Ashton arranged the choreography of *Pomona* to favour her injured foot (which did not, however, heal properly, causing her to retire early from dancing, though she has continued to teach and choreograph in Panama and the United States). 'Anna Ludmila,' wrote Haskell, 'has more than fulfilled all that I have always thought about her . . . She is as much an actress as a dancer should be, able to an extraordinary degree to feel and to suggest atmosphere. Frederick Ashton has understood her admirably, and at last she is presented as she should be.' And again, 'Ashton, who has admired and studied her work ever since her arrival in Europe, built the role round her personality and so created a work of art. I can conceive of other Pomonas, but I shall always remember Ludmila's. It belongs to her as truly as the role in *Biches* was Nemchinova's.' Ashton felt the same way: he wrote to Ludmila to express his delight that she would be available for a later performance: 'For me you are the only Pomona.'

The décor had originally been commissioned from Augustus John, but he was unable to carry it out, and it was designed instead by the Bloomsbury painter John Banting. His setting did not please Beaumont, who said it was 'in the sketchy manner affected by the Braque school'. According to the Dancing Times, it depicted 'fleecy clouds, shady trees, and amusing but anatomically impossible classic statues'.

Ashton's next assignment was to stage incidental dances and two short ballets for an entertainment called *A Masque of Poetry and Music*, subtitled 'Beauty, Truth and Rarity', presented by Arnold Haskell at the Arts Theatre Club. The main purpose of the evening seems to have been to display the diverse talents of Lydia Lopokova, who played in an adaptation of Shakespeare's *A Lover's Complaint* and excerpts from Milton's *Comus*, with a supporting cast that included George Rylands (who was also the director), Michael Redgrave, Robert Eddison and Geoffrey Toone. Ashton arranged the dance that concluded *Comus*, to music by Purcell, and two ballets, *'Follow Your Saint'* and *Dances on a Scotch Theme*, in which he and Harold Turner danced with Lopokova. The programme was given at the Arts from 10 to 16 December 1930.

The musical director was Constant Lambert; the original announcement of the programme in the Dancing Times stated that one of the ballets would be to music by Liszt, and it would be interesting to know what music Lambert and Ashton thought of using, since that composer had an important place in their later collaborations, but Ashton has forgotten. *'Follow Your Saint'*, subtitled *The Passionate Pavane*, was danced to music taken from John Dowland's *Lacrymae, or*

47

Seven Teares, figured in seven passionate Pavans, which had become known through a transcription by Peter Warlock; Lambert's arrangement was for small orchestra. The title of the ballet was taken from a poem by Thomas Campion, quoted in the programme as an epigraph:

> Follow your saint, follow with accents sweet!
> Haste you, sad notes, fall at her flying feet!
> There, wrapt in cloud of sorrow, pity move,
> And tell the ravisher of my soul I perish for her love:
> But if she scorns my never-ceasing pain,
> Then burst with sighing in her sight and ne'er return again!

Again, Ashton was praised for bringing out the dancer's personal qualities – 'the very essence of Lopokova's unique charm', one reviewer said. The piece was a series of more or less formal dances, solos, duets and trios, with those not dancing taking up poses at one side; to some extent it was an extension of the idea of the Pavane in *Capriol Suite*, with the important difference that Lopokova danced on point. *Passionate Pavane* was revived by the Ballet Rambert in 1936, when The Times wrote that the dances were 'modern commentaries on the ancient forms . . . Mr Ashton has a happy knack of borrowing just as much of classical technique as he wants, and using *arabesques* and *pointes* not as ends in themselves but as subservient to the style he has in hand at the moment. He further has a surer perception than some choreographers of the style required by the music which he chooses . . . Dowland's *Lachrymae* was a bold choice, yet he caught its English note and its gentle formalism, and so added yet one more to the repertory of miniatures which is growing naturally out of the conditions of the Ballet Club's work'.[3] The critic of The Daily Telegraph said that the ballet 'conveys the melancholy of the music in a kind of desperate gaiety. . . The dancing line is flowing, and the grouping emerges naturally out of the movement of the performers, so that the dances appear to flower from the sad and lovely airs.'

In complete contrast were the merry *Dances on a Scotch Theme*, to selections from the symphonies of William Boyce, another of Lambert's enthusiasms (he later arranged the score of de Valois's *The Prospect Before Us* from the same source). *Dances on a Scotch Theme* went into the repertory of the Ballet Club shortly afterwards – where it was more often given under the title *The Tartans* – and became a great favourite. Lopokova's part was taken by Markova, who describes the ballet as 'hilarious' – she wore a Scottish costume with flat shoes and 'a huge busby thing' that made it difficult to maintain her balance: 'On certain steps I would almost topple over, the antics that went on with the three of us, people used to be doubled up.' She also recalls that at the end of her solo she abruptly sat down on the floor of the stage.

❋

'*Follow Your Saint*': Harold Turner, Ashton and Lydia Lopokova

Group from
A Florentine Picture:
Rambert as the
Madonna, centre, with
Angels (Maude Lloyd
directly behind her,
Pearl Argyle kneeling
on her right; also
Elisabeth Schooling,
Prudence Hyman,
Andrée Howard and
Diana Gould)

The Dancing Times for December 1930 proclaimed the year that was coming to a close an *annus mirabilis* in the development of British ballet, for in addition to the formation of the Camargo Society and the first season of the Marie Rambert Dancers, the year had seen the establishment of the Vic-Wells Ballet as a permanent organisation and also the foundation of the Ballet Club by Rambert, Haskell and Ashley Dukes. They felt that the Marie Rambert Dancers, or Ballet Rambert, as the company came to be called, needed a permanent home and that their growing audience should have the opportunity to see regular performances. Ashton wanted to call it the Capriol Club, after the ballet that had consolidated his own position and that of the company as professionals to be taken seriously, but it was felt that this sounded too much like Camargo, and so they decided on something that was simpler and more to the point.

A prospectus had gone out, stating that the new theatre (it was the remodelled church hall adjoining Rambert's studio in Ladbroke Road) would be 'the only Repertory Theatre entirely devoted to ballet in the world'. There would be four seasons of three weeks each year, plus special recitals. The theatre would seat less than 200 people; the stage was tiny but boasted a cyclorama and 'very modern lighting'. Membership cost ten shillings a year. It was emphasised that the new organisation was not in competition with the Camargo Society – rather, their activities would 'dovetail'.

The December Dancing Times announced that the first performance would take place on 12 January 1931, with a programme including a series of 'Diaghilev Memories' with choreography by Petipa, Fokine and Massine, and a new ballet, *The Rape of the Lock*, with music specially composed by Anthony Bernard, but no choreographer mentioned. In the meantime, the Rambert Dancers gave another short season at the Lyric Theatre, Hammersmith, three weeks this time, over the Christmas holidays. Karsavina was again guest artist, joined by Woizikovsky, and they revived and danced in Fokine's *Le Carnaval*, with Ashton as Eusebius.

Ashton also choreographed a new ballet suitable for the season, *A Florentine Picture*, to music by Corelli, first given on 20 December. There had been a great exhibition of Italian painting at the Royal Academy that year, which Kenneth Clark had helped to organise. Ashton had seen it, and took his groupings (the subtitle of the piece was 'Groupings by Frederick Ashton') from those in some of the Florentine paintings. The Times critic spoke of the 'dissolving groups of six angels'[4] and Punch of their 'celestial patterns'.[5] At times the angels leaned out from the wings so that only their upper bodies were seen, and the emphasis was all on their gestures. A dissenting voice was the critic of the Nation, who said the piece was 'conceived on a wrong principle, [showing] just that tendency to "arti-ness" which is a menace to the future of Ballet in this country'.[6]

According to Mary Clarke, the dancers hated *A Florentine Picture* and called it 'Flossie',[7] but it was popular with the audience and remained in the repertory for some years, with Diana Gould, Maude Lloyd and Peggy van Praagh all taking Rambert's role of the Madonna. As usual, the production was done on the cheap: Rambert's costume from her early dance *Pomme d'or* again did duty for the Madonna, as it had in *Our Lady's Juggler*, and the angels' costumes, Ashton says, were made from some of her old curtains, which she dyed in the bathtub herself.

On 25 January 1931 the Camargo Society gave its second performance: Ashton's contribution was *Capriol Suite*, as it had been given at the Lyric. He also danced in a work by Ninette de Valois, *Rout*, to music of Arthur Bliss. Oddly enough, Dame Ninette now says that there were no men in *Rout*, which may have been the case when it was first done at her studio in 1928 and later at the Abbey Theatre in Dublin, but it seems to have been rearranged for the Camargo Society and Ashton's name is certainly in the programme. Like much of de Valois's work at this period, it had a strong Central European flavour, with movements 'based on those of fly-wheels and piston-rods, synchronised with the music, the rhythm being emphasized by the beating of the dancers' feet'[8] – the latter element was very troublesome for Ashton, in spite of his experience of dancing to counts with Nijinska.

The date originally announced for the opening of the Ballet Club proved to be somewhat optimistic, and the first performance actually took place a month later, on 16 February 1931. The repertory for the inaugural programmes included *Carnaval* and *Les Sylphides* (with Ashton), and Dances from *Aurora's Wedding*, including Nijinska's version of the *pas de trois* of Florestan and his Sisters, which was danced by Ashton with Pearl Argyle and Andrée Howard. One of the many ways in which Rambert was a pioneer was in her recognition of the importance of Petipa at a time when even Balanchine found his conventions 'intolerable'[9]: before the opening of the Ballet Club she had given a lecture on Petipa, illustrated by excerpts from his ballets danced by her pupils, at which she spoke of the revelation of dancing for its own sake afforded by his works. It was only later, when he was exposed to those works in their entirety as performed by the Vic-Wells Ballet, that Ashton was consciously influenced by the master, but Rambert's untiring advocacy must have had its effect on Ashton no less than the other ways in which she, as he later said, 'cultivated' him.

The Rape of the Lock did not materialise until several years later (1935), when it was choreographed by Andrée Howard to Haydn's 'Clock' Symphony, but the first programme did include yet another new Ashton ballet, *La Péri*, to the music of Dukas. Once again Ashton was inspired by the pictures in an exhibition at Burlington House, this time of Persian painting. Horace Horsnell described the ballet as 'an engaging pseudo-Persian affair of posing peris, faint-tinkling sequins and heavenly vapours', in which Markova 'danced divinely'.[10]

Encouraged by the success of their collaboration in *Marriage à la Mode* Ashton suggested to Markova that she might like to come and work at the Ballet Club. She was delighted, since the death of Diaghilev had left her without a permanent company in which to dance, and was moreover excited at the thought of being part of a lively new project. Certainly she did not take the job for the money – 'Fred and I,' she remembers, 'had the top salary, ten shillings and sixpence a performance!'

According to her, Ashton looked at her one day and said, '*La Péri*, Persian, come along, we're going to the exhibition,' and together they studied the pictures to get ideas for both movement and make-up. They drew their eyebrows in a straight line across, and Markova had purple nail-varnish specially made. The Péri was the first of many important roles he was to make for her, 'an inhuman figure,' Haskell wrote, 'whose very charm lies in mystery and distance'.[11] The groupings for the little corps of six Companions, while no doubt also derived in part from the paintings, showed the strong influence of Nijinska.

Even at the top salary, Ashton and Markova could not live on what they made at the Club, and had to look for other, more gainful employment. On 9 March Ashton gave the first of six performances in the *Scène de ballet* in Gounod's *Faust* at the Old Vic and Sadler's Wells, partnering Ninette de Valois in her own choreography. Many years later, Ashton wrote, 'I imagine I must have been a pretty rickety partner; but in those days male dancers were scarce and I dare say she was grateful for me to lift her even a mere inch off the floor'.[12]

He was also recommended to the producer of the stage shows at a new super-cinema at Marble Arch, the Regal, where an attempt was being made to combine films with spectacular shows in the style of the Roxy in New York. A new show was put on every week or two, with titles like *Festival Russe, The Dance Through the Ages* and one originally advertised as *Gypsy Love*, hurriedly changed the next day to *Gypsy Life*. Ashton was engaged to do a ballet that would run for three weeks, three times a day, to the *Dance of the Hours* from Ponchielli's opera *Gioconda* (it shared the bill at first with the film version of Sutton Vane's *Outward Bound*), and brought in Markova and William Chappell, who also did the costumes, to dance in it, with a corps de ballet of thirty-two girls. Markova's salary was £20 a week. She remembers coming down on a crescent moon, as the Spirit of the Night.

The ballet was a big success, and the producers asked her to stay on for two more shows. She insisted that Ashton should again choreograph her numbers. The next show was *Cabaret français* – this title notwithstanding, Markova recalls that she was the fox in a hunting scene, being chased by hounds which according to Anton Dolin were real.[13] 'To tell you the truth,' she says, 'I hated it – I used to come off black and blue, I was in tights all over with a tail and a headdress with little ears, and Fred gave me a lot of *pirouettes*, I used to *chaîné* with the hounds after me right across the stage, and all sorts of things down on the knees, almost acrobatic; Freddie was able to experiment on all kinds of things with me because I never said no, and it had to be spectacular for that kind of audience.'

This second show ran for two weeks; the third consisted of excerpts from the *Faust* ballet. Unlike de Valois's version which he had recently danced in, this was a

Group from *La Péri*: Markova as the Péri, Ashton as Iskender, centre; with Companions, from left to right, Andrée Howard ?, Elisabeth Schooling, Pearl Argyle, Maude Lloyd, Suzette Morfield, Betty Cuff

spectacular ballet, again with a corps of thirty-two: 'The whole thing was done in white, and all the corps came up on elevators out of the floor, and I came on in a short tutu and did a beautiful variation Fred did for me, very spectacular, it used to bring the house down.' This also ran for two weeks, and concluded Markova's engagement at the Regal. The schedule was gruelling, with early morning rehearsals at the Regal as well as performances, between or after which Markova was often dancing at the Ballet Club. Indeed, two days after the *Faust* ballet went on the Adagio from the second act of *Swan Lake* was added to the programme at the Ballet Club, with Markova as Odette and Ashton as Siegfried. (Dolin paid Ashton the compliment of saying that he preferred to see Ashton in this role to many better dancers – 'He has used his knowledge of line so cleverly. I have often watched him partnering, but never have I seen a bad line of arms or body'.[14])

Rehearsals were also going on for the next performance of the Camargo Society, the third, which took place on 26 April 1931 (before Markova had finished at the Regal – but the Camargo Society performance was on a Sunday, her day off). The programme included the première of another new Ashton ballet, *Façade*. This had been announced as early as the previous December, in the programme of the Masque at the Arts Theatre Club. Ashton had heard a performance of the 'Entertainment' *Façade*, with Edith Sitwell and Constant Lambert reciting her poems to the music of William Walton, either at the Chenil Galleries in Chelsea or in Paris a couple of years earlier, and asked Lambert to get Walton's permission to use the music for a ballet. Walton was willing, but Edith Sitwell refused to have anything to do with it – otherwise, Ashton now says, he might have choreographed it from the beginning to the original version of the music instead of to the orchestral suite. The programme at the first performance carried a note rather elaborately disclaiming any connection with the poems. When Ashton later went to stay with Osbert Sitwell at Renishaw Edith was rather unpleasant to him, and it turned out that the reason was that she regretted her refusal to collaborate, and wished to be associated with the ballet after all. After the ballet was revived at Sadler's Wells a subtitle was added to indicate the music's origin.†

An earlier ballet to Walton's music, with choreography by Günter Hess, had been presented in 1929 by the German Chamber Dance Theatre in Hagen, Westphalia. Hess visited London the following winter and was said in the Dancing Times to have met and 'exchanged ideas' with Ashton, who in fact took little or nothing from Hess's conception, which had a complicated scenario loaded with social significance. Ashton's ballet was, as the original programme stated, a divertissement satirising various kinds of folk, social and theatrical dance. No doubt at the time of its creation he would have been surprised to be told that it would prove to be one of the most durable of his ballets, and that it does survive is surely due not to the kind of performances it gets – usually quite crude – but to the fact that the dances are very well made and witty in themselves.

† In 1972 the Royal Ballet New Group briefly tried the experiment of performing *Façade* with the music in its original version for chamber ensemble and narrator (Peter Pears).

Façade: Markova in the Polka

The Scotch Rhapsody, for instance, manages to burlesque not only Highland dancing but also the classic *pas de trois*, as in the moment when the man lifts his two partners and they collide in the air in front of him. The Polka, in which the dancer enters, removes her skirt and performs a cheekily insouciant solo in her underwear, is a brilliant variation, ending – as originally danced by Markova – with a *double tour en l'air*, an unusual step for a woman to perform. In its first form the Waltz focused more on the patterns made by the dancers' arms and legs than on the vacuity of the girls' expressions, as nowadays. (Ashton has said that the idea was actually a parody of 'those groups of girls that there used to be at that time, the Hoffman Girls and all that sort of thing'.[15]) Although the 'smelly feet' joke of the Yodelling Song may embarrass one by the schoolboy level of its humour, the one about milking the cow, with the udder made by the hands of one of the men and the tail by the arm of another, can still raise a laugh by its ingenuity. The Popular Song remains the absolute epitome of all dead-pan music-hall soft-shoe double acts, and the Tango, in which a gigolo, clearly bent on seduction, instructs a Debutante, who is not quite sure what is happening to her, used to be funnier when its comedy was more subtle and its social comment slyer.

Façade: Alicia Markova and Ashton in the Tango, Ballet Club production

Façade: Lydia Lopokova and Ashton in the Tango, Camargo Society production ▷

One has come to suppose that the general tendency to broaden the humour is of a later origin than the first performance – a 1944 review in the Dancing Times said that Ashton had managed to be 'flamboyant, yet distingué' in the Tango while, 'As danced by Helpmann today it is merely a display of flaming eyes and cheap tricks, designed to get easy laughs.' Yet even at the first performance several critics found that Lopokova's portrayal of the Debutante verged on low comedy, though they agreed that she was enchanting as the Milkmaid. Beaumont was particularly disapproving and said that it was the kind of thing better left to Nervo and Knox.[16] The censure was not universal – the Manchester Guardian critic said of Lopokova, 'No other dancer has ever been able to assume for comic ends an expression quite so vacant, like a doll in a dream, and to belie it so richly by the subtlety of her dancing.'

The ballet was a great audience-pleaser and further established Ashton as a choreographer to be reckoned with. It was taken immediately into the repertory of the Ballet Club – indeed, Rambert had paid for the costumes for the Camargo production (£40) and in return acquired the rights to it; Ashton's fee for the choreography was £5. The original cast were all Ballet Club dancers, except for Lopokova. The question was, who would take her place in the Tango? 'Fred was going round like this,' Markova says, making that characteristic Ashton fists-to-temples gesture, 'and suddenly he said to me, Why don't you do it? I said, I couldn't possibly be Lopokova, I would have to do it my own way, and he said, I think that'll be marvellous, let's try it.' Certainly the Polka was tailor-made for her needle-sharp technique and her wit.

John Armstrong's set incorporated references to some of the numbers in the ballet. It showed the front of a Swiss chalet in pale grey and blue, with a Dutch door on which was painted the figure of a young woman dressed like the Polka dancer (Ashton used to make great play with this in the Finale, standing behind it and opening first the top, then the bottom half). Above the door were drawn, in white outline, male and female nudes, with arms linked. On one wing there was a pier on which a cow stood gazing out to sea.

On the same Camargo Society programme with *Façade*, two other Ashton ballets were given, *Mars and Venus* and '*Follow Your Saint*', as well as an important new ballet by de Valois, her version of Milhaud's *La Création du monde*, and a short piece by Karsavina to Glinka's *Valse-Fantaisie*, in which she was partnered by Ashton. The theme was a reversal of that of *Le Spectre de la rose* – a young man (Ashton) dreamed of dancing with his beloved (Karsavina) at a ball.† The Manchester Guardian commented that Ashton 'had never danced better'. He again partnered Karsavina when the Rambert Dancers gave another 'short summer season' at the Lyric, opening on the 15 June. This time he danced with her in *Les*

† It may have been the memory of this ballet that prompted Lambert to choose the Glinka piece as a prelude to *Spectre* when it was revived by Karsavina for the Sadler's Wells Ballet in 1944.

Sylphides, which he had already danced at the Ballet Club, and in a new ballet by Susan Salaman, *Waterloo and Crimea*, in which Woizikovsky also danced. The ballet was short-lived (although its theme, from a poem by Thomas Hardy, was used again by Walter Gore in an early ballet, *Cap Over Mill*) – its choreographer lacked the authority and experience to be able to make dances for such distinguished guest artists. *Les Sylphides* was another matter: Ashton again learned a great deal from Karsavina, who gave him a real understanding of its style and taught him the choreography in its correct, original form, without such corrupt later accretions as the *danseur*'s stroking of his leg in *développé* front instead of the simple *posé*, in his Mazurka.

Ashton has written of this experience: 'I remember my alarm at being allowed to touch her, let alone partner her, knowing that she had danced with all the great of her generation. Her attitude towards me was one of complete patience and encouragement, nevertheless demanding my absolute dedication and understanding of the technicalities of the roles. They were days of inspiration and absorption on my part, and the knowledge I acquired of the real meaning of dancing was invaluable for my future work. I drenched myself in her presence – I learnt the meaning of gesture, "nuance", the drama of movement inherent in the dance – and, watching her performance, the immense importance of the *"épaulement"*, now almost a lost aspect in most dancers. . . Karsavina on stage was a queen: her beauty, radiance and charm filled the theatre: her gesture extended its very walls – a great and unique dancer with an immense range of interpretation (the Duse of the dance)'.[17] He danced *Les Sylphides* many times afterwards at the Ballet Club and Sadler's Wells – in fact, he partnered Fonteyn in it at both theatres. One of the greatest compliments he has ever been paid, he considers, came from Anna Pruzina, a Russian teacher who gave company classes at the Wells during the mid-30s: she said of Ashton in this ballet, 'I must say he didn't absolutely ruin it.' Many years later he rehearsed the Royal Ballet when he felt they had lost the feeling for it, and gave them the benefit of what he had learned from Karsavina.

For the Lyric season Ashton also made a new ballet for Karsavina, which went on in the second week, a version of Erik Satie's *Mercury*, originally composed for Massine in 1924. 'Alas,' he wrote, 'I was young, and in awe of my privilege, and could hardly have done justice to her great qualities as a ballerina, but she was divine and beautiful as Venus: she greatly furthered my career by her trust and encouragement'.[18] Ashton devised his own synopsis, which was not printed in the programme at the first performance, but added later: 'Venus flees from Mars, borne by Apollo. Mars sends Mercury to intercept their love, and the messenger of the gods bears Venus away. Apollo, lamenting, is consoled by the Graces, and Mercury comes back to mock at him. Now Venus returns to seek Apollo, but finds Mercury too, and the dance ends in joyous abandon.' It will be seen that this was more a pretext for some dances than an authentic piece of mythology, and when Markova took over the role Ashton cheerfully substituted Terpsichore for

Venus in the argument when she protested that she was 'no beauty' and could not appear as Venus.

Once again, *Mercury* seems to have been an exercise in the late Diaghilev mode, and as such irritated Beaumont, who complained that 'there was not so much dancing in it as poses and arm movements', while admitting that some of these were 'pleasing'. 'The solo Mr Ashton had arranged for himself was most disappointing,' he went on, 'for his imagination did not seem to rise beyond a pose *en attitude* after Bologna's statue. And why on earth should Mercury wear a white jacket and tight-fitting trousers which suggested an attendant at a cocktail-bar or a *comique* out of a Montmartre revue!'[19]. The answer may have been Ashton's awareness of a physique not exactly that of a Greek god, with very thin legs – his mother, once she became resigned to her son's choice of career, used to say, 'If you want to find Fred, look for a pair of insteps and two profiles stuck together.' But he was, he says, 'very fleet' if nothing else, and covered a lot of space as he rushed about the stage.

Agnes de Mille vividly describes a fragment of *Mercury* in rehearsal at the Ballet Club: 'There were four or five of Mim's "lumpy, woolly" girls on the floor of the stage undulating, lifting, settling arms and legs. "It is the Adriatic," said Mim. "It is *Mercure* by Ashton." And by God, it was the Adriatic. "Watch," said Mim. "Venus will rise from the sea." And Venus did, in a yard-square space. Venus was Alicia Markova, the stringiest girl I ever saw, a darling little skeleton, with the great eyes of a moth at the top, and a butterfly blur at the bottom where normally feet would be, and in between shocks and flashes of electricity. When she paused there was the most beautifully surprising line I had ever looked at'.[20] (This would have been in 1933, after Markova had danced it both at the Ballet Club and the Camargo Society, with the change of nomenclature, but suggests that Ashton saw no inconsistency in having Terpsichore rise, like Venus, out of the sea. Just to add to the confusion, when Diana Gould danced it at the Ballet Club on 12 November 1931, she was called Venus, not inappropriately, but when it was danced there by Pearl Argyle, who of all dancers was best endowed to be the goddess of beauty, the role was still called Terpsichore.)

Haskell continued to champion Ashton and called *Mercury* 'in many ways his finest achievement. It is a perfect interpretation of Satie's music, flippant, laughing at itself, but often, and in the least expected places, strangely beautiful'.[21] In general, the ballet got a bad press: P J S Richardson said that 'even the artistry of Karsavina could not raise it above the mediocre. A striking exception, however, is the really brilliant entry and dance arranged for Mercury himself, which appealed to me as one of the best bits of detail Ashton has either arranged or danced'.[22] Many years later Karsavina wrote in a tribute to Rambert that 'Freddie Ashton in these early days already foreshadowed his talent for imagination and logical fluency of choreographic theme'.[23]

During the season at the Lyric many of the Rambert Dancers were also working in a film for which Ashton did the choreography, *Dance Pretty Lady*, directed by Anthony Asquith from his own screen-play based on the novel *Carnival* by Compton Mackenzie. It is a romantic film of great charm and lyricism that deserves to be better known. The rather novelettish story – about a ballet-dancer in the London music-halls of the Edwardian era, who falls in love with an aristocratic young artist – is handled with such delicacy of feeling that it never becomes sentimental. The photography is exquisite (the lighting cameraman was Jack Parker): the opening shots of the heroine as a child, dancing in the street to the music of a barrel-organ, are reminiscent of the work of such Victorian photographers as Paul Martin, and later there are backstage scenes with Degas-like compositions of ballet-skirts hanging on racks (and a dresser in black with a white apron), and a scene in a restaurant that also recalls Degas or Lautrec.

There were two ballet sequences, which were shot at night at the old Metropolitan music-hall in the Edgware Road. The first is a very funny patriotic music-hall number with Britannia seated upstage and a chorus-line in military uniform doing high-kicks in various formations. At one point four girls dressed as mermaids come forward doing something like the Dance of the Little Swans. In the finale, festoons of Union Jacks descend from the flies.

The other ballet plays a crucial part in the story and also in the poetic handling of it – a brief pastiche of *Les Sylphides* danced to the Prelude to Act II of *Swan Lake* (later another fragment is danced to part of the Valse des fleurs from *The Nutcracker*). Anthony Asquith has described this sequence and its editing in an article on 'Ballet and the Film':

> The dramatic point of the scene was that at the end of the number the heroine, who is a member of the *corps de ballet*, and the hero, who is sitting in the stage box, see each other for the first time and fall in love. For this reason I did not use any close-ups until that moment, for a close-up is the most emphatic kind of shot there is. The ballet scene itself was purely lyrical, and my object was to translate it into film terms. . . It was a kind of metaphor preparing us by anticipation for the love of the two main characters. I therefore treated it quite straightforwardly as a ballet scene, but in a way only possible in sound film.[24]

Chapter Four

1931–1933

One of the legacies of the Diaghilev company, in England at any rate, was a fairly large popular audience for ballet. In the second decade of its existence, especially, the company had frequently performed as part of the regular music-hall bill at the London Coliseum, and although balletomanes formed the habit of dropping in for that part of the programme only, one must assume that such engagements would not have been as frequent or extensive if the public at large had not also continued to attend.

The Ballet Club and the Camargo Society, by their very nature, were able to satisfy only a small part of the ballet audience, and that part was drawn on the whole from the ranks of society and the intelligentsia. It was not until the advent of the de Basil company in 1933 that the general public once more attended ballet performances in large numbers, attracted by the publicity given to the 'baby ballerinas', Baronova and Toumanova, and by the many revivals of standard ballets from the Diaghilev repertory. In the meantime, however, a public that would never have dreamed of going to the Russian Ballet in the old days was being built up in very unfashionable surroundings by the Vic-Wells Ballet, the company that grew out of a small group of students from Ninette de Valois's Academy of Choreographic Art, originally engaged by Lilian Baylis to provide incidental dances in plays and operas at the Old Vic and Sadler's Wells.

Baylis had followed in the footsteps of her aunt, Emma Cons, who had leased the Old Vic, originally the Victoria Theatre, in a working-class district south of the Thames, and reopened it as the Royal Victoria Coffee Music Hall, a strictly temperance institution, in 1888. When Baylis took over the management she gradually extended the entertainment offered there (and, from 1931, at Sadler's Wells) to include drama, especially Shakespeare, and opera, but although the productions were of a much higher quality than anything the Vic had aspired to in her aunt's day, 'Art, for Lilian Baylis, was from her childhood inextricably entangled with good works and social service, a kind of medicine dispensed to the poor and needy'.[1] She was never concerned to attract a fashionable audience, though she suffered their attendance because they paid to sit in the more expensive seats; much more important to her were the less well-off, especially the people from the neighbourhood, who sat in the pit and gallery for less than it costs to buy a programme in London theatres today.

It was not long before de Valois was able to persuade this formidable woman that she should be bringing ballet to her audiences as well, and occasional evenings of ballet began to be given at both theatres, with the resident group of dancers augmented by guest artists like Markova, Lopokova and Dolin, as well as less celebrated male dancers such as Ashton, who were in demand because at that time they were in short supply.

Both the Vic-Wells and the Ballet Club produced their ballets on a shoestring, but while Rambert's always looked elegant, those at the Wells were often painfully dowdy. But it was not for nothing that de Valois, like Rambert, had been a member of the Diaghilev company. Rambert may have had a more profound understanding of Diaghilev's artistic principles, but de Valois gained a more complete knowledge of how to run a company. Rambert always lost the artists she developed because she could afford to pay them so little and because inevitably they wanted the wider scope offered their gifts by larger companies. De Valois's great strength lay in her vision of what British ballet could become in five, ten, twenty years if plans were carefully laid and systematically carried out. Lilian Baylis was prepared to back her with such meagre financial resources as she could command – this was long before the days of generous public and private financial support for ballet companies, and Baylis had no compunction about browbeating her audiences in curtain speeches and exhorting them to attend as many performances as they could, bring their friends and 'pay for your seats, you bounders!'

So when de Valois invited Ashton to make a new ballet for her company at the beginning of the 1931–1932 season, the event had a significance beyond its intrinsic importance, and possibly de Valois knew it. The ballet, *Regatta*, with music by Gavin Gordon, was slight enough, in all conscience. First given on 22 September 1931, the ballet took place 'on board the steam yacht "Old Vic" off Cowes'. The cast included de Valois and, later, sometimes Ashton himself. Although the Times review said that the new ballet was derived from *Le Train bleu*,[2] it appears to have been a little heartier in its humour than that suggests. It featured such incidents as 'life-belt drills, deck flirtations, callisthenics and inevitable symptoms of *mal de mer*',[3] and the action culminated in a shipwreck and rescue. De Valois appeared as 'an orchidaceous foreign visitor' in high-heeled sandals, and the dances for the Three Yachting Girls (Freda Bamford, Sheila McCarthy and Joy Newton) made great use of the strong personalities, if not particularly strong technique, of the three dancers, though their graphic portrayal of the qualms of sea-sickness was a little much for some tastes.

Two days later the Marie Rambert Dancers opened another Short Season of Ballet, two and a half weeks, at the New Theatre this time, again with Karsavina and Woizikovsky as guest artists. It was so successful that Howard Wyndham and Bronson Albery, the managers of the theatre, booked the company into the

Regatta: At front, Ninette de Valois as A Foreign Visitor, with Walter Gore and William Chappell as Two Young Men; at rear, Freda Bamford, Sheila McCarthy and Joy Newton as Three Yachting Girls

Regatta: Ashton, right, rehearsing Stanley Judson, Ninette de Valois, Walter Gore (back row), William Chappell, Joy Newton, Sheila McCarthy, Freda Bamford (front row)

Palace Theatre, Manchester, for a week. Ashton made no new ballets for these engagements, but was preparing one that was given on the opening night of the Ballet Club's winter season on 12 November, together with Antony Tudor's first ballet, *Cross-Garter'd*, *Mercury* (with Diana Gould) and the second act of *Swan Lake* with Markova and Ashton. Ashton's work was based on Tennyson's poem *The Lady of Shalott*, which had been suggested as a subject by Ashley Dukes's sister Irene. Ashton himself devised the scenario, which reduced the characters and incidents of Tennyson's poem to terms that could be dealt with on the tiny stage of the Ballet Club. By this time he was learning to use its limited resources to the full. At the back of the stage there was a short flight of stairs, leading to a dressing-room; these stairs were already familiar to audiences from their use in *Le Boxing*, one of Susan Salaman's *Sporting Sketches*. In *The Lady of Shalott* they were used for the Reapers to make their exit, creeping up 'not daring to turn their backs on the haunted island'.[4]

For the mirror in which the Lady watches the 'shadows of the world', Ashton made use of a familiar device, a gauze stretched across the front of the stage, with Pearl Argyle on one side as the Lady and Maude Lloyd on the other as her Reflection, their movements being synchronised. At a rehearsal one day Argyle was sitting with her back to the audience, and Rambert suggested to Ashton that it would be better if they changed places so that Argyle's face would be seen, even though strictly speaking this reversal made her the reflection.

The ballet began with the Lady's spinning dance, then the Reapers entered: the Lady looked with longing at their carefree dance, but never entered into it. Two Lovers (Andrée Howard and Walter Gore) did a *pas de deux*, then Ashton appeared as Sir Lancelot, with a spear – his solo, the Dancing Times rather unkindly said, suggested the so-called 'Revived Greek' Dance, as taught by Ruby Ginner and Irene Mawer. With this one reservation, the reviewer called the ballet 'a little masterpiece': at the moment when

'Out flew the web and floated wide;
The mirror crack'd from side to side',

Pearl Argyle 'rose to heights I had never thought her capable of reaching'. The stage was in darkness for a few moments, and then came her drowning dance. A film exists of this very brief solo, from which one can see that Ashton used, perhaps for the first time, a kind of *plastique* that may have been derived from his memories of Isadora Duncan. There is a recurring rippling gesture of the fingers, to suggest the water streaming from her hair. At the end she falls to the floor, and the ballet closed with Sir Lancelot, the Lovers and the Reapers returning and gazing down at her body.

The Lady of Shalott was a success with both audience and critics – even Beaumont said it was Ashton's best so far, representing 'an overdue reaction from the Nijinska–Massine–Cocteau–Kochno influence'.[5] Haskell put it another way: 'his

Pre-Raphaelite *Lady of Shalott* is true English Romanticism, owing nothing to foreign influences'.[6] The ballet also revealed Ashton's growing sensitiveness in the use of music – the ballet was danced to a selection of piano pieces by Sibelius; a review of a later performance said: 'The choreographer's achievement may be judged by the almost irresistible impression one had that the music had been written for it'.[7]

In subsequent performances at the Club *Mars and Venus* returned to the repertory, as did the Dances from *Aurora's Wedding*, in which Argyle and Ashton led the *Grand Pas de sept*. At the end of the month came the first Camargo Society performance of the new season. In its October issue the Dancing Times announced that Ashton would present a new work to the *Two Suites for small orchestra* by Igor Stravinsky, but this idea was abandoned.

Instead, he did a ballet to Constant Lambert's choral work on a poem by Sacheverell Sitwell, *The Rio Grande*. Although the ballet was called by that title in the list of repertory, the programme was a little more ambiguous, reading as follows: '*Rio Grande*/Music by Constant Lambert/A setting of a Poem by Sacheverell Sitwell for Chorus, Orchestra and Solo Pianoforte/Produced as a Ballet entitled/*A Day in a Southern Port*/By Frederick Ashton'. It was given at the Savoy Theatre on 29 November, with Lydia Lopokova as the Queen of the Port and Markova as the Creole Girl; the principal male roles were taken by Walter Gore and William Chappell.

It is easy to see why Lambert's jazzy score appealed to Ashton: *The Lady of Shalott* did not by any means represent any permanent renunciation of modernism on his part, and the music also gave him an opportunity to express his nostalgia for the heat and languor of the tropical summers of his boyhood.

The Times review, which like most of the others condemned the piece with some vehemence, said that Ashton had 'so completely misunderstood the character of Constant Lambert's music that it is astonishing that he, Mr Lambert, the composer, can bear to stand up in front of this crude travesty and conduct it', but in fact Lambert himself had devised the scenario, which no doubt reflected among other things his attraction towards exotic women. For the Vic-Wells revival in 1935 he wrote a programme note stating that, 'The present production is not intended to be a literal interpretation of the words of the poem: the theme is suggested by the music.'

The ballet's depiction of the seamy side of life in a tropical seaport was too strong for many people at that time. Instead of treating the subject frivolously, as in an 'exotic' revue number, Ashton attempted to create a genuinely *louche* and erotic atmosphere.[8] It was not quite what people expected to see in a ballet, especially danced by classic ballerinas like Lopokova and Markova, supported by a corps de ballet of well-brought-up English girls, some of them barely out of their teens. And Edward Burra's décor and costumes were equally uncompromising: he was not given, in his paintings and drawings, to the sentimental portrayal of prostitutes, and Beaumont was shocked by the women's costumes, with their 'skin-tight

Rio Grande: Opening night group: left to right, Constant Lambert, Lydia Lopokova, Ashton, Edward Burra, Walter Gore (kneeling)

bodices, dresses about six inches long when seen from the front, bare thighs and stockinged legs'.[9]

Only a fortnight later the Camargo Society presented yet another new Ashton ballet, *The Lord of Burleigh*, in which he returned to the Tennysonian mode of *The Lady of Shalott*, though in a lighter vein. The synopsis for the ballet was devised by the music critic Edwin Evans, apparently after he had chosen the music.† Feeling that Mendelssohn's formal elegance was a neglected element in his work, he chose twenty-two numbers and arranged them in a sequence that was suitable from the point of view of key-signatures and the contrast of mood and rhythm, making a few cuts and actually writing one transitional bar himself. Casting around for a suitable theme, he hit on the idea of bringing together various personages from Tennyson's poems.

The plot was not exactly well developed, and the nature of the score Evans had put together more or less dictated that in form the ballet would be a series of divertissements. As Horace Horsnell put it, reviewing the 1937 revival at Sadler's Wells, the ballet 'takes these Tennysonian characters from several poems, and pairs or parts them with less regard for poetic justice than for the permutations of the dance',[10] something that resulted, we may assume, as much from Ashton's inclinations as from the vagueness of the synopsis.

† See Appendix B.

Rio Grande in rehearsal: Markova and William Chappell centre, with, left to right, Doris Sonne, Antony Tudor, Marie Nielson, Hedley Briggs, Sheila McCarthy, Travis Kemp, Ursula Moreton, unidentifiab[le]

As might be expected, most of the critics complained that what story there was disappeared as the ballet went on – only Haskell found this to be actually in the ballet's favour, noting with approval that Ashton 'had not been sidetracked into illustrating a scenario. . . In this way the dancing stood on its own merits, and to me, at any rate, there was a very close parallel with Tennyson'.[11] The ballet avoided the more pathetic overtones of the poems – it will be remembered that in the title poem the 'village maiden' was wooed by 'a landscape painter' who turns out, like Albrecht, to be a nobleman in disguise, the eponymous Lord, in fact. Unlike Albrecht, he reveals himself and marries the maiden, but she is unable to overcome the strain placed upon her by marrying out of her class, and eventually dies. Occasionally, however, Tennyson's comments on his characters are rather sly: for instance Lady Clara Vere de Vere 'slew' a suitor with her 'noble birth'. Ashton, as he reworked the ballet over the next few years, brought out the humorous side more and more.

It began with a tableau of the painter at his easel, surrounded by a group of young women, his models, in crinolines, pantalettes and bonnets. The costumes, in lemon-yellow, apple-green, and vari-coloured stripes stood out against George Sheringham's tapestry-like décor, in olive-green and brown, depicting a 'Park with oak and chestnut shady'. Then came the various solos, duets, trios, etcetera, culminating in a final romp to the last movement of the violin concerto. Beaumont made the sardonic comment that it would be immensely popular with dancers, 'to whom it offers a glimpse of Paradise in that it affords not only a solo apiece to

Group from *The Lord of Burleigh*: at centre Alicia Markova as Katie Willows, Walter Gore as Eustace, Diana Gould as Lady Clara Vere de Vere; among the other dancers, Elisabeth Schooling, Maude Lloyd, Andrée Howard and Betty Cuff

every member of the large cast, but often several'.[12] According to Diana Gould, in order to avoid confusion it was necessary to have a list of the numbers posted in the wings; Lopokova, she recalls, came backstage after the first performance and said, 'Freddie, I loved the first three days!'

Even critics who complained of the absence of dramatic interest had to admit that Ashton revealed his usual ability to show off each of the dancers (originally they were all from the Rambert company) to the best advantage, especially Markova with her brilliant footwork. As Katie Willows, she had two *pas de deux*, one with Chappell (in the title role) – described as 'beautiful and original' by P W Manchester – and the other with Andrée Howard as Lilian. Beaumont wrote that the Lord of Burleigh 'made love in a manner more fitted to represent a courtship of prehistoric days than one of the Victorian era' and that Ashton gave some of the ladies hip-movements that made 'their crinolines [swing] from side to side in a wide arc'.[13]

The first performance was at a midnight charity event in aid of Queen Charlotte's Hospital, attended by the Prince of Wales. Debutantes, including Cecil Beaton's sisters Baba and Nancy, sold programmes. The occasion was also the opening of the Carlton cinema in the Haymarket, and in addition to the ballets presented by the Camargo Society (which also included *Capriol Suite* and *Façade*, *The Dancer's Reward* by Ninette de Valois to Lambert's incidental music for Wilde's *Salome*, and Chopin's *Ballade in A flat* choreographed by Phyllis Bedells) there was a film, *Mischief* by Ben Travers (with Ralph Lynn and Winifred Shotter), imitations by Ann Penn, songs from *The Geisha* sung by the Marchioness of Douro, and dancing on the stage by the guests until the small hours.

Pompette: Andrée Howard in an early BBC television performance, 5 November 1936

On the evening after the 'Midnight Ballet Party' at which *The Lord of Burleigh* was first given, 16 December 1931, Ashton appeared as guest artist in the title role of a new ballet by Ninette de Valois, *The Jew in the Bush*, given at the Old Vic as a curtain-raiser to *Hansel and Gretel*, and again a week later at the Wells with *The Daughter of the Regiment*. The year ended with the Ballet Club revival of *The Tartans* on New Year's Eve. Early in the New Year, on 9 January, members of the Rambert company danced in a Farewell Benefit Performance of the Moscow Arts Theatre at the Kingsway Theatre – the evening began and ended with the actors in short sketches by Chekhov and Dostoyevsky, with a divertissement in the middle devised by Arnold Haskell, including Karsavina in a Russian Dance and Markova and Ashton in the *pas de deux* from Act II of *Swan Lake*.

In addition to revising *The Lord of Burleigh* for the next Camargo Society performance at the end of February, Ashton found time to arrange a new divertissement, a solo for Andrée Howard entitled *Pompette*, first danced by her at the Ballet Club on 4 February. 'One evening after a performance,' Rambert recalls, 'Andrée came out of the dressing-room on her way to a party, wearing a beautiful Edwardian-style evening-dress, black with a flower at her hip. Fred and I were in the studio and I said, Fred, you must make a dance for Andrée in that dress. The music was a French popular song that I sang to him and that Hugh Bradford arranged, *j'avais mon pompon*, and Fred called the dance *Pompette*, as a feminine equivalent of *pompon* – it's *argot* for being a little bit tipsy.'

A film exists of this number, a witty little character study of a coquette who tipples out of a champagne glass during the dance. It is performed on and around a chair, which she spins on one leg. At another moment she lies back across it and kicks one leg in the air. The costume has a bustle, which she waggles provocatively.

❋

Almost inevitably, Ashton's growing success as a choreographer of witty, elegant ballets brought him to the notice of the commercial theatre. The most important producer of musical shows in London's West End was Charles B Cochran. Anthony Asquith's mother, the redoubtable Countess of Oxford and Asquith, was a frequent visitor to the Ballet Club and one evening she brought Cochran to a performance. He was about to produce *The Cat and the Fiddle*, a new musical comedy by Jerome Kern. The story of the musical had to do with a conflict between modern jazz and traditional operetta, as exemplified by the American heroine (Peggy Wood) and the Rumanian hero (Francis Lederer), respectively. The conflict is resolved when he composes a new operetta blending both styles, and they realise that they are in love. There were problems with the first-act finale, a show-within-the-show, *The Passionate Pilgrim*. Shortly after Cochran's visit to the Ballet Club Ashton received a summons to go and help stage the scene.

Ashton's first rehearsal was alone with Alice Delysia, who was to sing 'Poor Pierrot'. Delysia, the French actress and singer, was an international star of many years' standing, and Ashton was understandably in awe of her. She arrived, he remembers, in a black satin dress, pearls and furs, but gradually divested herself of the fur coat, at least, and got down on the floor in response to his instructions. At the end of the afternoon she invited him to her dressing-room and gave him champagne, and he knew that he had passed the test, she had accepted him.

When the whole scene was put on the stage a member of Cochran's staff came over to Ashton at the back of the stalls and said, 'We've never discussed terms with you – how much do you want?' Ashton was accustomed to receiving a pound a minute from Rambert for his ballets, but feeling that Cochran could afford a bit more he took a deep breath and said, '£50.' The man went back to where Cochran was sitting and a moment later, he and the people sitting with him started roaring with laughter. Ashton felt sure that he had gone too far, and waited miserably for word to come back that he would get £15 or £20, but when the assistant returned he said, 'Mr Cochran says he'll give you £100.' At the end of the run Delysia sent Ashton her Pierrot costume, made by Norman Hartnell, and he used to wear it at fancy-dress parties.

The Cat and the Fiddle: 'The Passionate Pilgrim' – Alice Delysia, left, as Pierrot, ▷
with Muriel Barron as Pierrette and Eric Marshall as Harlequin

The Cat and the Fiddle opened in Manchester on 20 February 1932, and at the Palace Theatre in London on 4 March. Although the review in The Times called the *Passionate Pilgrim* scene 'weak in the composition of its movement',[14] A E Wilson in the Star said it was 'an enchanting scene . . . a fragment of delicate beauty, a fantasy of poor Pierrot which Delysia most delicately sings and mimes'.[15]

Cochran was evidently pleased with Ashton's work, because he gave him another job right away, staging dances for his next production, *Magic Nights*, one of his late-night cabarets in the Grill-Room of the Trocadero. In these he used performers who were also working in his other shows – for instance, while Massine and Eleanora Marra were in *On With the Dance* at the London Pavilion in 1925, dancing in *The Rake* and other ballets, they also danced in *The Picnic*, after Goya, to music by Albeniz, at the Trocadero. Ashton was not appearing in any other Cochran production, but he danced in *Magic Nights* – working at the Trocadero, he says, was like serving a prison sentence, you signed for a year. The performers who were in other shows rushed over to the Trocadero, where the show began at 11.30, as soon as the curtain fell. Pearl Argyle and Eve, the dancer and contortionist (a Scotswoman whose real name was Isabel McMurray), were both in *Helen!* at the Adelphi. The Friends of Mme Récamier in *An 1805 Impression*, the little ballet Ashton made for Argyle and himself, were members of Mr Cochran's Young Ladies. The producer's famous chorus girls were not selected on the strength of their ballet technique, and Ashton made the choreography

Magic Nights: Pearl Argyle as Récamier and Ashton as Her Suitor in *An 1805 Impression*, later renamed *Récamier*

Magic Nights: Rita Elsie, Kathleen Gibson and Mary Barlow as Récamier's Friends

elegant but simple – the ballet was not on point. It was a great success, 'a perfectly beautiful thing, most beautifully danced',[16] and it went into the Ballet Club repertory in December 1933, under the title *Récamier*, again with Argyle in the title role, and Antony Tudor in Ashton's role of Her Suitor.

Ashton also arranged a tango for Argyle and a rumba for Eve, and a duet for himself and Eve to the St Louis Blues called *The Bell Boys Stampede*. This may have been a later addition to the show – a review in the Evening Standard for 6 September 1932 said, 'Novelties are introduced this week at the Trocadero. . . *Magic Nights* . . . welcomes the return of Eve, notably in a new number with Frederick Ashton'.† In their number she and Ashton were identically dressed by William Chappell in bellhop uniforms with musical notes across the chest and running down the side of the trousers. The show's finale, *The Changing of the Guard*, was arranged for the full company by Buddy Bradley, and was mostly tap, which Ashton says he 'faked'.

The association with Cochran was important for Ashton for several reasons: employment in the commercial theatre made him known to a wider public and was certainly better paid than his work for the Ballet Club, the Camargo Society or the Vic-Wells. He and his mother were still by no means well off, but they were

†The only programme for *Magic Nights* I have found is dated 11 February 1933, from which the information here is taken; by that time Aimee Gillespie had replaced Pearl Argyle as Récamier.

able to move first to a flat in Clarges Street off Piccadilly, and later to 9 Guilford Place, at the northern end of Lamb's Conduit Street, in the Bloomsbury district.

Even more to the point was the fact that this kind of work gave Ashton further experience in practising his craft: as he puts it, working for producers like Cochran and, later, André Charlot, 'you had to deliver the goods'. In particular he learned a great deal from collaborating with Buddy Bradley, who had arranged the dances for *The Cat and the Fiddle* as well as *Magic Nights*. Bradley was born in Harrisburg, Pennsylvania, and later moved to New York, where he worked as a freight elevator operator in a building on West 46th Street where Billy Pierce had a dancing school; they got to know each other because Pierce ran the passenger elevator at night to help keep the studio open in the daytime. Bradley had taught himself to dance, and when Pierce asked him to teach some classes he said he was afraid because the students probably knew more than he did. Pierce said, 'Go back in there – even if they are better they don't know it.' Bradley proved to be a gifted teacher and choreographer, inventing routines to jazz records that he listened to on the Victrola after hours.[17] He began to stage dances for Broadway shows – including the Ziegfeld Follies, George White's Scandals, Earl Carroll's Vanities and, most notably, Lew Leslie's Blackbirds – and arranged numbers for Ruby Keeler, Eleanor Powell and Adele Astaire. He later went to London and was even more in demand as a dance director for both theatre and films, working with such stars as Jessie Matthews and Jack Buchanan. He opened a school there and went on working until the mid-60s, when he returned to New York. He died in Harlem in 1972.

In 1932 the Camargo Society decided to present a four-week summer season at the Savoy Theatre, in conjunction with the Vic-Wells Ballet and the Ballet Club, with a repertory including the most successful productions of their previous performances, plus revivals of the second act of *Swan Lake* (in a décor by Duncan Grant) and *Giselle*, both with Spessivtseva and Dolin; Ashton was Hilarion. As a novelty for this engagement, Ashton invited Bradley to collaborate with him on a ballet with music by Spike Hughes, the British jazz composer whose record *Six Bells Stampede* Ashton had heard in Bradley's studio. Because Hughes did not have time to compose an entirely new score, he took existing pieces, including the *Stampede*, and reorchestrated them for the London Symphony Orchestra (augmented by nine jazz musicians), adding an overture.

High Yellow was presented on the opening night of the season, 6 June 1932. The programme carried the following synopsis:

Tropical Island. Mammy and Pappy preside over family content. Mammy's big baby obliged, by circumstances too numerous to mention, to take his leave. His elegy of departure plunges the Island into general woe. But the dismay of his abandoned sweethearts (he has loved in duplicate) is dissipated at sight of two new fellows disgorged by the ship. Choreographic elation and orchestrated joy prevail.

High Yellow: ABOVE William Chappell, Doris Sonne and Walter Gore; BELOW Markova as Violetta, Ashton as Bambu; RIGHT three of the characters in the same ballet

Ashton himself was Bambu, the son, and Markova and Doris Sonne were Violetta and Cleo, his sweethearts.

Constant Lambert wanted to call the ballet *Coral Gables*, in the belief that that was the name of an island off the coast of Florida, but when someone pointed out that it was in fact a smart resort on the mainland, he suggested the title *Pink Palms* instead. 'Next,' writes Spike Hughes, 'the intellectual element in the Camargo Society came forward with the title *Sorrow in Sunlight*', after one of Ronald Firbank's novels. Although the story of the ballet bore no relation to that of the book, that was how the ballet was announced. Finally Hughes's friend Hyam Greenbaum said that if the ballet was supposed to be a cross between black and white, they should call it *High Yellow* and have done with it.[18]

In the programme the choreography was credited to Buddy Bradley, 'assisted by' Ashton, who seems to have helped Bradley shape it and teach it to the dancers. Elisabeth Schooling remembers Bradley going along the line to see who had the best idea of a movement he had demonstrated, and when he got to the end he just burst out laughing, but according to Hughes 'the dancers took to his typical smoothness and languid hand movements with remarkable ease and skill'.[19] Markova had a private lesson with him every day for six weeks before the ballet went into production, and has been known to demonstrate the snake-hips on occasion in more recent years. She recalls that at their first session Bradley said she reminded him of Florence Mills, whom she had never seen. Ashton, like Constant Lambert, was a great admirer of that artist, whose tragic quality impressed him so deeply that he says he can still see her vividly in his mind's eye. He told Markova, 'You couldn't wish for a greater compliment – come on, let's get to work!' The three of them spent a lot of time together; Bradley, she says, 'adored the same things we did, dance and the arts'.

High Yellow fulfilled the Camargo Society's ideal of a Diaghilev-type collaboration: the décor was by Vanessa Bell, Virginia Woolf's sister. It depicted the beach of a Caribbean island, with palm trees, sailing-boats on the sea and, in the distance, a steamer. The costumes were by William Chappell. Wendy Toye, who was in the corps de ballet at the first performance, remembers it as a 'super' ballet, and P W Manchester says that it was amusing and charming, much more so than *Rio Grande*. Unlike that ballet, *High Yellow* did not survive beyond the Camargo season at the Savoy, during which it had a total of six performances.

The conservative wing of British critics, Beaumont and P J S Richardson of the Dancing Times, hated the new ballet which, Beaumont wrote, 'begins with Mammy busy at the wash-tub and Pappy defying old age by working out a few hip and foot movements.' The Lament, he said, was boring, and most of the choreography consisted of the 'snakyhips repeated ad nauseam'.[20] The most Richardson could find to say was, 'It has one thing in its favour, it has nothing objectionable about it'.[21] Haskell, as usual, took the opposite view and said the elegy was 'quite obviously a creation that is big, original, and moving'.[22] The headline to the Sunday Referee's review called it 'A Feverish, Lovely Thing',[23] and a review in the Yorkshire Post said: 'The vividness of the colour and the fierce gaiety of the scene make an irresistible entertainment, restoring ballet to what it should be, dancing for its own sake'.[24]

During the Camargo season Ashton and Rambert were asked to play Job and his wife in Ninette de Valois's *Job*, but after a few rehearsals they found the roles, for all their simplicity, impossible to learn. They both got very depressed and ashamed, and finally had to withdraw. (Later, at Sadler's Wells, Ashton sometimes appeared as the figure described in the programme as 'Job's Spiritual Self', it being considered unsuitable at that time to identify him as God.)

Summing up Ashton's career to date, Haskell wrote: 'Frederick Ashton more than anyone in England today possesses those gifts of assimilating "atmosphere" that can turn ballet from an entertainment into an art with something significant to say. He possesses an unusual versatility, rare in ballet history. . . It may be argued that this is because Ashton has not yet found himself, and has nothing deep to say, but this is not true. His works show no trace of immaturity. *Mercury* . . . the wittiest and most subtle of his ballets, reveals a very deep understanding of the spirit of the French art of its period. . . Ashton is . . . supple enough to make fun of himself, dancers and dancing in *Façade*. . . He can turn from the sweetness of *A Florentine Picture* . . ., a remarkably effective reconstruction of pictures in the Pitti and Uffizi, to the sordid ballet-realism of *Rio Grande* . . ., and I have not yet exhausted his works or his moods. At his worst he is fond of pastiche, at his best he can create, but he is always entertaining and absolute master of his medium'.[25]

Clearly in this piece Haskell was defending Ashton against some frequently-made criticisms, and certainly at this time Ashton was revelling in his facility, turning his hand to whatever opportunities presented themselves. The positive side of this is that he was more and more pursuing the *métier* of choreography, just like his contemporary George Balanchine. But facility can be the enemy of real development, and in this respect the limitations imposed on Ashton by the tiny stage of the Ballet Club were salutary in that they forced him to pare away inessentials. At all events, Ashton continued to work in both spheres – the commercial theatre and the strictly non-profitmaking Ballet Club, Camargo Society and Vic-Wells – and at the same time continued to fulfil his contractual obligation to perform every night at the Trocadero.

It is unlikely that he and his colleagues at the Ballet Club had any sense of making ballet history: they were too concerned with making ends meet, for one thing. At the Club everyone had to do everything – those who were not involved in whatever ballet was being rehearsed were expected to help make costumes and paint scenery. No one had any money: Andrée Howard recalled, in an article in Dance and Dancers, that she once asked Ashton, 'Freddie, do you think there will ever be a time when we don't eat at the Express Dairy?' But they were, as he wrote in the same issue, 'very happy days'.[26] Ashton could always be relied on to entertain the rest of the company after the performance by doing his imitation of Pavlova taking a bow or, with a tutu on his head, of Mistinguett.[27] His Pavlova imitation somehow found its way on to some spare footage at the end of a film of one of Rambert's ballets, made shortly before the ballerina's death, and Ashton was very contrite when he saw it not long afterwards.

One of the ballets in Cochran's 1930 Revue was *Luna Park; or, the Freaks*, with music by Lord Berners, libretto by Boris Kochno, choreography by George Balanchine and décor by Christopher Wood. This had been considered as a possible item for an early Camargo performance but, for whatever reason, was never given in the Society's programmes. The score, however, was played as an interlude during the 1932 summer season, and it may have been then that Ashton decided to use it for a ballet of his own, though not with Kochno's story. Instead he made a miniature genre ballet called *Foyer de danse*, whose atmosphere was inspired by Degas's paintings of the ballet. This was given at the Ballet Club on 9 October 1932.

Once again the set incorporated the familiar staircase, which served in the ballet its actual purpose of leading to a dressing-room. The curtain went up on a group of *coryphées*, in long white ballet-dresses, each with a different-coloured ribbon, preparing for class – arranging one another's hair, tying their shoe-ribbons, stretching at the *barre* – a scene that led the Times critic to wonder 'whether this is to be a ballet poking fun at ballet. The fun is certainly there... But, though this is a work of art whose inspiration is three removes from real life, the comment of a dancer on the work of a painter who himself went to the art of ballet for his subject, it has a first-hand freshness entirely its own'.[28] At the time of Degas, the male dancer was in eclipse at the Paris Opéra, and rarely makes an appearance in the paintings, though both Perrot and Mérante figure in them as teachers. Ashton's role as the Maître de ballet, however, did not recall either of them – fussy and dapper in a yellow waistcoat and blue tailcoat and trousers, he looked more like a character in a Massine ballet, but performed with such precision and finesse that it was saved from being a mere caricature of a 'typical' Frenchman.

Under his instruction, the dancers went through a brief *barre*, towards the end of which the ballerina (Markova) arrived, late, receiving a rose from an admirer at the door. She went up to change while the *coryphées* removed the portable *barre*. Markova returned, in a ballet-dress of orange-crimson, to join in the rehearsal. Ashton showed her some steps, and danced with her. There was a *pas de trois*, then a solo by Ashton showing off his very neat *batterie*. Markova performed an *adage* supported by four girls, beginning with a figure that anticipated Balanchine – the two outside girls went under the arms of the two inner ones who held Markova's hands; then she had a solo typical of his choreography for her, ending with a diagonal of *pirouettes*, the last of which she finished facing upstage – realising her mistake, she quickly turned to face front. The rehearsal was interrupted by the

Foyer de danse: Five frames from Marie
Rambert's film, showing Markova as
L'Etoile, Ashton as Le Maître de ballet, and
the Coryphées

A Kiss in Spring: Markova and Harold Turner in the *pas de deux*, with corps de ballet ('Anyone who could get up on two legs')

arrival of Un Abonné, who flirted with the ballerina and chucked some of the other girls under the chin before being thrown out by the Maître de ballet. Rehearsal was resumed and completed. At the end the Maître kissed each of the girls, admonished one who had not done well enough and left with one of the others, who looked back and made a face at her colleagues. The Etoile was left alone: the Abonné returned and embraced her as the curtain fell.†

In its combination of classic with *demi-caractère* movement, *Foyer de danse* looked forward to more ambitious ballets as well as being a success in its own modest way. 'The dearest little pastiche imaginable,' wrote Horace Horsnell. 'It reflects, in its decoration, the pastel genius of Degas, and translates a classic idiom into the happiest, most intimate modern terms. The bevy of *coryphées* – period peaches every one, and Degas models to the life; the nimble, expert ballet-master, sketching and conducting each sally in a new divertissement; the careless, unmistakable star; the intruding patron with bouquet, and the sweet technical and human by-play, are details in a composition as graceful as it is true. Here are none of the angularities that check the ripples of tradition, and raise the amateur's eyebrows; but understanding smiles exchanged between past and present; new wine that enhances, not shames, an old bottle'.[29]

Just over a week later, at the Old Vic on 17 October 1932, *The Lord of Burleigh* entered the Vic-Wells repertory, with Markova as Katie Willows and Anton

†This description is based on Marie Rambert's film of the ballet.

Dolin in the title role. It became a mainstay of the repertory, with much shuffling of the various roles: Diana Gould made a rare guest appearance in her original part of Lady Clara Vere de Vere (which had been danced by Ursula Moreton at the Vic), on 24 January 1933; at the same performance Ninette de Valois was Katie Willows, a role Ailne Phillips also danced on occasion. One month after this revival (17 November 1932) Ashton danced the *Aurora pas de deux* from *The Sleeping Beauty* with Argyle at the Ballet Club. Meanwhile he continued to be more and more in demand in the commercial theatre, staging dances for two new shows in as many months. The first was an operetta called *A Kiss in Spring*, presented by Sir Oswald Stoll at the Alhambra on 28 November 1932. Ashton's main contribution was the ballet in the third act, which was danced by Markova and Harold Turner, supported by a corps de ballet that included, says Elisabeth Schooling, who was in it, anyone who could get up on two legs.

The review in The Times advised 'discreet' members of the audience to have a late dinner and arrive in time for a number called 'Carrambolina' danced by Prudence Hyman and Walter Gore, and then 'possess themselves in patience' until the ballet proper. 'All else in this lamentable tale of three artists, a street-singer, and a model is unspeakably dull'.[30]

In its staging the ballet seems to have been an extension of the idea of *Foyer de danse*, as is indicated by a description in G E Goodman's 'Notes on Décor' in the Dancing Times for January 1933: 'Beyond can be seen the brightly-lit stage, between the wings of which stand dancers awaiting their moment. Dwarfed by the high flats, they adjust their costumes, smooth their skirts, while one or two test their shoes with a swift experimental point. It is a picture that Degas might have painted.' The scene then changed to the stage itself by means of a revolve, and Markova and Turner danced the ballet, including a *pas de deux* and variations (for which the orchestration was by Constant Lambert). According to Elisabeth Schooling, the choreographic style was closer to that of the old Empire Ballets than to the Paris Opéra of the period of Degas.

Walter Gore was succeeded by William Chappell when he left to be in Ashton's next show, a revue called *Ballyhoo*, which opened at the Comedy Theatre less than a month later, on 22 December. The cast included Hermione Baddeley, George Sanders and Richard Murdoch, and marked the London début of the American dancer Walter Crisham. Once again Ashton shared the assignment with Buddy Bradley; he staged several numbers for Pearl Argyle, a 'Matelot' solo for Walter Gore that was similar to his dance in *Rio Grande*, and two fairly ambitious ballets, *Far Beyond the Crowd* and *Ballet for Four Pianos and Orchestra*. The former was an unusual number for Ashton, to judge from photographs, in that it was in 'modern' style, with the dancers in basic leotards and trousers or skirts, and poses and movements apparently deriving from the Central European school.

Ballyhoo: Far Beyond the Crowd: At left, Pearl Argyle with Walter Crisham

On 17 January 1933 *Pomona* entered the repertory of the Vic-Wells Ballet, with Beatrice Appleyard in the title role and Dolin in his original role of Vertumnus. (At the same performance he also danced his famous, or infamous, solo to Ravel's *Bolero*.) Reminiscent as it was of late Diaghilev ballets like *Apollo* or *Zéphyre et Flore*, *Pomona* brought a degree of sophistication to the repertory that it previously lacked and that attracted a more fashionable audience than the theatre in Islington had seen before. 'Ballet nights at Sadler's Wells are very smart nowadays,' said the Evening News, 'the assembly of motor-cars last night in the streets round about the theatre half suggested Covent Garden!'[31] The Ballet Club had from the beginning attracted a sophisticated public, as we have seen, and Ashton's next ballet there was aimed at what Horace Horsnell described as 'an audience of connoisseurs'.[32]

Les Masques; ou, Changement de dames was done to a score by Francis Poulenc composed in the year of *A Tragedy of Fashion*. It will be remembered that Ashton had wanted Poulenc to compose that ballet and *Les Masques* was very much the kind of piece that Ashton wished his first ballet to be – urbane, witty, sophisticated, quintessentially of its time. But now Ashton was fully in command of the resources that could enable him to realise such a work, and *Les Masques* was in its way a perfect ballet.

The story is sufficiently indicated by the names of the characters – it was like an ironic version of Tudor's *Jardin aux lilas*: a Personage goes to a masked ball, or perhaps a nightclub, with His Lady Friend, where they encounter another couple who prove to be His Wife and Her Lover. They switch partners and end up, as

84

they discover when they unmask as the curtain falls, with husband and wife re-united, to their surprise and delight, lover paired off with mistress.

Once again the dimensions of the stage of the Mercury (as the Ballet Club theatre was called later in the year) forced Ashton into understatement: there was not a wasted movement in *Les Masques*. The gestures were sharply stylised, with the hands held flat; at one point Ashton smoked an imaginary cigarette. At another the diplomat and his mistress had a brief altercation in pantomime, after which she left him; the Two Young Girls consoled him in a trio in which the 'Fred step' occurred, disguised by the *port de bras*, arms interlinked, bent upwards at an angle from the elbows.

By this time Ashton could not have wished for a designer more in sympathy with his ideas than Sophie Fedorovitch, and the work was a true collaboration, with the added participation of Matilda Etches, who executed the costumes, and Beatrice Dawson, who made the accessories – such as Markova's hat and muff – out of talc (clear plastic). The décor and costumes were all in 'cinematic' black and white, incredibly chic. Once again the staircase was incorporated into the set, with its banisters concealed with silver foil. To the left of the steps was a pillar, and there were curved opera-boxes with black curtains at each side of the stage (pillar and boxes were made of corrugated iron – according to Rambert the whole thing was done for £60).[33] Markova's white costume was like one of Ginger Rogers's dancing dresses; Pearl Argyle, as the Wife, was in Fedorovitch's favourite accordion-pleating, in black and white with an ostrich-feather fan; Ashton's black dress uniform had ostrich-feather epaulettes and the white ribbon of an order across the chest; Walter Gore wore a black tailcoat with white lapels and white trousers with a black stripe down the side – he also wore a tightly-curled black wig. The dancers even wore dark blue lipstick – the whole thing was pure Art-Déco.

Group from *Les Masques*: centre, Ashton as A Personage with Markova as His Lady Friend; Walter Gore as the Wife's Lover leaning on staircase at back

Markova's costume had a short fringed underskirt and a long train; at one point her evolutions left her with the train wrapped around her ankles, making further movement impossible until two of the young women watching from one of the boxes came out, unwound it, and returned to their places. At the end of their *pas de deux* Markova and Gore retired upstairs; when they re-emerged the train was caught up and closed across the front, as though to suggest that her favours were no longer to be freely bestowed: the whole ballet had this ironically erotic atmosphere, but mysterious and beautiful too – it was, as Markova says, 'much deeper than people thought'.

Gore's movements especially may have been inspired by Ashton's work with Buddy Bradley and suggested that quintessential line of 1930s' poetry, Edith Sitwell's 'allegro Negro cocktail-shaker'. Subtly hinted at, in fact, but not made explicit, was the idea that the Lover (Gore) was meant to be a black man (in conversation, Markova confirmed this).

Ashton was helped in the realisation of this ballet by the closeness of his friendship not only with Fedorovitch but with his cast as well. Shortly after Pearl Argyle's death he wrote: 'At that time it was my policy, whenever possible, to create opposing yet complementary roles for Markova and Pearl Argyle; it was a perfect partnership – one was a brilliant diamond, the other a flower, and in no ballet was this partnership shown to better advantage than in *Les Masques*'.[34] (The validity of this observation is not lessened by the fact, which escaped

Les Masques: Markova as the Lady Friend

Group from *Les Masques*: left to right, Walter Gore as the Lover, Markova as the Lady Friend, Ashton as A Personage, Pearl Argyle as His Wife; in rear, Anna Brunton, Elizabeth Ruxton and Tamara Svetlova as Three Ladies with Fans

Ashton's attention when he wrote it, that *Les Masques* was the only ballet in which he made roles for both dancers.)

Poulenc's *Trio* could not have been more perfect for the ballet if it had been written to order, and the composer was very pleased with it. As Horace Horsnell wrote, 'Music, décor, and dance are (as they should be) equal partners in this pure, if not so simple divertissement'.[35]

Ashton was still in no position to turn down commercial jobs; his next offer came from another famous producer of revues, André Charlot, who engaged him to stage two ballets for *How D'You Do?*, starring Frances Day and Douglas Byng. This opened at the Comedy Theatre, where *Ballyhoo* had not lasted very long, on 25 April. The first ballet, *The Legend of Berenice*, actually featured Miss Day: an 'ornate' mediaeval ballet, according to The Times, in which she looked 'like the conventionalized figure of some wild creature of Norse legend',[36] but her dancing ability was limited – the Dancing Times said that 'there is no more fascinating artiste in revue . . . but she is not suitable to play the lead in a ballet' and that Ashton was clearly trying 'to make bricks without straw'.[37]

The other number, a Rumba, was evidently more successful and Ashton remembers it as being very effective. It was led by Anna Roth and Walter Gore. The décor was described as follows by G E Goodman in the Dancing Times:

HAZELDEN.

Les Masques: A Punch caricature of
Maude Lloyd and Ashton

'. . . The inner stage was partially covered by a sloping sheet of red and orange striped material through which the light was projected from the rear of the stage. I have never seen anything that so approached the stifling heat of tropical lands'.[38]

Several choreographers tried to do something with Ravel's *Pavane pour une infante défunte* at the Ballet Club – Antony Tudor, whose version was first given on 1 January 1933, then Ashton, who did two different versions, using the décor and costumes that Hugh Stevenson had designed for Tudor. Both of Ashton's versions were danced by Diana Gould and William Chappell, the first on 7 May 1933. This was described in Time and Tide as 'a formal pas de deux of Infante and courtier . . . But in attempting to add to the formal movements a programme – less a story than a shaping and directing of mood – the choreographer is pouring into his mould more than the form can comfortably hold. Diana Gould and William Chappell move beautifully in the green dusk'.[39] Horace Horsnell enjoyed it 'both for its own funèbre, and Miss Diana Gould's impressive, graces',[40] but the Dancing Times, after wondering if Ashton had been influenced by Kurt Jooss's dance to the same piece of music, said that the new ballet was inferior to Ashton's own *Passionate Pavane*: 'The way Chappell peeped round the corner holding on to Diana Gould's *pannier* at times came perilously close to the ridiculous'.[41] The revised version, first given on 29 October 1933, was found by the Dancing Times to be 'an improvement',[42] if only because of the distinction Diana Gould brought to it, and it lingered in the repertory for a little while.†

†Two more versions were done later, one by Bentley Stone in 1937, and the other by Frank Staff in 1941.

Group from *Coppélia*, Camargo Society performance, 1934; left to right, Lydia Lopokova as Swanilda, Stanley Judson as Franz, Hedley Briggs as Dr Coppélius, Ashton and Ursula Moreton as Czárdás dancers

After a visit to Copenhagen in September 1932 by an 'English Ballet Company' whose personnel and repertory were drawn from the Camargo Society and the Vic-Wells Ballet, the Society had suspended operations, but now its committee accepted an invitation to give two Gala Performances at Covent Garden in honour of the World Economic Conference being held in London. The performances took place on Tuesday and Thursday 27 and 29 June, the programme consisting of the two-act version of *Coppélia*, in the Vic-Wells production, with Lopokova and Stanley Judson, and the second act of *Swan Lake*, danced by Markova and Dolin, who also did his solo *Espagnol* between the two ballets. Most of the dancers were from the Vic-Wells Ballet, with one interesting exception – Frederic Franklin (billed as Fred Franklyn), who danced in the corps. Ashton, with de Valois and Ursula Moreton, led the Mazurka and Czardas in the first act of *Coppélia*. The Tatler, reviewing the performances, said that it was 'a pity some of Frederick Ashton's work could not have been seen. The development of British ballet will owe so much to this young man'.[43]

At all events, the proceeds wiped out the Society's deficit. Even so, no further performances by the Society itself were to take place: at a subscribers' meeting on 30 November it was explained that such performances were no longer financially possible, that members should instead give their patronage and support to the Vic-Wells Ballet, and that whatever money remained at the Society's disposal would be donated to that company to help defray production costs of new ballets. In February 1934 an appeal was launched for 4000 half-crowns for that purpose.

Ashton had hoped to be asked by C B Cochran to stage the dances for the new Cole Porter musical, *Nymph Errant*.[44] In the event this commission went instead to Agnes de Mille, then making a reputation for herself in London as a concert dancer. But Ashton in the meantime was working on a new show, once again with Buddy Bradley, a revue by Ronald Jeans called *After Dark*. With Nelson Keys and Louise Browne in the cast, this opened at the Vaudeville on 6 July 1933. Miss Browne danced in a ballet by Ashton, *The Orchid and the Cactus*, in which she was partnered by Harold Turner. She was an excellent dancer, an American who came to London to appear in the Rodgers and Hart musical *The Girl Friend* in 1927, having danced in the Ziegfeld Follies and other shows in New York; she was said to hold 'the record for pirouette dancing (sic), of over eighty consecutive spins'.[45] (She is now chairman of the Yorkshire Regional Centre of the Royal Academy of Dancing.) Although her mother told Ashton that the Orchid and Cactus ballet was 'a masterpiece', he remembers it as being 'ghastly'. His other ballet in the show was called *Wall Street*, danced by Turner, Audrey Acland and Claude Newman, and that, he says, was full of rather pretentious symbolism – The Times, however, praised its 'ironical comment'[46] while the Sketch said it was 'cleverly invented but clumsily expressionist'.[47]

Lincoln Kirstein mentions meeting Ashton at a party given by Mr and Mrs Kirk Askew, apparently on the opening night of *After Dark*, at which they discussed the possibility of a Ballet Club in New York 'along the lines of The Mercury or the Camargo Society'.[48] Although such a project was not to be realised until the formation of Ballet Society in 1946, the first steps towards it were in fact taken that summer, a significant one in the history of modern ballet.

On 4 July the first London season of the de Basil company (still called the Ballet Russe de Monte Carlo) opened at the Alhambra, and on 8 July Edward James's company, Les Ballets 1933, with a repertory of new works by Balanchine, opened at the Savoy. (Both companies had previously played in competition in Paris.) Ashton and his friends were tremendously excited by the Balanchine season and, short-lived as it was, this company was to have an important influence on the development of ballet during the next three decades, not least because at the end of its run Kirstein concluded arrangements to bring Balanchine to the United States to found the School of American Ballet and its performing company, the American Ballet, precursor of Ballet Society and the New York City Ballet.

Several of Rambert's girls danced in Les Ballets 1933 – Pearl Argyle, Diana Gould, Prudence Hyman, Betty Cuff (Vera Nelidova) and Elisabeth Schooling – as well as Tilly Losch, then James's wife, the prodigy Tamara Toumanova, Nathalie Leslie (Krassovska) and Roman Jasinski. Constant Lambert and Maurice Abravanel conducted the London Philharmonic Orchestra. But it was not a financial success –

the public was more attracted by the de Basil company with its combination of 'baby ballerinas' and a repertory largely inherited from Diaghilev. To boost the flagging business at the Savoy, James brought over Lifar and company from Paris to share the season. Lifar was already maître de ballet at the Opéra but this seems to have been an *ad hoc* group, with Nikitina and Dubrovska as *premières danseuses*, and Pierre Vladimirov, the latter's husband, as *régisseur*. Lifar was to give his version of Beethoven's *Prometheus* as well as *L'Après-midi d'un faune* and *Le Spectre de la rose*. Dubrovska danced a solo arranged for her by Balanchine to music of Offenbach, *Dans l'Elysée*. The whole occasion seems to have been informed by a spirit of cooperation that, however fragile, was unusual in the annals of contemporary ballet – Dolin, for instance, was announced at one point to appear in Balanchine's *Errante* (in the event, Balanchine himself danced the role).

This apparent *rapprochement* was shattered when Lifar refused to dance on the evening of 11 July – he was supposed to dance *Spectre* with Markova, also a guest artist, and the *Blue Bird pas de deux* with Dubrovska. Ashton was called upon to save the day by appearing that evening with Markova in the *pas de deux* from *Les Sylphides*.

It was possibly during that summer that Ashton and Tilly Losch, for whom Balanchine made two of the most striking works in the repertory of Les Ballets 1933, *Errante* and *Les Sept péchés capitaux*, danced together in a charity gala that took place either at Grosvenor House or the Dorchester – neither of them could remember the date or the exact location of this event. The one thing that is certain is that they danced to the *Perpetuum mobile* of Johann Strauss. When Ashton first mentioned this to me, he said the choreography was his; Miss Losch was positive that it was hers. Ashton's reaction to this information was, 'We probably mugged it up together.'

The autumn of that year found Ashton working in the North of England, on two assignments that he must have accepted purely for financial reasons. The first was a musical, *Gay Hussar*, presented by Julian Wylie at the Palace Theatre, Manchester, on 30 September, starring Gene Gerrard. It never made it to the West End, but toured for several months in the North of England and Scotland, finally closing in Edinburgh. The main action was set in Tsarist Russia. As part of a sequence in 'the Imperial Opera House' when, by means of a revolving stage, the scene shifted from a dressing-room to the wings, the stage, and back to the wings (the same device as in *A Kiss in Spring*), Ashton staged 'an exquisite ballet . . . with dainty Miss Mary Honer. . .'.[49]

After completing his work on *Gay Hussar* Ashton moved on to Liverpool to produce the dances for a charity show in aid of the Royal Babies' Hospital and Child Welfare Association, *Nursery Murmurs*, which opened at the Empire Theatre on 6 November. This was one of a series of annual entertainments on behalf of the same cause: Frederic Franklin remembers one called *Heart Murmurs*. Ashton staged four short ballets: *Cavalcoward*, a Glazunov waltz, *Triptych* and *Perpetuum mobile*, in addition to several shorter numbers. In spite of their brevity, there was

Les Rendezvous: Markova in a rare action photograph of the original production

quite a lot of work involved, since most of the cast were amateurs, pupils of the Audrey Butterworth School, who were presumably of varying degrees of proficiency. At any rate, the November Dancing Times reported that rehearsals had been going on 'day and night' since 15 October, and that Ashton 'had introduced, especially in the musical comedy numbers, some extremely novel and clever ideas'. One of these was to inject 'satirical comment on everyday events' wherever possible, no doubt to make the show less like a display by a provincial dancing school and more like a topical revue.

Cavalcoward was inspired by the works of Noel Coward and performed to a selection of his music; Ashton danced in this, at any rate on opening night, perhaps impersonating Coward himself – his performance was said to be an inspiration to the other members of the cast, which included a chorus of twenty 'Murmur Young Ladies'. This number seems to have taken the place of one Ashton had originally planned to do to a piece of music by Victor Hely-Hutchinson, *The Young Idea*. 'This modern ballet,' said the Dancing Times, 'with its lighting, its masks, and its Coward music played on stage by Mr [Alfred] Francis and Miss Nancy Smith on two pianos, received perhaps the greatest appreciation, but Mr Ashton's other three ballets . . . were all of a novelty and originality that called forth a very warm reception'.[50]

Group from *Les Rendezvous*: unidentifiable, Gwyneth Mathews, Ninette de Valois, Travis Kemp?, Freda Bamford, Stanley Judson, Antony Tudor, Nadina Newhouse

The Glazunov *Valse de concert* was a classical number, and Ashton's first choreography to music of this composer, but he cannot now remember if he used the same one as in *Birthday Offering*. *Triptych* was to music of Corelli and may be presumed to have been similar in style to *A Florentine Picture*, though again he cannot remember if he used the same piece of music for both ballets. *Nursery Murmurs* ran for seven nights. Even if Ashton left after the first performance, as seems likely, it gave him very little time to work on his next ballet, another creation for the Vic-Wells Ballet. The October issue of the Dancing Times had announced that 'very possibly a new ballet by Frederick Ashton on an Italian theme' would be given during the season, 'but this is only a rumour'; next month the Vic-Wells advertisements listed 'Ballet-Divertissement', but no proper title as yet.

The ballet was *Les Rendezvous*, whose first performance took place at Sadler's Wells on 5 December 1933, with Alicia Markova partnered by Stanislas Idzikowski, and Ninette de Valois, Stanley Judson and Robert Helpmann in the *pas de trois*. The music, from Auber's opera *L'Enfant prodigue*, was arranged by Constant Lambert, and the décor and costumes were by William Chappell.

'*Les Rendezvous* has no serious portent at all,' Ashton said at the time of its creation, 'it is simply a vehicle for the exquisite dancing of Idzikowski and

93

Les Rendezvous:
Markova and Stanislas
Idzikowski as the
Lovers

Markova'[51] – a characteristically modest assessment of a ballet that is in fact of seminal importance in his work. Although it is in a sense a *demi-caractère* ballet, *Les Rendezvous* is closer to *Les Sylphides* or *Les Biches* than to, say, *La Boutique fantasque* or *Le beau Danube*, which is to say that it is a classic ballet with the dances linked by the slender thread of an idea, indicated by the title. It is one of the earliest and clearest statements of Ashton's personal classicism, and in this respect, for all its light-heartedness, it looks forward to works like *Symphonic Variations* and *Scènes de ballet*. And in its use of modest 19th-century ballet music in a way that is entirely fresh and free from condescension, it anticipates *Sylvia*, *La Fille mal gardée* and *The Two Pigeons*.

At the time, *Les Rendezvous* perhaps seemed no more than a delicious addition to the Wells repertory, but even as such it had an importance – at a time when people were again being encouraged to think of ballet as something that had, at its best, to be Russian, it showed that British ballet too could be dazzlingly brilliant and precise. Of course Markova and Idzikowski were both products of the Diaghilev company, but once again Ashton had revealed a new side to Markova, a gaiety and warmth and wit added to her familiar virtuosity – and she looked marvellously elegant in her grey costume decorated with roses and lilies of the valley, and headdress *à la* Taglioni. (The later costumes, white decorated with pink ribbons for the girls and blue sashes for the boys, are simpler than the originals but people who remember those say the new ones are not an improvement.)

In general Ashton made greater technical demands than before, on his dancers and on himself. The men's *pas de six*, for example, was something quite new for a company that had hardly possessed a male corps up to then, and Ashton used the ensemble, male and female, with much greater assurance than hitherto. The ballet has undergone many changes over the years, both in choreography and design (see Appendix D).

Once again, on the night of 5 December 1933, Ashton had attracted a fashionable audience to the Wells – it included Mme Elsa Schiaparelli, Mrs Somerset Maugham, and Benn Levy and his wife, the actress Constance Cummings. The next day Ashton set sail for New York on the *Ile de France*, steerage. During the final rehearsals for *Les Rendezvous* he had received a cable from New York inviting him to come to stage the Gertrude Stein/Virgil Thomson opera *Four Saints in Three Acts*; having no further immediate commitments, he accepted.

Chapter Five

1934

Virgil Thomson had asked Gertrude Stein to write an opera for him. Among the saints there were two saints whom she had always liked better than any others, Saint Theresa of Avila and Ignatius Loyola, and she said she would write him an opera about these two saints. She began this and worked very hard at it all that spring [1927] and finally finished Four Saints and gave it to Virgil Thomson to put to music. He did. And it is a completely interesting opera both as to words and music.[1]

Virgil Thomson had completed the composition by July 1928. The scenario was devised by Maurice Grosser after both text and music had been written: he visualized it as 'both an opera and a choreographic spectacle. Imaginary but characteristic incidents from the lives of the saints constitute its action. Its scene is laid in sixteenth-century Spain'.[2] Thomson had set all of Stein's text to music, including the stage directions, which were to be sung by a compère and commère in contemporary evening dress. According to Grosser, 'the ballets . . . were suggested' by Gertrude Stein herself.[3]

The opera had to wait more than five years for its first performance. This was to take place in Hartford, Connecticut, in the small theatre of the new Avery Memorial Wing of the Wadsworth Atheneum. The director of this museum was A Everett Austin Jr, co-sponsor with Lincoln Kirstein of the School of American Ballet and its projected performing company, which were to be located in Hartford. The production of *Four Saints* was conceived as part of this project, but when Balanchine arrived in the United States and saw that a school of the kind he and Kirstein envisaged could not succeed anywhere but in New York, any idea that he might have staged the opera himself had to be abandoned, and the production was taken over by The Friends and Enemies of Modern Music, a Hartford organisation.

Thomson engaged John Houseman to supervise the staging of the opera, but soon realised that although Houseman was a very efficient producer, what the piece needed was a choreographer, not only for the short ballet sequences, but to direct the entire action. Houseman agreed, and suggested Agnes de Mille who was in London at the time (it will be remembered that she had been given a job Ashton had hoped to get, that of staging the dances for Cochran's production of *Nymph Errant* – anyone who has read her account of that experience in *Speak to Me, Dance with Me* will agree that Ashton came off better). Thomson had met Ashton in the early summer of 1933; ever since he had completed the opera he had been in the habit of giving one-man performances of it in drawing-rooms in Paris, New York and London, and on one such occasion, at the London house of the art dealer Kirk Askew, Ashton had been present and discussed the music with him, making a few suggestions about how it could be put on the stage. Thomson had not seen any of Ashton's ballets, but felt that they could work together, and suggested that he be invited over to stage the opera. Constance Askew paid for the cable, and Everett (Chick) Austin agreed to pay his fare; the Askews said that Ashton and Thomson could share the guest room in their New York apartment.

When Ashton arrived in New York, on 12 December, the opera was already in rehearsal in the basement of St Philip's Episcopal Church in Harlem – that is to say, the singers, members of the Eva Jessye choir, were learning the music. The scenario had been worked out and the décor and costumes designed – as Ashton says, 'I had no say in anything like that. But we needed six dancers, and it was impossible at that time to find six Negro dancers who had ballet training; eventually we found three girls who'd had extremely elementary, well, *fancy* dancing was all you could call it, and for the boys I had a kind of black ADC, so to speak, who came everywhere with me as a kind of liaison officer, and we used to go to the Savoy Ballroom and pick out boys there who danced the Lindy Hop, or whatever it was at that time, marvellously, and ask them if they'd like to come and do it, and eventually we got three – but at first they thought we were pulling their legs. None of them was trained, but naturally like all Negro people they were very plastic and knew how to move, so it was a question of adapting.'

No doubt Ashton's experiences in revue and musical comedy, working with chorus dancers whose training might be limited, stood him in good stead. In any case, he always worked on the same principle, then as now, whether choreographing for brilliant technicians and great artists, or dancers whose gifts were not so great, or as yet undeveloped – he found out what they could do best, and used that, showing them always to the best advantage. The black dancers in *Four Saints*, he says, 'had a kind of delicacy that was very touching'.

In the first act the dancers, dressed as angels, were to perform such tasks as handing the singers their props and pulling the curtains to reveal a series of seven tableaux. In the second act there was a brief ballet in which the angels practised their flying exercises, and in the third a tango of sailors and their girls, performed in the garden of a monastery (at the end of which St Ignatius said, 'Thank you very much'). Gertrude Stein had seen French schoolboys playing football in the Luxembourg Gardens, watched over by their Jesuit schoolmasters, and Thomson

Four Saints in Three Acts: Beatrice Robinson Wayne and Bruce Howard as St Theresa I and II, with dancers

BELOW *Four Saints in Three Acts*: the procession

ABOVE Group from
*Four Saints in Three
Acts*

*Four Saints in Three
Acts*: Caro Lynn
Baker, Elizabeth
Dickerson, Mable
Hart, Floyd Miller,
Maxwell Baird, Billie
Smith

toyed with the idea of having a scene like that, but Ashton rejected it and instead had St Ignatius drilling the monks – as Thomson says, he had 'complete confidence in Ashton's perspicacity and inspiration'. In an interview, Ashton told H T Parker of The Hartford Courant that his choreography 'would be a combination of "snake hips and Gothic"',[4] which would seem to indicate that he drew on what he had learned from working with Buddy Bradley.

Even more helpful to Ashton in staging *Four Saints* was his Peruvian background. Someone came up to him after the opening and said, 'It's very strange, but the whole thing reminds me of Peru.' 'And I said, It's not surprising because that's where I came from and that's where I witnessed all these ceremonies.' One of his most striking inventions was the 'devotional and expiatory' procession in the third act, a combination of wedding and funeral. 'I did that in a way that gave the impression that they were moving the whole time but actually they were only swaying backwards and forwards, then every now and again they took one step, and it gave the impression of a procession moving when actually they weren't.' Gertrude Stein later wrote in *Everybody's Autobiography*, 'he does know what it is to be a Peruvian and that made it possible for him to do what he did with *Four Saints* to make a religious procession sway and slowly disappear without moving.'

Virgil Thomson went back in his score 'not to Spain, which I had never seen, but rather to my Southern Baptist upbringing in Missouri',[5] and it was his idea to use a black cast, who he felt would be able to sing the music and enunciate the text with unaffected clarity, but at first the idea rather horrified the fastidious aristocrat Florine Stettheimer, who feared that their skin tones would not blend with her brilliant palette. She even thought it would be necessary to use white or silver make-up, but was fortunately persuaded to abandon this scheme, though an attempt seems to have been made to eliminate the variations in the performers' pigmentation by using a standardized tan make-up.

It had been a stroke of genius, nonetheless, to commission the décors from this painter whose visionary and fantastic canvases depicted her own family circle, city- and landscapes, and still-life, in a manner that suggested a combination of Redon, Rousseau and Bonnard. Some of the features of her designs had been foreshadowed in a 1930 painting on the theme of Virgil Thomson and *Four Saints*, and were realised on stage with such materials as 'lace, feathers, gold paper, glass beads, cellophane, tarlatan and tulle'.[6] She was, Ashton says, 'the most refined and delicate woman I ever met in my life – she was so petite, and her gestures were so precise and exact. She was tiny and frail and yet at the same time capable of doing these terrific paintings with great passion and observation, and these brilliant colours.'

Ashton has written of his work on the opera, 'I did *Four Saints* well, because the action was not operatic but ritualistic and ordered, and not balletic but ceremonial, and never has any production had the beautiful leisure of a procession with its pauses, when the lifting of a hand and raised eyebrows were dramatic. It was the strangest and most beautiful production, I say this though I made it, because I am devout and the Negroes are devout and I am plastic and they are plastic. At first I had to make them copy me exactly and then I found it a great mistake, so I did a pose or gesture and said Now do that, and they would do something quite different but full of the beauty of their own skinny plasticity, and their heads would fall always harmoniously and they were never gawky, and though strange always harmonious'.[7] Thomson describes Ashton in rehearsal, 'standing, as choreographers like to do, in center-stage and moving the singers around him, at first with their music scripts in hand, so that movements and music and words all came to be learned together . . .'.[8]

It was not an easy task for Ashton: some of the singers had been in *Run, Little Chillun'*, directed by Rouben Mamoulian, one of the few previous all-Negro musical productions (aside, that is, from such revues as the 1921 *Shuffle Along* and the various editions of *Blackbirds*), but otherwise their lack of training and experience made some of the work heavygoing. 'One would get a whole scene set, and then one would come to lunch-time, and I'd say, Let's do it once more to make sure, and they would do it, and they would do it perfectly, and then come back after lunch, and I'd say, Now we'll go through Scene 2, and they'd never heard of Scene 2, and I'd have to start all over again, and so it was a terrible test for me, I had no assistant or anything, I had to remember everything all the time because they always forgot, which made it frightfully exhausting. And I remember at the dress rehearsal, when they got their costumes and everything, these brilliant costumes, they were all very thrilled, and they forgot everything, the whole thing was chaos. And I remember I was so tired by then, I came up on to the stage to give them my notes, and I started on the notes and I just burst into tears. And I remember one lady coming up to me and saying, Don't worry, Mr Ashton, we made Mamoulian and we'll make you. And then an extraordinary thing, the first night came and a miracle took place, they seemed to remember everything, they did it all marvellously, with their wonderful vitality, you know, and the fact that they had an audience and the audience were with it, made all the difference.'

The conductor of *Four Saints* was Alexander Smallens, who was Stokowski's assistant in Philadelphia and had, among other things, conducted for Pavlova during the First World War (he may well have conducted the performance of Pavlova's company that Ashton saw in Lima in 1917). Nevertheless, it seems that he and Ashton did not hit it off – Thomson thinks it unlikely that they talked about Pavlova, or much about anything at all (Smallens was not often present at the early rehearsals), and readers of *Run-Through*, John Houseman's memoirs, will remember his story of their disagreement during the dress rehearsal in Hartford, when Smallens yelled at Ashton, who left in tears after shouting back, 'I have worked with Sir Thomas Beecham, a genius! And he never spoke to me as you have'.[9]

Houseman says that Ashton received $10 a week pocket money as his only remuneration during the rehearsal period (Thomson thinks he may have got a small salary, $20 or $30, once the opera moved to New York). 'He was a delight to work with: except for occasional brief spasms of homesickness, he was gay, free,

A portrait of Ashton taken in New York at the time of *Four Saints in Three Acts*

self-confident, infinitely resourceful and imaginative and dearly beloved by everyone with whom he worked'.[10] The homesickness was somewhat mitigated by the presence in New York of two of his closest friends, Sophie Fedorovitch and Edward Burra, who were actually living in Harlem that winter. Since Ashton was staying with Kirk and Constance Askew he attended their *salon* on Sunday afternoons: painters, composers and writers met to drink tea and, after six o'clock, cocktails. Ashton remembers that the appointed moment for the switch was strictly observed: 'this was during prohibition so it was bathtub gin', on which the guests used to get decorously drunk. Also on Sundays at that time Martha Graham was performing at the Guild Theatre on West 52nd Street (now the ANTA), and Ashton went, in the cheapest seats, to see her. And, with Fedorovitch and Burra, he went to Harlem – still a fashionable thing to do in those days, but Ashton, perhaps because he was British, gained admittance not only to night-clubs (among his friends was the great blues singer Mildred Bailey) but also to the houses of Harlem society, where white people were rarely invited. Very often he walked home in the small hours from Harlem to the Askews' house on East 61st Street.

Work continued throughout the month of January, except for two days when Ashton had the 'flu and John Houseman took over his chores as well 'and staged the vision of the Holy Ghost to Virgil's satisfaction',[11] then at the beginning of February the company moved to Hartford. The opening of the Avery Memorial Wing of the Atheneum was a gala occasion, celebrated not only by the première of *Four Saints* but also with a great Picasso retrospective and the first showing of the designs for the Diaghilev Ballet that Chick Austin had bought from Serge Lifar in the previous year. The audience was so smart that in addition to the New York music critics the society columnist Lucius Beebe went to review the intermissions.

After six performances in Hartford the company returned to New York and, following a week of rehearsals during which Ashton had to adapt his choreography for a larger stage, opened at the 44th Street Theatre for a two-week run. In spite of bitterly cold weather and a taxi strike, 'everybody came' to the New York opening, Thomson wrote, 'from George Gershwin to Toscanini'.[12] (Among others, Cecil Beaton escorted Tilly Losch, and Robert Benchley was with Dorothy Parker.) Some of the critics were convinced that the whole thing was what is now called a put-on, and few of them, it seemed, could resist the temptation to attempt a more or less clumsy parody of Gertrude Stein. Even The New York Times had come out with the following headlines after the Hartford première:

FOUR SAINTS' ACTS
IS ACTS IN 30 ACTS
There is a Difference Between
Steinse and Nonsteinse,
What Difference.

Words Prosody Pattern
So Stein Negro-Sung Cellophane
Opera is Fantastic Melody in
Hartford Premiere[13]

The New York Sun, under a headline that read:

FOUR SAINTS IN THREE ACTS
Or a Saint and $\frac{1}{3}$ Per Act
Pink Cellophane Opera It Makes It Well
Fish Four Saints It Makes It Well Fish
Read Em and Weep

went so far as to print lengthy excerpts from the libretto. The Sun's art critic, Henry McBride, was one of the work's staunchest defenders: 'The work, like most successful new things, seems a miracle . . . That is why so many people weep for joy during the entr'actes, out in the lobby. They can't explain it, any more than they can ever "explain" any enduring work of art, but they felt it, and therefore they weep'.[14]

Some who came to scoff were won over, and there were many people who went back to see it more than once, and some who went night after night. The run was extended for a further two weeks, during the second of which the theatre was sold out, and 'by public demand' Harry Moses, the producer who had brought the show to New York, reopened it two weeks later at the Empire, where it played for a further fortnight. Moses hoped to take it to Paris and London, and announced plans to keep the company together and build a repertory of more conventional operas, but these projects came to nothing. The opera was revived for a few performances in Chicago the following November, when Gertrude Stein, who had returned to the United States for a lecture tour, saw it for the first time. Since Ashton had long since returned to England, the production was reassembled with the help of a prompt-book made by Thomas Anderson, one of the singers.

All in all, then, *Four Saints* had less than fifty performances in New York, and less than a dozen elsewhere, but it had an impact that was out of all proportion to its commercial success, which, limited though it may seem, was certainly remarkable for a work of such an avant-garde nature. Both the Hartford and the New York performances received an enormous amount of publicity, nation-wide. Two days in advance of the Broadway opening, Carl Van Vechten, who as might be expected was one of the opera's most enthusiastic champions, gave advice to the spectator on how to approach 'this rather miraculous music drama ... take your seat in the theatre ... without expecting or desiring or hoping for anything'.[15]

The New York critics returned to the piece in follow-up articles to their original reviews. Stark Young, in his first review in The New Republic, said, 'Only now and then in the theatre can we hope for something of the quality of a thing in nature (a tree, a melon, a sheet of water, a flight of birds)'.[16] In a later article, he defended the work's lack of 'meaning' saying that most plays on Broadway 'suffer from aboutness', and went on, 'This may sound to some like a plea for art without sense, but it is really only an objection to sense without art'.[17]

The following month Young contributed a rather more abstruse piece to Theatre Arts that analysed Ashton's use of images from paintings by Giotto, Goya and El Greco, though not, he emphasized, in the manner of *tableaux vivants* – 'All Mr Ashton's derivations were alive, which means they were entirely free of their pictorial originals. . . His derivations, or at times pictorial borrowings, were elusive, touch and go; and one's pleasure out of them lay not in mere recognition . . . but in the freshness of their precision, their fluency of imitation, and the light vitality of their departure. It was not so much a case of imitations as of the contagious life in the art tradition'.[18]

John Martin in a Sunday article suggested that the whole work used the methods of dance in the sense that it was 'the method of abstract dramatic action'. *Four Saints*, he said, was 'a synthesis of the theatrical arts such as we have all been waiting for and talking about for years'. At the same time, Martin felt that Ashton had been hampered in the realisation of his ideas by the performers' lack of training, and he objected to moments when the action pointed up colloquial references in the text to comic effect, something that was of course done quite deliberately by Ashton ('one of the saints had to say, Please be coming to see me, and I made her do it a bit like Mae West, and things of that sort – I made similes, with the nonsense of the words sometimes making sense, which gave it a kind of amusing quality'). But Martin too defended the work's lack of conventional meaning 'in this day of social struggle' – 'It is of the utmost importance that new theatrical forms be developed for the expression of concepts that are not to be expressed through reason and logic. . . What if experiments of this sort have no meaning? It is the easiest thing in the world to mean something'.[19]

Ashton enjoyed a tremendous personal success, all the more serious writers recognising the importance of his contribution to the piece, though several of them were aware of the technical limitations of the dancers. 'Especially funny,' wrote Bernard Sobel in The New York Herald Tribune, 'were the attempts of the dancers to balance themselves gracefully in some of the grotesque postures provided by Frederick Ashton'.[20] H T Parker in The Hartford Courant found the two brief ballets 'highly amusing' but added 'as dancing it was very very ragged'. 'Mr Ashton's real triumph, however,' he went on, 'was the ballet-like scene where the company of lesser saints weaves in and out under the joined arms of their mates, each carrying a lighted candle upon the night-darkened stage'.[21] Theatre Arts for April 1934 gave Ashton credit for 'a considerable share of the success of *Four Saints,*' saying that he 'was responsible not only for the slight dances but for the lovely patterned movement of the whole work, the flow of gesture that accompanied the song, the rhythm that fused the music and the action and gave life to the designs. There was no external evidence of Mr Ashton's labors, only the achieved style of the thing itself.' The writer related this style to the productions of the Ballet Club in London.

For a while, Ashton considered staying in New York. He had some offers, and even went to seek the advice of John Martin. 'He advised me against it – he said that there was really no place for me there, that the American dance wasn't classical, as indeed it wasn't in those days, it was before the full impact of the de Basil company, which changed everything, was felt so maybe he was right, I don't know.' Perhaps an even stronger compulsion to return to Britain was a personal one – for all the intoxication of his New York success, Ashton was still homesick. Sophie Fedorovitch and Edward Burra had been present at the Hartford première, but had since gone home, and now Ashton 'suddenly got a sort of mad desire to see an English spring'. On 22 March 1934 – after the show had closed at the 44th Street Theatre, but before it reopened at the Empire – Ashton sailed for Europe on the *Berengaria,* paying a supplement out of his own pocket so as not to have to go steerage this time. There was some idea in his mind that he might return for one or other of the projects that had been offered to him. 'But you know how it is in America, you've got to be there, and if you're not, you're just forgotten. . . It would be interesting to speculate what my future might have been if I had stayed there,' Ashton said in conversation recently.

Chapter Six

1934-1935

Or, he might have added, the future of British ballet. The importance of Ashton's part in that future was to be even more decisively established within the next two years, with his engagement as a permanent member, and principal choreographer, of the Vic-Wells Ballet. Success abroad might have been expected to result in a more immediate improvement in his prospects at home, but such a change is rarely automatic, and Ashton's case was no exception, and for the moment he returned to the Ballet Club. Another event that took place at the Wells very soon after his return was of momentous importance in the history of British ballet: the début, as a Snowflake in *Casse Noisette*, on 21 April of Peggy Hookham. The name seemed unsuitable to Ninette de Valois, and the young dancer, after using her mother's maiden name of Fontes for a while, finally settled on Margot Fonteyn.

At the Ballet Club, de Valois was rehearsing her only work for Rambert's company, *Bar aux Folies-bergère*, based on the Manet painting in the Courtauld collection, to Chabrier piano music selected by Lambert. This ballet, first presented on 15 May, reunited Ashton (as a dancer) with Markova, who appeared as La Goulue, and Pearl Argyle, who was the Barmaid. The story was trite enough – the Barmaid loves the waiter, Valentin, who in turn is infatuated with La Goulue – but Ashton made him a real person, not a caricature. The Rambert company gave a summer season at the Mercury that lasted until the end of June, during which month Ashton presented his first new ballet since returning from the United States, *Mephisto Valse*. Constant Lambert was a great admirer of Liszt, particularly of the late, 'diabolical' piano music, at that time little appreciated. He had discussed the idea of a Liszt ballet with Ashton before, and now suggested the first *Mephisto Waltz* as a ballet for Markova, who he felt was the ideal interpreter for the role of Marguerite.[1]

The action of the ballet followed fairly closely that of the episode from Lenau's version of *Faust* depicted in the music: 'The scene is . . . a village inn which Faust and Mephisto enter, in search of love, on hearing the music from inside. The peasants are dancing, and the attention of Faust is taken by the landlord's daughter, who comes in to carry drinks to the dancers. Mephisto seizes the violin and his

Ninette de Valois's *Bar aux Folies-bergère*: Ashton as Valentin with Markova as La Goulue

playing intoxicates the audience, who completely abandon themselves to love-making under the influence of the music. As the dancing reaches its climax, the singing of a nightingale is heard in the starlit woods, through the open doors. Mephisto goes on playing, while, two by two, the dancers disappear into the night. The village maiden throws herself into the arms of Faust, and . . . they, too, vanish into the woods.'

This description is taken from Sacheverell Sitwell's book on Liszt, in which he describes the work as 'one of the great documents of Romanticism', and Ashton's was a perfect Romantic ballet in miniature, both in scale (nine dancers on the tiny Mercury stage) and length (about eleven minutes). Again he and Sophie Fedorovitch made ingenious use of the architecture of the stage – not only was the famous staircase incorporated into the set, but the ballet began with Faust and Mephisto passing across the narrow apron in front of the curtain and knocking at the door to the left of the proscenium to gain admission to the inn.

Ashton added a few details of his own to the action: when the curtains opened some young men were discovered playing dice. Mephisto entered and apparently (judging by their amazed reaction) rolled a double six at the first throw, as if by magic. More important, the part of Marguerite, within the small compass of the work, became a role in the tradition of Giselle and other heroines of the Romantic ballet, the innocent maiden who falls in love and then suffers the agony of betrayal.

Mephisto Valse:
Markova as
Marguerite, Ashton
as Mephisto

BELOW *Mephisto Valse*:
Markova as
Marguerite, Walter
Gore as Faust

In many ways the ballet was very simple and austere – again, under the influence of Fedorovitch, Ashton pared away inessentials. There were moments of stillness, which on a stage the size of the Mercury were often more telling than any violent movement could be (perhaps the best example of this is the famous frozen tableau at the biggest climax of the music in Antony Tudor's *Jardin aux lilas*): for instance, when Mephisto brought Faust and Marguerite face to face they stood quite still gazing into each other's eyes, while the couples danced in the background. Slowly Faust raised his arms, and then fell at Marguerite's feet, at which point she backed away, then ran upstage. The stage cleared, and Faust had a passionate solo. Marguerite danced a solo with spiralling turns into *pas de bourrée* backwards – this to the four corners of the stage – finally coming face to face with Faust again; this time she fell at his feet. Mephisto took Faust's place, raised her up, and whirled her around the stage.

At the end of the ballet, when the nightingale's song is heard, the three principals moved upstage, Marguerite leaning on Faust's shoulders as Mephisto drew him back. Mephisto again changed places with Faust, separating the lovers, and took Faust up the stairs to watch her through a 'mirror' (a gauze panel in the backcloth) in her brief final dance of despair.[2] Here, according to Markova, Ashton carried the story a stage further than indicated in the music's programme and gave her a gesture of placing her hands on her belly, after which she looked up with her eyes filled with the realisation that she was with child – 'there was no big climax, nothing, just the realisation'. A last *grand jeté en tournant*, then she fell in a swoon as Mephisto tore the 'mirror' from top to bottom.

Group from *Mephisto Valse*: at rear, Markova, Gore and Ashton; at front, Elisabeth Schooling, Doris Sonne, Peggy van Praagh, Hugh Laing, Rollo Gamble, Frank Staff

The treatment of the role, and Markova's performance of it, gave a depth to the ballet, whose general atmosphere of macabre melodrama matched what Sacheverell Sitwell calls the 'haunted and evil' tone of the music. Gore was Faust, and Ashton himself Mephisto, and the three were so used to working together that they were able to create a powerful dramatic impact with the simplest means. The choreography for the three supporting couples somehow gave them the weight of a full corps de ballet – there was a moment when they fairly surged on to the stage from the stairs.

Fedorovitch's design for the décor was in brick-red, with the costumes for Marguerite and Mephisto in black and white, and Faust's in grey. Markova danced the role in white character-shoes – Fedorovitch's idea, according to Rambert, though the drawing clearly shows her on point.[3]

In the autumn of 1934 Kyra Nijinsky, the daughter of Vaslav, joined Rambert's company and took over the role of Marguerite, in which she was, according to Rambert, 'deeply touching'.[4] (Her father had planned a ballet to this music during the American tour of the Diaghilev ballet under his direction in 1916; this was never performed though, according to Richard Buckle, its choreography was completed.[5] Lincoln Kirstein says that de Basil considered producing a version for Kyra Nijinsky in 1933, perhaps with choreography by Balanchine.[6] In 1945 Kyra Nijinsky was dancing in Florence with a small company of her own and included a version of *Mephisto Valse* in her repertory, but I have no idea whether or not this bore any resemblance to Ashton's ballet.[7] In the summer of 1948, Bronislava Nijinska choreographed a version which Markova and Dolin danced at Lewisohn Stadium in New York.) Kyra Nijinsky also danced the role in heeled slippers, but at a later date when Ashton was teaching it to Pearl Argyle, Rambert asked him if there were any particular reason for this, and he said no, so she danced it on point and thereafter it was always done that way.

As we have seen, the Camargo Society had ceased to function as a performing organisation and planned in future to devote its energies and whatever funds might have accrued to sponsoring new productions by the Vic-Wells Ballet. In August the first of these was announced by the Dancing Times. One idea had been to invite Michel Fokine to mount a new work for the company, but there was not enough money for that, 'so Frederick Ashton has been engaged and he will be afforded more scope than he has had in the past'. There was talk, the story said, of doing William Walton's choral work *Belshazzar's Feast* as a ballet, perhaps in the late autumn, after the production of the full-length *Swan Lake*.

There was no further word on this project. At the beginning of the Wells season Ashton revised *Les Rendezvous*; among other things he added the *pas de quatre* of the four 'little girls'. This was Margot Fonteyn's first creation of an Ashton role (she was still listed in the programme as 'Margot Fontes'). At this first encounter with the young dancer – she was fifteen years old – he found her, he has said, 'stubborn, difficult, but musical and elegant'. *Le Lac des cygnes* was given on 20 November, with Markova and Helpmann. Fonteyn also danced as a Peasant Girl and a black cygnet in *Lac*, and later in the season (5 February 1935) appeared as 'airy, fairy Lilian' in *The Lord of Burleigh*. According to P W Manchester, 'that was the night everyone knew she was going to be the one'. Ashton, meanwhile, was in no better financial shape than before he went to America: Rambert's habit of paying her choreographers one pound a minute for their ballets meant that he had received £11 for *Mephisto Valse*, so he was obliged to accept a couple of commercial jobs. *Jill Darling!*, a musical comedy by Vivian Ellis, started life as *Jack and Jill*, which opened at the Opera House, Manchester, on 5 March 1934, with Arthur Riscoe: it toured for a while but never came into London. In its revised form it opened at the Saville on 19 December 1934, when Ellis and Riscoe were able to fulfil their original plan of casting Frances Day in the starring role, which she played as a Hungarian.[8]

Ashton arranged only one number, 'I'm Dancing With a Ghost', which he himself danced with Frances Day, at her insistence. Ashton, wrote Ellis, 'managed to relax between rehearsals by lying full-length in the stalls gang-way. It looked very professional'.[9]

Jill Darling!: Frances Day and Ashton in 'I'm Dancing with a Ghost'

At one point the management decided to save money by dropping Ashton from the cast, since he was being paid something like £15 a week to do just one number. But Frances Day threatened to quit if he were fired, and he was retained. When she had to leave in the summer of 1935 to fulfil a film contract, and was replaced by a real Hungarian, Irene Palasty, the producers actually offered to increase Ashton's salary if he would only stay in the show.

Also in December 1934, Ashton was at Drury Lane filming the ballet sequences for the film version of *Escape Me Never*, which had opened as a play the year before. It was a preposterous piece whose *raison d'être* was to provide a vehicle for Elisabeth Bergner.

The ballet sequences, when they finally arrive, are brief, and mostly notable for the glimpses they afford, in long-shot, of the young Fonteyn. At other moments we see Beatrice Appleyard as the ballerina's understudy. The choreography is conventional enough. In a rehearsal scene Fonteyn (or is it Appleyard?) does *grands jetés en tournant* and *assemblés en tournant*, and later, in the performance, the inevitable 'Fred step'. At first Ashton had arranged some abstract choreography that he remembers as being 'rather good' (the music was by William Walton), but he was asked to alter it for various reasons that seemed to him unconvincing, so he refused, saying he wanted to know the real reason. Finally he said he thought he could guess what it was – that the star objected to playing her big emotional scene in the middle of a really interesting ballet. This was admitted to be the case, at which Ashton said that was something he could understand, and agreed to make the change.

At about this time Ashton met W B Yeats, who thought highly of his work and of his judgment in artistic matters – he even wanted Ashton to come to Dublin and take over the Abbey Theatre (where de Valois had worked with the poet in the late 1920s, performing in the Plays for Dancers among other things), but Ashton did not take this offer very seriously. He now feels that he treated Yeats rather frivolously, impertinently criticising his portentous manner of delivery when reading his own verse aloud and preferring the company of younger friends to that of the venerable and distinguished poet.

In the early months of 1935 Ashton continued to work at the Ballet Club. On the 6 January a new ballet was given, *Cinderella*, by Andrée Howard, to music of Weber, with Ashton as the Prince, partnering Pearl Argyle. It was a classic ballet scaled to the size of the Mercury stage, used with the ingenuity characteristic of all Rambert's choreographers – the stairs were once again in evidence, and before the last scene there was an interlude before the curtain with three courtiers trying the glass slipper on feet that appeared from beneath it.[10] Ashton cut an elegant figure as Prince Charming.

Andrée Howard's
Cinderella:
Pearl Argyle as
Cinderella, Ashton as
Prince Charming

At the end of the month the Rambert company moved to the West End for a season at the Duke of York's, for which Ashton produced a new ballet, *Valentine's Eve*, to the *Valses nobles et sentimentales* of Ravel – announced in the January issue of the Dancing Times under the same title as the music; it was also said that Markova would dance in it, but in the event the leading role was taken by Pearl Argyle, and later by Maude Lloyd.

Ashton's synopsis read as follows:

It is Valentine's Eve. They are waltzing. Constant is a poet, Phryné a coquette. He hands her a keepsake and with it his heart, for he still believes in love.

Lightly she parts with the token to her very next partner. She has never understood about a heart, and so in turn it circles the ballroom, until it reaches Solange. She too believes in love, and it is the poet whom she loves. She gives him the token. He recognises it. He is broken-hearted, as he traces it from dancer to dancer, and throws it at the feet of the heartless one. His

Group from *Valentine's Eve*: Elisabeth Schooling as Bette, Walter Gore as Robert, left; Maude Lloyd as Phryné, seated centre, with Hugh Laing as Constant kneeling at her left; also, Ann Gee, John Andrewes, Andrée Howard, John Byron

fellows laugh. They are men of the world. As the curtain falls he is seated on a conversation-chair with Solange, together and apart. In silence each one is nursing his sorrows.

True love is out of place amid the waltzing of Valentine's Eve.

About this ballet, Peggy van Praagh has said, 'Fred never explained ballets as Antony Tudor did – before doing a ballet with Antony you were sent off to do your homework and given six books to read, to get the character right, as in *Jardin aux lilas*, but Fred just said, follow the music. . .

'We had a *pas de trois*, I think it was Schooling, Frank Staff, and myself, and we came into rehearsal one morning and Fred sat down and said, I've got a terrible hangover, I'm not going to be able to think of a step today. Then he said, Get up, do some Cecchetti *enchaînements*, just dance, get yourselves warm. I was very much the Cecchetti girl in those days, trained by Margaret Craske, and I just went through all the Saturday morning steps, because I thought they were rather pretty, and he was sitting there with his hand over his eyes, he wasn't even looking, and suddenly he said, Yes, that'll do. And I said, What do you mean, that'll do? And he said, Can you do it again? And then he took a series of these Cecchetti *enchaînements*, and twisted them, and put different arms, or different head, and different rhythm, but the basic steps were there, and that became the whole of that *pas de trois*. . . .

'That was the first time I'd worked for him, and I didn't know that this is what he does – he gets the people that he's going to create for to move in the way that's natural for them, and then he takes it and moulds it to his own uses. And he always in those days used to come and watch a lot of classes when he was creating, because he always wanted to base it very much on the classic technique and he always said unless he'd seen class, or been doing class, he couldn't get into the feeling – he had the basis first, and then would add his own style afterwards. . . . He always takes his dancers and pushes them about in the torso, and I don't know any other choreographer who actually makes them *feel* the movement – I think he likes them to get a physical feeling of movement, of the exact movement he wants. Whereas some people like you to copy them doing it, Fred gets hold of the dancers and really pushes them into it, to get the angle he wants.'

The story of the ballet, which somewhat resembled Schnitzler's *La Ronde*, though without the harsh realism that underlies that play, was well suited to the perfumed atmosphere of Ravel's score (an actual cardboard heart was passed around among the dancers), as was Fedorovitch's exquisite décor, achieved by gauze screens in rose and claret with shadows of ferns – 'as if in some expensive conservatory where amorous intrigue might take place during a fashionable ball'.[11] There was also the conversation-chair, which, as The Times noted, played an important part in the action, 'being hurriedly wheeled about to catch Mr Ashton's dejected form, whenever he sees Phryné flirting with another man'.[12]

Besides Argyle and Lloyd, who was the rejected Solange in the original cast (when she took over Argyle's role van Praagh moved up into hers), the cast included Ashton's old friends Gore and Chappell, as well as Schooling, Staff and Hugh Laing, who later replaced Ashton as Constant. 'The dancing and the story are one,' Haskell wrote, 'There is both sentiment and irony here'.[13] The ballet, though well received, did not remain in the repertory.

Up to that time Markova had been dividing her time between the Ballet Club and the Vic-Wells, but now she let it be known that she wanted to move on. De Valois was faced with the necessity of taking another big step forward and finding a ballerina within the ranks of her own company. By then the choice was obvious – the young Margot Fonteyn, who was given Markova's role in a revival of *Rio Grande* on 20 March. Markova had not yet left the company, but no longer cared to dance the Creole Girl. It was perhaps an odd choice for Fonteyn's first major role – she was not quite sixteen – but it set the seal on her position as the future ballerina of the company.

Markova and Dolin were preparing to form their own company under the management of Vivian van Damm, who ran the Windmill Theatre, home of Non-stop Revudeville, a fairly decorous kind of 'burlesque' show with carefully stationary nudes. As a sort of trial run, van Damm presented the Vic-Wells Ballet, led by Markova and Dolin, for two weeks at the Wells at the end of the regular opera and ballet season; and then moved the company into the West End for a week at the Shaftesbury Theatre, where it could be seen by a public that would not dream of taking a bus-ride out to the mainly working-class district of Islington. The engagement at the Wells opened on 20 May with a new ballet by de Valois,

Group from *Rio Grande*: at front, Margot Fonteyn as th Creole Girl, William Chappell as the Creole Boy

Rio Grande dress rehearsal, Sadler's Wells, 1935. In centre, William Chappell as the Creole Boy, Margot Fonteyn as the Creole Girl, Beatrice Appleyard as the Queen of the Port, Walter Gore as the Stevedore, with corps de ballet; Ashton may be seen standing to the right of the proscenium arch

The Rake's Progress, based on Hogarth's series of paintings and with a score by Gavin Gordon. (This was originally offered to Ashton, but he turned it down, saying it was 'not for him'.)[14]

Meanwhile Ashton had been busy with yet another West End musical, *The Flying Trapeze*, starring Jack Buchanan (whose numbers were arranged by Buddy Bradley). For this production the Alhambra Theatre was transformed into the interior of a Parisian circus in the 1860s, with a background formed by tiers of seats and the orchestra in an elevated box in the middle of them. The principal dancers were Pearl Argyle and Hugh Laing. Laing had a reputation at the Mercury for doing the most dangerous physical stunts, apparently without fear. Ashton made use of this in a number simulating a tightrope act on a platform eight feet above the stage. The platform was painted black and the stage was in darkness except for a spotlight on the two dancers: one of the things Laing had to do was to run the length of this platform, of which he could not see the edge, carrying Argyle in an arm's-length lift. To add to the difficulty and danger, the chorus surrounded the platform wearing costumes that were covered in red and white sequins that shimmered as they caught the light, with dazzling effect. For all its elaborate staging, the show was not a success, and in general the dancing was considered the most distinguished element. One critic said that Argyle and Laing in their tightrope number 'ravished the senses'.

Teddy Knox as 'Danilo' and Jimmy Nervo as 'The Widow' *in* "The Very Merry Widow." A Scene from "ROUND ABOUT REGENT STREET."

Ashton's willingness to turn his hand to any kind of work that came within the province of a choreographer is shown by his next assignment: *Round About Regent Street* was one of the long series of musical extravaganzas that played before the Second World War at the London Palladium, and after it at the Victoria Palace, featuring the Crazy Gang, three pairs of music-hall comedians who had joined together as a team, with immense success: Bud Flanagan and Chesney Allen, Jimmy Nervo and Teddy Knox, and Charlie Naughton and Jimmy Gold. Rather unsophisticated company for Ashton, it might be thought, yet he appreciated the professionalism of the Gang and their producer, George Black. 'He was so marvellously precise – when I went to discuss the show with him he had the whole thing there; he said, I want a chorus and a half, or two choruses, and here is the set, and the amount of room you'll have, and here is the costume (in came a chorus-girl) – and the whole thing was like that, nothing ever deviated from that, there was never any question of doing fifty-five choruses unendingly, and then being told, Oh, it's much too long, it must be cut – he knew exactly, and he'd got the whole thing timed out, so that I never had to do anything in excess of what he wanted.'

All the same, working with the Gang was no easy matter, since they too had equally positive ideas of what they wanted to do – and of what everybody else on stage should be doing, or not doing. For them, Ashton staged a burlesque of *The Merry Widow* (Ernst Lubitsch's film version with Jeanette MacDonald and Maurice Chevalier had been made in the previous year), beginning with a waltz by the dancing chorus, done 'quite seriously – and then on came Nervo and Knox' as the Widow and Prince Danilo, who did their own version, also arranged by Ashton – a 'frantic dance,' said the Tatler, 'that has its climax in bitings and rhythmic clawings on an Edwardian settee'.[15]

Also featured in the show was another American dancer, Jeanne Devereaux, 'a sort of human top . . . people used to say she had ball-bearings in her toe-shoes', for whom Ashton arranged several numbers.

Chapter Seven

1935-1939

De Valois, as well as being faced with the necessity of finding a ballerina, was aware that she also needed another resident choreographer besides herself if the Vic-Wells Ballet were to continue to develop into a major ballet company. With her usual farsightedness, she knew that any decision she made in that respect would have consequences beyond the immediate one of strengthening the current repertory: it was a question of nothing less than developing, over the next twenty years, a native style of ballet. As a basis for this, she was systematically adding the great 19th century classics to the repertory, and there was now a coming generation of dancers trained in the Vic-Wells School to provide the necessary raw material. De Valois's own tendency as a choreographer was towards dance-drama. Although a fine classic dancer herself, with a strong and precise technique, and although her early choreography had been influenced by Nijinska and the other choreographers whose works she had danced as a soloist in the Diaghilev Ballet, more and more she was working on similar lines to modern 'Central European' choreographers like Kurt Jooss.

De Valois saw that it was necessary to develop the classic, pure dance aspect of the ballet along with the dramatic. Antony Tudor had been a member of the company for some time, and had arranged a couple of opera-ballets. At the Ballet Club, he had choreographed *Lysistrata* and *The Planets* and several smaller works. Now he was anxious to try something more ambitious at the Wells. De Valois was dubious; in the first place, she felt that Tudor needed the kind of experience of working with great choreographers that she had had with Diaghilev and Ashton with Ida Rubinstein, and advised him to join the de Basil company for a couple of years. She promised him that there would still be an opening for him at the Wells at the end of that time, and the opportunity to choreograph, but Tudor rejected her advice and in the next two years made two mature, important ballets for Rambert, *Jardin aux lilas* and *Dark Elegies*, before leaving to form his own company. In the second place, and more important, de Valois realised that Tudor was not the classic choreographer she needed, and so she invited Ashton to join the Vic-Wells ballet as a regular member of the company, both a principal dancer and

Fokine's *Le Carnaval*:
Ashton as Pierrot

resident choreographer. Ashton had received a similar offer from the Markova-Dolin Ballet, then in process of formation: perhaps perceiving that de Valois's company was built on a firmer foundation, he accepted her offer. Whatever hopes de Valois might have had for Fonteyn's future, she also knew that the young dancer would not become a fully-fledged ballerina overnight, and further strengthened the personnel of her company with the addition of Pearl Argyle who, though not a great technician, brought a touch of glamour to the company, and Mary Honer,

Constant Lambert and Margot Fonteyn, backstage at Sadler's Wells before a performance of *Façade* 1935

Final group from *Façade*, 1935 revival: back row, left to right, Beatrice Appleyard, Mary Honer, Harold Turner, June Brae, Pearl Argyle, Peggy Melliss, William Chappell, Elizabeth Miller, Pamela May; front row, Robert Helpmann, Fonteyn, Ashton, Gwyneth Mathews, Richard Ellis

who *was* a brilliant technician but until then had danced mostly in musical comedy.

Ashton immediately began work in both capacities. The 1935–1936 season opened on 27 September with a programme including *Les Rendezvous*, with Fonteyn now promoted to Markova's role, and Fokine's *Le Carnaval*, in which Ashton appeared for the first time as Pierrot (at the Ballet Club he used to dance Eusebius). This became a favourite role of Ashton's; Lopokova once said that he was its best interpreter since Adolph Bolm. Other ballets Ashton went into included *Les Sylphides* and de Valois's *Douanes*, newly redecorated by Sophie Fedorovitch, in which he played the Passport Officer (Tudor's old role).

Ashton's agreement with the management was to produce 'at least' three new ballets during the first season[1]; he was free to accept outside engagements that did not interfere with his work for the ballet company. On 8 October *Façade* – not strictly a new ballet – was added to the repertory. The revival was given some semblance of novelty by the addition of a new item, the Country Dance, put in chiefly to give Argyle something to do in the ballet (she also led the Tarantella instead of Molly Brown, who, as the Debutante, would normally have done so). The Country Dance also featured Robert Helpmann, by now the company's *premier danseur noble*. He had partnered Markova in *Swan Lake*, and although never a very strong technician, he cut a very romantic figure and was a superb partner. His role in *Façade*, as the wicked Squire who exercises his *droit de seigneur* and lures the Maiden away from the Yokel, was intended to exploit Helpmann's talent for comedy, but in spite of some droll by-play with a shooting-stick, the number was only mildly funny. But in general, *Façade* was a useful and stylish acquisition for the Vic-Wells. Ashton was also preparing a major new work, Stravinsky's *Le Baiser de la fée*.

This score was commissioned by Ida Rubinstein; as we have seen, Ashton danced in the original version choreographed by Nijinska for her company. At the suggestion of Alexandre Benois, who was to design the ballet, Stravinsky based his music on works of Tchaikovsky, mostly piano pieces and songs. The rather whimsical notation 'inspired by the muse of Tchaikovsky' that appears on the score refers both to the fact that the earlier composer's themes underwent a typically Stravinskyan metamorphosis and to Stravinsky's idea that the allegorical significance of the fairy story he chose as a subject related to Tchaikovsky himself, who was marked at birth by his muse and then claimed at the height of his powers.

Both in its length and its musical complexity, *Baiser* was an ambitious project for Ashton. The story, too, was not without its problems: in an article in the Old Vic and Sadler's Wells Magazine at the time Ashton wrote that he intended to interpret it in his own way, 'by taking the necessary liberties for the construction of a choreographic spectacle emanating directly from the character and style of the music – which in no way will be a realistic treatment'.[2] Perhaps this was Ashton's way of saying that he would ignore the story if it got in the way of the dancing. Both libretto and score do present almost insurmountable problems for the choreographer, particularly in the final tableau, whose length is too protracted for a really satisfactory conclusion to the ballet.†

Ashton wanted to do the ballet because he loved the score, and felt that Nijinska's version had been doomed to failure by the obligation to let Ida Rubinstein appear as the Fairy. Although he had danced in that production, Ashton feels that his own was not particularly influenced by Nijinska, nor was he at that time consciously influenced by Petipa, even though he was praised for having found a choreographic equivalent to Stravinsky's adaptation of Tchaikovsky.

According to Margaret Dale, each of the four scenes was in fact in a different style, and for this reason she feels that the seeds of various later Ashton ballets were to be found in *Baiser*. Thus, the Prologue was 'modern' in style, almost Wigmanesque (and here we may remember his visits to Martha Graham's performances in New York the year before). 'The tempest was all suggested by the mother's

† For synopsis, see Appendix B.

Façade: Harold Turner
and William Chappell
in the Popular Song

Façade: Molly Brown
and Ashton in the
Tango

Le Baiser de la fée Tableau III: Margot Fonteyn as the Fiancée, with Bridesmaids, Harold Turner as the Young Man, Pearl Argyle as the Fairy

body movements, her swaying torso, and by Sophie's décor.' This statement of Miss Dale's is supported by the Dancing Times review: 'There is no evidence of the tempest that is raging save in her movements, and through these one almost hears the wind howl as she is buffeted from side to side. The Spirits who pursue her also give the effect of being borne on the wind. Equally fine is the entry of the cloaked villagers, who bear away the dead mother and the living child in the calm that has followed the storm'.[3] Ashton's treatment of the storm Spirits, one assumes, was strikingly different from that of Balanchine, who first choreographed the ballet in 1937: a *ballabile* similar to the waltz of the Snowflakes in Ivanov's *Casse Noisette*, even to having the dancers wave sticks with clusters of white pompons on them. Sophie Fedorovitch costumed the Spirits in grey-green draperies, and there was, Ashton says, 'a lot of swirling – the sort of thing one imagines a snowstorm to be like.

'Where I fell down – where I think everybody falls down – was in the village scene, because I didn't break it up enough'. Margaret Dale remembers an ensemble number that was almost like a *Schuhplatteln*, 'more like a de Valois ballet, very early Vic-Wells!' Ashton attributes the failure of this scene partly to the perversity of Stravinsky's instrumentation – what sounds on the piano like a robust rustic dance proves to very sparsely orchestrated. Fedorovitch also seems to have been less successful here, putting Fonteyn (the Fiancée) in a long white dress, Harold Turner (the Young Man) in white shorts, and the village men either in top hats or wide-brimmed white straw ones.

The third scene, on the other hand, was very beautiful, with Ashton's first big classic *pas de deux* (impossible in *Les Rendezvous*, for instance, as P W Manchester has pointed out, because Idzikowski was too small to partner Markova in that way). As for the dances of the group of bridesmaids, Margaret Dale feels that these embodied a kind of distortion of the classic that foreshadowed the style of Ashton's later Stravinsky ballet, *Scènes de ballet*, with its syncopated toe-steps matching the fragmented rhythms of the music.

Ashton feels that his solution to the problem of the final scene worked very well, with the dancers grouped behind a gauze curtain, and Turner carrying Argyle, as the Fairy, in slow, floating lifts, or dragging her along the floor; at other moments she would jump over a group of dancers lying on the stage, and he would catch her. Finally she was carried along a line of dancers and off into the light, as though into eternity. The effect of this scene was greatly heightened by Fedorovitch's designs – 'the grey-pink mysteries and dark, finely-conceived shadows of the "Eternal Dwellings".'[4]

The role of the Fairy was perfectly suited to Argyle's cool, aristocratic beauty and exquisite line. Ashton cast Harold Turner as the Young Man: though a less accomplished partner than Helpmann, he was technically a virtuoso, and Ashton wanted to make the dance element of the ballet as strong as possible. The Fiancée was Ashton's first important creation for Fonteyn, and not achieved without difficulty. Ashton was still not completely convinced about her – for instance, he preferred Elizabeth Miller in *Les Rendezvous*. When de Valois first suggested that

Le Baiser de la fée
Tableau IV: Pearl Argyle as the Fairy, with corps de ballet

Le Baiser de la fée:
Margot Fonteyn
as the Fiancée

he use Fonteyn in *Baiser*, his reaction was, 'I don't see anything in her', and early rehearsals with her were marked by a conflict of wills. 'I felt,' Ashton has written, 'a great frustration in being unable to mould her precisely as I wanted. Her performance needed to be much more precise. I got very cross with her at times and went on and on at her, relentlessly. One morning after I had been particularly severe, she suddenly rushed and threw her arms around my neck and burst into floods of tears. I knew then that I had won the battle; that I would be able to work with her'.[5] The result was not only lovely choreographically but also a completely believable characterisation. One critic wrote, 'Mr Ashton has had the wit to create an original romantic figure – and Miss Fonteyn the inspiration to body it

Le Baiser de la fée:
Margot Fonteyn and
Harold Turner in the
pas de deux

forth with poignant ecstasy and pathos through the medium of her attested virtuosity. This person really lives – so much so that it is difficult to allow the superior allurement of Miss Pearl Argyle's Fairy, graceful but shadowy as she is'.[6]

Thus in his first important work as resident choreographer Ashton had established a partnership with a ballerina that was to be of even greater importance than his collaboration with Markova, and had also shown that he was indeed the classicist that de Valois had sought. Even Rayner Heppenstall, who was not by any means without reservations in his admiration for Ashton's work, wrote in his *Apology for Dancing* that the *pas de deux* 'was certainly the loveliest piece of unmixed classicism in English ballet or, for that matter, in a good many years of any Ballet. Mr Ashton is honest enough – and it is a very high virtue – to accept his limitations and neither to strain at more than he can encompass nor to play for loud and obvious theatrical effects. And above all, everything he does is eminently grateful to dance. It fits the classically trained dancer's body as a Bellini aria fits the vocal apparatus of the classically trained singer.'

Even though Ashton was to follow *Baiser* very shortly with another ambitious work, he had not by any means given up the commercial theatre. Such work, though very much a sideline, continued to be an important additional source of income for him, since his salary at the Wells, though regular, was by no means large – £10 a week, with no royalties for performances of his ballets. By the time *Baiser* went on at the Wells, on 26 November, Ashton was already working on dance numbers for C B Cochran's 1936 revue, *Follow the Sun*. Rehearsals were in progress in several London theatres at once: Buddy Bradley was working with Claire Luce and the chorus at the Adelphi, Ashton on the ballet at the Palace, while book rehearsals were going on at the Shaftesbury. After a while Ashton and Bradley had to move to the Stoll when other shows took over the theatres they were in, and in the meantime, Arthur Schwartz was coaching the principals in his songs at home. *Follow the Sun* was very much a dancing show. Claire Luce, the leading lady, had danced with Fred Astaire in *Gay Divorce*, his last stage show, in both New York and London; there was a whole contingent of Cuban dancers, Ciro Rimac's Rumbaland Muchachos, who introduced the Conga; another featured singer and dancer was Jeni Le Gon, a black artist who had been in the first Astaire-Rogers film, *Flying Down to Rio*; and Miss Luce's partner in two of Ashton's numbers was to be Nick Long Jr, another American.

Ashton's principal contribution was a ballet entitled *The First Shoot*, a distinguished collaboration: the libretto was by Osbert Sitwell,† the music by William Walton and the décor by Cecil Beaton. The ballet, in which the wife of an Edwardian peer, an ex-chorus-girl, was accidently killed at a country-house shooting-party, was a great success. In spite of the sad story, it was very amusing, and although only ten or twelve minutes long, very lavishly produced.

The choreography consisted mostly of very simple steps: the Manchester

† See Appendix B.

Follow the Sun:
Claire Luce as Lady de
Fontenoy, Ashton
as Lord Charles
Canterbury in
The First Shoot

Guardian said that Ashton found 'a rhythm and a pattern for the strutting of the pheasants, the loading and discharge of guns, the squatting upon shooting-sticks, and the rest of the routine of the moors'[7] – not particularly promising material, but as always in this kind of assignment Ashton was obliged to cut his cloth according to his measure. At the end of the ballet, pheasants covered the heroine's body with leaves. For the pheasants, Beaton originally designed conventional ballet skirts, following Sitwell's instruction, 'We want to observe in everything that *faint* line of parodied resemblance to the *Lac des cygnes* (pheasant feather opposed to swans)',[8] but Ashton said, 'No tutus!' and so they were removed from the design.

Ashton evidently thought highly enough of the possibilities of *The First Shoot* to consider reviving it later, presumably in an extended form – it is included in a list of titles in a notebook that he kept during the 1940s, with the notation 'for America' – possibly New York City Ballet.

When the show opened in Manchester just before Christmas, Ashton had to dance the leading role of Lord Charles Canterbury, 'the comparatively poor but fascinating younger son of the Duke of Dashton', when Nick Long's arrival was

delayed because he was in Hollywood filming *Broadway Melody of 1936*, with
Eleanor Powell. Ashton danced in the show for the first two and a half weeks, and
Long finally made his first appearance on 8 January 1936. The London opening
was set for the 24th of the month, but on the 20th King George V died, and the
opening had to be put off, to allow for a period of national mourning, until 4
February. On 11 April Cochran started running the show on a twice-nightly
schedule; some time later Nick Long left and was replaced in the dance numbers
by another member of the cast, Robert Linden. Apparently he and the leading
lady did not get along very well, and soon afterwards Linden also abruptly left the
show. At very short notice, Ashton was called in to dance opposite Claire Luce not
only in *The First Shoot*, but also in two other numbers he had choreographed but
not danced before, 'Nicotina' and 'Dangerous You', and he continued to appear in
the show for the remainder of the run (from 21 May to 27 June).

Even before *Follow the Sun* opened, Ashton found time to choreograph another
short dance to music by Walton, and was presumably already hard at work on his
next important ballet for the Vic-Wells. *Siesta*, the Walton piece, went on, in
spite of the national mourning, on 24 January, the day that was to have seen the
London opening of the revue – but this too was a postponement, from the
21st. *Siesta* was not a new work by Walton, and had in fact been played as an
interlude at the same Camargo Society performance as the première of *Façade*.

Ernest Newman described the new *pas de deux* in The Sunday Times: 'On the
rise of the curtain we saw Pearl Argyle and Robert Helpmann recumbent on the
stage, looking so comfortable that one almost felt inclined to call out to them
not to dream of disturbing themselves on our account. But slowly as the music
went on, the conscientious couple seemed to realise that rather more than this was

A rehearsal discussion
of *Siesta*: left to right
Pearl Argyle, William
Walton, Ashton,
Robert Helpmann

expected of them. They rose to their feet, felt the urge of life returning to their sluggish limbs, treated us for two or three minutes to a few dance movements and then, apparently tiring of it all quite soon after we had done, wisely lay down again and seemed to share our relief that it was all over'.[9] The dance was described in The Times as 'a languorous pas de deux . . . with a few tango steps to suggest a South American locality'.[10]

It will be remembered that about eighteen months previously there had been talk of a ballet based on Walton's *Belshazzar's Feast* at the Wells, sponsored by the Camargo Society. Although that had fallen through, presumably because there was not enough money to pay for the performance of a large choral work as well as the scenery and costumes, the officers of the Society – at any rate, J M Keynes and M Montagu-Nathan, who as treasurer and secretary respectively continued to take an active interest in its affairs, still wanted to sponsor an important new ballet, and had asked Constant Lambert to think of a substitute.

Lambert's intimate connection with British ballet in its early years will be evident from the frequency with which his name has been mentioned as composer or arranger of music. His activities were in fact ubiquitous and indefatigable: not only was he musical director of the Vic-Wells Ballet and one of the greatest conductors of ballet anywhere, he also frequently played one of the two pianos that provided the accompaniment at the Ballet Club. But his influence was even more profound than all of this implies – many ballets owed their conception artistically as well as musically to Lambert; as a witty and erudite companion he was responsible for cultivating the taste not only of Ashton but also of Fonteyn and other members of the company.

On 16 September 1935 Lambert wrote to Keynes to tell him that after considering and rejecting various possibilities, including ballets to music by Berlioz and Chabrier, 'I have at last hit on a scheme which I really think is good and . . . ideally suited to Fred.' The argument, he said, was 'a mingling of romantic themes from Berlioz, Gautier, Villiers, etc.' Ashton was excited about the idea and wanted to do it after Christmas, and Lambert wanted Pavel Tchelitchev, or failing him Sophie Fedorovitch, to design the décor. He warned Keynes that the project would be costly: all the music, to be selected from late piano works of Liszt, would have to be scored, a task he intended to entrust to Gordon Jacob – but 'I don't know how he can be offered less than £50,' and Tchelitchev was also likely to be expensive. He asked Keynes to consider using the funds available to the Society for the ballet, and to call a committee meeting soon to discuss the idea.†

Keynes replied approving the suggestion, but adding that no money had actually been collected for *Belshazzar's Feast,* and that he would have to get permission from 'the Income Tax people' to use the Society's remaining funds for such a

---

†This letter and the ensuing correspondence are preserved in the library of the Royal Ballet School at White Lodge; I am indebted to Miss Joan Lawson for drawing my attention to their existence.

purpose. He also rejected Lambert's suggestion for a designer.[11] A meeting of the committee was held and it was agreed that an appeal should be sent out to members.

On 8 December 1935 Keynes wrote to Cecil Beaton asking him to consider designing the new ballet: 'We think it might suit your taste and fancy very well.' He told him that there was not much money available and that the work would have to be done very quickly, since the first night was only two months away. The sets would have to be very simple, not only for reasons of economy but because of the limited space for storage at the Wells. Both scenery and costumes would have to be executed in the theatre's own workshops, but Keynes realised that Beaton would want to supervise the work and assured him of his support 'in insisting on . . . proper standards'. In making this pledge, Keynes probably had in mind Lilian Baylis's notorious determination to cut costs by whatever means she could muster. As Ashton has said, 'when one was doing a new ballet, she always tried to palm off on one old costumes, ancient clothes, second-hand evening dresses, peers' robes and other oddments that people had given her'.[12]

Beaton accepted the commission and proposed a fee of £50. He also asked that a few of the principals' costumes be made by Karinska (who was also working on his designs for *The First Shoot*). He was equally anxious to complete the work quickly, and in fact promised to deliver the designs in ten days. On 13 December Lambert, Ashton, Beaton and de Valois met to discuss the production, which had been given the title *Apparitions*. Meanwhile Lilian Baylis was keeping close watch for possible extravagances – she wanted to know exactly what expenses the Camargo Society was prepared to assume, and did they include 'possibly (although we hope not) extra rehearsal?'[13] As for Karinska, 'Of course I have no objection to an outside dressmaker making some of the frocks, provided they are not very elaborate, and not out of the picture when taken with those made in our own workrooms'![14]

Beaton also asked if some of the scenery could be executed by a professional studio, that of Alick Johnstone, rather than in the Vic-Wells workshop, and Keynes wrote to Miss Baylis to ask if there were any old cloths that could be used.[15] Her reply[16] was that two scenes were being painted at the Old Vic, at a cost of £43 six shillings, and that all the old Camargo Society cloths had already been used. Expenses were mounting – four stronger lamps needed for the Cave Scene would cost seven pounds ten shillings each; Keynes pencilled in the margin of her letter the sums of £53 for Alick Johnstone, £50 for Beaton, £75 for music, and £43 for the Old Vic – a total of £221. He had already written to Samuel Courtauld,[17] suggesting that they each donate an additional £50 to cover the costs of the ballet, and Courtauld had agreed;[18] Keynes replied to Miss Baylis that the Society would contribute a total of nearly £250.[19] Miss Baylis objected to Beaton's idea of sewing beaded designs on to the 'tarleton' (sic) skirts for the Ballroom Scene because it would cause quicker deterioration,[20] and Beaton agreed to scrap the beads; then again, the tassels he wanted for the Funeral Scene would cost too much, would not looped ribbons serve the purpose?[21]

In spite of such economies, by 19 February the total cost had risen to £300, and Keynes's personal contribution was £75.[22] Gordon Jacob was being paid £75 for his orchestrations, and Constant Lambert had asked for £5 for his own personal expenses – 'I am not asking anything for the scenario or the arrangement of the music – but for expenses of buying music, etc.'[23] Ashton, of course, was on salary as dancer and choreographer. Beaton gave back his fee of £50 to go towards Karinska's bill (she ended up making all the dresses for the Ballroom Scene). Finally the Society received a donation of £100 from Lord Rothermere to help defray the increased cost of the ballet.

Even so, it is almost absurd in these times, when one of the ball-dresses could not be made for Beaton's original fee of £50, to think that a ballet on the scale of *Apparitions* could be put on for a few hundred pounds. The collaborators were quite happy to work, quite literally, for love – those were the 'years of happy comradeship' that Ninette de Valois wrote of in an obituary piece on Lambert fifteen years later.[24]

After the opening Lambert wrote to Beaton, who had had to leave for New York before the final stages, to tell him of the great success of the première which, according to time-honoured theatrical tradition, followed a chaotic dress-rehearsal. As usual with Karinska, the costumes were not ready; 'the atmosphere was dead, and one felt the awful weight of middlebrow opinion against the whole thing'. But at the first performance everything came miraculously together, the costumes were rushed, ready or not, to the theatre by taxi during the first ballet of the evening: 'It was a real collaboration,' wrote Lambert, 'and everyone agrees that it knocks spots off any ballet since *Cotillon*'.[25]

Since Ashton says that he remained in Manchester throughout the engagement of *Follow the Sun* – putting in changes, rehearsing Nick Long in the dances, and so forth – he cannot have had much more than four weeks of actual rehearsal time for *Apparitions*, an astonishing fact in view of the scale and complexity of the new ballet, greater even than *Baiser* and hence more ambitious than anything he had attempted so far. A certain amount of preparation had of course been done in advance – 'Constant and I had wanted to do a Liszt ballet for ages, we had been through all the music that we liked long before that, and Constant did the whole of the libretto, which was based on Berlioz's *Symphonie fantastique*.'†

Lambert made some changes: the protagonist became a poet rather than a composer, and he emphasized the motif of the chase – first the poet pursuing his beloved and then the woman, transformed, pursuing him.[26] The Epilogue of *Apparitions*, in which the woman, who has up to then been a figment of the Poet's fevered imagination, returns to lead her companions as they bear away his dead body, is an important addition by Lambert to the story: Berlioz's symphony ends with the orgy, and there is no redemption. *Apparitions* predated by some five months the production of Massine's choreographic version of *La Symphonie*

† See Appendix B.

fantastique: Massine's ballet was first given by the de Basil company on 24 July 1936, and Ashton's on 11 February.

Apparitions was no doubt conceived primarily as a vehicle for Helpmann. As I have said, he was not a virtuoso, and as a consequence the ballet relied heavily on his acting ability and glamorous stage presence. The Prologue was essentially a mime-scene for Helpmann with a few *tours en arabesque* to express his mounting agitation. The first two apparitions who were revealed behind the stained-glass windows of the Poet's study, the Monk and the Hussar, were motionless, menacing figures, but as the third, the Woman in Ball Dress, Berlioz's *idée fixe*, Fonteyn presented an unforgettable dance image, even in the narrow confines of the space behind the window, twisting and turning her body, with enticing movements of her arms and coquettish flutterings of her fan.

The first tableau, the Ballroom Scene, is generally regarded as one of Ashton's masterpieces. Beaton's décor was unusual in that it had wings only on stage right, with a flat wall of white gauze on the other side. Shadows of chandeliers, music-stands and a 'cello were projected on to the scenery from behind. As the scene opened, the corps de ballet moved in and out of the wings, giving the impression of a larger space beyond. As the music ('Polnisch', from *The Christmas Tree*) worked up to a series of ever more feverish climaxes, the men carried their partners across the stage in a succession of big lifts, moving in parallel lines and diagonals along which the Poet vainly pursued the Woman. 'Jadis', also from *The Christmas Tree*, was a more poignant piece that at last brought him face to face with her, still in coquettish guise; during this section the corps couples were frozen in exquisite poses that suggested the elasticity of time in the Poet's dream. Music and choreography together vividly created the feeling of entering deeper levels of the dream-state as the scene passed into the frantic vortex of the *Galop* and then into another encounter with the Woman (to the second *Elegy*), no longer an elusive, taunting figure but transformed into the Poet's loving, comforting muse.

The following scenes, on a snow-clad plain, with maddening bells personified in a *ballabile* and a sinister funeral procession, and in a cavern where a diabolical orgy was led by the woman, now hideously masked, were generally held to be weaker, though the procession was certainly very effective dramatically. The bells' dance was technically and rhythmically complex, and was led by two of the strongest technicians in the company, Mary Honer and Elizabeth Miller. At that time company classes were being taught by two totally contrasting teachers, Margaret Craske, then as now the high priestess of the strict Cecchetti method, and Anna Pruzina, a Russian who exhorted her pupils to lift their legs as high as possible without worrying about such considerations as the correct placement of the hips. According to Michael Somes, some of Pruzina's rather slapdash style of movement found its way into *Apparitions*, particularly in the Bells Scene. Margaret Dale, who danced in it a little later on, said the *ballabile* was difficult musically as well as technically: 'You never did anything four times, there would be three, then seven. The costumes were dreadful to dance in, very tight, straight-cut bo-

dices that didn't allow you to breathe, and the tutus had a layer of stiff cellophane under the tarlatan that glinted in the light – it probably looked very effective, but it made a terrible clatter. Then there were terrible horsehair wigs and masks that cut into your eyes so you couldn't see the next person, and great antennae that if you weren't careful got locked in those of the girl next to you. Everybody hated doing it, but it was a very good dance, I think.' A characteristic feature of this number, together with the irregular rhythms, was the punctuation of the steps with brief sudden pauses, the rhythmic accent marked with just a nod of the head.

Twenty-six members of the opera company were brought in to provide the procession of monks in the Funeral Scene, and at first they even chanted the dirge-like music (*Unstern*) though this was later eliminated. On tour without the singers anyone who was available, including de Valois herself and the rehearsal pianist, Hilda Gaunt, would be pressed into service to swell the ranks.

The set for the Cavern Scene consisted of a series of cut-cloths of diminishing sizes, to give a kind of forced perspective, but this created problems for the choreographer – 'the moment anyone fell to the floor they went out of sight, it was like dancing in a tunnel'.[27] Musically, too, this scene was difficult because the action, instead of being tailored to a series of short pieces of music, had to be fitted to one longer piece, the third *Mephisto Waltz*, with its many repeats.

137

Apparitions ballroom scene: Fonteyn and Helpmann in the 1949 revival

For all its imperfections, *Apparitions* originally had a tremendous power, and further strengthened Ashton's claim to be taken seriously, rather than as a confectioner of amusing trifles. Arnold Haskell in particular singled out an important aspect of the ballet, and of Ashton's talent, that was to become more and more notable as he grew into maturity – that it was not just a pastiche: 'with extraordinary sensibility and an obvious knowledge [of] and feeling for the period, Ashton has made it live. He has conceived it as a romantic and not as a modern looking back upon a quaint period'.[28] Similarly, Haskell realised that Fonteyn's performance had a significance beyond this ballet – 'In her, Ashton has undoubtedly found someone who can evoke and reveal the deeper sides of his art.' *Apparitions*, indeed, may be said to have defined Ashton's future relationship with Fonteyn – that of the creative artist and his Muse.

One incidental criticism of the ballet was that the scene-changes necessitated rather lengthy interludes, and even Jacob's wonderful orchestration of the sinister *Ungarisch*, for instance, did not stop audiences from becoming restless. When he returned from the United States Beaton tried to solve the problem by designing a drop-curtain, suggested by illustrations in a German edition of *Peter Schlemiel*: it depicted the Woman, 'wearing the mask of a death's head, in the act of gathering up the shadow of the Poet . . . against a vivid yellow background'. So far from beguiling the audience, it caused them to recoil 'in horror', and the curtain was scrapped after only a few performances.[29]

When the ballet was revived at Covent Garden thirteen years later, the changes could be made fast enough for the interludes to be cut. But the ballet did not work any more. Even the ballroom scene was less effective when the vast space was actual and not illusory. All the dresses, it seemed, were made twice as voluminous: Fonteyn's original lilac costume was replaced by an elaborate black one that was inappropriate for the tender side of the role. This change of design, indeed, re-flected a change in her interpretation: as Clive Barnes wrote, 'The girl needs the unremitting cruelty of the very young: once make her a *grande dame à la* Touma-nova and half the ballet's poignancy evaporates. She should be immature: all life, all youth, all fancy, a thoughtless beauty killing in innocence'.[30] Helpmann's role seemed weaker than in the intimacies of the Wells: Mary Clarke wrote, 'It is neither purely mimed . . . nor really danced, but an odd compromise between the two. It would be more convincing balletically if the tantalising bells . . . drove the poet into a brilliant and terrifying dance'.[31]

Later, an attempt was made to restore the original intimacy by masking down the stage and replacing the cyclorama with a skycloth; in the revival for Sadler's Wells Theatre Ballet in 1957 the new sets were further cut down, which gave the production a distressingly second-hand look. Moreover, Anne Heaton and John Field could not supply the youthful allure that Fonteyn and Helpmann themselves had failed to recapture.

It might be thought that after this prolonged period of activity Ashton would have taken a rest, but the 'passionately lazy' Ashton (in Rambert's famous phrase) went straight to work on another revue. The fact is, of course, that people who are by nature lazy either do nothing or drive themselves to work very hard, and so it was with Ashton at this period of his career. The new revue was originally to be called *London in the Season*, but the death of the king meant that there would be no 'season' in the social sense that year, and so the title was changed to *The Town Talks*. Like *How D'You Do?*, it was produced by André Charlot, and opened at the Vaudeville on 11 March.

Vivian Ellis wrote, and Ashton choreographed, *The Hat* for June, 'as a dancing vendeuse trying to sell a hat to an infuriatingly difficult customer'.[32] (June, née June Howard Tripp, and later Lady Inverclyde, was a former pupil of Pavlova who

Apparitions: Ashton
with Gwyneth
Mathews and Pamela
May in the ballroom
scene

became a musical comedy star.) In general, however, the revue received only faint
praise from the critics: for example, The Times said, 'If one were to imagine a
typical revue, light, competent, empty, amusing now and then, but without
special challenge of wit, satire, or spectacle, this is what one would imagine'.[33]

At the Wells, Ashton continued to dance both in his own ballets – *Façade* and
Apparitions, in which he sometimes went on as one of the Dandies, and later as
both the Hussar and the Monk – and in those of de Valois, the above-mentioned
Douanes, for instance, and a new ballet that went into the repertory on 17 April
1936, *Barabau*. This was a new version of a ballet originally done by Balanchine
in 1925, his first for Diaghilev; de Valois's version was designed by Ashton's
friend Edward Burra. Ashton played the part of a boorish sergeant of the Fascist
militia; when it was revived early in the Second World War he exaggerated his

ABOVE *Les Sylphides* at
the Ballet Club, with
Margot Fonteyn,
Ashton and Elisabeth
Schooling; Sally
Gilmour is in the
corps de ballet, directly
behind Schooling

RIGHT *Passionate
Pavane*:
Maude Lloyd, Walter
Gore and Frank Staff in
the 1936 revival

characterisation to the point where it became a broad caricature of Mussolini himself, which gave the ballet a certain popularity on the same level as songs like 'We're Going to Hang Out Our Washing on the Siegfried Line', but not enough to give it a permanent place in the repertory. Later in the same month he danced at the Ballet Club in *Les Sylphides*, partnering Margot Fonteyn in one of her rare guest appearances there.

The success of Ashton's first ballets at the Wells brought wider recognition both to himself and to the company, which had not previously been considered to be in the same league as the Russian companies. There were now two of these, the 'Original' (as it was later called) Ballet Russe headed by Colonel de Basil with Massine as choreographer, and a new one just formed by de Basil's former partner René Blum, under the artistic direction of Fokine. Blum approached Ashton to do a ballet for this company, the Ballet de Monte Carlo. Its title and collaborators were even announced in the Dancing Times for May 1936, in which month the company was due to open its first London season, at the Alhambra. The ballet was to be called *Epsom*, with music by Marcel Delaunay and décor by Raoul Dufy. It is easy enough to imagine it, a *demi-caràctere* ballet *à l'anglaise*: perhaps fortunately, the project came to nothing, though Ashton did get as far as visiting Dufy in Paris to discuss it.

At the beginning of the new season, Ashton produced his final work for the Ballet Club, the revised version of *Passionate Pavane* (*Mars and Venus* was revived at the same performance, 11 October 1936). A few days later at the Wells, he added an important new role to his repertory when he danced the title role in de Valois's *The Rake's Progress*. His duties as resident choreographer were not limited to the production of new ballets – he also had to take his turn at arranging the ballets for the operas, most of which had been done in the past by de Valois herself. Early in the autumn of 1936 Ashton did a new ballet for the existing production of *Die Fledermaus*.

He was also working on another important ballet, *Nocturne*, to music of Delius, which was presented on 10 November. The idea of a ballet to Delius's *Paris* had been suggested to Ashton by Edward Sackville-West, the distinguished music critic, though it is not clear how much of the actual story was devised by him. Ashton says that it was he himself who worked out the details and, with Lambert, planned the relationship of the action to the music; he also says, without elaborating, that the scenario was to some extent autobiographical. Lambert was against 'symphonic' ballets and even objected at first to the use of Delius's tone poem. It is true that the piece does not immediately strike one as being suitable for a ballet, but the dances and the action were so perfectly tailored to its structure that it worked marvellously.

The title was originally announced as *Paris*, but changed to *Nocturne*, presumably because the collaborators wished to avoid any reference to a specific locale, as they stated in a programme note: 'Delius's Paris is described by the composer as a Nachtstück or Nocturne. It is this aspect of the music, rather than the purely

RIGHT *Nocturne*:
Fonteyn as the Flower
Girl, Ashton as the
Spectator

BELOW Group from
Nocturne: Fonteyn as
the Flower Girl, on
floor at right, Robert
Helpmann as the
Young Man, June
Brae as the Young
Girl, left of centre

Home and Beauty: Mr Cochran's Young Ladies in 'Dressing for Dinner'

local aspect, that has been stressed by the artists responsible for the present production. They have made no attempt at a realistic evocation of Paris itself. Instead, they have concentrated on a human drama to which the night life of a great city forms the background.' In accordance with this, Fedorovitch's décor consisted merely of a low balustrade against a night sky and pillars at each side with posters advertising a ball. Against this monochrome background the costumes made a sumptuous effect – the brilliant colours of the evening dresses, the men's evening suits, not in black but colours like plum or bottle green, the maskers in black and yellow, Fonteyn in grey and white. The 'human drama' was a simple, even novelettish, one: a rich young man, escorting his fiancée to a ball, is momentarily attracted by a beautiful flower-girl, but abandons her when the rich girl returns and claims his attention; the poor girl, genuinely in love, is heartbroken.

As a theme for a ballet this had the great advantage that it could be told entirely in terms of dancing: the solos and duets of the main characters are set against the ensembles of the revellers (fashionable young men and women), with a secondary group of maskers who function as a kind of ironic and sinister chorus, weaving in and out of the action, preventing the flower girl from reaching the man she loves, mocking her in her betrayal – a deliberately artificial device that has become something of a cliché, but then was still fresh. There was one more character: an older Spectator who at the beginning and end of the ballet gazed out over the balustrade at the city of light, and remained on stage throughout, standing apart from the action but observing it closely, until the end when he tried in vain to console the flower girl. The introduction of this compassionate yet detached figure was something of a stroke of genius on Ashton's part (and his performance of it was unforgettable): when asked what gave him the idea, he said, 'Well, I suppose I wanted to put myself into it, and I've always liked ballets that begin and end the same way – that's why I always adored *Thamar.*' A few images remain: Fonteyn's incomparably expressive *arabesque*, the interlacings of the arms and heads in Helpmann's duet with June Brae, like a stylised ballroom dance, some of the women being lifted by their partners to gaze down curiously at the abandoned flower girl, and, indelibly, Ashton slowly walking to the back and raising his arms in a gesture of resignation on the last phrase of the music.

Nocturne, according to Haskell, was 'the first of [Ashton's] sophisticated ballets to have depth and to show a really serious confrontation with his material'.[34] It also demonstrated his growing assurance in handling a work on a large scale, and above all reflected his deepening relationship with Fonteyn, who under his guidance was able to create a real and touching portrayal of the idealised figure of the Flower Girl. Even with her, it was never Ashton's habit to go deeply into such matters as motivation and character; he preferred to work with her by example. Indeed, Ashton's facility in imitating dancers of the past whom he admired often served a very serious purpose when he would show Fonteyn how Pavlova or Karsavina would have performed a certain movement. Helpmann was a thoroughly convincing philanderer; Ashton suggested a greater depth to the character in a beautiful solo to an adagio passage in the score, with sustained arching jumps from side to side.

As a *ballet d'atmosphère, Nocturne* was second only to Tudor's *Jardin aux lilas,* but it has long since disappeared from the repertory.

Ashton maintained his activities at a level of intensity equalling that of the previous year: he seems to have been involved in several projects more or less simultaneously, both at the Wells and elsewhere, and it is indeed hard to understand how he managed to fit them all in. Once again he was staging numbers for C B Cochran's annual revue, which ended up being called *Home and Beauty.* Just as the previous year's show had been delayed by the death of King George V, this one had the ill-luck to coincide with the abdication of Edward VIII, so that the designation 'Coronation' Revue proved to be inappropriate. It was much less of a dancing show than its predecessor, but it had a new gimmick of its own: it was not quite a 'book' show, but all the scenes and lyrics (by A P Herbert) were linked by a central idea, a weekend house party given by the Earl and Countess of Mulberry. Most of the featured players were the same characters throughout – only Binnie Hale and Nelson Keys appeared in various guises.

The main dance-number was 'Twilight Sonata', in which 'a shadowy procession of belles and beaux in the fashionable costumes of 1800, 1840, and 1880' were seen in a series of lovers' trysts at a sundial, watched over by Greta Gynt and Frank Staff as a pair of statues.[35] *Home and Beauty* had a successful run in spite of every-thing, but more than one critic complained of the lack of dancing in the show – James Agate, for example, asked why did Mr Cochran 'entirely cold-shoulder Terpsichore, the muse to whom he has ever been most beholden'?[36]

Less than a week after the London première of *Home and Beauty*, on 8 February 1937, there opened in Cambridge a production of Molière's *Le Misanthrope*, starring Lydia Lopokova, who had pursued a double career, as dancer and actress, ever since 1914. This was presented by her husband, J M Keynes, who invited Ashton to choreograph a short ballet, *Harlequin in the Street*, as a curtain-raiser, with theme and décor by André Derain, who also chose the music (from the works of Couperin).† Constant Lambert arranged the pieces for two pianos, and later for small orchestra when the production was moved into London.

Lopokova did not dance in the ballet, though several other members of the cast of the play did. It was very short, no more than ten minutes, and simply intended, Ashton says, 'to establish the atmosphere – a French market-scene, with marvel-lous costumes by Derain, full of character'. (They were executed by Karinska.) Harlequin was danced by Stanley Judson and the Gossips by Peggy van Praagh, Susan Reeves and Mary Skeaping. The show came into the Ambassadors' Theatre in London on 23 February. Judson left the cast at this point and Ashton gave his role to Alan Carter, then sixteen years old and recently accepted by de Valois into her company.[37]

Another week later, a ballet that was to become a classic went on at the Wells. (Somehow, Ashton managed to find time and energy during all this to dance in the Ballet Rambert's February season at the Duchess Theatre.) *Les Patineurs* could be called a companion-piece to *Les Rendezvous*, another ballet-divertissement to music originally composed for an opera-ballet, in this case Meyerbeer's *Le Prophète*.

Originally, *Les Patineurs* was not intended for Ashton at all, but for de Valois, and 'a new Ballet-Divertissement' by the latter was even announced in the Dancing Times as late as January 1937. Lambert had arranged the music, and was playing it for her after a matinée in a dressing-room adjoining Ashton's. He heard it, and 'I said to myself: "My goodness, that ballet is much more suited to me than to her; can't I possibly do it?" As luck would have it she was so busy that I was then able to take it on'.[38] It is hard to see how de Valois could have been much busier than he was at that time, though in early January she was occupied with preparing Fon-teyn for her first *Giselle*, on the 19th. Another motive for the exchange may have been in return for his relinquishing *The Rake's Progress* eighteen months before.

Like *Les Rendezvous*, the new ballet was set in a park, in winter rather than

† See Appendix B.

Les Patineurs: Mary Honer, Harold Turner and Elizabeth Miller in the *pas de trois*

spring, and the dances were based on the idea of skating. *Les Patineurs* also resembled the earlier ballet in that it presented a new technical challenge to both choreographer and dancers. In Harold Turner and Mary Honer, the company boasted two virtuosi who could stand comparison with any in the Russian companies, and *Les Patineurs* was specifically designed to show them off, with Fonteyn and Helpmann somewhat less prominently featured in the romantic *pas de deux*. The four men in the *pas de huit* also showed a marked improvement in technique; everyone particularly noticed the remarkable elevation of the young Michael Somes, who had lately graduated to the company from the Vic-Wells School, where he had been the first male scholarship student.

'The chief aim I had was to show the virtuosity of the then growing English ballet,' Ashton wrote. 'Actually, when I was doing the last part, I had 'flu, with a temperature of 103, so the last entry of the Blue Boy was Harold Turner's choreography. I was too ill to do it. I left that piece out and said, "You must fill it in." I just did the Finale and left that piece for him to do.' (This refers to Turner's several entries during the finale, but not the actual conclusion of the ballet, where the Blue Skater spins as the curtain falls and rises and falls again.)

'The ballet was based on skating, although in the days when it was done, ice skating was not so fashionable. I have never really seen any skating, that is apart from championships on Movietone News. But one girl, Elizabeth Miller, had actually done some and she gave us some hints. In a sense it was a new development in my style, because I had never before really set out just to do something that was simply for virtuosity, just to show dancers off. I had never done anything that went at that speed, mounting and mounting to a tremendous climax at the end. Somehow it all poured out. I didn't give it much thought, because knowing it was about skating, I just did choreographic patterns to such skating movements as I knew. You see, there is nothing really behind it. There is naturally a construction in it, but it does not require dramatic impact or anything of that sort. It is a show piece'.[39]†

The première of *Les Patineurs*, on 16 February 1937, was a triumphant occasion. Many people must have realised that its success had a wider significance in terms of the development of the company and British ballet as a whole. It was not only at Covent Garden in the summer seasons of the Russian Ballet that great dancing was to be seen, but also right there at Sadler's Wells. Even the critics for once did not write off a pure-dance ballet as being inherently unimportant. The Times, for instance, said:

> *Les Sylphides* is the most perfect example of the [divertissement] form, and if *Les Patineurs* does not equal that masterpiece it at least has the same coherence and unity. Mr Frederick Ashton has devised a brilliant choreography based upon the classical technique modified by the movements of skating. The re-

† For a description of *Les Patineurs*, see Appendix D.

sult is novel and beautiful, lit up by flashes of wit, for he has not forgotten the limitations and danger of dancing upon ice in his pre-occupation with its grace and swiftness.

> The most striking dance in the ballet is a variation for Mr Harold Turner, which one is not afraid to call the most brilliant characteristic solo in the classical style since the dance of Harlequin in *Carnaval* . . .[40]

Les Patineurs has remained a perennial favourite in the repertory of the company, in all its manifestations. Unlike *Les Rendezvous*, the basic design of Chappell's décor has remained unchanged: there have been more or fewer arches according to the size of the stage, and a few modifications in the details of the costumes (in the beginning Helpmann, in the *pas de deux*, wore a rather summery-looking broad-brimmed white hat, quickly replaced by a fur-trimmed pillbox of the same shape as the other men's), but in general there has been no attempt to improve on designs that always seemed just right for the ballet. Without claiming credit for this, Ashton does say that 'I told William Chappell I only wanted to use two colours – which it is mostly, except for the Red Girls which I gave him as a concession'.[41] It is a pity that Cecil Beaton did not follow Ashton's directions in designing American Ballet Theatre's production, in which the principals are all dressed in different, *fondant* colours, and the corps de ballet in bright red and blue against a rather bleak décor.

Naturally there have been many changes of cast over the years: one rather curious one was that, according to Ashton, Ninette de Valois sometimes danced the 'white' *pas de deux* on tour, which would have been shortly before her retirement from dancing.

These were the early days of BBC television, and *Les Patineurs* was among the first ballets to be transmitted in its entirety from Alexandra Palace (on 3 May 1937 and again 7 December 1938.) Ashton also choreographed a solo for Margot Fonteyn to Debussy's *First Arabesque*, which she performed with the harpist Sidonie Goossens on 20 March 1937 and on subsequent occasions.

Again, it might be thought that Ashton would have been justified in resting on his laurels, but before the season was over he had given the Vic-Wells Ballet another of its classics and also revived an earlier work that had been in and out of the repertory over the years. That done, he went ahead and did yet another revue. *A Wedding Bouquet* was announced as forthcoming in the January 1937 issue of the Dancing Times, but without a title, simply as a 'New Choral Ballet'. The idea for it was Lord Berners's; he began to compose the music before actually entering on the collaboration with Ashton. Indeed, his original intention was simply to write a choral work, with words by Gertrude Stein, and only later did he decide that it should be a ballet.[42] The scenario was concocted by Berners, Ashton and Constant

Lambert, in weekends at Berners's country house. He did not, as Virgil Thomson did with *Four Saints*, take a text of Gertrude Stein and set the whole thing to music, but chose various passages, mostly from *They Must. Be Wedded. To Their Wife* (the riddle, 'What is a clever saucer?' etc., is from *What Happened* and seems to have been a later interpolation by Lambert), and arranged them in an order to suit his musical ideas. Occasionally he did not scruple to change a word or two, as in the sentence 'So the month of July opens and closes,' where he substituted 'August' to accommodate the rhythm of his musical phrase.

It is not a narrative ballet, but rather a series of incidents at a provincial wedding in France around the turn of the century, one of those ghastly occasions where everything goes wrong – Julia, one of the guests, who is a little demented, appears to have been seduced by the Bridegroom at some earlier time, and is probably not the only one of his conquests to be present (indeed, if it is not actually a shotgun wedding, it certainly appears to be a *mariage de convenance*); another guest, Josephine, gets drunk, and has to be removed.

The striking thing about *A Wedding Bouquet* is that it is not, like de Valois's *Douanes*, say, a character ballet in the manner of Massine, but essentially a classic ballet, and it is full of dancing. Ashton was handling his medium with ever-increasing assurance, especially in the ensembles (there is no corps de ballet as such) – for example, the waltz with its beautiful double 'Oranges and Lemons' formation, a circle bisected by a straight line. Several passages look like class *enchaînements* that Ashton incorporated into his choreography, with some editing; Harold Turner,

150

A Wedding Bouquet:
three photographs of
Mary Honer and
Robert Helpmann in
the *pas de deux*

when he was reproving the tipsy Josephine, had a brief but brilliant classic variation. In this context the places where classic ballet is parodied serve a more important function than mere 'in' jokes – for example, the *pas de deux* for the Bride and Groom, for which she changes into a tutu, with a pale blue corset and one garter. If the marriage of Aurora and her Prince is celebrated by a *grand pas de deux*, what more fitting than that *this* wedding should be similarly celebrated? The dance becomes, in fact, a witty metaphor for the wedding night and perhaps their whole married life to come – everything still going wrong, somehow she keeps ending up facing the wrong way, but he gamely carries on. Not to be outdone, Julia's dog Pépé also dons a tutu to dance a *pas de trois* with two of the male guests – and here the humour becomes more surreal; at another moment, when Webster, the maid, is photographing the wedding group, Pépé runs in to complete it by taking up the pose of the reclining girl in the centre of the opening tableau of *Les Sylphides*.

During the course of rehearsals the ballet seems to have become more farcical than was originally planned. Helpmann, for instance, was clowning at rehearsal one day and this gave Ashton the idea of making the Bridegroom much more of a comic figure. Helpmann evidently enjoyed greatly the opportunity to exploit this side of his talent, especially when it involved making fun of his own *persona* as *danseur noble*, as in the *pas de deux* with all its inversions of familiar supported adagio. Ashton also gave him a tango solo, in which he danced with top hat and cane like a rather seedy, raffish version of Fred Astaire.

The role of Webster, who runs the whole household with iron discipline, similarly made hilarious play with de Valois's noted strictness, as when she examines the hands of the peasant boys and girls, turning the palms over to see if both sides are clean and delivering a characteristic slap to a hand that proves to be grubby. (The lucky 'Fred Step' was assigned to her.) The whole ballet, in fact, was a remarkable gallery of portraits of very real people, brought to life with an extraordinary sense of character by the various members of the company. Gertrude Stein told Ashton they all looked and behaved exactly like the people she had in mind when she wrote her play, and when he visited her later at Bilignin would point out to him the originals of Josephine, or Julia, or Ernest. Miss Stein was presumably prepared to stretch a point in the case of Webster, since it would seem to have been Daniel Webster that she was thinking of when she wrote, 'Webster was a name that was spoken.' Pépé, however, was certainly taken from life, since Miss Stein and Alice B Toklas had a Mexican terrier with that name: 'Pépé the little Mexican dog is going to be on the stage not in person of course but a little girl to play him but even the littlest little girl is going to be a very large little Mexican. Alice Toklas wanted them to put a little one on wires little like the real Pépé but they said it had to be a little girl'.[43]

Some critics at the time felt that the figure of the mad girl Julia, Fonteyn's role, was disturbingly real and therefore a flaw in what they saw as an entirely farcical piece, but the poetry of the ballet lies in the occasional unsettling glimpses of reality below the surface frivolity. In any case, Fonteyn learned to maintain the essential objectivity of comedy in her performance, so that her Julia, though utterly single-minded in her dotty determination to be a member of the wedding, stayed within the framework of the piece.†

Ashton used again his favourite device of beginning and ending the ballet the same way: at the rise of the curtain Webster is standing alone, making a gesture with her forefinger as the narrator says, 'This is now scene one,' and at the end it is Julia who stands alone, with a similar gesture on 'only one' (Pépé comes in to curl up at her feet, and Julia pulls her hair down over her face as the curtain falls).

His treatment of the words was somewhat similar to what he had done in *Four Saints*, a kind of choreographic gloss on the text, sometimes letting the words give a flash of illumination of character, at others interpreting them literally so that what might seem nonsense on the printed page would suddenly appear startlingly apt – as when Violet, to the phrase 'Thérèse, I am older than a boat', does a rowing movement that expresses her weary desperation. At first the words were sung by a chorus wearing period costumes, but during the war when that was impossible Lambert hit upon the idea of reciting the words, which he did seated at a table to one side of the stage, sipping champagne and keeping an eye on the action. This was much more successful because the words, in his clear and caustic delivery, were finally audible; when the ballet was revived at Covent Garden after the war it was

---

† It is interesting to note that at the matinée on 8 May 1937, Fonteyn danced Giselle *and* Julia, two mad heroines.

Group from *A Wedding Bouquet*: Webster (Ninette de Valois) taking the photograph of the wedding group, including Mary Honer and Robert Helpmann as Bride and Bridegroom, centre, Fonteyn as Julia, at right

again possible to have the singing chorus, but soon afterwards the spoken narration was restored, from choice rather than necessity.

Lord Berners had visited Gertrude Stein and Alice B Toklas at Bilignin, discussed the ballet with them, and played the music. He saw there a rug 'made by an old woman in Virginia', given to them by Sherwood Anderson: 'everybody especially French people admire it every time they see it, the pale colors are so American and the river and the house and the simple harmony of it and the taste in it . . .' Its American origin notwithstanding, Berners 'made a drawing of this carpet and is going to use it as the back drop . . .'[44] And so he did, with a false proscenium like looped-back lace curtains. There was also a front-curtain showing the bouquet itself, with wedding-cake figures of bride and groom on either side. The costumes, whose execution was supervised by William Chappell, were extraordinarily successful simplifications of period costume to ballet purposes, especially Julia's dress (black over pink) and Josephine's (lilac-pink).

Miss Stein and Miss Toklas came to London for the final rehearsals and the première at Sadler's Wells on 27 April 1937:

We met Fred Ashton. I am always asking Alice Toklas do you think he is a genius, she does have something happen when he is a genius so I always ask her is he a genius, being one it is natural that I should think a great deal about that thing in any other one.

He and I talked a great deal on meeting, and I think he is one. More likely than any one we have seen for a long time . . .

And then we went to the Sadler's Wells Theatre for the rehearsal I had never seen a rehearsal a dress-rehearsal, and there were so many there, not only on the stage but everywhere and they do make them do it again and I liked hearing my words and I like it being a play and I liked it being something to look at and I liked them doing it again and I like the music going on . . .

I did like the ballet. It was a play and well constructed and the drop-curtain had a bouquet that was the most lovely bouquet I have ever seen painted and Pépé the dog was charming and they were all sweet and kind and English, and the characters were real even if they were French and the music and all went together and really there is no use in going to see a thing if you have not written it no use at all, anyway that is the way I feel about it . . . Tomorrow is another day and we will go to the theatre again and see how it is done when there is an audience there. Tomorrow then.

It was tomorrow which was yesterday and it was exciting, it was the first time I had ever been present when anything of mine had been played for the first time and I was not nervous but it was exciting, it went so very well. English dancers when they dance dance with freshness and agility and they know what drama is, they like to dance and they do know what drama is, it all went so very well. . . .

And then gradually it was ending and we went out and on to the stage and there where I had never been with everything in front all dark and we were bowing and all of them coming and going and bowing, and then again not only bowing but coming again and then as if it was everything, it was all over and we went back to sit down.

I guess it was a great success.[45]

Once *A Wedding Bouquet* was finished Ashton worked on the revival of *Pomona*, in John Banting's original décor. Fonteyn was learning the title role and at a Gala

Pomona: Pearl Argyle
as Pomona, Robert
Helpmann as Vertum-
nus, in the 1937
revival

Matinée in aid of Vaslav Nijinsky on 28 May 1937, she danced the *pas de deux* with Helpmann; in the following month she danced a solo called *Pastorale* in a television programme. Although this was described in the Radio Times as 'an extract from a new ballet by Constant Lambert, on which he is now working,' and the piece was said to be dedicated to the dancer by the composer,[46] it seems more likely that the dance was from the forthcoming revival of *Pomona*. The ballet as a whole re-entered the repertory when the company was in Cambridge during its summer tour, the first week in June. At the first performance of the revival at the Wells on 28 September 1937, Pearl Argyle, rejoining the company after a season's absence, danced the title role. From 15 to 26 June the company was in Paris, giving the première of de Valois's *Checkmate* at the Théâtre des Champs-Elysées on opening night, with Ashton as one of the two Players in the prologue (later on he sometimes took Helpmann's role of the doddering Red King). The repertory in Paris included the revived *Pomona*, *Apparitions*, *Nocturne*, *Les Patineurs* and *Façade*. Presumably Ashton returned to London for the première of his new revue, *Floodlight*, written and composed by Beverly Nichols, which opened at the Saville Theatre on 23 June.

Once again Ashton was sharing the dance numbers with Buddy Bradley, and the revue starred Frances Day, John Mills and Hermione Baddeley. It seems, nevertheless, to have been rather a disaster.

Ashton arranged a number called 'Dancing with the Daffodils' for Frances Day in which she first recited the Wordsworth poem, then sang a Beverly Nichols song based on it, and finally danced with The Girls. The result was too much for one reviewer: 'Lightly she floats, gently she plucks, delicately she fondles; and here are the Girls, yellow-petalled on the top, more or less like daffydowndillies. Well, Miss Day dances with floral grace, and there is undeniably a public for it. But oh, dinkums and pinkums! – oh, Albertina! – Aw, shucks!'[47]

Ashton's main contribution was a satirical ballet called *Sir Thomas Beeton in the Kitchen*, and this was more kindly received: the same critic said it was 'well planned as to pattern, deftly malicious as to music, hilariously mimed by Hermione Baddeley's Cook and Cyril Wells's Chef'. Miss Baddeley danced on point in this ballet, two years before her celebrated appearance as Mme Allova, partnered by Cyril Ritchard as Harold Helpmeet, in 'The Creaking Princess' in Herbert Farjeon's *Little Revue*.

Ashton was again being courted by one of the major international ballet companies. When the de Basil company came to Covent Garden that summer, *The Triumph of Neptune*, the Lord Berners-Sacheverell Sitwell 'English Pantomime' ballet first presented by Diaghilev in 1926 with choreography by Balanchine, was listed among the new productions, in a new version by Ashton. As with the

Floodlight: Hermione
Baddeley as the Cook
and Cyril Wells as the
Chef in *Sir Thomas
Beeton in the Kitchen*

Les Rendezvous:
Fonteyn, lifted, and
Harold Turner, at
right, in the 1937
revival

previous year's *Epsom*, this did not materialise – a pity in this case, because both
score and subject would have been ideally suited to Ashton's talent.

In the new season at the Wells the revival of *Pomona* (which Fonteyn danced
with Somes on 9 October) was followed, on 16 November, by a new production
of *Les Rendezvous*, redesigned by Chappell, with Fonteyn and Turner in the leads
and Ashton himself in the *pas de trois* with Jill Gregory and Claude Newman.
Continuing this series of revivals, *The Lord of Burleigh* went back into the repertory
on 7 December, also redesigned (by Derek Hill). Horace Horsnell described the
new décor as 'a landscape that might have been painted by a pre-Raphaelite who
had seen Russian days'. Pearl Argyle danced the role of Lady Clara and Helpmann
the title role (which he had sometimes done in the old production); Julia Farron,
then in her teens, scored one of her first successes in Lilian's *pas de deux* with Katie
Willows (Elizabeth Miller), as Andrée Howard and Fonteyn had before her. On
the 21st of that month Fonteyn finally did her first complete *Swan Lake*, having
shared the role with another ballerina until then (dancing Odette to the Odile of
Ruth French or Mary Honer – she had, however, done Act III by itself a year
before).

During the previous summer Ashton and Constant Lambert had spent part of
their holiday working together on a new ballet, *Horoscope*. This was given for the

The Lord of Burleigh: Pearl Argyle as Lady Clara Vere de Vere, Leslie Edwards as Edwin Morris, Richard Ellis as Eustace, in the 1937 revival

Final group from *Horoscope*: Fonteyn and Somes, lifted, with Pamela May as the Moon, below, Richard Ellis and Alan Carter as the Gemini, left and right

first time on 27 January 1938, marking another milestone in Ashton's development and in the history of British ballet. Lambert was interested in astrology long before it was the cult it has become in the 60s and 70s. The theme of the ballet, as given in the programme, was as follows:

> When people are born they have the sun in one sign of the zodiac the moon in another. This ballet takes for its theme a man who has the sun in Leo and the moon in Gemini, and a woman who also has the moon in Gemini but whose sun is in Virgo.

> The two opposed signs of Leo and Virgo, the one energetic and full-bodied, the other timid and sensitive, struggle to keep the man and woman apart. It is by their mutual sign, the Gemini, that they are brought together and by the moon that they are finally united.

This programme note was signed with Lambert's initials.

Although *Horoscope* was compared with Massine's 'symphonic' ballets it was certainly very different musically. Lambert's score, dedicated to Margot Fonteyn,

160

was divided into nine movements (1 Prelude – Palindrome; 2 Dance for the followers of Leo; 3 Saraband for the followers of Virgo; 4 Variation for the Young Man; 5 Variation for the Young Woman; 6 Bacchanale; 7 Valse for the Gemini; 8 Pas de deux; 9 Invocation to the Moon and Finale). It is probably his best ballet music, but it is not at all weighty. The theme worked better than the high-powered allegory of a ballet like *Les Présages* – even without a belief in astrology one could accept the idea of two people in love being kept apart by the differences in their personalities and finally brought together by the qualities they have in common. A rather mystical note on the composition of the ballet was Lambert's assertion, quoted by Richard Shead,[48] that the palindromic Prelude was dictated to him by Bernard van Dieren after that composer's death. On the other hand, Ashton himself gave Lambert the melody for the Invocation to the Moon.

According to Margaret Dale there was a general air of seriousness about the rehearsals of *Horoscope*, as though everyone knew that they were engaged in the creation of a major work of greater depth than anything Ashton had hitherto attempted. It was not altogether an easy ballet for him; the score presented some problems (he felt that the Saraband was rather static and repetitive) and also he found it difficult to portray the tension between the Leo and the Virgo characteristics in dance terms. To some extent it was embodied in the choreography for the corps de ballet, the men representing the followers of Leo and the women the followers of Virgo.

Ashton's choice for the Young Woman was naturally Fonteyn, whose position as the chosen interpreter of Ashton's most important ballets was by now firmly established. As the Young Man he cast Somes, who was gradually being promoted to leading roles. The variation Ashton made for him in *Horoscope* was rather different from the kind of dance Ashton had been making for his male soloists – that is to say for Helpmann and Turner, the one a consummate actor and the other a brilliant technician – Somes was still young and comparatively unfledged, and Ashton used this somewhat raw quality, as of tremendous energy as yet unchannelled.

The ballet began with a 'frozen' tableau of Somes standing isolated against a background of the male corps, his arms in a *demi-seconde* position, fists clenched, head tilted slightly back in his characteristic way: on a musical cue, all broke into movement, Somes turning his head and his fists this way and that. All this was very fine, and so were the turbulent dances for the corps, the double variation for the Gemini, and the Moon's beautiful serene entrance, which featured Pamela May's exquisitely pure line, her draperies stirred by a faint breeze as she held the crescent of her arabesque, and then came slowly forward with the hands of her attendants making a shimmering path like the reflection of the moon in water. Only Fonteyn's variation was less felicitous – The Times found it 'trivial' and lacking 'the character of sensitiveness it was supposed to represent'.[49] But there was – again – a lovely *pas de deux*, with the lovers' interlocking *attitudes*; they ended

Horoscope: LEFT Fonteyn as the Young Woman, Somes as the Young Man; RIGHT Fonteyn and Somes, with Pamela May lifted by Richard Ellis and Alan Carter

in an embrace on the floor – at one performance Somes's shirt got hooked to Fonteyn's costume and they had to improvise an exit together; Ashton, thinking they had wilfully changed the choreography, was furious.[50] The ending of the whole ballet, the piling up of the dancers into a massive architectural group, reflected the continuing influence of Nijinska.

Fedorovitch's designs created an atmosphere of mystery from the very beginning with the drop curtain of the zodiac against a cloudy sky. The main décor too repeated this motif of clouds in a monochrome sky, with the lighting suggesting the cool grey of moonlight. The costumes were simple and also mostly in shades of grey, except in the Bacchanale when, as Arnold Haskell described it, 'introduced by the brass, the hot, coloured costumes mix like the devouring flame of a prairie fire with the pale, moonlit costumes already on the stage'.[51]

The company's feeling that *Horoscope* was an important event was shared by the audience and most of the critics. One dissenting voice was that of P J S Richardson, whose reservations were expressed in terms that fairly accurately defined the difference between Ashton and de Valois at that time: 'Mr Ashton's choreography seems to have many loose ends and seldom to be tidied off and well balanced like that of Miss de Valois. [Her] ballets . . . always give me the impression that before she starts to arrange she visualizes the effect she wishes to produce as a whole, with the result that when she has arranged each detail these fit together perfectly. Mr Ashton, except in one or two notable cases such as *Nocturne* or *Les Rendezvous*, gives me the impression that he has arranged the parts before thinking of the whole. One perhaps gets the most brilliant moments, but when they are all put together they do not always seem to fit'.[52]

It is doubtful whether *Nocturne* or *Les Rendezvous* were any more the result of careful planning on Ashton's part than *Horoscope*: the fact is that he has always relied to a great extent on intuition, for better or worse, while de Valois's ballets were rather the product of an intellectual process. Of Ashton it might be said that he creates in the way described by E M Forster: 'He lets down as it were a bucket into his subconscious, and draws up something which is normally beyond his reach. He mixes this thing with his normal experiences, and out of the mixture he makes a work of art'.[53] In Ashton's case there was also the fact that, as has been noted, telling a story was never his main concern. In the early days, de Valois has said, he often used to lose interest in a ballet before he got to the end of it: 'I used to have to say, Come on, you're going to finish it!'

Horoscope was short-lived, for an unhappy reason: it is the only ballet that was lost in the Nazi invasion of Holland in 1940 which was never revived. The full score was lost as well as the scenery and costumes, so that immediate restoration was impossible. There was talk of reviving it for the 25th Anniversary Performance of the Sadler's Wells Ballet in May 1956 – an attempt may even have been made to start putting it back together again, but there proved to be too many gaps in people's memories; also, according to Michael Somes, some bits of choreography had found their way into other ballets. In any case, the plan was dropped.

As we have seen, the revival of the great 19th-century classic ballets in the most authentic versions possible was fundamental to de Valois's artistic policy for the Vic-Wells Ballet. To accomplish this aim she had secured the services of Nicholas Sergeyev, a sometime régisseur of the Maryinsky Theatre who had managed to get out of Russia after the Revolution with a number of notebooks containing scores of several of these ballets notated by the Stepanov method. Only Sergeyev could read this notation, and in rehearsal he used to pore over the notebooks and then tell the dancers what to do. Occasionally he was a little vague but, in general, what he came up with was close enough to traditional versions presented by Soviet companies to suggest that the notation, and his interpretation of it, were fairly accurate. Having presented *Giselle*, *Casse Noisette*, *Swan Lake* and *Coppélia* with his help, de Valois was preparing to attempt the greatest of all the works of Marius Petipa, *The Sleeping Beauty*. Diaghilev's London revival in 1921, in spite of Bakst's sumptuous *mise-en-scène* and a cast that included most of the surviving ballerinas of the Maryinsky company, was not a financial success.

Action photograph of a group from *The Judgment of Paris*: Pearl Argyle as Venus, left of centre, William Chappell as Mercury, on steps, Helpmann as Paris, right, with Elizabeth Miller and Mary Honer as Juno and Minerva

De Valois felt that the public she had been so carefully building up and educating was now ready for *The Sleeping Beauty*, even though a revival on a scale as lavish as that of Diaghilev was impossible, both because of the limited funds available and the small size of the stage. Even so, plans to present the ballet at the end of the 1937–38 season were postponed so that the stage could be somewhat enlarged to accommodate the new production.

As a stop-gap to supply a novelty in its place, de Valois rather hastily put together a new ballet, *Le Roi nu* (*The Emperor's New Clothes*), to a score by Jean Françaix composed for Lifar two years earlier. This was presented on 7 April, with Ashton, William Chappell and Claude Newman as the three Tailors. This ballet, like *Horoscope*, was also short-lived, in this case because it simply was not very good.

To pay for the new extension to the stage, which was to be a memorial to Lilian Baylis, who had died in the previous November, a Gala Performance was given on 10 May 1938: Ashton also whipped up a new ballet for this occasion, *The Judgment of Paris*, with music by Lennox Berkeley. It was a trifle, a throwback to the neo-classical manner of *Pomona*. Another reason for doing it was that Ashton had not made a new ballet for Pearl Argyle since *Le Baiser de la fée*, though the revivals of *Pomona* and *The Lord of Burleigh*, and de Valois's *Le Roi nu*, had provided her with new roles. But to some extent she had been overlooked in the preoccupation on the part of de Valois, Ashton and Lambert with grooming Fonteyn for the position of prima ballerina.

Argyle was indeed a natural for the role of Venus – as Horace Horsnell wrote, she looked 'divinely fair' and also 'condescends to the splits, a graceful feat her emblem-trammelled rivals do not essay'.[54] In fact the other goddesses gave Venus very little competition for the golden apple: they always danced as a pair (in this respect the ballet somewhat resembled Balanchine's *Apollo*, whose eponymous hero makes clear his preference for Terpsichore over the other two muses), and as Horsnell indicates did not expose very much of their beauty, while Venus at a crucial moment removed her skirt, revealing the short tunic she wore as an under-garment.

This ballet also began with a frozen tableau. Both choreography and music were in the neo-classical vein – The Times said that Berkeley's score sounded like Rameau with modern harmonies.[55] It was prettily designed by Chappell – the set had a flight of steps leading up to three columns, with a backdrop showing a ruined temple on a hillside overlooking the sea. Chappell's own part consisted mainly of sitting on the steps looking on and handing the golden apple to Helpmann when required, but he gave himself a very handsome, brief white and gold costume to do it in. The two lesser goddesses were in purple and blue. Even though the ballet was done for Argyle, Fonteyn also danced it, with Somes as Paris, but there were very few performances with either cast.

In the late summer Ashton worked on his last show for the London musical stage – bringing to an end a secondary career that had supplemented the some-times meagre income he earned as a dancer and choreographer during the 1930s. The show was called *Running Riot*, presented at the Gaiety Theatre on 31 August 1938, a sequel to *Going Greek*, given at the same theatre and with the same stars (Leslie Henson and Fred Emney) in the previous year. Ashton choreographed a Chinese Ballet for Louise Browne, a number that Vivian Ellis, the composer, says in his autobiography he 'cannot, for the life of me, recall'.[56] The Times said that it was 'the most ambitious turn', but 'not very efficient in spite of the fact that it is produced by Mr Frederick Ashton'.[57] A programme dated three weeks after the opening night no longer lists the ballet among the musical numbers, so it was pre-sumably dropped.

Once again Ashton began the new season at the Wells with an opera-ballet, followed just over a week later by a revised and enlarged version of *Harlequin in the Street*. The opera was *Tannhäuser*, first given on 2 November 1938. Of Ashton's Venusberg Scene, F Bonavia wrote in The Daily Telegraph, 'The Sadler's Wells Ballet rose nobly to the occasion. If the choreography was on a more modest scale than that of the most luxurious European theatres, it was, nevertheless, effective and in good taste'.[58]

J M Keynes gave the décor and costumes for *Harlequin in the Street* to the Vic-Wells Ballet and the augmented version entered the repertory on 10 November 1938. Lambert devised a new scenario, said to be 'after Jean-François Regnard', a minor 17th-century playwright who was presumably chosen because he was

Scene from *Harlequin in the Street*, second version: Alan Carter as Harlequin, left; June Brae as La Superbe and Somes as Monseigneur, centre; Palma Nye, Jill Gregory and Patricia Garnett as Commères, right

roughly contemporary with Couperin. The new scenario dealt in typical *commedia dell'arte* style with various cases of mistaken identity, supervised by Harlequin.† Lambert also made a new selection of music and had it orchestrated by Gordon Jacob. The greater part of the choreography must also have been new, though the enlarged version retained the Gossips, restyled 'Commères', and it seems likely that some of their choreography and that for Harlequin himself was retained from the original.

Alan Carter again played Harlequin: even at that age, he was an unusually brilliant technician and Ashton made full use of his ability to jump, turn and beat – indeed, the solo that was taught by Carter in 1973 to one of the dancers in the Royal Ballet's Ballet for All company is extraordinarily difficult and taxing even by today's standards ('a sprint', as Carter called it).* The solo was only part of a role in which the dancer 'never stopped', as Carter says, since 'he was the linking figure in the whole of the action.' The other leading roles were also given to relatively junior members of the company: June Brae and Michael Somes as the lovers, Frank Staff the Bread-boy and Richard Ellis the Bird-catcher. In the following two years both of the latter made single appearances in the title role.

Harlequin in the Street was perhaps a minor ballet but it was in its way a perfect

† See Appendix B.

* It begins with the following *enchaînement* repeated three times: *entrechat six, pas ciseaux,* bending the knees and bringing the feet together before landing; followed by a *pirouette* and going on into more *entrechats, brisés, révoltades,* all done equally to right and left. At one point the dancer is called upon to turn eight *pirouettes* with the arms going from fifth position *en bas* to the waist to the shoulders to fifth *en haut,* changing on every other turn. It ends with a *double tour en l'air* to the knee, deep *croisée* position.

166

Harlequin in the Street: June Brae, Alan Carter, Michael Somes

one, a true collaboration in the Diaghilev style. Its *commedia dell'arte* theme inevitably invited comparison with Massine, but it could certainly have held its own with, say, *Les Femmes de bonne humeur.* The particular flavour of the piece probably came mostly from Derain. This was the first time that the Vic-Wells Ballet had had a décor by one of the painters of the School of Paris who had designed for the Russian Ballet of Diaghilev and his successors.

The ballet survived into the early seasons at the New Theatre during the war. The main reason it was dropped was that after Carter was called up the company lacked a dancer of sufficient virtuosity to fill the title role, though at one point there was the talk of reviving it for Deryk Mendel. Some time later the décor was painted over because of the shortage of canvas, and a small masterpiece of wit, gaiety and elegance was lost forever.

During the first half of the 1938–1939 season everyone in the ballet company was preoccupied with the production of *The Sleeping Princess*, as it was then called, following the nomenclature adopted by Diaghilev: the première was on 2 February 1939, with Fonteyn and Helpmann as Aurora and the Prince, June Brae as the Lilac Fairy, John Greenwood (a member of the opera company who sometimes played mime roles in ballets) as Carabosse, and Honer and Turner in the Bluebird *pas de deux*. Ashton was the Second Prince in the Rose Adagio, and danced Puss-in-Boots in the last act to Molly Brown's White Cat. It is astonishing now to realise that the company danced Petipa's masterpiece on the stage of the Wells, which even with its new extension was still tiny – equally hard to imagine how the ballet could have been rehearsed in the Wells Room (the room in which coffee is served to patrons in the intervals), where most rehearsals were conducted at that time, and where Ashton's important ballets of this immediately pre-war period were created. 'It was,' Margaret Dale recalls, 'very informal at the Wells in those days. We used to go there about 10 o'clock in the morning for class and stay all day until after the performance. We used to watch all the rehearsals – we'd sit around the side of the room like part of the furniture.'

Curiously enough, a report appeared in The Sketch on the day before the première that negotiations were in progress for the Vic-Wells Ballet to visit New York during the World's Fair the following year. The outbreak of the Second World War put a stop to these plans, if indeed they were very far advanced. It is doubtful, though, that the Vic-Wells Ballet could then have taken New York by storm, as the company did a decade later with a much greater production of *The Sleeping Beauty*. But that such a visit could even have been contemplated is evidence of the company's – and Ashton's – growing reputation abroad.

Once *The Sleeping Princess* was completed, Ashton started work on a new ballet, *Cupid and Psyche*, in which he renewed his collaboration with Lord Berners, who wrote both music and libretto, the latter based on Apuleius's version of the Greek legend of Cupid's love for the mortal, Psyche.†

There was a deliberate policy in the Vic-Wells Ballet at that time of developing the younger dancers. Fonteyn's position as prima ballerina was firmly established after the addition of Aurora to her repertory; Somes was 'coming on' and so was Alan Carter. Now it was to be the turn of Julia Farron and Frank Staff. Farron had already danced Columbine in *Le Carnaval* and the Polka in *Façade*, and made a strong impression in the 'Finger' variation in the Prologue of *The Sleeping Princess*. Staff was potentially the best British male dancer so far, as strong technically

† See Appendix B.

as Turner. The logical next step then was to make a ballet around the two of them, and it was bad luck that that ballet should have been *Cupid and Psyche*.

For the new ballet was a mistake both in conception and in execution. Ashton says that Bernard Shaw put his finger on it when he came to see it: 'You've made the same mistake that I once made – you've been frivolous about serious people.' The first part of the ballet was lyrical but in the final scene Ashton attempted a kind of *ballet-bouffe*, following the lead of Berners, who wrote that scene somewhat in the manner of Offenbach. Horace Horsnell wrote that it had a 'catholicity of rhythms and enthusiasms that would probably not find even Ta-ra-ra-boom-de-ay a solecistic intruder'.[59] Jupiter and Juno entered as if drunk, hiccuping and falling over backwards: the former was depicted as a goose-stepping Fascist leader giving a Mussolini salute. Venus was a blowsy burlesque queen. Apart from the fact that this kind of vulgarity overwhelmed the poetry of the love story, it was already, in the spring of 1939, too late for jokes about Fascism – it was not funny any more, and to introduce that kind of humour made it seem that the collaborators were out of touch with the temper of the times.

Equally clumsy and gratuitous, if not a confession of failure, was the device of having the story declaimed before each scene by 'members of the Old Vic Dramatic School'. The ballet was booed from the gallery on the first night, and was taken off after four performances. It had been intended that Staff and Somes would alternate as Cupid and Pan, but they never got the chance. The failure of the ballet was a real blow to the two young dancers whose careers it was intended to advance: eventually Farron recovered from it and became one of the company's most mature and valuable artists, but Staff left to rejoin the Ballet Rambert, where he would have the opportunity to choreograph as well as dance.

And yet – it is hard to believe that *Cupid and Psyche* was without redeeming features. The dance of the Tanagra figures finally brought to the stage an idea Ashton had had several years before in the early days of the Ballet Club. According to Maude Lloyd he had started to sketch out some movements but was unable to get anywhere with it and abandoned the idea, at least temporarily – it is in fact typical of Ashton to drop an idea in this way but store it away somewhere in the back of his mind for later use. More important, the *pas de deux* in which Cupid swept Psyche off her feet introduced, according to Margaret Dale, the 'walking on air' motif that was to become an Ashton hallmark, and similarly the Zephyrs' dance was composed of wafting, airy movements. Horace Horsnell remarked that 'empyreal finesse is more happily suggested' by such choreographic means 'than by the young god's later flights on a wire, or the too frequent and laboured resort to pick-a-back'.[60]

Even at the time, *Cupid and Psyche* had defenders – Haskell thought it could be salvaged and turned into a success: 'All the material is there, and Ashton's handling of the dancers is a pleasure to watch. He is now amazingly sure of himself'.[61]

An amusing story of how Ashton choreographed one section of the finale was told to me by Julia Farron: 'Like everything else in those days, the ballet was rehearsed in what is now the Wells Room, and when Fred was doing the finale he got stuck. He looked out of the window and saw some children in a playground across the street, joining hands and dancing round, only they didn't make a proper circle, but, the way children do, made it a bit lop-sided, more or less kidney-shaped. When he saw that, Fred said, That's the formation I want, so we all had to copy it, and after that whenever he rehearsed it he kept shouting, Keep the kidney, keep the kidney!'

❋

It may have been early in the summer of 1939 that Muriel Stuart, the English dancer who had been a soloist in Pavlova's company until her marriage, and after that for many years resident in the United States, and a distinguished member of the faculty of the School of American Ballet, returned to Britain to visit her mother. She saw Ashton at Margaret Craske's studio in West Street and asked him to arrange a dance for her. Ashton readily agreed – Miss Stuart believes that his motive was the opportunity it gave him to talk to her about Pavlova. They worked together in Miss Craske's studio: the dance was difficult, using all of Miss Stuart's flair for *plastique*, but also a lot of very swift movement. Neither of them can now remember anything more about it – for instance, what music he used ('probably a bit of Chopin', says Ashton) – and Miss Stuart is fairly certain that she never actually performed the dance in public.

Although neither *Epsom* nor the revival of *The Triumph of Neptune* ever materialised (the latter was announced a couple of years in a row), Ashton was still receiving invitations from the 'Russian' companies. The one he finally accepted was from the Ballet Russe de Monte Carlo, now under the artistic direction of Léonide Massine. Ashton went to Paris during the summer and rehearsed the ballet, then called *Le Diable s'amuse*, there. Both libretto and score were the work of Vincenzo Tommasini, whose principal claim to fame was to have adapted the scenario (from Goldoni) and the music (from Domenico Scarlatti) of an earlier ballet also set in Venice, Massine's *Les Femmes de bonne humeur*. According to Grove, *Le Diable s'amuse* was composed in 1936, though part of the score may have an earlier origin, for also listed among his compositions is *Il carnevale di Venezia*, variations in the manner of Paganini for orchestra, first performed in New York under Toscanini in 1929. Certainly the score of the ballet included such a set of variations, as well as adaptations of Paganini's *La Chasse*, *Moto perpetuo*, many of the twenty-four *Caprices* and his arrangement of Rossini's 'Di tanti palpiti', an aria from *Tancredi*. (The description of the music as being 'on themes by Paganini' is a little imprecise, since the melody of 'The Carnival of Venice' variations is by Sir Julius Benedict.)

The ballet was first announced at the time of one of the periodic reshufflings of the two Russian ballet companies in 1938, when Fokine left the Blum company and went back to de Basil, switching with Massine, who took with him to Blum Danilova and Toumanova. At the same time the Markova-Dolin Ballet came

Group from *Cupid and Psyche*: Julia Farron as Psyche, Frank Staff as Cupid, centre, with Zephyrs

apart, Markova going with Massine and Dolin with de Basil. (For a time there was talk of a grand *rapprochement* of the two companies, with Fokine, Massine, Balanchine, Nijinska, Lifar and Ashton as choreographers. The June 1938 Dancing Times said 'it almost seems too good to be true' – and how right they were.) Massine's company announced that Balanchine would choreograph 'a new ballet on the life of Paganini, with music by Tommasini', a subject that Balanchine had already dealt with in his *Transcendence*, to music of Liszt, in 1934. At the end of the year (1938) it was announced again, only this time Ashton was named as the choreographer. By the time Ashton was ready to start work on it, during the summer of 1939, Fokine was preparing his own *Paganini*, to the Rachmaninov Rhapsody, and that may have been a factor in the decision to change the story of *Le Diable s'amuse*.

Paganini, because of his superhuman virtuosity and sinister appearance, was popularly supposed to have been in league with the devil. As the title suggests, in the final version of *Le Diable s'amuse* the devil himself became the protagonist. In holiday mood, he causes a young beggar to disguise himself as a prince, with whom an unsuspecting young lady falls in love.† (Paganini did not entirely disappear from the ballet – he was depicted on the drop-curtain for the entr'actes,

†For a full synopsis, see Appendix B.

'perched on a tombstone sawing a fiddle against a night sky of a lyre of clouds'.[62])

The ballet seems to have been completely planned, and the décor and costumes designed, before Ashton was brought into it, though as he says it was Eugene Berman's habit to make several different versions of each design, which at least afforded Ashton the possibility of choosing the one he liked best. Berman had designed, also for Ballet Russe de Monte Carlo, a revival of Lifar's *Icare* in the previous year – his first work for ballet – but *Le Diable s'amuse* gave him 'his first opportunity to work in the grand Italian manner, and . . . he created a world rich in the festive aspects of Venice, yet lighted by a disconcerting, infernal glare. . . The Prologue presented a monumental doorway in ruins, with the inside of the bright palace shown most effectively through gaping holes and tumble-down walls. It opened the eye for the diabolical ballroom scene which was brilliantly lighted from within by a shocking-pink and red glare . . . Scene 3 was a hunting ground of fields, stones and a rocky bridge. The Finale, a glowing scene of the Venetian piazza with its Palladian architecture crowned by a gymnastic statuary and sumptuous azure ducal banners. The costumes and masks were most inventive in grotesqueries: the beggars, the wood-gatherers, the vegetable-vendors, the wandering minstrels of Berman's easel painting came to life . . .'[63]

The décor, libretto and score with which Ashton was presented as *faits accomplis* were the components of a ballet on a far more lavish scale than he had so far attempted, a ballet designed to be seen in great opera houses. Ever the professional, he decided that his best course was to regard the ballet as a commission that he would carry out to the best of his ability. He rehearsed three ballerinas in the leading role: Danilova, Markova and Mia Slavenska. Markova, being familiar with the dancers of the company by then and of course with Ashton's work also, was able to advise him which dancers he would find easy to work with, who might be suitable for a particular role, and so forth.[64]

The experience Ashton had gained from his major works of the last few years enabled him to handle the larger canvas of *Diable s'amuse* with assurance. It was a tricky combination of *ballet d'atmosphere* and *ballet à grand spectacle*. Ashton was by now a master at creating atmosphere by choreographic means, whether the feverish excitement of the ballroom scene, reminiscent of the similar episode in *Apparitions*, or the quietude of the more lyrical moments. Equally confident, though, was his composition of the finale, a spectacular series of divertissements to the variations on 'The Carnival of Venice'. As always, Ashton used the technical capabilities and personal qualities of his dancers, and indeed sought their active collaboration. Danilova's role acquired something of a soubrette quality; she had one solo that was similar in its broken rhythms to the variation in *Les Rendezvous*. When Ashton got stuck in her solo in the finale, he asked her to show him a step, and she gave him one from an old Petipa ballet, a series of *relevés* in *arabesque* and *attitude*

Devil's Holiday: Alexandra Danilova as the Daughter, Marc Platoff as the Devil ▷

Devil's Holiday: Danilova as the Daughter, Frederic Franklin as the Young Lover

on alternating feet, travelling backwards *en diagonale*. Similarly at a loss in an ensemble passage, and seeing Franklin doing a step from the Mexican hat dance, which he had learned from another English dancer and choreographer, Wendy Toye, Ashton told everyone to learn it, and put it into the ballet.[65]

Franklin, in whom Ashton had shown an interest when he danced with the Markova-Dolin Ballet, was to be the Young Lover, and the Devil was to be danced by Marc Platt (Platoff), an American who was one of the leading character dancers of the Ballet Russe. Both men were given brilliant solos, Platt's being rather jazzy, and Franklin's acrobatic, not at all the kind of thing Ashton would have made for Helpmann or even Somes – as Franklin says, Ashton, in characteristic fashion, drew it out of him, while at the same time pushing him to the limits of his technique and beyond. At one point Franklin had to circle the stage with a movement in which he went up on his toes and over on to his knees, followed by a kneeling walk forward – repeated several times. The dance ended with a series of pirouettes during which he had to go down into *demi-plié* and rise again several times, finishing on the knee. This solo was intended to express the young beggar's love for the girl; in rehearsal, Ashton said to Franklin, 'I don't like that pained, soulful look,' and told him to let the emotional expression come through the use of his whole body.[66]

As might be expected, Ashton made two exquisite *pas de deux* for the lovers. As seen in a rather fragmentary rehearsal film,[67] the duet in the dream interlude has some movements that are startlingly similar to those in Balanchine ballets of a later date, as when Danilova turns one knee across the other in *passé*; there is a series of these with alternating legs, arms in opposition across the body, with Franklin taking her hands from behind and finally promenading her in *arabesque*. This dance ended with Franklin lifting Danilova at arms' length and turning as he lowered her to the floor. In another *pas de deux* she was required to do supported *pirouettes* facing her partner, with her back to the audience, a reversal of the usual procedure that Danilova found very disconcerting.[68]

Ashton completed the choreography of the entire ballet, of some forty-five minutes' duration, in two weeks of rehearsal. When Ashton finished the last scene the entire company broke into applause. Frequently an elderly gentleman would sit and watch rehearsals, Ashton told me: 'He used to sit very discreetly and during breaks come and offer me little cakes, and he was charming; I would take them, and then he'd go back and never say anything more, and then finally one day he came and said to me, Monsieur, je vous admire beaucoup, votre chorégraphie se déroule comme une chaîne. And so I was terribly pleased, I thought what a marvellous thing for somebody to say, so I went over to Danilova or someone and asked who he was, I thought he was probably some old White Russian duke or something, and she said, But don't you know, that is Matisse – who was at that time designing *Rouge et noir* for Massine – and I said, Thank God I *didn't* know, because I wouldn't have been able to do anything.'

The première was to have been at Covent Garden on 7 September 1939: Ashton, his work completed, had rejoined the Vic-Wells Ballet for their tour of the North of England. The tour ended on 2 September in Leeds, and Ashton was on his way back to London the next day to conduct the final stage rehearsals of his new ballet. On that day, war was declared. The Ballet Russe de Monte Carlo season was cancelled, and the members of the company, preparing to assemble in London, had to make their way to New York instead, by whatever means they could. Half of them, including several principals, sailed over on the SS Rotterdam and arrived on the morning of 26 October, the day the company was to open at the Metropolitan Opera House, with *Devil's Holiday*, its title having been Englished on the bill for the benefit of American audiences.[69] The dancers went more or less straight to the theatre for a hurried rehearsal, and somehow the performance went on as planned.

The critics were accordingly prepared to make allowances; John Martin wrote the next day that the ballet was 'not in any condition to be subjected to review', but wrote later that 'a reasonable interval . . . finds the work just about what it seemed to be at its première, namely, an extremely weak effort. Ashton is fairly swallowed up as choreographer by the music, the scenario (which is a pointless one, to begin with) and the décors, and seems, indeed, to have put up no fight at all. His composition is thin and static, and markedly ungrateful to the dancers who struggle to give it life'.[70]

This negative opinion was by no means shared by all the New York critics.

Grace Roberts, in her *Borzoi Book of Ballets*, after characterising 'one critic's' review as 'clumsily patronizing', noted that the story, while 'complicated on paper . . . is admirably clear in the theatre, and moves on to its end dancing all the way'. Although she felt some of the divertissements in the last scene were lacking in interest, in other respects, '*Devil's Holiday* need not give place to any contemporary work in a similar genre. The use of the *corps de ballet* in the ballroom scene, the tender *pas de deux* of the dreaming lovers, and the solos devised for Devil and the Beggar are marked with distinction.' Albertina Vitak, in the American Dancer 1939, wrote that Ashton's 'choreographic phrasing . . . often gave new twists to some quite ordinary steps'.[71]

A better idea of the ballet than one can form from watching the inadequate record of the film is given in Edwin Denby's review at the time of the first performance:

> The Monte Carlo, which I am always happy to see, began the season with a new ballet Diaghileff would have been proud of: *Devil's Holiday*. And Massine, who has been the Diaghileff for this production, deserves equal praise. I have seen it three times and I like it better each time. Everything about it is full of zest, sincerity, freshness, and charm . . . Berman, from whom we had wonderful drops for *Icare* last season, has given us five more which are as brilliant as any baroque Burnacini, but full of a contemporary intimate and personal sentiment, and also scenically discreet; and his costumes are the most wonderful imaginable – just look at the two Servants of the Devil, at the Devil's horrible disguise, or the farandole in the last scene, like a fashion show in heaven . . .

> And I am delighted too with the new choreographer, Frederick Ashton, the young Englishman who several years ago did the dances for *Four Saints*. His style is original, and originality usually looks awkward at first or unnecessarily complicated, or arbitrary, or something. His at first looks jerky, and you miss the large simple phrases you have come to like in Fokine, or the expert mass climaxes of Massine, or the incredibly long moments of extension and tenderness of Balanchine, like speech in the silence of the night. But you can praise all that and still praise Ashton too. If he derives from anyone it is, I think, Nijinska, with her hasty almost shy elegance, her hobbled toesteps. He derives too it seems to me from the kind of awkward and inspired dancing that young people do when they come back from their first thrilling ballet evening and dance the whole ballet they have seen in their own room in a kind of trance. The steps do not look like school steps (though they are as a matter of fact correct), they are like discoveries, like something you do not know you can do, with the deceptive air of being incorrect and accidental that romantic poetry has. But how expressive, how true to human feeling the dances are. The perverse solemnity of the betrothal guests, the noble and pathetic stiffness of the betrayed betrothed, the curious frenzy of

cruelty after the scandal; these are real emotions. The lovers' dream dance is restlessly hurried like a dream in which you know you are only dreaming; and what a final and brief conclusion it has into a deeper sleep. Like a Sitwell poem, the Hunting number is fussy and witty to heighten the lonely and frantic despair of the lost lover, interrupted by a diabolically hysterical substitute love. And the last scene is a whirl of inventions, of young eagerness that can hardly stop for the tenderness it dreams of, and that is tender without knowing it. A choreographer who can call up so many sincere emotions, who keeps a steady line of increasing interest (and animation) throughout a long ballet, and does not fall into conventional tags at important moments is a real rarity who is worth being enthusiastic about... Personally the only part I do not care for is the fox's dance, which however gets a laugh and a hand.

Devil's Holiday is probably difficult to dance and it is danced very well by everyone. The type of expression is not mimetic, but like that in classic ballet, in which the entire personality illuminates a role that the dancer has to conceive without the aid of detail. Danilova is particularly fine, of course; Krassovska is brilliant; and Franklin is magnificent. Platoff, of whom I think very highly as a dancer, was good but not as good as he generally is. All the dancers in the divertissement of the last scene were splendid.[72]

(An amusing footnote to Denby's remark about 'a fashion show in heaven' is provided by a Bonwit Teller advertisement in The New York Times for 12 November 1939 depicting 'Debutante Clothes derived from costumes [for *Devil's Holiday*] by Berman... All the Satanic gaiety in the world,' with outfits with names like Venetian Gallant, Satan Is a Gentleman, Dream of Love, Fox Hunt Suit and Betrothed's Coat.)

Ashton never saw *Devil's Holiday*. It remained in the Monte Carlo repertory for a while: there were only two performances in the spring season the following year, at one of which Markova danced the leading role. Later on Eglevsky danced Platoff's part, and Youskevitch Franklin's. But then the ballet was dropped, and the décor and costumes got used in other productions – for instance, a revival by Danilova of a scene from *Paquita* in 1949.

Ashton might have seen his ballet if he had accepted an offer that he received from America to join a new company that was being formed with the old Mordkin Ballet as a nucleus, to be called Ballet Theatre. He decided not to go, but suggested that they invite Antony Tudor and Andrée Howard instead – both of whom accepted and went over to revive ballets they had done in England for the new company's inaugural season in January 1940.

Chapter Eight

1939–1945

With the outbreak of war, the plans for the new season at Sadler's Wells, which had been due to open on 18 September, were drastically revised. Ashton abandoned a projected ballet on the subject of Pocahontas, the American Indian princess who was brought to England by her lover, Captain John Smith, for which Rex Whistler was to design the décor and costumes and Constant Lambert had selected music from Henry Purcell's works for the theatre. (In preparation for this ballet, Ashton had been studying George Catlin's monumental work on North American Indians.) In the late 1930s, Ashton had moved to an elegant house at 24 Wharton Street, near Sadler's Wells. This was not then a fashionable neighbourhood, as it became after the war, but several members of the company lived there, as well as other artists and theatre people. Ashton's mother died in that house shortly before the war, and he gave it up once war broke out and moved to a smaller one in Wharton Cottages, nearby.

The Vic-Wells Ballet went on a tour of the provinces with a reduced repertory and no orchestra – the music was played on two pianos by Constant Lambert, who made the arrangements, and Hilda Gaunt. People had expected that the outbreak of war would be followed soon after by heavy air-raids, but these did not materialise – then. So on 26 December the company returned to the Wells, with an orchestra, for a month's season, towards the end of which, on 23 January 1940, a new ballet by Ashton was given that was in many ways a radical departure from any of his pre-war works, *Dante Sonata*.

In a BBC broadcast at a later date, Lambert described his collaboration with Ashton on this ballet: 'As we were touring the provinces for weeks on end, with a fairly established repertoire, all our spare time could be devoted to the endless discussion of new creations. In the case of *Dante Sonata*, the first of our war-time ballets and one whose symbolism is clearly inspired by the outbreak of war, Ashton suggested the theme of Dante's *Inferno*. I, after various ideas, settled on the Liszt piano piece which is used. The general layout, by which I mean not the dancing as such, but the association of various characters with various themes, and the general dramatic sequence were then established mutually by Ashton and myself. I played the piano at almost all the rehearsals while the choreography was being created, so that when it came finally to orchestrating the ballet, I had the whole stage picture in my mind. I am certain that, apart from whether people like *Dante Sonata* or not, it has a visual-cum-musical unity which could only have been achieved by this form of collaboration.

'The longer I work in ballet, and I have been doing it now for twenty-three years, the more convinced I am that the ballets which endure are those in which no one collaborator can say, "This is my ballet." Nightly quarrels round the supper table are far more fruitful in the long run than polite letters from a distance'.[1]

Dante Sonata was in fact not only discussed and planned, but rehearsed, during the provincial tour in November and December of 1939. It has often been said that the ballet was 'inspired by the agony of Poland', but Ashton says that the inspiration was not as particular as that – it was his 'reaction to the whole stupidity and devastation of war'. Whether or not he originally thought of a literal treatment of the idea of the *Inferno*, Lambert's suggestion of Liszt's *Fantaisie, quasi Sonate* immediately meant that the treatment would be more abstract because of the intensely compressed nature of the music, whose duration is about twenty minutes. Sacheverell Sitwell says of the piece, 'The air of damnation hangs over it and the images are of the Vortex and the Whirlwind'[2]; a programme note discouraged too literal an interpretation of the ballet:

Liszt's *D'après une lecture de Dante* (After Reading Dante) is not, like his Dante Symphony, an illustrative work. It was intended to represent in musical form his reactions after reading Dante's *Inferno* and *Purgatory*.

The artists responsible for the present production have adopted the same attitude towards Liszt as Liszt did towards Dante. The ballet is therefore a freely symbolical interpretation of the moods and form of the music and, though it represents the warring attitudes of two different groups of equally tortured spirits, it tells no set story.

These two groups were identified in the programme, after the first performance, as Children of Light and Children of Darkness.

Sophie Fedorovitch derived her monochrome designs from Flaxman's line engravings illustrating Dante. Ashton too studied both Flaxman's and Gustave Doré's illustrations for the *Divine Comedy*, and used them as a source of choreographic ideas. He decided to work in an idiom that was very different from the way he had been working – except, perhaps, in some of the corps de ballet sections in *Horoscope*. Consciously or not, he went back to his memories of Isadora Duncan and invented a free or 'modern' style in which the dancers went barefoot, the women's hair unbound.

What one mostly remembers from *Dante Sonata* are its images of shame and suffering, turmoil and torment: Pamela May's solo in which she circled the stage

Group from *Dante Sonata*: at centre, Robert Helpmann above and June Brae crouching, as the chief Children of Darkness, with Michael Somes and Margot Fonteyn below as the chief Children of Light; Pamela May is directly above Fonteyn

in a series of triplet runs on half-toe, with a whiplash movement of her torso, hair tossing back and forth, hands to her shoulders and flung down before her body, first one, then the other; the seething, writhing groups of figures, piling up and dissolving again; Fonteyn and Somes advancing towards each other, covering their faces with one hand – pausing every few steps to extend that hand, then again covering the face in shame. There were two tableaux of crucifixion, the first when Somes was 'nailed' to the stage by Helpmann, followed by a sorrowing entry of the 'Light' women, Fonteyn with a grey veil over her head (this too came from Flaxman), their enormous shadows cast on to the backcloth; the second came at the closing moments of the ballet, a double crucifixion of both Somes and Helpmann, the leaders of the two opposing groups: here Ashton was unmistakably making the point that neither side 'wins', a rather bold notion at that particular patriotic stage of the war.

Another moment that returns to the memory occurred at a prolonged treble trill in the piano part: a beam of light shone on to the stage, and for a moment gave some of the Children of Light a glimmer of hope that they might escape from their torment, but as they advanced towards it, arms outstretched, it was extin-

Dante Sonata: ABOVE John Flaxman's Earthquake illustration for Dante's *Inferno*, from which Sophie Fedorovitch took the design for the backcloth; BELOW Flaxman's illustration of the Lovers Punished, from which Ashton derived movements for his ballet

guished and they were once more lost in despair. The lighting throughout played an important part in creating the atmosphere, and was of an unusual design: at times the main side lighting came from one side of the stage only, and there were also 'special' spots in the footlights that sometimes threw large shadows on the backcloth.[3]

Dante Sonata created a sensation. Some of the critics had a few reservations – Beryl de Zoete complained that some of the dancers portraying the Children of Darkness overdid the grimace of agony that contorted their features[4] – but in general the critics were at least respectful, and The Times went so far as to say that 'the ballet . . . certainly enlarges once more the expressive possibilities of dancing', while Miss de Zoete called the ballet as a whole 'a real contribution to the spirit of the time'.

The Times review began by saying that Ashton 'has always been a versatile and resourceful choreographer, but hitherto his work has mostly been of the light and deft kind upon entertaining and elegant subjects. . . *Dante Sonata* makes an advance into quite new territory'.[5] The critics had been making this kind of comment about every one of his 'important' ballets since he had become resident

Dante Sonata: Pamela May, Michael Somes and Margot Fonteyn as Children of Light, in the 1946 revival

choreographer at the Wells: the critic who could see that 'seriousness' is not to be measured only in terms of content was a rarity at that time. One such was Miss de Zoete, who made the very important point that 'the lightness of his touch and his extreme cleverness have, perhaps, inclined some people to discount his serious artistic aims. Yet a ballet like *Harlequin in the Street*, though it may be a trifle, is not *trifling*, but on the contrary a composition of great subtlety, complexity and variety of mood'.[6]

There was no doubt of its effect upon audiences, which was positively cathartic. The cast, led by several of Ashton's most devoted interpreters, performed with fierce intensity. Fonteyn, Somes and May were the principal Children of Light, while Brae and Helpmann personified the leaders of the Children of Darkness with a sense of their torment as well as their malevolence. When *Dante Sonata* was revived at Covent Garden after the war, its power seemed to have evaporated, and one felt a little sheepish at having once been so wiped out by it. It would be interesting, though, to see it again and look at it purely as a dance work.

Ashton's next ballet, *The Wise Virgins*, was also in its way a product of his reaction to the war. He and Constant Lambert both undertook to occupy their time while on tour with the ballet company – on train calls and other such tedious occasions – by reading the whole of the Bible. According to Richard Shead this exercise was conducted 'not always in a devout spirit',[7] but Margaret Dale recalls that Ashton was determined to read it all the way through, with the superstitious notion that when he had finished the war would be over. In any case we may assume that Ashton's attitude was likely to be more devout than Lambert's: though not a Roman Catholic, Ashton has often said that it is his habit to go to the Brompton Oratory, the church near the Victoria and Albert Museum, to pray for guidance before starting work on a new ballet.

He had heard an orchestral arrangement of the aria 'Sheep may safely graze', from Bach's Cantata No 208, and decided he would like to make a ballet using that and other such pieces. A Biblical subject was obviously appropriate, and he decided on the parable of the wise and foolish virgins from the Gospel according to St Matthew, Chapter XXV, which had previously been used for a ballet in the early days of the Vic-Wells Ballet by de Valois, to a score composed for the Ballets Suédois by Kurt Atterberg. Lambert played Ashton a lot of other pieces from the Bach cantatas and chorale preludes, and a selection was made, to be orchestrated by William Walton. *The Wise Virgins* was presented at the Wells on 24 April 1940. Though never stated in the programme, the ballet was dedicated to Edith Sitwell.

The décor was by Rex Whistler, whose work as a designer, illustrator and muralist was distinguished by its meticulously rendered architectural fantasy. His drop-curtain depicted two parallel pink walls, going off in perspective, with an open doorway in one, and in the other a closed, studded gold door. In the fore-

Scene from *The Wise Virgins*, showing Rex Whistler's set and one of Ashton's baroque groupings, with Somes as the Bridegroom, left, Fonteyn as the Bride, right, Annabel Farjeon and Claude Newman as her Mother and Father, to left and right of portal, Margaret Dale as a Cherub, lifted centre

ground was a lamp of the kind seen in illustrations to the story of Aladdin: smoke curling from it surrounded a drapery supported by angels; on the drapery were inscribed the opening verses of the parable: 'Then shall the kingdom of heaven be likened unto ten virgins, which took their lamps, and went forth to meet the bridegroom. And five of them were wise, and five were foolish.' The main set was a pink wall with a huge portal, also with a gold-studded door, flanked by figures of winged male angels. The women's flesh-coloured tights and painted nipples showing through their draperies were considered rather daring at the time.

The ballet began with the mounting of an androgynous cherub guard before the gates – four dancers, one male, three female, all identically costumed in pink tights with short black velvet tunics decorated with stars. Their choreography consisted mostly of small *batterie*. They were reinforced by a group of male angels, and the bride arrived with her parents, attended by the five wise virgins. The foolish virgins had a pert, tripping entrance, saucily led by Mary Honer. Fonteyn danced a solo that again was not in the least balletic in style – at the time it was said to be influenced by Hindu dancing (Ram Gopal was appearing in London at about the same time), but Ashton says that the gestures and arm movements of which the dance was chiefly composed, together with *soutenu* turns and kneels, were derived from his observation of Baroque art.

The verse in the parable, 'While the bridegroom tarried, they all slumbered and slept,' suggested to Ashton a kind of *berceuse* in which, as Horace Horsnell said,

The Wise Virgins:
Fonteyn and Somes

'the swooning lovely bride is dream-wafted to her glowing bridegroom'.[8] Somes had little to do except stand in statuesque attitudes as the object of Fonteyn's demure devotion, and indeed except for the cherubs and the foolish virgins there was very little dancing – in the way of steps – in the ballet. Much of the choreography consisted of slowly piled-up groupings that, in contrast to those in *Dante Sonata*, spiralled upward – Ashton says that he may have taken books with him to rehearsal and attempted to reproduce configurations from actual Baroque paintings and sculpture. There was, of course, an apotheosis of Bride and Bridegroom united in glory, with the foolish virgins cast out.

The atmosphere of the ballet was serene and genuinely devout. One may suppose that, as with *Four Saints*, the ritualistic, sometimes positively static choreography owed much to Ashton's boyhood exposure to Catholic ceremony. To this the entrées of the nubile foolish virgins provided a necessary, frivolous contrast, yet there were those who found them almost vulgar, and others who found the more devotional passages tedious. Ashton was also attacked for his use of Bach for theatrical purposes: 'Ballet', said The Times critic, 'lays violent hands on whatever it would have nowadays, and we steel ourselves not to be shocked even when Bach's lovely organ prelude on the Passion Chorale is used to accompany the pirouettings of the languishing bride'.[9] Such disapproval may seem excessive today, but in 1940 the controversy aroused by Massine's 'choreographic symphonies' was still very much alive, with its implicit assumption that dancing was an inferior, even frivolous form of entertainment – it should be remembered too that in most newspapers ballet was still reviewed by the music critic rather than by a specialist. Although Ashton was defended by Horace Horsnell (a rare exception to that rule), who averred that 'Bach . . . would have been pleased with his collaborators', The Times returned to the attack in a later article: 'Mr Ashton elaborates (as perhaps he legitimately may) and sophisticates (as he assuredly may not) the simple story to music with all sorts of close associations quite out of keeping with those here imposed on it. Even Mr Whistler's charming but opulent décor fits with nothing else. A scrupulous taste, while recognising many features of merit, can only be offended by their discordant conjunction'.[10]

The Wise Virgins only gradually became an audience favourite: it was exquisite as a spectacle, one of the most beautiful the Vic-Wells Ballet had ever presented. Above all, the ballet reflected Ashton's faith in Fonteyn as an interpreter: although her role had very little dancing in the conventional sense, she was able to remain the focus of the whole work by virtue of her quiet conviction and the sheer beauty of her presence. Unfortunately the main set was too heavy to be transported away from the Wells and when the company left later in the year the ballet had to be performed in draperies; without the décor, and without Fonteyn, the ballet inevitably seemed a little vapid; ultimately it was dropped from the repertory.

⁂

In May of 1940 the company went through one of the most dramatic chapters in its history, when it was sent by the British Council to perform in several towns in Holland, Belgium and France. Granted the importance of this kind of cultural propaganda in wartime, it does seem rather rash to have subjected the dancers to the risks of going so close to the German border and to the line of battle. According to Alan Carter one date was in a town a few kilometres from the border, where the local orchestra played so badly that Constant Lambert became convinced that they were members of the Fifth Column.[11] As it turned out, the company was caught in the Nazi invasion of Holland, and managed to escape only after spending four days within earshot of the bombardment. It crossed the North Sea in a cargo-boat, a voyage that lasted twenty hours: de Valois wore Ashton's dinner-jacket in addition to her own clothes in order to salvage it, but the scenery, costumes and orchestral parts of the entire repertory of six ballets had to be abandoned.

Of the Ashton ballets, *Horoscope* was never revived; *Les Patineurs* and *Dante Sonata* were fairly easily remounted (the latter had to be performed to a recording that had luckily been made, until such time as Lambert could reconstitute the score); *Façade* was redesigned, and went back into the repertory soon after the company's return, on 23 July (at which performance Fonteyn danced the Polka and the Tango after having danced Giselle).

Façade, 1941 revival: Robert Helpmann, June Brae, Ashton, Joan Sheldon in the Foxtrot

At this time, further new numbers were added: Ashton's own solo, Noche Espagnola, in which he once again recalled his Peruvian origins, really added nothing that was not already there in his Tango characterisation, and the Foxtrot, a 'twenties' number incorporating elements of the Charleston, Black Bottom and other popular dances of the time, predated *The Boy Friend* and other pastiches of the period. But in general the coarsening process was hastened by this new version, a fact emphasised by the new décor, which showed the front of a house, again with a Dutch door (though with no figure painted on it), and a window in which stood a woman in Edwardian dress, holding a flower. To the left, above a railing, was a clothesline with long underwear hanging out to dry. Some of the costumes made blatant what had formerly been subtle: for instance, the corset and bloomers that replaced the short knickers revealed when the Polka dancer removed her skirt. Others altered the point of the original joke – the Waltz dancers' new evening dresses and the Debutante's hobble-skirt, which made her seem much more soignée and sophisticated than before.

The dancers, in other words, took their Dutch experience in their stride and went right back to work. De Valois produced a new ballet, *The Prospect Before Us; or, Pity the Poor Dancers* – if the title had a topical ring, the action was in fact based on incidents in the history of the ballet in late 18th-century London, and any satirical reference seemed to be to the shuttling back and forth of dancers in the immediately pre-war Ballet Russe rather than to the British dancers' own recent trials. This ballet, in which Ashton impersonated his great forebear Noverre, was given on 4 July.

Even though the 'phoney war' was over, performances continued at the Wells throughout the summer with a large repertory of classic and modern ballets: the prolonged season finally closed on 6 September, the evening before the 'blitz' began in earnest. Further performances in London were out of the question for the moment, especially when bombs fell in the vicinity of the theatre, which for a time was used as a shelter for people who had been bombed out of their homes. Classes and rehearsals continued to be held there, however. But for the time being the company went on the road again, and the Vic-Wells administrative offices were moved to Burnley, Lancashire.

In December Mr and Mrs L K Elmhirst, the American philanthropists who had endowed the school of arts at Dartington Hall in Devon, invited the company for a brief stay – a period of needed rest and rehearsal during which Ashton worked on a new ballet. It had been announced that he was planning a work to Tchaikovsky's incidental music for *The Tempest*, drawing upon Shakespeare's play and also the *Notebooks* of Leonardo da Vinci, which had lately been re-published and which Ashton read with great fascination. This was to be designed by Graham Sutherland. In the event, the third ballet of this early wartime trilogy was rather different, though his choice of artist remained unchanged. The new ballet would seem to

Façade, 1941 revival:
Fonteyn and Ashton in
the Tango

have been performed, at least in part, as a work in progress during the stay at Dartington, but the first complete public performance was at the New Theatre (now the Albery) in the West End, where the company opened on 15 January 1941 for a month's season of matinée performances (the blitz being now in full swing), with music played on two pianos by Hilda Gaunt and Constant Lambert. *The Wanderer* was given on the 27th.

Here Ashton returned to torment, this time psychological rather than spiritual: the despairing inner journey suggested in Schubert's song was translated into a kind of surrealist imagery, given pictorial form by Sutherland's designs. Perhaps because people found the meaning of the ballet obscure, later programmes carried a note initialled by Constant Lambert:

Although Schubert's great Fantasia in C, opus 15, quotes a theme from one of his songs, The Wanderer, it has no romantic programme attached to it by the composer. It is an abstract sonata in four connected movements whose moods and rhythms have dictated the symbolism of the present ballet. The Wanderer in this ballet is not the physical traveller of the 19th century, but a mental and emotional traveller who belongs to all time. In the first movement we see him as a young man, turning his back on love and compassion, fascinated only by the glittering prizes of the external world. The second movement shows him, in an internal world of doubts, despair, and distracting visions which clog his progress. The third movement shows him in the external world again, but this time he finds only disillusion in the prizes now within his grasp. In the fourth movement he summons up all the elements in his life, and conquers both the external and internal worlds by a supreme effort of the will.

The Wanderer, final tableau: Helpmann lifted, with Patricia Garnett and Mary Honer to left and right; Fonteyn downstage at right, Margaret Dale and Deryk Mendel seated at left, Pamela May and Somes kneeling centre

As this synopsis suggests, *The Wanderer* had something in common with Massine's symphonic ballets: although the dancers were not identified as such in the programme, the personified abstractions of *Les Présages* – the Hero who struggles with Fate, Folly, Passion and Temptation – were not very far away. Helpmann's performance in the title role, however, emphasised the neurotic nature of the conflict, and was a remarkable *tour de force* in itself – he was on stage throughout. The ballet may well have been prompted by Ashton's own attempts to find himself, both as an artist and in a personal sense: if the final resolution was in the vein of

The Wanderer: LEFT Pamela May and Michael Somes as the mature lovers; RIGHT Margaret Dale and Deryk Mendel as the adolescent lovers

rather facile optimism that he significantly rejected in *Dante Sonata*, this was most likely dictated by the unequivocally major-key conclusion of the music.

There were indeed superficial resemblances to the actual choreography of the earlier Massine symphonies here and there – the Hero lifted in triumph at the end, as in *Les Présages*, the mourning chorus of women in the slow movement as in *Choreartium* – but in many parts of the new ballet Ashton further extended and developed his own style. There was a new brilliance and virtuosity in Fonteyn's role as the personification of worldly success, and her acrobatic double work with Helpmann was a sensation at the time – he lunged with one arm akimbo, and she ran, jumped, and landed with her knee in the angle of his arm. There were striking lifts for the corps, too – particularly one in which the men carried the women in a kind of spreadeagled position across their shoulders like birds of prey (Ashton intended here a specific reference to dive-bombing aircraft), which occurred at the ominous rumblings that interrupt the sorrowful calm of the slow movement.

Even more important in terms of his future work – in both their poetic imagery and their movement – were the two pairs of lovers personifying innocence and experience. The choreography for the adolescent couple (Margaret Dale and Deryk Mendel) was conventional enough, but that for the adults (Pamela May and

Michael Somes) was original in several ways. Ashton had been criticised for some of the erotic movement he gave to the Children of Darkness in *Dante Sonata*, and again he was rebuked for 'an unhealthy and childish sexual preoccupation'.[12] One cannot entirely exclude the suspicion that at times Ashton was motivated by a desire to shock, yet an important fact about the new *pas de deux* was that its explicit eroticism for once did not convey a sense of guilt about sex but on the contrary expressed, with great beauty, the tenderness of two people physically engrossed in one another. Certainly the dance was composed with less than his usual facility; according to Michael Somes, stormy scenes accompanied its creation, often ending with Pamela May reduced to tears. Choreographically, Ashton here explored further the 'walking on air' lifts that he had begun to use in *Cupid and Psyche* and that were to become a hallmark of his style.

More problematical, perhaps, was the invention of a series of 'significant' gestures for the ballet's opening – Helpmann, flanked by two pairs of young men wearing shorts (one of the most unfortunate costumes in modern ballet, with its suggestions of the Boy Scout movement or even the Hitler Youth), advanced from the rear of the stage with his hands held before his face in a wing-like position, then went into a series of semaphoric, angular gestures – significant, but of what? At any rate, they became a recurrent motif in the ballet. Undoubtedly the symbolic element in *The Wanderer* was given emphasis by Sutherland's two décors (essentially enlarged canvases in his customary style) and the costumes, many of which were downright ugly. There was often talk of giving the ballet in practice costume, which would have been an interesting experiment, for no doubt it would have been easier to see the choreography and judge it on its own merits.

Opening scene from *The Wanderer*: Helpmann, centre, with, left to right, John Hart, Alan Carter, Leslie Edwards, John Field

Once again, Ashton came in for severe criticism over his choice of music. He had a great admiration for Balanchine's *Errante* to the same music (in an orchestration by Charles Koechlin), with its extraordinary décor by Tchelitchev, given in the season of Les Ballets 1933 – a very different kind of piece – but had for some time wanted to do a ballet of his own to the Schubert *Fantasia*. Its Lisztian connections were presumably not lost on Ashton and Lambert – the work is generally regarded as a precursor of the Liszt Sonata, which Ashton was to choreograph many years later, and it was Liszt's arrangement for piano and orchestra that was used when the ballet company was able to perform with an orchestra again. James Agate, the drama critic of The Sunday Times, who did not normally lower himself to take notice of ballet, attacked *The Wanderer* two weeks running, and the critic of The Times professed not to understand why the ballet retained the title of the music, for 'The only thing which Mr Robert Helpmann and his colleagues never do is wander. They dance, they run, they perform callisthenics of a vigorous kind; they fall in heaps on the stage, writhe over one another, and pile themselves in strange figures and shapes'.[13] Horace Horsnell, as usual more sympathetic, preferred not to attempt any interpretation of the action – 'It is better recommended and enjoyed as pure dancing. . . The interest of this new work lies in its economy of statement and inventive detail'.[14] Ashton's staunchest defender was again Beryl de Zoete, who found that *The Wanderer* 'justifies our belief in the advancing genius of Frederick Ashton, both intellectually and aesthetically. . . There are moments when the dance groups actually seem to take mobile form from within the canvas [of Sutherland's sets]'.[15] Neither Horsnell nor de Zoete was shocked by the *pas de deux* of the lovers, whose roles, she said, were 'the loveliest . . . of all: tenderly intertwined, absorbed in mutual delight, they dance the exquisitely composed love episodes with entrancing beauty'.

London seasons at the New Theatre continued to alternate with provincial tours: the company was now officially called the Sadler's Wells Ballet, finally acknowledging the fact that for many years now the Vic-Wells organisation had been clearly divided between the two theatres from which its name derived, plays being given at the Old Vic, and ballet and opera at the Wells. There, in pre-war days, the ballet and opera companies had appeared concurrently, with ballet performances only two or three times a week. Their wartime separation, and the constant performing on tour or in town, meant that the ballet company was reaching a wider public, and attaining a higher degree of popularity, than ever before.

At the New there was at first a daily matinée at two o'clock with another immediately following it on Thursdays (4.15) and Saturdays (4.30). In the five-week season beginning on 19 May the performances were at 7 pm, with three matinées a week. (Darkness, and air-raids, came at a later hour as summer advanced.) A further season of three weeks began on 21 July, again with evening performances

On tour during the war: waiting for a train. Ashton as Queen Alexandra with Fonteyn paying homage; Helpmann, Chappell and Ashton as the Three Graces

at 7, a matinée on Thursdays, and *three* performances each Saturday, at 2, 4.45 and 7.30 pm: on the first Saturday Fonteyn danced *Giselle* and *Les Patineurs* at the first, rested while *Coppélia* was given at the second, then did *Les Sylphides, The Wise Virgins* and *Façade* in the evening.

Robert Helpmann did not enjoy any such luxury – his only rest came in the second act of *Coppélia* when Franz falls asleep, for he danced every ballet, having inherited the role of the Bridegroom in *The Wise Virgins*. Some balletomanes were hardly less indefatigable: the author, then a ballet-struck schoolboy, was not the only one who on more than one Saturday ran down St Martin's Lane from the Arts Theatre Club, at the end of the combined Rambert and London Ballet's hour-long lunchtime programme, to arrive just as the curtain was going up on the two o'clock matinée at the New.

The April 1941 issue of the Dancing Times announced that Ashton would produce a new ballet during the summer season, but it was not to be, for his call-up notice came at the end of the May–June season, on the last night of which (21 June) he had to go on as one of the Children of Light in *Dante*, in place of Leslie Edwards, who had already gone. At the end of the performance Ninette de Valois made a speech in which she told the audience that Ashton, Somes and Carter were all leaving. Many of the dancers were in tears.

Ashton received a brief reprieve when he was given special leave to appear in the first fortnight of the July season; his last performance was on 2 August. Back in the RAF, he was made an intelligence officer with the task of interpreting aerial photographs, and after a while was posted to the Air Ministry in London. During this time, he lived near Regent's Park, in the gardener's cottage of Hanover

Lodge, the London residence of his friend Alice Astor, then Mrs von Hofmanns-thal. The Sadler's Wells Ballet had a further season at the New in September during which *The Sleeping Princess* was restored to the repertory. Performances were at 6 pm, since the evenings were drawing in, but this was subject to altera-tion at short notice.

Early in 1943 Ashton was again given special leave, more extended this time, to choreograph a new ballet, *The Quest*, a patriotic spectacle that dealt with the same subject matter as his earlier wartime ballets, the conflict between good and evil, though in a more literary way. During the war, it was Fonteyn and even more, Helpmann who kept the Sadler's Wells Ballet going – Helpmann, moreover, was the undisputed star. After Ashton's departure, Helpmann was obliged to add to his other responsibilities that of providing new ballets for the repertory; he had for some years been pursuing a parallel career as an actor and when he finally had to produce full-scale ballets this inevitably influenced his choice of subject. In his first ballet, *Comus*, the action actually stopped while he delivered two speeches from Milton's masque, and the second, *Hamlet*, was built around his perfor-mance of the title role which he subsequently played in a production of Shake-speare's tragedy. These two ballets were cleverly adapted from their literary sources and benefited from Helpmann's highly developed sense of theatre. The continual depletion of the ranks of male dancers and the fact that Helpmann him-self (who, as an Australian, was spared the call-up) was no virtuoso, added to the necessity of emphasising this aspect of ballet rather than pure dance, the aspect to which Ashton was more and more drawn.

With *The Quest*, however, he found himself saddled with an unwieldy scenario drawn from Spenser's *The Faerie Queene*, which did not succeed in condensing its subject into a form that easily lent itself to choreographic treatment. Time was short, and it was not possible for him to collaborate with Doris Langley Moore, the author of the libretto, on a less episodic distillation of the theme, though he did manage to simplify her original scenario considerably, eliminating a Lion who personified Loyalty, and one or two unnecessary incidents.† Even so, the finished ballet lasted forty-five minutes.

Ashton's first idea was to use music of Delius, but then it was thought more suitable to commission a score, and the obvious choice of composer was William Walton. The Dancing Times had lately been publishing serially Joan Lawson's translation of Petipa's notes to Tchaikovsky for *The Sleeping Beauty*, a typescript of which she had supplied to Ashton, and this seems to have prompted him to prepare a detailed minutage for Walton, though without specifying actual tempi and numbers of bars as Petipa did.*

The creation of *The Quest* was not an easy task. The ballet was rehearsed on tour. Walton composed very slowly and the music came to Ashton a page or two at a time. Frequently he was obliged to telephone Walton and plead for more music,

† See Appendix B. * See Appendix C.

sometimes only to be told that the composer was stuck. On occasion Ashton had to go to meet a train at the local railway station to collect the latest pages of manuscript which Walton sent to him via the guard. Still the music did not arrive fast enough and when he got to the finale Ashton had to ask Hilda Gaunt to improvise at the appropriate length and tempo and then adjust his choreography to fit when the music finally got there.

Not unnaturally the completed ballet showed signs of this piecemeal composition, both musically and choreographically. Walton made use of leitmotivs for the principal characters. For instance, the lilting Siciliana for Una, the personification of goodness, was transformed into 'a sensuous and seductive waltz' when she was impersonated by the evil Duessa. The dances of the Seven Deadly Sins were musically a set of variations whose theme was not stated.[16] In spite of all this ingenuity, the score was not Walton's most distinguished composition; sometimes it sounded like his incidental music for morale-boosting films of the same period. But if the ballet was a failure as a whole there were some arresting passages. The many fights and duels taxed Ashton's invention: he managed to translate them into dance terms and introduce considerable variety. Thus, in the margin of Doris Langley Moore's scenario, at the fight in Scene 3, Ashton made the notation, 'Court take part in fight, mask it (back to audience) and shift about with it to add excitement'.

The Quest: Helpmann as St George surrounded by Hermaphrodites in the Palace of Pride

The Quest: Jean
Bedells, Julia Farron
and Moyra Fraser
as Charity, Faith
and Hope

The Quest, final
tableau: Helpmann as
St George, Fonteyn as
Una, with the Virtues
and their Attendants

OPPOSITE *The Quest*:
Moira Shearer as Pride,
surrounded by Celia
Franca as Wrath, Ray
Powell as Gluttony,
Gordon Hamilton as
Avarice, Nigel
Desmond as Sloth

The scene of the Seven Deadly Sins gave him an obvious chance to make a set-piece divertissement, and the result was appropriately brilliant and even comic in a repellent way: Sloth, for instance, could hardly stay on his feet and had to be propped up by courtiers. There was an interesting solo for Alexis Rassine as Sansloy, using arabesques and 'a falling movement on to the knees'[17] – possibly a variant of the movement he had given Frederic Franklin in *Devil's Holiday*. Beryl de Zoete wrote of 'one particularly exciting moment' in the *pas de deux* after Una and St George are reunited, in which 'she flows to and fro across the stage with immensely quick tripping movements, in a rising flood of delight'[18] – clearly another variation on the 'walking on air' motif. Perhaps the most beautiful passages were those for Faith, Hope and Charity and their attendants, consisting of slowly assembled groupings rather in the ritualistic style of *The Wise Virgins*, which no doubt can be traced back through *Four Saints* to such an early work as *A Florentine Picture*. In addition to providing roles for Fonteyn and Helpmann, Ashton choreographed for the first time for two young dancers who were coming into prominence and indeed beginning to share ballerina roles with Fonteyn and Pamela May – Beryl Grey and Moira Shearer – discovering a notable dramatic talent in the former. He managed to take time off from his RAF duties to make some revisions after the first performance – for instance, instead of a static grouping at the finale Helpmann was seen walking slowly across the stage with his banner behind a white gauze curtain.

The Quest was not John Piper's first work for the stage – he had designed Stephen Spender's verse play *Trial of a Judge* for the Group Theatre in 1938 – but it was the first in which he adapted the topographical style he developed during the war to theatrical purposes. The décors were of varying quality, the most successful being the last scene – not surprisingly, since it was taken from Inigo Jones's design for Night in Sir William Davenant's masque, *Luminalia* (1638).[19]

Ashton returned to active duty – ironic term for what was for him a fallow period that, however difficult to endure at the time, eventually bore fruit. In September of 1944 the Sadler's Wells Ballet temporarily moved its London home to the Princes Theatre, and there on 28 November *Nocturne* was revived. Ashton, on leave, conducted final rehearsals and appeared in his old part of the Spectator. The audience gave him an ovation and he made a short speech: 'I want to thank you for the affection with which you have remembered my ballet and to tell you how pleased I am to discover that, after three and a half years' absence, I can still raise my arms'.[20]

Soon after that he again managed to get away from his RAF duties long enough to arrange some dances for John Gielgud's production of *A Midsummer Night's Dream*, which opened at the Haymarket Theatre on 25 January 1945. This production was in the style of a Jacobean masque, and therefore did not use the Mendelssohn music; instead, there was music composed and arranged by Leslie

Bridgewater. There was no corps de ballet of fairies and the dances were in fact kept to a minimum. Ivor Brown, in The Observer, approvingly noted that 'Little People [were kept] decently few and decently in hand, instead of permitting them to run interminably amok with vast irrelevant ballets'.[21]

At most the *Dream* provided Ashton with an opportunity to flex his muscles, as it were. On 17 April, the Ballet returned to the New Theatre; the war in Europe ended early in May and Ashton was released from the Services. He took a house at 25 Yeoman's Row, off the Brompton Road, and at once set to work rehearsing his ballets. The season ran until 23 June, and a month later the company returned to Sadler's Wells. On the opening night, 24 July, Ashton again appeared in *Nocturne*, but not in his old role in *The Prospect Before Us*. It was announced that he would shortly be at work on a new ballet. He received an offer from the Paris Opéra which he refused, preferring to devote himself to his own company. On 21 August *The Wanderer*, which had dropped out of the repertory, was revived. After a season of eight weeks, the company went on a ten-week tour of Germany for ENSA (Entertainments National Service Association), the organisation that provided entertainment for the armed forces.

Chapter Nine

1946-1949

During the war the Royal Opera House at Covent Garden had been converted into a dance hall, but in the autumn of 1945 it was announced that performances of opera and ballet would resume in the following year. As early as 1937 there had been talk of a fortnight's season by the Vic-Wells Ballet at the Garden, talk that came to nothing, though the company had danced there in Gala Performances, in 1933 under the auspices of the Camargo Society, and again in 1939 when two acts of *The Sleeping Princess* were given at a Command Performance in honour of the President of the French Republic. But in those days the Opera House was generally reserved for the great international opera seasons and the annual visits of the Russian Ballet. Now, in the access of patriotism that followed the end of the war, it was decided that Covent Garden should become the home of British opera and ballet companies. The Sadler's Wells Ballet was named resident ballet company, in tacit recognition of the fact that it had become, as a result of its war-time tours all over the country, Britain's National Ballet in everything but name.

It was decided that the most appropriate vehicle for this translation would be a new production of *The Sleeping Beauty*, under its proper title, and on a grand scale, with décor and costumes by Oliver Messel. This production reopened the Opera House on 20 February 1946. As in the 1939 production, Margot Fonteyn was Aurora and Robert Helpmann the Prince, doubling as Carabosse, the wicked fairy. Ashton choreographed a new Garland Dance in Act I to replace the old version of the famous waltz, danced by twelve couples in 1939 (and therefore presumably somewhat rearranged by Sergeyev from Petipa's original, in which there were children as well). During the war this had been dropped because of the shortage of men, then restored as a dance for twelve girls. Ashton arranged a new dance (also for women) that has not been improved upon in subsequent revisions, with such felicitous inventions as a formation of two concentric circles of dancers moving in one direction, while a single figure moves between them in the opposite direction, under the arches of their garlands.

Another addition by him was the *pas de trois*, 'Florestan and His Two Sisters', danced by Moira Shearer, Gerd Larsen and Michael Somes, replacing the Jewel

Fairies' *pas de quatre* in Act III. In fact the first girl's variation is from the earlier divertissement and is therefore by Petipa, whose authorship was acknowledged when the programme was later amended to read 'by Frederick Ashton after Marius Petipa'.

During this first season Ashton performed the role of Carabosse for the first time, one of many such character parts that he was to undertake at Covent Garden. Incredibly malevolent, his impersonation still contained many comic touches that almost made the wicked fairy endearing, as in his gleeful little dance with the attendant rats. In his time Ashton had observed many formidable dowagers, and this no doubt enriched his characterisation.

He made further additions and revisions in later years: on 9 January 1952 Beryl Grey danced a new variation for Aurora in the Vision Scene, also described as being 'after Marius Petipa'. In the 1939 production Sergeyev had given her a solo danced to the waltz variation from the Jewel *pas de quatre*; now the proper music was restored, with choreography that seems to have been based by Ashton on Violetta (Prokhorova) Elvin's memories of the Bolshoi version, which may or may not have been authentic Petipa. In any case, it was a beautiful variation, with its series of *battements raccourcis* (a step that also occurred in the 1939 solo). There was no variation for the Prince in Act III in Sergeyev's notes, probably because the role was created by Pavel Gerdt when he was too old to perform one. It had not been thought necessary to insert one for Helpmann, but on 23 February 1955 Ashton finally put one in for Somes, similarly credited as 'after Petipa'.

At first the dancers seemed dwarfed by their new surroundings and only gradually did they learn to fill the stage of the Opera House: *The Sleeping Beauty* proved to be an inexhaustible masterpiece that they could grow into as they acquired greater strength and authority. For the first few weeks at Covent Garden it was given nightly, but on 18 March there was a triple bill that included *Nocturne*. Sophie Fedorovitch pronounced herself dissatisfied with the way the ballet looked on the larger stage, and after a while it was dropped from the repertory, to the regret of its many admirers. It was not the only pre-war ballet that did not survive the transfer. Those that failed to do so were nearly all ballets whose dramatic or emotional impact did not come across in the larger theatre; ballets which made their effect through dancing, such as *Les Patineurs*, were far more likely to be successful.

Two nights later there was another triple bill that was to have included *Symphonic Variations*, the long-awaited new ballet by Ashton, but Somes sustained an injury and it was postponed, *Dante Sonata* being given in its place, along with *Les Patineurs*.

The new ballet was postponed for five weeks, which gave Ashton time to make radical revisions, and was finally given on 24 April 1946. 'While I was in the RAF,' Ashton says, 'I suppose through unhappiness and frustration, I became interested in mysticism, read lots of mystical books, St Theresa of Avila, St John of the Cross, and so forth. I used to listen to Franck's *Symphonic Variations* a great deal and when

The Sleeping Beauty: Ashton as Carabosse

I originally wanted to do it as a ballet I had a very elaborate idea for it, a kind of mystical marriage and I don't know what.' In a programme of a concert at which the Variations were played, Ashton scribbled an outline for his projected ballet:

(1) The lover excites the love of the spouse.
(2) The wound of love.
(3) Rapture caused by spark of love.
(4) The call of the Bridegroom.
(5) Before the spiritual nuptials.
(6) The heart's joy in union.

An elaboration of this original scheme may be found in entries in a notebook Ashton kept at the time†:

Woman – Winter – 12 or 6 girls

Man – Summer – 6 men or 12 men

or 6 + 1 Man

Fertility   6 + 1 Girl

Woman – Winter – Shadow

Man – Summer – light, Fertility

The Women, the Winter, mourn the departure of the Men.

The waiting period, the earth robbed of the sun.

The moon period, the Underworld, darkness. . . .

The arrival of the Men, the sun's rays. The search for the male. The summer.

The Earth, the light . . . the dance of Union . . . the Festival.

(a) *Poco allegro* – Part 1. The Women, Winter, the period of waiting, the Moon period, the Underworld, the Darkness. The Earth, Venus mourning. The Virgin's faith.

(b) *Allegretto* – Part 2. The arrival of the Men. The Sun's rays, the Summer, the World, the Heavens, the Light, Adonis returns to the Earth, Life, Love, the Lover excites the love of his Spouse.

(a) *Molto piu lento* – Part 3. The Search. The Wound of Love and Rapture caused by spark of love. The Dance of Union, Fertility.

(b) *Allegro non troppo* – Part 4. The Call of the Bridegroom. The Festival. The Summer. The Marriage. The Heart's joy in union. 'Art and Faith united in one unseverable bond.'

Discussing these notes with Richard Buckle in a conversation reported in Buckle's magazine Ballet, Ashton said, 'I was interested in the idea of "dedication" and absorption in divine love; and I also considered the notion of introducing a suggestion of a nun taking the veil into the ballet. But perhaps the dominant

†The same notebook contains, among other things, a list of possible ballets, including *Symphonic Variations*, Britten's *Les Illuminations* and *Variations on a theme of Frank Bridge*, *Les Sirènes*, *Don Juan*, 'Stravinsky' (possibly *Scènes de ballet*), all of which he was to realise, and others that he did not: *Pocahontas* and *The Tempest*, which as we have seen had been considered earlier, the latter now with the notation '(for Lincoln [Kirstein])', as well as *Agamemnon*, Sibelius's *7th Symphony*; 'Classical Theme (Judgement of Paris)' – apparently a more serious treatment of this subject than he had done in 1938, judging by a brief synopsis that appears on another page; *Matinée Musicale* (presumably Britten's second suite arranged from late works of Rossini); *The First Shoot* 'for America'; and Saint-Saëns (*Concerto*). On another page, under the heading 'Music', Ashton has jotted down Schoenberg's *Gurrelieder*.

theme of the ballet was the seasons. At the beginning I meant it to be winter with the three women moving alone coldly, unfertilized. When the man begins to dance he introduces the spring; and the last part of the ballet represents to a certain extent the fullness of summer and the plenty of harvest . . .

'All these things were only "put into" the ballet, if they *were* "put in", to be eventually refined and eliminated. I did not want to load the work with literary ideas; and I was quite willing for people to read whatever they liked into it. For instance, someone said to me, "I see *Symphonic Variations* as the morning of the world," and I said, "Quite right!"'[1]

It may have been the original scenario that made Constant Lambert object at first to the use of César Franck's music for a ballet – in general he disapproved of the use of symphonic music and had, for instance, vetoed an earlier suggestion of Ashton's for a ballet to Debussy's *La Mer*.

As Ashton thought more and more about the ballet, he first of all decided to eliminate the corps de ballet and told Sophie Fedorovitch, to her surprise, 'I'm going to take all those people out, don't bother designing costumes for them' – he was just going to use six dancers. As he continued to work, the shape the ballet assumed was that of a pure dance in which the original mystical content was almost completely submerged. Even so, some passages were still, as he puts it, 'overcharged', especially the finale, and the postponement of the opening gave him a rare opportunity further to pare away whatever was inessential. Ashton continued to make changes right up to the last moment, especially to the ballet's final moments, of which there were several versions, including one that had all the dancers lying on the floor. Indeed, he continued to revise the choreography even after the first performance. Perhaps because, after so long a hiatus, Ashton no longer composed with his old facility – or was as easily satisfied – *Symphonic Variations* was the first Ashton ballet to be rehearsed behind closed doors – before that the company had been free to watch whenever they liked, but thereafter closed rehearsals became the rule.[2]

More than any other ballet Ashton had created, *Symphonic Variations* was the product of deep thought and careful revision, so that the final result attained an absolute economy of utterance. It is true, no doubt, that a residue of the ideas that Ashton had considered and rejected as subject-matter remains as a kind of sub-text. Richard Buckle, in the discussion quoted above, objected that there would have been no harm in giving 'a hint of your intentions', but Ashton replied, 'Perhaps I was afraid that if I put my thoughts into words, even to myself, I might deflect myself from creating the work in terms of dancing, and that it might become too literary, and that the final nature of my inspiration might crystallize into something I did not really intend'.[3] Whatever meaning an individual spectator might choose to read into it, the ballet stood as Ashton's choreographic credo.

During the war the tendency of the repertory had become increasingly literary – Ashton himself had contributed to this development, willy-nilly, with *The Quest* – and even now the first new ballet to be given at Covent Garden was a

Ashton with Sophie Fedorovitch, about the time of the creation of *Symphonic Variations*

new work by Helpmann, *Adam Zero*, in which dancing was subordinated to symbolic paraphernalia and elaborate stage machinery. Ashton wanted to counteract this tendency and to reaffirm the position of the classic dance as ballet's most important element. It was not his intention in *Symphonic Variations* to display ingenuity of invention but simply to set three men and three women dancing on the vast expanse (as it seemed then) of the Opera House stage, uncluttered with scenery and effects. *Symphonic Variations*, and not *Adam Zero* with its elevators, moving cycloramas and complicated lighting, was the ballet with which the Sadler's Wells Ballet took possession of its new theatre. It was a turning-point in the history of British ballet, and Ashton's coming-of-age as a choreographer, twenty years after his first tentative steps. With it he asserted his claim to be considered Petipa's rightful heir, as Balanchine had in *Apollo*.

This claim was defined by A V Coton in an article in Ballet Today: 'It is not possible to rate *Symphonic Variations* as anything other than this century's third great monument of classical choreography... This ballet satisfies exactly the same conditions as do *Les Sylphides* and *Apollo*, and is dependent to a lesser degree than either of them on plot, setting or musical reference. The curtain rises on a vast stage, and before the deep-set backcloth of sprayed white-and-green are seen six immobile and minute dancers, clad all in white, with a little black relief here and

207

there. Nothing whatever is stated of place, person, condition or circumstance; here we have six living bodies within a prescribed area of space which, throughout the duration of the music, move in splendour and heroism, creating solo, duet, and ensemble dances of a fascinating variety of shapes, emphases, and configurations. The disparity between these persons and the vast area of their action proposes an imagery of infinities . . .; so that, not too fantastically, we can catch the imagery either as planetary bodies moving with subtle rhythm against cosmic vastness, or as the geometric complexities revealed in watching the rapid formation of crystals under a microscope. . . On analysis it can be seen that no step or movement-sequence is daringly new – every part of every pattern is something that one could quickly isolate in that laboratory where a dancing class takes place. Yet the majesty and splendour of this ballet [are] made out of the same kind of simplicities that Fokine and Balanchine both used in their master works. . . In each of these instances a choreographer of assured mastery, moving perhaps to some degree deliberately, and to some extent intuitively, has re-stated the primary function of theatrical dancing by re-shaping its basic material into a new and exciting assemblage of images'.[4]

Symphonic Variations was not, of course, a ballet without precedent in Ashton's former work: it was rather a summation, and indeed a consummation, of his career up to that point. Movement ideas and motifs that went back at least as far as *Les Rendezvous* and had continued to be explored in such ballets as *Le Baiser de la fée*, *Horoscope*, *The Wanderer* and even *Dante Sonata*, were extended still further: skimming lifts with *batterie* or *pas de bourrée* just off the floor, sculptural groupings in supported adagio by one man and two or three women. The basic classical positions of feet, arms and torso were modified in ways that defined the style – the dancers when at rest stand with one foot crossed over the other, resting on the point; there is a characteristic *port de bras* with the arms making parallel lines, one above the head, one across the chest; in low *sissonne* lifts, the woman curves one arm around her partner's head. Above all Ashton found the courage to be simple: to allow the dancers to stand motionless before the final passage of vigorous dancing – necessary, he says, so that they could catch their breath since they never left the stage during the whole ballet, but from such practical considerations may come the most poetic, human moments in a dance. Equally beautiful in their calm simplicity are the transitional passages when the dancers take hands and run round the stage.

Even though *Symphonic Variations* more than any other ballet creates a feeling of serenity, for the dancers, in the beginning, it was 'an absolute marathon'[5] and made demands on them such as had never been made before. They had no characters to hide behind, and no chance to go into the wings to gasp for air. It was a test of sheer stamina that very few British dancers could stand at that time. The women had to maintain an absolute purity of line, and the men were called upon to perform multiple *entrechats six*, *doubles tours en l'air*, *pirouettes* that finished deliberately off balance without losing control, and steps of elevation, all while continuing to preserve the essential, almost reflective lyricism of the piece. The original cast rose magnificently to the occasion. Fonteyn remains incomparable – her stamina at least was never in question after all the gruelling years of touring, and her performance established her once and for all as the exemplar of the national style that Ashton was beginning to create. The fair Pamela May and the red-headed Moira Shearer, who had both danced Aurora in the new *Beauty*, were the obvious, perfect complements to Fonteyn, and her equals in the purity of their classicism. The men, Somes, Henry Danton and Brian Shaw (the last two replaced in the following season by John Hart and Alexander Grant), gave promise of a new strength in British male dancing, which not unnaturally had suffered more than anything else as a result of the war. At the time of writing, when the Royal Ballet can present casts with the calibre of Antoinette Sibley or Merle Park, Ann Jenner, Jennifer Penney, Anthony Dowell or David Wall, Michael Coleman and Wayne Eagling, *Symphonic Variations* retains all its pristine freshness.

Sophie Fedorovitch's contribution was more than just the design of the décor and costumes. Ashton used constantly to discuss the ballet with her and no doubt she was in some degree responsible for the simplicity of its final form. Ashton has described how he used to go bicycling with her on spring evenings through the Norfolk countryside where she lived: 'One day we came up a hill and suddenly there was the most marvellous glade, filled with sunshine, and this had the most terrific effect on us; I said, This is the colour it's got to be, a sort of greenish-yellow.' Christian Bérard described the décor as 'a lily-of-the-valley'[6] and Marie Rambert wrote that it 'seemed to flow out of the music and into the dancing'.[7]

For the most part, the ballet's beauty and importance were recognised from the beginning. It is true that one critic found it 'prim and dull . . . this is plotless ballet, dancing in a vacuum, and nature abhors it'.[8] In America the ballet was dismissed as 'watered-down Balanchine' when first shown there, but in recent years New York audiences have begun to recognise its quality. In any case, the place of *Symphonic Variations* as the Royal Ballet's signature work seems assured.

That first season at Covent Garden, extended several times, lasted for a record 131 performances, of which seventy-eight were of *Beauty*. The company then had a holiday followed by a provincial tour and a visit to Vienna. The new audience they had built up in Britain during the war knew of the pre-war Russian companies only through such books as Arnold Haskell's *Balletomania* and the reminiscences of older ballet-goers, many of whom still refused to accept British ballet as the real thing. However, during the summer of 1946 London had its first visits from foreign companies since the end of the war: Les Ballets des Champs-Elysées, with ballets by Roland Petit and others, and Ballet Theatre from New York, which danced at Covent Garden.

These were not the fabled 'Russian Ballet', but still gave an opportunity to

LEFT *Symphonic Variations*: Fonteyn and Somes

BELOW *Symphonic Variations*: Left to right, Moira Shearer, Henry Danton, Fonteyn, Somes, Pamela May

ABOVE *Symphonic Variations*:
Left to right, Shearer,
Danton, Fonteyn, Somes,
May

RIGHT Group from
Symphonic Variations:
Fonteyn, Somes, May, with
Shearer partly hidden behind
Somes; Brian Shaw in
background

compare the native product with companies which in one way or another had had more recent contact with certain representatives of the pre-war companies: the Ballets des Champs-Elysées had the artistic collaboration of Boris Kochno, and many dancers of Ballet Theatre had been trained by émigré teachers now resident in the United States; the latter company's repertory included two or three works by Balanchine. The French company was exciting for the elegance of its décors, even though few of the ballets were of much choreographic substance. In this respect the American company was stronger, with its new works by Antony Tudor and Jerome Robbins, and audiences were completely won over by the charm and vitality of the dancers.

For the dancers, too, exposure to the work of their colleagues from overseas could only be beneficial. Ashton made many friends among the members of the visiting companies, and his work received due admiration from them. Ballet Theatre acquired Ashton's *Les Patineurs*, rehearsed under his supervision during the London season, though not presented until the company returned to New York in October, with new décor and costumes by Cecil Beaton.

In the same month, the Sadler's Wells Ballet reopened at Covent Garden; the September issue of Ballet had mentioned the possibility of a collaboration between Francis Poulenc and Ashton who, it said, 'would certainly be the composer's choice as choreographer'. This never came to anything, though for a while Ashton considered *Les Animaux modèles*, a ballet Poulenc composed for Lifar during the war. The first new ballet of the season reunited Ashton with two of his collaborators of former years, Lord Berners and Cecil Beaton. The ballet, *Les Sirènes*, was first given on 12 November.

For some time, Ashton had had the idea of a ballet that would evoke the world of Ouida, using her novel *Moths* as a basis.[9] According to Cecil Beaton, Ashton was walking on the beach one day and 'stopped to watch the movements of the seagulls, wheeling, strange and remote, above the beach. He decided to combine *Moths* with the seagulls, introduce certain characters from the novel, such as the opera singer and Lady Kitty, gather them together on the *plage* at Trouville together with La Belle Otero, a Maharajah, a handful of mermaids, the first balloon – and see what came of it'.[10]

Ashton worked out a scenario on these lines – the characters to be impersonated by Fonteyn and Helpmann were identified as actual personages in this first draft,† though later disguised by fictional names: the Spanish dancer, La Belle Otero, became La Bolero; and the tenor, D'Ardath, Adelino Canberra of the Adelaide Opera – a reference to Helpmann's Australian origin. His first title for the ballet was *La Plage; ou, les Sirènes*.

The ballet was, in Cecil Beaton's blunt term, a flop. He says that he, Ashton and Berners wanted 'to create an atmosphere that was mysterious and vaguely sinister; it was to be a foggy day on the beach and there should be a sense of desolation

† See Appendix B.

Les Sirènes: Ashton as King Hihat of Agpar, with his Suite

behind all the *mondaine* high jinks'.[11] Unfortunately, they lost sight of that idea in the effort to make the ballet amusing – in fact it seems to have gone wrong in the same way as *Cupid and Psyche*. The result was described by one former member of the company as 'an expensive, indulgent folly' that suggested the collaborators were out of touch with things. Beaton's set was elaborate and ugly, his period

Les Sirènes: Fonteyn
as La Bolero with
Helpmann as Adelino
Canberra

costumes insufficiently adapted to the purposes of ballet: in his own words, 'the general effect was too near that of a musical comedy'.[12]

At one point, indeed, Helpmann actually broke into song. As suggested in Ashton's draft synopsis, Berners's music used themes from Waldteufel: it was not his most successful score, but like all his ballet music, it was never less than serviceable – as Ashton said of him in an interview with The Times, 'He wasn't Brahms or anything, but his music was always competently delivered. His waltzes are lovely; they are evocative of governesses sitting at upright pianos, tinkling away'.[13]

Ashton was so enchanted with the idea of descending from the flies in a balloon as the Eastern potentate, King Hihat of Agpar, that he quite forgot that he was afraid of heights and therefore would not enjoy it at all. After the première he decided not to make the entrance again, whereupon Helpmann, thinking it too good to lose, appropriated it for himself. Alexander Grant's first created role in an Ashton ballet was as one of the children who jumped through a hoop; he doubled as one of Ashton's attendants, in which capacity he frequently had to tell the choreographer what came next in performance, Ashton having been too preoccupied with the ballet as a whole to have had time to become thoroughly familiar with his own role.

A page in Ashton's notebook shows that he tried – rather desperately – to think of ways in which the setting and story could be made to suggest pretexts for movement, including:

Side jumps to avoid waves
Floating, swimming
Drying as a dance
Touching sunburn
Shivering
Playing ball?
Photographing
Pas de promenade for smart world making and changing formations.
Zarzuela.
Daily dozen.
Paddling (old people).

Clearly none of these provides much occasion for sustained choreographic invention, and it was probably the lack of dance interest that gave the piece such a short life (only nineteen performances). All the same, there were some good jokes, and some beautiful moments in the *pas de deux* for Helpmann and Fonteyn, who looked very glamorous in her Spanish costumes. But she soon relinquished the role to Violetta Elvin, the first Soviet dancer to have emigrated to the West after the war, who had made a sensational début in the Blue Bird *pas de deux* on the second night of *Beauty*.

❉

On 12 December, a month after the première of *Les Sirènes*, came that of an even more elaborate production in which the ballet company joined forces with the opera, *The Fairy Queen*. It will be remembered that one of Ashton's earliest choreographic efforts, almost twenty years before, was the dances for an undergraduate production of Purcell's masque based on *A Midsummer Night's Dream*, which was a favourite work of Constant Lambert's – in fact an early Vic-Wells ballet, *The Birthday of Oberon*, with choreography by Ninette de Valois, had been based on the Masque of the Seasons from the fourth act, in an arrangement by Lambert. Now he had the resources for a full-scale production of the complete work, using actors, singers and dancers. For this new revival Lambert reduced the spoken text to a minimum, but what there was consisted as far as possible of Shakespeare and not his 17th-century adaptor, and concentrated on the quarrel between Oberon and Titania over the changeling boy. The final version was the result of a close collaboration among Lambert, Ashton, Michael Ayrton (the designer) and Malcolm Baker-Smith (the co-director), who all 'sat up night after night playing through the music and exchanging ideas until no one knew which idea was whose'.[14]

They decided 'to place the [chorus] singers in boxes, two tiers each, on either side of the stage'[15] to allow Ashton unrestricted space. He had about three weeks in which to rehearse his dances; as before, he decided against 'a slavish reproduction' of 17th-century dance style and put the female dancers on point.[16] Since Michael Ayrton based his designs on the work of Inigo Jones, also strictly speaking an anachronism, period authenticity was not the most important consideration. Ashton's choreography for the Echo Dance elaborated on the idea he had used in his 1927 version: 'The foremost dancer (Beryl Grey) executes a long passage of broad, sweeping movements which are echoed by the middle dancer (Gillian Lynne) in a shorter and less sweeping form. This is followed by the furthermost dancer (Margaret Dale), who gives a mere suggestion of the opening movement'.[17] The final *chinoiserie* introduced a modification of the classic technique with 'gestures which are a brilliant reconstruction of ancient Chinese and Cambodian sculptures'.[18]

Otherwise the most successful passages were the dance for the Followers of Night, 'especially the winged grouping with its curious effect of foreshortened bodies and gently breathing arms',[19] and the *pas de deux* for the Spirits of the Air, danced by Fonteyn and Somes to the Chaconne from *Dioclesian*, in which Ashton further explored those 'walking on air' movements that he had developed in *The Wanderer* and *The Quest*. The production was necessarily short-lived (it was revived five years later with new choreography by John Cranko), and there were suggestions that Ashton should make a suite of dances from it to preserve his best choreography without all the elaborate trappings, but in the end what happened was that some of the floating lifts from the *pas de deux* were incorporated into *Symphonic Variations* and others used later still in a *pas de deux* with a similar theme in *Homage to the Queen*.

✻

The Fairy Queen:
Fonteyn and Somes as
the Spirits of the Air

De Valois had long looked forward to the day when her policy of repertory-building could be extended to include works from the Diaghilev era in addition to *Les Sylphides* and *Le Carnaval*, which had been revived in the early thirties. To dance ballets like Massine's *Tricorne* and *La Boutique fantasque*, hitherto considered the exclusive property of the 'real' Russian dancers, would be an acid test for her company. Accordingly, she invited Massine to mount these two ballets, as well as a revised version of *Mam'zelle Angot*, which he had previously done for Ballet Theatre. These revivals left the company with no rehearsal time for new ballets by its resident choreographers, so Ashton for a while turned his hand to directing operas, both at Covent Garden and for Benjamin Britten's recently-formed English Opera Group. With characteristic self-deprecation, Ashton says that one reason he undertook this new work was that if he 'dried up' as a choreographer it would give him another string to his bow.

The first was Massenet's *Manon*, presented at Covent Garden on 30 January 1947. Ashton tried to inject more movement into the opera than was common at the time – he found the chorus singers a little difficult to work with at first but he managed to arouse their interest and they soon began to enter wholeheartedly into the work. Looking back, he feels the gambling scene was very successful. Again there are entries in his notebook that indicate how he worked out various ideas for movement and for introducing variety into the crowd scenes:

> Old lady, funny man, porter.
> Canary lady, 2 men, 3rd woman. . . .
> Porters and coachmen
> Manon appears on 'Lo'
> Act III Scene 1: General commotion (Petrouchka) up to entrance of Smart
>   Ladies.

The Benjamin Britten work was *Albert Herring*, given at Glyndebourne on 20

Scene from *Albert Herring*, with Peter Pears, centre

June 1947. This opera was freely based on Maupassant's story *Le Rosier de Madame Husson*, with the locale moved to Loxford, 'a small market town in East Suffolk, in the year 1900'. Ashton heightened the comic element, not always with the approval of the librettist, Eric Crozier. Britten, however, told him years later that he regarded *Albert Herring* as the most perfect production of any of his operas. There were several notable comic characterisations, especially those of Peter Pears in the title role and of Joan Cross as Lady Billows.

At the time of the transfer to Covent Garden a smaller company had been formed to dance in the operas at Sadler's Wells and also give one or two ballet performances each week. This was originally called the Sadler's Wells Opera Ballet, but the title was soon changed to Sadler's Wells Theatre Ballet when it became clear that the company could also serve a useful function as an autonomous touring group, performing in theatres too small for the main company and giving experience to young dancers and choreographers. The director of the 'junior' or 'second' company, as it was sometimes called, was Peggy van Praagh, who suggested that Ashton might like to revive *Valentine's Eve*. He felt, however, that the original idea would now seem too sentimental, and decided instead to make a completely new ballet to the same music, Ravel's *Valses nobles et sentimentales*, presented under that title at the Wells on 1 October 1947. Again the designs were by Fedorovitch, very similar to those she had done for the earlier ballet.

Ashton threw out the story in favour of a much vaguer pretext of shifting relationships among a group of young people at a ball. However, he did admit to Richard Buckle that 'the ballet was suggested by actual people and events', without going into detail. Buckle's description of the action was as follows: 'Two (boys) were both attracted by the same girl, at least she was always present in their thoughts, even when they were dancing with other girls. At the end she returned to them after an absence, and I was left in doubt as to which of them, if either, she would eventually choose'.[20]

Just as *Symphonic Variations* in some ways recalled *Apollo*, filling an equivalent place in Ashton's œuvre as a kind of manifesto, so *Valses nobles et sentimentales*, with its intimations of romantic intrigue, suggested a parallel to the Balanchine of *Le Cotillon*, whose aura of heady, perfumed decadence had made it the prototype of a whole genre of ballets. The style of supported adagio similarly recalled Balanchine, as in a moment when one girl leaned in *arabesque penchée* on a boy's shoulder, with a second girl leaning on *her* shoulder and echoing the line of the *arabesque*. (Ashton's ballet was of course made before Balanchine's version of the same music.)

A new motif that occurred in the *Valses* and was to reappear in several later ballets was that of having one woman partnered by three or four men, who would, for example, pass her from hand to hand in a promenade or lift her, two holding her by the arms, while her legs were extended across the shoulders of two others.

Group from *Valses nobles et sentimentales*

Formally speaking, the structure of the ballet was determined by that of the music and not by the relationships, which were simply pegs on which to hang the dances. Ashton did not use the first waltz as an overture as did Balanchine later, but raised the curtain at once on the waltzing dancers. The last waltz, Ravel's 'epilogue', drew together fragments of the preceding choreography as the composer did with the musical themes.

Sadly, the ballet is lost – it was before the days of notation. It was a perfect vehicle for young dancers (its original cast included Anne Heaton, Elaine Fifield, Maryon Lane, Jane Shore, Donald Britton, Michael Boulton, Kenneth MacMillan and Peter Darrell). If Ashton's three early war-time ballets formed a trilogy that reflected a search for the solution of an inner conflict, so *Symphonic Variations*, *Valses nobles et sentimentales* and his next ballet formed a trilogy of another kind – one might say that they show how in his creative life at any rate that conflict was resolved. By no means incidental to this development was the revival of *Les Rendezvous*, also for the junior company, a definitive version of a ballet that embodied Ashton's earlier steps along the paths of classicism on which he was now firmly set.

Ashton tells the story that he was sitting in the bath with the radio playing and heard some music that he did not recognise: 'I was fascinated by the rhythm of it, so I rang up the BBC to ask what it was. After they told me I had great difficulty in locating it, but finally got someone in the States to send me the record.' The music was Stravinsky's *Scènes de ballet*, written for Billy Rose's revue *The Seven Lively Arts*, which was presented in New York in 1944; the ballet was danced by Markova and Dolin, with the latter's choreography.

Ashton discussed the music with Richard Buckle, who proposed a rather complex scenario for it somewhat in the manner of Boris Kochno. 'I wanted to suggest,' he has written, 'that every end is a beginning; that after the events of the day we enter a new world in the solitude of our own minds and in sleep; that death may be a new birth; and that when a ballet finishes it begins a new life in our thoughts after we have ceased to see it with our eyes'[21] – any one of which rather metaphysical conceptions would have been more than enough to deal with in a ballet of less than seventeen minutes' duration. Stravinsky had a very different kind of choreographic action in mind, as indicated by his programme note: 'A classical ballet which I composed in 1944. This music is patterned after the forms of the classical dance, free of any given literary or dramatic argument. The parts follow each other as in a sonata or in a symphony, in contrast or similarities.' Ashton decided to approach the music in that spirit rather than using Buckle's scenario.

Specifically, *Scènes de ballet* was the first time that he consciously paid homage to Petipa. A strange thing about its creation, he says, is that 'I, who at school could

Valses nobles et sentimentales: Donald Britton, Elaine Fifield, Maryon Lane

Scènes de ballet: LEFT Fonteyn in the ballerina's first variation; RIGHT opening tableau with Donald Britton and Alexander Grant in foreground, Somes in rear; the other two men who complete the group in the opposite corner from Britton and Grant are not shown in the photograph (compare with the opening tableau of *The Wanderer*, page 193). The photographs show the set as it appeared at the first performance only

never get on with algebra or geometry, suddenly got fascinated with geometrical figures, and I used a lot of theorems as ground patterns for *Scènes de ballet*. I used to drive the girls mad trying to solve these theorems, moving them from one position to another. I also wanted to do a ballet that could be seen from any angle – anywhere could be front, so to speak. So I did these geometric figures that are not always facing front – if you saw *Scènes de ballet* from the wings you'd get a very different, but equally good picture. We would get into terrible tangles, but when it finally came out I used to say, QED!' Margaret Dale confirms this, saying that it was an uncomfortable experience – the ballet was rehearsed in a very dirty, dingy hall where Ashton would come each day with his volume of Euclid and set the dancers to working out theorems.

The music was unlike any score Ashton had used before, with its broken rhythms, constantly shifting time-signatures, and fragmented phrasing. *Baiser de la fée*, after all, because of its Tchaikovskyan origin, has a certain romantic feeling. The use of such music as this was perhaps a necessary departure for him at the time, dictating a stricter, more astringent technical approach than César Franck and Maurice Ravel. In this too he sought the cooperation of the dancers, who would suggest to him movements that might go with the music, which he took and moulded according to his own conception of it. Michael Somes believes that Ashton learned a great deal about music from the experience – from the necessity to break down a complex score into its components.

Scènes de ballet: LEFT Fonteyn supported by Alexander Grant, John Field, Donald Britton and Philip Chatfield (hidden); RIGHT Fonteyn in the ballerina's second variation, with Somes kneeling at right

The ballet was made for a principal couple, Fonteyn and Somes, with a group of four male soloists and a corps de ballet of twelve women. The curtain rises on a tableau of the five men, the *premier danseur* standing centre and the others in pairs at opposite corners, in austere, heroic dual groupings. As they alter these poses on a series of annunciatory chords, he does *entrechats six*. This opening strikingly recalls that of *The Wanderer*, with classic *pas* and noble *attitudes* replacing the symbolic, even neurotic gestures of the earlier ballet – one movement that is common to both is the abrupt turning of the head from side to side, which indeed is a recurrent motif in *Scènes de ballet*. The corps de ballet enter in two lines and there is an ensemble passage in which they are broken up into groups of four; *enchaînements* are passed from one line or one group to another (a compositional device derived from Petipa), and there are occasional incursions by the men. The excitement quickens as the ballerina enters and dances a brief, brilliant solo that is this ballet's equivalent of Aurora's entry into the first act of *The Sleeping Beauty*. At the end of it two of the men present her to her partner in a high lift; there follows a *pas de deux* that introduces further variants of Ashton's by now familiar lifts – a run on point lifted barely off the ground, or low *cabrioles* forward and back. A particularly happy invention is a series of low lifts from side to side in *passé* that occur on piercing notes by the flute, echoed by the corps de ballet who also pause in *passé* as they *bourrée* out to the side from their lines down the centre of the stage. At the end of this passage the ballerina is carried off by her partner in an *arabesque*, her head thrown back. In Ashton ballets the *pas de deux* is always a metaphor for sexual union but

223

here, as befits the music, its expression is cool, not impassioned, except for one moment when the ballerina breaks through her reserve to embrace her partner.

The most specific reference to Petipa comes in the adagio to the 'C major trumpet melody, imitated by a horn at two bars' distance, which sounds like a tune played outside a celestial pub', to quote Desmond Shawe-Taylor's description[22] – in Ashton's choreography a *grand pas d'action* in the manner of the Rose Adagio from *The Sleeping Beauty*, with the men replacing each other as they support the ballerina in a promenade or, towards the end, a series of *pirouettes*, in which she takes the preparation with one partner who, by the time the turn is completed, has changed places with the next, and so on all along the line of five men. Another passage has the men standing in a line, each one lifting her in a high *jeté* over to the other side and then lunging into *arabesque à terre* as she is lifted by the next man. As the adagio finishes, the ballerina is again carried off in *arabesque*, as before.

After another short ensemble both principals have variations: first the man, who is joined at times by the other four – he does a series of double air turns with the others again changing their poses in between, and finally the five dance in unison. The woman's solo, to the duet for two solo cellos which (to quote Shawe-Taylor again) 'play in thirds against a feathery string accompaniment', is notable for its almost oriental arm movements, contrasted with the precision of the toe-steps; while she dances the four men recline at the right of the stage, one knee drawn up with an arm resting on it, with her partner kneeling amongst them.

224

In the finale there is a great series of *grand jeté* lifts, first by the ballerina and her partner, then, as they go from side to side, one supporting couple after another joins in and drops out again (a typical Ashton device, this, going at least as far back as *Les Patineurs*), with the principals running to the back to begin another series. The apotheosis finds the four men in their opening poses, with the *premier danseur* supporting the ballerina in the centre. This ending was perhaps the last remnant of Richard Buckle's suggested treatment – he had wanted the entire corps de ballet (and possibly the ballerina) to leave the stage, with the hero '[enjoying] his apotheosis in magnificent solitude'.[23] Even this disappeared when, later, Ashton added the twelve corps de ballet women to the final group.

But although Ashton had rejected Buckle's scenario, he accepted his suggestion for a designer – André Beaurepaire, who had designed *Concert de danses* for the Ballets des Champs-Elysées. It is possible that Beaurepaire listened to Buckle's ideas, but he had several of his own to add to the mixture. As was his habit, he turned out many versions of the décor, none of which pleased Ashton, who kept suggesting that he listen to the music. Beaurepaire in his turn insisted that his drawings expressed its quality exactly. 'Faced with the task of bending André to his will,' wrote Buckle, 'Ashton was in turn confident, determined, diplomatic, despairing, plaintive and resigned to the worst'.[24] There were endless problems: the main décor was a kind of viaduct going away in false perspective on either side, which was supposed to disappear at the apotheosis, to be replaced by 'a spiky Gothic pavilion'. At the dress rehearsal this transformation did not work and in any case the two sets were seen to be in ludicrously disparate styles. On opening night the pavilion was used throughout as the only set, but thereafter it was scrapped and the viaduct restored.[25] On occasion the ballet has been performed without any décor at all.

The costumes have also undergone slight modifications, though, except for the male soloist's, which is now similar to that of the other men, the designs have not basically been changed – tutus for the women (ballerina in yellow and black, corps in blue and black), the men in tunics with geometrical designs in appliqué. At one time the girls were given new wigs and hats inspired by headgear worn by a woman Ashton saw in a restaurant.[26]

At first Fonteyn seemed ill at ease in the ballerina role – a situation that was always betrayed by her adoption of a rather glassy, fixed smile, but as she grew in authority in the great classic roles she began to understand this one and to grasp that its essential quality was elegance rather than mere *chic*. (It is important to recognise that Fonteyn grew enormously in assurance as a result of a guest season with Roland Petit's Ballets de Paris in May 1948, when she danced both in his *Les Demoiselles de la nuit* and in excerpts from *The Sleeping Beauty*.) It has been danced by nearly all of the company's ballerinas, by none more brilliantly, perhaps, than Antoinette Sibley, who told me that she considers it one of the greatest of all ballets, 'I don't care if the audience doesn't understand it, or if it gets no curtain calls – one always finds something new in it.' Jennifer Penney, too, with her elegant line and *port de bras*, gives a ravishing account of it. *Scènes de ballet* was also a landmark in the development of British male dancing – the original quartet of soloists, presented by Ashton with a new challenge, aspired to a prowess that was quite unaccustomed – even though today we take it for granted.

In one way that was significant, *Scènes de ballet* established a pattern for many of Ashton's subsequent ballets – it was slow to win popularity or even critical recognition. As we have seen, Ashton was deeply concerned to restore the dance element to its rightful place as the primary subject-matter of ballet, but in spite of the success of *Symphonic Variations*, he was still in advance of many of the critics. British listeners were not used to the acerbity of late Stravinsky and there was still a feeling that a ballet without a message must lack seriousness. There were honourable, predictable exceptions: Richard Buckle, Mary Clarke ('any ballet lover worth his salt should be prepared to wrestle with choreography that is not superficially titillating for the sake of the rewards that will come when he has sought out the heart of its mysteries'[27]), Beryl de Zoete, ('a geometric, dispassionate harmony which is indeed something new and strange and altogether admirable'[28]). But The Times was uncompromisingly negative ('Mr Ashton has [not] been able to contrive anything noteworthy'[29]), and so was Punch ('Take it down and bury it'[30]).

Fortunately the ballet has been retained fairly consistently in the repertory, not always in perfect condition: one may say that both dancers and critics have grown into it, as witness a recent review by Clement Crisp – 'at every viewing its grandeur of image, the clarity of its planning, the momentum of its incidents, excite the imagination as do few other ballets . . . We are . . . involved with the central matters of the classic dance, as Ashton offers us a commentary and a masterly summation of the attitudes and incidents of the Petipa tradition in which he was educated and was to extend in his own big ballets. . . The succinct structure of the piece is in itself a marvel: the dance incidents are often epigrammatic, but their pulse, the swift changes of emotional and dynamic tempi are so sure that there is never any feeling of haste or of ideas not fully explored'.[31]

It must be added that, in recognition of its right to be considered as one of Ashton's greatest masterpieces, *Scènes de ballet* should be redesigned: the décor and costumes seem more irrelevant and dated each time one sees them – it is a ballet that could stand the test of being seen in the most austere setting and dress (as it was performed by the Berlin company under Kenneth MacMillan's direction).

With good reason, *Scènes de ballet* is one of Ashton's own favourites among his ballets: apart from its intrinsic quality, it gave him an added confidence in his powers that enabled him to make the next important step in his career, a necessary one both for himself and for British ballet, a full-length work in the tradition of the Maryinsky classics. This was done at Christmas-time in the following season, but first there was another new one-act ballet, *Don Juan*, given a month before, on 25 November 1948. (At this time Ashton and Lambert, who had resigned as musical director in the previous year, were officially appointed as joint Artistic Directors of the company with Ninette de Valois.)

Ashton had been considering the subject of *Don Juan* for several years: during the war he had corresponded with his old friend and collaborator Edward Burra, who had drawn up a rather complicated scenario, in several scenes, and made preliminary sketches. Then Ashton heard the tone-poem by Richard Strauss at a concert and decided that it would be better to use this score and condense the story into its essence rather than following the play by Zorillas, as Burra had suggested. Ashton communicated this decision to Burra, who replied, 'I think the Essence is a much better idea than some ungainly plot.' Ashton also wrote to Edwin Evans, who had written the programme note for the concert he had attended: 'I gather there is nothing you don't know about the Don. I also have a play by Zorillas, *Don Juan Tenorio*. I would like very much when the occasion arises to do a ballet on this subject, the only thing that holds me back is that I was so bored by Fokine's version [to Gluck's ballet score], for once the great master failed to interest me. I wonder if you would give me more fully the "programme" of Strauss' version and the quotations from Lenau's poem. I like the poetic and episodic treatment of Strauss rather than a logical development of the plot à la Fokine. Will you put your great knowledge at my disposal? I shall be most grateful and keep it all under your hat or rather under your beard! I shan't be active again for some time I suppose but I must occupy my mind by planning for the future. I am also very interested in Franck's Symphonic Variations and can visualize a ballet to them of a more abstract sort. Can you suggest a way of treating them? Forgive my bothering you but I would be most grateful for your help'.[32]

Strauss's tone-poem is based on Nicolaus Lenau's version of the Don Juan legend, in which he seeks the ideal woman in vain, and is finally killed in a duel. Ashton, when he finally came to produce the ballet, did not follow this outline, but rather produced a kind of abstraction of the story, and indeed in style the ballet was somewhat in the same severely classical vein as *Scènes de ballet*. The music proved to be rather unsuitable, being too short to allow for even this abstract treatment, and Ashton extended the length of the ballet by adding a brief silent prologue in which the Don was seen surrounded by six of his former loves, each of whom he passionately embraced before Fonteyn entered as the personification of La Morte Amoureuse (named after a poem by Théophile Gautier, from which a quotation was given as an epigraph to the ballet, in the translation by Algernon Charles Swinburne: 'The love that caught strange light from Death's own eyes'). He pursued her throughout the ballet, temporarily diverting his attention to a Young Wife (Shearer); when La Morte Amoureuse finally returned and embraced him, her kiss proved to be fatal and he died in the arms of his other amours. Ashton was undecided in the beginning whether to use only one dancer to represent the women in Don Juan's life, or several; he finally settled on the latter alternative.

He now says that certain elements in the ballet defeated him and that he did not, therefore, fully bring it off, though there were lovely things in it. Anyone who saw it would agree that these included the two *pas de deux* (with Fonteyn, and with

Don Juan: Centre,
Fonteyn as La Morte
Amoureuse, Helpmann
as Don Juan

Shearer) and the Carnival Scene. The *pas de deux* with Fonteyn, particularly, continued in the same line of development as others of that period, though in a more
percussive, even violent, mode – there were, in particular, many striking inventions based on the *pas ciseaux*, such as a lift in which she was carried across Helpmann's shoulder with legs open almost in a split. In the Carnival the corps de ballet
was used 'to heighten the atmosphere and draw attention not only to the confusion
in Don Juan's mind, but also to his heartless and ruthless quest. This continually
swirling mass of dancers in high revelry matches the increasing passion and tempo
of the music. . . It fills the stage almost to overflowing, and a climax of sound and
movement is reached . . .'[33] The corps de ballet danced well, the reviewer quoted
said, 'as they always do in an Ashton ballet because they are part of a whole'.
On the other hand, the writer felt, not without justice, that the ballet as a whole
lacked the lyricism and passion that both the music and theme demand. The
critic of The Times said that a great part of Ashton's invention was 'devoted to
devising novel ways of transporting the female body', which he described as 'a sure
sign of strain', offering the conjecture that Ashton had been going too often to the
Ballets des Champs-Elysées.[34]

Undoubtedly a cause of weakness was the casting of the title role. Helpmann
was by now severely limited technically and also failed to generate the personal
magnetism that would have enabled him to be the dominant figure in the ballet.
Don Juan was in fact the last romantic role that Ashton made for Helpmann, and
for the next fifteen years or so Fonteyn's regular partner both in the classics and
new ballets was Somes.

Burra's décor and costumes had an appropriately sinister quality, even though the idea of a partly ruined viaduct was getting to be rather overworked; the costumes were fairly conventional, except for the beaked masks worn by the Carnival dancers, which also appear in some of his paintings on similar subjects.

Fonteyn tore a ligament on the opening night of *Don Juan* and her part was taken over at subsequent performances by Violetta Elvin. More seriously, it meant that she was out of *Cinderella*, at least at the beginning, but the new full-length ballet went on as scheduled, on Christmas Eve, with Moira Shearer in the title role. Ashton had envisaged the production of an evening-length ballet as early as 1939 but clearly such a project was impossible in war-time.[35] With the move to Covent Garden it could again be considered, and he thought of doing Delibes's *Sylvia*. This was shelved, temporarily at least, in favour of Prokofiev's *Cinderella*, which had been composed during the war and presented first at the Bolshoi, with choreography by Zakharov, in 1945, and then at the Kirov, with choreography by Sergeyev, in the following year. Iris Morley had seen one of the Soviet versions and P W Manchester took Ashton to meet her and hear her description of it.[36] He decided to omit the third act episodes showing the Prince's journey in search of Cinderella, which afforded excuses for a divertissement of national dances ('I didn't like any of the places he went to, nor the music for them'). The only other cut of any consequence he made in the score was a dance of Grasshoppers and Dragonflies following the variation of the Fairy Summer, though it is clear from his notebook that he originally intended to include them. Otherwise, Ashton's scenario follows fairly closely that of the composer.†

It is not surprising that what inspired Ashton most about *Cinderella* were the lyric and comic aspects of the story, the characters of Cinderella herself and of her two stepsisters. At first, these were to be played by women – Moyra Fraser the dominant one and Margaret Dale the passive one, but Fraser accepted another engagement, and so Ashton decided to have them played *en travesti* by Helpmann and himself.[37] Originally, following Perrault, he planned to have a stepmother as well, but she must have been eliminated very early on. Although this kind of female impersonation was not without precedent in ballet history, the inevitable comparison was made with English Christmas pantomimes, though Ashton says he had always hated them and never went to see any. It will be remembered that he had danced the role of the Prince in Andrée Howard's *Cinderella* at the Ballet Club early in 1935, and his own ballet recalled her treatment of the story in several particulars, including the characters of the Ugly Sisters. In more important aspects the structure of Ashton's *Cinderella* derives from the Petipa-Ivanov classics, notably the divertissement of the fairies of the four seasons at the end of Act I, the *ballabili* of the Stars, and the big waltz and *pas de deux* in Act II, although this is not

† See Appendix B.

Cinderella: Shearer as Cinderella, attempting to leave the ball as midnight strikes; Somes as the Prince at right

set in the traditional form with variations and coda (the two solos precede the *pas de deux* proper).

Prokofiev wrote, in a 1945 essay,[38] 'What I wanted to express above all in the music for *Cinderella* was the poetic love of Cinderella and the Prince, the birth and flowering of that love, the obstacles in its path, and finally the dream fulfilled.' It was to be expected that this aspect of the story would appeal equally strongly to Ashton. The waltz in the ballroom scene, a concerted number for Cinderella and the Prince, the Fairies and their cavaliers (the Prince's Friends), the Stars and the Courtiers, followed by the two solo variations and later the *pas de deux* – all these dances exquisitely express 'the birth and flowering' of love. They do so, as one might suppose, in terms of the kind of choreographic motif that Ashton had been exploring in all his recent ballets, including the scissor- or compass-like movements that occurred in Fonteyn's role in *Don Juan*, here converted to lyrical effect when interspersed with feathery *petite batterie*. Dale Harris has written of the 'gently, subsiding close'[39] of the *pas de deux* – Cinderella leans forward in low supported *arabesque*.

It has often been said that the brevity of the *pas de deux* in Act III makes the end of the ballet disappointing as an expression of love's fulfilment. Perhaps more is

230

needed to say 'and they lived happily ever after' than the ballet's quiet finish (hardly an apotheosis), with Cinderella and the Prince getting into a boat and sailing away or, in the later revision, simply walking off together as the Jester forlornly covers his face. Perhaps, as has been suggested, the Kirov ending is better – the curtain coming down as the lovers dance around the stage by themselves.[40] But the fact remains that there is no music for an extended *pas de deux*, and Ashton anyway always seems to prefer 'a dying fall'. At all events, he did not feel impelled to include an enlarged *pas de deux* among his many revisions – he had, he says, 'used up' the emotion that the story evoked in him.

There can be no disputing the brilliance of the Seasons divertissement and the *ballabili* of the Stars. Ashton has said, 'I always return to Petipa over everything . . . people sometimes find me at a matinée of *The Sleeping Beauty*, which I have seen literally hundreds of times. And they ask me what I'm doing and I say "having a private lesson".'[41] These dances show how well that lesson has been learned. The *ballabili* are built on simple combinations of steps (especially *pas de chat*), star patterns, and pointing gestures that suggest a sparkling radiance. Each of the four variations uses steps and, especially, *port de bras* that portray the characteristics of the various seasons and, equally, reflect the qualities of their original interpreters: the lightness of Nadia Nerina's elevation, punctuated by little flicks of the wrists, as Spring;[42] Elvin's voluptuous languor as Summer, undulating and stretching; Pauline Clayden's impetuosity in the stormy solo for Autumn, with its vertiginous off-centre turns and pointing fingers; the stately detachment of Grey as Winter, her arms straight out to the side as she spread a thin film of ice with her *ronds de jambe à terre*. In a coda, led by the Fairy Godmother, each of these is quoted in turn. The Godmother's own variation, earlier in the act, was less satisfactory, though graciously danced by Pamela May. For a while it was omitted altogether, then later different music was substituted which enabled Ashton to choreograph a new dance whose 'drifting lyrical flow'[43] continued the feeling of her lovely theme music (which Ulanova was so fond of that she wanted Profokiev to give it to Cinderella instead).

The mention of these original interpreters brings us to the question of Fonteyn's replacement by Shearer in the title role. *Cinderella* was put together very quickly, in about six weeks, which meant that it was started even while he was still making *Don Juan*, but Ashton says that he had done hardly any work with Fonteyn herself on the longer ballet before her injury. So that it was Shearer who, he says in a revealing phrase, 'dragged it out of me,' and the role was clearly made to exploit her best features, the brilliance of her technique and her lightness. Many people have said that only when Fonteyn finally appeared in the ballet (which did not happen until 25 February 1949) did the character come fully to life. Undoubtedly she was, then and for many years afterwards, its ideal interpreter, but Ashton says that he was very pleased with Shearer, that she was an underrated dancer, perhaps because of her great personal beauty. But it was left to Fonteyn to fulfil the pathos of the character, especially in the first act where, as Mary Clarke has said, 'she was

Cinderella, 1965 production: the dancing lesson; Ashton and Keith Martin, as the Dancing Master, perform the 'Fred step' with Helpmann looking on

not afraid to look a drab and frightened waif . . . (which) lent her transformation an added radiance'.[44] She brought out the playfulness, too, as in the dance with the broomstick when she imagines herself going to the ball and imitates her Step-sisters' ungainly attempts to master the gavotte (appropriately enough, both the Ashton-sister and Cinderella do his 'lucky' step from the *Gavotte Pavlova* here). No other dancer has been as exquisite in the variation in Act II, especially the magical moment when she balances in *relevé passé derrière* and looks back over her shoulder. Above all there was an unaffected simplicity and sweetness of nature, which made her farewell to the Stepsisters, especially Ashton, the most emotionally charged moment in the whole ballet.

Whether or not Ashton cared for pantomime, his creation of the sisters' roles is in the great tradition of clowns like Dan Leno who always appeared as 'dame' in those Christmas extravaganzas. Both Ashton and Helpmann were brilliant mimics, who frequently entertained their friends and colleagues with impromptu turns at parties or to enliven the tedium of train-calls or backstage waits. Helpmann had put this talent to professional use in a series of impersonations of famous actresses in a wartime revue, *Swinging the Gate*, while Ashton was one of several celebrities who posed for the illustrations for 'My Royal Past, by Baroness von

◁ *Cinderella*: Cinderella (Fonteyn) says goodbye to her Stepsisters (Helpmann and Ashton)

233

Bülop, as told to Cecil Beaton', an elaborate spoof of aristocratic memoirs, published in the autumn of 1939 (a time when such a book must have seemed even more of an anachronism).[45] Ashton appears in wig and choker as a minor duchess, complete with Edwardian monobosom. Both Ashton and Helpmann, as we have seen, gave notable performances as Carabosse, but the Ugly Sisters were their crowning achievement in this genre.

Ashton's own role, which turned out to be the biggest hit of the ballet, came about almost by accident ('the sort of accident that happens to geniuses',[46] as Denby said) – because of the pressure of time, Ashton had to leave his part until last, and he told Helpmann that he would make himself the foil to Helpmann's more domineering sister, and further decided to be 'addled and forgetful' so that if in fact he forgot what came next in performance it would just seem like part of his character. Though he used some characteristic gestures of his own, some aspects of the character, and even the wig and make-up, recalled Andrée Howard's performance in her own ballet. The solo in the ballroom scene (where she forgets her steps and does Ashton's 'racking his brains' gesture) came to look more and more like an affectionate parody of Pavlova, and the hilarious circuit of the stage that the two sisters make with their oranges, heads nodding, the steps getting bigger and bigger, was taken from his memory of the Oompah Trot performed by Fred and Adele Astaire in *Lady, Be Good!* Funny as Helpmann's performance was, he relied largely on received comic effects (for instance, swinging his beads around his neck in the manner of Beatrice Lillie), whereas Ashton created a real character, selfish, weak and vain, but genuinely pathetic. Not only was his farewell to Cinderella touching, the exit that followed – 'limping off to a bleak and dreary old age' as Peter Williams wrote[47] – was heartbreaking. What was also remarkable, in a performance so hurriedly put together, was the particularity of the detail – the way he bit the thread in the opening scene with the shawl, for instance – nothing was generalised or just sketched in. Naturally things were added as the ballet was performed more and more – for instance in the ballroom scene first Helpmann added a fish-dive with *his* suitor, then a little later Ashton 'retaliated with a Bolshoi-style leap' on to his partner's shoulder.[48]

For many years *Cinderella* was regularly revived at Christmas-time at Covent Garden and was danced by a succession of ballerinas and their partners. When the sisters were played by women in later years (Moyra Fraser finally played the role intended for her, with Margaret Hill; on another occasion Andrée Howard appeared in Ashton's role) it did not work – as with the female impersonators in the Kabuki Theatre, the kind of observation of the female character that lay beneath these comedy performances could be achieved only by men.

The original décor and costumes by Jean-Denis Malclès, who had designed for the Ballets des Champs-Elysées, seemed very stylish at the time, but what Peter Williams called their 'heavy-handed post-war French tapestry approach'[49] dated rapidly. For some reason the opportunity to introduce a series of transformations at the end of Act I – pumpkin into carriage, mice into horses – was not taken.

Cinderella: Trying on the shoe: Ashton and Helpmann, with the Jester (Alexander Grant) in the middle

The ballet was redesigned for the revival at Christmas, 1965, with décor in the far more appropriate tradition of Victorian scene-painting by Henry Bardon, and costumes by David Walker. One error of judgment in Bardon's designs was that at first the staircase at the back of the ballroom scene was divided into two: it was soon converted to a single flight, restoring Cinderella's entrance, with its quality of a magical visitation, as she walked on point straight down the steps and continued to the front of the stage in *pas de bourrée*.[50]

Of all the reviews, it was Edwin Denby's (originally published in Richard Buckle's magazine, Ballet) that was the most perceptive and the most illuminating: while pointing out weaknesses in both overall design and in specific detail, he says, '*Cinderella* hasn't the disharmony of a piece that can't do what it wants to do, and impact and drive are not its method of being interesting. The fun of the farce

235

Le Rêve de Léonor: John Gilpin as an Ephebe, with Belinda Wright and Joan Sheldon as Two Bouquets, Milorad Miskovitch as the Sombre Seducer

Ashton rehearsing *Le Rêve de Léonor*

keeps relaxing the hold of the central story and in the story the dances don't try for intensity and fail, they don't look silly, they look agreeable . . . The spell it creates doesn't crystallize in a climax or a specific dance image but no mean gesture breaks the continuity of it. English in the lightness of its fragrance, the charm it holds is a grace of spirit, an English sweetness of temper . . . To keep in a three-act ballet such a tone, to sustain it without affectation or banality, shows Ashton's power, and he shows this in doing it as simply as possible, by keeping the dancing sweet . . . The dance impetus of his piece, mild though it is, is open and confident. The variety of ballet styles blends without a blur, each springing as fresh as the other from the score, and the spell of being inside the imaginary world of music, where dancing is natural doesn't break all evening . . .'[51]

In the New Year Ashton was occupied at first with the revivals at Covent Garden of *A Wedding Bouquet* (17 February 1949) and *Apparitions* (24 February 1949), the latter of which Lambert returned to conduct. In April Ashton took leave from the Sadler's Wells Ballet to do the first of a series of ballets that he was to make for other companies in the next decade, *Le Rêve de Léonor*, for Roland Petit's Ballets de Paris, first given at the Princes Theatre in London on 26 April 1949. This ballet has a curious history. The libretto concocted by the painter Léonor Fini (who also designed the décor and costumes) was, if not autobiographical, at any rate auto-mythological, to coin a word, as the name of the protagonist suggests.† This scenario was originally to be used as the basis for a ballet choreographed by Petit to the Liebestod from Wagner's *Tristan und Isolde*. After he and Fini had a falling-out this was presented without décor as *Grand pas d'action*, and the libretto and designs were handed over to Ashton to see what he could make of them (he says he was more or less 'bullied' into doing it). He decided to use Britten's *Variations on a Theme of Frank Bridge*, which he had had in mind for some time – music that at least had the advantage of cutting the intended length of the ballet by one half – but Ashton had a hard time reconciling the rival claims of synopsis and score, and their incompatibility was only made more obvious by moments when ghostly voices called out the eponymous heroine's name, or a 'Sphynx' sitting in a bathtub gave out a cackling laugh.[52]

Even so, Ashton found some stimulation in working with dancers like Renée Jeanmaire and Milorad Miskovitch. Unfortunately, he fell into the trap of trying to emulate other ballets in the French company's repertory in which the dancers rolled around on the stage in what were intended to be graphic representations of the act of love. Perhaps the kindest comment came from Miss Manchester: 'As Ashton was the choreographer it would have been almost impossible to have entirely excluded beauty from some of the movements'.[53]

† See Appendix B.

Chapter Ten

1949–1951

Over a year elapsed before the presentation of Ashton's next new ballet, but during that time an event took place that marked the beginning of a new epoch in the history of the Sadler's Wells Ballet – the company's first New York season and tour of the United States and Canada. Such a venture had been discussed in the previous year but at that time the old Metropolitan Opera House was not available, and the company's administrator, David Webster, had rightly decided that the New York City Center was unsuitable, so the visit was postponed until the situation changed. The first New York season accordingly opened at the Met on 9 October 1949, with a performance of *The Sleeping Beauty* danced by Margot Fonteyn and Robert Helpmann, with Ashton as Carabosse and Beryl Grey as the Lilac Fairy, and conducted by Constant Lambert. The repertory also included Ashton's *Façade* and *A Wedding Bouquet*, which were both very successful, and *Symphonic Variations* and *Apparitions*, which were not. *Cinderella* was also given, and gradually became an audience favourite.

But it was of course with *The Sleeping Beauty*, and Fonteyn's performance in it, that the conquest of New York was accomplished. For New York audiences Fonteyn was the company's star, its *prima ballerina assoluta*, even though Helpmann's greatness as a partner was acknowledged. Then, as now, the American public had a more immediate response to dancing itself, the physical activity, than audiences at home, and there was keen appreciation of the British style, its lyricism, reticence and refinement, in contrast to the more extrovert qualities of American, and Russo-American, dancers. The company's style of performing *The Sleeping Beauty* (of which Fonteyn was the exemplar) was the evolving British classic style. Each country in which ballet has taken root has developed a national style through the modification of the academic technique by the admixture of indigenous characteristics (both of physique and personality) and, equally important, by the discoveries of a master choreographer (not always a native of that country): a Frenchman, Marius Petipa, in Russia; the Franco-Danish August Bournonville in Denmark; a Russian, George Balanchine, in the United States; and in Britain, Frederick Ashton, the Anglo-Peruvian – particularly in his post-war ballets and for that matter his additions to *Beauty* itself which helped to shape the way in which the whole ballet was performed. It should not be forgotten, however, that the company's experience in America was itself an important factor in determining the way its style developed, if only because, having adapted themselves over the last few years to the larger stage at Covent Garden, the dancers now had to enlarge their way of performing still more so that it would 'read' in the even wider expanses of the old Metropolitan Opera House. After a month in New York the company went on tour, returning to London in time to reopen at Covent Garden on 26 December 1949 with *Cinderella*.

While in New York Ashton had received an invitation to choreograph a ballet for Balanchine's New York City Ballet, and a month later, therefore, he sailed back to the States on the SS America. On arrival he was met by his old friend Alice Astor, then Mrs David Pleydell-Bouverie, and had to give a press conference at which he was asked by a reporter from the Hearst newspapers, 'Mr Ashton, do you authorize me to say you do not teach Princess Margaret Rose the can-can?'[1]

The ballet he chose to do for New York City Ballet was *Illuminations*, to Britten's song-cycle on poems by Arthur Rimbaud, an idea Ashton had had in mind for several years, having become fascinated by Rimbaud during the war. He read the poems, Enid Starkie's biography, and various French books on the poet: 'I found him one of the most tragic human beings, and I used to weep when I read about him.' When he heard Britten's setting of the poems at a concert he asked the composer if he could use it for a ballet. He discussed the idea with Christian Bérard when he was designing Massine's *Clock Symphony* for the Sadler's Wells Ballet in 1948; Bérard made some drawings on the brown-paper covers of a recording of the music Ashton got from the BBC; the ballet was even announced for production at the end of that year,[2] but Bérard died before the project could be realised. The idea came to Ashton's mind again when Lincoln Kirstein, director general of the New York City Ballet, asked him for a ballet, and they agreed to invite Cecil Beaton to design it.

Lincoln Kirstein discussed the ballet with Cecil Beaton even before Ashton's arrival in New York and they agreed that there was no point in imitating Bérard, but that 'It must have a child-like quality, it must be as provocative and daring as Rimbaud's poetry itself . . . To begin with we agreed everything should be extremely poor, patched, darned, mended and torn again . . . We looked at the paintings of Klee . . .'[3] Kirstein kept arriving with armfuls of books, and they came up with the idea that the set should be erected by children in front of the audience, using an enlarged version of a construction toy.

Not unnaturally, Ashton vetoed much of this when he arrived, producing instead postcards of Picasso *saltimbanques* and a Van Gogh night scene. The three of them went away for the weekend and Kirstein brought with him children's books of Rimbaud's time. One of these had illustrations showing children dressed as pierrots, and it was this that gave the collaborators the clue they were seeking: 'A troupe of pierrots are disguising themselves as Rimbaud, as his townspeople, as

239

his muse, and as kings and queens'.[4] In its final form this concept was simplified – the idea of its being a ballet within a ballet was more or less eliminated – but the pierrot costumes were retained, for everyone except Rimbaud himself, who was in a stylised version of a black velvet jacket and striped trousers, but also with white pompons that relate his costume to the others. Apart from the basic irrelevance of the pierrot costumes, their use had the unfortunate effect of prettifying the ballet; Beaton's designs were in his most bloodless manner. The painted scrims that constituted the set, following his conviction that 'everything should be transparent', were in black and white, with a spattering of inkblots, rather in the manner of Eugene Berman.

Ashton wanted the ballet to have realistic elements, with allusions to episodes or personages in the poet's life as well as to the poems, and he wrote out a kind of outline in his notebook that suggests this kind of combination, a good example of his method of plotting the action in accordance with the music, jotting down ideas for the actual movement at the same time.†

The finished work followed Ashton's outline in many respects, though as usual with him the rehearsal process involved cutting out extraneous material – for instance such notions as the dancers 'helping themselves' to properties from a stall on stage, the family going to Communion with umbrellas, and the 'Marine' motifs did not find their way into the ballet, but the opening in a frozen tableau was kept in (it was a device that Ashton had used before to good effect), and also the handful of confetti thrown into the air, a gesture apparently intended to signify masturbation. Other incidents were added as rehearsals progressed or perhaps as a result of discussion among the collaborators (Kirstein must clearly be considered one of these, although as usual he remained anonymous).

As might be expected when Ashton was working with dancers who were not familiar with his methods, the ballet does not look like any of his others. Even though the dancers saw that Ashton was quite clear about what he wanted, his way of choreographing was very different from Balanchine's, at any rate in regard to the music. Ashton's method was to compose a fairly long phrase of movement whose relation to the musical phrase might initially seem vague to them (they had a similar experience when working with Antony Tudor), while Balanchine, with his profound technical knowledge of music, always counted everything out very precisely. Tanaquil LeClercq tells of trying to teach her role to Diana Adams, who kept asking, 'What are the counts?' and she could make only some such reply as, 'When you hear this in the music, you do *that*, then if you move a little faster on this next thing, you'll make it.'

Miss LeClercq was familiar with Rimbaud's work and Ashton did not spend time talking to her about it, but with Nicholas Magallanes, who was to impersonate the poet, he did, also giving him books to read – all of which was an unusual procedure for Ashton.[5] Magallanes had had comparatively few roles demanding

† See Appendix C.

Illuminations: Nicholas Magallanes as the Poet, centre

this degree of dramatic interpretation, and the performance Ashton drew out of him was an extraordinarily compelling one. Similarly, Melissa Hayden's role of Profane Love gave her a rare opportunity to express a passionate sensuality, an opportunity that she made the most of. To increase the possible range of movement for this character, Ashton decided that she should have one foot bare, the other on point. However, he did not inform her of this until late in the rehearsal period, when he asked her one day to remove one shoe. When she protested, Ashton told her that she would find that he had choreographed her part in such a way that all the steps calling for the use of the full point occurred on one foot only, and so it proved. Another dancer who revealed unsuspected talents both technically and interpretively was Robert Barnett, who presented Ashton with brilliant *pirouettes* and *petite batterie* as the raw material for his virtuoso *demi-caractère* role as the Dandy.

It has been said that *Illuminations* is closest in style to *A Wedding Bouquet* among Ashton's other ballets, but this is true only in the sense that both comprise a series of character vignettes rather than a coherent story. *Illuminations* may well be the most 'literary' of his ballets, apart from *The Quest*, but as with *The Lord of Burleigh*, for instance, its literary source is only the peg on which the dance fabric is hung. In a perceptive review at the time of the first performance, John Martin wrote that 'The more one knows about its cruel and turbulent hero, Arthur Rimbaud, the more vivid are Ashton's images, and the more brilliant is his weaving together of the poet's life and the fantasy and voyance [sic] of his poetry.

'Approaching the ballet, however, with no special background whatever . . . what one sees is perhaps something like this: A passionate and rebellious poet views

Illuminations: 'Being Beauteous'; Tanaquil LeClercq as Sacred Love, with Shaun O'Brien, Roy Tobias (seated), Arthur Bell and Dick Beard

his life as a grim and vulgar side-show, a world of dirty and bedraggled Pierrots who have no idea what he is up to; he hangs his beautiful visions defiantly on the stars. Pulling him in opposite directions are two women – the white-clad figure of what is called in the program Sacred Love, and the voluptuous and overwhelming figure of Profane Love. The latter he yields to totally but rejects ultimately with violence. The former he visualizes as a queen, and tearing the crown from the head of her king, dons it himself and overturns the pattern of his society. In a vision he sees her as a "Being Beauteous" borne aloft, but amid "whistlings of death and circles of muffled music;" and from the ranks of the barbaric side-show of Pierrots the figure of Profane Love emerges to direct his murder. Following still the dream of his pure vision, he walks entranced into immortality.

'So far, so good; but under this lovely, romantic exterior Ashton has packed stuff of harsher and more violent character. He has told us much of the essential story of Rimbaud's actual life, including his virulent personal relationship with the older poet, Paul Verlaine, a relationship which all but destroyed them both, before the world and in their inmost natures. By lifting the whole theme into terms of high abstraction, Ashton has managed to tell an untellable story, and to do it without the slightest color of offence, with passion but with dignity.

'As the figure of Profane Love is not merely a symbolically bowdlerized version of Verlaine but represents elemental forces much deeper than any single individual, so the figure of Sacred Love must be considered as representing less a person than the idealisms of Rimbaud – his Muse, in short. We are dealing thus with im-

242

personalized symbols but without sacrificing the brutal facts of a highly personalized actuality, and this is where Ashton has done a supremely subtle and impressive job'.[6]

It is possible to hold the opinion that the various elements of the ballet are in fact less successfully integrated than this suggests, and that the piece attempts to exist on too many levels: there is the choreographic embodiment of imagery from the poems – itself filtered through the sensibility of Benjamin Britten – overlaid by the references to Rimbaud's life; and the Pierrot-metaphor only adds a further layer that, as I have indicated, introduces an element of chi-chi. Moreover, the 'realistic' incidents do not always fit appropriately into the abstract fabric of the dance – such moments as the shooting of the Poet (an actual pistol-shot, followed by the shedding of synthetic blood), his pantomime of relieving himself behind a *pissoir*, or the 'Après-midi like' gesture with the scarf (actually he pulls it between his legs) are graphic to the point of grossness – the symbol of the handful of confetti is at least ambiguous. More seriously, the treatment of the two aspects of love is done with unequal success in dance terms.

The most beautiful and sustained choreographic invention occurs in 'Being Beauteous', an adagio for the woman personifying Sacred Love supported by four men, one of whom was, in the original cast, a black dancer (Arthur Bell) recruited for the purpose from Katherine Dunham's school in New York – he was intended to refer to the period Rimbaud spent in North Africa and in particular to his devoted Ethiopian servant. Ashton could not, of course, choreograph such an adagio without its being a further development along the lines of similar passages in two of his previous ballets, *Valses nobles et sentimentales* and *Scènes de ballet* – there were lifts, promenades and supported turns in which the dancer was passed from one partner to another.

On the other hand the *pas de deux* of the Poet with Profane Love, while it has fascinating intertwinings of arms and legs, finally falls back on the kind of grapplings and rolling about that depict sexual activity in a way that is usually called 'explicit'. Here and elsewhere in the ballet it was hard not to feel that these were the last vestiges of Ashton's immaturity – that he felt he could get away with things in New York (and previously in Paris) that he would not be allowed to do in the Establishment atmosphere of Covent Garden. It is not offensive, but one wishes that Ashton had found a way to translate it into dance terms.

One intensely personal image remains in the ballet that links it to other Ashton works, before and after *Illuminations*, in which he did achieve such a transformation – the pair of young lovers who appear towards the end, at the moment when the Poet 'hangs the stars in the heavens', totally engrossed in one another, oblivious of what is going on around them. They are the lovers from *The Wanderer*, and they foreshadow other couples in ballets still to come. Locked in each other's arms and eyes, they suggest the possibility of joining together the spiritual and the physical, the Sacred and the Profane, into one whole that one would have to call simply 'Love', and they give the lie to that false dichotomy.

The opening night of *Illuminations* (2 March 1950) was a gala event with British and United States flags prominently displayed, marking the opening of an International Theatre Month sponsored by UNESCO.[7] The ballet was a great success and has been revived in recent years by the New York City Ballet under the supervision of Nicholas Magallanes. John Martin's review made the familiar comment that it showed that Ashton was capable of more than 'light, whimsical, witty inventions' and added that it was probably not a ballet Ashton could have done for his own company[8] – and indeed when it was shown in London by the New York City Ballet the following summer the Dancing Times pronounced it 'sordid and unhealthy'.[9]

Ashton returned to London immediately after the first performance and Balanchine followed soon afterwards to stage his *Ballet Imperial* (now known as *Piano Concerto No 2*) for Sadler's Wells Ballet – as part of an informal exchange. On the 15 May there was a sentimental occasion at the Wells itself, announced as being in honour of the twenty-first anniversary of the first full evening of ballet given by the Vic-Wells Ballet (in point of fact it was only the twentieth, but nobody noticed the mistake until too late). Among other things, *A Wedding Bouquet* was given with its original cast.

In the Birthday Honours that year Ashton was made CBE. Early in September the company set off for their second New York season, again followed by a tour of the United States, with a repertory including *Dante Sonata*, which did not fare any better than *Apparitions* or *Symphonic Variations* the year before, although *Façade* was again a big hit.

Before crossing the Atlantic again Ashton had been occupied with an elaborate but rather disastrous film, as both performer and choreographer. *The Tales of Hoffmann* was an attempt by the team of producer-writer-directors, Michael Powell and Emeric Pressburger, to repeat their success with *The Red Shoes* a couple of years before – which in commercial if not artistic terms had been considerable. They reassembled several elements of the earlier film – the same dancing stars (Moira Shearer, Ludmilla Tcherina, Léonide Massine, Robert Helpmann), and the same designer (Hein Heckroth) – but although the new film was certainly superior musically and, in Ashton, engaged the services of a great choreographer, the element of kitsch was too strong to be overcome. As Gavin Lambert wrote, 'The total ensemble of striving romanticism, of Offenbach, of expressionist theatrical décors by Hein Heckroth, of rich Technicolor photography, of simultaneous opera and ballet with dubbed voices issuing from the dancers as they pirouette, and of camera tricks, results more in overwhelming confusion even than incongruity. . . The most spectacular failure yet achieved by Powell and Pressburger'.[10]

Ashton did try to do something interesting with some of the sequences he worked on. A Dragonfly ballet was interpolated in the Prologue – Hoffmann was seen watching it at the Opera House in Nuremberg, and it led into the flashback of the three Tales: Ashton had seen some nature films of the predatory dragonfly that kills its mate after coupling and wanted to use the idea for a ballet. Such a theme has become one of the more tedious commonplaces of contemporary ballet, and is not made very interesting in the film: the actual killing is very mild, not at all like Robbins's *The Cage*, for instance – Shearer just pushes Edmond Audran away and he disappears under the water. The dance is trickily filmed – it experiments with a process in which the dancers seem to float against the background, and in time-honoured cinema fashion ignores the fact that the performance is meant to be taking place in a theatre – but except for Shearer's beautiful *jetés*, the dance interest is small.

The Ballad of Kleinzack has Ashton in the title role, as a hunchbacked jester who loves a beautiful maiden (Shearer). The sequence is done in pantomime rather than dance. As a performer Ashton is seen to better advantage in the first story, as Dr Coppélius's assistant, half-human, half-puppet: he plays it with some subtlety, managing to inject a little pathos as well as humour. There is a quite amusing marionette ballet, with Ashton supposedly manipulating the dancers, and Shearer does a variation to Olympia's *coloratura* aria – when the 'machinery' runs down she starts to keel over, but Ashton hurriedly winds her up again. In the Epilogue, Shearer and Audran dance a Romantic *pas de deux*, to the famous Barcarolle – more *Les Sylphides* than *La Sylphide* in style – the excuse for which is that all of Hoffmann's loves merge into one. This dance is seen simultaneously from four angles on a divided screen. One can hardly blame Ashton for not attempting any kind of period authenticity in his choreography since the style of the film as a whole is late 1940s' kitsch. Ashton's own comment on this assignment will suffice: 'It was like going back to the old days – a sort of *stint*.'

On the Sadler's Wells Ballet's return from America Ashton started work on a major ballet, *Daphnis and Chloe*. Ravel's 'choreographic symphony' was originally commissioned by Diaghilev for Fokine as early as 1909, but the ballet was not produced until 1912, when for various reasons it did not have a great success – it was overshadowed by Nijinsky's *L'Après-midi d'un faune* and the accompanying scandal, a month earlier, for one thing. Fokine's libretto adapted from the pastoral by Longus is so closely tied to Ravel's score that it hardly permits of alteration, at least in terms of incident, though a change of emphasis is certainly possible. Ashton was very aware that he was inviting comparison with the older version – 'In England,' he has said, 'the Russian Ballet died very, very hard – people's memories go back and back and back, and they always come and say it's not as good as it was in the old days. I was afraid of that, but fortunately in London we have Tamara Karsavina who was the original Chloe, so I asked her to lunch and I said to her I'm thinking of doing *Daphnis and Chloe*, because I think it's a great piece of music, and I'd like to rescue it from the concert hall and bring it back into the theatre where it belongs. And she said, quite right. . .'[11] He had, in fact, thought of doing the ballet as early as 1935, when he first joined the Vic-

Wells Ballet: he saw it then as a possible vehicle for Markova, but the project was too ambitious for the company's resources at that time, especially musically.[12]

Ashton spent a holiday in Greece in the summer of 1950, where he had a strong feeling that the tradition of the old gods was still alive; he had had a few preliminary rehearsals even before this, but his visit convinced him that he must approach the subject in the light of that experience, and besides he was 'bored with Greek ballets with people running around in tunics and veils and scarves', and so he wanted to do *Daphnis* in modern clothes, 'as though it could still happen to this day.' Karsavina, so far from being shocked by such an approach, supported him fully: to handle it the other way would only invite comparisons with Fokine, and besides 'would not have the life force that it had'.[13] Ashton accordingly commissioned the décor and costumes from John Craxton, a young English painter who lived in Greece and was concerned precisely with the portrayal of ancient mythology in contemporary terms. (The first announcements stated that the designs would be by Oliver Messel, a choice that must have been considered before Ashton's concept was fully developed.)

Fokine's version of Longus, to judge by the scenario he gave Ravel, is a somewhat laundered one; it smacks of the sentimental eroticism of Somov's illustrations,† with which he may have been familiar. For instance, a key incident in the story is the seduction of Daphnis by the young woman from the town, which Longus treats as a necessary part of his education, making possible the consummation of his love for Chloe. In Fokine, however, he spurns her and she leaves, mocking him. Ashton treated the incident in a way that was closer to the original at least in the sense that the seduction does take place – if Lykanion mocks him, it is because of his lack of expertise. It seems that for a while, according to Ashton's notations in his copy of the piano score, he considered introducing the character of Cupid, who was to shoot his arrow at one of the lovers from the top of the grotto of Pan. Fortunately, he had second thoughts and Cupid did not appear in the finished work. One important change was the substitution of a solo for Chloe, leading into a *pas de deux*, for the pantomime of Pan and Syrinx that Fokine had intended to be accompanied by the flute solo in the third scene.

Perhaps the most significant decision was to put the ballet on point. The result is as far from the modish neo-classicism of the early mythological ballets – *Pomona* and the rest – as it is possible to imagine: the transformation of *Daphnis and Chloe* into a classic ballet (in the balletic sense of the term) gives it a timeless quality in addition to the contemporaneity that Ashton sought. Gordon Craig, in his marginal notes in his copy of *Commoedia Illustré* on the Ballet Russe, said of the Diaghilev ballets of the first, 'exotic' period, 'They thought they could imitate so well as to deceive us into believing it was creation. . . They had no belief in themselves and principles. . . They disguised everything and created nothing'.[14] It is impossible to form an opinion now of the justice or injustice of Craig's stric-

† Larissa Salmina-Haskell: *Russian Drawings in the Ashmolean Museum*, Ashmolean Museum, Oxford 1970.

Daphnis and Chloe, finale: Fonteyn as Chloe, centre, with Christopher Gable as Daphnis, left

tures as applied to the original *Daphnis*, but I believe that Ashton's creation of his own version came out of his growing faith in his own powers and in the principles of classic ballet, its viability as a means of expression for his chosen score and story. This gave him the courage to be simple, to work against the lush impressionism of the score, creating a tension that gives the ballet its structural strength. A moving example of this is the quartet of the two lovers and their would-be seducers in the first scene, in a line across the front of the stage like the principals in a Mozart opera, doing a simple combination: *ballottés* to front and back, *coupé ballonné, pas de chat* – and the sequence ends with the 'Fred step'.

Simplicity was the key too to the solution of the problem of the finale. 'In working on *Daphnis and Chloe* I found the music so wonderful and so beautiful and so overwhelming sometimes that I felt that it was like waves that were going

247

to submerge me, and I had great difficulty in keeping my head above it, especially in the last scene, where there's a great surge of music – I found it is difficult to match it up with movement, because it seemed to me that perhaps it was almost better to stand still. And I find that often the better the music is, the stronger it is, and the more emotional, the more you can stand still and do nothing. It's when the music is bad and inferior that you must exert your whole choreographic ability. And I found at the time in watching Wagner's operas that same quality of standing still – when Tristan turns and sees Isolde and for what seems like half an hour they just stare at each other – I wanted to bring that quality into it somehow, because I think it has a wonderful theatrical benefit to one . . .'[15] Constant Lambert's advice was on the same lines – he told Ashton that he didn't have to worry too much about the great climaxes of the score, which could take care of themselves, as it were. So after trying several different versions of the finale – 'piling people up', he found, did not work, 'because if you pile people up they've got to get down again' – he again resorted to simplicity. The dancers advance in lines doing small prances and *renversé* turns; as in the finale of a Petipa ballet the principals have individual entries – unfortunately there is no music for Lykanion to have one, but both Dorkon and Bryaxis return when their musical themes recur. At the moment of the greatest musical climax Ashton's master-stroke is to empty the stage of everyone except Daphnis and Chloe; he turns in the centre and she circles him in *chassé coupé jeté* (the fact that Ashton says he did this 'in desperation' does not make it any less masterly); the chorus all leap on again and as the ballet ends everyone is jumping up and down, fluttering scarves; one last *pirouette* – but the curtain is down by the time they finish it.

Of course there is an admixture of other elements to achieve the idiom: Ashton studied *The Antique Greek Dance* by Maurice Emmanuel and took certain poses and suggestions for steps from it (the book had been in his possession since 1936, when he found it in Cyril Beaumont's shop); there are figures from Greek folk-dance in the opening ensemble of the shepherds and in the last scene they take up 'archaic', frieze-like poses. The dances for the pirates in their lair have often been called the weakest part of the ballet: though Ashton says that he used to wish he were Fokine when choreographing this scene, the similarity to the latter's *Prince Igor* dances is, as Clive Barnes points out, not nearly as marked as some critics have claimed[16] – in fact, given the nature of the music at that point, the dances are at least thoroughly workmanlike, and with the general improvement of the male corps, convincingly ferocious.

The two 'competition' solos in the first scene have similarly come to serve their purpose more and more convincingly as they have been better performed: Dorkon's solo proves that he is a formidable rival to Daphnis, but he loses the contest because the other shepherds find him lacking in grace and, laughing (it's in the score), they literally throw him out. Daphnis's solo, on the other hand, is limpid and unassertive in its virtuosity – *doubles tours en l'air* with the crook held in front of him, *pirouettes* with it across his shoulders, jumps with rapid changes of the feet in parallel position. There are moments in this solo that seem to refer to Nijinsky – the pose with the crook across the shoulders recalls photographs of Fokine's version, and others are reminiscent of the archaic poses of the Faun – there is even what Ashton notes in the score as the '*Sylphides* step'. The dance of the Nymphs of Pan embodies two of the most important influences on Ashton's work – Pavlova and Duncan: at one point they do a step that is straight out of Pavlova's solo *La Nuit*, and at another they run forward on point, 'leaving themselves behind,' to quote Ashton's memorable description of how Isadora used to run. (This dance, incidentally, succeeds remarkably, in combination with the music at that point, in evoking a sense of the numinous; so too in a different way does the brief dance of panic, in the literal sense, at the end of the second scene, when the pirates find their bodies and limbs jerking involuntarily this way and that just before the apparition of Pan. A small but significant criticism to be made of the ballet is that the shepherds at the beginning of the next scene, on the other hand, do not acknowledge his presence in their midst at all.)

Above all, the *danse d'école*, underlying all these stylistic elements, represents an equivalent of the innocence and purity of the love of Daphnis and Chloe, and of the 'early morning of the world' quality of the music. If, as I have suggested, *Illuminations* contained the last vestiges of Ashton's immaturity, *Daphnis* may be considered his first fully mature work, and the first of a series of great ballets about love that he was to make in the next two decades – that recognise the fact that sexuality and innocence are not mutually exclusive. For this reason it is really unimportant that Daphnis himself is a passive character in terms of the story – the ballet is about love, not the rescue of a young maiden from her abductors. Ashton's Daphnis, unlike Fokine's, even if he knows that he should repulse the older woman, is young and hot-blooded enough to succumb to the temptation: the fact of his seduction – even, one might say, the moment of orgasm – is absolutely clear, but it is all done as a dance, the sexual climax is also a choreographic one: as he lifts her and turns she does a series of *battements* forwards and backwards, culminating in a *frisson* through the legs and body as she arches back.

There is moreover no suggestion that his love for Chloe is only 'spiritual' – that it is not as sexual as his attraction to Lykanion. The ballet reaches its highest point of poetry in Chloe's solos and in the exultant *pas de deux* at the beginning of the third scene. Chloe only pretends to flirt with Dorkon, to get Daphnis away from Lykanion, but recoils from his touch when that becomes bolder. Her solo in the pirates' lair, her clothes torn and her wrists tied with a rope, has an inviolate purity and pathos, and yet she is like a wild thing in defence of that purity. When she is returned to Daphnis she at first hangs on his neck and then as the music swells he turns and gradually raises her out into a horizontal position. Following this there is a series of low lifts back and forth – he raises her in *arabesque* to one side and she does a *cabriole*; finally there is a breathtaking moment when she finishes a *pirouette* arched across Daphnis's back leg as he lunges forward. In the solo to the flute music her steps seem again to refer to folk dance, as she slaps her foot before and behind her; when he joins her there are further variants of Ashton's favourite skimming lifts.

Of this ballet, Ashton has said: 'I enjoyed almost more than anything working on *Daphnis and Chloe* because it was all so very, very difficult and I had to dig deeply into myself to do it'.[17] Not surprisingly, therefore, he gave his greatest interpreter one of her most personal roles – indeed, in conversation recently he said that he misses Fonteyn more in *Daphnis* than in any other ballet. In attempting to describe the role of Chloe one is inevitably seeing Fonteyn in one's mind's eye, however beautifully it has been performed by Antoinette Sibley, for instance. Daphnis too was one of Somes's best roles; later Christopher Gable also partnered Fonteyn with a sweetly solicitous regard – though perhaps for sheer beauty of dancing neither of them approached Anthony Dowell, the poetry of whose phrasing makes the tricky 'competition' solo work better than it ever had before.

Daphnis and Chloe:
Fonteyn as Chloe
captured by the pirates

Group from *Daphnis and Chloe*, Scene 3: Antoinette Sibley as Chloe, Anthony Dowell as Daphnis, with corps de ballet

The sensuality of Lykanion made it a perfect role for Violetta Elvin, and later Julia Farron and most recently Deanne Bergsma have made a strong impression in it.

Craxton's scenery, with its grass banks and trees, evoked 'a bare, sun-baked landscape'[18] that matched the spare clarity of Ashton's conception. His clothes were less successful, though considerably modified over the years – the basic idea, of trousers and open-neck shirts for the men and dirndl skirts for the women, is fine, but marred by the decorations on the former and the rather too vivid colours of the latter. Only the immortals wear costumes that do not have the 'contemporary' look – Pan and his entourage of Nymphs, Dryads and Fauns (the last two were later omitted), whose costumes, at Ashton's suggestion, were taken from the same source-book as some of the choreography, Emmanuel's *The Antique Greek Dance*.[19] The worst part of the décor is the hideous drop-curtain with the huge head of Pan.

Ashton feels that the contemporary look of the ballet was what 'masked' its beauties for many people at the time of its first performance, on 5 April 1951.[20] For whatever reason, *Daphnis and Chloe* was received with a coolness bordering on incomprehension by the critics, with a few honourable exceptions (notably P W Manchester, then editor of Ballet Today, and Clive Barnes and Peter Williams of Dance and Dancers). Gradually the ballet gained acceptance, but its first unanimous recognition as a masterpiece came from the New York critics, led by John Martin and Walter Terry, in the American tour of 1953.

Chapter Eleven
1951–1956

The Sadler's Wells Ballet was now firmly established at Covent Garden. Follow-ing the triumphant tours of North America its international status was unquestion-ed. Inevitably, perhaps, a reaction set in, and the cool reception of *Daphnis* was symptomatic of it. There was a general feeling that the company had gone into a period of artistic decline, especially when the dancers returned exhausted by transcontinental touring. Creative juices seemed to be drying up, important roles were frequently undercast, performances in general were often lack-lustre. Critical comments to this effect were none the less justified for being made by those who had been wrong about *Daphnis*, though all the more resented, perhaps, at Covent Garden. Particularly unfortunate, and indeed tragic in its sequel, was the failure of Ashton's next ballet, *Tiresias*, also on a subject from Greek mytholo-gy, though far removed from the idyllic mood of *Daphnis*.

The theme of *Tiresias* was one that had fascinated Constant Lambert for many years, and he had in fact proposed a ballet on the subject to the Camargo Society as long ago as 1930. At that time he visualised it in satiric terms, it being the fashion then to handle such subjects in that way, and indeed this was still the intention when the idea was again taken up twenty years later, to fulfil a commission by the Arts Council as part of the celebrations of the Festival of Britain,[1] as may be seen from Lambert's first draft of the synopsis.† Somehow as Lambert worked on it he handled the subject with increasing seriousness, even portentousness.

The libretto was based on the Greek legend of the seer, Tiresias, who was changed into a woman and back again to a man, transformations triggered by his disgust at witnessing the copulation of a pair of snakes. After these experiences he was called upon to decide an argument between Zeus and Hera over whether men or women derive greater pleasure from the sexual act. Tiresias, having stated that the greater pleasure was on the part of the woman, was struck blind by Hera, but given the gift of prophecy by Zeus in recompense. This story, difficult enough to convey in dance terms, was summarised in a notably evasive programme note that was no help to the audience at all.† No mention was made of Tiresias's

† See Appendix B.

Tiresias, closing scene: Somes as the male Tiresias, centre, flanked by Pauline Clayden and Brian Shaw as the Snakes; Gerd Larsen as Hera, Alfred Rodrigues as Zeus at rear

reason for striking the snakes with his staff; the dispute of the gods was said to be over the relative 'happiness' of the two sexes.

By 1951 Lambert was a sick man, but he worked with great intensity on the score. Even so, the major portions of the orchestration had to be farmed out among other musicians, mostly friends of his. Worse still, Lambert's musical ideas became diffuse, and what was intended to be a thirty-minute ballet lasted twice as long on the opening night. However intractable the theme might be, it is just possible that Ashton might have been able to do something with it if he could have handled it with the light touch that Lambert originally intended, but the score in its final form gave him no chance to do so. He had to call on all the resources of his professionalism, to say nothing of his loyalty, to realise his friend's conception, and made a conscientious effort to find an appropriate choreographic style.

But Ashton was not by temperament fitted to devise the kind of heroic action Lambert visualised for the outer scenes of the ballet. The gymnastic and Pyrrhic dances of the first scene looked disconcertingly like photographs of the epic ballets Serge Lifar did at the Paris Opéra in the 1930s – *Alexandre le Grand* and the rest – with their preposterously grandiloquent attitudes, an effect to a large extent inherent in the material. Ashton found the third scene, the dispute between Zeus and his consort, particularly difficult to translate into movement, and was finally reduced to giving them a series of more or less unintelligible, hieratic gestures: the result was, inevitably, absurd – like an opera without singing. There was, however, a memorable final image as the blinded Tiresias tapped his way into old age.

Only in the second scene did the dramatic situation and its implications draw

253

Tiresias, Scene 2:
Fonteyn as the female
Tiresias, with John
Field as Her Lover

from Ashton choreography of a really personal nature, in Fonteyn's solo with a scarf and a *pas de deux* of wonderfully ambiguous eroticism (which was also the best, because most intimately felt, part of the score). More acrobatic than any Ashton had done since *The Wanderer*, the latter was in other respects on similar lines to his other recent duets, with the familiar 'walking on air' motif, but given a different flavour by the use of attitudes and gestures derived from Cretan sculpture. Less distinguished were the duets for the two copulating snakes, 'who writhe and coil around each other'.[2]

Isabel Lambert, Constant's wife, painted a drop curtain featuring fish-bones that seemed to have nothing to do with the rest of the work. Her first and last act décors were in a rather monumental, operatic style, while the middle act had the look of a Chinese water-colour. More successful were some of her costumes, particularly those for women deriving from Minoan painting, with bared breasts and bell-shaped skirts.

The critical reception for *Tiresias* was almost overwhelmingly negative. It is possible that some of the critics overreacted against it because they felt, rightly or wrongly, that the ballet was symptomatic of a general decline in artistic standards. Six weeks after the première, Constant Lambert died, and the totally unwarranted assertion was made by some of his friends that he had been 'killed' by the adverse reaction to his last work – unwarranted because Lambert was already very ill before the ballet was put on, and finally such considerations are irrelevant to the assessment of a work of art. Even so, Lambert's death was a great blow to the artistic, and not alone the musical, side of the Sadler's Wells Ballet, and a grievous loss to his friends and collaborators of many years. At performances after his death, both Fonteyn and Somes danced their roles as the two aspects of Tiresias with fiercer intensity in tribute to him, though Fonteyn in subsequent revivals relinquished hers to Violetta Elvin. When the ballet was revived early in 1952 considerable revisions were made, and some twenty minutes were cut from the ballet.

Tiresias was not given in New York until 1955, and there, although in general poorly received, it found a champion in John Martin, who praised choreography, music and décor, and called the ballet 'a delicate psychological fantasy with profoundly philosophical overtones'. In particular he called the second scene 'such a ravishing blossoming of experience that Tiresias as a man could never match it for delight'[3] – though one might make the comment that it was only as a woman that Tiresias was seen experiencing love; the only incident relating to the man's experience of it was his disgust at the sight of the copulating snakes.

In 1952, there was no American visit for the main company: instead, Sadler's Wells Theatre Ballet went over for a short New York season and a tour, neither of them very successful, chiefly because it was made insufficiently clear that it was not the 'fabulous' Sadler's Wells Ballet itself, as Sol Hurok had taken to advertising it, but the 'junior' company. For this tour Ashton produced a one-act version of *Casse Noisette*, so that the repertory would include another classical ballet in addition to *Coppélia*. This had its première at the Wells before the tour began, on 11 September 1951.

Ashton's predated by several years the recent universal proliferation of new versions of *The Nutcracker*, and while most of them have been concerned to make sense of the story by making the action part of the pre-adolescent imaginings of the heroine of the original story, or by some other means, Ashton's solution was to dispense with the story altogether, including the whole of the party scene and the nightmare that follows it, and simply present a series of divertissements. Clive Barnes described the choreography as being 'freely based on Ivanov' – certainly, unlike some other choreographers Ashton realised that it is difficult to improve on the original choreography for the *grand pas de deux*, and left it as it was. He also did not change the Chinese dance. According to Barnes, 'It was . . . by far the most satisfying version of the ballet yet produced in England'.[4]

A new *pas de deux* was made for Beriosova in the Snow scene, and Ashton also devised new Spanish, Arabian and Russian dances, a *ballabile* of Snowflakes and a new finale. He made a new male variation for the *pas de deux*, since none existed in the Sergeyev version previously in the Wells repertory: David Blair began this with two double turns in the air in quick succession, an unusual feat for a British male dancer at that time.[5] The result was called in the Dancing Times 'a rich, almost indigestible spectacle relieved only by passages of magnificently austere classical

Casse Noisette, Scene 1, the Kingdom of Snow: Svetlana Beriosova as the Queen, Robert Lunnon as the King

Casse Noisette, Scene 2, the Kingdom of Sweets: final group, with Elaine Fifield as the Sugar Plum Fairy, David Blair as the Nutcracker Prince, centre

dance . . . Beriosova . . . excelled herself . . . in a dance which provided full scope for her magnificent extension, flowing line and purely Russian nobility of style'.[6]

What made the spectacle indigestible was mainly Beaton's designs. The costumes for the flowers, with enormous headdresses, were inspired by the designs of Charles Wilhelm for the old Empire ballets and also perhaps the engravings of Grandville – a good idea, but the resulting confections were difficult to dance in. The costumes worn by Beriosova and Robert Lunnon in the Snow *pas de deux*, on the other hand, were in the rococo manner. The first décor was again in the splotchy black and white style he had used in *Illuminations*, while the second suggested to the critic of The Times 'the nightmare one might expect after a surfeit of green Chartreuse, claret and scallops'.[7]

A few days before the première of *Casse Noisette*, at a matinée on 8 September, Ashton gave his first performance as Dr Coppélius, at Covent Garden. His characterisation was less grotesque, more believable than Helpmann's, for instance, and even managed to be quite touching. Early in 1952 *The Sleeping Beauty*

was revived and refurbished, with Ashton's new variation for Aurora in the Vision scene. Otherwise Ashton's services were again not very much in demand at Covent Garden, because the company was engaged in rehearsals for ballets by Massine, Andrée Howard and John Cranko, and he took the opportunity to accept assignments elsewhere. In January and February, he was in Hollywood arranging some dances in a film for Moira Shearer. *The Story of Three Loves* was a trilogy of short stories, of which *The Jealous Lover* was no doubt another attempt to repeat the success of *The Red Shoes*: a story of a young dancer who auditions for a Diaghilev-style impresario but succumbs to heart-failure before she can achieve fame. The suggestion of a triangle in the title is misleading – the conflict is between her love for dancing and her frail health. Shearer had originally been named for the role of the ballerina in Samuel Goldwyn's *Hans Christian Andersen*, starring Danny Kaye, with choreography by Balanchine. In the event Renée Jeanmaire played that part and her husband, Roland Petit, did the choreography, while Shearer went to MGM to do *Three Loves*, and at her suggestion Ashton was brought over to arrange the dances.

Ashton told John K Newnham of the Dancing Times, 'Don't expect very much ballet. . . Moira doesn't appear in the ballet scenes at all, except as a spectator. Her dances are restricted to three solo variations, one at an audition, one in a studio, and another when she goes on [a deserted] stage in evening dress'.[8] The 'ballet scenes' he mentions were a few glimpses of a ballet called *Astarte* being performed by the impresario's company, with Shearer in the audience. He surprises her dancing alone on the stage afterwards and invites her to his house to dance for him in his private studio. This was the main dance sequence, with Shearer supposedly improvising to the Rachmaninov Paganini Rhapsody while James Mason, as the impresario, says things like, 'Hold it!' and 'Higher, higher!' The film was summed up in a review by Karel Reisz in the Monthly Film Bulletin as 'a simple piece of kitsch'.[9]

From Hollywood Ashton went to New York to mount *Picnic at Tintagel*, his second ballet for the New York City Ballet (it had been announced in the previous October that he would produce two new works for the company, but in fact he did only one). This, incidentally, enabled him to be present at the New York opening of the Sadler's Wells Theatre Ballet. A ballet on the theme of *Tintagel* had actually been announced for production during the New York City Ballet's summer season at Covent Garden in 1950; when later it was announced again the title was variously given as *Iseult at Tintagel* and *Tintagel*. The original intention had been to use Bax's tone poem on the subject but as Ashton worked out his ideas that music proved to be unsuitable, and it was Robert Irving, Constant Lambert's successor as Musical Director of the Sadler's Wells Ballet, who suggested using *The Garden of Fand* by the same composer instead, and together they mapped out

Coppélia: Ashton as Dr Coppélius ▷

the action in an hotel in Blackpool on tour during November of 1951.[10] The theme of the ballet (as given in the programme) was as follows:

> To-day a mist-swept ruin, the Cornish Castle of Tintagel has been considered for centuries as the scene of the love story of Tristram and Iseult, which has inspired writers from the time of Geoffrey of Monmouth to Tennyson, Swinburne, Richard Wagner, Thomas Hardy and Jean Cocteau.
>
> It is imagined that a party of tourists in 1916 (the date of the composition of the score), visits the castle. Overcome by the atmosphere that lurks among the ancient stones, they find themselves involved in an echo of the famous tragedy. When they recover their sense of time and are recaptured by the present, the power of the legend persists.

Apart from the obvious sources of the story, which was one that Ashton had always loved ('I liked the idea of two people falling desperately in love against their own volition, so to speak'), he got the idea for his flashback treatment of it from reading *An Adventure* by the Misses Moberly and Jourdain, an account by the two ladies of a visit to Versailles in 1901 during which they believed themselves to have been transported back to the 18th century.[11] Ashton and Beaton visited Tintagel together 'to get the proper atmosphere'.[12] Beaton devised a kind of transformation scene that could change the set in a few seconds from ruins to mediaeval castle and back again, by means of a kind of vertical panorama. The costumes, too, were devised to allow for an almost instantaneous change, with Edwardian motoring clothes – Inverness capes or dusters, goggles and (for the women) huge hats with veils – that could be flung off to reveal the stylised mediaeval costumes underneath. Actually these costumes for the framing action were of the Edwardian era rather than 1916, at which time Britain was in the middle of the First World War.

The ballet began with a brilliant, diabolical solo by Merlin, in the shape of the caretaker of the castle ruins. The party of tourists arrived and spread out their picnic. As the Wife and her Lover raised their glasses to one another, they found themselves transported back to their previous incarnations as Iseult and Tristram. The Husband, King Mark, departed for the hunt, and there followed the *pas de deux*, 'at once lyrical and sensual', which Lillian Moore described as 'the *raison d'être* of the ballet . . . the mood is that of passionate and earthy, but transfigured, love'.[13] At the climax of this dance, the King returned to confront the lovers, betrayed by Tristram's jealous rivals. Just as Iseult and Tristram were to be put to death, Merlin broke the spell and the characters were restored to their original guise. As they left the scene of these mysterious events in terror, the caretaker picked up the swords that still lay on the stage, 'relics of the dream or omens of what is to come'.[14]

Edwin Denby took a different, less respectful view than his colleagues: '*Picnic at Tintagel* has a fine mystery story opening and very pretty indecent lifts in the *pas de deux*. To me it seemed that Ashton's Isolde behaved like a Potiphar's wife with a willing young Joe. She appeared in the lobby of her Central Park apartment building in her slip, found a big schoolboy there, seduced him instantly, and then again. A couple of bellhops peeked. And King Mark and some flags murdered the poor punk. Whether young Tristan ever noticed what it was he was doing with the lady – that is left in doubt; and that is the private poignancy of the piece'.[15]

As in *Illuminations*, Ashton gave the American dancers roles that exploited talents they were not usually called upon to display – Diana Adams's dramatic ability as well as her cool, patrician beauty (Melissa Hayden was originally announced as Iseult and danced it later); Tristram was the first important part created by Jacques d'Amboise, who was then only seventeen; Merlin, like the Dandy in the earlier ballet, was a virtuoso role for Robert Barnett; Francisco Moncion was a menacing and powerful King Mark.

Perhaps Lincoln Kirstein's claim in an opening night speech, at the New York City Center on 28 February 1952, that *Picnic at Tintagel* represented 'the first fruits of a new Elizabethan Age' was a little premature, but the ballet was at least

Picnic at Tintagel: Left to right, Diana Adams as Iseult, Yvonne Mounsey as Brangaene, Jacques d'Amboise as Tristram

Vision of Marguerite:
Belinda Wright as
Marguerite, Oleg
Briansky as Mephisto,
John Gilpin as Faust

a useful addition to a repertory lacking in dramatic works and certainly more successful than Antony Tudor's *La Gloire*, given at about the same time. It remained in the repertory for a few seasons, but ultimately was lost. For the *pas de deux* if nothing else it would have been worth preserving.

Before leaving for the United States Ashton had fulfilled another outside commission, for the London Festival Ballet, though the piece, *Vision of Marguerite*, did not receive its first performance until after his return, on 3 April 1952 at the Stoll Theatre. It was done at the suggestion of Alicia Markova, who wanted Ashton to revive his earlier ballet *Mephisto Valse* for her. She was present at the first few rehearsals, but then left the company, and the role of Marguerite was given to Belinda Wright. It seems likely, though, that the idea of reconstructing the old ballet was abandoned earlier than that, and instead Ashton made a totally new one, eliminating the corps de ballet and concentrating on the three principals.†
This time the action did not follow Lenau's *Faust* as closely: the ballet began with Faust and Mephisto before a scrim, behind which there appeared a vision of Marguerite at her spinning-wheel, conjured up by Mephisto. He tells Faust that he will take him to her, and the scrim rises to reveal Marguerite with her maid. Mephisto and Faust enter and Faust begins to court Marguerite, but Mephisto intervenes and the dance becomes a *pas de trois* in which the lovers are continually

† By a coincidence, *Mephisto Valse* itself was revived in its original form by Ballet Workshop, in tribute to Sophie Fedorovitch, about a year later.

being separated by Mephisto. Finally he casts a spell on Marguerite, who falls dead, and he leads Faust away.

In form the greater part of the ballet was essentially an extended *pas de deux* with the lovers being manipulated like puppets by the evil force of Mephisto, though within that framework the three dancers each had solos. The Dancing Times spoke in its review of the 'floating lifts', which indicates that the piece was linked to Ashton's other ballets of that time rather than to the earlier *Mephisto Valse*.[16] Richard Buckle said the new version was 'altogether less direct, more delicate, and prettier than the old. With uncanny ease Ashton unfolds within fifteen minutes the tale of Faust's temptation, the seduction and betrayal of the unhappy Marguerite. Not only is the story clear, but is told almost entirely in dancing . . . So smooth a flow is perhaps something of a drawback: the drama of the situation tends to be ironed out, leaving no more than a sad little story. . .

'The part of Marguerite was to have been danced by Markova. . . Belinda Wright was touchingly light and fragile, but she lacks the experience which would bring out the full pathos. John Gilpin danced, as always, exuberantly, though he made a rather extrovert young Faust, only too glad, one may guess, to leave his books on any excuse. Briansky was outstanding in his devilish solo. The part of the maid must surely be one of the least demanding in any repertoire'.[17]

It seems evident that in one respect *Vision of Marguerite* was inferior to *Mephisto Valse*, and that was in the décor. James Bailey's new designs were pretty enough, but conventional, whereas Fedorovitch's for the old ballet expressed with her usual telling simplicity the conflict between the innocent purity of Marguerite and the diabolical evil of Mephisto.

According to Julian Braunsweg, Ashton's fee for this work was £50, but 'I don't think he was ever paid'.[18]

In P W Manchester's *Vic-Wells: A Ballet History*, under the heading 'Frankly Wishful Thinking', the author had expressed the wish that Ashton would in the future choreograph both *Daphnis and Chloe* and *Sylvia*. Whether or not Ashton was consciously heeding this advice, he had considered the Delibes score for his first three-act ballet in 1947, when he had consulted Richard Buckle about it, and Buckle had again presented him with a treatment. He proposed 'transferring the action . . . to the Second Empire. Sylvia, instead of being a nymph of Diana, would become Lady-in-Waiting to the Empress, and her lover Amyntas . . . would now be the Duc de Marseille, who was only snubbed because Sylvia thought from his clothes that he must be a gamekeeper. Orion, the wicked Huntsman, would become an amorous Baron, owner of the country house and park in which the action took place, from whose tipsy advances Sylvia must be saved by the young Duke in Act II.' All this was to be given 'a vague poetical atmosphere' by having the characters throughout in 'classical fancy-dress, preparing as they were a masque for the entertainment of the Empress'. It is not clear why Buckle thought that such

Sylvia, Act I:
Alexander Grant as
Eros, left, Fonteyn as
Sylvia, right, with
Attendant Nymphs,
John Hart as Orion,
above

Sylvia, Act II: Sylvia
(Fonteyn) rescued from
Orion (John Hart,
lying on floor) by Eros
(Grant)

a treatment would 'hold the attention of a modern audience' better than the original libretto, but in any case Ashton at first accepted it and asked Buckle to approach Jean Hugo to design the ballet.[19] Then he had second thoughts and laid the project aside in favour of *Cinderella*. Later he again considered *Sylvia*, as a possibility for the Sadler's Wells Theatre Ballet, treated 'tongue-in-cheek', but again the idea was dropped – as was another project of Ashton's for that company, a new version of *La Sylphide*.

He seems also to have discussed *Sylvia* with Sacheverell Sitwell, from whom there exists a letter to the choreographer, undated, in which he says, 'Since we talked the other day I have been looking at Mr Beaumont's account of *Sylvia*. I have seen it, years ago, once in Paris and once in Nice, but have practically forgotten it, except for the music. . .

'The plot, I imagine, wants to be made as simple as possible, so that all the accent can be on the music and the dancing, and the décor which, I do feel, would be an opportunity for lovely, large simple effects. . . I feel so certain *you* could do something beautiful with the music . . .'

Now, after several months away from his own company, Ashton on his return finally decided that the time had come to do *Sylvia*, which was announced at the end of the season in July for production at the beginning of the next, and was in fact given for the first time on 3 September 1952, at Covent Garden. The libretto followed fairly closely the original by Jules Barbier and Baron de Reinach, for Louis Mérante – though he also conscientiously read the poem by Tasso from which it was drawn.† Sylvia, as the original subtitle of the ballet indicated, is one of Diana's nymphs who, having taken a vow of chastity, rejects the love of Aminta, a shepherd. Eros intervenes and causes her to fall in love with Aminta, but Sylvia is abducted by the evil hunter, Orion. She is rescued by Eros and restored to her lover; Diana forbids their union until she is reminded that she too once loved a mortal, Endymion, at which she relents.

The story is very similar to that of *Daphnis* – both ballets have an ineffectual hero who does nothing to save the heroine from a fate worse than death; instead he passes out and the rescue has to be made by a *deus ex machina*. This similarity was not lost on Ashton, and to add to his difficulties he found a lot of the music very banal at first. Fortunately he made the wise artistic decision not to make fun of either the music or the story, but to introduce a legitimate humorous element by building up the role of Eros. 'In the first act,' he told Walter Terry, 'there is supposed to come on quite seriously a sorcerer to that very silly tune. I couldn't do that seriously – I tried very hard, I cast someone for the sorcerer and we behaved with great solemnity, and it became to me more and more ridiculous: unfortunately I have a sense of humour that *will* come out on occasions. But then I thought, well, in mythology the God of Love is always up to pranks, so I decided to combine those two characters. After I had done that, after I'd thought, I'll make

† See Appendix B.

that slightly comic and keep that spirit of what the music was to me . . . that was one step further.

'After that it became very difficult to know how to dress it, whether to dress it in a modern way . . . or whether I would get somebody who would recreate for me the Second Empire. And I decided that was the best way to do it'.[20] Since he had never seen a production of *Sylvia*, Ashton considered going over to Paris to see Albert Aveline's version at the Opéra, but finally decided it was better not to be influenced by someone else's approach.

The score still presented difficulties: 'I find that in the last act there isn't enough drama – you get the drama right at the end but in the middle there's a lot of music that's rather thin, it's charming but it doesn't really give you a great climax until the moment when Diana appears at the end and pardons her, and is shown that she's not so good as she pretended to be either'.[21] Working with Robert Irving, Ashton made certain changes in the order of the musical numbers and they interpolated four numbers from *La Source* into the third act (one was a combination of two others).[22]

In spite of Ashton's misgivings, Sitwell's conviction that he would do 'something beautiful' with it was justified. As early as *Les Rendezvous* Ashton had shown a remarkable feeling for ballet music of the 19th century, and in *Sylvia* he let this intuitive understanding guide him in his choice of the appropriate style of movement: 'Hearing this 19th-century music, it's impossible for me when I'm doing choreography to depart from the spirit of the music. Probably I'm guided subconsciously in this – I don't know that I deliberately set out to do so. I try to be inventive, but I think I have a very adjusted sense of what the music is trying to say to me'.[23] (Ashton had a dream at the time in which Delibes came to him, kissed him and said, 'Vous avez sauvé mon ballet.')

Sylvia, even more than *Cinderella*, was full of dancing, and not least for the ballerina. The role was perfectly tailored to display the increasing assurance and virtuosity that Margot Fonteyn had acquired since her recognition abroad; in each act she was called upon to perform in a different style – the cool Amazon of the first act, in the second act first spurning Orion's advances and then feigning seductiveness, finally in the third act appearing as the fully classic ballerina in her *pizzicati* variation and in the *pas de deux* with Michael Somes.

This *pas de deux* was perhaps the greatest Ashton had yet composed, beginning with a beautiful lift in which Sylvia was carried on supported upright, half-kneeling on her partner's shoulder. P W Manchester wrote that Ashton 'never forgets that a *pas de deux* is also a love scene, [and] he has this time invented a miraculous moment when Aminta places his hands on either side of Sylvia's head and gently draws it back against his cheek'.[24]

Although Ashton felt that the third act was unsatisfactory, he managed to create a brilliant set of divertissements for it, with a fine variation for Somes, who had spent part of the summer studying with Volinine in Paris and was able to do it justice.[25] Less happy was the *pas de deux* of the sacrificial goats – this was a

Sylvia, Act III:
Fonteyn and Somes in
the *pas de deux*

period in which nearly every ballet seemed to have its pair of animals, usually danced by Pauline Clayden and Brian Shaw, and inevitably reminiscent of the embarrassing poodles from *La Boutique fantasque*. Alexander Grant contributed a marvellously mischievous Eros, especially funny in his entrance as the sorcerer – to say nothing of his feat of standing motionless through the first half-hour or so, as a statue.

The décor, by Robin and Christopher Ironside, though not exactly consisting of 'large simple effects', was exquisite in detail and opulent in overall design, with a wonderful transformation at the end of the second act – as lavish and loving a re-creation of the period as Ashton's own, made possible in each case by a total act of identification with the sensibility of another time.

In spite of all this, *Sylvia* was another ballet that got some lukewarm reviews at first – again it was left to the American critics the following year to recognise its quality. Even so, the feeling continued that the ballet did not work, and various changes were made. At first these were minor and for the better – for instance, the vision of Diana and Endymion was at first a painted one, but Ashton later replaced this with a *tableau vivant* that was far more satisfactory. Another addition at the same time was to show Aminta asleep at the feet of Eros after the transformation scene at the end of Act II. More important, after the first season of the Bolshoi Ballet in London in 1956, Ashton made certain changes that showed the influence of that company – for instance, an almost acrobatic dive by Sylvia into Aminta's arms. But, later, wholesale cuts were made, first in the third act divertissements, then finally the whole ballet was cut down to one act, consisting of most of the original first act, with a new goats' dance at the beginning instead of the Dryads and Sylvans, omitting all reference to Orion, and ending with the *pas de deux* and a general *galop*. This was a mistake – like all the great 19th-century classics (and *Sylvia* must be included among these by virtue of its score), *Sylvia* needs the amplitude that the three-act form affords. Its many devotees would be happy to see this ballet returned to the repertory in its entirety.

Just before Christmas 1952 the Sadler's Wells Ballet presented a new production of *Swan Lake* – the second they had given at Covent Garden, with revisions to the standard choreography by Ninette de Valois and two important additions by Ashton. The first was a *pas de six* to the Waltz from Act I – previously used only as a prelude to the third act in Wells productions, if at all – and the second a Neapolitan Dance in Act III, a tarantella danced by Julia Farron and Alexander Grant. This dance, with its swift footwork and its brilliant finale in which the dancers spin around the stage, now face to face, now back to back, was a showstopper and

Scene from *Orpheus*, Act I: Kathleen Ferrier as Orpheus, centre

has been retained in the various subsequent revisions of *Swan Lake* presented by the company.

More than a quarter of a century had passed since Ashton's first ballet and first collaboration with Sophie Fedorovitch, who remained one of his closest friends: now they entered into another project together that was to be their last – a production of Gluck's *Orpheus* in which, as in *The Fairy Queen*, the opera and ballet companies joined forces. Early in their friendship Fedorovitch had formed the habit of telephoning Ashton in the morning to wake him up in time for class or rehearsal, and she continued to do this during the rehearsals of *Orpheus*. He, for his part, used to call her nearly every night when he got home, no matter how late. Someone had once said of her that 'her friendship given immediately had an element of challenge in it', and this element had always been very important in Ashton's relationship with her – the 'gentle bullying' he spoke of in a tribute to her, by means of which Fedorovitch used to force him to think his ideas through and eliminate whatever was superfluous.[26] For some time Fedorovitch had been on the Board of Advisors at Covent Garden, a position that recognised and extended her influence on British ballet.

The production of *Orpheus* was to open on a Tuesday, 3 February 1953. Rehearsals had been strenuous, and on the previous Friday evening the company was dismissed until the dress rehearsal on Monday morning. Ashton was nearly late for that rehearsal because he had not received his usual call from Fedorovitch; when she failed to appear, he sent her assistant, Alan Tagg, to see what was the matter. He found her dead in her studio – there was a gas-leak there, and she had been dead for two days.[27] She left the bulk of her estate to Ashton, enabling him to buy his country house at Eye, in Suffolk.

Fedorovitch's death was not the only tragedy connected with the production of *Orpheus*. Kathleen Ferrier, who sang the title role, was, as Ashton knew, suffering from cancer; she died soon after the première.

Ashton was responsible not only for the dances but the general *mise-en-scène* of *Orpheus*; he was able, Richard Buckle wrote, 'to unite singers and dancers in a single pattern. Turning his back on the 18th century he has staged the opera in an austere and "abstract" style . . . Ashton's opening tableau, with the chorus grouped on two staircases and with a few dancers tending Eurydice's tomb in the foreground, sets a noble Isadora Duncan-ish tone which is maintained throughout'.[28] These stairs were the most important feature of Fedorovitch's décor – they led up to a platform, enclosing the space in which the action took place, and were set against a cyclorama on to which clouds or flames were projected. On the stairs stood large symbols that were changed to suggest the location of each of the acts – 'the Gates of Hell, the Heavenly Harps, the void through which Orpheus brings Eurydice back to earth'.[29]

The opera, conducted by Sir John Barbirolli, was given in a version that combined parts of both the original (1762) and the revised (Paris, 1774) versions. The grotesque dance of the Furies was led by Alexander Grant, while the Dance of the Blessed Spirits was done by Svetlana Beriosova who, Buckle said, 'runs most touchingly up and down stairs, in and out, with a dove on her hand'.[30] Ashton abbreviated the celebrations added to provide a rather incongruous ending for the Paris production, but even so the final act was rather tame.

The 2nd of June, 1953, was the night of the Coronation of Queen Elizabeth II, and to celebrate the occasion Ashton made a new ballet, *Homage to the Queen*, that was also intended to show off the whole company at its best. This raised the question of protocol: as Ashton said, 'If you want to keep a company happy, you can't always look after the talented dancers, the ones with gifts – you have to look after people who've been loyal, who've been useful, who happen to be good partners, good mimes – they all have to be considered, they must also be treated decently, and if you do that I think you can hold a company. It's when you start abusing them and only looking after the talented ones that a company falls to pieces. In this instance I was guided entirely by protocol – naturally I favoured the ones I thought were more gifted, I gave them a little bit more to do.

'Also we had a limited time, we had only forty minutes in which to do the whole thing . . . I made a very detailed plot: first of all we had four ballerinas, and I racked my brain and thought, what can I do with four ballerinas? There are four seasons, four this, four the other, and so I finally hit on the elements – I've used the seasons many many times! – and I cast each ballerina suitably as I thought.

'Now within that framework, I devised the idea of making four separate little ballets, in which I would use so many different members of the company in each one, and thereby give them all a chance to show themselves, and supposedly pay their own homages, large and small'.[31]

It was decided that the ballet should be done with a commissioned score, and Ashton followed his usual practice of making a detailed minutage for the composer's guidance. Before he decided on the format of the four elements, Ashton had thought of naming the divisions of the ballet after the four queens, Elizabeth I, Anne, Victoria and Elizabeth II, and the first plan he drew up for Malcolm Arnold followed this scheme.†

Malcolm Arnold produced a score according to Ashton's specifications, though the order of the numbers was changed somewhat after he decided to use the idea of the four elements as the framework. Ashton, having 'divided all the company and put them into what I thought would be the best things . . . set to work . . . I had to do a parade at the beginning to show off the whole company, the size and the strength, and for everybody to come and bow to Her Majesty'. The ending was a problem, which Ashton solved by having an apotheosis 'in which the old

† See Appendix C.

Queen Elizabeth hands her sceptre and orb, which unfortunately you can never see, but still, that's what she's supposed to be doing, the old Queen hands the young Queen the sceptre and orb – the lighting always goes wrong at that moment'.[32]

Each of the entrées was arranged to demonstrate the particular qualities of its dancers. The Queen of Earth (Nadia Nerina, partnered by Alexis Rassine) was, appropriately, given *terre à terre* steps – *batterie*, *sauts sur les pointes*, and poses on point with the supporting knee bent. Water (Violetta Elvin with John Hart) 'exploits Elvin's beautifully sinuous arms and body to the full and conveys the falling of cool running water by . . . soft *bourrées*, *pirouettes*, *temps levés*, and lovely *port de bras*. At a change in the music he gives the effect of pattering rain in brilliant solos for Julia Farron and Rowena Jackson, and a tempestuous passage of aerial leaps for Brian Shaw'. Fire (Beryl Grey with John Field) 'is designed to give the impression of dangerous beauty by the use of swiftly changing *épaulements* [and] brief *élancé* movements'. In this section Alexander Grant, as the Spirit of Fire, had a characteristically brilliant solo with leaps and sudden falls. Finally, the Air section contained yet another superb *pas de deux* for Fonteyn and Somes, full of lifts that transmuted acrobatics into poetry.[33]

Homage to the Queen: Fonteyn as the Queen of the Air, lifted by her Consort, Somes, with Attendants

Final group from *Homage to the Queen*: Fonteyn as Queen of the Air, centre, with Violetta Elvin as Queen of the Waters, Beryl Grey as Queen of Fire, Nadia Nerina as Queen of the Earth, and company

After all of this, the apotheosis was something of an anti-climax, however necessary in such a *pièce d'occasion*. Both Ashton and his designer, Oliver Messel, were aware of this problem – Messel wrote to Ashton after the first night that 'the profile effect turned out in the end a little Miss Liberty . . . if she remained like a Spanish Madonna suppliant to the Queen of the Past [it] might be more simple and effective, keeping full back view until the end picture of her facing the audience and blessing the dancers'. It must be added that Messel's designs in general did the ballet a disservice – it was suggested on at least one occasion by Peter Williams, in Dance and Dancers, that if it were redesigned *Homage to the Queen* would have been very useful as a *défilé* for the presentation of the company on galas and other special occasions, but this was never done and in due course the ballet was dropped from the repertory.

In September the Sadler's Wells Ballet went to the United States for the third time, opening in New York on the 15th. The repertory included *Sylvia, Daphnis and Chloe, Don Juan* and *Homage to the Queen*, none of which had been given in New York before, and the season was a personal triumph for Ashton. The quality of the first two works in particular was recognised as it had not been by most of the London critics, and an all-Ashton night was sold out completely. Ashton himself felt that he was being taken more seriously as a creative artist than ever before, a recognition that was all the more important to him after the loss of such valued friends and mentors as Lambert and Fedorovitch. All the same, the next year was not a particularly productive one for him, partly because after a coast-to-coast tour of the States lasting more than four months de Valois was determined that the company should not be overworked on their return. During the year Ashton again played Dr Coppélius, in a new production by de Valois of *Coppélia*, and added a new role to his repertory – Kostchei in Fokine's *The Firebird*, revived for Sadler's Wells Ballet by Grigoriev and Tchernicheva as part of the Homage to Diaghilev in the 1954 Edinburgh Festival (23 August 1954) – the year of Richard Buckle's memorable Diaghilev Exhibition. Ashton's Kostchei was a remarkable impersonation with two unforgettable moments: the gesture of pointing at and beckoning to Prince Ivan, with an amazingly crooked finger, and his falling asleep during the Firebird's Berceuse, his head shaking slightly and his eyes never quite closed, as though he were afraid to close them completely in case he never woke up again. These were examples of the particularity of detail that is in all great acting – incredibly subtle and yet so accurately observed that they were legible even in a large theatre. (The first performances were conducted by Ernest Ansermet, one of Diaghilev's conductors, who told Ashton that, watching him go to sleep, he momentarily lost his place in the score.)

During the summer Ashton had gone with a small group of dancers led by

Fokine's *The Firebird*: Ashton as Kostchei, with his followers

Fonteyn and Somes to the Granada Festival in Spain, where Fonteyn danced a new solo, *The Entry of Madame Butterfly*. Thirty years before, Vera Trefilova, one of the great ballerinas of the Maryinsky Theatre, had danced a solo in the 1924 'Sunshine' matinée, called *Spring Flower of Japan*, to music by Puccini (presumably from *Madame Butterfly*), wearing a costume designed by Constantin Korovin, a tutu whose bodice was cut like a kimono; she carried a fan in one hand and a parasol in the other. Ashton had seen this number and 'adored it'; both the dance he arranged for Fonteyn and her costume by Dior were inspired by Ashton's memories of Trefilova's, though the music he used was from *The Mikado*. 'A tame and self-consciously coy affair,' Peter Williams called it when it was revived at Covent Garden a couple of years later (under the title *Entrée japonaise*), 'and the Sullivan music made it all the more "titipu". The manipulation of fans ill becomes a great ballerina. . . Dior's costume in pink and lime green was ugly'.[34]

It might be thought that when Ashton did get to work again on something more considerable he would have done so with renewed self-confidence after his recent success in America, yet although he made three new ballets in quick succession during the following season, none of them quite succeeded, for a variety of reasons. The first two were given on 6 January 1955: *Rinaldo and Armida* and *Variations on a Theme of Purcell*. These ballets were rehearsed during a provincial tour in November and December, and were specifically designed to display the talents of younger members of the company. They were dedicated to the memory of Sophie Fedorovitch – ironically, since they demonstrated Ashton's need for a little of the 'gentle bullying' she used to give him. He still felt, too, the lack of advice in musical and artistic matters that he used to get from Constant Lambert.

Rinaldo and Armida, based on an episode from Tasso's *Ierusalemme Liberata*, was, like *Homage to the Queen*, done to a commissioned score of no great distinction by Malcolm Arnold. The role of the enchantress, Armida, who lures the warrior Rinaldo to her domain but surrenders to his love, thus ensuring her own death, was perfectly suited to Svetlana Beriosova's mysterious personality, and needless to say Ashton tailored the choreography to show off her statuesque beauty, but the idea of the 'kiss of death' seemed to be a throwback to Ashton's old preoccupation with 'decadent' subject-matter, though no longer handled with much conviction. The action was reduced to what was essentially a series of three linked *pas de deux* – as Clive Barnes wrote, 'It is like a duel in which each contestant has a second', Gandolfo for Rinaldo, and Sibilla for Armida. 'The three *pas de deux* are split up by the intervention of the "seconds", and each represents a phase in the story's development. At first Armida is the ice-cold seductress of legend, later she is faltering, finally yielding . . . The mounting passions . . . are particularly well conveyed by three lifts spaced out through the work. The preparation for each lift is the same, Rinaldo turns to Armida and holds up his arms. Armida approaches from the front left of the stage. In the first lift she jumps at him and sinks to the

Rinaldo and Armida:
Svetlana Beriosova as
Armida, Somes as
Rinaldo

ground, in the second she clings to his neck, in the third, at the climax of their love, she rises high on his shoulder'.[35]

Such passages notwithstanding, the treatment was somehow fatally chic – reflected in Peter Rice's designs in black, white and grey, the one colour-note being the red rose carried by Armida. The décor was of bare trees against a snowy landscape, with black leaves continually falling; at the beginning the stage was filled with mist, and at the end a black wall rose at the back of the stage through which Rinaldo burst his way. (This ending was later changed so that he did not escape.) The costumes of the two men, Michael Somes and Ronald Hynd, suggested evening dress uniform of a much later period than that of Tasso's warriors.

One's imperfect memories of this ballet inevitably prompt the uneasy feeling that perhaps it was one of those Ashton ballets that would have grown in stature with time and greater familiarity – except that one essential ingredient was certainly lacking, a score that might have inspired Ashton to a poetic handling of the subject which would avoid falling into cliché. It is only fair to mention that *Rinaldo and Armida* had a faithful champion from the beginning in Clive Barnes, who called it 'a tiny understated masterpiece . . . this simple *pas de deux* of the destructive power of love is exquisitely carried out . . . the ballet wastes nothing, and rises above the level set by its rather conventionally ordinary décor and music, to say something worth saying about people'.[36]

If the score for *Rinaldo and Armida* sounded like film-music, that for the second new ballet that evening, *Variations on a Theme of Purcell*, actually was written by Benjamin Britten for a film, *Instruments of the Orchestra*, though it has had a separate existence as a concert-piece, usually played, as in the ballet, without the explanatory narration used in the film. The programme carried a quotation from Ovid as an epigraph: 'If you have a voice, sing; if soft arms dance – and with whatever gifts you have for pleasing – please!' Ashton originally planned to make a comedy ballet, 'with fire-engines' according to Alexander Grant, whose role, a combination of jester and master of ceremonies, had its funny moments (a parody of Dolin's *Bolero*, a bit of the old soft shoe), but on the whole *Variations* ended up as a pure classic ballet with three female soloists (Elaine Fifield, Nadia Nerina and Rowena Jackson), Grant, a group of six men and a corps de ballet of twelve women. To some extent the dancers were identified with the various musical instruments pinpointed in the different variations – Grant, for instance, had a solo to the percussion section – and there was an attempt to make a distinction between the formal 17th-century style of the opening and closing statements of Purcell's theme (from the incidental music to *Abdelazar*) and the contemporary style of the intervening variations. To underline this, Peter Snow's décor (a semi-circular garden wall that restricted the performing space) featured a pedestal on which stood a bust of Purcell which was turned round at a certain point to show a bust of Britten on the reverse, but this device was omitted after the dress-rehearsal. His costumes, basically conventional ballet tutus and tights, were given 'period' additions for the two processional sections (trains for the women, feathered hats for the men).

Again, one problem was that the music failed to spur Ashton's inventive powers. Another factor that prevented the success of the ballet was that it received an indifferent first performance. But even later when the work was danced more adequately it failed to make a strong impression. The two new ballets served their purpose of 'bringing on' the dancers who at that time were considered most promising, but nearly all of them were better served by the choreographer in future ballets.

Fifield's turn came very soon, again in a ballet that was not destined for a very long life, though more deserving of it – *Madame Chrysanthème*. Ashton had read the novel by Pierre Loti, and what appealed to him about it was the fact that the eponymous heroine was not sentimentalised, as in *Madame Butterfly*, which is presumably partly derived from the same source. In collaboration with Vera Bowen he devised a scenario, in its first form rather complex, but gradually he eliminated incidents and characters that were not essential to the main theme – the French sailor who, stationed in Nagasaki, finds a 'temporary' Japanese wife, and the nature of their relationship. So far from being a tragic, abandoned heroine,

Variations on a Theme by Purcell: Alexander Grant with Rowena Jackson, Elaine Fifield, Nadia Nerina

Madame Chrysanthème: Chrysanthème (Elaine Fifield) presented to Pierre (Alexander Grant) and Yves (Desmond Doyle) by M Kangarou (Ray Powell)

'she is always absolutely charming, but he never feels that he can get through to her, never knows what she is thinking, but at the same time she always does her part impeccably towards him'.[37] Underlying this was the more general theme of the inability of East and West really to understand each other.

Ashton cut out the character of Chrysanthème's Japanese lover, and a nightmare scene in which Pierre dreams that he is tormented first by insects and then by apparitions of Chrysanthème and his rivals for her love, among other incidents. At one point he wanted the different scenes to correspond to the four seasons, but wisely decided to concentrate the action into the course of a single summer. The final scenario made its points very clearly, especially the end in which Pierre, before sailing, returns for an amorous farewell, only to find Chrysanthème testing the coins with which he has bought her, tapping them with a little hammer and dropping them into a bowl to test their genuineness.†

Again Ashton commissioned a score, this time from Alan Rawsthorne, who worked very slowly and indeed delivered the orchestration only at the last minute.[38] The score began and ended with 'an unaccompanied woman's voice

† See Appendix B.

wailing a wordless poem'.[39] Rawsthorne was married to Isabel Lambert, Constant's widow, who designed exquisite décor, using screens and windowshades against a Japanese landscape in pale colours. The scene-changes were made, Kabuki-style, in view of the audience by black-clad figures. There were references too to the Japanese print-makers, for instance in the opening scene with people wearing straw capes as protection from the rain. The balletic stylisation of Japanese costume (kimonos that were whisked away to reveal very brief tutus) matched the choreographic style, with toe-steps suggesting, as John Martin wrote, not only the dainty walk of the Japanese women but also 'an air of wilful subterfuge'.[40] In contrast was a Samurai-like dance for the Japanese men and Alexander Grant's hornpipe, which expressed a more European virility. To some extent, the Japanese solo Ashton had made for Fonteyn the year before was a preliminary sketch for this ballet, for instance in the use of the two small fans. A Japanese dance company had appeared in London during the previous year, and Ashton's memories of their repertory also contributed to the style of *Madame Chrysanthème*, transmuted by his unfailingly classical approach. The *pas de deux* subtly expressed the submissiveness of the Oriental woman to the male, as well as their passionate love-making, and as so often with Ashton, ended on a quiet note: Chrysanthème knelt at the side of the sailor, and, 'all fears overcome . . . pattered gently towards him on her hands'.[41]

The ballet was presented on 1 April 1955, during a newspaper strike, but was favourably reviewed in some of the weekly magazines: C B Mortlock in Punch said 'never before can the charm, the delicacy, and the exotic mystery of legendary Japan have been so subtly proposed for acceptance in the theatre as in the choreography of Mr Ashton and the dresses and settings of Isabel Lambert . . . I should be surprised to hear that there is a genuine note detectable anywhere in this exquisite work. None the less, or perhaps for that reason, I felt that a magic casement had been opened on the inscrutable and romantic East and that its hitherto elusive spirit had kindled answering emotion'.[42]

Madame Chrysanthème gave its ballerina, Elaine Fifield (and later Maryon Lane), a role perfectly suited to her both dramatically and technically. In America that autumn John Martin, on a second viewing, called it 'a major Ashton creation'. Yet it somehow never caught on, and was not to remain very long in the repertory. Ashton believes that this may have again been because of a lack of real distinction in the score, but even more because the rather sardonic conclusion of the ballet did not appeal to the public, which would have preferred something less cynical.

As soon as *Madame Chrysanthème* had had its première, Ashton left for Copenhagen, where he was to choreograph a version of Prokofiev's *Romeo and Juliet* for the Royal Danish Ballet. He had earlier suggested to Ninette de Valois that he might do this for the Sadler's Wells Ballet, but she felt that one full-length ballet by that composer was enough. This was not only before the proliferation of

Romeo and Juliet:
Mona Vangsaa and
Henning Kronstam

versions of *Romeo and Juliet*, but before the first visit of the Bolshoi Ballet to the West, and Ashton's was therefore done without the benefit (or otherwise) of exposure to the powerful *verismo* Soviet version. His natural instinct was both to follow Shakespeare's play as closely as possible and at the same time towards formalisation, to make it, in fact, a classic ballet in which the most important elements were the *pas de deux* and other pure dance passages, with the mime scenes forming an essential contrast. It was not surprising, therefore, that Ashton should once again have looked to Petipa for guidance in choreographing the ballroom scene, with its formal ensembles, a *pas de trois* for Romeo and his companions (in Ashton's version this took place at the moment of their uninvited incursion into the Capulets' ball), the dance for Paris and his eight kinsmen, and particularly the dance for the six friends of Juliet, who fulfilled here and elsewhere a function similar to that of such groups in classic ballets like *Coppélia* and *The Sleeping Beauty*: particularly lovely was their dance, ironic in its lyricism, with three troubadours who came to awaken Juliet for her marriage, only to find her apparently dead. Even so, the choreography was flavoured almost as much by Bournonville as by Petipa, since as always Ashton was very much influenced by the dancers he was working with, products of the Danish school.

Other choreographers, following Lavrovsky's example, have set the story against the background of the feud between the two families and the street life of Verona, and in some productions this background even tends to overshadow the figures of the lovers. For Ashton, the focus of the story was the intimate tragedy of the two young people caught up in an all-consuming passion, and he did a certain amount of cutting to eliminate extraneous material, but the score is so closely matched to the Soviet libretto that only a limited amount of modification is possible. As John Martin wrote, Ashton recognised both the intractablenesss and the inherent grandeur of the music and 'by his very humility . . . conquered the problem'.[43]

The Royal Danish Ballet is famous for its great mimes, many of them former dancers who graduate to character roles in middle age, and Ashton made full use of their gifts: roles like the Nurse, Friar Laurence and Lord and Lady Capulet were played by such artists. At the other extreme, he used a ten-year-old boy, Bjørn Madsen (son of a famous dancer), as the Nurse's impudent page, who imitates her behind her back. The ballet began with brief danced and mimed 'soliloquies' for some of the principals, to establish their characters – for instance Niels Bjørn Larsen, as Tybalt, did movements that were 'svelte and smooth, like a cat'.[44]

Ashton's fight scenes were carefully choreographed dances rather than realistic brawls, and differentiated according to their place in the narrative – the slight skirmishes of the feuding servants with hand-to-hand wrestling by individuals (which Ashton felt was more authentic than the more usual sword-fights), then later the two big duels between Mercutio and Tybalt, and Tybalt and Romeo, which were set against a counterpoint of movement by the crowd. 'The first,' wrote one critic, 'is rather slow in a heavy, violent way, but the other is very fast; Romeo and Tybalt fight furiously up and down the steps on either side of the stage and across the terrace, until Tybalt is killed at the top of the steps and rolls down them with terrific effect'.[45] The choreographic device Ashton used in Mercutio's death scene derived from the mad-scene in *Giselle*, quoting fragments of the character's earlier choreography.[46]

It is a familiar paradox that it takes a mature actress to portray Juliet's growth from carefree innocence to tragic transfiguration, and Ashton cast Mona Vangsaa, an established ballerina, in the role. On the other hand, for Romeo he chose Henning Kronstam, who had only recently been promoted to soloist rank. Their *pas de deux* were again typical of Ashton's work at that period: in the balcony scene most of Juliet's movement was based on the *arabesque* – for instance, she did fast supported *soutenu* turns into *arabesque penchée*; together, the lovers did a diagonal of *arabesque posée, grand jeté en tournant* landing in a kneeling position, then sitting back on the heel with the head bent over to the front knee. Typically, too, they were shown as being very much in love physically: before they started to dance they kissed each other hungrily on face and neck, and the dance was an enlargement, an intensification, of their passion. The most beautiful, and most Ashtonian, passage is a sequence of lifts in which she barely skims the surface of the floor in little hops in *arabesque*, alternating with repeated hops in *passé derrière* and little runs – all in a circle around the stage, a kind of ecstatic shimmer of movement.†

At first Ashton's handling of the final scene in which Romeo dances with what he believes to be Juliet's corpse came in for some criticism on grounds of taste: he later toned it down, but this was after all a familiar balletic device, used, for example, by Balanchine in the *pas de deux* in *Jones Beach* in which a girl was rescued from drowning (and many years earlier in the *Slaughter on Tenth Avenue* ballet in *On Your Toes*). At this point, Ashton omitted any reconciliation of the two houses – with the lovers' deaths the ballet was over for him.

As befitted his concept, the décor by Peter Rice was much less elaborate than most other versions, using a basic set of a wide platform across the back of the stage, with steps descending to floor level, the rest being suggested by curtains. Undeniably, the décor seemed unnecessarily sketchy at times, and Peter Williams's criticism that the décor and more particularly the costumes could have made a more effective contribution in terms of colour was well taken.[47]

The première of *Romeo and Juliet* on 19 May 1955 was a great success – there were nine curtain-calls, virtually unprecedented in a theatre that traditionally had none at all – and the ballet stayed in the Danish repertory for ten years; subsequent attempts to revive it have been unsuccessful, partly because of the unavailability of the choreographer. Its loss is regrettable but apparently irretrievable since the

†Comments based on London Festival Ballet's revival of this *pas de deux*, 1973.

Danish company has now acquired another version. The Balcony *pas de deux*, recently revived by London Festival Ballet, is less effective out of context.

In the autumn of 1955 the Sadler's Wells Ballet began its fourth tour of the United States, during which, as we have seen, both *Tiresias* and *Madame Chrysanthème* were given for the first time in New York with more favourable critical response than in London, though neither became a great audience favourite. In December the company took part in a colour-telecast of the full-length *Sleeping Beauty*, edited by Ashton, who himself appeared in his familiar role of Carabosse.

Soon after their return to London, on 23 January 1956, there was a midnight matinée at the Stoll Theatre to commemorate the twenty-fifth anniversary of the death of Anna Pavlova. The programme ended with the Water and Air sections from *Homage to the Queen*. Ashton was in charge of the general arrangements for this performance, including the traditionally delicate task of dealing with the various ballerinas involved. Several of them dropped hints to the effect that they might be persuaded to perform Pavlova's famous solo *The Dying Swan*, but Ashton is said to have settled the question by announcing, 'If anyone dances *The Dying Swan* at this performance, it will be me'.[48]

Ashton had always liked Dukas's score for *La Péri*, which he had choreographed for Markova at the Ballet Club in 1931; indeed in 1950 it was announced that he would make a new version for her and Dolin to dance in a series of performances they were to give at the Royal Albert Hall in June of that year, with costumes by Oliver Messel. These were cancelled when Markova had to undergo an operation, but Ashton now took up the piece again when he was asked to choreograph a new *pas de deux* for Fonteyn and Somes that they could perform both with the Sadler's Wells Ballet and in their frequent guest appearances elsewhere.

The new *La Péri*, then, was essentially a display piece for Fonteyn (though Svetlana Beriosova also danced it), and became even more so when the publishers of the score suddenly decided to exercise their right to insist that Ashton adhere to the composer's wishes and restrict Somes's role to pantomime and partnering. This meant that Ashton had to cut out all the dancing he had arranged for him, with some resentment because other versions of the ballet were not subjected to the same capricious restrictions. It was only because Ashton was able to produce a photograph of Bakst's costume design for Trouhanova and say, 'You don't think Fonteyn will dance in *that*, do you?' that he was able to evade a similar demand that he use the Bakst designs.

The movement for the Péri was basically classic with a slight Eastern flavour, provided by such things as the lateral shifting of the head found in Oriental dancing (in which Fonteyn was said to have had lessons with Ram Gopal) and also, Clive Barnes interestingly suggested, elements of Uzbek dancing as well.[49] Fonteyn's interpretation seemed to be an extension of her remarkable performance as the Firebird. The most striking moment was her *arabesque* held and slowly stretched into deep *penchée* as Somes sank to the ground – although he was supporting her by one hand the effect was rather that she was gradually forcing him down as she pleaded with him to return to her the flower of immortality.

Clive Barnes, as preface to a not particularly enthusiastic review, wisely commented that first impressions of Ashton's ballets were apt to be even more misleading than in the case of other choreographers: '[His] choreography is usually so simple and apparently familiar that its originality is only obvious after the first disappointment of being neither startled nor bewildered has worn off'.[50] It might be added that in this respect Barnes had a better record than some of his colleagues, some of whom would have done well to take his words to heart. But he was right in saying that *La Péri* was in fact far from being Ashton's best: as he justly pointed out, it is easier to distinguish between Iskender's wish for immortality and his desire for the Péri herself in a programme note than in dance terms.

The ballet began with the stage in darkness, with Somes picked out in a spotlight and a few waning stars overhead. As the lights came up, they revealed a décor that was an enlarged painting by Ivon Hitchens, whose connection with the subject of the ballet was obscure. Nor did it have much in common with Levasseur's striking but chic costumes. Later, Levasseur himself provided a new set, an 'arrangement of ramps, ropes, and steps',[51] that was neither more appropriate nor more beautiful.

Another, happier twenty-fifth anniversary was to be celebrated on 5 May 1956. On that date in 1931 the first full evening of ballet had been given by the then Vic-Wells company at the Old Vic; now the company was about to receive the royal charter that would designate it the Royal Ballet, conferring on it officially the status it had in all but name of the National Ballet of Great Britain. For the anniversary performance, as a tribute to Ninette de Valois, Ashton made a new *pièce d'occasion*, *Birthday Offering*, a divertissement in the style of Marius Petipa, or rather in Ashton's personal extension of that style. Robert Irving chose pieces by Alexander Glazunov, mostly from his ballet *The Seasons* – nothing from *Raymonda* because at that time Ashton was considering a production of the complete ballet.

Formally the ballet was a *grand pas de quatorze*, and offered convincing proof of the enormous progress the company had made in the decade of its residence at Covent Garden. *Birthday Offering* was a ballet in the grand manner, a comparable work to Balanchine's *Ballet Imperial* in its definition of a classic style derived from the masterpieces of the 19th century. The ballet began with an entrée and grand adagio for the seven ballerinas of the company and their partners (the ballet was known in the company as 'Seven Brides for Seven Brothers'). The entrée, to the first *Concert Waltz*, established the style, as with serene dignity the dancers swept around the stage in a wide circle, the men supporting the women in *attitudes posées en avant* and *en arrière*. Each of the *danseuses* had a solo variation, the men danced a Mazurka, there was a *pas de deux* for Fonteyn and Somes, and the Finale

La Péri: Fonteyn and
Somes

was a reprise of the opening. The variations were tailored to the individual qualities of each ballerina – particularly memorable were Beriosova's gracious solo,
Nerina's with its brilliant leaps and double turns in the air, the languor of Elvin's
and the amplitude of Grey's; Fonteyn's variation exploited her exquisite *batterie*, as
when she travelled backwards with a *frisson*-like *frappé* of the working foot, punctuated by a little shrug of the shoulders. To have given the men individual solos
as well would have made the ballet unwieldy, and British male dancing had not
quite attained the level of development at which it could stand that kind of exposure, but the Mazurka showed that there had been a decided improvement –
Ashton set them leaping and spinning at the climax, 'with Somes executing a
series of fast *doubles tours en l'air*, flanked by Blair and Doyle flashing round in a
pirouette *à la seconde*, while the four other boys circle round this trio, also spinning,
all this gives a new meaning to centrifugal force'.[52] In 1965 Ashton was to add a
single male variation for David Blair, and another in 1968 for Rudolf Nureyev,
both to music from *Raymonda*, having given up the idea of choreographing that
ballet.

Birthday Offering: Left to right: Bryan Ashbridge and Svetlana Beriosova, Desmond Doyle and Rowena Jackson, Brian Shaw and Elaine Fifield, Somes and Fonteyn, Nadia Nerina and Alexander Grant, Violetta Elvin and David Blair, Beryl Grey and Philip Chatfield

The *pas de deux* was one of Ashton's most beautiful, introducing yet another of the seemingly endless variations on his skimming lifts – Fonteyn entered doing tiny *pas de bourrée*, with Somes lifting her just barely off the ground as she travelled across in a diagonal. Otherwise the *pas de deux* was remarkable for being entirely without lifts – a deliberate omission, for Ashton had seen a recent *pas de deux* by a younger colleague consisting of practically nothing else, and decided to show that it was possible to make a duet without any.

Birthday Offering offered the most convincing proof of how richly the company deserved the accolade Royal: a demonstration such as only classic dancing can give of human beings at their most noble and aristocratic. To Ashton himself, it probably did not seem a very important ballet when he was actually engaged in putting it together – its subtitle indicates that it was not intended to outlast a couple of performances, and although it was elaborately costumed by André Levasseur, with three-quarter length tutus in late 19th-century style, there was no décor except for a few chandeliers from Fedorovitch's set for *Veneziana*, a ballet by Andrée Howard, and some standing candelabra from *Homage to the Queen*.

Ashton was probably therefore quite surprised when the ballet received a more enthusiastic press than any he had done for years, and was recognised as a major creation in line with those other ballets that had formulated his own particular brand of neo-classicism. It went into the regular repertory, raising the question of what was to happen when it was no longer danced by its original team of ballerinas. Undeniably, when performed by dancers of lower calibre, *Birthday Offering* loses its point. There were suggestions that Ashton might be well advised to recast the material in a different form, such as a production of *The Seasons* that would incorporate the variations taken from that ballet. He preferred to leave it unaltered, however, except for such minor changes as the new men's solos and a slight reshuffling of the women's on occasion – thus in 1962 when Nerina or Beriosova alternated in Fonteyn's place as leading ballerina each retained her own variation, with the other's being danced by Monica Mason. Otherwise, Ashton felt he had made the statement he wished to make, and for the moment had nothing to add to it.

Birthday Offering:
Fonteyn and Somes in
the *pas de deux*

Chapter Twelve

1956–1963

There followed a period of some eighteen months in which Ashton produced no major new works. The charter of incorporation that conferred the title of Royal Ballet on the Sadler's Wells and Sadler's Wells Theatre Ballets, and the School, was dated 31 October 1956. At that time, few companies from the West had visited the USSR, though one or two individual dancers had appeared there as guest artists. The company's success in America was by now an accomplished fact, but to gain acceptance in Russia would be an achievement of even greater significance. Plans for the company to visit Russia in the autumn of 1956, however, had to be abruptly cancelled in the wake of the Soviet invasion of Hungary. For that tour Ashton had prepared the so-called 'mirror' version of *Les Patineurs* with double corps de ballet, and this was taken into the repertory early the next year. On 26 March 1957 Fokine's *Petrouchka* was revived, under the direction of Serge Grigoriev and Lubov Tchernicheva, with Ashton as the Old Showman, a role that he played with his usual sense of the grotesque, though it was not as extraordinary a portrayal as his Kostchei in *The Firebird*.

In September the company again visited the United States, and late in the year Ashton went to Italy to mount two productions for the Scala in Milan (the original plan had been for him to revive *Cinderella* there, but for whatever reason this was dropped). On 31 January 1958 there was an evening of works by Maurice Ravel, the two one-act operas *L'Heure espagnole* and *L'Enfant et les sortilèges*, and the ballet *La Valse*, choreographed by Ashton. He had danced in Nijinska's original version, the first of two she choreographed for Ida Rubinstein. According to Ashton it was somewhat reminiscent of *Les Noces* in its massive building up of groups, with the men and women dressed almost identically in lamé tunics, and completely counter to Ravel's ideas for the ballet. Ashton had always wanted to make his own version, keeping as close as possible to Ravel's description, 'a kind of apotheosis of the Viennese waltz'.

Both Ashton and his designer, Levasseur, followed Ravel's directions for the opening of the ballet: 'Through whirling clouds couples of waltzers are faintly distinguished. The clouds disappear gradually; a huge ballroom is seen peopled

Ashton rehearsing *La Valse* at La Scala, Milan

with waltzing couples,' and this brief description of the action was printed in the programme. The effect of 'whirling clouds' was achieved with projections on a scrim, with isolated couples picked out behind it by a follow-spot, then the scrim was raised to reveal the main décor, which, as Ashton described it in an interview 'was in tobacco colour with the sky showing through at the back'.[1]

Ashton's version was like Nijinska's inasmuch as it was essentially an ensemble ballet for twenty-one couples, three of them being used, in Clive Barnes's phrase, as a solo *concertante* group.[2] With some ingenuity he overcame the danger of monotony in the unrelenting three-quarter time, using actual waltz steps only rarely, and the difficulty of the prolonged climax ('I just made everybody run on at that point and take up positions' – also as in *Daphnis* he sometimes emptied the

La Valse: Royal Ballet production

stage of all but the soloists). But the choreography, as seen in the 1963 film, *An Evening with the Royal Ballet,* is still repetitious and musically not very enterprising – certain steps are introduced each time the musical phrase they originally accompany recurs, with very little variation. Early on there seems to be an attempt to create a slightly sinister atmosphere by having the men and women advance towards each other in two parallel lines, reaching out their arms and then turning away with heads averted, hands over their eyes, but it looks generalised and therefore meaningless. The macabre incidents invented by Balanchine for his version may also be clichés of this kind of ballet, but at least they work theatrically.

La Valse was a success in Milan, and Francis Poulenc, who was present, told Ashton that it was the first time he had seen a successful realisation of the score. It was revived by the Royal Ballet at a Gala Performance on 10 March 1959, when Ashton cast younger members of the company in the principal roles.

The second assignment at the Scala was to stage the dances for a production of

Gluck's *Orfeo*. He did not, as he had five years before at Covent Garden, handle the overall staging, which was done by the German actor and director Gustav Gründgens. This, and the fact that the designer was Hein Heckroth, suggest a Teutonic approach totally alien to Ashton's idea of the opera – he says that it was hideous to look at, in a kind of 1930s' kitsch style. Moreover, it was a painful experience for him, with all the tragic associations the opera inevitably held for him. It was given only five times, and perhaps the most notable thing about it was that the soloist in the Dance of the Blessed Spirits was Carla Fracci, who was promoted to ballerina status at the Scala during that year.

One reason that Ashton produced only minor works during the second half of 1956 and 1957 was that he was occupied with preparations for what was in many ways his most ambitious project so far – his first full-length ballet with a score commissioned from a contemporary composer, *Ondine*, which after several post-ponements was finally given its première at Covent Garden on 27 October 1958. (One reason for the delay was that at the end of the 1957–1958 season he was driving to the country with Alexander Grant when their car was involved in an accident in which Ashton received serious facial injuries.)

He had been casting about for several years for a suitable subject: once again he had considered *The Tempest* but dropped it because Fonteyn was not attracted by the character of Miranda.[3] Very serious consideration was given to *Macbeth*: Ashton produced a detailed scenario and minutage for a score to be composed by William Walton,† and he wanted Georges Rouault to design décor and costumes. At the end of the 1954–1955 season de Valois had announced in a curtain speech that there would be a three-act ballet by Ashton and Walton in the following year, though she gave no hint of the subject. It is rather surprising that Ashton got as far as he did with a subject that seems so unsuited to the nature of his genius, and it is evident that he did falter, for the original scheme of a three-act ballet was drasti-cally abridged to a long single act (forty-five minutes) before being abandoned altogether.

However, it is clear that Ashton was always looking for suitable subjects, some of which might be in his mind for many years. For instance, late in December 1930 he and Marie Rambert had attended a performance by the Habima Players, whom C B Cochran was presenting at the Phoenix Theatre, of Salomon Ansky's famous play *The Dybbuk*, preserved in their repertory in the production Vakhtangov had directed in 1922. He was deeply impressed by the play and by the performance of the actress Rovina in the role of Leah. Many years later, after the war (he is not exactly sure when), he thought of this as a possible idea for a ballet, and discussed it with Zvi Friedland, then the director of the Habima, who as a young actor had played, in the performance Ashton saw, the part of Chanan, Leah's lover, whose

† See Appendix C.

spirit, or *dybbuk*, returns to possess her body after his death. It seems that Ashton's discussions with Friedland reached a fairly detailed stage before he decided not to do the ballet.

Likewise, Ashton had long been intrigued by the story of *Ondine*, the water sprite who loved a mortal. He had seen Louis Jouvet's famous production of Giraudoux's play in Paris before the war, with its magical décor by Pavel Tchelit-chev, with whom he had discussed the idea of a one-act ballet on the theme. He considered it again in 1950, and then in 1956, after discarding both *The Tempest* and *Macbeth*, proposed it to Fonteyn, who found it 'ideal from my point of view'.[4] He again approached Walton, but the composer was too busy to undertake the score, and suggested instead the German composer Hans Werner Henze. Ashton knew Henze, who had written an enthusiastic letter to him after seeing *Scènes de ballet* when the Sadler's Wells Ballet was on tour in Germany in the late 40s; they had subsequently met and talked of a collaboration.[5]

Henze accepted the commission and he and Ashton went to Italy together to discuss the project. Ashton read the libretti of two 19th-century ballets based on the story, Jules Perrot's *Ondine; ou, la Naïade* and Paul Taglioni's *Coralia*, but decided to base his own on the original novel by Friedrich de la Motte Fouqué, retaining only the idea of the *pas de l'ombre*, Fanny Cerrito's famous solo, from Perrot's version. Ashton prepared a rather complex libretto that underwent many changes and simplifications before the ballet reached the rehearsal stage, including the renaming of most of the characters: Undine became Ondine, Hulbrand, the hero, became Palemon, Bertalda was shortened to Berta, and for the Lord of the Mediterranean Sea, oddly named Uncle Kuhleborn, Ashton, after rejecting various inventions such as Tresondino, finally came up with Tirrenio.†

Ondine was to be in three acts; in the first Palemon, the hero, is captivated by Ondine and follows her into the forest, deserting his fiancée Berta. Ondine and Palemon are married and she becomes a mortal being with a soul. Act II finds them on a ship on which Berta is also a passenger. Tirrenio, the Lord of the Mediterranean Sea, causes a storm that wrecks the ship, and carries Ondine back to her native element. In the last act Palemon and Berta, having been rescued, are celebrating their nuptials. The festivities are interrupted by Tirrenio and his creatures, including Ondine. Palemon begs forgiveness, but because of his betrayal, her kiss is fatal to him. She carries his body back with her to the sea.

In the earlier drafts of Ashton's libretto, the dancers for the third act divertissement were brought on by Tirrenio disguised as a Neapolitan ambassador, a needless complication, though its removal robbed the entrée of any dramatic pretext. This act was indeed rather overloaded with divertissements, since there was also a *grand pas classique* earlier. In a later revision Ashton took two numbers out of the latter section and used the music to give Palemon and Berta each a solo, feeling that their roles were somewhat undeveloped. Also in earlier drafts Berta's vanity

† See Appendix B.

Ondine: The fatal kiss;
Ashton rehearsing
Fonteyn and Somes

was demonstrated by having her wash in the waters of the fountain from which Ondine first appeared, supposed to have magical properties, and there was even a passage in the third act where Tirrenio complimented her on her beauty, and she explained that 'the water of the magic fountain keeps her lovely' – one of those notions that defy exposition in classical mime (better suited, perhaps, to the television commercial). As was his habit, Ashton drew up a detailed minutage for the guidance of Henze, reproduced in Appendix C.

Henze came to London early in 1957 to begin work, and stayed in Alexander Grant's house, where there was a piano; Grant recalls that Ashton would often ask him anxiously, 'Have you heard a tune today?' When rehearsals began Ashton worked in the usual way with a pianist but soon found the piano reduction unsatisfactory, so he asked Henze to have a recording made of the full score. This was done by a German orchestra under Robert Irving's direction, and after that Ashton

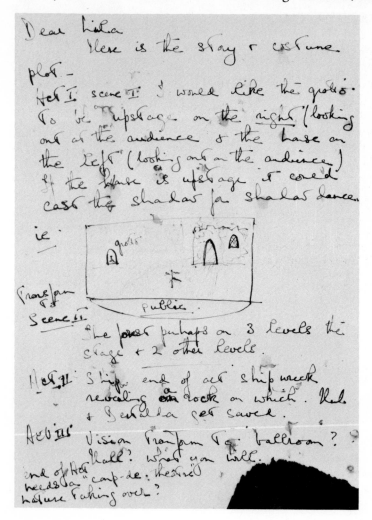

Ondine: A page from a letter from Ashton to Lila de Nobili, with a sketch for the décor of the first scene

OPPOSITE *Ondine*, Act I Scene 1: Fonteyn in the 'Shadow' dance rehearsed to a tape, finding that he had to throw out most of what he had already set.

Ashton was determined that *Ondine* should be the product of close collaboration with both composer and designer. For the latter, he chose Lila de Nobili, to whom he gave careful instructions and even a sketch of his requirements for the first act, which she followed closely. In his letter he wrote that the third act 'needs a *coup de théâtre* – nature taking over?' He asked her to bring him rough sketches 'to inspire me and so that . . . we can be in harmony of spirit . . . I must tell you how very sympathetic I found you on meeting you and I feel that my instinct was right and I long for all three of us to make something beautiful and lasting.' He had been able to discuss the ballet with her in person while working at La Scala, since she was there designing an opera for Zeffirelli. Later, he invited her to watch rehearsals, and de Nobili also listened to the score before starting her work.

In an interview with Peter Brinson, Ashton said, 'I wanted the movement to be fluid like the rhythm of the sea rather than set ballet steps. In general, all the choreography has been inspired by the sea. I spent hours watching water move and have tried to give the choreography the surge and swell of waves. This is why I use the corps as an expressive instrument now more fully than before. In a sense, too, the water episode of *Homage to the Queen* . . . was a first attempt at the style . . .'[6] Elsewhere, Ashton stated that he tried to suggest 'the ebb and flow of the sea: I aimed at an unbroken continuity of dance, which would remove the distinction between aria and recitative'.[7] As well as looking at the sea itself, Ashton studied Leonardo's drawings of waves. Clive Barnes, in his review of *Ondine*, suggested that the ballet represented a new development in Ashton's choreography, adding 'a new, rhapsodic element', whose origin he traced back not only to *Homage to the Queen* but also to *Orpheus* and, interestingly, *Dante Sonata*.[8]

The heart of the ballet was of course the role of Ondine and Fonteyn's performance of it – the critic of The Times described it as 'a concerto for Fonteyn'.

Ondine: Fonteyn as Ondine playing with her shadow

Ondine: Fonteyn as
Ondine, Somes as
Palemon, showing a
variant of the
characteristic *port de
bras*

Ondine, Act II: Fonteyn and Somes on board ship

She flickered and darted about the stage in swift rivulets of *pas de bourrée*, with rippling arm movements as though shaking drops of water from the ends of her fingers, the very personification of a water sprite, playful, wayward and captivating. As he has often done, Ashton devised a characteristic *port de bras* for Ondine and the other water sprites, arms stretched forward or upward with the hands crossed at the wrist, fingertips together making a fish-like shape. If it is true that choreographically *Ondine* was a new departure this was both prompted by, and furthered, Fonteyn's growth as an artist and dancer as she absorbed the lessons learned from the first visit of the Bolshoi Ballet two years before – a broader utterance and a deeper identification with the character.

The actual choreography was as much an act of collaboration as any of the preliminary work with composer and designer, and modification of the scenario continued as a result of discussions held in the rehearsal room between Ashton and the principals. 'Sometimes,' Fonteyn said in an interview with Peter Brinson, 'Henze's score . . . just didn't seem to say the same thing as the scenario. Take, for example, the little mime scene about Palemon's heart in the first act. Ondine comes out of the water. Palemon sees her and loves her. After this, in the original version, Ondine was attracted by Palemon's amulet and snatched it away. When he took it back she became petulant and angry.

'But when we did that scene it seemed false, especially musically. So now Ondine replaces the amulet round Palemon's neck because she is newly interested in him rather than the amulet. At that moment he presses her hand to his heart. She is frightened by his heartbeat (Ondines don't have hearts, you know) and jumps back with surprise. Then, overcome by curiosity, she puts her hand over his heart to feel it beat again'.[9]

In the Shadow Dance she first discovered her own shadow, then that of the mortal, Palemon, and their *pas de deux* used Fonteyn's lyrical line in *arabesque* to the full. The long second *pas de deux*, in Act I Scene 2, after Palemon has pursued Ondine into the forest, expressed their growing love for one another – a typical Ashton touch was the simple gesture of Ondine caressing her lover's hair.[10] At the end of the ballet, when Ondine vainly tries to resist her desire to bestow the kiss that will cause her lover's death, the choreography rose to tragic heights.

Ondine, Act I Scene 2: the marriage of Ondine (Fonteyn) and Palemon (Somes), with Leslie Edwards as the Hermit; the corps de ballet grouping may be compared with that from *La Péri*, page 53

Ashton showed himself to be the master of theatrical effect in the second act when the movement simulates the rocking of the ship. Earlier, the ship appeared to set sail – the scenery representing the harbour was moved off and replaced by a seascape. The set for this act was framed in an oval false proscenium as though seen through a telescope.[11] Another cunning illusion was the apparition of Ondine in the third act, when she seemed to be dancing in the water, actually supported by four unseen partners. De Nobili painted much of the scenery herself, faithfully reproducing the subtlety and delicacy of her original designs.

Ashton has said that the choreographic structure, as opposed to the texture, of *Ondine* was based on his old model, Petipa, and certainly the fact that the second act is largely pantomime or, more correctly, *pas d'action* (there are no extended dance passages, save the *pas de trois* for Ondine, Berta and Palemon, and that too is part of the overall fabric), recalls old ballets like *Le Corsaire*, and also perhaps Bournonville's *Napoli*. But in the second scene of Act I Ashton often showed once again the influence of Nijinska in the corps de ballet groupings – indeed, one of them recalls a grouping from his own early version of *La Péri*.

For all the high seriousness of Ashton's aims and the painstaking preparations, *Ondine* was not a completely successful work. The scenario, even after all the revisions, is far from satisfactory. Too much of the action is unexplained – where are they going on that ship, and why? – and the subsidiary characters are inadequately motivated, Berta a one-dimensional, peevish 'other woman' and Tirrenio, however brilliantly choreographed for Grant, a kind of demon king with no real function in the story (as Fonteyn pointed out in the interview quoted above). Palemon, too, was an ineffectual hero. These faults might not have been so obvious if *Ondine* had been a one-act ballet, a choreographic poem in which the details of the plot would have been of less consequence.

More seriously, much of the score is emptily eclectic, page after page evoking only the most mechanical response from the choreographer. Weakest of all are the third-act divertissements, which constitute two separate, self-contained ballets-within-a-ballet – indeed the second, *commedia dell' arte* section is actually a complete miniature piano concerto, but this is merely ingenious, no substitute for sustained lyric invention.

Like many of Ashton's ballets, *Ondine* underwent revision even after its première. The title role was danced on occasion by others, notably Beriosova, who succeeded in giving a very personal, 'pre-Raphaelite' (in Peter Williams's phrase) interpretation: Lynn Seymour learned the role but never danced it. It remained indissolubly identified with Fonteyn, and when she decided she could no longer dance it, *Ondine* disappeared from the repertory – though fortunately her performance is preserved on film in Paul Czinner's *The Royal Ballet* (1959), along with her *Firebird*.

Soon after the première of *Ondine*, Ashton moved into the house he now occupies in Chelsea. More than a year passed before his next new work, though during that time he mounted *La Valse* for the Royal Ballet and revived *Les Rendezvous* in an enlarged version for the Opera House stage. As has been noted, Ashton had considered the possibility of a complete *Raymonda*, and Karsavina urged him to do it, but he was worried about how to make the story work, and even though she offered to help him solve the problems, he remained unconvinced, much as he loved the score. As a kind of test-piece, perhaps, he choreographed a short *pas de deux* from the first act under the title *Scène d'amour*, for Fonteyn and Somes to dance at a Gala Performance she arranged for the Royal Academy of Dancing on 26 November 1959, at Drury Lane. This dance depicted Raymonda's passionate leave-taking of Jean de Brienne on the eve of his departure for the Crusades, and thus preserved some reference to the story of the complete ballet; it began with Fonteyn 'standing on some steps looking out into the night' in an attitude of 'yearn-

ʹing and expectancy' (when it was revived by the touring company of the Royal Ballet recently, she was discovered, instead, sitting in a chair in reverie).

Ashton's debt to Petipa was once again very clear, in such passages as a supported balance in *attitude* with several rapid changes of the hand and a series of supported *pirouettes*, the first finishing facing front, the second in *arabesque*, and the last, surprisingly, again in *arabesque* but facing the partner. But the dance was also typically Ashtonian, as when the ballerina did little runs on point lifted just off the ground. Typical too was the moment when the music reached the height of its crescendo and instead of some *grand développé* or spectacular lift, the lovers sank to the floor in a last embrace – she tries to make him stay, then seeing that it is impossible gets his cloak, puts it round his shoulders, and as he walks off holds on to it until it too leaves her grasp and she is left alone, kneeling on the stage.

At the time of *Ondine*, Alexander Bland wrote in The Observer of a 'basic fallacy' in the piece – 'the belief that you can take the myths of another age and present them as living, emotion-rousing symbols to a new generation. This is aesthetic taxidermy... In spite of the superimposition of contemporary music, Ondine, with her grottoes and amulets, is rooted in the dead past... One day ballet will sink altogether if it does not shed its cargo of Victorian clichés'.[12] It is unlikely that Ashton intended his next ballet to be an answer to this kind of criticism, and yet it was a work whose contemporary validity was beyond any question, and at the same time, with the kind of paradox typical of genius, derived from a source even earlier in origin than *Ondine*. The idea of a new version of *La Fille mal gardée* came from Karsavina, who again enthusiastically encouraged Ashton's proposal.

In an article on 'My Conception of *La Fille mal gardée*', Ashton has explained why he chose to recreate the old ballet, which dates from 1789, instead of doing something new. 'It happened ... that at the time I was reading Dorothy Wordsworth's Journals and I was swept by a longing for the country of the late eighteenth and early nineteenth century: the country of today seems a poor noisy thing by comparison ... There exists in my imagination a life in the country of eternally late spring, a leafy pastorale of perpetual sunshine and the humming of bees – the suspended stillness of a Constable landscape of my beloved Suffolk, luminous and calm.

'At some time or another every artist pays his tribute to nature: my *Fille mal gardée* is my poor man's *Pastoral Symphony*, for it was to Beethoven's symphony that I constantly returned during the period of preparation. From him I got the accumulative waves of movement that I tried to put into my ballet, and the moments of serenity and noble simplicity were also derived from him and imposed on poor Hérold – the thrill of arrival in the country and the days of contemplation and distant, endless staring and dreaming to a *musique concrète* of farmyard noises, all to end in a storm ...'[13]

La Fille mal gardée, Act II: Widow Simone (Holden) falls asleep and Colas appears at the transom window (Blair with Nerina)

La Fille mal gardée, Act II: 'When I am married . . .' Nerina as Lise

Ashton copied Dauberval's original libretto in longhand one morning in the British Museum, and one sunny afternoon, sitting in a small Gothic ruin in the grounds of his house in Eye, wrote out his own version of the simple story of the maiden in love with a young farmer, who contrives to outwit her mother's plans for a more advantageous marriage. Ivor Guest found not only the score of the 1828 Paris production, by Hérold, in the library of the Paris Opéra, but also, in the Municipal Library at Bordeaux, the score written by an unknown hand for the original production in that city in 1789. Also in existence was the score composed by Peter Ludwig Hertel for Paul Taglioni's revival in Berlin in 1864, which, with various interpolations, was used by Petipa and Ivanov in their 1885 revival at the Maryinsky Theatre, and is still heard in current productions, more or less derived from that version, in the USSR, the United States, and elsewhere. Ashton felt that he would need to have a new score, based on music from these sources, and approached first Alexander Goehr, then Malcolm Arnold, both of whom turned down the commission.

With time running short, Ashton finally asked John Lanchbery, then principal conductor of the Royal Ballet, to undertake the task. Together they went through the older scores and quickly rejected Hertel's as too heavy-handed. Lanchbery's arrangement, therefore, drew on three sources: the original (1789) score (which came to light after he had started work), Hérold's and the *pas de deux* on themes from Donizetti (mostly from *L'Elisir d'amore*), that had been interpolated for Fanny Elssler in 1837 and was also discovered at the Paris Opéra. A great deal of this material was very sketchy and lacking in variety, and Lanchbery found that he had to compose a great deal of new music as well as making radical changes in the old.[14] Ashton followed his usual practice of making a minutage and breakdown of the action into dance sequences, though this was less detailed than usual,† probably because the two men worked in close collaboration, planning the action together in thrice-weekly meetings when Lanchbery would play over what he had written, then make any alterations that Ashton felt to be necessary, orchestrate it, and send it to the copyist. In the course of these meetings various modifications were made to the scenario, some of them suggested by Lanchbery – for instance, the episode of Alain's snatching away the flute and attempting to play it, in the second scene of Act I, Ashton having said he needed an excuse to get Alain and his father off to clear the stage for the 'Elssler' *pas de deux*.[15]

Karsavina not only explained to Ashton the ballet's historical significance – it was one of her own favourite roles and she remembered Zucchi's performance of it – but taught him Lise's mime scene in the second act. No doubt Karsavina also supplied other details, such as Lise opening a drawer as a possible hiding-place for Colas when they hear the mother returning, that are common to Ashton's version and the Petipa/Ivanov and perhaps go back even further. Ashton possesses a small book published in Leningrad in 1937 concerning the ballet (called *Vain Precautions*

† See Appendix C.

in Russia), on whose cover is a colour picture of the set for Act I, very similar in lay-out to that of his production (including the chicken-coop); another picture shows a maypole dance in progress, in the Soviet Scene 3, and another Lise trying to steal the key from the sleeping Simone, who holds a tambourine.

Typically of Ashton, he took other ideas from various sources: the cock and four hens who begin the ballet so hilariously, and their realistic costumes, from seeing Walter Felsenstein's production of Janáček's *Cunning Little Vixen* at the Komische Oper in East Berlin; Clive Barnes has made the point that the role of Alain closely parallels that of the stammering oafish Vašek in Smetana's *The Bartered Bride*;[16] the Maypole Dance in Act I Scene 2 is genuine, from a folk dance taught at the Royal Ballet School; the idea for the pauses in Lise's solo in the 'Elssler' *pas de deux* Ashton got from hearing Spohr's *Nonet* on the radio one evening; he went with Nadia Nerina and David Blair, his Lise and Colas, to the Georgian State Dancers, who performed in London late in 1959, and the next day in rehearsal tried ways of adapting one of their steps – it ended up as one of the choreographic leitmotivs of *Fille*, Lise's fast little prances *sur les pointes* that she does *en diagonale* in the coda of the *pas de deux* (earlier in the same number, she and Colas perform a version of it together, and she reprises it in the finale of the whole ballet).[17]

Throughout, as can be seen from Dmitri Romanoff's production in the repertory of American Ballet Theatre – whose choreography is attributed to Dauberval, via Mordkin and Nijinska (and hence presumably derived from Petipa/Ivanov) – Ashton took hints from tiny incidents in earlier versions and expanded them in typically poetic ways. For example, Colas's appearance in the transom window while Simone is at the spinning wheel became a short but exquisite *pas de deux* in which he spins Lise from above in 'finger' turns, then lifts her into an embrace and swings her pendulum-like from side to side. The dreadful gossiping neighbours, on the other hand, Ashton omits entirely.

Perhaps the greatest of all Ashton's inspirations was to take the motif of the ribbon, which certainly goes back as far as the first Paris production in 1803 and may be presumed to originate in Dauberval, and extend its use through the whole of the action until it becomes one of the most resonant metaphors in the whole of ballet. In the 1803 libretto Lise hangs the ribbon on a tree (in Ashton she ties it in a bow through a ring in the wall of the barn) as a sign to Colas, who finds it and ties it to his stick; later it is used as a prop in their first duet. In Ashton this is only the beginning, and when one knows his version the moment when Colas takes the rolled-up ribbon and throws it out to Lise sends echoes through the whole length of the ballet to come. Some of the uses of it certainly derive from Petipa/Ivanov – such as Lise's spinning out along the ribbon and then turning back to Colas as he winds it in again (also remembered by Karsavina), and the 'playing horses' passage. Others are Ashton's own: he came into rehearsal one day with a dozen 19th-century prints of different ribbon designs that he wanted to experiment with, and asked the dancers to help him work out the 'cat's cradle' – Nerina and Blair got

La Fille mal gardée:
Cat's cradle, with
Nadia Nerina as Lise,
David Blair as Colas

LEFT AND OPPOSITE
La Fille mal gardée,
Act I Scene 2: Nerina
and Blair in the
'Elssler' *pas de deux*

stuck and it was the understudies, Merle Park and Brian Shaw, who finally figured out how to complete it.[18]

The cross-over between the scenes is also Ashton's invention, when Lise's friends make a coach with ribbon wheels and Alain as the horse, with a ribbon for a bridle. But it is in the 'Elssler' *pas de deux* that the metaphor reaches the most poetic heights: after the friends, in a rather Nijinska-esque grouping, have made X's (for kisses) with the ribbons, they use them as the spokes of a wheel with Lise at its centre, supporting her as she turns *en attitude*. Colas runs in to her, lifts her, and as he does so the ribbons flutter down – the lovers have relinquished all other ties except their love. But we are not done with ribbons, even so – there is still the Maypole Dance to come, and Lise's wedding dress has ribbons crossing the bodice. Strangely enough, Ashton never saw Pavlova dance this ballet (he saw it danced by her company in 1927, but with Butsova and Oliveroff) – if he had, one might suppose that her use of the ribbon had stayed in his mind for all those years. (Needless to say, the 'Fred step' occurs in *Fille*, during the finale.)

Marie Rambert has said that when Ashton has found music that is sympathetic, his invention takes off and soars from the moment he hears the first few notes; in *Ondine*, as I have suggested, this did not happen and he was often forced to rely entirely on his craft, but the humble and unpretentious tunes that Hérold wrote (or borrowed) for *Fille*, in Lanchbery's not particularly subtle but eminently danceable arrangement, released in Ashton a flow of his most personal and profound poetry. It has been said of Ashton that he is in love with love – that he has so

307

true a sense of the compatibility of young people that he is able to suggest without sentimentality a combination of sexuality and innocence – as opposed to the 'decadent' view of sex to be found in earlier ballets. Lise and Colas are romantically in love – there is a moment in the first act when she is so busy day-dreaming about him that she doesn't notice that he's standing in front of her – but they are physically in love, too. One of the notations in the score, at the end of the ribbon *pas de deux*, reads 'Love is upon them' – it is a quotation from the 1803 libretto – and we know that Ashton means it to be love in its fullest sense of tenderness and desire; again in the second act when Colas has surprised her, he kisses her along her arm up to her throat and her head falls back in rapture – they sit on the wheatsheaves and there is a long, passionate kiss at the music's climax, but this does not seem like a failure of imagination on Ashton's part, since he has already shown us their love in so many ravishing dance images that by then we want them to kiss as much as they do themselves. There is, finally, no doubt that there is a bed in the room where they have been unwittingly locked in together by Simone, and that they have lain in it.

The actual choreography of *Fille* was done in less than four weeks of rehearsal. Very unusually for Ashton, he gave the dancers a full scenario before starting work, so that they knew who they were meant to be. Both Nerina and Blair had always been very concerned to extend the limits of their own technique, and by implication that of British dancers in general – Blair had started something called 'The Club' among the male dancers to which the entrance 'fee' was the ability to execute eight *pirouettes*, later increased to twelve. Ashton had previously exploited Nerina's speed and elevation in her solo in *Birthday Offering* two or three years before, and Blair had contributed to the men's mazurka in that ballet; now Ashton wanted to push the possibilities of this new virtuosity still further. He worked in a state of high excitement, with very little revision. During rehearsals, Blair's wife, Maryon Lane, gave birth to twins, and one day, Blair recalls, he had to go to visit her in Queen Charlotte's Hospital after class, then go to Drury Lane to dance the *Don Quichotte pas de deux* with Nerina at a gala matinée. Impatient to continue working, Ashton insisted they rehearse after that, and was waiting for them in the studio at the Royal Ballet School in Baron's Court when they arrived in a taxi. He wanted to work on their scene in the second act, when Colas surprises her as she imagines their married life – and set the whole thing in about fifteen minutes.

As always, the dancers presented him with material out of which he fashioned his choreography, and he continually spurred them to ever greater feats of technical brilliance. At that time Errol Addison – himself a very strong dancer in his day, a favourite pupil of Cecchetti – was teaching the men's classes, and many of the steps used in Colas's solos came directly from these. His solo in the 'Elssler' *pas de deux* was put together in about ten minutes – Ashton asked for some kind of jumping turn, and Blair suggested a *saut de basque* travelling backwards on a diagonal; Ashton asked for a double, with an interlacing movement of the legs, finishing in 4th position looking down, then going into a *relevé en arabesque*: a typical example of how he would take a simple classroom step and embroider it. Similarly, it was natural to Blair after performing this *enchaînement* three times to round it off with a *chassé coupé assemblé* into a *double tour en l'air* to the knee, but Ashton told him to land in a crouching position, then again suddenly come up into *arabesque*, so there was an element of surprise. Elements of the Bournonville style gave this solo an individual flavour, as in the fast little *pas de bourrée couru* circling backwards and in the *enchaînement* that ends the dance: *cabriole* in *arabesque*, followed by a *grand sauté à la seconde en tournant* going immediately into a *grand jeté en tournant*, again finishing with a *plié* and *relevé en arabesque* (this is similar to the step performed by Fadeyechev in the Bolshoi *Swan Lake*, first seen in London in 1956, and which may have been taken to Russia from Denmark by Johansson, the great Danish teacher of the Imperial School).[19]

The swinging movement of this step was echoed by Nerina's jumping combination in the coda, another example of the way Ashton varies an ordinary, basic step – she does *grand fouetté sauté*, but in reverse, with *battements en cloche* going from front to back. All these movements, Blair says, sat easily on the body because they were based on the classic technique, the dancers' daily vocabulary. One reason that everything went so easily was that Nerina and Blair were used to working together and were on the same wavelength – to which Ashton quickly 'tuned in'. Their main problem, in fact, came when they had to go back and remember what they had done and set it.

The ballet's choreographic felicities are seemingly inexhaustible, and certainly too numerous to describe. According to Blair, Ashton was never at a loss when choreographing for the corps de ballet, whose work is full of exquisite figures, such as the sequence in which Lise goes along the diagonal line of friends, doing a *jeté en tournant* holding hands with one, then a *posé* leaning on the shoulder of the next, and so on down the line, with each girl as she leaves her following in the same alternation of steps. Or again, in the second scene the friends come one after the other in quick succession to take Colas's hand and do a *jeté en tournant*. The *pas des moissonneurs* that immediately precedes this passage is built on a very simple step, just a *chassé* and *point tendu* from side to side accompanied by a circling gesture with the sickle – the four lines pick up this step and its variations one after the other. The *pas de trois* of Lise, Colas and Alain, in which the latter is blissfully unaware of his rival's presence, is a little like a comic version of the *pas de trois* of the Sylphide, James and Effie in Gsovsky's production of *La Sylphide* for the Ballets des Champs-Elysées; Alain is terribly conscious of his function as partner, thrusting his arm stiffly up at not quite the right angle to complement the line of her *arabesque* (the Bridegroom performs a similar action in the *pas de deux* in *A Wedding Bouquet*).

Ashton reserves for the final *pas de deux* his most characteristic images: as Blair points out, at the most joyous moments the lifts are high – Colas literally throws Lise up into the air at the apex of a *grand jeté* – while at the most tender they are low and skimming; one of Ashton's most daring surprises occurs when Lise *bourrées* towards Colas, who looks as if he is preparing to support her in some spectacular turn or dive, and all that happens is that she nestles against his upraised right arm. One of the happiest strokes in the whole ballet is the singing exit at the end, which most poignantly expresses the feeling that they are dancing out of doors, out into the rest of their lives – it is only the ballet that is over.

Ivor Guest quotes a contemporary review of an 1828 revival: '[Dauberval's] genius has fertilized the subject to such a degree that after the first scene one does not notice the similarity of the others and at the end one is as moved and touched as though all these incidents of a little village love affair were events of the greatest importance',[20] and it can stand as an equally apt comment on Ashton's re-creation, as can Alexandre Benois's famous description of Zucchi's performance as Lise, which he said 'seemed actually to exude the fresh fragrance of fields and meadows'.[21] The poetry of Ashton's version derives from the fact that it is rooted in the reality of English country life: the comedy of the cock and hens at the beginning is all the funnier for being the result of very precise observation.

Dale Harris has spoken of Ashton's charity towards his characters: Alain is no mere figure of ridicule, and the choreographer finds a lovely way to give him a happy ending too, as he tiptoes back into the deserted farmhouse to retrieve his beloved red umbrella. In this role Alexander Grant has been for many years unbeatable – incredibly, fifteen years after the première he is as nimble, funny and touching as ever. Originally Ashton had cast Robert Helpmann as Widow Simone, but he withdrew before any of the choreography was created. Helpmann may well have regretted his decision, but we do not, since we would otherwise have been deprived of Stanley Holden's superb performance. He reminds one of the great comedians of the British music-hall, such as Nellie Wallace or Dan Leno, the famous 'Dame' of late Victorian pantomime – artists whose comedy depended not on telling jokes but on characters created out of close and loving observation. Holden has the impeccable timing of such performers: hearing the approach of Thomas and Alain, Widow Simone goes to the mirror to fix her hair before opening the door – then darts back for one extra look of pure self-approval. Like so much else in this ballet whose origin is French, the role is quintessentially English, especially in her clog-dance – Holden was able to furnish Ashton with all the colloquial, Lancashire steps for this number (with enough left over for an unauthorised but very enjoyable encore on special occasions). The salient characteristic, though, of this irascible, much put-upon dame is her underlying love for her daughter, which is never in doubt.

La Fille mal gardée was created in an atmosphere of great happiness, and shows it. Ashton has been known to be physically sick on the opening night of a new ballet, but not that of *Fille*. The première took place on 23 January 1960: as though to forestall any criticism such as Alexander Bland's of *Ondine*, the programme carried a note by Karsavina that described *Fille* as 'a charming period piece singularly compatible with the artistic trends of today – artistic reaction to contemporary

La Fille mal gardée: Ashton rehearsing Nadia Nerina and David Blair in the final *pas de deux* ▷

life'. It was a great success from the beginning – at home, though it has taken a while for New York audiences to realise that it is *not* the same ballet as the version given by American Ballet Theatre, and that they can buy tickets for it with the expectation of a wonderful evening. When the Royal Ballet finally went to Soviet Russia the audiences, in Leningrad especially, were overwhelmed by it; fresh wild flowers wrapped in newspaper were thrown from the gallery,[22] and the critic Natalia Roslavleva called it 'a perfect re-creation of Dauberval's master-piece as seen by a contemporary eye, and a thoroughly British ballet'.[23]

Many dancers have danced the roles of the lovers: Merle Park appeared as Lise soon after the first performance, though Brian Shaw, Blair's understudy, never danced Colas (in more recent years he has been one of Holden's successors as Simone). Ann Jenner's gaiety and the lightness of her jump make her an ideal Lise, and Lesley Collier too captures both the mischief and the tenderness of the charac-ter. Of all the successors to Blair, who was every inch a gentleman farmer (it was presumably only his lack of wealth that made him an unacceptable suitor), one may feel a slight preference for Michael Coleman, though it is a role that all the male principals seem to undertake with pleasure, perhaps because it gives them at least as much opportunity to dance as any of the classic ballets and is a real character into the bargain – David Wall and less predictably Anthony Dowell are both great

La Fille mal gardée:
Stanley Holden as
Widow Simone,
Alexander Grant as
Alain, Leslie Edwards
as Thomas

La Fille mal gardée: Stanley Holden in Widow Simone's clog dance

in it, and recently it has been danced by Nureyev. (When it was first offered to him he seemed dubious, saying to Ashton, 'What happens to me in second act?' Later when he decided he wanted to dance it, Ashton reminded him that the second act was the same as it had always been.)

There is, unfortunately, one element in *Fille* that is inferior to the rest. One cannot quarrel with the score, even if it is not of the highest calibre of ballet music, because it has triggered choreography of genius in a way that more 'important' music could not have done – a suggestion made at the time of its creation that Poulenc should have written it shows a lack of understanding of the nature of Ashton's musical responses. The weak partner in the artistic collaboration was the designer, Osbert Lancaster, even though his choice of models – French popular prints and children's books – would seem appropriate. Somehow along the way he lost what he called the 'freshness and naïveté' of these sources.[24] While many of the costumes are pretty enough, there is a kind of jokey condescension in the décor that comments on the ballet and its period in a way that neither Ashton nor Lanchbery ever do – the cows and dogs drawn on the backcloth, the pictures on the walls, all these things hit precisely the wrong note. Again, at the time it was said that Derain (had he been still living) or Jean Hugo would have been ideal designers

313

– but British painters like Stubbs or George Morland are closer to the kind of look it should have. When the ballet is redesigned, as it should be – the money would be well spent, for obviously it is going to stay in the repertory a long time – the décor should give as strong a sense of place and period as the choreography.

Of all Ashton's ballets, *Fille* most clearly illustrates the truth of Edwin Denby's comment: 'The more trivial the subject, the deeper and more beautiful is Ashton's poetic view of it'.[25] Another American critic, Nancy Goldner, has written 'I like *La Fille* best because of its answer to the question: what is more profound, smiles or frowns, fulfilled or unrequited love? The either/or construct is unfair of course, but in *La Fille* Ashton gives tragedy a definitive run for the money and certainly extends one's notions of what profundity means'.[26]

Following *La Fille* it was rumoured that Ashton was going to undertake a new production of *The Sleeping Beauty*, but when that ballet was revived on 10 June it was the familiar Oliver Messel version, somewhat refurbished but still looking a little the worse for wear. During the summer, however, he did rehearse a new production of *Giselle*, which was first given at the Metropolitan Opera House in New York on 30 September 1960 – the company's sixth American tour. Again he had the benefit of Karsavina's crystal-clear memories of the ballet as she had danced it in St Petersburg, especially of the mime-scenes. Many cuts were restored and Karsavina taught Gerd Larsen Berthe's important mime passage in which she tells the legend of the Wilis and warns her daughter that she will be overtaken by a similar fate if she does not curb her enthusiasm for dancing.†

Ashton's contribution to the production was chiefly to supply new choreography to fill the gaps made by the restoration of previously omitted music; he also arranged new groupings for the corps in the second act, very much in the spirit of the Romantic ballet, and a new solo for the girl in the 'Peasant' *pas de deux* to music composed (presumably by Adam and not by Burgmüller who wrote that interpolated divertissement) for a variation by Giselle that has long since disappeared from the ballet. This was a charming solo somewhat reminiscent of the girl's variation in *Les Rendezvous* – perhaps therefore not entirely suitable for *Giselle*, but worth preserving as an individual number.

The new *Giselle* was not completely successful but had the great advantage of being informed by a knowledgeable and sympathetic point of view; Ashton in any case made revisions later, some of them when Nureyev danced for the first time with the Royal Ballet, as Albrecht to Fonteyn's Giselle. Peter Wright's

---

†In passing one may note that this aspect of Giselle's character tends to be underplayed nowadays, but it was in a performance of Ashton's new production that season in New York that Lynn Seymour gave an unforgettable interpretation, making it very clear that Giselle is dance-mad, so that the second act became a real conflict between her love for Albrecht and her love for dancing, both strong enough to survive beyond the grave.

serviceable but pedestrian production is not an improvement, and certainly James Bailey's designs were preferable to Peter Farmer's.

Ashton's next work was another two-act ballet, somewhat in the same vein as *Fille* but on a smaller scale, *The Two Pigeons*. This was choreographed for the touring section of the Royal Ballet and first performed by them at Covent Garden on 14 February 1961. The ballet, with music by André Messager and choreography by Louis Mérante, was originally presented at the Paris Opéra on 18 October 1886. Messager was musical director at Covent Garden during the early years of the 20th century and the ballet was revived there on 21 June 1906, with new choreography by François Ambroisiny, maître de ballet of the Théâtre de la Monnaie at Brussels – the same Ambroisiny who had been choreographer for the Royal Opera season in 1928 when de Valois was *première danseuse* and Ashton was in the corps de ballet. Although it was probably his reading of the original libretto in C W Beaumont's *Complete Book of Ballets* that gave Ashton the idea of doing a new version, he decided to discard the story by Mérante and Henri Régnier in favour of a new one of his own devising, inspired by the fable by La Fontaine that gives the ballet its name. The fable is quoted at some length in the programme in Edward Marsh's translation, but it provides the merest pretext for Ashton's story. In Mérante's ballet the action took place in Thessaly in the 18th century: the 'pigeons' were two lovers, Gourouli and Pepio. When Pepio leaves in search of adventure his fiancée follows him, and the gypsy girl with whom he becomes infatuated turns out to be Gourouli in disguise, giving the ballerina a dual role. The original libretto was in three acts, but Ashton decided to restrict his own to only two, having taken a vow, he says, to do no more three-act ballets – he always felt the difficulty of resolving the third act, with the necessity of a divertissement for which the music might not be good enough ('one needs a Tchaikovsky for that'); no doubt the success of *Fille* confirmed him in this determination.

Ashton brought the action forward to the period of the ballet's composition and set it in Bohemian Paris. His hero and heroine are identified simply as The Young Man and The Young Girl, who are living together (married or not) in his studio, where at curtain-rise he is seen attempting to paint her portrait and being continually frustrated by her inability to keep still. She fidgets, she rubs her back against the chair, she treads on a crawling insect – does everything to distract his attention: what she wants to do, clearly, is make love. In exasperation he makes her take her pose again, sits her down, crosses her arms, and arranges her hands in a wing-like position on each side of her face. She is really getting on his nerves and we begin to realise that they are in worse trouble than at first appears: like the pigeon in the fable, he is bored with domesticity. As always happens in such situations, every time she tries to make things better she only makes them worse: she tickles him and he laughs, but is annoyed with himself for doing so. When she pulls a chair over for herself it is the one he was about to sit down on, and he lands on the floor – she can't do anything right. He sits down with legs outstretched, she goes to sit on his lap and he lets her fall with a bump, then leans backward until his body is arched over with his head touching the floor. They are found like this by a neighbour,† who arrives together with some of the girl's friends (the traditional group of eight *coryphées* who, in the ensemble that follows, do the 'Fred step'). At first he pretends nothing is wrong but soon begins to express his irritation in a very funny mime passage.

Up to now everything has been treated humorously, but soon we realise that the ballet is deeper than at first appears. The boy stands in an attitude of resignation surrounded by the kneeling friends. Suddenly, through the skylight, we see the two pigeons of the title flying past – a moment that, like the first unfurling of the ribbon in *Fille*, makes the spectator catch his breath: it occurs at exactly the right place in the music and presages the ballet's dominant choreographic metaphor. The *pas de deux* that follows uses a series of bird-like movements, and this is not the only instance where something that was used for comic effect in *Fille* is adapted to poetic purposes in the later piece. Many of the movements are indeed still humorous: the girl puts her hands on her hips and moves her elbows backwards and forwards, with a pecking motion of the head, and does a kind of turned-in *passé relevé* with the foot flexed, suggesting a pigeon's preening and strutting. The quaintness of these steps hardly prepares us for the poetry with which the metaphor will be developed later.

It begins to look as if the couple are getting along a bit better, but the improvement is only temporary, and everyone is relieved when a group of gypsies is heard out on the street, and they are invited in to provide a welcome diversion. But it turns out not to have been a good idea – the boy is immediately attracted to a gypsy girl.

This leads into a theme with variations that fills a similar function, formally and dramatically, to the one in the first act of *Coppélia*: the Girl is trying to win back her lover, with the help of her friends who try to prevent the gypsy girl from reaching him. The Girl has a solo that expresses her anger, her decision to put up a fight, and then the rivalry actually takes the form of a dance competition, with the Gypsy performing a sequence of steps that the Girl attempts to copy. But she is no match for the other's uninhibited sensuality and even though she sends the gypsies about their business, she cannot prevent the boy from taking up his cloak and his sketch-pad and going after them. The Girl leans against the banister, one hand on her hip, the arm moving like a broken wing, while her friends try to comfort her. She goes to the window and sees one of the white pigeons flying away across the rooftops.

† Originally described in the programme as 'His Mother', but according to Lynn Seymour she was always referred to in rehearsals as 'Lady Bountiful' – a rather nosey neighbour who brings them baskets of food; Ashton confirmed this and said it was a 'mistake' to call her 'His Mother' in the programme – certainly if she were she would be an absolute cipher, who fills no function in the plot except for the rather strange moment when she stands Nemesis-like at the top of the stairs before the boy leaves. The cast list was corrected in the 1974–1975 season.

The Two Pigeons,
Act I: Christopher
Gable as the Young
Man, Lynn Seymour
as the Young Girl

The Two Pigeons,
Act I: Elizabeth
Anderton as the
Gypsy Girl and Lynn
Seymour as the
Young Girl,
competing for the
Young Man
(Christopher Gable)

*The Two Pigeons,
Act II Scene 1: pas de
trois* of the Gypsy Girl
(Elizabeth Anderton),
Her Lover (Robert
Mead) and the Young
Man (Christopher
Gable)

The first scene of the second act takes place in the gypsy camp. The gypsies, led
by a young boy who is an accomplished pickpocket, are dancing for some sight-
seers, who begin to get nervous and leave. The young artist arrives and is treated a
little roughly by the gypsy leader and the other men, but the gypsy girl again
behaves seductively towards him. The leader, however, is also her lover and there
is a *pas de trois* in which she is lifted first by one, then the other – the young man
will obviously not win her easily. The revels continue – the girl dances a pizzicato
solo with *pas ciseaux* and the young man a variation somewhat recalling Colas's
in *La Fille mal gardée*. In the ensemble *danse hongroise* that follows they have a duet
section, and further brief solos in the finale, but then the atmosphere begins to grow
hostile and sinister; the girl's amorousness turns to mockery – she incites the two
men to a bout of Indian wrestling, in which the gypsy is the victor, and the young
man is tied up with ropes, manhandled and left unconscious by the gypsies. In a
short entr'acte some of them cross the stage, quarrelling amongst themselves or
going off to make love. The boy enters, sobered by his experience, the ropes still
tied to his wrists and around his waist. One of the pigeons flies on to the stage, as
if to lead him home.

The last scene, 'Back to the studio', finds the girl alone in her sorrow. The boy
returns, with the pigeon on his shoulder: full of remorse, he begs her forgiveness in
a *pas de deux* that reaches poetic heights that have only been hinted at earlier, particularly in the development of the bird metaphor. It begins with the girl sitting

The Two Pigeons, Act II Scene 2:
'Back to the studio' – Seymour
and Gable in the final *pas de deux*

on the floor, her body bending forward with her hands on her hips. He stands behind her and reaches down through the crook of her arms to her extended foot, like someone who gently caresses a wounded bird. There are images of flight in high or swooping lifts; she extends her leg in a *développé* front then lowers it with a little beating movement (she has already done this in a brief solo that begins the scene); he lifts her above his head and she flutters her hands and feet as she descends, like a bird alighting from flight. At one moment she takes an *arabesque penchée* and he, facing in the opposite direction, echoes the line of it with his arm – again, a comic device from *Fille* turned to poetic effect. At the last they walk together towards the rear of the stage: she turns her head to look behind her and he tenderly brings her cheek back to rest on his shoulder again. The dance, and the ballet, end with a typical Ashton diminuendo, the lovers sitting on the floor, one on each side of the large wicker armchair on which she had posed at the beginning. The pigeon is perched on the back, and finally its mate flies in to join it.

The Two Pigeons is an almost perfect ballet: it tells its story with complete clarity and entirely in terms of dancing. Like *Fille*, it is only superficially a light comedy ballet: beneath that surface it is another of Ashton's profound and poetic statements on the nature of love. At the end one believes, not that they will live happily ever after, but that they have grown up and reached a level of maturity at which their love will be able to survive future difficulties. The gypsy dances have been called unconvincing but they are certainly adequate to the ballet's need for local colour and consistent with the general style – the girls are on point, with ankle-bracelets of coins. It is Ashton's natural instinct, and a sound one, to formalise this kind of ensemble.

As always, Ashton handles a humble 19th-century score with consummate tact and trust, knowing exactly how much weight it can be made to bear. Messager's music may not be the equal of that of Delibes or Lalo, but it has ravishing tunes. (Interestingly, one of his operettas was *Madame Chrysanthème*, written in 1893 – Ashton, when told of this, remarked that he wished he had known it when he did his ballet on the same subject.) Again, Ashton worked with Lanchbery on the score, re-arranging the order of the numbers and making cuts, and Lanchbery re-orchestrated some parts, including the finale, which existed only in the piano copy. He also interpolated one number from *Véronique*. Much of the preliminary work was done during the previous year's American tour, from which Ashton returned early to work with the dancers of the other company on the new ballet. For this reason his collaboration with Lanchbery was not as close as it had been on *Fille*. The subsequent discovery of the score that Messager had prepared for the shorter version of the ballet that had been given in London in 1906 emboldened Ashton and Lanchbery to be a little freer in making their own adaptation, since Messager himself had made many manuscript alterations. Lanchbery even felt justified in adding a few transitional bars of his own to make their ending work.[27]

In the case of *The Two Pigeons* Ashton made a wise choice of designer: Jacques Dupont's décors are among the best the Royal Ballet has had in recent years, atmospherically exactly right and exquisitely painted. As Peter Williams pointed out, Dupont in his first set solved the problem that Osbert Lancaster failed to in the second act of *Fille*, to design an interior with plausible dimensions and yet adequate space for dancing, giving the studio height by means of the huge skylight, with a view across the rooftops of Paris beyond.[28] In the second act ingenious use is made of a wooden fence that is pulled across the front of the stage by the gypsy men to form a 'curtain' behind which the change can be made. As for the costumes, those for the women are particularly successful – the girl's white dress, a long tutu incorporating elements of period costume, the Degas-like dresses of her friends, and the gypsy girls' multi-coloured skirts and blouses, which avoid garishness by the careful choice and juxtaposition of colours.

Ashton created the ballet for members of the younger generation of Royal Ballet dancers. Lynn Seymour had already made a remarkable début in *Swan Lake* and revealed extraordinary talents as a dance-actress. Although British dancers were continually improving in both technique and projection, few of them – not even Fonteyn at this stage of her career – had yet acquired that sense of total commitment to movement that was so impressive in the Bolshoi dancers at their first appearance in London. Seymour, especially in two ballets by Kenneth MacMillan, *Le Baiser de la fée* and *The Invitation*, had shown this kind of willingness to subordinate technique to total expressiveness. Ashton chose her for *The Two Pigeons* which, she says, represented a total reversal of gear from her roles in MacMillan's ballets, though she had experience of Ashton's way of moving, through being rehearsed by him in the repertory.

Ashton, his part, was as usual thinking of Pavlova – Seymour, he said, had feet like hers, and he showed her tricks that Pavlova had used to show them off. Once again, he worked very quickly, sketching in the general pattern, which remained virtually unchanged as he filled in the detail. He would strut around the studio doing birdlike movements and getting her to copy them or elaborate on them: she says that he continually encouraged her to hurl herself about, to wring as much movement as possible from her body, preferring always that she go too far so that he could correct her, rather than not go far enough, saying things like 'Don't be so stiff and English!' She found that she got her ideas about the character – that she was no mere vapid ingénue, but impetuous and huffy – from the movement as they worked it out. The humour too emerged as they rehearsed: at the beginning it was all done quite seriously but gradually became lighter and more amusing, bearing out Ashton's conviction that one cannot set out to do a funny ballet – it is something that happens or not, a lesson he had doubtless learned over the years from failures like *Cupid and Psyche* and *Les Sirènes* as much as from successes like *A Wedding Bouquet*.

The part of the Young Man was originally created for Donald Britton, who was prevented from dancing the first performance by an injury he sustained on the day of the dress rehearsal. It was therefore danced by Christopher Gable, the understudy. This change made a great difference to the ballet – Britton was a virtuoso and by then in his early thirties, whereas Gable was very young and not fully formed as a dancer, so that instead of being about an older man not quite ready to settle down with a younger woman, the ballet became a story of a young man who had to sow his wild oats before learning the nature of true love. One feels bound to say that the latter is more moving and seems more 'right', though when Seymour danced it in New York with Alexander Grant and later with Britton himself the ballet reverted to Ashton's original conception.

Over the years *The Two Pigeons* has firmly established itself as an audience favourite, partly because of having been performed for many years by the touring company, but it took both public and critics a while to see its quality. Indeed at the beginning several of the critics, apparently still not having learned their lesson from so many other Ashton ballets, dismissed it as inconsequential – again with the honourable exceptions of Clive Barnes and Peter Williams in Dance and Dancers. Thus Alexander Bland called it 'a sad affair, one of those barley-water ballets with gently pretty music . . . and gently pretty décor . . . to which we are temperamentally all too prone'.[29] Even now some of the reviewers can be quite patronising ('silliness and sentimentality'), but judging from the success of a recent revival the ballet seems assured cf its place in the repertory. Doreen Wells and David Wall, who had performed it many times in the days of the touring company, danced it again, bringing out all of its comedy, pathos and passion. This was just before Wells's decision to leave the company – like so many Royal Ballet dancers, she had found her greatest fulfilment in an Ashton role.

The Two Pigeons has been performed for only one season in New York, and was not a great success: on tour the company was persuaded to perform only the gypsy scene from the second act, which cannot have made very much sense out of context.

In June 1961 the Royal Ballet's visit to Russia, cancelled five years earlier, finally took place. The company performed in both Leningrad and Moscow; Fonteyn, as might be expected, had a personal triumph in both *Sleeping Beauty* and *Ondine*, but the latter was otherwise received with respect rather than heartfelt enthusiasm. *Fille* on the other hand was an unqualified success. The visit was in exchange for the first visit to London of the Kirov Ballet from Leningrad, and it was at the moment of that company's departure from Paris en route to London that Rudolf Nureyev became the first of its famous defectors. In the autumn Margot Fonteyn invited him to perform at her Gala Matinée in aid of the Royal Academy of Dancing, at the Theatre Royal, Drury Lane, on 2 November. For this occasion Ashton arranged a solo for him to music of Scriabin (the choice was Nureyev's), *Poème tragique*. The beginning of it, as described by Margot Fonteyn, may have been inspired by Ashton's memory of Isadora's dance to Chopin's *Funeral March*: Nureyev stood motionless, wrapped in a long red cloak which he flung aside[30] (when Isadora did this, Ashton recalls, it revealed an enormous sheaf of lilies she

Poème tragique:
Rudolf Nureyev

was carrying). The dance was described by Mary Clarke as 'A great outpouring of passion and sadness. Arms flung wide, he leaped and soared about the stage; it was a hymn to freedom and at the same time a tragic realisation of the responsibilities and conflicts freedom can bring'.[31] Richard Buckle called it 'a dance in the modern Moscow style, a dance of despair... [with] splendid swinging *pirouettes en attitude*, tragic clutching arms, falls on the knees, hair all over the face – thrilling!'[32]

This was its only performance: at the time Nureyev was officially a member of the International Ballet of the Marquis de Cuevas, and at the matinée he also danced the *Black Swan pas de deux* with the company's ballerina Rosella Hightower, but very soon afterwards he began his long association with Margot Fonteyn and the Royal Ballet.

Meanwhile Ashton was preparing another ambitious production for the Royal Ballet, which was presented at Covent Garden on 12 December. Whether or not his choice of Stravinsky's melodrama *Persephone* was made in answer to the critics of his last ballet, it was certainly very different from it, or indeed any work he had undertaken before. Like *Le Baiser de la fée*, *Persephone* was originally commissioned from Stravinsky by Ida Rubinstein, though it was not one of the ballets Ashton had danced in. The music was an elaborate setting of a poem by André Gide, adapted from Homer's hymn to Demeter, mother of Persephone. Presumably to satisfy Ida Rubinstein's pretensions as an actress as well as a dancer, the title role involved the declamation of portions of the text, the rest being sung by a tenor who impersonated Eumolpus, the High Priest, and a chorus. According to Lincoln Kirstein the original plan was that Balanchine should choreograph it,[33] but as finally presented by Rubinstein at the Paris Opéra on 30 April 1934 the choreography was by Kurt Jooss, with décor and costumes by André Barsacq. This production was given only three times, and subsequent performances of the score have usually been without stage action. Stravinsky himself made it clear that he regarded the work as a hybrid, and an unsuccessful one at that: when Robert Craft asked him, 'What is your feeling now about the use of music as an accompaniment to recitation?' he replied, 'Do not ask. Sins cannot be undone, only forgiven'.[34]

Ashton was no doubt prompted to attempt the difficult score in part because of the opportunity it gave to display the talents of Svetlana Beriosova, who had proved herself a gifted interpreter of his choreography with her assumption of the title role in *Ondine* and was moreover possessed of a beautiful speaking voice. (In the first performances she wore a Japanese transistor microphone concealed in her costume, but in a revival six years later her speaking part was pre-recorded.) Ashton's solution of the problem of how to stage *Persephone* was the one that might have been expected of him – he made a classic ballet out of it. This approach worked well enough for the scenes on earth, but the middle scene was more of a problem – 'scenes in hell *are* hell to do'.

Persephone: Ashton, centre, rehearsing Svetlana Beriosova, right, and corps de ballet

As Clive Barnes commented at the time, 'Just as Stravinsky regarded the Gide as almost an abstract arrangement of syllables, so Ashton has apparently regarded the Stravinsky as almost an abstract arrangement of notes.' Ashton also used another element that has recurred frequently in his work, the element of ritual, in keeping with the occasionally static quality of the music and also echoing Gide's Christian interpretation of the myth (Persephone returns to the underworld at the end of her own free will, out of compassion for its denizens). Thus Ashton sought to unify the disparate ingredients of the piece by the very simplicity of his approach – so that, to quote Barnes again, 'The feeling of a disintegrating medium, those disconcerting grinds of gear changes as the score slips from speech to song and then to orchestra, which I was strongly conscious of in the concert hall, has been swept away . . . For this Stravinsky should be grateful, for to a surprisingly large extent Ashton seems to have unflawed a flawed masterpiece.

'Where Ashton has not been so felicitous . . . is in some of the detailing of the dance. Should he, for example, have selected quite such a gamine strut, with bouncing hips and flouncing thighs, to suggest the vernal innocence of *le premier matin du monde*? Pluto's variation, raped from the score, and itself a mixture of Lifar and originality, seems out of place in its context, while the conception of Mercury, not that untrue to the music, is hardly mercurial.

325

'If some of the details raise doubts, with others one is immediately content. The small things of fluttering hands, and arms bent just so in instinctively correct Grecian angles; the larger things of completely untroubled craftsmanship in the big ensembles, as the huge cast walk and dance through their interweaving patterns with a joyful certainty. There is the pleasure of seeing old tricks (that lovely Fokinian touch at the end when the girls fall back in sequence into their partners' arms) exquisitely used by a master choreographer.'[35]

Other reservations that Barnes had concerned the acrobatic and erotic *pas de deux* for Persephone and Pluto, which he felt was a shade too lush for the music, a crossover in the entr'acte when a line of girls hopped across in front of the act-drop holding on to one another's toes, and the characterisation of Demeter, which was reminiscent of Hera in *Tiresias* (also impersonated by Gerd Larsen) with her haranguing gestures. Noël Goodwin, the music critic, made the comment that Ashton sometimes followed Stravinsky's score too slavishly, especially in the dances for the corps de ballet – 'By mirroring the dotted rhythms and displaced accents Ashton seems not only to verge on the banal choreographically, but transmits that back to the music'.[36]

But these were minor criticisms of a work that Ninette de Valois has described as 'a very noble ballet, Ashton in the fullness of his maturity',[37] and that Marie Rambert said at the time was his best work. We may assume that Ashton found himself very much in sympathy with the philosophic content of Gide's poem, its insistence on the complementary nature of good and evil, and even more perhaps with its more concrete imagery of nature, of the rebirth of spring after winter's death:

Il faut, pour qu'un printemps renaisse
Que le grain consente à mourir
Sous terre, afin qu'il reparaisse
En moisson d'or pour l'avenir.

Beriosova had a great personal success as Persephone: her physical appearance was never more beautiful, and exquisitely as she spoke the verse, her dancing was even more expressive. Keith Rosson was a 'passionate and powerful' Pluto,[38] while Derek Rencher projected 'an almost radiant nobility'[39] as Demaphoön, Persephone's earthly lover. If Gerd Larsen was unable to make much of Demeter, this was no doubt because of the limitations of the role itself; Alexander Grant's Mercury was a kind of cross between his Eros in *Sylvia* and his Tirrenio in *Ondine*.

Ashton made the appropriate choice of a Greek painter, Nico Ghika, to design the ballet; like John Craxton in *Daphnis*, he rejected a conventional idea of Greece, cypresses, Doric columns and wine-dark seas, in favour of brilliantly coloured, sunlit landscapes with spiky rocks and vegetation for the first and last scenes, while the middle scene elaborated the theme of rock-strata. The overall look of it, according to Peter Williams, was like a combination of the tapestries of Jean Lurçat and certain paintings by Max Ernst. Williams found some of the costumes

Persephone: Beriosova
as Persephone, Keith
Rosson as Pluto

Raymonda pas de deux,
in performance and
rehearsal: Svetlana
Beriosova and Donald
MacLeary

successful individually but en masse there was too great a confusion of different colours, cuts, and silhouettes.⁴⁰

Persephone was by its nature not destined to be a great popular success – and in any case because of the problems presented by the score could not become a standard repertory item. It was never seen in New York, nor, for that reason, by the present writer. The ballet was given a dozen times in its first season, three the following year, and eight when it was revived in 1967 – a not very grand total of twenty-three. Now, presumably, it is lost.

Ashton's only new choreography in 1962 was also for Svetlana Beriosova, partnered by Donald MacLeary – a *pas de deux*, with variations and coda, from Glazunov's *Raymonda*. Although this was yet another *pièce d'occasion* made for a Gala Performance at Covent Garden (on 3 May 1962), it shows that he had not quite given up the idea of doing the complete ballet. Whereas the *Scène d'amour pas de deux* had encapsulated part of the story of *Raymonda*, the new one was typically the kind of number to be found in the third act of a long ballet, with many virtuoso tricks including an arm's length lift from which Beriosova swooped down into a fish dive.⁴¹ The *pas de deux* was dressed by André Levasseur, with Beriosova in a deep pink tutu trimmed with gold embroidery, and an ornate gold headdress, MacLeary in a dove-grey velvet tunic, with pink and gold panels and a wide white collar.⁴²

Official recognition of the progress of British ballet and of its role as a cultural ambassador, and of Ashton's part in all this, came in the Queen's Birthday Honours for that year, when Ashton, who had been made Commander of the British Empire in 1950, was knighted. At a reception to celebrate this event given by the London Ballet Circle on 15 October 1962, Ashton made a speech in which he said, 'Choreographers *must* be honoured in their lifetime – posthumous recognition is far too late'.⁴³

Ashton had not made a new ballet for Fonteyn since the *Scène d'amour*, and for some time he had been looking for a suitable subject for the ballerina whose career had been so closely linked to his own. He was divided between two heroines of French literature, Manon Lescaut and Marguerite Gautier: he had in his possession a copy of Eugène Scribe's libretto for Jean Aumer's ballet based on the Abbé Prévost's novel, presented in Paris in 1830, and John Lanchbery had found the score, by Fromental Halévy, in Paris, but after studying these Ashton came to the conclusion that neither was suitable for his purposes. As for *La Dame aux camélias*, a score for a two-act ballet on the subject had been composed by Henri Sauguet in 1957, and Ashton studied that, too, but again was not convinced.

Then one evening in April 1962, after he had been thinking about all this for over a year, he heard the Liszt Piano Sonata on a radio programme called Music at

Night, and realised that he had found what he was looking for – 'almost immediately,' he says, 'I could visualise the whole thing in it'. It was not his intention to make a narrative ballet that followed the outline of Dumas's play or of Verdi's *La Traviata*, but to concentrate the essence of the story into 'a kind of tabloid, a pillule', as he told Alexander Bland of The Observer, adding, 'But I would like it to be strong enough to kill.'

In the course of his preparations for the ballet, Ashton went back not only to the play but to Dumas's original novel: 'It's much better than the play. Much stronger; for instance, that bit where Armand has Marguerite's body dug up just to look at it again, and it's all wormy.' The character of Marguerite Gautier, he found, was based on a real person – Marie Duplessis, a courtesan with whom Dumas had been in love and who died of consumption at the age of twenty-three. Then he discovered that Duplessis had also had an affair with Liszt – 'I found this fascinating, I often wondered whether she could have inspired this very piece'.[44]

As is his habit, Ashton worked out the structure of the ballet with his pianist – the basic carpentry of how the incidents would fit into the score – though he left the actual creation of the steps until he worked with the dancers. 'In this case,' he told Bland, 'I even knew exactly when Marguerite would cough; she does it very discreetly behind her hand' (it goes with a recurring staccato figure in the music). Ashton decided on a flashback structure with a prologue showing Marguerite on her death-bed and the rest of the action represented as her feverish recollection of the events of her life – until Armand rushes in for the actual death-scene. This device is similar to that used by Helpmann in his *Hamlet* and in many of Martha Graham's pieces: whether or not these were in his mind, the structure is clearly indicated by the cyclical form of the music, a form which in any case has a strong appeal for Ashton. The only other important character would be Armand's father, but even he would be reduced to 'a symbol of duty and morality... When I was in Moscow with the company, there was a Kabuki troupe from Japan, and I was tremendously impressed. The way they just stand while the emotion builds up inside them, and then suddenly alter the fold of a sleeve or something that tells everything. The father is a bit Japanese...'[45]

By the time Ashton had reached this point, Fonteyn's new partnership with Rudolf Nureyev was established, and it was natural that he should come to think of *Marguerite and Armand* as a ballet for the two of them. At a press conference towards the end of the 1961–1962 season Ninette de Valois announced the ballet among the plans for the following year; Ashton, she said, would also stage a revised version of *Swan Lake* with décor by Georges Wakhevitch. The date of the new ballet was set for 13 December 1962.

Ashton entrusted the designs to Cecil Beaton; they decided to do away with painted backcloths and wings and use instead a semi-circular framework to define the stage area, and also to suggest the 'gilded cage' in which Marguerite is imprisoned by her way of life. Beaton took his design for this from a firescreen in his country house.[46] Similarly, Ashton got the idea for the curtain that frames the final episode from one that he saw looped over a rail in a drillhall in Hammersmith where the ballet used to rehearse. Otherwise scene changes would be indicated by lighting; there was to be a chaise longue around which much of the action would revolve, and some chandeliers – the only other decorative elements were a white curtain that floated down at the end of the prologue showing Marguerite on her deathbed, and some projections that Beaton decided to throw on the cyclorama – huge blown-up photographs of Fonteyn and Nureyev over which cloud and water effects would be superimposed.

After only four rehearsals Nureyev developed foot trouble and had to go into a nursing home for treatment, which meant the ballet had to be postponed until the early spring, when it would replace the projected revival of *Swan Lake*. Before Ashton could resume intensive rehearsals the two dancers had to fulfil dates in Australia and Panama, though he did manage to get a few sessions with them before they left. He prefers to start at the beginning of a ballet and work his way through to the end, but circumstances dictated a different method, and he started with the scene of their first meeting. This change of his habits did not ease his usual nervousness at beginning a new ballet, but the work went well. 'The next day,' he told Bland, 'I did one of the scenes with the Father. Michael [Somes] was standing with Margot, very stern and stiff, and I saw the door open a crack and Rudi looking in very cautiously, in his scarf and everything. I could see him tiptoe round behind me as we went on working and when we began to come to the end of the scene he started stripping off his coat and things, and just at the right moment he flew out from behind me into Margot's arms; it was wonderful'.[47]

When Fonteyn and Nureyev returned from overseas, work could be resumed, and the ballet was completed in fifteen rehearsals. The first performance took place on 12 March 1963. The programme did not offer a synopsis of the story, but simply said, 'In the last stages of her fatal illness, The Lady of the Camellias re-lives some incidents of her tragic life,' and named the various sections of the ballet: Prologue – The Meeting – The Country – The Insult – Death of the Lady of the Camellias.

In the Prologue (in which Fonteyn's place is taken by a double, Ann Jenner in the first performance), Marguerite, lying delirious on her couch, sees a vision of Armand, first in the form of one of Beaton's projections, then in the flesh as Nureyev dances the only extended solo passage in the ballet. The white curtain billows down and through it we see Marguerite, sitting on the chaise longue in a scarlet ball-dress, surrounded by admirers, among them a Duke, her current protector. (The other men were made up to resemble portraits of famous men of the time, including Franz Liszt.) Ashton has said that this scene was suggested by an incident in the life of Anna Pavlova, who went to a reception in her honour in Lima, Peru (presumably at the time when Ashton saw her dance there), attended only by the local gentlemen, but it inevitably recalls the exquisite film fragment of Pavlova in *Christmas*. In any case, it is clear that Pavlova was as always very much in Ashton's mind when he was working on this ballet, and that it is as much a homage to her as to Fonteyn herself: he said to Alexander Bland, 'How she would have torn the

Marguerite and Armand: Fonteyn as Marguerite surrounded by her admirers

part to pieces!'[48] (It is reasonable to suppose that Beaton, at least, thought also of Garbo, whose costumes in *Camille* were all in black and white; Fonteyn's first costume was crimson, but for the country scene she was dressed in white, with floating ribbons, and for her return to the demi-monde in black and white.)

Armand enters; they are both transfixed as their eyes meet for the first time. Left alone, they dance together. Although this *pas de deux* expresses the first rapture of their falling in love, her behaviour when the others return is still coquettish. She throws him a camellia, and one of the other men makes as if to pick it up, but Armand prevents him, snatches it up and rushes off, pressing it to his lips. Their *pas de deux* in the country scene is in a different key – the playful happiness of fulfilled passion, in ironic contrast to the scene with Armand's Father that follows. Although he appears as an abstract figure of authority, he also shows a momentary tenderness towards Marguerite in her anguish at his demand that she renounce Armand. Clive Barnes, in his review of the opening performance, wondered if there was to be detected in this scene an allegory of the situation that then existed in the Royal Ballet, with Somes, Fonteyn's former partner, relegated to a character role and disapproving her new rhapsodic freedom of movement and the un-

Marguerite and Armand:
Fonteyn as Marguerite,
Nureyev as Armand,
in the final *pas de deux*

inhibited ecstasy of her acting, both released by the younger dancer and typified in the following duet with Armand, after Marguerite has made her decision to leave him, expressing both her despair and her passionate hunger for his love.[49]

A brief ensemble for the male corps leads into the scene at a gambling party – they seem to be excitedly telling each other of Marguerite's imminent return into their midst. She arrives, once again accompanied by the Duke, who makes it clear that he expects her to limit her attentions to himself, indicating the diamond necklace she wears, presumably a recent gift. Armand appears, stung by what he sees as her betrayal, and insults her by tearing the necklace from her throat and contemptuously throwing a handful of banknotes at her feet. Marguerite is left alone as the Father enters; although he can offer no comfort he does again show some compassion. In despair, she goes off – a tottering, trembling walk on point that is one of the most heartrending moments in Fonteyn's performance.

The final scene rises to fever pitch as the action catches up with itself, so to speak. Again we see Marguerite ill and alone, tormented by memories. Armand arrives – and Nureyev's spectacular entrance, running all around the stage with his cloak flying behind him, was surely inspired by Ulanova's running to Friar Laurence's cell in *Romeo and Juliet*. The final *pas de deux* has a kind of raw passion and desperation that are so real that one is almost embarrassed to watch. It contains the ballet's most unforgettable dance image, when Marguerite, in her last death-throes, seems to climb up Armand's body as her spirit tries to escape from the prison of the flesh. In a final gesture, she puts her hand to his face then falls back lifeless, and the ballet is over.

If *Fille* and *Two Pigeons* were in their different ways celebrations of fulfilled sexual love – and it is this that gives these ballets their depth and poetry – *Marguerite and Armand* released this undercurrent of passion in tragic terms: with his usual perception Ashton saw that Nureyev had found the key to unlock Fonteyn's final reserve as an artist, and he gave their partnership its perfect vehicle. The word has been used in denigration of the ballet, but is not so intended here; for one thing *Marguerite and Armand* extended Fonteyn's interpretative powers rather than merely exploiting her as did Cranko's *Poème de l'ecstase*. And as Ashton has said, 'Who is to say that *La Sylphide* wasn't a vehicle for Taglioni, or *Giselle* for Grisi? And besides, there's nothing wrong with a vehicle provided it goes.' Some people compared it with Ashton's earlier Liszt-Beaton ballet *Apparitions*, but that work remained within the conventions of its period, the beloved was an ideal and when she finally personified physical passion she turned into a monster – it belongs to the time when Ashton still equated sex with guilt and shame. Clive Barnes made the interesting suggestion that the new piece was closer to Ashton's more recent Liszt ballet *Vision of Marguerite* (the new version of *Mephisto Valse*) – it had, he said, 'the same pulse, the same speed, the same compression and . . . the same urgency',[50] which suggests that whatever he did for Fonteyn, Nureyev did not open up this new creative vein in Ashton, even though he undoubtedly provided the means for its most complete expression.

Indeed, as Dale Harris has pointed out, *Marguerite and Armand* 'gave Fonteyn the opportunity to be uniquely herself but gave Nureyev something far less personal. Armand is a generalized portrait of the young, handsome lover. Marguerite is the summation of Fonteyn's entire career. With infinite skill and tact it seizes on her power to excite and move the audience. *Marguerite and Armand* is a tribute to everything that Fonteyn had achieved, a fable of her attainments and inevitable decline. Unlike many of the ballets Fonteyn has appeared in during the last seven years – *Paradise Lost, Pelléas et Mélisande, Poème de l'ecstase* – *Marguerite and Armand* is seemly. Like the *Dying Swan* for Pavlova it projects an ultimate truth in metaphorical form about Fonteyn as dancer and human being'.[51] There were those who said that Ashton was again indulging in a kind of Romantic pastiche, yet, to quote Barnes once more, 'Ashton's originality...finds no particular outlet in modern techniques as such...He has pushed his branch of the lyric theatre to a degree of personal expressiveness that is entirely contemporary in its feeling'.[52]

As it proved, *Marguerite and Armand* was Ashton's ultimate homage to Fonteyn, the last complete ballet that he has created for her, and as durable as the ballerina herself – since the role calls as much for acting as for dancing, it remains one that she can continue to perform with no lessening of conviction. It has also been a ballet that she and Nureyev have danced in many places and not only with the Royal Ballet – at the Paris Opéra, La Scala in Milan, the Rome Opera, and in North and South America. No one else has ever danced it – though curiously (as it seems now) in the beginning Lynn Seymour and Christopher Gable were the understudies. It would have been interesting to see them do it, but almost immediately the ballet became so identified with its stars that for anyone else to attempt it would have been unthinkable. Fortunately their performance is recorded in the Nureyev film *I Am a Dancer*, directed by Pierre Jourdan. There is a certain amount of 'cinematic' adaptation but it is fairly unobtrusive, and has the advantage of doing away with Cecil Beaton's décor (the projections turned out to be a mistake, an attempt to introduce a 'trendy' theatrical device that was not organic to the work); also the film used the Liszt Sonata in its original form, which would surely be equally acceptable in the theatre now – both the orchestrations that have been used have the effect of making the music seem more melodramatic than need be.

Some time previously de Valois had announced her intention of retiring at the end of the 1962–1963 season: Ashton was her obvious successor as director of the company, a position that he looked forward to filling with mixed feelings. However, de Valois postponed her retirement when it was decided that Ashton should mount his version of *Romeo and Juliet* with the company early in the following season – then, for whatever reason, he changed his mind, and de Valois stepped down as previously planned, which meant that he had to turn down an offer to choreograph the dances for the film of *My Fair Lady*.[1] (At the end of the visit of the Bolshoi Ballet that summer a suggestion was made that the companies should make a swap – Ashton's *Fille mal gardée* for Lavrovsky's *Romeo and Juliet* – but unfortunately that too came to nothing in spite of enthusiasm on both sides: the addition to the Bolshoi repertory of a contemporary choreographic masterpiece might have had an enormous effect on that company. In the end, Ashton entrusted the choreography of the Prokofiev score to Kenneth MacMillan, whose version has assumed warhorse status since its creation early in 1965.)

As director, Ashton delegated much of the actual administrative work to his assistants, Michael Somes and John Hart, with John Field taking charge of the touring company. As far as the repertory was concerned, he was anxious to do justice to other choreographers besides himself, and in his first season there were revivals of de Valois's *The Rake's Progress*, Andrée Howard's *La Fête étrange*, and Helpmann's *Hamlet*; Balanchine's *Ballet Imperial* was also restored to the repertory, joined by two other Balanchine works to music by Tchaikovsky – *Serenade* and the *Pas de deux* to some music composed for the original Moscow production of *Swan Lake*. An even more important addition to the repertory was Nureyev's reconstruction of the fourth act, the Kingdom of the Shades, from Petipa's *La Bayadère*, with its opening *défilé* by the corps de ballet, an astoundingly audacious piece of choreography. Under Ashton's direction, the Royal corps was to become the finest in the world, and no ballet has displayed them more magnificently than *Bayadère*, which although based on Nureyev's recollection of Petipa's choreography as given (and revised) in Soviet Russia, has come to exemplify the Royal

Ballet's classic style in its most dazzling form – a style that is essentially Ashtonian. It was Ashton's intention to make the company as a whole more important than any single dancer: one of his directorial acts was to change the order of curtain-calls, so that if the applause warranted it there would be another full company call after the principals' solo bows.[2]

The old production of *The Sleeping Beauty* was freshened up, and as the season went on Ashton made one or two changes; most significantly, on 29 February 1964 he put the Awakening scene back where it belongs, at the end of Act II, instead of beginning Act III with it as had been done since 1946. On 12 December 1963 the much delayed new production of *Swan Lake* was finally unveiled. It was rather different from what had been planned earlier: Ashton was responsible for most of the choreographic additions, but the overall production and staging were the work of Robert Helpmann. The décor was not by Wakhevitch but by Carl Toms. Nureyev arranged the Polonaise in Act I and the Mazurka in Act III (now called Act II), and there was a new Czárdás in the same act by Maria Fay. The ballet opened with a Prologue, choreographed by Ashton, that purported to show Odette's transformation into a swan (an event better left to the audience's imagination), using some of the same music that Balanchine used in his *Pas de deux*. In the first act proper Ashton arranged a new Waltz for six couples, to replace his old *pas de six*, and a *pas de quatre* to music originally composed for the *pas de deux* in Act III. In Act II (now known as Act I, Scene 2) he made a new dance for the four leading swans; his contributions to the 'Black' act, in addition to the Neapolitan Dance retained from the old (1952) production, were a Dance of the Guests and a new Spanish Dance; the last act (Act III in this production) was entirely his choreography.

The new Waltz was not an improvement on the old one: in spite of some felicitous moments, it had a tendency to fly off in all directions. The *pas de quatre* is a series of divertissements in Ashton's most brilliant classical style – actually Merle Park's variation was based on the Charleston and Antoinette Sibley's on the Cha-cha,[3] but these origins are not evident in the results: the steps are transformed in a typically Ashtonian way, especially in the Sibley solo, with its rather sinuous movements of the arms and upper body in counter-rhythm to the syncopated steps of legs and feet. The two men have a double variation, and the finale of the whole sequence is very exciting, with the dancers passing each other in mid-air as they do *fouetté sauté* into *arabesque*.

The Dance of the Guests lacks the slightly sinister atmosphere suggested by the music (called *Danse des nains* in the score) and that one remembers in the old Bolshoi version. The Spanish Dance, on the other hand, is very Bolshoi in feeling, with the two women snapping into low back-bends, and the Neapolitan Dance (again danced by Alexander Grant, partnering Merle Park this time) as rousing as ever.

Ashton's last act was a kind of homage to Ivanov, though with at least one typically Ashtonian device, the peeling off of the corps de ballet in diagonal lines led by Odette, who returned each time to Siegfried's embrace. In its dramatic aspects, Ashton's arrangement – or Helpmann's – was no more successful than the old, except that one did see Odette and Siegfried plunging to their deaths from a promontory above the lake rather than running off upstage right (where, by some convention, such suicides always appear to take place); before this, the tug-of-war between Siegfried and von Rothbart, with Odette in the middle, was most unseemly.

This is not the place to enter into a lengthy discussion of the production as a whole: the original plans for it had been laid under de Valois's regime, though Ashton as her successor must certainly accept responsibility for it. It must be said, in any case, that it was a very misguided recension: it tried to improve the theatrical viability of the ballet by making sense of the dramatic structure, but in the process destroyed the poetry of the ballet by spelling out what does not need to be made explicit. The tendency of previous Royal Ballet productions of *Swan Lake* had been towards the elaborate and the literal rather than the simple, poetic and allusive, and Helpmann compounded these errors, particularly in the violence done to the score – and it is in the music if anywhere that the answer to the problem of what to do with *Swan Lake* lies. Ashton's last act was of a piece precisely because he returned to Tchaikovsky's original, without Drigo's later interpolations – the trouble is that in doing so he eliminated the music for the last *pas de deux*, and finally Ivanov's version works better in the context of the whole ballet because it does have that necessary ingredient. All the same, Ashton's was a beautiful elegiac choreographic poem in its own right and one wishes that the Royal Ballet would preserve it as a separate item, perhaps in the touring repertory, or at least for the annual school performances.

Swan Lake: Ashton's *pas de quatre*; left to right, Antoinette Sibley, Brian Shaw, Merle Park, Graham Usher

Fortunately the basic Petipa–Ivanov choreography did survive in the touring company production (revised in 1965) and after MacMillan succeeded Ashton as director in 1970 that became the only Royal Ballet production – at first with Ashton's fourth act but in 1972 the Ivanov was restored. Of Ashton's other additions, the new Waltz, the *pas de quatre*, and the Neapolitan and Spanish Dances were retained – the *pas de quatre*, in handsome new purple costumes by Leslie Hurry, was eventually moved to the third act, where it musically belongs and hence works much better, allowing for the restoration of the Petipa *pas de trois* (which it had supplanted) to Act I.

The quatercentenary of Shakespeare's birth fell in April 1964, and it was decided that the Royal Ballet should celebrate the event with a triple bill consisting of the revival of *Hamlet*, a new ballet by Kenneth MacMillan based on themes from the sonnets, *Images of Love*, and a third work by Ashton. He again considered the possibility of *The Tempest*, but finally settled on *A Midsummer Night's Dream*. He was of course very familiar with it, having been involved in productions both of Shakespeare's play and of Purcell's opera based on it, *The Fairy Queen*, at various times in his career. He decided to do his version in Victorian style, using Mendelssohn's music, as had the Old Vic production in 1954 for which he had choreographed the Nocturne – though both that production and Ashton's ballet owed much to Tyrone Guthrie's *Dream* at the Old Vic in 1937, with designs by Oliver Messel and choreography (to Mendelssohn's music) by Ninette de Valois, in which Helpmann played Oberon to Vivien Leigh's Titania.

Ashton had no idea when he set out of doing anything but a straightforward narrative ballet that 'followed the play very closely and tried to illustrate its meaning in movement'; he gave John Lanchbery a copy of Lamb's *Tales from Shakespeare* and asked him to prepare a synopsis – he would do the same and then they would compare the results and put together a libretto based on them. He also said that there was a lot of music by Mendelssohn that they could use to fill out any parts of the action not covered in the incidental music, but Lanchbery felt that they would lay themselves open to criticism by interpolating other material, and besides he found that Mendelssohn had written so much music for the play, both early and later in his life, that he decided to set himself the task of using music only from that source; working in close collaboration, with Ashton, he pieced together a score that satisfied this requirement, with the single exception of a few transitional bars that he had to compose himself. After the ballet was completed, Ashton asked him what other music he had used and was surprised to be given the answer, none.[4]

Ashton cast Antoinette Sibley, then moving up into ballerina status, as Titania, and opposite her a young dancer, Anthony Dowell, who had made a great impression a couple of years earlier in a variation from Bournonville's *Napoli* divertissements and was beginning to take such leading roles as the Country Boy in *La Fête étrange*. Ashton began with the pantomime scene of their quarrel (which

The Dream: Scherzo.
Keith Martin as Puck

begins the dramatic action of the ballet), without being specific about the reason for it – in fact they thought at first they were cast as one of the pairs of mortal lovers. Gradually it became clear who they were meant to be, but Ashton continued to be more concerned with the mime than anything else, showing the scene to outsiders to see if they could follow the action: Dowell in fact began to assume that he would not have very much dancing to do, but then quite late in the rehearsals Ashton made first the Scherzo with its virtuoso passages for both Oberon and Puck (Keith Martin), and then the *pas de deux* for Titania and Oberon to the Nocturne. When it came to the point he made this last dance with characteristic speed in two or three rehearsals – the only part that gave them trouble was something that Ashton had seen in a dream, the moment when Oberon promenades Titania in *arabesque* and she bends her torso down as she turns in towards him, which took them a whole day to figure out.[5]

Ashton worked hard to create the Victorian atmosphere without simply relying on the décor and costumes and the music. Much of the choreography is consciously in a 19th-century style: the dances for the corps de ballet are very clearly the product of his 'private lessons' from Marius Petipa, and there are also direct references to the iconography of the Romantic ballet – individual dancers take up poses from

340

lithographs of Taglioni and at one point four fairies form a famous group from *The Pas de Quatre* of 1845. The décor and costumes were commissioned from Henry Bardon and David Walker respectively, both of them students of Lila de Nobili: Bardon designed an elaborate woodland glade and Walker's costumes, especially those for the fairies, in greenish yellow, were beautiful.

When the triple bill was presented on 2 April the critical reception of *The Dream* followed the usual pattern for a new Ashton ballet, with occasional exceptions like *Fille*. The most notable event of the evening, it seemed, was Nureyev's double appearance in the other two ballets. Ashton was as always praised for his craftsmanship but oddly enough even Dance and Dancers, whose critics had an honourable record of appreciating such ballets as *Daphnis and Chloe* and *The Two Pigeons*, which their colleagues dismissed, underestimated *The Dream*'s other qualities. Dance and Dancers, in fact, had previously suggested, at the time plans for *The Dream* were first announced, that the Royal Ballet should acquire Balanchine's two-act version, and now Clive Barnes compared Ashton's unfavourably to it: Balanchine's, he wrote, was 'the more profound, and therefore the more Shakespearean. Probably the reason for this is simply that Balanchine was fulfilling an ambition whereas Ashton, I felt, was merely fulfilling a commission'.[6] Such was the general tenor of reviews at the time – that Ashton had come up with another *pièce d'occasion*, pretty enough, but without lasting value; and perhaps Ashton's own feelings about the ballet were not very different.

There is no need to belabour the fact that, at this writing, *The Dream* has lasted for over ten years and seems likely to become one of the perennial classics of the Royal Ballet, and of other companies into whose repertories it has passed. It has come to be seen as one of Ashton's masterpieces, another of the great ballets of his maturity on the subject of human nature. Comparisons with Balanchine's version are perhaps pointless – suffice it to say that in Balanchine there is no *pas de deux* for Oberon and Titania (who has to be content with a 'Cavalier' with no other function – the male dancer relegated once again to the role of a mere *porteur*), whereas in Ashton the Nocturne crowns the whole work, one of Ashton's most profound statements on the nature of love. In condensing the story he had made their quarrel and reconciliation the main action, with the misadventures of the two pairs of mortal lovers as sub-plot, but both serve to illustrate various aspects of the central subject – love, 'its confusions, its diversity, its changefulness, its power to educate and transform'.[7] The mortal lovers find it easy to transfer their affections from one partner to another under the influence of Oberon's magic; the same power teaches Titania where her love truly lies when she sees the foolishness of her temporary infatuation for the transfigured Bottom. The *pas de deux* encapsulates a whole relationship, 'the astonishment of sensual discovery',[8] the stormy conflict of wills, Oberon's subduing of Titania's rebellious spirit to his own, constancy attained in a final perfect union on equal terms – and all through dance imagery, sudden shifts in direction, an *arabesque* that melts from pride into submissiveness, Oberon's rocking of her horizontal body from side to side. 'All the comedic disruptions are brought

The Dream: Antoinette
Sibley as Titania,
Anthony Dowell as
Oberon in the
Nocturne *pas de deux*

into harmony by what the royal pair discover about themselves in that dance'.[9]

One should not, of course, forget the brilliance with which those disruptions are handled in the ballet, one of the few in which the audience actually laughs out loud. As in *Fille*, Ashton's wit is always tempered by his humanity; though the mortal lovers are foolish, they are not held up to ridicule. He makes hilarious use of supported adagio, turning its conventions upside down, so that movements normally used to bring people together seem to be flinging them asunder, the accepted shorthand for amorous fulfilment is distorted into petulant rejection. There is no funnier passage in ballet than the *pas de quatre* in which people keep getting picked up and put down again out of the way – one laugh tops another as Ashton rings the changes on this simple comic device. The 'Fred step' is also turned to comic effect when done, very fast, by the fairy who finds herself alone on the stage at the end of the Scherzo and does not know which way to turn.

342

Obviously in a one-act ballet, even an unusually long one, something of the original play had to go, and Ashton reduced the roles of the 'mechanicals' to the minimum, except for Bottom himself, who is strongly characterised (as might be expected in a role made for Alexander Grant). Once again Ashton used a balletic convention for a surprising and comic purpose, by putting him, when transformed into an ass, on point. The brief mime scene when he is returned to human form – 'I have had a dream' – brings to mind Ralph Richardson's unforgettable playing of that moment in the 1937 Guthrie production.

The Dream is sure of a place in contemporary ballet history if only because it initiated a new partnership, Sibley and Dowell, that was to become second only to that of Fonteyn and Nureyev in popular esteem. Many others have danced these roles – Nureyev himself has had a try at Oberon – but no one has managed to emulate Sibley's swiftness and her impersonation of a half-wild creature, nor the silken fluidity of Dowell's phrasing.

The Dream: Antoinette Sibley as Titania, Alexander Grant as Bottom

Monotones: Gymnopédies: Left to right, Anthony Dowell, Vyvyan Lorrayne, Robert Mead

In Ashton's second season he continued the policy of reviving works from the Diaghilev era with productions of *Les Biches* and the *Polovtsian Dances* from *Prince Igor*. Even with Nureyev as a Polovtsian Warrior the latter never came to life, but the revival of *Les Biches* was a project very close to Ashton's heart. He felt that Nijinska, who had influenced him so strongly, had not received due recognition as one of the great modern choreographers, and he personally invited her to come over and mount *Les Biches* for the Royal Ballet (Ninette de Valois had also wanted it for the repertory). He sat in on rehearsals, to ensure that a suitably respectful atmosphere was maintained – 'at first,' he says, 'some of the dancers were inclined not to take her seriously, but by the end they all adored her'. He also attended all the costume fittings to see that everything was done properly. Nijinska reminded him that in Paris many years ago he used to sit and watch all of her rehearsals, and said to him, 'Tu es mon fils'.

That season *Romeo and Juliet* finally entered the repertory, in the version by MacMillan, and the touring company did their new, but traditional, *Swan Lake*. Ashton himself had no time to embark on any major work, but when the annual gala performance in aid of the Royal Ballet Benevolent Fund came round on 24 March 1965, he did a short ballet for the occasion. He had always loved the *Gymnopédies* of Erik Satie, ever since he had seen Nemchinova and Dolin dance to the first of them in one of their seasons at the Coliseum in the late 20s, and that was the music he chose. In the summer of 1964 Merce Cunningham and Dance Company had made their first appearances in London, and Ashton had seen one programme in which they danced Cunningham's ballet to Satie's *Nocturnes*, with its pure white costumes by Robert Rauschenberg. Ashton had particularly enjoyed that piece – 'it was poetic', he told Cunningham, 'and I like dances to be poetic' –

and it may be that he had stored away his impression of it somewhere in his mind, and that in a way it inspired him to do a pure white Satie ballet of his own. Not that there is any other similarity between the works, and certainly no question of 'influence', but it is characteristic of Ashton that he is open to such stimuli. It may well have amused him to produce a work that was surely contemporary enough in flavour to satisfy his severest critics, and yet was as deeply rooted in the *danse d'école* as anything he had ever composed.

All the same, it again seems likely that Ashton thought of the new piece as a little *pièce d'occasion* that would serve the purpose of providing a novelty for a gala – no one was more surprised than he when the result turned out to be another masterpiece, however small in scale. The *pas de trois*, which he called *Monotones*, was danced by Vyvyan Lorrayne, Anthony Dowell and Robert Mead, three of the company's purest classical dancers, in white costumes – leotards and tights, with glittering belts and skull caps – designed by Ashton himself. The austerity of the piece was absolute – Ashton's personal classicism distilled to an even purer essence than in *Symphonic Variations*, with all superfluities eliminated.

As so often, Ashton took his cue from the music: 'The Gymnopédies,' writes Rollo H Myers in his study of Erik Satie, 'are three in number – each one representing a different "facet", as it were, of the basic idea which gives them unity but of which nevertheless each Gymnopédie supplies a variant'.[10] Choreographically, *Monotones* is similarly built on a basic motif, of *arabesques* and *attitudes*: the first *Gymnopédie* begins with the woman on the floor in a split, with her head bent over to her front knee. The two men raise her upright in this position and slowly turn her round between them (this time Ashton had been dreaming of 'a chicken on a spit'); later there is a variation with the woman being turned in the reverse position – extreme *arabesque penchée*, with the torso bending forward. Pursuing the idea still further, Ashton made a further variation, an extension of the new promenade he had introduced in *The Dream*: the woman takes a supported *développé à la seconde*, and is turned by one of her partners under her own arm into *arabesque* – the movement is almost impossible to describe, in fact you don't believe your eyes when you see it. A more complex variation still is the passage where the woman is turned *en attitude* at arm's length by one partner while the other moves backwards underneath the bridge formed by their arms, comes round to the front again and, taking her foot, elongates the leg into *arabesque* – and even this does not exhaust the changes Ashton rings on the basic idea: the woman is promenaded yet again in the same manner, with the other man coming through from the back this time, ending with the three of them in identical *attitude* positions. The sculptural groupings into which these movements resolve themselves seem to refer directly to similar ones in *Symphonic Variations*.

By the same token, *Monotones* explores other of Ashton's favourite movement themes. The woman 'walks on air' lifted just off the ground by one man while the other does a *pirouette* finishing off centre (again, compare *Symphonic Variations*), and the whole is repeated, switching partners. Yet another reference to the earlier

345

ballet comes in the moments when the three dancers run about the stage with hands linked (in which formation they do *fouettés* into *arabesque*, one of the men jumping). As always, Ashton uses the simplest steps to produce the most striking effects: for example, 'the simple *changement* from a left to a right diagonal, performed three abreast' described by Arlene Croce – the woman does hers on point. 'It comes, hair-raisingly, on a key-change in the second Gymnopédie, and the powerful effect it has is out of all proportion to the humility of its means. It's like a shock to the senses'.[11]

Miss Croce also mentions the 'there-you-have-it' gesture of the upturned palms that occurs several times in the dance (it's a less emphatic version of the Blue Skater's gesture in *Les Patineurs*) and that seems to confirm the 'saltimbanque' character of the costumes, as though Ashton thought of the dancers as celestial acrobats. The choreography shares with the music the quality of seeming to extend into infinity, in space and time: there is no attempt to build to a climax, the dance and the music both just stop, but with no sense of finality. (Alexander Grant, in conversation, suggested that it was no coincidence that the creation of the piece happened at the time of the arrival of the first astronauts on the moon.)

Any attempt to describe isolated events in the dance in this way inevitably violates one of its most salient qualities, its seamlessness. To quote Arlene Croce again, 'the continuity of [Ashton's] line is like that of a master draftsman whose pen never leaves the paper'.[12]

Monotones was an instant success and clearly had to be given a permanent place in the repertory. The problem was that except on gala occasions when the programme could legitimately consist of a number of short items it was too brief to stand by itself. Ashton therefore augmented it with a companion piece under the same title when it entered the repertory just over a year later, on 25 April 1966 – both sets were given, with the first in order of composition being danced second.

The obvious choice of music for the other set was the *Trois Gnossiennes*, Satie's next published composition after the *Gymnopédies* – another product of what Rollo Myers calls his 'Trinitarian' obsession, reflected also in Ashton's use of the *pas de trois* form, this time for two women and one man (Antoinette Sibley, Georgina Parkinson and Brian Shaw). In a contrast that Sibley calls typical of Ashton, the new dance was 'earthly', as opposed to the 'heavenly' feeling of the original set. The costumes, again by Ashton, were a sea-green version of the white ones for the first set – later the colour was changed to terra cotta, certainly more in keeping with the idea, but after a time reverted to the green again. The basic material, and the manner of its development, were similar to those of the *Gymnopédies*: in both, for instance, there are passages where movements are repeated in faster tempo. Indeed, the rhythmic subtlety of both *Monotones* is extraordinary – although one never loses the sense of the music's steady pulse, Ashton plays with it, and against it, using *rubato* and counter-rhythms. Again, there are echoes of *Symphonic Variations* in the groupings, and in the use of the 'at rest' position from that ballet, one foot crossed over the other, even a suggestion of the characteristic *Symphonic Variations port de bras.* There is also an almost direct quotation from Balanchine's *Apollo* when the dancers walk forward side by side with one hand under the next person's chin.

A slightly different note, however, from the first trio is introduced in the opening pose when the dancers are found with one hand held in front of their eyes, which led Peter Williams to detect a dramatic, or at any rate emotional, situation – 'the three seem on the brink of experience which will be climactic in their lives. . .

Monotones:
Gnossiennes: Left to
right, Antoinette
Sibley, Brian Shaw,
Georgina Parkinson

whereas in Gymnopédies there is a magnetic attraction between the three figures, in Gnossiennes there is a physical attraction which doesn't work out . . .'[13] It would be rash to suggest that Ashton, of all choreographers, wished to eliminate all emotional colouring even from such an 'abstract' work as this: he himself has written, 'I think that ballets without librettos, popularly known as abstract ballets, though appearing to convey nothing but the exercise of pure dancing, should have a basic idea which is not necessarily apparent to the public, or a personal fount of emotion from which the choreography springs. Otherwise, in my opinion, a cold complexity emerges which ceases to move an audience'.[14]† All the same, it seems unprofitable to try to figure out whether Ashton had in mind a contrast between spiritual and physical love, or whatever, when making the two *Monotones* – it is the dancers' spatial relations that absorb one's interest, things like their movement one after the other across the stage from *arabesque*, dropping across to a kneeling position, then coming up into *arabesque* again (this too may refer to a passage in *Apollo*), or such groupings as one where the man stands between the two women, holding each by the hand as she pulls away in a stretched *arabesque*, or another where he supports them both in *arabesque* as they stand in front of him, the lifted foot resting on his shoulder.

As before, the simplicity of the means is extraordinary, as in a walking step the dancers perform several times, sliding into a lunge forward with the arms coming down from above the head into a typically extreme *croisé* position (this is one of the steps that Ashton varies by accelerating and syncopating the tempo). Ashton's remarks about his use of the space in *Scènes de ballet* have already been quoted (see page 222): in that work the asymmetry of the geometrical figures overlays the constancy of the symmetry implied in the hierarchy of ballerina and partner, soloists and corps de ballet that is inherent in Stravinsky's score. In fact it was the earlier ballet, *Symphonic Variations*, that did away with the traditional imperial arrangement of the ballerina in the middle, with her male support, backed up by the corps – it is almost like a Cunningham piece in that it has no centre, the six dancers move freely in relation to each other and to the space as a whole, with each one remaining his own centre, so to speak. In *Monotones* Ashton explored this kind of spatial disposition still further – significantly, the dances work less well on a small stage like that of Sadler's Wells, they need the expanse of a large stage properly to make their effect.

On 21 April 1965, a month after the gala performance at which the first *Monotones* received its première, the company opened once again at the Metropolitan Opera House in New York. The new work was not included in the repertory but it was otherwise very rich in Ashton ballets – *The Dream*, the revived *Daphnis* and *A Wedding Bouquet*, as well as *Marguerite and Armand* and the perennial *Patineurs*;

† See Appendix A.

Les Noces: Beriosova,
Nijinska and Ashton
at rehearsal

the new *Swan Lake* was also given. As had happened with others of his ballets, *The Dream* got a more enthusiastic reception in New York than in London, a reception that set the seal on the new partnership of Sibley and Dowell, who began to dance Oberon (and other roles) with increased authority as a result. It was apparent in New York that under Ashton's direction a new spirit had emerged in the company as a whole and transformed it – a kind of generosity, a sense of fulfilment that went right through the company from the principals to the corps de ballet, reflecting Ashton's stated concern with each and every dancer as an individual.

In the year that passed before the production of the second *Monotones* Ashton continued to be preoccupied with his duties as director, which of course included the supervision of the repertory, his own and other ballets. The 9th of June 1965 saw the first performance at Covent Garden of the slightly revised *Sylvia* by the touring company. The following Christmas, *Cinderella* was revived with beautiful new scenery and costumes by Henry Bardon and David Walker. There were changes in the choreography too that were nearly all for the better. The following February *Les Patineurs* was restored to the repertory in a version closer to the original (that is to say, the 'mirror' version – see page 288 – was finally dropped).

More important than any of these was the revival on 23 March 1966 of Nijinska's *Les Noces*, last performed by the de Basil company some thirty years previously. Towards the end of de Valois's directorship, Jerome Robbins had been invited to produce a new ballet for the Royal Ballet, and had decided on *Les Noces*. Preparations for this had gone as far as the completion of designs, by Sean Kenny, but no further. Robbins finally did his version for American Ballet Theatre, in 1965. However his failure to fulfil the commission for the Royal Ballet made possible the restoration of Nijinska's masterpiece. On the opening night Ashton made a short speech as he brought the choreographer out for a bow, calling her 'one of the greatest choreographers of our day,' at which Marie Rambert called out from her seat in the stalls, '*The* greatest!' Not long ago Ashton attended a performance of *Les Noces* at Covent Garden and said afterwards, 'It still knocks me out.' Later in the year (15 November 1966) there was another significant revival from the Diaghilev era, Balanchine's *Apollo*, which meant that the Royal repertory now included two of the most revolutionary and influential works of the late Diaghilev era.

These additions to the repertory are further proof of how seriously Ashton regarded his responsibilities as director: he certainly could not be accused of running the company as a showcase for his own work. In this connection, Ashton was deeply aware of the fact that the other great British choreographer of our time, Antony Tudor, was not represented in the repertory. Apart from the injustice to Tudor himself, the company was the poorer for it, and Ashton now moved to repair the omission by inviting Tudor to mount an original work for them. The ballet, *Shadowplay*, first given on 25 January 1967, was not entirely successful but clearly the work of a distinguished mind; it was, moreover, even more important than *The Dream* in the part it played in Anthony Dowell's development.

Ashton also wished to choreograph an original work for the touring company, which had acquired its own production of *The Dream* in a new décor by Peter Farmer. For a while he considered returning to the music of one of his earliest ballets, Mozart's *Les Petits riens*, but finally he settled on a modern score, the *Sinfonietta* of the Australian composer, Malcolm Williamson, which had been commissioned by the BBC in 1965.

The ballet, also called *Sinfonietta*, was given at Stratford-upon-Avon on 10 February 1967. Choreographically, the most important section was the slow movement, subtitled Elegy, which, Ashton says, was a kind of extension of the possibilities he had been exploring in *Monotones*. Many choreographers have set themselves the problem of making a dance for a woman partnered by several men, in which she seems never to touch the floor: the first part of Ashton's adagio was such an exercise, but there was less emphasis on the sheer mechanics than appears in some solutions – the dance was poetic in its suggestion of 'creatures belonging to the air rather than the earth'.[15] Following this there was a passage in which the five men swung the ballerina (Doreen Wells) around in a stretched second position, with one partner after the other taking over and turning her into *arabesque*.[16]

Ashton feels that this middle movement carried the whole work: the first, he says, 'wasn't up to much' – subtitled Toccata, it was a double *pas de deux* for Brenda Last and Kerrison Cooke, and Elizabeth Anderton and Richard Farley. The fast, intricate rhythms of the first pair, with their 'brilliant supported turns and scissor lifts',[17] contrasted with the more *legato* entries for the second. The third movement, Tarantella, had several passages of virtuoso dancing, particularly the swift solo variations for David Wall, punctuated by double turns in the air.[18]

The décor for *Sinfonietta* was the work of the Hornsey College of Art Light/ Sound Workshop, derived from a multiple they had made for the Lisson Gallery[19] – a perspex ball with holes in it that projected light from an inner source. Ashton had gone to an exhibition at the gallery and seen this object and wanted to use a giant version of it for his décor. The result, he felt, was actually rather distracting. The costumes were by Peter Rice – pure white for the Elegy, and very reminiscent of the original *Monotones*, even to the skull-caps; those for the outer movements were more obtrusive – horizontally striped in garish colours, they clashed with the softly melting projections of the décor.

Sinfonietta was dropped after its second season: it may well be that the banality of the music prevented its survival. In 1971 the Elegy was given as a separate number in a gala performance, and its revival was announced in 1973, but did not take place.

❈

Sinfonietta: Elegy. Doreen Wells lifted; David Wall, right

Almost another year passed before Ashton's next ballet. In the spring of 1967 the Royal Ballet again went to the United States, giving its first season at the new Metropolitan Opera House in Lincoln Center, followed by a coast-to-coast tour. The repertory included the new productions of *Cinderella* and *Swan Lake* (and, for the last time, the old one of *Sleeping Beauty*), as well as *Fille*, *The Dream* and *Monotones*. *Les Noces* was also given, to be met with by almost total incomprehension by the Hurok subscription audience. In December of 1967 the abbreviated version of *Sylvia* was done. It was followed on 9 January 1968 by *Jazz Calendar*, Ashton's first large-scale ballet for the main company since *The Dream* nearly four years before. Even so, it seems to have been put together as a last-minute stopgap when a novelty of some kind was needed at Covent Garden owing to the postponement of a scheduled new production of *Aïda* by the opera company.

Richard Rodney Bennett's *Jazz Calendar*, like Williamson's *Sinfonietta*, had been commissioned by the BBC, in 1964, and was a 'third-stream' jazz composition based on the children's rhyme:

> Monday's child is fair of face,
> Tuesday's child is full of grace,
> Wednesday's child is full of woe,
> Thursday's child has far to go.
> Friday's child is loving and giving,
> Saturday's child works hard for his living,
> And the child that is born on the Sabbath day
> Is bonny and blithe, and good and gay.

This seemed to Ashton like a good basis for a light ballet that would give varied opportunities to the dancers.

At the suggestion of Nigel Gosling, art critic of The Observer (as well as being, with his wife, Maude Lloyd, ballet critic under the joint pseudonym of 'Alexander Bland'), Ashton invited a young painter, Derek Jarman, to prepare some designs. Jarman had been studying scenic design with Peter Snow and Nicholas Georgiadis at the Slade, and approached the project without any preconceptions of what a ballet décor should be like. Ashton talked to him a little about the idea and gave him a tape of the music to listen to, and told him to come back a week later with some sketches. Jarman did so, and Ashton accepted some of them, but rejected others. This all happened late in November, and by the end of the first week in December the work of executing the scenery and costumes had begun – none too soon, with the première only a month away, a month, moreover, that included the Christmas and New Year holidays.[20]

Jarman's designs were very original – the only décor that remotely resembles them is Miró's for Massine's *Jeux d'enfants*, which similarly consisted of free-standing abstract shapes against a plain backcloth. During a brief prelude that

Bennett added to the score for the ballet, the curtain rose on a front-cloth depicting a page of a calendar with letters and numbers stencilled in day-glow colours.

The first number was a solo for Vergie Derman, who was first seen seated between two enormous red circles – Jarman's idea had been that they would be mirrors, and he wanted the dancer to carry two hand-mirrors. There was still a multi-faceted mirror on stage right, and certainly the choreography suggested a certain narcissism, as the dancer preened herself and admired the beauty of her limbs, rather in the manner of a high-fashion model.

'Tuesday' was a *pas de trois* for Merle Park, Anthony Dowell and Robert Mead, which immediately suggested at least in its male casting and costuming the possibility that Ashton was parodying his own *Monotones*: the two men were in white all-over tights decorated with black lines round one leg, while Park wore a similar costume with many layers of white fringe – all three wore skull caps. The décor was a pyramid of transparent plastic spheres. Some of the choreographic material was reminiscent of *Monotones*, too – supported promenades in *arabesque*, lifts alternating between one partner and another (the men functioning as 'bookends', as Anthony Dowell put it), the same linear designs culminating in a final triple-*arabesque* pose – but with the difference that everything was done at top speed. Ashton in fact disavows any intention of parodying his own or other choreographers' work in this ballet, but it was only to be expected that he would explore thematic material similar to what he was using in other ballets of this period, however different the emphasis.

The main feature of the 'Wednesday' décor was another cut-out circle, this time in green with black blobs on it; above it was an ominous stylised hand-like

Jazz Calendar:
Tuesday *pas de trois*.
Left to right, Robert
Mead, Merle Park,
Anthony Dowell

Jazz Calendar: Friday *pas de deux*. Nureyev and Sibley

shape. The dance had been choreographed for Beriosova, supported by four men, but she was injured before the opening and the role was taken over by Vyvyan Lorrayne, her long hair hanging loose like that of a Charles Addams cartoon figure. The number was a soulful, parody-blues variation on the adagio from *Sinfonietta*, at the end of which the woman was sucked down into the circle of crouching men, with one arm remaining above to give a last despairing gesture.

The fourth tableau, 'Thursday', was for Alexander Grant and a group of six women; the décor consisted simply of a pale blue triangle at stage centre – at times Grant's shadow was multiplied on the yellow backcloth as in a Fred Astaire number. The dance was one of those big-city-bustle numbers, with everyone jogging and jigging (including a passing reference to Scottish dancing); sometimes Grant's fast, frenetic movements were contrasted with the girls in slow motion. Various forms of travel were represented in figurations – subway, boat, plane. At the end Grant, left alone, made a spiralling descent to the floor and threw up his hands.

The décor for 'Friday' was a love-knot of red and blue forms twisted together: the same description could be applied to the dance itself, which was, naturally, a *pas de deux*, danced by Sibley and Nureyev in parti-coloured tights, half-red, half-blue. In an interview with Oleg Kerensky, Ashton said that he wished to show two people enjoying the sexual act, rather than love in any 'spiritual' sense.[21] The languorous, sensual intertwinings ended with the two dancers lying at full-length on the floor, head to head: then they took hold of each other and slid into a cheek-to-cheek position, still horizontal. According to Antoinette Sibley, Ashton left the tape at home on the day he was to begin work on this *pas de deux*, and had to choreograph to the accompaniment of 'any old blues' which he and the dancers sang, and later fitted the dance to the proper music.

As for 'Saturday', Ashton, feeling that 'no one works harder for their living than dancers',[22] decided to cast that section in the form of a men's ballet-class, which gave him the opportunity to make several private jokes as well as showing off the virtuosity of dancers like Michael Coleman, Keith Martin and Wayne Sleep, with Desmond Doyle as ballet-master. The décor was a skeletal obelisk at rear, with portable *barres* on each side, all made of aluminium tubing. Wayne Sleep was the latecomer on whom the teacher picked but who worked harder than anyone. Coleman did a classical combination across the floor and finished it off with a jazz step. At one point they all did the famous 'cow-hop' – the slow progression across the stage in *arabesque* from the second act of *Giselle* – and the scene ended with everyone doing double air turns until, one by one, they collapsed.

'Sunday' was led by a soloist – it was Marilyn Trounson, a junior member of the company who went on for Ann Jenner, who had been taken ill – wearing a multi-coloured version of the Tuesday girl's fringed costume. The décor consisted of bits from the previous scenes; similarly, in the choreography everyone came back and did their own movements, with Trounson kibitzing. The finale had everyone circling the stage in an apparent reference to the popular television show of the time, 'Sunday Night at the Palladium'.

Jazz Calendar was a great success with the public, and most of the critics, for that matter. To me it is one of the few Ashton ballets that are not merely slight, but inconsiderable. His craftsmanship, of course, never deserts him, but there is a fatal lack of conviction in what seems to be an attempt to show that he could be 'trendy' – it looks rather as one imagines his revue numbers during the 30s might look if we saw them today (in this respect it is not without significance that, before Ashton, Wendy Toye, a successful choreographer of London musicals, had expressed an interest in Bennett's music). It may be, as Peter Williams suggested, that the Friday *pas de deux* would seem more important if danced to other music,[23] but the man's bumps and grinds would always look out of place in an Ashton ballet. It is probably true that the music makes the ballet seem more dated than necessary – even so, some of the choreographic devices, such as the figurations in the Thursday sequence, belong to an outdated mode of dance composition. All this is not to suggest that Ashton lacks the contemporary spirit, but as we have seen, its clearest expression in his work comes, paradoxically, in ballets whose superficial appearance is quite traditional, such as *Fille* and *Two Pigeons* and *Daphnis*.

The best thing about *Jazz Calendar* was certainly Derek Jarman's designs, which were truly original and effortlessly typified the spirit of 'swinging London' in the late 60s as well as relating to various current trends in the visual arts in general.

Perhaps one day the whole thing may turn out to have an unexpected validity as a period piece.

In the following spring the Royal Ballet again went to New York. The condensed *Sylvia* was given, and *Marguerite and Armand*; *Symphonic Variations* was brought back to America for the first time since the company's first visit and this time met with a more sympathetic reception; *Fille* was made acceptable to the subscription public by the inclusion of *La Bayadère* in the same programme.

Early in the 1950s, when Julia Trevelyan Oman was studying stage design at the Royal College of Art, she had the idea of a ballet based on Elgar's *Enigma Variations*, and made a series of sketches as a project. Her professor, Hugh Casson, was so impressed that he wrote to Ninette de Valois about them; she asked Miss Oman to leave the folder of drawings at the stage-door. She did so, then six months passed with no further word, at the end of which time she asked to have them returned, after which she considered the matter closed. Ashton, however, had looked at them and found them interesting, but he did not think the time was ripe for such a ballet. For one thing, Elgar's music did not appeal to him. But the idea remained in the back of his mind, and in 1966, when he was looking for a subject, he remembered the sketches – he says that he had particularly not forgotten Miss Oman's covering note, written in brown ink on green paper – and in the meantime he had seen some of her work for plays and films and been impressed by it, so he telephoned her and asked her to come and see him and bring the original drawings if she still had them. He decided that now he would like to produce the ballet, although she insisted that she would have to make entirely new designs.[24]

The ballet was to follow Elgar's scheme of a series of portraits of his wife and friends. An earlier ballet by Frank Staff, presented by the combined Rambert and London Ballets early in the war, was an abstract treatment of the music, but Ashton rejected this kind of approach in favour of the more difficult one of finding a choreographic equivalent for Elgar's musical character studies, which could easily have become a mere divertissement, even granted that with some ingenuity he avoided making them all solos. Julia Trevelyan Oman's style of designing was a highly detailed naturalism, and to handle the work in this manner was even more of a challenge to the choreographer: when dancers represent actual personages, dressed in everyday clothes, albeit of another period, it may make the conventions of ballet less easy to accept. (One concession that was made for practical reasons was that the women's skirts were shorter than they would have been in actuality – though still quite a lot longer than usual in ballet, making it necessary for the dancers to have rehearsal skirts, to get used to the length.)

Oman and Ashton decided that the ballet should be set in Elgar's Worcestershire, at the time of the composition of the music (1898). In a programme note, Ashton outlined the circumstances: 'Some time before the action of the ballet takes place, Elgar had sent the score of the *Enigma Variations* to the famous conductor Richter in the hope of interesting him in the work. The characters, intimates and friends of the composer dance their individual variations, at the end of which a telegram arrives from Richter, addressed to their mutual friend Jaeger, agreeing to conduct the first performance.'

The décor divided the stage into two areas, showing both the exterior and the interior of Elgar's house – the garden on stage right, with a gateway at the back, and a hall on stage left with staircase leading to the upper rooms. At the front there was a scrim through which the opening tableau could be dimly seen as the curtain rose – this, says Miss Oman, had the function of carrying the audience from the Opera House back into Elgar's world and time.[25] The kind of attention that she gave to detail is evident from a memorandum she sent to Ashton: 'The area . . . round the heavy fringed large checked linen hammock is secluded: a patterned carpet from the drawing-room has been placed on the grass, under the hammock. By the hammock, wicker chairs with patterned cushions, a small table covered with a dark thick fringed cloth and a lace cloth over it. The table is dressed with a silver tea pot, cups, saucers, and a tea tray.' She insisted on equally meticulous detailing on the costumes – the men's character shoes, for instance, had to have authentic broguing, and when it was pointed out that the audience could not see it, she replied, 'The dancers can, and it will help them with their characters'.[26]

Enigma Variations (*My Friends Pictured Within*) was first given at Covent Garden on 25 October 1968. At first sight it seems like a complete departure from Ashton's previous work, mostly because some of the details of the action as well as the overall staging are naturalistic, almost in the manner of a play. This is by no means a superficial quality, but an important part of the ballet's poetry; at the same time it has a meditative feeling rare in the work of any choreographer. It seems possible that Ashton at least conceived the action as being simultaneously interior and exterior in another sense – that it takes place in the memory of the protagonist rather than in actuality.

But *Enigma*, no less than any other of Ashton's ballets, is firmly based on the classic technique, and shows his belief in its expressive powers. It has been suggested that one work of his that it does resemble is *A Wedding Bouquet*, and this is true to the extent that both ballets comprise a series of character vignettes in an accurately observed social milieu: interestingly, however, Antony Tudor made the comment to me that *Enigma* reminded him very strongly of *The Lord of Burleigh*. Characteristically, Mr Tudor would not elaborate but, without first-hand knowledge of the earlier ballet, one may suppose that the similarity lies both in the episodic treatment and in the very English feeling of both ballets. One may add that there are moments when *Enigma* may remind one of Tudor himself, not just in its creation of period and psychological atmosphere, but even in movement (the way the two men in 'Nimrod' turn their upper torsos as they slide the foot forward into 4th position, arms held close to the sides). This does not stop *Enigma* from being one of Ashton's most personal ballets.

His preliminary research had been just as painstaking as the designer's – as always, he read all the relevant books, especially the memoirs of such people as Mrs Richard Powell (the original 'Dorabella'). The composer's own descriptive notes (from which I have quoted in the following paragraphs) were of course invaluable.[27]

The opening of the ballet finds some of the characters assembled in a frozen tableau, out of which Elgar (Derek Rencher) is the first to move as the music begins – he walks about studying his score while his wife, 'whose life was a romantic and delicate inspiration', (Svetlana Beriosova) watches anxiously from the top of the stairs. A few autumn leaves drift from the trees. Dorabella (Antoinette Sibley) arrives, interposes herself between Elgar and his score and embraces him before going into the house. Elgar's wife comes downstairs and hovers solicitously about him – typically, Ashton uses one of the most simple ballet steps for this (*pas de chat*, *pas de bourrée* from side to side); they dance a brief *pas de deux*, ending with Elgar standing, still preoccupied with his own thoughts, while she kneels beside him holding his hand against her cheek.

The next three numbers form a small gallery of English (or rather British) eccentrics: first, Hew David Steuart-Powell (Stanley Holden), 'a well-known amateur pianist and a great player of chamber music', who rides in on a bicycle (it came from the collection of the Victoria and Albert Museum, on condition that a replica would be made for the ballet if it were a success). Giving the bicycle to a gardener to hold, he lights his pipe, takes out his watch, realises he is late for an appointment, and remounts, riding off standing *en arabesque* on one pedal. Richard Baxter Townshend (Brian Shaw), the author of the 'Tenderfoot' books, comes in on a tricycle, laboriously pedalling in time with the music; slightly deaf, he has to use an ear-trumpet and is teased by some children who are playing in the garden. He too rides off and is followed by William Meath Baker (Alexander Grant), 'a country squire, gentleman and scholar', who rushes on to give everyone their instructions for the day (as was his habit), sliding on his heels like Widow Simone, before disappearing up the stairs. These three solos were character-dances almost in the Massine manner: it might be better if they were not bunched together in this way, but of course the sequence is dictated by the music.

The next two characters, Richard P Arnold (Robert Mead) and Isabel Fitton (Vyvyan Lorrayne), were brought together in a *pas de deux* by Ashton, though there is no evidence of their being romantically linked in real life – he was the son of Matthew Arnold and she 'a Malvern lady, an amateur viola player'. Ashton took his cue, perhaps, from Elgar's comment that her variation is 'pensive and, for a moment, romantic'. This is one of the passages that could be said to be reminiscent of Tudor (whose *Jardin aux lilas* was also in rehearsal at the time), except that Ashton instinctively casts his dance in a classic form, with the two having individual 'variations' (in the balletic sense), followed by another duet before they return to their places, she in the hammock and he at her side. And the idiom is Ashtonian, with lifts in which there are little skittering movements and sudden changes of direction. Again as they finish a few leaves fall: a familiar enough device

– indeed, as Ashton pointed out, he used it himself in *Rinaldo and Armida* – but in the context it is as potent as a similar image in an Ozu film, a kind of punctuation, linking one memory with the next.

The seventh variation, Arthur Troyte Griffith (Anthony Dowell), 'a well-known architect in Malvern', is an explosive solo with leaps that change direction in mid-air, brusque *chaîné* turns, and a final gesture with the hands to indicate his slamming down the lid of his piano in anger at what Elgar calls his own 'maladroit essays' to master that instrument.[28] In contrast is the solo for Winifred Norbury (Georgina Parkinson) with its spiralling turns, in which 'her gracious personality is sedately shown'. Her walk upstage, twitching her skirt from side to side, may indeed be a direct quotation from *The Lord of Burleigh* (the swinging of the ladies' crinolines that Beaumont found so objectionable).

This leads into the famous 'Nimrod' variation, named for Elgar's publisher A J Jaeger (Desmond Doyle), which Elgar called 'the record of a long summer evening talk, when my friend discoursed eloquently on the slow movements of Beethoven'. The dance begins as a duet for the two men, which Ashton says he tried to do 'like question and answer',[29] then becomes a trio when they are joined by Elgar's wife. Here the further distillation of the essence of Ashton's personal classicism in *Monotones* opened the way for its further use as a poetic resource: the dance is basically a simple sequence of *arabesques*, *tombés* and *pas de basque*; beautiful lifts in

359

which first one man, then the other, swings the woman round close to the floor
or picks her up just off the ground and puts her down on the other side of him;
the running motif from *Symphonic Variations* is used, too. With such simple
means Ashton achieves an eloquent statement of 'the voiceless language of sympathy'. (To complete the quotation, from E M Forster's *Howards End*, 'The
affections are more reticent than the passions, and their expression more subtle' –
which may be one reason why it is so rarely attempted in ballet.) At the end of the
trio the three walk forward and raise their hands in a questioning, or even im-
ploring gesture. According to Antoinette Sibley, Ashton wanted Dorabella to be
in this section, but she was ill at the time and could not rehearse. It is hard to imagine the dance with her in it – it would have been very different both in form and,
presumably, content. (It is not quite clear whether Elgar's feeling for her is meant
to be merely affectionate, or something stronger – he kisses her lightly on the lips
at her first entrance.)

It is Dorabella's variation that follows, one of Ashton's most captivating
pieces of choreography, with swift *batterie* and little *changements* – she continually
repeats the rhythm of the tripping, syncopated figure that Elgar uses to convey
the hesitation in her speech, even when it does not occur in the music. Both here
and in the Troyte solo Ashton has made dances that work as classical variations
as well as revealing character.

The ballet returns to its comic mood with the next entry, George Robertson
Sinclair (Wayne Sleep), 'late organist of Hereford Cathedral': the music refers to

an incident in which his bulldog Dan fell into the river Wye. Ashton at first wanted Sleep to wear a cap with a bulldog mask attached to it, but later gave up the idea. However, there are still suggestions of an intended identification of man and animal in such things as his little pawing gestures.

Ashton cheated a little in his use of the variation depicting Basil G Nevinson (Leslie Edwards), 'an amateur cello player of distinction [and] a serious and devoted friend', by having him sit at one side playing his cello as the accompaniment to a dance for Elgar and his wife, continuing the theme of their earlier duet – their mutual devotion, and her sadness in realising that her love for him cannot reach him in his essential isolation (she reaches out to touch him and misses by a finger-tip's length as he moves away, lost in thought).

The last solo is that for Lady Mary Lygon, represented in the score by three asterisks, 'a lady who was, at the time of the composition, on a sea voyage' (Deanne Bergsma). Her anonymity in the score may signify that she stands for several women whom Elgar had loved, and also for something more abstract – an ideal towards which the protagonist aspires, what used to be called in ballets about artists 'his Muse'. In dance terms, the solo rather recalls Loïe Fuller, as the dancer makes billowing shapes with her draperies. Ashton has said that he meant these to

Enigma Variations: taking the photograph

Enigma Variations:
Ashton rehearsing
Derek Rencher and
Beriosova

convey the idea of the sail of a ship, which, together with the rocking movements of the dance, would suggest that she was on a voyage.[30]

In the finale all the characters are brought together. Ashton invented an incident to provide a climax, the arrival of the telegram. Its content can of course, be conveyed only in the programme note, but it is in any case unimportant – the telegram is symbolic, a message from a higher power that will transform the actors' lives. A minor but real flaw, however, is the participation of Lady Mary Lygon in this scene – after it has been established that she is present only in Elgar's memory or imagination. Ashton agrees, but says her presence was necessary for the purposes of symmetry. The ballet ends with the taking of a group photograph (as in *A Wedding Bouquet*), again at least partly symbolic, recording the moment for ever in the memory of the protagonist. (The ending always sounds a little abrupt, because the ballet uses the original conclusion of the score and not the more extended one Elgar wrote at Jaeger's suggestion.)

Inevitably, *Enigma Variations* made people think of Chekhov – its combination of humorous character studies with the elegiac evocation of time past; certainly the ballet is extraordinary in the way it has several layers of meaning. It may well be said to deal with such larger matters as the essential loneliness of the creative

362

artist and the twilight of empire, but it does so in terms of intimate, domestic detail, a walk in the garden, the turning of the pages of a book, the arrival of a telegram, the photograph. Just as British actors seem to have an instinctive understanding of the life portrayed in Chekhov's plays, so the Royal Ballet dancers created an absolutely convincing circle of friends: Ashton says that Elgar's daughter came to see the ballet and said, 'I don't understand how you did it – they were all exactly like that. . . And I never liked any of them, except Troyte.' Yet these remarkable impersonations are achieved with the minimum amount of character make-up – a change of hairstyle, a moustache, a pair of glasses. Derek Rencher's Elgar, deliberately understated, with very little actual dancing to do, is still the focus of the whole ballet; Doyle's Jaeger is equally restrained, equally moving. The Lady, Elgar's wife, was certainly the greatest role Ashton created for Beriosova, and one that used to perfection her sad, reflective quality and her ability to make a simple gesture speak volumes, as when she stands at the table leafing through a book (or a score), closes it, and holds it up to her breast. The ballet is almost unimaginable without these three central performances, though in fact Monica Mason has frequently danced Beriosova's part – but, wonderful artist though she is, there is something about *her* personality that makes the character seem very forthright and managing. (John Percival mentioned that he had made a similar observation to a music critic, who replied, 'You mean that Mason dances the real person and Beriosova dances the music Elgar wrote'.[31]) Other roles have seen more successful replacements, but altogether the original cast had an ensemble quality worthy of a great acting company.

Only a poet could have conceived a ballet like *Enigma*, and only the audacity of genius could have brought it off, this use of the resources of classic ballet to achieve a nobility of discourse and carry a weight of metaphor that many would say are beyond its scope – but it is his faith in those resources that makes Ashton a great poet. In the spring of 1969 the Royal Ballet danced in New York for the third consecutive year, and *Enigma* made a great impression – it is the only Ashton ballet to be included in Lincoln Kirstein's *Movement and Metaphor*, which tells the history of ballet in terms of fifty seminal works. A film of the ballet was made at Covent Garden early in 1969. Directed by James Archibald, it is no more satisfactory than most filmed ballets, but does preserve some record of the performances of all of the original cast except Antoinette Sibley, whose part was danced, as often in the theatre, by Ann Jenner.

For some years there had been talk of a new production of *The Sleeping Beauty* to replace the 1946 version whose Oliver Messel décors had seemed so sumptuous after the years of wartime austerity but were beginning to look rather shabby. When the new one finally materialised, on 17 December 1968, the overall production was not by Ashton, but by Peter Wright, with 'new and additional choreography' by Ashton, décor by Henry Bardon, and costumes by Lila de

Nobili and Rostislav Douboujinsky. It was, on the whole, a failure, in spite of the very real beauty of some of Bardon's scene painting: the idea of placing the story in a kind of fairy-tale mediaeval period, rather in the Pre-Raphaelite manner (the idea, apparently, was de Nobili's) entirely contradicted the music.

The first of Ashton's additions was a new solo for one of the fairies (the Fairy of Joy – they were all given new names again) in the Prologue, to the 'Sapphire' variation in 5/4 tempo from the Jewel Fairies' *pas de quatre* in Act III, not used by Petipa in the original production. It was tailor-made for Georgina Parkinson, a brilliant number in which she circled the stage in swift jumps that changed direction in mid-air. In Act I Ashton made a new Garland Dance that was no improvement on the old, although it was now done by both men and women and given some dramatic point by serving as a background for the entrances of the four Princes, suitors to the Princess Aurora. In Act II the Prince was given the kind of moody adagio solo that has become mandatory in the full-length classics (to the Sarabande from Act III), and at the end of this act, after the Awakening, Ashton made a very beautiful *pas de deux* to the entr'acte music, also discarded by Petipa, that follows the Panorama – beautiful, but unsuitable, though it could be said to express in dance terms a passage from Perrault's tale:

> Then, as the spell had come to its end, the Princess awoke and, looking at him more tenderly than would seem proper for a first glance:
>
> 'Is it you, my Prince?' she said. 'You have been a long time coming.'
>
> Delighted by these words, and still more so by the tone in which they were uttered, the Prince hardly knew how to express his joy and gratitude. He swore that he loved her better than life itself . . .
>
> In short, they went on talking to each other for four hours, and still had not said half the things they wanted to say.[32]

The *pas de deux* bore a fleeting resemblance to the one from Act II of Nureyev's *Nutcracker* (first given in the previous season), with the two dancers both doing the same broad, sweeping steps, rather than the man supporting the woman, but as it went on the dance images became more typically Ashtonian, with *sissonne* lifts, swiftly reversing direction, in double time against the even flow of the music. Perhaps because it was first choreographed for Sibley and Dowell, it was also rather similar in style to the Nocturne from *The Dream* – another way of saying that it did not fit into *The Sleeping Beauty*, unlike Ashton's other additions which so carefully preserve the correct style. Especially now that the production as a whole has been supplanted, the *pas de deux* could perhaps be preserved as a separate item.

In Act III Ashton recast his 'Florestan' *pas de trois* under the title 'Gold and Silver' for two men and one woman (Jennifer Penney, Brian Shaw and Keith Martin), giving the men a joint variation and preserving the Petipa variation from 'Florestan' for the woman. This was not a very satisfactory arrangement and before long the old *pas de trois* was restored, though still under the new title.

Dramatically, the new production had as many inconsistencies as the old – for instance, the old woman who gave Aurora the fatal spindle did not turn out to be Carabosse in disguise. There were many cuts, some of them minor in terms of actual duration but still devastating to the structure – as Arlene Croce wrote, they shortened 'the clock-time of the ballet but not that other time in which the ballet happens in the imagination of the audience'.[33] In what was left, however, no actual violence was done to Petipa's choreography, which may have seemed a small mercy at the time but now would be cause for deep gratitude.

The new *Beauty* was taken to New York the following spring, and so was *Jazz Calendar*, which, predictably, did not travel well. Once again, there was no new Ashton ballet during 1969: his next work was another *pièce d'occasion*, made specifically for the Royal Ballet's Benevolent Fund Gala on 9 February 1970, a *pas de deux*, the first of several he was to choreograph during the next few years.

The dance was called *Lament of the Waves*, a translation of the title of the music by Gérard Masson, which Ashton had heard at a concert, and which attracted him because although it used many of the compositional devices common in contemporary music, it was still recognisably in the tradition of French composers like Debussy and Ravel. There was also, as Ashton says, his own 'fascination with

The Sleeping Beauty: Sibley and Dowell in Ashton's 'Awakening' *pas de deux*

water' – the subject-matter of the dance was simply stated in the programme as 'Two young lovers are drowned'. He decided to cast two very young dancers, Marilyn Trounson and Carl Myers, partly because if he used somebody better-known it would become a ballet 'about Sibley and Dowell drowning', for instance, and he wanted the dancers to keep the anonymity of 'dead bodies lying on a beach'.

At the beginning the illusion of their sinking down to the ocean-floor was achieved by having them descend on a lift, and later in more purely choreographic terms, as when they stood in double *arabesque* and slowly bent the supporting leg. Reaching stage level, they drifted about in eddying turns, but the dance images also suggested their love-affair that they re-enacted in memory just before dying – 'moments of tenderness, of passion, and of occasional antagonism'.[34] As well as the kind of lifts characteristic of his other *pas de deux*, Ashton used floorwork of the sort more often associated with the modern dance (and which he had previously introduced into the 'Friday' section of *Jazz Calendar*).

The dance was seventeen minutes long, but Trounson and Myers sustained their arduous roles with an intensity that was made even more touching by their youth and comparative inexperience, and as always Ashton was able to bring out their qualities as dancers and as people – as John Percival wrote, 'the way Trounson, held horizontally across Myers's shoulders in a typical Ashton lift, twice pushes back the loose hair that falls over her face is just one example of how Ashton has used their unspoiled naturalness to point his choreography'.[35]

In keeping with the subject and the music, the décor was the work of a young artist, Bill Culbert – actually, as in *Sinfonietta*, it was an adaptation of a multiple published by the Lisson Gallery, a 'light projection sphere' that emerged from the darkness of the background towards the end like a monstrous sea-anemone.

Lament of the Waves:
Carl Myers and
Marilyn Trounson

Farewell Gala, Metropolitan Opera House, New York, 31 May 1970: Ashton at front; John Lanchbery, Fonteyn, John Hart, Sol Hurok, David Webster, Somes, Nureyev, Sibley and Dowell may be seen in the front row behind him

Another decorative element was provided by a dappled gauze curtain that hung above the stage like the surface of the water and finally descended to cover the dead lovers – actually, this was borrowed from Jacques Dupont's décor for Petit's *Pelléas and Mélisande*, dropped after very few performances in London and New York the previous year. The very simple costumes were the work of Derek Rencher.

Once again, in his choice of collaborators and interpreters, Ashton had shown that he had an instinctive sympathetic understanding of the young, however rooted in the past his own imagination might seem to some observers. Yet there was another aspect to *Lament of the Waves* that was, as Ashton says, 'autobiographical'. As early as 1967 he had announced his intention of retiring at the end of the 1969–1970 season: he probably meant it at the time, yet it seems likely that he could have been persuaded to stay on a little longer. However, the administration of the Royal Opera House chose to take him at his word and he was informed by David Webster, then the General Administrator of Covent Garden, early in 1969 that he was expected to step down the following year. So that when he made *Lament of the Waves* retirement was imminent, and the ballet was to some degree informed by his own 'morbid feeling of being submerged by time', expressed by brief references to earlier works – as if not only did the lovers see their lives passing before them, but Ashton himself was reviewing his own creative life, although this was properly subordinated to the primary content. Be that as it may, the ballet was short-lived: Carl Myers was injured in a car accident soon after the première, and his role was taken in some performances by David Ashmole. But it was not shown in New York that spring, and not retained in the repertory after Ashton's retirement.

A Wedding Bouquet and *Daphnis and Chloe*, which had not been given in America for several years, were revived for that New York season, on the closing night of which (31 May 1970) there was a gala performance in Ashton's honour. At his own request, Nureyev's production of *La Bayadère* was danced 'as an honour to the corps de ballet', with Fonteyn and Nureyev in the leads, and the rest of the programme consisted of the final scene of *Daphnis*, *Symphonic Variations*, the *pas de deux* from *The Dream* and *Façade*. At the end Ashton received a warm personal ovation from the audience and the assembled company.

Less than a week later, on 6 June 1970, an ambitious full-length ballet by Ashton had its première in Bonn as part of the Beethoven bicentenary celebrations: *The Creatures of Prometheus* was choreographed for the touring company, although it was known that under the new régime to be headed by Kenneth MacMillan and

The Creatures of Prometheus: Doreen Wells and David Wall as the Creatures, with Hendrik Davel as Prometheus (back to camera), Paul Clarke as Apollo, centre

John Field the two companies of the Royal Ballet were shortly to be amalgamated.

Prometheus was composed by Beethoven for Salvatore Viganò, whose ballet, a grandiose allegorical spectacle, was first produced in Vienna in 1801. The original scenario no longer exists, but there are contemporary accounts and other historical records such as Beethoven's own notebooks: a libretto put together from these sources by Jean Chantavoine and Maurice Léna is printed in the Heugel edition of the score. Other modern choreographers who have tackled the ballet, notably de Valois and Lifar, have concocted stories of their own, but Ashton elected to follow Viganò's at least in its basic outlines, though with a lighter touch.

As conscientious as ever, Ashton studied not only the reconstructed libretto but other relevant texts that were brought to his attention, such as a translation of a verse commentary on the score by Johann Gabriel Seidl (1804–75) published in the *Weiner Zeitschrift für Kunst und Literatur, Theater und Mode,* 1841, and Goethe's poem *Prometheus,* written in 1775, which was set to music by both Schubert and Wolf and may or may not have been known to Beethoven himself. Ashton used a stanza of this poem, approximately in the translation by S S Prawer, as an epigraph to the ballet:

> Here I sit, forming them
> In my image,
> A race that will resemble me;
> To suffer, to weep,
> To enjoy and be glad,
> And not to heed you –
> Like me![36]

Ashton's synopsis was as follows (in his version, Act I became a prologue, and the main action took place in one scene rather than two):

> The ballet shows Prometheus as a maker of mankind proudly displaying before the Gods on Olympus two figures he has created from clay and water, adapting in them the best qualities of the various animals. With a brand of flame from the sun, he brings them to life. But they must also have mind and spirit and so he turns to Apollo, the Patron of the Arts, who produces music which charms the statues and awakens their sensibilities. The creatures give signs of emotion. The climax of creation has been reached. The man and woman are mutually attracted. Thalia, the Muse of Comedy, teaches them gaiety. Mars shows them the effects of warfare and Melpomene, the Muse of Tragedy, the gamut of tragic emotion. Bacchus initiates them in the pleasures of wine and Terpsichore teaches them to dance and so they become rounded creatures fit to embark on the voyage of life.

This summary does not quite make clear that in the Prologue Prometheus was first seen fleeing from the wrath of Zeus, to the section marked 'Tempesta' in the score, carrying the torch he had stolen from Olympus. After he had animated the Creatures, he led them to Parnassus, where the main action took place before the temple of Apollo. Ashton also introduced the character of Eros who, after Apollo had given the Creatures souls, awakened their tender feelings for each other by piercing their hearts with his arrows.

With John Lanchbery's help, Ashton made a few minor changes in the score, omitting No 13 (*Terzettino di groteschi*) entirely, reversing the order of Nos 6 and 7, and making both small cuts and some additional repeats in other numbers where necessary. Nos 11, 12, 14 and 15 were made into one sequence, Terpsichore's dancing lesson. As usual, Ashton drew up a minutage.†

The main problem with *Prometheus* was to devise a style that would preserve the allegorical nature of the ballet without using stereotyped mythological figures, and to make it light without traducing the nobility of Beethoven's music. Ashton decided to take as his cue the date of its composition, 1801. Prometheus himself, according to his notes, was to be made to look as much as possible like the young Beethoven (an identification earlier proposed by Seidl), while Apollo was to be dressed like Beau Brummel. Mars, according to this scheme, would be equated with Napoleon, and the War episode would recall the 'ragged retreat from Moscow'. Ashton even had the idea of a kind of apotheosis, a 'picture of Beethoven – seated and crowned with tomes all round him', but discarded it.

Unfortunately, this approach did not succeed: somehow the result did not look like an Ashton ballet at all, a sure sign that the music had not touched off any flow of invention in him. No doubt the fact that many of the dancers in the touring company were not used to working with him was also an inhibiting factor. The overtly comic parts were the most successful, such as Terpsichore's dancing lesson (like certain teachers of ballet, she wielded a stick), though the point was blunted by the fact that the Creatures had already had a lesson, at least in *port de bras*, from Prometheus himself, and later danced a pretty *pas de deux*, expressing the feelings with which they had been endowed by Apollo and Eros, without benefit of further instruction. Several critics commented on the unsuitability of giving the 'Eroica' theme in the finale to Eros rather than to Prometheus; the other dancers had brief solo entries to the variations on the theme, and the ballet closed quietly with a formal tableau (instead of the planned apotheosis) – one of the few characteristically Ashtonian touches. Individual numbers had some charm and wit – it was as a whole that *Prometheus* lacked conviction.

The dancers, too, seemed uncertain whether to play it straight or for laughs – at least this was so at the London première in the following November, though according to John Percival the first performance in Bonn had been greeted with 'gales of laughter'.[37] David Wall had not danced at Bonn owing to an injury, the part of the male Creature having been taken there by Kerrison Cooke; when Wall finally appeared in it at Covent Garden, one got the impression that he sensed that

† See Appendix C.

the audience was ready to laugh and opted for a comic interpretation on the spur of the moment. As the female Creature, Doreen Wells lacked warmth and lyricism. Sandra Conley, in Melpomene's mournful solo, and Brenda Last and Alfreda Thorogood as Terpsichore and Thalia, respectively, came off better, while Hendrik Davel (Prometheus) and Paul Clarke (Apollo) had little to do except pose.

But the general impression was of insipidity, not improved by the designs of Ottowerner Meyer, resident designer at the Theater der Stadt Bonn. *Prometheus* had its advocates, among them John Percival and Andrew Porter, in The Financial Times, but it was clear that audiences were puzzled by it, and the ballet did not survive beyond the 1970–1971 season.

On their return from the United States at the beginning of June, the main company began preparations for a second farewell gala, of a kind at once more ambitious and more intimate than the one in New York, to be held at Covent Garden on 24 July. These preparations took place in secret so that Ashton would not know what was being done – even on the night the programme was not given out until the end so that its contents would come as a surprise. The evening was to be nothing less than a retrospective of Ashton's entire career, consisting of excerpts from thirty-five of his ballets and one, *Symphonic Variations*, in its entirety. The programme was devised and produced by John Hart and Michael Somes, with the assistance of Leslie Edwards, with a narration written by William Chappell and spoken by Robert Helpmann. Dances from long-forgotten ballets were reconstructed by people who had danced in them years before, and in many cases roles were danced by their original interpreters – Fonteyn, for instance, appeared in five of her own – but in others they were taken by younger dancers who could never have seen the ballets concerned. Thus Alexander Grant danced Gore's solo from *Rio Grande*, Deanne Bergsma one from *The Lord of Burleigh*, Marilyn Trounson appeared as Psyche in a variation from *Cupid and Psyche*, Vyvyan Lorrayne as the Moon from *Horoscope*, Monica Mason danced Pamela May's solo from *Dante Sonata*, Vergie Derman and Donald MacLeary the Lovers' duet from *The Wanderer*, and Rudolf Nureyev was the Poet in *Apparitions* (Helpmann's ad lib was, 'My interpretation was *quite* different'). Nureyev also danced part of *Les Rendez-vous*, a ballet that has since gone into his repertory.

It was, needless to say, an emotionally-charged occasion – described by Peter Williams as 'the most enthralling and moving evening of dance-theatre that most of us have ever spent'.[38] After the Garden scene from *Marguerite and Armand* Fonteyn and Somes made a quick change and returned in the finale of *Daphnis and Chloe*, roles that they had long since relinquished. At the end every one danced the waltz from *A Wedding Bouquet* in whatever costumes they were wearing, until Helpmann reached the words 'They incline to oblige only one', at which point Ashton, who had been led backstage only a few moments before, descended to the stage on one of the lifts to take his bow.

Tribute to Sir Frederick Ashton, Royal Opera House, 24 July 1970: Fonteyn, in her costume as Chloe, lays a bouquet at Ashton's feet; also in front row, Alexander Grant, Merle Park, Michael Coleman, John Lanchbery, John Hart, Somes, Helpmann, Beriosova

Such a programme could never, alas! be repeated, though a few of the excerpts from early ballets were incorporated into Ballet for All's 'Birth of the Royal Ballet' programme two years later.

During the seven years of Ashton's régime he did much more than carry on where de Valois had left off. Even though his own choreographic output was necessarily reduced in quantity there were three works – *The Dream, Monotones* and *Enigma Variations* – that many people would count among his masterpieces. While delegating certain administrative responsibilities to others more capable of carrying them out, Ashton had conscientiously fulfilled other directorial duties and had put his personal stamp on the company more unmistakably than ever – he was no mere figurehead. The repertory was extended in important ways – above all, in his eyes, with the revivals of Nijinska's *Les Biches* and *Les Noces*. The corps de ballet became the finest in the world. Already, in 1960, Ashton had shown with *La Fille mal gardée* that it was possible for younger dancers to lead the company. Although Fonteyn, far from retiring, had further consolidated her position as *prima ballerina assoluta* through her partnership with Nureyev, under Ashton's direction new stars emerged from within its ranks – most notably, of course, Sibley and Dowell.

But to Ashton each and every member of the company was important, he took a personal interest in all of them, never missed a dancer's début in a role and was always approachable. 'I read somewhere,' he told me, 'that de Gaulle always made a point of standing up when anyone came into his office to see him, and that impressed me very much, I thought if de Gaulle does that, I should too, and I always did.' In recognition of his achievement as Director, he was made Companion of Honour in the Queen's Birthday Honours that year.

Ashton was given to referring to his régime as a 'caretaker government' – a designation that would be misleading if taken to indicate a mere interregnum, but correct in so far as it implied that he continued to build on the foundations de Valois had laid. The future was less certain: the new directors, Kenneth Mac-Millan and John Field, proposed a radical reorganisation of the company in which the old touring company would be disbanded, to be replaced by a smaller touring group that would be able to produce experimental new ballets. Such, at any rate, was the plan, and this is not the place to discuss its subsequent modifications.

The repertory, of course, remained, and so did most of the dancers. The most hopeful sign that continuity between past and present would be maintained was the assurance that Ashton would continue to choreograph for the company – not as prolifically as in the past, certainly, but it was understood that he would contribute 'one ballet a year'.

Chapter Fourteen
1970-1975

But it was not to be. On his retirement, Ashton said that he would no longer feel obliged to make a new ballet just because one was needed for a particular dancer or to provide a novelty for the repertory – he would do only things that interested him, that presented him with a challenge. He was asked to stage the dances for a new musical comedy based on J B Priestley's *The Good Companions*, but this did not appeal to him. He considered a number of ideas for ballets–among others, the Gershwin Piano Concerto, Tchaikovsky's String Sextet (*Souvenir de Florence*), Rachmaninov's *Rhapsody on a theme of Paganini*, Elgar's ballet score *The Sanguine Fan* – but pursued none of them.

Immediately before and after his retirement Ashton was engaged on a project that was certainly ambitious enough, the film *Tales of Beatrix Potter*. This was the brain-child of a young couple, Richard Goodwin, a producer, and his wife Christine Edzard, a designer who had assisted Lila de Nobili on Zeffirelli's film of *Romeo and Juliet*. They had shown some of Beatrix Potter's books to de Nobili at the time she was working on the 1968 *Sleeping Beauty*, and the three of them discussed the possibility of a ballet based on them. They approached Ashton, but his reaction was, 'If I did that just before my retirement, people would say, "The old man's gaga."[1]' Before long the Goodwins came to the conclusion that the idea would work better as a film, and this Ashton consented to. During the summer and winter of 1969 they developed their adaptation of nine of the stories and Christine Edzard made hundreds of sketches.

Early in 1970 John Lanchbery started work on the score, which was to be based on Victorian and Edwardian salon and theatre music (rather than on music-hall songs of the period, as was first intended). With Goodwin, Lanchbery went through quantities of music they found in secondhand shops and in the British Museum, by composers like Sullivan, Balfe and Jacobi; the 'Tale of Two Bad Mice' has one passage that may or may not be Minkus, and in another quotes the famous 'Apache Dance' that we now know, thanks to Richard Bonynge's recording, to be adapted from the *Valse des rayons* from Offenbach's ballet *Le Papillon*. As in other collaborations with Ashton, Lanchbery carefully tailored the music to fit the action and

Tales of Beatrix Potter:
Julie Wood as Mrs
Tittlemouse, Keith
Martin as Johnny
Town-Mouse

Tales of Beatrix Potter:
Lesley Collier as
Hunca Munca,
Wayne Sleep as Tom
Thumb

Tales of Beatrix Potter:
Frederick Ashton as
Mrs Tiggy-Winkle

indeed was largely responsible for the final shape of the film – it was he, for instance, who insisted that Peter Rabbit himself be included; accordingly, he composed a tarantella for him.[2] Eventually the film's director, Reginald Mills, decided to use Peter Rabbit as a linking figure throughout.

The work continued, with such major interruptions as the Royal Ballet's spring visit to America and Ashton's work on *The Creatures of Prometheus*. All the dancers in the film were to be members of the two companies of the Royal Ballet, and when rehearsals began during the summer, after they had returned from their respective tours, it was necessary for these to be scheduled around the companies' own rehearsals.

But Ashton had again found a congenial subject and worked with all his accustomed fluency. The dancers in the Mouse Waltz had to rehearse with ropes tied round their waists and hanging down at the back so that they would know what it was like to have a tail. Suzanna Raymond describes Ashton, similarly adorned, dancing round the studio saying, 'Wouldn't it be lovely to have a tail, think of all the things you could do with it, you could pick things up and carry them, you could skip rope with it . . .,' and she adds, 'That's how we found a lot of things for that dance. And in the Pigs' scene he made us all go around doing piggy things, and he'd say, "Yes, that's good, use that," then put all the bits together that he'd chosen.'

Inevitably, the film was not a complete success: the portrayal of animals by human beings is full of pitfalls, especially in a film. In particular, the masks created by Rostislav Doboujinsky, who made the animal masks for the recent *Sleeping Beauty*, were exquisite but lifeless, so that the dancers' heads, on top of their beautifully moving bodies, looked like examples of taxidermy. A more general criticism is that the film takes too much for granted the audience's familiarity with the books – some of the sequences don't bother to tell the stories, relying on instant recognition of beloved characters to do the work. Only the wonderful scene of the two naughty mice (Lesley Collier and Wayne Sleep) destroying the dolls' house is absolutely clear.

All the same, it is surely the only ballet film – the only one that originated as a film – that does not traduce or cheapen its choreographer's spirit. To Ashton the material was evidently just as worthy of his efforts as *Enigma* or *Fille*, and the result is just as rooted in the reality of English country life as those two masterpieces. And it is full of fresh and absolutely adorable dancing – the Mouse Waltz with its echoes of the Garland Dance from *Beauty*, the loving *pas de deux* of Pig-wig (Brenda Last) and Pigling Bland (Alexander Grant, who, together with the other male pigs, is on point like Bottom in *The Dream*), Michael Coleman's frog-leaps as Jeremy Fisher, and above all Ashton's own perfect characterisation of Mrs Tiggy-Winkle, with its typically dainty footwork.

However unimportant a work *Tales of Beatrix Potter* may be in Ashton's canon, it is clear that he felt a kinship with their author, of whose work her biographer, Margaret Lane, has written: 'Conveying truth by means of fantasy, enlarging our

Meditation from
Thaïs: Antoinette
Sibley and Anthony
Dowell

perception of life by poetic means, is one of the highest functions of art, and it is
not extravagant to say that in her small and special sphere Beatrix Potter performed it . . . She has made her books, like lyrics, out of emotional experience,
and it is this real feeling under the gentle playfulness of the fantasy that strikes so
directly home'.[3]

Ashton choreographed several short pieces during the early seventies. The first was
a *pas de deux* to the *Meditation* from Massenet's opera *Thaïs*, for Sibley and Dowell
to dance at a Gala Performance at the Adelphi Theatre on 21 March 1971. This
piece of music is included in Richard Bonynge's album Homage to Pavlova and
so was presumably in her repertory, though not, it seems, as one of her own solo
divertissements. At all events, Ashton says he never saw her dance it, yet the *pas de
deux* is one of his dances that unmistakably evoke her spirit – there is even one
gesture of Sibley's, when she coils her arm about her head, that recalls a specific
one of Pavlova's, in the film of her *Danse orientale*.

The dance bears no relation to the dramatic situation of the opera (in which the
music is called *Méditation religieuse*); rather, it reduces to its essence the kind of
vision scene of which the perfect example is that of the Kingdom of the Shades
from *La Bayadère*. At the beginning Dowell is alone on the stage, then Sibley
enters in a drifting *pas de bourrée* like some Oriental apparition, with a veil over her
head – the costumes were designed by Dowell himself, and when Ashton was talking to them about his ideas Dowell looked at Sibley and said jokingly, 'Maybe
you'd better have a yashmak,' and Ashton said, quite seriously, 'Oh yes, of course'.[4]

378

The *pas de deux* was put together in two or three rehearsals, and Sibley says they didn't take it terribly seriously – the kiss at the end, she says, was 'my fault'. But they soon found it to be extraordinarily difficult: whether being literally thrown through the air, lifted straight up from a kneeling position, or balanced on Dowell's shoulders, Sibley had to be like a disembodied, weightless spirit. Just as many of Pavlova's numbers would have been pure kitsch danced by anyone else, only Ashton could have got away with *Thaïs*, because he believes not only in the balletic conventions it draws upon, but in the idea of romantic love that is its real subject.

Rather to the dancers' surprise, the ovation at the first performance was such that Ashton had to announce that they would dance it again. The critic of The Daily Telegraph found it 'hackneyed'[5] and James Kennedy in the Guardian suggested it was 'lacking, perhaps, the quality of poetic surprise'.[6] Marie Rambert has said that Ashton has made three undoubted masterpieces – *Symphonic Variations*, *La Fille mal gardée*, and *Thaïs*.

The *pas de deux* has been performed by Sibley and Dowell both in Royal Ballet programmes and when they have appeared with other companies as guests; it was also filmed for BBC television, with a sequence showing Ashton rehearsing the dancers.

About a week later *La Fille mal gardée* had its first performance in Budapest, by the Hungarian State Ballet, and in May it was done in Munich, produced by Annette Page and her husband Ronald Hynd, director of the ballet company there. Meanwhile, in London, preparations were under way for another Gala Performance, organised by Richard Buckle. Buckle had conceived it to be his mission at that time to save Titian's *The Death of Actaeon*, then in the Harewood Collection, from being sold to America, and hoped to raise enough money for the cause by means of a gala, advertised as 'The Greatest Show on Earth', which would also serve to further his plans for a Museum of Theatre Arts. One of the ballets he wanted to present was to be called *Romance*, to songs by Franz Liszt, settings of poems by Victor Hugo, with choreography by Ashton for Margot Fonteyn and David Wall.[7]

The ballet, and the gala as a whole, did not work out quite as intended. In its final form the performance, at the London Coliseum on 22 June 1971, was described as a 'répétition générale' for The Greatest Show on Earth, rather than the Show itself. The Hugo–Liszt ballet was called *c. 1830* and only the last song, 'Oh, quand je dors', was choreographed by Ashton, and danced by Fonteyn and Desmond Kelly, he as a Poet, she as his Muse. The rest of the piece was choreographed by Geoffrey Cauley; one of the poems was performed in a setting by Berlioz and another was spoken, not sung. The décor was by Jean Hugo, great-grandson of Victor, based on the poet's own paintings, with costumes by Jean Hugo and his daughter Marie.

The gala also included performances of the *Meditation* from *Thaïs* and the Popular Song from *Façade*, which was danced by Doreen Wells *en travesti* and John Gilpin.

✤

The September number of Dance and Dancers announced that Ashton would create a new ballet for the Royal Ballet in December, but this turned out to be without foundation – or perhaps wishful thinking. In March 1972 Ashton went out to supervise the final rehearsals of the Australian Ballet's production of *Cinderella*, and to play his own role as one of the Stepsisters, opposite Robert Helpmann, at that time one of the artistic directors of the company. They played their parts again in the PACT (Performing Arts Council Transvaal) Ballet production in Johannesburg that September.

In between these two guest stints in *Cinderella*, Ashton, in July, had made another duet, for Vyvyan Lorrayne and Barry McGrath of the touring section of the Royal Ballet. This was another version of William Walton's *Siesta*, first performed at an evening of opera and ballet given at the Maltings, Snape, home of the Aldeburgh Festival, in honour of the composer's seventieth birthday. This anniversary had in fact fallen on 20 March but the performance did not take place until 28 July, the programme consisting of Walton's one-act opera *The Bear*, *Siesta* and *Façade* – the first performance of the ballet in the original musical version, with Peter Pears reciting the Edith Sitwell poems.

Siesta was, in other words, another *pièce d'occasion*, which Ashton called 'a birthday card for Willie Walton'. It took place on and around a large foam-rubber mattress in front of a slatted screeen through which could be seen the mid-afternoon sunlight. Lorrayne, in a filmy flowered skirt and bra, lay waiting for her lover, McGrath, who shortly entered, bare-chested, in white trousers. The dance was by turns playfully acrobatic and sensually entwining, ending with an arms' length lift, McGrath kneeling on the bed and Lorrayne descending to a horizontal position across his shoulders, turning this way and that; then they subsided on to the bed, rolled across one another, and finished lying side by side.

It is unlikely that the new *Siesta* bore any resemblance to the first one in 1936 – for one thing, no one would have remembered any of it, least of all Ashton. Although the new version was mild enough, it no doubt would have been thought rather shocking by the previous generation. But it was refreshing to see a dance that was actually lighthearted in its eroticism, suggesting that sex could be fun instead of the source of guilt and conflict, as usual in contemporary ballet. The atmosphere of a sultry, languorous afternoon in which a man and a woman prepare to make love led some people to compare *Siesta* with Robbins's *Afternoon of a Faun*, but the essential theme of that ballet is the dancers' narcissism that ultimately prevents any kind of amorous contact beyond the most chaste of kisses, while *Siesta* was about two people having a good time together.

A third *pas de deux*, also done for a gala, that for the Royal Ballet Benevolent

Siesta: Vyvyan Lorrayne and Barry McGrath

Fund on 15 November 1972, was *The Walk to the Paradise Garden*, from Delius's opera *A Village Romeo and Juliet*. Actually there are three dancers, Merle Park and David Wall as the lovers, and Derek Rencher as the stationary figure of Death who appears at the end. The programme note was reminiscent of that for *Lament of the Waves* in its laconicism: '*The Walk to the Paradise Garden* may be regarded as an orchestral *liebestod* for the doomed lovers.' The dance, in other words, did in this case refer directly to the theme of the opera from which the music was taken.

If *Siesta* was a playful prelude to love-making, *Paradise Garden* seemed to find the lovers in its rapturous aftermath, filled with happiness and sensual delight in

381

The Walk to the Paradise Garden: Merle Park and David Wall

OPPOSITE *The Walk to the Paradise Garden*: Derek Rencher as the figure of Death, with Merle Park and David Wall

each other, but with occasional moments of foreboding, premonitions of the approach of death. It begins with the lovers on the ground but soon opens up into large, rhapsodic movement as they rise and go into a series of typical Ashton lifts – at first low, with changes of direction, then gradually becoming more and more acrobatic, Bolshoi-style, as when Wall throws Park into the air and she spins horizontally before being caught in his arms again. Some of the lifts are familiar, not only the one- or two-handed overhead ones, but also an understated one where Wall lifts Park just off the ground and puts her down behind him, recalling a lift in the 'Nimrod' trio from *Enigma* (not to mention one in Act I of MacMillan's *Manon*). But others are quite new, like the amazing one where Wall holds Park vertically above him, upside down, and she literally almost dives headlong to the floor.

When Death finally appears he is not, as usual, dressed in black, but a chalk-white figure who simply awaits them, opening wide his arms and, in a striking *coup de théâtre*, swallows them up in the mazy folds of his cloak where they vainly seek each other, reaching out for one another's hands. At the last he spits out, as it were, their earthly remains and they fall dead at his feet after clasping hands for one brief instant. Like *Thaïs*, it was no mere divertissement but a ballet in miniature, saying as much in a few minutes as many full-length ballets. As John Percival wrote, Ashton 'caught the mood of the Delius music perfectly, although seeing deeper into it than his audience perhaps expected'.[8] Brief or not, this dance gave Merle Park the most important role that Ashton had ever choreographed for her,

and as with so many other dancers he brought out reserves of passion that had been hidden until then.

The designs were by one of Ashton's oldest collaborators, William Chappell; a décor with a pattern of flowers and leaves that also has something of the look of a mandala, and simple costumes that suggest exactly what the title of the opera says, a village Romeo and Juliet.

At the same performance an earlier *pièce d'occasion* was also revived, *Birthday Offering*, with Fonteyn, Beriosova and David Blair in the parts they created. Fonteyn's partner was David Wall, and the new galaxy of supporting ballerinas included Sibley, Park, Jennifer Penney, Ann Jenner and Georgina Parkinson.

A major event of the Aldeburgh Festival of 1973 was the production on 16 June of a new opera by Benjamin Britten, based on Thomas Mann's novella *Death in Venice*, with libretto by Myfanwy Piper. Presumably because it presented him with the kind of challenge he had spoken of, Ashton agreed to do the choreography. The dancers' roles in *Death in Venice* were to be far more closely integrated into the structure of the work than in the usual opera-ballet, whose performers look like denizens of another world than that of the singers. In fact Britten acknowledged that difference but used it to dramatic effect – the fourteen-year-old Polish boy Tadzio, with whom the aging writer Aschenbach becomes infatuated, his mother and the other children were all dancing roles. This device made it clear,

383

as Desmond Shawe-Taylor wrote, that 'Aschenbach's failure to speak to Tadzio, in the natural way of friendliness, and subsequently to the boy's mother, to warn her of the spreading cholera, [is] due in part to his sense of guilt, but also to the fact that they inhabit different worlds'.[9]

The role of Tadzio was danced by Robert Huguenin, a recent graduate of the Royal Ballet School, his mother by Deanne Bergsma, and the other children by pupils of the School. There were a couple of dance sequences, both based on the idea of children's games on the beach, the more extended one at the end of the first act being identified with the Olympic Pentathlon; otherwise Ashton was called upon to stage more or less fragmentary if not incidental passages of movement such as the hackneyed episode of the sinister strolling players in Act II. To have to stage not one but two scenes dealing with games would have been a strain on any choreographer, and Ashton was further hampered by having to use young students who were unused to his methods. Even though in the Pentathlon scene the offstage voice of Apollo and the on-stage chorus in their robes are drawing classical parallels ('Come, see where Hyacinthus plays/Basking in Apollo's rays', etc.), Ashton was still stuck with having to devise dances based on running, the long jump, discus throwing, the high jump and wrestling. Only Tadzio's own formal solo rises above the literal depiction of this kind of activity. At moments in the choreography one can notice quotations from earlier Ashton works such as *Monotones* and *Scènes de ballet*, but these only underline the lack of a sustained lyrical evocation of a halcyon vision, not only in the choreography but in the music as well – and without the one there cannot be the other.

The opera as a whole is misconceived. The real theme of the novella resists translation into dramatic terms: depicted on the stage, the relationship between Aschenbach and Tadzio becomes merely a pederastic infatuation, whereas in the book it at least starts as an adoration for a platonic ideal of beauty that happens to be personified in a boy. When the boy is played by a strapping teenager – as he must be if the dancer is to be capable of meeting the technical demands of the choreography – their encounters inevitably look flirtatious, since he is obviously old enough to know the score.

The most beautiful moment in the opera comes at the very end, a dance image that says it all, as Aschenbach sits dying while Tadzio, beckoning to him, swims out to sea – the libretto says that he is walking but Ashton heightens the image by giving the dancer a series of slow swimming movements in a deep *arabesque pliée*.

In 1974 the production went briefly into the repertory of the Metropolitan Opera in New York, again with Peter Pears as the protagonist. The choreography was slightly revised by Ashton in London and then reproduced from notation by Faith Worth (who similarly revived *Monotones* for the City Center Joffrey Ballet while in New York). Tadzio was danced by Bryan Pitts, a young dancer from the New York City Ballet.

❊

Ballet for All, the third company of the Royal Ballet, was founded by Peter Brinson in 1964 with the support of the Calouste Gulbenkian Foundation. The purpose of this small group was to introduce new, and especially young, audiences to ballet by means of 'ballet-plays' which would instruct as well as entertain. The first production was called 'Ashton and *La Fille mal gardée*', and the choreographer's work was further represented in a programme called 'The Birth of the Royal Ballet' in 1972. At the beginning of that year Alexander Grant had become director of the company, when Brinson relinquished the post to become director of the United Kingdom and British Commonwealth Branch of the Gulbenkian Foundation itself, although he still maintained his connection with Ballet for All ('The Birth of the Royal Ballet' was devised and written by him).

In all their years of working together Ashton and de Valois had never collaborated on an original ballet, although both had had a hand in editing their company's productions of the classics. (An early announcement of the ballet that became *Homage to the Queen* said that it would be a joint work.) In 1973 Grant persuaded them to provide choreography for a new Ballet for All production, 'World of Harlequin', which he had devised for presentation on the group's autumn tour. The first part was to show how ballet has been influenced by *commedia dell'arte*, in particular by inheriting such characters as Harlequin, Columbine and Pierrot, and in general in the use of mime. The second part was an original Harlequinade in nineteenth-century style, *The Wedding of Harlequin; or, Harlequin's Revenge*, with music of the time of Grimaldi and décor and costumes adapted from the

Death in Venice: Peter Pears as Aschenbach, right, watching Tadzio (Robert Huguenin) and his friends

Juvenile Drama prints of Benjamin Pollock. For this part of the entertainment Ashton choreographed the dances of Harlequin and Columbine and of a pair of skeletons, while de Valois arranged the clowns' dances, the pantomime sequences and the linking passages.

It was not, then, a collaboration in the strict sense of the word – they rehearsed separately and even when their rehearsals followed one another, each would wait until the other had left the room before starting work, not from any antagonism but more probably because of nervousness at being watched. Alexander Grant, as well as writing the story for the pantomime and finding the music in the British Library, acted as liaison man between the two choreographers.

The harlequinade made no great pretence of period authenticity. The word 'pantomime' when used to describe the traditional British Christmas entertainment is a misnomer since these extravaganzas have habitually included almost every theatrical element *except* mime. *The Wedding of Harlequin* was closer to a real pantomime, that is to say a play acted out in gesture and movement. Only the actor impersonating Grimaldi sang and delivered some authentic patter including, at the end, the speech written by Thomas Hood for the famous clown to make at his farewell benefit in 1828.

Otherwise it was a not very accurate pastiche, with some charming incidental dances. Graham Fletcher as Harlequin danced a brilliant, technically difficult solo with much small *batterie*, and a lovely *pas de deux* with Columbine (Belinda Corken). The skeletons' dance, in which the male dancer was mostly invisible so that the girl, lifted, seemed to be jumping, turning upside down, and so forth, without any support, was amusing but the use of ultra-violet light to achieve these trick effects was an anachronism. Altogether it was very minor Ashton.

Around Christmas-time members of the opera and ballet companies usually stage a cabaret for the Friends of Covent Garden – during his tenure as director Ashton appeared as Britannia in one of these. The 1973 Christmas Party, on Sunday 16 December, was called *Tonight at 8.30* and was mostly in the currently popular vein of nostalgia, with Wayne Sleep appearing as Shirley Temple, Laura Connor and Christopher Carr as Ginger Rogers and Fred Astaire, and so forth. In one number four girls danced the cygnets' *pas de quatre* from *Swan Lake* wearing the hens' costumes from *Fille* – '*Les Petites cygnes mal gardées.*'

In a Grand Finale Ashton danced the waltz from *The Merry Widow* with Margot Fonteyn, she in a black ball dress by Christian Dior: a sentimental occasion of some historic importance, since it seems unlikely that they will ever dance together on a stage again. Fonteyn gave Ashton a new recording of Lehár's operetta that Christmas and as he listened to it he began to think about doing a ballet based on it, but finally decided that it was impossible – 'too many waltzes' – and too complicated a plot.

Ashton and Fonteyn
dancing the *Merry
Widow* Waltz at the
Friends of Covent
Garden Christmas
Party, 1973

On 1 April 1974 there was a Fashion Show in aid of the Royal Ballet School, at the Royal Society of Arts, in which the clothes were modelled by pupils of the School. The show was divided into seventeen numbers which Ashton staged, with the assistance of Michael Pink, then a student of the Senior School and a young choreographer of some promise. To judge from a film of this event made by Derek Jarman, the dances were rather in the style of *Jazz Calendar*. The music was a *pot-pourri* of popular tunes ranging from a Scott Joplin rag through 20s' and 30s' songs like 'Singin' in the Rain' and 'These Foolish Things' to rock numbers, and Ashton approached the task with some misgivings as to his ability to find an appropriate style for the more contemporary music. However, he became more interested as he went on working – characteristically, it was the dancers he became excited about, even though he had trouble teaching some of the girls to walk like mannequins.

387

In addition to the lack of experience of the performers, another limitation was imposed by the dimensions of the stage, which was very wide and very shallow. He used fairly simple steps to get his effects, including, of course, the 'Fred step', and varied them with such time-honoured devices as parasols used à la *Floradora* sextet (of 1899), some elementary tap and acrobatic routines, and mime sequences (as in 'These Foolish Things'). He let Michael Pink arrange a Kung-fu number for the boys for 'Enter the Dragon', and for 'Journey Through Dawn' choreographed a typically *plastique* solo for a girl in which she knelt and did sweeping movements with the arms, rather like the male soloist in *Les Rendezvous*.

For the young dancers, it was a marvellous experience to work with a great choreographer and to see his straightforward approach to such a routine assignment. Ashton was, as ever, the complete professional, practising his craft without any nonsense about 'inspiration', and in the process seeking out the particular qualities of his dancers and showing them, as always, to the best advantage.

He continued to receive invitations to arrange small numbers for special occasions, and in 1975 accepted three of these. First he made another *pas de deux* for Merle Park and David Wall, this one for a programme put together by Petrus Bosman, a member of the Royal Ballet who often organised gala performances (including the one at which *Thaïs* was first given) and tours by small groups of dancers from the company, usually under the rubric 'Artists of the Royal Ballet'. Such was the case for this performance, which was to take place at the Maltings in Snape on 16 March.

Some three years earlier, the Australian Ballet had announced that Ashton would choreograph a ballet for them to music by Offenbach. This was the only ballet score by the composer, *Le Papillon*, in its original production in 1860 also the only ballet choreographed by the great Romantic ballerina, Marie Taglioni. The music had recently been recorded by Richard Bonynge and Ashton did indeed consider it as a possibility for the Australians. But, as happened at other times during the first years of his retirement, the announcement proved to be premature, and though Ashton did go to Australia it was only for the revival of *Cinderella*.

One reason that *Le Papillon* did not materialise was that Ashton came to the conclusion that the score as a whole was not sufficiently interesting. But there was enough for a *pas de deux*, certainly, and he chose some excerpts for the number he made for Park and Wall, which he called *Scène dansante*. The selection included the *Valse des rayons* which occurs in a different form in *Tales of Beatrix Potter*. Although musically not divided into separate numbers, the *pas de deux* took the traditional form of an entrée, adagio, variations and coda, and displayed the dancers' virtuosity to the full.

Both Anna Pavlova and Isadora Duncan occupy honoured places in Ashton's personal pantheon of muses, together with Karsavina, Markova and Fonteyn. Of Pavlova he has said, 'I never lose the vision of her',[10] and he has always retained vivid memories of Duncan, too: 'The way she used her hands and her arms, the way she ran across the stage – these I have adopted in my own ballets'.[11] No other contemporary ballerina is as well suited as Lynn Seymour to impersonate Duncan – indeed, Ashton had thought that she should have played her in the film Karel Reisz made several years ago. 'Vanessa Redgrave,' he is reported to have said, 'could never look like Isadora. Isadora was small, round, feminine, voluptuous. She was round, appealing – everything I thought, and think, dance should be'.[12] When one sees reconstructions of Duncan's dances today, such as those taught by Julia Levien to Annabelle Gamson, one is struck most of all by the fact that the movement does not attempt to conceal the weight of the body, as much ballet dancing does – the impulse is down into the floor, even in the many skipping jumps. One of the things that make Seymour unique – in addition, that is, to her extraordinary gifts as a dramatic actress – is precisely this sense of gravity.

Five Brahms Waltzes in the Manner of Isadora Duncan: Lynn Seymour

In the summer of 1975 Ashton arranged a very short dance for her, an impression of Duncan, which Seymour performed on 22 June at the State Opera House in Hamburg, as part of a gala performance to honour the memory of Nijinsky, organised by John Neumeier, director of the ballet company there. The dance was to one of the most famous of Brahms's Waltzes, one which Duncan herself used to dance, opus 39 No 15. Unlike Julia Levien, Ashton was unable to attempt an authentic reconstruction, but the piece did begin with something he remembered Duncan doing – walking forward with her hands cupped together before her, letting fall a stream of rose-petals between her fingers as she advanced.

Seymour wore, as Duncan did, an almost transparent shift over her otherwise nude body, a costume that apparently shocked some of the audience in Hamburg. The dance was only two minutes long – 'two minutes,' wrote one German critic, 'of transfiguration, of time rediscovered, of deep penetration into European cultural history . . .'[13] If there has been in some quarters a tendency to take Duncan less than seriously, the *Brahms Waltz*, Horst Koegler wrote, was danced by Seymour 'with such rapturous dithyrambic élan that she swept away all our scepticism about Isadora. This choreographic miniature not only made it clear how much both Fokine and Nijinsky profited from Isadora, but through her Sir Frederick achieved a sort of vindication of the often maligned pioneer of modern dance, which could not have been more aptly timed for Women's Year'.[14]

On two or three occasions during the following season Seymour repeated this dance in gala performances presented by American Ballet Theatre. Ashton, however, felt that it was too short to stand by itself and decided to choreograph further waltzes, making a short suite which Seymour performed for the first time at Sadler's Wells on 15 June 1976, on the occasion of the gala performance to celebrate the fiftieth anniversary of Ballet Rambert – actually, of *A Tragedy of Fashion*, in which the company had its origin.

Floresta Amazõnica: Margot Fonteyn and David Wall

Floresta Amazŏnica: Margot Fonteyn and Rudolf Nureyev

Five Brahms Waltzes in the Manner of Isadora Duncan, to give the work its full title, is, like the single one Ashton arranged first, presumably based as much on a study of the iconography and contemporary accounts of the dancer as on his own memory of her. The little pantomine of trailing her fingers in the water and playing at knuckle-bones, the use of the scarf and the rose-petals, the skipping and running steps, the extraordinarily plastic arm movements – all these are certainly authentic, and though Ashton would not claim that he has created anything more than an impression of Duncan, one American who saw Seymour dance the complete *Waltzes* at another ABT gala and who remembered seeing Duncan in the early 20s said without equivocation, 'It was just like that.' Certainly Seymour's performance, now lyrical, now tragic, now tempestuous, was an extraordinary act of intuitive identification with the spirit of another dancer whom she had never seen.

Later in the summer of 1975 Ashton choreographed another short piece, a *pas de deux* for Margot Fonteyn and David Wall. This originally formed part of a longer ballet by another choreographer, Dalal Achkar, artistic director of the Ballet do Rio de Janeiro, called *Floresta Amazónica*, first performed on 8 August in the opening programme of the First Winter Festival of Dance in that city. The music was adapted from Heitor Villa-Lobos's score for the MGM film of W H Hudson's *Green Mansions*, a book that Ashton had often considered as a possible basis for a ballet, and indeed one that would provide a role for Fonteyn. His *pas de deux* seemed to encapsulate the theme of the novel, with Fonteyn as a nature spirit in love with a mortal. As this description may suggest, the dance was a little reminiscent of Ashton's earlier writing for Fonteyn in *Ondine*, with the technical demands necessarily reduced. As in others of his recent duets, there was quite a bit of floorwork; otherwise, most of the time Fonteyn was being lifted or supported in *arabesques* or *pirouettes*. The dance clearly pleased Fonteyn, who has performed it frequently since as a separate number both on tour in Brazil and later in Europe and in New York, where she was partnered by Ivan Nagy and Rudolf Nureyev, respectively. Out of context, it seems slight enough, but it displays Fonteyn's most touching quality, her vulnerability.

Ashton himself went to Rio for the Festival and even toured with the dancers in the interior of Brazil. No doubt the opportunity of revisiting South America, after more than fifty years, was a temptation, though he did not go so far as to cross the continent to Peru. As it was, the travelling and the social life were exhausting for him – performances begin late in South America and were often followed by parties, with early departures the morning after. It took Ashton several weeks to recover once he got back to England, and he had a busy winter ahead of him.

For – at last – Ashton had decided that he was ready to embark on a new ballet. Not only that, he had agreed to appear in the Royal Ballet's Christmas revival of *Cinderella*, which had not been performed by the company since 1973. Of the many ideas that he had been turning over in his mind, the one he had settled on was Turgenev's play, *A Month in the Country*. He had spoken of this project to Julia Trevelyan Oman during the rehearsals of *Enigma Variations*, and told her that he wanted her to design it. The idea may have originated much earlier, in 1936 or 1937 when he saw a production of the play at the Westminster Theatre with an actress called Gillian Scaife as Natalia Petrovna. Certainly he had liked the play – better, he says, than any of the Chekhov plays he saw around the same time. It is not surprising that Ashton should have felt an affinity with Turgenev, with whom he shares the qualities 'of romantic melancholy and ironic humour, of serenity and disenchantment, of stoicism and tenderness', ascribed to the novelist by John Hayward.[1]

For various reasons, Ashton did not pursue the idea following *Enigma* – for one thing, he was afraid people might say the two ballets were too much alike. More important, he had not decided what music to use. At first he thought of Tchaikovsky piano pieces, but after Kenneth MacMillan's *Anastasia* it seemed unwise to attempt another Russian subject with music by that composer. He went through music by other 19th-century Russians, Glinka, Borodin, Balakirev, even Cui, but nothing seemed suitable. Then one day at a party he asked Sir Isaiah Berlin, the authority on Russian literature, who would be the right composer. Berlin said, 'Give me five minutes,' and at the end of that time came back and said 'Chopin'.

Ashton's first reaction was, 'Oh no, not again.' The Royal Ballet had within the last few years presented three ballets by Jerome Robbins to Chopin piano music (to say nothing of *Les Sylphides*). To make yet another selection of such pieces seemed to be asking for trouble. Nevertheless, Ashton conscientiously went through a great many of them, without getting anywhere. Then one day, by coincidence, Michael Somes lent him a record of some early Chopin works for piano and orchestra: the *Variations on 'Là ci darem'* (from *Don Giovanni*), the *Fantasy on Polish Airs*, and the *Andante spianato* and *Grande polonaise*. Still with no thought of using them for the Turgenev, Ashton went to buy a recording of the pieces for himself, but the version Somes had lent him had been deleted, so Ashton bought another, by Claudio Arrau, who plays them in the chronological order of their composition. That, Ashton says, was the 'right' order – all at once, he saw how the ballet might work.

With the help of his friend Martyn Thomas, Ashton set about making his usual detailed outline, fitting the action to the music.† He indicated many cuts, reducing the running time to about thirty-three minutes: 'I cut out of nerves, because it seemed endless.' (In the end, he reinstated about seven minutes of music, both for the sake of the overall shape and to accommodate the action without rushing through it.)

Ashton's collaborator on previous ballets, John Lanchbery, now musical director of the Australian Ballet, came back to London to work with him on the new one, and to conduct the first performances. They spent a week together in September 1975, making a kind of collage of the three pieces. Lanchbery persuaded Ashton not to add two of the Preludes (one of them the 17th, which he had choreographed twice before, earlier in his career), suggesting instead ways in which various passages could be transplanted or reprised, preserving the organic nature of the whole. As they worked, the two men were continually amazed at how well the music supported the dramatic structure. Lanchbery's adaptation – what Ashton calls his 'welding job' – is extraordinarily ingenious and tactful, creating what is almost a seamless entity out of the three works, with no question, as he put it, of 'composing several bars in the manner of . . .'

In the meantime, Ashton had talked again with Julia Trevelyan Oman. At one dinner party he told her the idea had come up again, and at another they sat next to each other and started 'moving knives and forks and things about the table', as Oman recalls. They decided to set the ballet in 1850, the year the play was written, rather than in the early seventies, when it was first performed, since the clothes of the earlier period could more easily be adapted for dancing. Oman had been to Russia in preparation for designing *Eugene Onegin* at Covent Garden a few years before, and had collected a card-index of details of design and architecture that she was able to draw on when she started work on the new ballet.

Ashton, for his part, prepared himself by reading as many books by and about Turgenev as he could find, especially the more romantic short novels like *First Love*, *Smoke* and *Spring Torrents*. These helped him with the general atmosphere and with the actual realisation of the characters of the play: 'I took certain gestures Turgenev describes different characters doing, and gave them to the people in the ballet.' In a book of Turgenev's letters to the actress Marya Gavrilovna Savina, one of whose favourite roles was the young girl, Vera, in *A Month in the Country*, he

† See Appendix C.

found a description by a friend of the author's, A F Koni: 'Your action when you put your head on the knees of your "benefactress", movingly and without words confessing that you are in love, affected me deeply and is still before me'.[2] Ashton gave this gesture to Denise Nunn, the dancer who played Vera in the ballet.

It was necessary, of course, to condense the action of the play considerably. For one thing, a five-act play had to be reduced to a one-act ballet whose final duration was about forty minutes. Moreover, there are dramatic incidents and psychological complexities that cannot be translated into dancing. Ashton concentrated on the central situation, revolving around the young tutor and his effect on the various members of the household and their relationships, which could be so translated. Characters that are essentially extraneous to this were eliminated.

Undoubtedly one of the factors influencing Ashton's choice of the subject was the presence in the Royal Ballet of the ideal dancer for the role of Natalia, the *femme de trente ans* who already has a husband and an admirer, but falls in love with her son's young tutor. Lynn Seymour had gone through a difficult period in which she had danced only intermittently, but in the last year had made a remarkable come-back, dancing both old and new roles with all her accustomed intensity and musicality, and greater technical assurance than before. After renewing his collaboration with Seymour in the Isadora Duncan solo, Ashton knew that she was the perfect choice for Natalia.

For most of the other roles he chose dancers he had worked with before – Dowell for Beliaev, the tutor, Rencher for Rakitin, Natalia's lover, Wayne Sleep for Kolia, her son, Grant for her husband. As the maid he cast the beautiful Marguerite Porter, who had succeeded Vyvyan Lorrayne in the role of Isabel Fitton in *Enigma Variations*. The part of Vera, he felt, had to be played by a young, inexperienced dancer, and he chose Denise Nunn out of the corps de ballet, because she had 'the right quality of innocence'. This, plus a footman (Anthony Conway), was the entire cast.

Even though Ashton was occupied at the same time with preparing for *Cinderella*, rehearsals for *A Month in the Country* went very easily – the choreography flowed out of him, a good sign, Ashton says, that he is on the right track. In spite of the effects of an influenza epidemic that removed first Denise Nunn and then Lynn Seymour from the final rehearsals, and indeed threatened to prevent Seymour from dancing on the opening night, the ballet went on as scheduled on 12 February 1976.

In the course of rehearsal, Ashton restored certain incidents from the play that had been omitted in the original synopsis, making his treatment of the story both more developed and more subtle. For instance, the scene between Natalia and Rakitin became somewhat closer to Turgenev: Rakitin enters unseen by Natalia and puts his arms round her. She melts at his touch, then turns to find it is he and not Beliaev, and registers, 'Oh, it's you.' Then follows her confession of her love for Beliaev and Yslaev's discovery of Rakitin consoling Natalia in an embrace whose nature her husband does not understand. (In the play, he enters with his

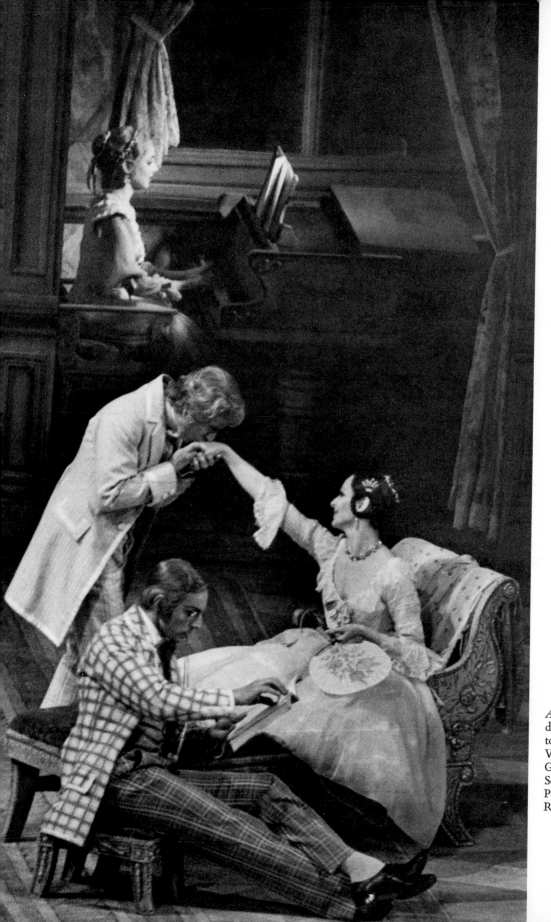

A Month in the Country: domestic scene. From top, Denise Nunn as Vera, Alexander Grant as Yslaev, Lynn Seymour as Natalia Petrovna, Derek Rencher as Rakitin

mother, one of the characters eliminated by Ashton.) All this kind of action is told by the simplest means; Ashton said he wanted to avoid 'the pomposity of conventional mime', and though he is not afraid to use the most obvious gesture for 'I love him' – hands on heart – most of the drama, here and elsewhere, is conveyed in terms of silent acting.

Ashton had sufficient faith in his ability to make the action clear to refrain from giving a complicated synopsis in the programme, which simply states: 'The action takes place at Yslaev's country house in 1850. Beliaev, a young student, engaged as a tutor for Kolia, disrupts the emotional stability of the household. Finally Rakitin, Natalia's admirer, insists that he and the tutor must both leave in order to restore a semblance of calm to Yslaev's family life.'

Ashton has said that the structure is operatic, almost Mozartian, with passages of dance ('arias') alternating with the interludes of 'recitative'. This conception was no doubt prompted by the first piece of music, the variations on a theme from *Don Giovanni*, which Ashton loves because 'it brings together my two favourite composers'. The ballet opens with one of Ashton's tableaux – a family group with Rakitin reading to Natalia as she languidly fans herself, Yslaev, her husband, buried in a newspaper, Kolia at a desk working on his lesson, Vera playing the piano, and the footman, Matvei, in attendance – establishing the somewhat uneasy calm of life in the Yslaev household before the advent of Beliaev, the tutor. The group unfreezes as Katia, the maid, enters and tells Yslaev that he is wanted on the estate; he leaves. This is done to Chopin's statement of the theme (most of his long introduction is used at the end of the ballet). As he moves into the actual variations, Ashton introduces some of the characters with variations in the balletic sense. Natalia dances to the first (Brillante) variation, then Vera to the second (Veloce). The third is taken up by an incident invented by Ashton: Yslaev returns to look for his keys, the search for which proceeds all over the stage and develops into a comic episode somewhat reminiscent of the *pas de quatre* of the lovers in *The Dream*, with people bumping into one another or being lifted out of the way. Another variation follows, marked *con bravura* in the score, and Kolia's variation is just that – he bounces a ball and passes it over and under his leg and behind his back as he spins in multiple *pirouettes*.

The *ritornelli* linking the variations are used for brief passages of 'recitative' rather than the 'mock minuet' indicated in Ashton's draft. The longer, more dramatic *ritornello* preceding the fifth variation introduces an abrupt change of mood as Beliaev comes in, bringing a kite for Kolia. The sky outside darkens, a sudden breeze stirs the curtains, and there is a distant roll of thunder (this too is in the music). Beliaev, apparently unaware of the effect his arrival has had on the women of the house, dances the fifth, *adagio*, variation, which leads into the *alla polacca* finale, beginning as a *pas de deux* for Beliaev and Natalia, joined first by Vera and then by Kolia – each has brief solo passages.

The rest of the ballet is built on a series of *pas de deux* which carry the narrative forward to its conclusion (in spite of the mimed interludes, the overall impression is of a ballet in which the dancing hardly pauses for a moment from beginning to end). The first *pas de deux* is for Natalia and Rakitin, who comes to declare his love for her but is taken aback when she in turn confesses that she loves Beliaev. Rakitin is obliged to play the role of sympathetic confidant. At Yslaev's interruption she runs off weeping, leaving Rakitin to explain as best he may.

The second *pas de deux* is that for Beliaev and Vera, in which it is made very clear that the romantic feelings are all on her side (as he says in the play, 'I love you as I would a sister'). At the end she pulls his head down into an embrace, but he stops short of kissing her. They are discovered by Natalia, who dismisses Beliaev and demands an explanation. (Ashton was particularly pleased by the fact that her opening and closing of the doors on her entrance go exactly with a repeated, drawn-out *arpeggio*.) She tells Vera that such love is impossible, becomes angry and slaps her face, then at once is contrite. Rakitin enters and Vera runs out; noticing Natalia's agitation, he suggests a walk in the garden and they go off, doing the 'Fred step' as they move upstage, facing the rear.

The third *pas de deux* is in complete contrast – a peasant dance (Chopin's Kujawiak) for Beliaev and Katia. He has entered, evidently in some confusion, and is glad enough to enjoy an uncomplicated flirtation with the maid. All the same, his thoughts are on Natalia, and when Katia leaves he picks up Natalia's scarf from a chair. She enters and sees this, though he tries to hide the scarf as he turns to her. She puts a rose into his buttonhole and he takes her hand; as the *Andante spianato* begins they go into the last, passionate *pas de deux*. Natalia tries, but not very hard, to cool his ardour, and they end in an embrace.

The finale – the *Grande polonaise* with interpolated reprises of sections of the other pieces – moves swiftly. Vera enters and summons the rest of the household to witness what is going on. Natalia tries to shrug it off, but Vera insists and runs off hysterically, pursued by Natalia and Yslaev. Rakitin indicates to Beliaev that it is time for them both to take their leave, and they go off to pack. Natalia re-enters to find the room empty – her husband follows her and she half-swoons in his arms, and he helps her to her room. Rakitin and Beliaev come to say goodbye to Yslaev and Kolia; the boy cannot understand what is happening and his father tries to console him. Again Natalia, now in a négligée with two long blue ribbons at the back, returns to the empty stage. She dances a last despairing solo, ending with her head buried in her arm as she leans against the armchair. Unseen by her, Beliaev steals back for a last farewell – again, this incident is invented by Ashton, to replace the scene in the play where Beliaev gives Vera a note for Natalia. He goes to her, hesitates, then picks up and kisses the end of first one ribbon, then the other, throws the rose at her feet, and rushes off. She raises her head, sees the flower, and looks around, but he is gone. Natalia is alone as the curtain falls.

Whether or not *A Month in the Country* will ultimately receive general recognition as one of Ashton's masterpieces, it is too early at this writing, shortly after the first performances, to say. Certainly, unlike his last full-scale work, *The Creatures of Prometheus*, it is unmistakably an Ashton ballet, and in the direct line

A Month in the Country: Lynn Seymour as Natalia, Anthony Dowell as Beliaev

BELOW *A Month in the Country*: Lynn Seymour and Derek Rencher execute the 'Fred step' as they exit

of development that may be traced through his major works, not just in recent years, but from earlier in his career. Thus, while it is possible to compare the new ballet with *Marguerite and Armand* and *The Dream* in the way it reduces a story to its essential components and conveys it in dance terms, it should not be forgotten that Ashton learned this aspect of his craft many years ago when he was making ballets for the tiny stage of the Mercury Theatre, where choreographers, 'guided and goaded by Marie Rambert', (in A V Coton's marvellous phrase) had to learn 'the most effective way in which to utilise duration of dance-phases; impact of the music; dramatic tensions between the several characters. . .'[3]

Not for nothing, moreover, did Ashton dedicate *A Month in the Country* 'to the memory of Sophie Fedorovitch and Bronislava Nijinska, Chopin's compatriots and my mentors'. It was Fedorovitch who helped him to apply the lessons learned at the Mercury to ballets designed for larger stages, first Sadler's Wells and later Covent Garden. Nijinska's theories of movement have always informed Ashton's choreography, and it is evident from the beginning of *A Month in the Country* that they continue to do so, in Seymour's first variation, with its basically simple steps accented by twists and bends of the torso. (The way in which her arms weave about her head in a later solo passage once again recall Pavlova.)

There are elements, motifs, from many previous Ashton ballets to be found in the new piece. Vera's solo reminds one of the woman's variation in *Les Rendezvous* (which Denise Nunn had danced in Royal Ballet School performances) in its swiftness, its punctuating gestures, and the *pirouettes* immediately augmented by a further rotation. Yslaev's entrance, when he is looking for his keys, is similar to the several solos in *Enigma* in which eccentricity of character is graphically delineated in a few steps. The *pas de deux*, of course, has always been Ashton's most eloquent form of utterance – at least as far back as *Leda* – and here there are four in succession, each of them completely differentiated in the kind and degree of feeling that they convey. Ashton has always been careful to use lifts, even the most acrobatic, for expressive purposes, and not for their own sake. There are, as we have seen, several kinds of lifts that have become trademarks of his style; he uses them here in their familiar forms but also extends and develops them in quite new ways. For instance, in Dowell's duet with Denise Nunn there are two lifts that can be said to have their origin in those in *Enigma* (for instance) in which the man picks the woman up only a little way off the ground. Here Dowell first does this and then very slowly raises her to his arms' length, turning as he does so: the result is breathtaking in its virtuosity but even more in its poetry.

There are also variations on the familiar lifts that change direction in mid-air or in which the woman swoops down towards the floor in a *ciseaux* position; another in which Seymour does a little *battement* with the front foot as she is lifted in a *grand jeté* recalls a motif from *The Two Pigeons*. At the most passionate moments in her *pas de deux* with Dowell he tosses her into the air, Bolshoi-fashion, and catches her in a kind of fish-dive.

All this is not to suggest that *A Month in the Country* is a mere anthology of

moments from previous ballets. On the contrary, it offers the most encouraging
evidence that Ashton's creative powers continued to renew themselves during the
'fallow' period following his retirement. None of this evidence is more convincing
than the fact that, rather than pursuing originality at all costs, he has found fresh
new ways to use the simplest steps and movement ideas. For instance, one might
suppose that all the possibilities of the *pas de bourrée* had long been exhausted, yet
the final moments of the *pas de deux* between Natalia and Beliaev, in which she
drifts from side to side, echoing the movement with her raised hands, while he
slowly propels her forward, supporting her under her upper arms, are a perfect
image for her tremulous advance into a new and dangerous romantic entanglement.
Again, it might be thought that Ashton had said all there was to say about ribbons,
decoratively and metaphorically, in *La Fille mal gardée*, yet the closing moments of
the new ballet could not express more poetically the notion that Beliaev is not
only saying goodbye but setting Natalia free again.

As with *The Dream*, Ashton had started out with a limited intention of translating a well-known play into movement, and had ended up creating something entirely his own. Some people, among them certain American critics, judged the ballet as an adaptation, failing to recognise the fact that the original had undergone a typically Ashtonian transformation. His ballet is another of his statements on the subject of love, in this case love that for various reasons does not come to fruition and yet transfigures those whose lives it touches.

As always, Ashton found inspiration in the talents of his dancers. It is possible that if he had made the ballet earlier in his career he might have choreographed the role of Natalia for Fonteyn or perhaps Beriosova, investing the character with their personal qualities as dancers and people. With Seymour, Natalia certainly emerges as vulnerable, passionate and inscrutable – as she might have with the others – but Seymour also brings to her a kind of wilfulness that is both amusing and exasperating: she is not afraid, in creating a whole character, to show her unsympathetic side. Most notably, Ashton responded to Seymour's development into a mature woman and artist – as Oleg Kerensky said, Natalia differs from her previous created roles, which 'have required her to impersonate a teenage girl'.[4]

In the male roles, most of the actual dancing is given to Beliaev and Kolia, both of which give full scope to their creators' virtuosity. The solo passages for Wayne Sleep, indeed, are among the most brilliant Ashton has arranged for a male dancer – in one diagonal *enchaînement* he does a jumping turn with his legs flying out in a split, reminiscent of one of Baryshnikov's specialities. The choreography for Dowell is more innovative, extending the vocabulary of male adagio dancing with its deep *chassés* and sustained leaps; a particularly arresting movement is the *chassé* into *arabesque* after which he immediately turns and faces in *arabesque* in the opposite direction, which Ashton develops into a signature step for the character. As I have said, Grant's role as the husband is rather similar to the eccentrics in *Enigma*; Rencher's, while hardly reminiscent of his role in that ballet, is almost entirely an acting part, and his character is indeed less subtly delineated than the others precisely because it is not portrayed in dance terms. As so often before, Ashton's sympathetic understanding of young dancers showed itself in his choreography for Denise Nunn. The role of Vera challenged her both technically and dramatically, but under his coaching she rose to its demands and created a touching portrait of the innocent victim. Marguerite Porter's beauty is perhaps a little too delicate for the earthy Katia, but her duet with Dowell was exhilaratingly performed.

It must be said that, as with *La Fille mal gardée*, the weakest element in the collaboration is the design. Julia Trevelyan Oman's decision to place the Yslaevs in a grand, indeed palatial residence is not helpful to the creation of the proper atmosphere for the ballet, nor are the set's extreme symmetry and naturalism. Her notion of decorating the walls of the salon with many paintings based on contemporary engravings of scenes from *Don Giovanni* is simply mystifying. The connection between the décor and the score must be lost on the spectator since the paintings do not 'read' beyond the first rows of the orchestra stalls, if that far, and so the idea must seem like self-indulgence on the designer's part. None of this, in any case, helps to create that sense of provincial ennui, of summer lassitude, fertile ground for imprudent or unrequited infatuations, which pervades Turgenev's play. Another aspect of Turgenev's writing that had a strong appeal for Ashton was his love of nature, of the Russian landscape: passages like the description of a summer day that begins 'Bezhin Meadow' in *A Sportsman's Notebook* would have evoked a deep response in the Ashton who wrote, in an article quoted earlier, of 'the days of contemplation and distant, endless staring'. The landscape depicted in the backdrop seen through the window at the back of the set is a poor equivalent indeed for such writing. Ideally, perhaps ,the décor should have had the feeling of a painting by Fedotov or another of the 19th-century Russian realists. Failing that, one could at least have wished for something like Tania Moiseiwitsch's designs for the memorable Old Vic production of *A Month in the Country* by Michel St Denis in the late 40s. Oman's work is all the more disappointing when one remembers the importance of her contribution to *Enigma*.

It remains to be seen whether Ashton will be encouraged by the success of *A Month in the Country* to go on and create more ballets on a similar scale. Certainly it should have been enough to show him that he is indeed 'wanted', and also that, as Alexander Bland said, 'the creative flow is running free and strong',[5] two matters on which Ashton claimed to have some doubt before he went back to work. At Ashton's age, Petipa had yet to produce *Swan Lake*, Acts I and III, and *Raymonda*, and one may hope that Ashton too still has further masterpieces to give the world.

The story is told that Ashton had once advertised for a new housekeeper, and when he was interviewing applicants, he said to one woman who seemed a promising candidate that he didn't really mind how well she cleaned and cooked, 'but I have to be *loved*'. Love is clearly the subject of most of his ballets, however lightly treated, and it is important to him to be loved not only by those around him, but by the dancers he works with and the public he works for. As Maude Lloyd said, 'He made a friend of you when he worked with you, drew it out of you, even leaned on you.' In a similar vein, Suzanna Raymond of the Royal Ballet observed that the warmth of human feeling in his ballets reflects Ashton's friendly relationship with his dancers. There can be no doubt in Ashton's mind of the love of the dancers of the Royal Ballet when he goes in to rehearse one of his ballets, nor that of the audience when he takes a call after a performance. Even during the period of relative inactivity in the first half of the 1970s, Ashton frequently came before the curtain, as though in need of the reassurance he derived from the ovation that always ensued. Although he takes pride in his craftsmanship, if only because he feels he learned it from the best teachers, he is almost chronically self-deprecatory: when he asks a friend 'Was it all right?' after one of his own ballets, his anxiety seems completely genuine. He would never say, like a certain young choreographer on being told that his latest ballet was his best, 'What's wrong with the rest of my work?'

Like Jane Austen with her 'little bit (two Inches wide) of Ivory on which I work with so fine a brush',[6] he has tended to avoid what is often thought of as 'important' subject-matter, and though it is at least as true of dance as of poetry that, as Auden said, 'it does not have to be great or even serious to be good',[7] Ashton sometimes expresses the belief that this tendency puts him in a minor category as an artist. When he read the review of *La Fille mal gardée* by the American critic Nancy Goldner quoted on an earlier page, he said, 'I'm not sure about all this talk of profundity.' One may say of the characters in *Fille*, as David Robinson wrote of those in a film by Yasujiro Ozu, 'The people are foolish, comic, but above all *loved*.' Robinson goes on to quote Ozu's biographer, Donald Richie: 'What remains after an Ozu film is the feeling that, if only for an hour or two, you have seen the goodness and beauty of everyday things and everyday people . . . beautiful because real'.[8]

I have quoted a few pages earlier Ashton's comparison of the structure of *A Month in the Country* with that of a Mozart opera. No one would claim that operas like *Le nozze di Figaro* or *Così fan tutte* offer a view of human relationships that is anything less than profound, even though the plots are farcical, even contrived. It is not the plot of a Mozart opera that matters, but the music, and it is the music that conveys the essential seriousness of the work's meaning. (This is equally true of much humbler works of musical theatre like Jerome Kern's *Very Good Eddie*. There are, on the other hand, many dances, operas, and other works of the lyric theatre whose 'importance' lies only in their subject-matter, or 'concept', and not at all in the choreographic or musical content.)

In precisely the same way, the dancing in an Ashton ballet conveys the seriousness, the poetry of his vision of human life. Some twenty years ago, he wrote in a letter: 'I am afraid that the older I get the less interested I am in ballets of the pests, persecutions and cynicism of contemporary life, and frankly I only like ballets which give an opportunity for real dancing, and after all that is what the whole thing is about. A re-statement of one's own personal idiom of the classical ballet is all I ask to be able to achieve'.[9]

Increasingly during the last two decades, this has been Ashton's concern – what he has called 'the purity of the dance expressing nothing but itself', being careful to add, 'and thereby expressing a thousand degrees and facets of emotion, and the mystery of the poetry of movement'.[10]

Ashton has not generally been regarded as an innovator; indeed, there are those who may regard the return to the evening-length ballet, a development which he initiated in the West, as a retrograde step. Yet his preoccupation with the material

Sir Frederick Ashton receiving an Honorary Doctorate of Music
from the University of Oxford, 23 July 1976 ▷

of dancing was surely unique among British choreographers until a new generation grew up under his influence. He is of course widely acknowledged to be the creator of the native British style in classic dance, but the originality of many of his ballets in formal terms (*Les Rendezvous, Scènes de ballet, Monotones*, to name a few) has often gone unrecognised because of their deceptive conventionality, and their seemingly unimportant thematic content.

He is not in any case the kind of artist who sets out to be an innovator: any discoveries he has made have happened because his work has taken him in that direction, without any deliberation on his part. By the same token, a more obviously experimental choreographer like Merce Cunningham may come up with something that looks startlingly classical, through a similar process. With Ashton, as I have tried to show, choreography has always been a craft, a profession that he has been proud to follow for fifty years: in that time he has produced a body of work as impressive in its extent, and as likely to survive, as any of his contemporaries.

Yet he always resists any attempt to pin the label of 'genius' on him. When Mary Clarke told him that an admirer had used the word in connection with a revival of *The Two Pigeons*, he wrote back to her: 'The word genius is bandied about too frequently these days. People forget Shakespeare, Mozart, Michelangelo . . .'[11] When being interviewed on BBC radio about *Enigma Variations*, he said that he had 'tried to bring out the loneliness of genius'. Ian Horsbrugh, the interviewer, asked, 'Is that something you share?' and Ashton replied, 'Well, the loneliness perhaps, but not the genius'.[12] But like Gertrude Stein answering her own question, 'Is he a genius?' one may say, ignoring his own disclaimers, 'I think he is one. More likely than any one we have seen for a long time.'

APPENDICES

CHRONOLOGY

NOTES

BIBLIOGRAPHY

INDEX

Appendix A: *The Subject Matter of Ballet*

Contribution by Frederick Ashton to a symposium in *Ballet Annual 1959*

A ballet does not necessarily require a libretto, but it seems that most of the greatest ballets of the past have had librettos of a kind that supplemented choreographic expression and enabled the direct emotions that lend themselves best to ballets to move and excite a poetic response in the audience and yet were understandable dance dramas, clear and true in all purposes, i.e. *Giselle* and *Le Lac des Cygnes*. I think that ballets without librettos, popularly known as abstract ballets, though appearing to convey nothing but the exercise of pure dancing, should have a basic idea which is not necessarily apparent to the public, or a personal fount of emotion from which the choreography springs. Otherwise, in my opinion, a cold complexity emerges which ceases to move an audience.

Poetic evocation when sensitively handled can lead to masterpieces such as *Les Sylphides*, *Serenade*, etc., and leave an audience suspended in a trance-like response (that a story ballet can never achieve) because of their very directness and delicacy of poetic potency that needle-like reaches the heart.

A choreographer must have a firm grasp of the style of movement he is using or the result will lack a synthesis and be diffused. It must convey something very definite to him which gives it form and cohesion.

Unsuitable stories are generally of a complexity that requires words to make them understandable and thereby aspire to another medium. Situations must be direct and fundamental and understood through the plastic statement which must be clear and portray the situations with clarity, truth and dramatic understanding.

I think that all choreographers need guidance of some sort or other. If they are established masters, they may get this from the composer or designer with whom they collaborate or from influences that surround them and should constantly during the rehearsal period submit their work to criticism and revision to people whose opinions are of value to them; a fresh eye can do wonders when one's own nose is too deeply embedded. The young, I think, should serve an apprenticeship to a master, thereby learning the craft and technique, enabling them later on to revolt against the principles they have learnt and to clarify their own statement. Alas, it was given to few to have a Diaghileff and Kochno at their elbow.

The type of subject is surely a personal matter. One instinctively chooses the subject best suited to one's credo and devises a form that suits one's inspiration. Personally, I do not believe that everything can be expressed in ballet. It has its limitations like any other art and nothing is achieved by breaking the bonds of its very stylisation.

I find it incompatible when a dancer 'on point' is endeavouring to express realistic and pedestrian emotions of an overcharged nature. Here, I almost agree with the modernist school – the point shoe is incongruous.

I do not think that choreographers have necessarily to be 'engaged' or 'committed' or to write ballets about current social happenings. These subjects are as likely to date as quickly as yesterday's newspaper. Some say, and I think rightly, that if ballet is to be taken seriously, it must deal with serious matters. I believe simply that a ballet must be a good work of art; that it must express the choreographer's vision of experience as truthfully and as beautifully as possible. Insofar as it does this, it will express his most profound sense of values and thus be likely to concern itself with matters of more permanent significance than topical issues. He should deal with that which is spiritual and eternal rather than that which is material and temporary.

Appendix B: Synopses

A Tragedy of Fashion

Original synopsis by Ashley Dukes

Dances:

1 Monsieur du Chic indicates his joy at the creation of his new model, which will mark the summit of his achievement in the world of fashion.

2 He summons Orchidée and they rejoice together over the launching of the new model.

3 Orchidée celebrates the triumph of fashion.

4 A young beauty brings her decrepit old beau to watch her choose her clothes. Mannequins enter and display some of the costumier's former creations, which are rejected.

5 Monsieur du Chic is undismayed, in the conviction that his latest creation will prove irresistible.

6 Orchidée appears in the latest model, Volupté du Désert. The lady laughs at it. In her opinion it is fit for a mummy. Orchidée protests that it allows full freedom of movement. She turns cartwheels and performs the split by way of proving its flexibility. The lady is still contemptuous. In despair, Orchidée spins upon her belly like a top, upon which the scandalised customers withdraw.

7 Despair of Monsieur du Chic, who cannot endure the shame of seeing his work of art rejected. He appeals for sympathy to Orchidée, who laughs and hands him his scissors. With this instrument of his glory he stabs himself to the heart. Orchidée sheds two tears over his corpse, but she is already late for an amorous appointment, and therefore sheds no more.

The End.

Pomona

Synopsis by Thomas McGreevy (from the programme of the Camargo Society)

INTRATA – At the rise of the curtain, Pomona, goddess of fruits, and her nymphs are discovered in an orchard in a wood near Rome, the nymphs in little groups, Pomona apart.

No 1 CORANTE – The sound of a hunting horn is heard. The god Vertumnus and his train of immortals, all wearing hunting attire, enter. Vertumnus makes attempts to gain favour with Pomona, but she repulses him and then, frightened by the bolder advances of Vertumnus and the immortals she and her nymphs fly into the wood, Pomona with the eldest. Vertumnus watches her departure; then disgusted with the failure of his disguise expresses his chagrin in a dance. But it is with new decision that he leads his train away.

No 2   PASTORALE – Pomona comes back timidly and expresses her sense of isolation in a dance. She goes.

No 3   MENUETTO – The nymphs re-enter timidly, but are disappointed to find the hunters gone and dance with melancholy. They are interrupted by the return of the immortals, who, having discarded their hunting attire, make a gentler entry this time. Pomona comes back quietly, and unnoticed, looks on while the immortals succeed little by little in gaining favour with the nymphs and leading them away, one by one. At the end she is again alone.

No 4   PASSACAGLIA – Vertumnus returns disguised as a lady of uncertain age. He endeavours to comfort Pomona. He succeeds, and casting off his disguise follows Pomona into the wood.

No 5   RIGADOON – Divertissement danced by the nymphs and immortals.

No 6   SICILIANA – Vertumnus comes back to the orchard with Pomona. They dance a *pas de deux* expressive of their love for each other.

No 7†   MARCIA (FINALE) – Joyous return of nymphs and immortals. Nuptial dance.

† Added to synopsis at first Vic-Wells revival.

The Lord of Burleigh

Argument by Edwin Evans

In the poems of Alfred Lord Tennyson are many charming people whom the poet has neglected to introduce to each other. Some of them are not even named. In this ballet a few of them are identified and made mutually acquainted. Here, for instance, is the Lady Clara Vere de Vere, who is described as proudly disdainful of an unnamed suitor. Why should he not be the Lord of Burleigh, who, roaming the country as an obscure landscape painter, would obviously be unworthy of her Ladyship's serious attention? His Lordship, according to the poet, woos a nameless village maiden who is unaware of his high estate until he presents her to his vassals. Why should she not be Katie Willows, who, appropriately enough, comes from 'The Brook'? The plight of Mariana, waiting for a lover who cometh not, is known to all, and so is that of Edward Gray, who mourns a dead love. Surely every humane feeling demands that they should be brought together and find mutual solace in that emotion which, we are told, is akin to love. Of the other characters, some are paired, some left unattached; for in the realms of poetry, as of the ballet, there are inevitably more women than men, yet none of them 'superfluous'.

Le Baiser de la fée

Synopsis as given in the programme of the Vic-Wells Ballet

1st Tableau (Prologue) – The Lullaby of the Tempest

A woman carrying a child in her arms is making her way through the tempest.

She is pursued by spirits, loses her way, and dies of exhaustion.

The Fairy appears and seals the child with her mysterious kiss. Peasants enter, find the dead mother and bear her and the child away with them.

2nd Tableau – A Village Festival

The child of the prologue, now a young man, is dancing with his friends and with his fiancée. As evening falls they leave him.

The Fairy enters disguised as a gypsy, takes his hand and tells his fortune. She speaks to him of his love and promises him a supreme happiness. The Young Man begs her to lead him to his fiancée.

3rd Tableau – The Bridal Chamber.

The Young Man, guided by the Fairy, arrives at the bridal chamber where his fiancée, surrounded by her companions, is preparing for her wedding. After a pas de deux the fiancée goes out to put on her bridal dress. The Fairy reappears wearing a bridal veil, and the Young Man, mistaking her for his fiancée, speaks to her of his passionate love. She throws aside the veil and he perceives his mistake. He tries to escape her but her supernatural power is too strong for him.

She bears him away to the eternal dwellings where once again she seals him with her mysterious kiss thus preserving the happiest moment of his life for ever unaltered.

4th Tableau (Epilogue) – The Lullaby of the Eternal Dwellings

The First Shoot

Synopsis by Osbert Sitwell

The action takes place in a woodland glade, during a fashionable Edwardian shooting party, the first given by Lord de Fontenoy since his marriage to the lovely Connie Winsome, late of Musical Comedy. After an opening dance of pheasants, Lady de Fontenoy enters, soon followed by her admirer, Lord Charles Canterbury, who performs a dance for her pleasure, but they are interrupted by the rest of the party, who march round, firing in the air, and then dance off to luncheon. Lord Charles lingers, fires at another bird, and accidentally wounds Lady de Fontenoy. Dragging herself on to the stage, she dies in his arms, to the intense interest of the other guests.

Apparitions

Synopsis by Constant Lambert

Prologue

It is the Romantic Period. A young poet is sitting in his study working at a sonnet entitled 'L'Amour Suprême'. But its final form eludes him. Suddenly lights spring up in the windows and strange figures appear before his tired eyes – a dandified hussar, a monk of menacing aspect and, finally, a woman in ball dress who looks at him alluringly. She becomes the symbol of the supreme love which he is trying to enshrine in his poem and he is obsessed by her image. The figures vanish as mysteriously as they came. The poet, fired by his vision, tries to complete his poem but he is too overwrought. In a despairing attempt to soothe his nerves he takes a dose of laudanum and falls into an uneasy sleep.

Tableau I

In his first dream the poet finds himself in an enormous ballroom. Ladies of fashion are dancing with young dandies, amongst them the hussar he had seen in his vision. He tries to join in the dance, but they disregard him. At the end of a mazurka the guests draw aside and the woman of his vision enters and dances alone. The ball ends with a *galop general* in which they change partners. At times he finds himself dancing with the woman but it is only by chance and it is clear that the hussar occupies her interest. As the galop finishes the guests leave.

For a moment it seems to the poet that the woman returns to him with words of love, but it is only a dream within a dream and as the vision fades he is alone.

Tableau II

In his second dream the poet finds himself on a snow-clad plain. It is the evening and the bells are chiming. The spirits of the bells take visible form and dance round him mockingly. Their jangling ceases only to give way to a more sombre note. A chant is heard and a funeral procession appears led by the monk of his vision. Drawn by a morbid curiosity he rushes up to the bier and tears the cloth away. Lying there is the woman in ball dress. The monk thrusts him aside and the procession passes on leaving the poet praying in the snow.

Tableau III

In his third dream the poet finds himself in a cavern. The guests from the ball-room are there but dressed in a strange uniform as though members of some unholy cult, and this time their revelry has a sinister quality. The poet throws himself into the orgy with abandon until, to his horror, he sees that a new figure has arrived. It is the woman in ball dress but transformed into a hideous and vicious creature. This time it is she who pursues and her companions force her on him against his will. He falls to the ground in exhaustion and she removes the mask which has hidden her beauty. But he does not see the transformation. The unholy revels continue.

Epilogue

He awakes in despair realising that his dreams are but a reflection of his own tragic life. He dashes to the centre window but no vision is vouchsafed to him. He kills himself.

Gently and sorrowfully the woman in ball dress and her companions enter and bear him away. 'L'Amour suprême' is achieved at last.

Harlequin in the Street

First version; synopsis by André Derain, as given in the programme of the Arts Theatre, Cambridge.

A grave and serious overture, before the curtain rises on a street scene in Paris, serves to prepare the audience for what is to follow. Three gossips, who should be better employed, are urged into gay steps by the scandal which they are exchanging about their neighbours. They are properly rewarded by the arrival of Harlequin, brought to the city by the approaching carnival, who shakes them as they deserve and, having thoroughly upset their complacency, disappears in a bound. As the gossips are beginning to recover themselves, there enters a bourgeois gentilhomme, and, a little later, an ancient marquise carried by two porters in a shabby sedan-chair. Again the Harlequin, surmising that her thoughts are no better than they should be, upsets her chair and throws the dame into confusion. Fortunately there returns at this moment the bourgeois gentilhomme who feels himself fully commissioned by his proper importance to chastise all the world with his cane, and courteously to put the good lady back again into her chair. The porters continue on their journey, the street scene continues as before, and the Harlequin, satisfied that all these foolish thinkers are dispersed, returns to celebrate in a pirouette the true purposes of life.

Second version; synopsis (by Constant Lambert), 'after Jean-François Regnard'.

A street at dawn. Two clandestine lovers, La Superbe and Monseigneur, take a sentimental farewell and arrange to meet later. They are too engrossed in their love-making to notice the mocking of Harlequin until he jumps between them, sends them off in opposite directions and robs the young man of his coat.

Seven o'clock strikes and the street comes to life. Porters, still putting on their coats, say goodbye to their wives and go reluctantly to work. A bird-catcher tries to sell his wares, but has them stolen. A cheerful bread-boy passes on his round. Finally a flustered messenger arrives with a letter from La Superbe to Monseigneur. Harlequin pretends to be the recipient, steals the letter and re-writes it. When Monseigneur re-enters Harlequin presents him with a letter apparently from his mistress telling him that he must disguise himself as a porter in order that their meeting shall be unknown. The two porters re-enter and the young man pays one of them to lend him his clothes. Meanwhile Harlequin disguises the bread-boy in the other porter's clothes.

La Superbe re-enters to meet her lover and is shocked and bewildered to receive gallant advances from first one apparent porter, then another. When the real porter comes in dressed in her lover's clothes she is deceived by the disguise and flies to his arms. On discovering her mistake she faints. When she recovers, a general unmasking takes place. Lovers and husbands are restored to their rightful partners, and Harlequin, having deceived both high and low, expresses his derision in a care-free dance.

Cupid and Psyche

Synopsis by Lord Berners

Scene I

In a certain city in Greece there lived a king who had three daughters. The two elder sisters were fair to behold, but such was the loveliness of Psyche, the youngest, that the townsfolk carried her in triumph through the streets. The altars of Venus were neglected and the people worshipped Psyche in her stead.

Now this aroused the anger of the Goddess. She sent for her son Cupid and said to him 'Go, seek out this presumptuous maid and let her become the slave of an unworthy love. Thus shall your mother be avenged.'

Cupid hastened to obey his mother's commands. Putting on the mask of invisibility, he set forth on his mission of vengeance. But the beauty of Psyche was proof even against the wrath of the Gods, and the God of Love himself fell a victim to his own weapons.

Casting aside his bow and arrows, he bore her swiftly through the air, over the high mountain tops and set her down among the flowers of a valley in his own domain.

Scene II

Cupid has built a fair palace for Psyche and here, attended by the Zephyrs, she lives happily awhile. Yet Cupid himself remains invisible and comes to her only under cover of the night. Such, he tells her, are the conditions imposed on the union of Gods and mortals. And he warns her that she must not seek to look upon his face or to discover what manner of being he is, for undue curiosity would surely bring disaster in its train.

After a time Psyche begins to long for the company of her sisters. She begs of Cupid so earnestly that she may be allowed to see them that he at last consents, and they are transported by the Zephyrs to Psyche's palace.

At first they greet their sister tenderly, but when they hear of her good fortune and see the magnificence of her habitation, envy turns their hearts to evil and they seek how they may best destroy her happiness. They discover, by cunning questions, that Psyche has never looked upon the visible form of her lover.

'Alas,' they cry, 'this is hardly a satisfactory situation for a young girl. This vaunted God of yours is without doubt some monster so hideous that he dare not show his face. And when his lust is satisfied he will in the end devour you.'

Scene III

Distracted by doubt and fear, Psyche listens to the evil counsels of her sisters and, taking with her a lighted lamp, she draws aside the curtain of the bedchamber. But lo! instead of some fearful monster there is revealed to her the sweetest and most gentle of all creatures, the God of Love himself lying asleep on the couch. As she gazes upon him in rapture a drop of burning oil falls on his shoulder. At the touch of fire the God starts up. Reproaching her bitterly for her want of faith, he rises upon his wings and takes flight into the sky.

After wandering through many countries in search of Cupid, Psyche returns once more to her native land. Meanwhile Venus, as punishment for his disobedience, holds Cupid captive in her palace, and she pursues the luckless Psyche with her vengeance, subjecting her to many trials and persecutions.

At last, driven to despair, Psyche determines to put an end to her sufferings. As she makes her way to cast herself from a high rock into the sea, the God Pan appears to her. Touched by her misery, he calls upon the Gods to help her. Ceres, Minerva, Apollo, Diana, Jupiter and Juno all plead in turn with Venus, and by their powers of persuasion induce the angry Goddess to relent. Cupid is restored to Psyche, and all the Gods join in the marriage feast. Apollo sings to the lyre, Pan plays on his reeds, Ceres scatters her flowers, even Venus herself dances to the music. Thus, with due rites, does Psyche pass into the power of Cupid.

Devil's Holiday

Synopsis by Vincenzo Tommasini

Prologue: The devil disguised as a rich stranger in search of amusement strolls the streets of Venice. He encounters a group of creditors and bailiffs at the door of a ruined palace demanding payment from the old lord. The noble and his daughter beg for patience, and are answered with threats. The devil ends the dispute by distributing generous purses of gold. The grateful old lord invites the devil to his daughter's betrothal ball in the palace. Noticing a young beggar raptly admiring the daughter, the devil signals him to follow, and promises to fulfil his desires.

Scene One: At the ball, the young girl, surrounded by guests, dances with her fiancé. The devil enters, followed by the beggar in princely costume. The young girl, responding to the devil's will, abandons her fiancé to fall in love with the beggar. But this intruder is surprised at his amours by the fiancé and the old lord who indignantly turn the beggar out of the palace.

Entr'acte: The beggar and the young girl in a lover's dream.

Scene Two: In a forest clearing a band of hunters rest and dance about the fox they have killed. Their merriment halts suddenly, and they scatter when the devil rises in the place of the dead fox. The beggar enters seeking the young girl whose image obsesses him. To make him forget this love, the devil causes a young gypsy girl to appear and whirl the beggar away in a dance. Thus the young girl, in search of her lover, encounters him dancing with the gypsy. The beggar sees her, recovers his memory, perceives the devil's trickery, and decides to fight him. Drawn by the noise of battle, the hunters come to the beggar's aid, but the devil flees at their approach.

Entr'acte: The devil prepares for the carnival and dons a disguise with the help of two servants.

Scene Three: The old lord, his daughter, the beggar, the hunters, all under the devil's influence, mingle with the carnival masqueraders in the square of Venice. The devil circulates among the crowd but the people penetrate his disguise and surge upon him ominously. They tear off his domino, whereupon they are petrified by the sight of the devil incarnate. At that moment, the clock strikes midnight, and the devil vanishes. The atmosphere cleared, the carnival comes to life.

The Quest

Synopsis by Doris Langley Moore

Scene 1   Outside the House of Archimago

St George and Una, lost in a storm, fall under the spell of Archimago, who transforms his female servant into an evil semblance of Una. St George is deceived and leaves in disgust.

Scene 2   Near the Palace of Pride

Duessa chooses Sansfoy as her cavalier. St George challenges him to battle and kills him. Duessa throws herself at St George's mercy, and they leave together. Una, searching for St George, is deceived by Archimago, who enters disguised in similar armour.

Scene 3   The Palace of Pride

St George enters the Palace of Pride with Duessa. Sansjoy follows him and they fight. Duessa takes the side of the Saracen knight and reveals her love for him when he is killed. St George, doubly disillusioned, sees the Palace of Pride and Duessa in their true light.

Scene 4   Near the Palace of Pride

Sansloy is mourning for his two brothers. Archimago enters, still disguised as St George, and Sansloy kills him. Una realises that she has been deceived by the Magician. Sansloy makes violent love to her. St George enters, kills Sansloy and is re-united to Una.

Scene 5   The House of Holinesse

St George brings Una to the House of Holinesse. After pledging himself to England, St George bids farewell to his beloved Una and departs on his quest.

Les Sirènes

Draft synopsis by Frederick Ashton†

It is dawn on a French watering place and Sirens are sitting on a rock combing their hair and singing the latest waltz. Two Seagulls are picking about on the beach, they are frightened away by the arrival of children with large hoops, their nurses flirt with the local police. The sirens in terror slide off the rock on a piercing colora-

† A slightly different version is given by Cecil Beaton in his book *Ballet*.

tura top note, leaving their combs behind them. The gulls take possession of the rock and comb out each other's feathers. The children play around till the arrival of the smart world who parade themselves on the beach in elegant beach wear with enormous hats. Lady Kitty enters more elegant than anybody and very blonde and accompanied by an asinine Guardsman and the latest fashionable tenor; they dance and flirt and everybody dances.

At the climax of gaiety La Belle Otero, the rage of the moment, enters. She is persuaded to dance, she steps on to the rock and does a mock Spanish dance *comme une vache espagnole*, all are ravished, especially the Tenor and Guardsman, *she* has eyes only for the tenor.

Excitement grows as an oriental carpet seller rushes on and proceeds to lay down his carpets. The gay world line the length of carpet and a foreign royalty in morning clothes, orders, decorations, jewels, white spats over oriental shoes, and a fez, appears. He walks down the carpet an attendant holding a sunshade over his head and all curtsy. As he comes to La Belle Otero she throws out her hip in Spanish allure, which gains his immediate attention and awakens his desire. Lady Kitty is ignored and flounces off. The Royal Personage makes advances to Otero who already is attended by the tenor and Guardee. They do a dance of rival claims. The Guardee offers her marriage, the tenor his false heart, and the Royal personage his jewels, which naturally win her but not her love which has gone to the tenor. As Otero and personage exit she throws a kiss to the Guardee, a flower or garter to the tenor and a note of assignation. The gay world leave for lunch. The tenor is left alone with his memories and the seagulls who peck interestedly around him.

Otero eventually steals back and does a swooning love dance with the tenor, during the lunch hour, as she gets more carried away and abandoned she drops the jewels given to her by the Royal personage. They decide to bathe to cool off their passion, and disappear into wheeled cabins and while undressing sing a duet, the seagulls listen with great interest and applaud – but suddenly see the jewels glistening on the beach, they bite at them, and eventually take them on to the rock and sit on them and nod off, rest their eyes, have a little siesta.

Otero and Tenor emerge in bathing dresses and as they appear, the corps de ballet also in bathing dresses come on pulling the sea. All bathe and the Sirens rise up out of the water singing (coloratura) and confusing everybody. After bathing they take off the sea and Otero and tenor D'Ardath remain to sun bathe. The royal personage suddenly appears looking for Otero, who is caught in an embrace, he indignantly demands back his jewels, a search is made, they cannot be found, the police are called by Lady Kitty, general scandal, all scorn Otero encouraged by Lady Kitty, the tenor included; afraid of his career he exits with Lady Kitty, as does everybody else. Otero escorted by police and followed by Royal Personage and Guardee determined to 'see it through, Old Boy'.

As evening draws near the Sirens reappear on the rock, the gulls wake up and the male gull lifts the *collière* and puts it round the female's neck with pride and affection, she preens herself and the orchestra softly play the opening bars of Les

Patineurs Waltz which the Sirens take up in the background, and comb their hair. Slow curtain.

Cinderella

Synopsis, as given in the programme of the Sadler's Wells Ballet

Act I   A room in the house of Cinderella's father.

Cinderella's step-sisters are busy embroidering a shawl to wear at the court ball to which they have been invited. Cinderella is seated at the fireside. The sisters quarrel among themselves and leave the room. Left alone, Cinderella recalls the happy days when her mother was alive. Her father wants to be kind to his daughter, but is afraid of his bad-tempered step-daughters who scold him angrily when he tries to comfort Cinderella. A mysterious old beggar-woman appears in the midst of this scene and begs for alms. The sisters drive her out but Cinderella gives her bread. The old woman casts a gentle look at the kind girl and disappears.

Purveyors arrive – dressmakers, a hairdresser, a jeweller, etc. – and the sisters dress for the ball. A dancing master and two violinists enter and the sisters practise the gavotte. Cinderella's father and his step-daughters set out for the ball, and Cinderella is left sadly alone.

Again the mysterious beggar woman appears and, throwing off her disguise, reveals herself as the Fairy Godmother. She summons the fairies of the seasons, Spring, Summer, Autumn and Winter and their attendants to dress Cinderella for the ball, as a reward for her kindness.

All is ready, but the fairy points to the clock, warning Cinderella that she must leave the ball before the clock strikes twelve, or all the magic charms with which she is invested will fade away and Cinderella, the Princess, will once more be a scullery maid. Escorted by the Seasons and the Stars, Cinderella drives to the ball.

Act II   A ball at the Palace.

The ball has begun, courtiers move about in a formal dance and the jester dances. Cinderella's father and the step-sisters arrive. A fanfare, and the Prince is announced. Mysterious music is heard and Cinderella appears, so beautiful that they all take her for a princess; even her step-sisters fail to recognise her. The Prince, charmed by her beauty, offers her three oranges, the rarest fruit in his land, which she gives to her sisters. The scene empties and the Prince and Cinderella, left alone, declare their love for each other. The waltz is resumed and, caught up by the dance, Cinderella forgets the fairy's warning. The clock strikes twelve and Cinderella rushes from the palace, losing a slipper on the way. The Prince, dismayed, picks up the lost slipper and swears to find the girl he loves.

Act III   *Scene i.*   After the ball. A room in the house of Cinderella's father.
         Scene ii.   An enchanted garden.

Cinderella awakes at her own fireside. Was it all a dream? The slipper she has hidden in her apron convinces her that she really was in the palace and danced with the Prince. The sisters run in, tell Cinderella about their conquests at the ball and show her their oranges. Women rush in to say that the Prince is looking everywhere for the girl who lost the slipper. The Prince appears and the sisters try on the slipper. Cinderella kneels to help, and the second slipper falls out of her apron. The Prince recognises in the modest Cinderella, the beautiful Princess of the ball and the Fairy Godmother appears to reunite the lovers, who live happily ever after.

Le Rêve de Léonor

Synopsis by Léonor Fini

Asleep, half-hidden in the darkened countryside, surrounded by the weird creatures of her imagination, Léonor, possessor of beautiful golden hair, dreams. In her dream she sees herself devoid of hair, pursuing her own golden tresses. She is caught up in the midst of voluptuous, derisive creatures. This phase of her dream fades and passes to a remembrance of the occasion when she went to a Ball as Proserpine, who, for the sake of a pomegranate, was cast back into Hades. As Proserpine, she is again tempted by greed. This time it is a mass of rich sweetmeats and whipped cream in which she is engulfed. The dream again changes and Léonor becomes a little white owl playing gaily among beautiful feathered beings who come to her rescue when a large black bird tries to carry her off. She finally slays the black bird as the first light of dawn awakens her to a new day.

Tiresias

Two versions of the synopsis are given, an early draft prepared by Constant Lambert for Frederick Ashton, and the final version as printed in the programme:

Tiresias
Ballet in one act and 3 scenes (after Lemprière) by Constant Lambert

Scene I 'In Crete there lies the scene.'
An open air gymnasium in the outskirts of Knossos. Columns either side. Large Bull (flat) centre stage.

Dance I Young girls (nasty smelly little adolescents but don't tell this to the corps de ballet) are miming the old Cretan sport of vaulting in the nude over the horns of a bull. Fun, games and girlish laughter. At the climax of their hideous pranks Tiresias enters in a carefree and slightly contemptuous manner. Executes a rather exhibitionist step. After which the little beasts run off half ashamed half mocking.

Dance II Tiresias slightly puzzled by his mingled reception pulls himself together and performs a dance of male triumph. (He is at this stage the typical athletic hearty of about 20.)

Dance III He is joined by a gang of other hearties who execute a 'danse guerrière' in his praise. Spears and double Minoan shields if possible. GLOIRE! The triumph of T's youth.

Dance IV Sudden change of key and lighting. A revolting young virgin (but revolting my dear!) enters and tells T that the priestesses are arriving. Solemn cortège of priestesses (this is a long number). In the middle the young virgin presents him with a wand of honour (sex symbols etc) which he accepts with slight apprehension. More GLOIRE. The captains and the queens depart. T (by now about 28) is left in a state of bewilderment.

Dance V Enter two snakes copulating. Tiresias for reasons known only to himself dashes at them in a puritanical fury and beats the female snake with his wand. Thunder and lightning! From behind the bull appears the figure of the female Tiresias wearing the mask of the young Tiresias. T is terrified. Margot takes off her mask and T disappears down trap. Black out.

Scene II (Pastoral Intermezzo)
Landscape with rocks and flowers. The Dove Goddess constructed by flat near the backcloth. Tiresias (by now an attractive girl of 30) discovered alone. Romantic solo. (Dance I.)

Dance II Entrance of shepherds and shepherdesses. Ensemble. Solo for T in middle. Ineffectual passes by shepherds. Exit of shepherds and shepherdesses. Short solo for T.

Dance III From behind the Dove Goddess (sex symbol again) appears a luvlly man. Grand pas de deux starting off slowly but ending up in a state of erotic frenzy. Climax of T's sex life.

Dance IV T now a handsome woman of 40 invites her friends to a Bacchanale. 'A frenetic rumpus supervenes' (literal quotation from the Opera House, Palermo). Passes made all round but none to the hostess. At climax of orgy enter two gate crashers The SNAKES, and they're *at it again*. The disillusioned Tiresias seizes her wand and beats the male snake. The female Tiresias disappears as the elderly Tiresias appears as a man with a beard and breasts. (We must work out the technical details of this together.)

Scene III An open courtyard in a Palace. Yellow backcloth. Two pedestals on which are placed Jupiter and Juno. Grouping of corps de ballet to be discussed later.

Argument between Jupiter and Juno on relative pleasure of being man or woman. Juno saying man and Jupiter saying woman. Tiresias is called in as only living authority. A man dances to his tune from Scene I. A girl dances to his tune from Scene II. T unhesitatingly says 'woman'!

Juno furious at losing her argument strikes him blind. (Thunder, lightning etc.) Jupiter as compensation gives him the gift of prophecy. Semi-religious finale. At the very end Michael and Margot enter in the same costumes as the snakes to form a triptych. END

Scene I In Crete, There lies the Scene.

Young girls in a gymnasium are attempting to somersault over the horns of a bull. The youthful Tiresias enters and displays his superior prowess. The young girls leave in mockery.

Tiresias executes a dance of athletic triumph. He is joined by his warrior friends who pay him homage. Their dance is interrupted by a young Neophyte who tells him that priestesses wish to give him a wand of honour. He accepts it with reluctance and is left alone.

Two snakes enter. Tiresias strikes the female snake with his wand and is transformed into a woman.

Scene II In the Mountains.

Tiresias, now a woman, is discovered alone. She is joined by a group of shepherds and shepherdesses but the shepherds do not appeal to her.

From behind a statue appears a stranger. They fall in love. The shepherds and shepherdesses celebrate the happiness of Tiresias and her lover. The Neophyte re-enters with the wand and the bacchanale is interrupted by the presence of two snakes. Tiresias strikes the male snake with her wand and is changed back to a man.

Scene III A Palace.

Zeus, the God, and Hera, the Goddess are disputing the relative happiness of the two sexes each maintaining that the other is the happier of the two. Tiresias is called upon for a decision. He states firmly that he preferred his life as a woman. Hera, furious at being contradicted strikes Tiresias blind. Zeus as recompense gives Tiresias the gift of prophecy.

Sylvia

Act I A Sacred Wood.

Nymphs and Sylvans are dancing in the moonlight. At the approach of the shepherd Aminta, they disperse. The intruder is left to muse in solitude over his illicit passion for the leader of Diana's huntresses, the chaste Sylvia to whom, though he has seen her only once, his heart is irretrievably lost. The sound of a horn is heard in the distance. Aminta recognises the music of Diana's hunt and hides behind the shrine of Eros. Sylvia and her attendant nymphs appear. They dance in honour of the chase. In the arrogance of her virginity, Sylvia taunts the image of Eros.

Meanwhile, Orion, the robber Khan, whose depredations are the scourge of a terrorized peasantry, has secretly been observing the scene. The beauty of Sylvia enflames his senses and he determines to possess her. The discovery of Aminta's cloak, inadvertently discarded on the approach of Sylvia, betrays the presence of her lover. Incensed by the notion that a man should have presumed to spy upon her, Sylvia commands her attendants to bring forth the culprit. Perceiving the tender motive of his conduct, she blames the machinations of Eros and seeking to avenge the affront, turns with drawn bow towards the statue of the god. Aghast at the intended sacrilege, Aminta shields the statue with his body. Sylvia's arrow strikes him through the heart. Unmoved by this act of devotion, Sylvia anathematizes the love god. As she does so, an arrow loosed by the god himself pierces her to the heart. Though trembling from the wound, she affects a disdainful indifference and gathering her companions vanishes into the wood.

Dawn breaks. Peasants, on their way to the fields, pause to make obeisance before the shrine. One of their number, a young shepherd, lingers behind. On the approach of Orion, he takes cover. The Khan advances towards the prostrate Aminta and gloats over the fate of his rival. Suspecting that Sylvia will return, he awaits her in hiding. Sylvia, transformed by the miraculous effects of the love god's arrow, re-appears in compassionate quest of the lover to whose mortal plight she had lately been indifferent. Emerging from his hiding place, Orion seizes the unsuspecting nymph and carries her off to his grotto palace in the remote depths of the forest.

The young shepherd summons his friends. They leave their furrows to weep with him over the body of Aminta. An old sorcerer appears mysteriously in their midst. They explain to him the cause of their grief; in reply, he plucks a rose from a nearby bush and presses its petals to the lips of the inanimate Aminta. Gradually the lover revives. His first thoughts are of Sylvia. Her torn mantle is found and the sorcerer tells of her abduction. Aminta turns in prayer towards the shrine. Casting off his cloak the sorcerer reveals himself as the god and charges Aminta to set forth in search of Sylvia.

Act II   Orion's Grotto.

Orion's concubines entice Sylvia with luxurious raiment and precious jewels. He declares his love but Sylvia repulses him. He summons slaves to dance for her pleasure, and tempts her to refresh herself with rare wines and exotic foods.

She performs a Bacchic dance, ostensibly for the delectation of her captor, but in reality a ruse to postpone the odium of more intimate endearments. While dancing she plies him with repeated draughts of wine. He vainly pursues her in the dance and at last falls to the ground in a drunken stupor. His slaves, who have been following the bibulous example of their master, sink into insensibility from the same cause.

Though she is momentarily free to depart, Sylvia's efforts to find a way out of the grotto are fruitless. In desperation, she invokes Eros. The god appears; at his bidding, the grotto vanishes and he beckons Sylvia forth into the freedom of the woods.

Act III   A Sea Coast near the Temple of Diana.

A festival of Bacchus is due to take place. The revels are exalted by the participation of Ceres, Apollo, the Muses and other Divinities. They dance, with groups of peasants impersonating Spring and Summer, before the statue of the wine god.

The disconsolate Aminta, still in quest of Sylvia, intrudes upon the festivities. Suddenly, a ship is sighted. On the prow stands Eros; Sylvia, veiled, and surrounded by her attendant nymphs, accompanies him. Aminta is irresistibly impelled towards the veiled stranger. Eros lifts the veil and the shepherd, in an ecstasy of relief, greets his beloved.

A divertissement ensues in which Apollo, the Muses and other deities celebrate the rescue of Sylvia. The sacrificial goats destined for the altar of Bacchus join in the celebration. The entertainment is arrested by the arrival of the enraged Orion. He menaces the lovers. Aminta engages him in combat, while Sylvia takes refuge in Diana's temple. The appearance of the goddess herself, surrounded by armed attendants and followed by the distracted Sylvia, interrupts the fight. Orion in a last attempt to re-capture his prey, is struck by an arrow from Diana's bow and reels back mortally wounded. Her wrath is now deflected upon the lovers. She refuses to pardon the profanity of their attachment. Eros angered by her severity, causes the clouds to part revealing a vision of the infatuated goddess leaning over the prone Endymion on Mt Latmos. Diana, mortified by this reminder of her own passion for a simple shepherd, is driven to relent. She pronounces her forgiveness and in the midst of ceremonious rejoicing accepts with Eros the grateful homage of the lovers.

Madame Chrysanthème

Synopsis by Frederick Ashton and Vera Bowen

Scene I A Quay at Nagasaki.

Pierre and Yves, two sailors from the French warship *Triomphante*, land in Nagasaki.

They are accosted by Djinns offering their services, amongst whom is Mr Kangarou, who entices them with coloured postcards of various mousmés. They show a decided interest, and depart together in search of the realisation of Mr Kangarou's pictures.

Scene II The House of Indescribable Butterflies.

Kangarou welcomes the sailors. Pierre is looking for a temporary wife. They are greeted with joy by mousmés, young maidens who seek to delight them and gain their approval. They fail to please however, and Kangarou beckons for Mlle Wistéria and Mlle Pluie d'Avril to display their charms, but they too do not succeed in pleasing Pierre. Suddenly Yves calls Pierre's attention to a young girl seated apart. Pierre is enchanted, and will have none other. A price is agreed with her parents, and Chrysanthème leaves ceremoniously with her family and friends to await her forthcoming marriage.

Scene III A Government Office.

Pierre and Chrysanthème are united before a Dignitary, Government officials and her parents, and the agreed sum of silver dollars is handed over.

Scene IV Chrysanthème's and Pierre's House. Evening.

A procession of Chrysanthème's friends arrives at the house, and the festivities commence. After gaiety and dancing, the friends depart, leaving Pierre and Chrysanthème alone together. As night has fallen, Pierre and Chrysanthème retire.

Scene V Chrysanthème's House. Morning.

The *Triomphante* has been ordered to sail. Yves comes to take Pierre back to the ship. His own parting with his two mousmés is no less sad than that of Pierre and Chrysanthème. Failing in her attempts to make Pierre stay, Chrysanthème gives him a bouquet of her name flowers, and begs Pierre to return for a last good-bye before setting sail, and he promises. Mr Kangarou attempts to extort more money from the sailors as they leave. Chrysanthème is left alone in her house – counting her blessings, when Pierre returns as promised, silently so as to surprise her. Disillusioned at finding how she is occupied, he leaves forever.

> 'O Ama – Teracé – Omi Kami
> Wash me clean from this little marriage of mine,
> in the waters of river Kamo'

Ondine

Synopsis by Frederick Ashton

This is the story of Palemon and Ondine telling how Palemon wedded with a water-sprite and what chanced therefrom and how Palemon died and she returned to her element beneath the Mediterranean Sea.

Act I Scene 1 Outside Berta's Castle

Berta, returning from a hunt, is being courted by Palemon, who offers her an amulet, which she scorns. She rejoins her friends. Palemon is left alone in meditation. A strange being – Ondine – appears mysteriously and Palemon is immediately captivated. She is alarmed and disappears into the forest, where Palemon – already in the clutches of his destiny – follows her.

Berta sees Palemon disappear with Ondine; cries alarm and orders their pursuit.

Scene 2 A Mysterious Forest

Tirrenio and the sprites lie in wait for the lovers. He endeavours to separate them and warns that should Palemon be unfaithful he must forfeit his life. Ondine, defying Tirrenio, together with Palemon seeks out a hermit who marries them. She gains her soul.

The act ends with Berta distraught at the acts of Tirrenio who tries to impede her pursuit of the lovers.

Act II A Port

Palemon and Ondine, after their marriage, come to a Port where, seeing a ship, they decide to embark. Berta, following, sees the lovers and bribes the captain to take her unseen on board. She, not knowing of their marriage, is moved by jealousy when Palemon, in a transport of love, offers the amulet to Ondine.

She reproaches Palemon and reminds him that he had previously offered it to her.

Ondine immediately gives the jewel to Berta. The enraged Tirrenio rises from the sea and snatches the amulet from Berta. Ondine runs to the side of the boat and dipping her hands into the water produces an exquisite magical necklace which she presents to Berta, who, horrified by the supernatural gift, throws it at Ondine's feet. The sailors regard Ondine with awe and doubt and threaten her. Tirrenio, rising from the sea to protect Ondine, beckons to her. He creates a storm and, rising on the crest of a wave, seizes her and drags her to the bottom of the sea. The storm increases.

Act III   Palemon's Castle

Palemon and Berta, who have been saved from the shipwreck, arrive from their wedding ceremony. Berta shows her present to him, a magnificent portrait, and then leaves to prepare for the guests. Palemon, in a reverie, has a vision of Ondine under the water. Berta returns and disturbs his dream. The guests arrive and the festivities begin: at their height strange and sinister happenings occur.

Tirrenio appears seeking vengeance – the festivities are disrupted – Berta is dragged out by the Ondines and Ondine reluctantly appears.

Palemon now realises that Ondine is his only love. She warns him that, owing to his lack of faith, her kiss can only mean his death. Finally, sadly, she kisses him and he falls dead. She takes his body back to her own element there to hold him in an eternal embrace.

Appendix C: Ashton's Notes on His Ballets

The Quest

Ashton's instructions to William Walton for the score:

Scene 1

1   St George and Una in storm approach home of
Archimago as Archimago sees them servants take off
his magician's robe and two bats fly from under it
and dance round him. Archimago then walks up and
down telling his beads devoutly. $1\frac{3}{4}$ min. storm.

2A   Archimago makes them welcome, drinks passed round? $\frac{1}{2}$ min.

2B   Una exhausted does dance suggesting fatigue, lullaby?   1 min.

3   Bats flutter round Una and St George and make them
sleepy. They fall asleep. $\frac{1}{2}$ min.

4   Archimago whirls around in an ecstasy of malice. $\frac{1}{2}$ min.

5   Archimago summons his female servant, changes her
into Una and leads her to St George   1 min. or less.

6   St George awakes and rises, does dance with false
Una, at end of which he rejects her and retires into
the chapel.   1 min.

7   Archimago, angry at his failure, calls his male
servant and makes him lie with false Una. Brings St
George out to watch spectacle. $\frac{1}{2}$ min.

8   St George takes his helmet and exits in disgust.
Archimago retires. $\frac{1}{2}$ min.

9   Interlude suggesting dawn bats in belfry, at end
of which Una comes out of the house and searches for
St George unable to find him goes on her way. $\frac{3}{4}$ min.

10   Archimago comes out of hermitage to find Una gone,
curses servants for letting her go. Servants bring
him armour like St George. He exits preceded by bats
and with noise of distant thunder like in Symphonie
Fantastique?   1 min.

                                                        Total   9 mins.

Scene 2

1   Sansloy and Sansjoy on stage, are joined by
Sansfoy and Duessa all knights compete for hand of
Duessa and should each do a dance suggesting their
various characters. Sansfoy most appealing Sansloy
heartiest and most brutal Sansjoy poetic and most
attractive but unscrupulous.   3 mins.

2   Enter St George challenge and fight and kill [Sansfoy]
and exit with Duessa.   1 min.
3   Enter Una searching for St George, weary and
falls asleep.   ½ min.
4   Bats flutter preceding Archimago who enters dressed
like St George (St George theme distorted here) closes
his visor wakes Una and exit together.   1 min.
                                              Total   5½ mins.

Scene 3
1   Curtain rises on Pride sitting on throne surrounded
by Deadly Sins, and six hermaphrodites standing ready to
begin dance.   1 min.
2   At conclusion of Hermaphrodite dance each sin does
short dance.   About 4 mins.
3   At conclusion of Sixth Sin Queen Pride does her
dance, at end of which she is joined by other Sins, so
as to finish the Sins in a grandiose fashion.   1 min. or more.
4   Small fanfare and entrance of Sansloy.   ½ min.
5   Rhapsodic dance for entire court.   ¾ min.
6   Fanfare for St George. Intro challenge, separation
by Queen who descends from throne and begs them to
fight like Gents.   ¾ min.
7   Fight.   1 min. or ¾.
8   Defeat of Sansloy, Duessa throws herself on his
body. St George disillusioned. Cobwebs descend.
Music here should be harsh and discordant to suggest
disgust (dust and ashes) and then slow down as St. George
exits slowly and sadly.   1 min.
                                              Total   9¼ mins.

Scene 4
Scene same as scene 2 a rocky place towards evening.
1   Sansjoy (poetic one) alone dance of mourning
(like the beginning of Pathetic symphony last movement
lacrimoso strings and slow?)   ½ min.
2   Enter Archimago preceded by bats, gets killed by
Sansjoy Una runs away is caught.   ¾ min.
3   Sansjoy does impassioned dance with Una of seduction.
(towards end of dance St George enters and
watches Una defending her virtue, is moved)   ¾ min.

4   St George rushes to Una's defence and kills
Sansjoy, and is re-united with Una their themes come
together in the most movingly lyrical passage you have
ever written.   1¼ mins.
                                                    Total   3¾ mins.

Scene 5 House of Holinesse
1   Short prelude to scene perhaps a single bell tolling.
2   Curtain rises on Faith, Hope, Charity and their
attendant virtues.
3   Half a min of Faith and Virtues aspiring,
religious music.
4   ½ a min of Hope and Virtues, Broad visionary music.
5   ½ a min of Charity and her Girls. Compassionate
music.
6   Combined effort of virtues leading to Entrance of
Una and St George who are welcomed by F H & C.   1 min.
7   Pas de deux of Una and St George (wonderful music
high spot of ballet)   2 mins.
8   At end of pas de deux Una and Saint George are
separated and he is reminded of his duties to his
country.   ½ min.
9   Music for Virtues who dress St George in his
Armour again.   ½ min.
10   Farewell of Una and St George.   ½ min.
11   Exit of St George with banner, triumphant exalted
music.   ½ min.
12   Apotheosis. 1 min sense of suspended action like
your March with all the bells in England ringing.
                                                    Total   7½ mins.

Illuminations

From Ashton's notebook:
Basic costumes
To which etc are added?

I   Fanfare (Light)
      Curtain up on 2
      4 Trumpeters
      Lights
      Open on everybody in wooden poses. Lights up slowly on them.
      Fête de la Nuit

Villes II (Light)
<u>6 men 6 girls + soldiers</u>

Animate.   Stall of all properties for ballet.
                    Just help themselves.
Soldiers to drag boy away from mother?
Church parade of 1st Communion of R. family with umbrellas.
2 lovers on lamp post all through.
Saltimbanques.
Juggler? A fair?
A bacchanal?
Frozen poses & then much movement then freeze again.
Ending drunk & lazy amorous poses.

Phrase (Light)
<u></u>Hanging garlands
confetti out of Pocket at the end.
Solo.

IIIB   Antique (Light)
<u>Pas de trois</u>
1 Boy 2 Girls or 2 Boys
Suburban Bacchantes
flute flowers, garlands
Love   Sex
Leave garment behind
'Après midi like'
3   1 man & 2 girls
    or 2 men

IV   Royalty (day)
<u>6 men 6 girls</u> & soldiers
2 soap boxes
1 Trains tied on like children
3 Streamers
Tough to knock off crowns at end.
drum boy. Trumpeters.
Cushions with crowns
Sceptres – bowing heads
canopy? home made
paper hats   swords
all done on stage
Train to be used for Sail

V   Marine (afternoon)
<u>Cart like boat</u>
rocking movements
Material for waves

or sail & all behave like in a boat
or swimming movements
Carnaval de fleurs
one pizzicato movement (girls)
against adagio (men)
<u>lighthouse lighting</u>
6 girls & 6 boys
+ soldiers now sailors

VI   <u>Interlude</u> (sunset)
6 ~~voices~~ Men   Enter in fugue
Men with bare torsos
+ soloist
Bestial poses, caresses

Aube (Moonlight & dawn)   VII   Being Beauteous
The Queen metamorphosed parmi les Toughs
on backs movements with legs – Lullaby (Dante)
      →   ←
                   back & forward
     ✕
                   Ophelia
Queen veiled – she is desire
round changing light
6 men & girl   Dream quality
                   veiled lids (?)

VIII   <u>Parade</u> (Red amber)
Start with R & men later everybody
sort of march to gallows
form 4 etc
children paper hats
swords
Torches – parade
lanterns, leaves – as for celebrating departure

IX   <u>Depart</u> (Light)
climb up on people fr back stage
or ladder
small bundle
shot in Arm?
Apotheosis?

<u>Villes II</u> continued
Light suddenly at end 'It is Spring' amazed crowd exaltée.

Homage to the Queen

Ashton's instructions to Malcolm Arnold for the score:

Distant Fanfare developing into loud fanfare as curtain rises.
Entrée of entire company. (March Allegro e Maestoso 2 min
developing into Adagio $2\frac{1}{2}$ mins developing into coda
Allegro Vivo $\frac{1}{2}$ min.)
1st Entrée (Elizabethan) 6 girls   1 min.
Solo (Grant)   1 min. Jig.
6 girls few bars $\frac{1}{4}$ min into Pas de deux Pavane. 2 mins.
Var. Girl $\frac{3}{4}$ min & Var. Man $\frac{3}{4}$ min.
Coda All 1 min.

$6\frac{3}{4}$ mins.

2nd Entrée (Anneish) Pas de Quatre Allemande 2 mins.
Pas de deux Moderato Allegro 2 mins.
Variation Girl Corante $\frac{3}{4}$ min Gavotte Joyeuse for man $\frac{3}{4}$ min.
Coda Gigue all $\frac{1}{2}$ or $\frac{3}{4}$ min.

$6\frac{1}{2}$ mins.

3rd Entrée (Victorian) Pas de Trois (Shaw, Farron, Jackson)
Waltz flowing 1 min. Variation Shaw $\frac{3}{4}$ min. (Allegretto-
pesante 2/4 time.) Coda $\frac{3}{4}$ min Presto 2/4 time. $2\frac{1}{2}$ mins.
Introduction to pas de deux 6 girls pas de deux (Songs
Without Words) 2 mins.
Var. Girl $\frac{3}{4}$ min. Var. Man $\frac{3}{4}$ min. Coda (all) $\frac{3}{4}$ min.

$6\frac{3}{4}$ mins.

4th Entrée (Modern) Grandiose Introduction Moderato
Cantabile 12/8 or 4/4 6 boys & 6 girls & Fonteyn & Somes
$1\frac{3}{4}$ mins.
Var. Fonteyn brillante 1 min. Var. Somes $\frac{3}{4}$ min Allegretto
Pesante 3/4 or 6/8. Pas de Six Scherzo $1\frac{1}{2}$ mins.
Pas de Deux grande Adage (mit harps doing overtime) 3 min.
Grande Finale (Heraldic) & Apotheosis in 2 parts.
Brisk for 1 min. then slow grand Climax for $\frac{3}{4}$ min. Finis.
All this is merely an indication for you and can be
departed from at will, and anything altered to suit
your musical conception.

Macbeth

Ashton's draft synopsis and instructions to William Walton for the score of a projected ballet based on Shakespeare's tragedy (never produced):

Synopsis:

ACT I

Sleep-walking music; Lady M enters as later in sleep-walking scene; or discovered on; movement as in sleep-walking; lifting of the hands to the imagined crown 'the golden round'. Porter or dwarf enters with letter. As she reads it we see behind a gauze the meeting of Macbeth, Banquo and Fleance with the Witches who offer a crown first to M and then passing by Banquo to Fleance; as they vanish, Duncan, Malcolm and Macduff enter; Macbeth and Banquo kneel and are raised up and embraced by the King who then presents Malcolm to them placing the coronet he is wearing upon Malcolm's head. They depart and we see Macbeth alone for a moment before the dumb show fades. A short pas seul by Lady M on whom the lights come up is followed by the entry of Macbeth and a very powerful pas de deux in which she demands the murder of Duncan; this is interrupted by the 'knocking on the gate' motif and the entry of the King, Malcolm, Macduff and attendant Lords; short ceremonial dance leads to the King being lighted by torches to his bedchamber (with 2 grooms in attendance?). Sleep music. Macbeth and Lady Macbeth alone; she fetches the daggers; he refuses them; she mounts the stair to do the deed but fails – Macbeth alone for a moment while she is off stage – 'Is this a dagger that I see before me' – she returns with the daggers, forces them upon him and leads him to the stair – alone her movements anticipate the sleep walking scene – he returns with bloody hands – the sleep music works up to nightmare – she cannot control his hysteria – 'knocking on the gate' motif. Dwarf opens to Macduff; Macbeth enters and directs him to Duncan's chamber; the murder discovered; entry of Malcolm and Banquo and courtiers; (alternatively Macduff and Banquo enter and discover the murder and Macbeth only enters with the Lords and attendants when the alarm is raised) (This is better.)

The close of this Act is difficult and important. When Macbeth goes up to Duncan's chamber and returns he might bring the body of a murdered groom and throw him down the stair as the criminal; then he should meet Malcolm face to face and blench with terror so that Malcolm knows that he is guilty; Macbeth is on the point of striking Malcolm dead in his rage and terror when Lady M seeing the whole situation saves it by intervening and swooning away; in the commotion we see Malcolm escape; after Lady M has been carried off they realise that Malcolm has fled and the three Thanes then make a solemn vow upon their swords – one with another and each with all, Macbeth, centred between Banquo and Macduff, to avenge the murder. This is the proper curtain but it is conceivable that for simplification of plot Macduff, the true avenger should be left alone and that Malcolm should reenter to him cloaked and disguised, reveal his suspicions and make a pact. This would strengthen the last Act and elucidate the whole.

434

ACT II

This movement should be shorter and should be more of a single entity than the rush of events and variety of Act I; in fact, just the Banquet as a great set piece with corps de ballet – richly coloured and set, as against the gauntness and night of the first movement.

Macbeth and Lady Macbeth as King and Queen, robed and crowned.

Homage done by all the thanes (Macduff missing) ending up with Banquo and Fleance – Lady M makes much of the boy and Macbeth of Banquo; Banquo asks leave to retire; is urged not to fail the feast; Macbeth and Lady Macbeth; he blenches at the murder; she exerts her will, bids an attendant bring in the assassins (I think that more than 4 or 6 might be a bit silly; as it is in the opera). The King and Queen exit; short dance of the assassins; as they depart the feast is brought on and the guests; when all is ready the King and Queen enter; greetings – they retire to sit in state – Macbeth comes down – points to Banquo's chair and bids them fill their cups to drink to Banquo; as he raises his to his lips Banquo appears in the chair and raises a cup to pledge him in return. Macbeth's hysteria as the Ghost vanishes; Lady M intervenes – forces him to repeat the ceremonial dance with which they had welcomed their guests – again in the middle of one of the figures the Ghost intervenes – Macbeth collapses; the guests arise and depart; King and Queen left alone – he rejects her efforts to comfort and strengthen him, withdraws from her; she is left alone; and as she muses and becomes a prey to strange fancies, old hags or witches steal in and gather up scraps of food from the banquet, scavengers. (Possibly 2 murderers might enter and show her Fleance's coat so that she knows her plot has failed – this might come directly the guests have departed.)

ACT III

A Witches sabbath of warlocks and witches of all kinds – full corps de ballet. The Cauldron in the Cavern. To them enter Macbeth. They conjure up first of all Macduff; then Fleance crowned; then Malcolm with a branch in his hand. (I think the show of Kings might be omitted – one could have the blood boltered Banquo with Fleance.)

Macbeth defies the witches – the cauldron vanishes as they dance round him – he is left alone: 'Tomorrow and tomorrow and tomorrow'.

Sleep-walking scene repeating earlier figures and effects.

The Heath. Macduff and Malcolm and soldiers; the army with branches; dance of the trees; they take up position; Macbeth and soldiers enter; the trees begin to move; Macbeth's soldiers fly; he stands awe-struck; the trees divide and Malcolm and Macduff come upon him as from an ambush. Macduff makes Malcolm stand aside; Macduff and Macbeth fight; as Macbeth falls the trees surround him; Macbeth's head raised aloft(?); stage empty; Lady M enters in a sleep walking trance; she kills herself; witches enter and rifle the body; they are scattered by the entry of Malcolm and his army with banners; Macduff and other Lords do homage to Malcolm.

435

Instructions to the composer:

ACT I

1.	Lady Macbeth alone, musing	1½ minutes
	Messenger, soldier, brings letter from Macbeth	½
2.	(Back, behind gauze). Three Witches. Sinister hag music. Starts andante, working up to agitato, quicker and more agitated, and slowing again with percussion for entrance of Macbeth, Banquo and Fleance, who accost the Witches	1
	Quick music for Witches who fuss round the cauldron	1
	Slow mysterious music for prophecies:	1
	(a) Crown for Macbeth	
	(b) Crowned Child for Banquo	1
	Scene ends with a puff of smoke and crash of cymbals. Music should suggest disappearance and smoke. Vision disappears	½
3.	Lady Macbeth and Ladies. Preparation of toilet. Ceremonial slow music. Andantino(?) 3/4 Grazioso in quality(?)	2
4.	Fanfare. Arrival of King and Party, with Macbeth, Banquo and Fleance. Processional music. Presentation of ring. Drinks brought in. Carousing. General exit.	4
5.	Interlude. Dance of Sleep. (As in Faerie Queen, dance of Spirits, in 1st half)	3
6.	Short introduction	½
	to Pas de Deux between Macbeth and Lady Macbeth, ending with a Pas d'Action, which includes murder and smearing of attendants' faces	5
7.	Dance of Sleep, turned to Nightmare. 'Macbeth has murdered sleep.'	1½
8.	Interrupted by Knocking. Entrance of Macduff, who discovers murder. Escape of Malcolm. Macbeth kills attendants.	3
9.	Coronation of Macbeth and Lady Macbeth Spurning of Fleance	2½
		30

ACT II

1.	Briefing of Assassins. Music should start slow and sinister, accelerating like a train up to the murder of Banquo. Animando to murder and anger of Lady Macbeth	3 minutes
2.	Blackout and interlude to	$\frac{1}{2}$
3.	Banquet. Set scene	1
4.	Ceremonial Court Dance. Minuet	2
5.	Dance of Warriors. Sword Dance (better not Scottish)	2
6.	Dance of Fool. Scherzando	2
7.	Short Dance of Lady Macbeth and Ladies. Molto grazioso, allegretto 6/8	2
8.	Macbeth rises from his throne to greet Lady Macbeth, and when he returns to it, the Ghost of Banquo is there	$\frac{1}{2}$
9.	General consternation at Macbeth's curious behaviour	1
10.	Reprise of Court Dance, with Ghost appearing among the Courtiers. Fool again	$1\frac{1}{2}$
11.	Macbeth breaks up the Dance	$\frac{1}{2}$
12.	Lady Macbeth jumps into the middle of this, and executes a brilliant solo. Quick 2/4 rhythmical time. The Ghost rises out of the trap behind her at the end of the dance.	$1\frac{1}{2}$
13.	General consternation, and break-up and exit of the Party	$\frac{1}{2}$
14.	Macbeth slumped on his throne. Lady Macbeth is alone, a prey to Phantoms	2
		20

ACT III

Scene 1

1.	Quick Dance of Witches	2 minutes
2.	Visions.	
	Vision 1, dance of Witches	1
	Vision 2, dance of Witches	1
	Vision 3, dance of Witches	1
	March of Kings, cortège macabre	2
	Distraction of Macbeth	$\frac{1}{2}$

437

	Dance of Comforting Spirits	$2\frac{1}{2}$	10
	Scene 2		
1.	Lady Macbeth alone, sleepwalking	5	5
	Scene 3		
1.	Macbeth, Dance of bravado	$1\frac{1}{2}$	
2.	Trees advancing, Corps de Ballet		
	Lady Macbeth stifled		
	Macbeth finds her dead		
	Macduff rises out of the Trees		
	Macduff kills Macbeth	5	
3.	Apotheosis of Malcolm		
	Trumpets on stage, blaring		
	State trumpeters	2	$8\frac{1}{2}$
			$23\frac{1}{2}$

Note: This 'minutage' was subsequently revised and considerably reduced in length, the first act to sixteen minutes, the second to fifteen, and the third to fourteen. Ashton was evidently concerned about the lack of opportunities for dancing offered by the story, and in the second version tried to remedy this defect by adding dances for the protagonist in Acts II and III, with the following comments: (Act II) 'I feel that here Macbeth should have at least one good strong dance and possibly a big pas de deux with Lady M. This is pretty well his last chance of doing anything before he cracks up. This could perhaps be what the IIIrd act is to Swan Lake, brilliant and realistic in contrast to the other two acts which are pretty eerie.'

(Act III) 'A short danse noble for M – the last noble note in a man – a hark back to a heroic movement before final disintegration.'

It was no doubt this defect that finally decided him to abandon the project, as well as the fact that Fonteyn did not see herself as Lady Macbeth.

Ondine

Ashton's instructions to Hans Werner Henze for the score. The three acts are taken from different copies that seem to represent different stages of planning:

Act I

		Minutes
PRELUDE		
1	Washing and dressing (allegro)	$1\frac{1}{2}$
2(a)	Guests arrive (bustling)	1
	followed by dance of guests	$1\frac{1}{2}$
	interrupted by Hulbrand's entrance	

(b) Hulbrand—definite theme $\frac{1}{2}$

(c) Approaches Bertalda, offers her amulet, which
she brushes aside and exits to prepare for
Hunt (cellos for offering amulet, violins
for refusal; quicken to 2/4 or 6/8) $\frac{3}{4}$

3 Hulbrand meditative dance (melancholy quasi
saraband) leading to entrance of Ondine $1\frac{1}{2}$

4(a) Appearance of Ondine out of fountain
(glissandi—harps, taken over by violins),
interruption as maid sees her and rushes
out (agitato staccato—woodwind) 1 ?

(b) Introduction (elusive coquetry) 1

5 Shadow Dance (3/8 or 6/8 slow in varying
tempi (slow-quick-slow-quick) 2

_____

12

6 She begs for amulet, he refuses her, she
rushes off in huff, he pursues her as maid
enters and sees him disappear after nymph:

(a) amulet scene (pleading music) $\frac{1}{2}$

(b) Huff (pettish music and exit) $\frac{1}{2}$

(c) ~~Maid~~ Bertalda sees him pursue $\frac{1}{2}$

    Calls others (exit) $\frac{1}{4}$

_____

7 Guests re-enter followed by Bertalda and
maids, who orders pursuit—~~maids close
fountain?~~ (agitato) 1

_____

2

8 Transform to forest—hermit seen to
establish him 2

9 Kuhleborn dance (strong and sinister—
mephisto)—quick 3/8 $1\frac{1}{2} = 2\frac{1}{4}$

10 Lovers enter back stage, H in pursuit $\frac{1}{2}$
Seen by K, who starts his tricks, confusion,
horrors, lights, etc. Fear, separation at
end of which K reconciled—horrors abate $2\frac{1}{2}$ $(3\frac{1}{2})$

11 Introd. and pas de deux (adagio—more
movement in middle)

  Adagio—2 mins.   Solo Hulbrand ⎫
      1 min quicker, gather speed and sound ⎬ $4\frac{1}{4}$ $(5\frac{1}{2})$
  Adagio—1 min quiet ⎭

12   Seek hermit who marries them—~~K appears~~   1.40
      ~~and interrupts ceremony—departs—marriage~~
      ~~proceeds~~   2
                                                    ———
                                                    3.40

13   Forest fury again—confusion of guests, K
      frustrating all and sundry—guests disperse—
      Bertalda in despair $2\frac{1}{2}$
14   Hermit emerges from hermitage, comforts her
      and indicates the way the lovers have taken, 3.55
      she rushes after them, $1\frac{1}{2}$
      Storm increases   1
                                                    ———
                                          $(34\frac{3}{4})$ $31\frac{1}{4}$

END OF ACT

OVERTURE?

Act II

1 ⎧Port—Melodie Pescal while fishermen mend
   ⎪nets—sentimental, nostalgic song   2
2 ⎨Ondine and H arrive and observe the scene
   ⎩(theme of marriage re-introduced)   1
3   Arrival of Bertalda who throws herself on their
    mercy—embarkation (more moved but not fast)   1
4   Boat leaves—Transformation music.   1
 (a) Once on board, etc (guitar tune)   1
 (b) Rocking dance—ending with quieting of waters $1\frac{1}{2}$
     slow—quick—slow   1
5(a) Pas de trois
     Pantomime of amulet
     Recitative gracioso (viola solo) dance
     Bertalda variation   3
 (b) At end of dance, she leans on side of boat.
     K rises from water and snatches amulet from her.
     Mysterious water music—crescendo and snatch. $\frac{1}{2}$
6   Bertalda furious etc recitative pantomime $1\frac{1}{2}$
7   Dance distraught of Ondine, more and more
     calling, increasing shouts.   1
8   K causes storm—Dance of everybody (dance of
     confusion) at end of which K seizes her on
     crest of wave and disappearance of Ondine—
     H tries to leap in water—shipwreck   5

Act III
Prelude and vision under water   5

Pas de supplication   2
Bertalda and Kul interrupted by entrée and promenade
of guests etc   1

Grand pas classique   6½
    Adagio boys and girls   ⎧ 2
    Var Girls   ⎪ 1½
     ,, Boys   ⎨ 1½
    Coda General fast   ⎩ 1½
Entrée of Kuhleborn   ¼
followed by rush of Neapolitans   ½

Divertissement   11
    The divertissement consists of
    12 boys 12 girls corps de ballet
    + 3 principal boys & 3 principal girls
        Part One—all 12 boys & 12 girls   1
        into which enter the soloists
        pas de six   1
        pas de trois 2 boys & girl   1
        pas de trois 2 girls one boy   1
        12 boys & girls   1
        var 3 girls   1
        var 1 boy   1
        var 2 girls & 2 boys   1
        All six for finish   1
        All 12 boys & girls
        + all pas de six   2

Solemn dance interrupted by Ondines—fright of Bertalda
All exit pas d'action   2

Pas de deux   3
& apotheosis   1

La Fille mal gardée

Excerpts from Ashton's notes:

Act I Scene 1
  1) Overture. Hens waking—farmyard noises. Dawn.
  2) Peasants going to fields.

3) Enter Lise awakening dance with ribbon? & business.
   Enters house or dairy.
4) Enter Colas & harvesters, finds ribbon etc.
   dances blows kisses etc.
5) At Balcony & Simone appears etc.
6) Villagers apply for work. S gives sickles etc.
7) Colas re-appears & hides in stable.
8) Scene with Colas & Lise.
9) Pas de deux Ribbon dance.
10) Village girls.
    A Entrée few bars
    B Dance of Village girls
    C Dance of Lise
    D Coda
11) Return of Simone
12) Enter Thomas & Alain—Scene
13) Dance of Alain
14) Off to Harvest

Beginning of Act II:†

1. Entrance of Simone and Lise—tired sad theme.
2. Simone busies herself with spinning wheel,
   then locks door and flops down.
3. Spinning diminuendo to sleep—orchestral snores.
   Lise tiptoes to get key but Simone wakes with a start.
4. Tambourine dance ending in Simone sleeping again,
   wakes again and bangs tambourine—Lise dances.
5. Simone does little dance herself (variation on
   clog dance). Knocks at door.
6. Harvesters appear and are paid.
7. Simone dresses and goes to see notary; locks Lise in.
8. Lise climbs staircase but does not see Colas—
   despondent—does mime scene 'when I am married I
   will have children, three etc'—sentimental music.

The Creatures of Prometheus

Ashton's 'minutage':
Overture
Prologue
Tempesta   5
Unveil Statues

† Quoted in John Lanchbery and Ivor Guest: 'The Scores of *La Fille mal gardée*'

Scene of flowers
Exit to Apollo   9

Act I
  4   Presentation of Creatures   2.35 sec
  5   Pas de deux—pas d'action $6\frac{1}{4}$
  7   Prometheus solo & Apollo—
          gratitude of creatures   1
  6   Laughter—Thalia   1.10 sec
  8   War (Scena) $3\frac{3}{4}$
  9   Tragedy $3\frac{3}{4}$
 12   Revival $1\frac{1}{2}$
 10   Pastoral $2\frac{1}{2}$
 14   Lesson $4\frac{3}{4}$
 15   Finale $4\frac{1}{4}$
                                          ―――――――
                                              42 mins

          $40\frac{1}{2}$ of dancing
                                              $1\frac{1}{2}$ curtain down

A Month in the Country

Ashton's notes:

From very beginning which is the overture until immediately before the first piano note. Repeat.

Then orchestrate piano part, or orchestrate bits omitting piano. Cut. Procession music.

Piano returns with the waterfall of orchestral notes on which curtain rises to see Vera having completed the chord with brother standing turning pages. Vera then plays Mozart theme. Nat[alia] is sitting with boy friend who is reading to her whilst she fans herself.

When orchestra takes up theme Nat rises and does mock minuet with boy friend. Next. Natalia does variation (1) with fan. Children get up to admire Nat. At end when orchestra comes in all four do mock minuet. No repeat?

2nd variation Vera then when orchestra comes in all four do mock minuet. No repeats?

3rd variation is entry of father looking for plans. All tease him and he exits and four go into mock(ing him) minuet on orchestra. & mock father. No repeats?

Variation 4 Wayne joined by other 3 when orchestra enters (with ball)

Finish. No repeats?

Mood music begins   possible cuts

Awareness of Tutor.

Natalia introduces Tutor to Boyfriend. Disapproval.

Boyfriend sits and buries himself in a book. Cut.

Adagio for Tutor with rapt admiration from remaining three.

443

Variation 6.

Pas de trois.   2 children together
                    Tutor with Boy
                    Tutor alone
                         with girl.
                    3 together.

Boy dances to Tutor. Vera is jealous and cuts in and also dances to Tutor. ?
Develops into pas de trois. Cuts.

Pas de trois ends as the end of Là ci darem, as Nat packs the two children and Tutor
into the Garden. (Kite flying?)

Beginning of Polish airs is Boyfriend's declaration to Natalia. She laughs it off
and leads him into garden to right.

pause   Vera pulls Tutor into room from garden left, and then begins their pas de
deux. CUT

End of pas de deux on three cadences. Natalia has returned and observed through
garden entrance. $\frac{1}{3}$ way through 2nd Band.

Side Two Cut 1st Band.

Anger orchestra beginning of Band Two. DRASTIC CUTS

Tutor is chased into garden by boy (flies kite in background).

Mother guiltily remonstrates with Vera

Such love is not possible

Vera declares undying love for Tutor

Mother tries to reason. Cuts.

Vera rushes off in tantrum followed by Nat into house? (Natalia slaps Vera's face
& the latter rushes out.)

Slow movement is tutor's entry followed by maid with strawberries. Repeat
bridge. They enter into a peasant spirited mazurka, which ends with Tutor
shushing maid out of French windows. Then Tutor alone has two repeats of
Russian music. (Nat watches him.) Played slower, orchestrated.

Nat comes in from garden—with flowers. CUTS.

Into pas de deux (Spirito) with Nat peters out into trickle then Prelude 3 in G
major.

Repeat before Theme. Then Orchestra follow on which is Vera entering from
garden, horrified, rushing through room and calling rest of the party to witness
what has been happening. Nat unsuccessfully tries to explain away her behaviour.
More orchestration.

Scene with daughter, followed by husband

Exits pursuing daughter leaving Boyfriend to dismiss Tutor and go himself (on
strong chords)

Nat re-enters with husband. Sort of pas de deux in which Nat gets hysterical and
husband leaves Nat alone.

Passionately. Heavily orchestrated.

17th Prelude with Tutor kissing ribbons.

Appendix D: 1 Comments on *Les Rendezvous*

There have been so many changes in both the choreography and the design of this ballet that it is almost impossible to record them all. In the original production (1933) there were a principal couple, then called 'Lovers' (Markova and Idzikowski), the three dancers in the *pas de trois* (de Valois, Judson and Helpmann), and a corps de ballet, the 'Walkers Out', consisting of six women and six men (one of whom, Helpmann, was also in the *pas de trois*). The programme would seem to suggest that there was a women's *pas de six* immediately following the Entrance, but no one I have spoken to has any recollection of this. In any case it would have been supplanted a year later by the new *pas de quatre* of 'little girls', one of whom was Fonteyn. At this time the woman in the *pas de trois* (Ailne Phillips) was given a partner for the Entrance (William Chappell) who did not appear in any of the succeeding numbers, except presumably the finale – again, this is according to the programme, but Chappell has no recollection of being in the ballet at that time. In the 1937 revival this extra man was left out and all three of the *pas de trois* dancers led the Entrance. However, in a programme dated 10 January 1940 the extra man appears again (it was Claude Newman, partnering Jill Gregory) – but this was evidently not a permanent change and may indeed have been an error in the programme. The more usual arrangement at that time seems to have been as in the original – one of the *pas de trois* men did not dance in the *pas de six* and thus was reserved as a partner for the woman.

Further changes were introduced into the version presented by Sadler's Wells Theatre Ballet in 1947: the *pas de quatre* girls were given more to do – they took part in the Adagio, for instance. At this point the Lovers were renamed, or translated into, 'Amoureux', and the Walkers Out became 'Promeneurs'. The Entrée was led as before by two of the *pas de trois* dancers. In the Royal Ballet revival of 1959 the corps de ballet was enlarged to ten couples. When the Theatre Ballet became the touring section of the Royal Ballet its production of *Les Rendezvous* was retained, but sometimes given in the enlarged version, depending on the size of the stage. However, the definitive version, if such a thing can be said to exist, would seem to be the 1937 version as revised in 1947. With minor modifications, it is the version included in the repertory of the newly-constituted touring section since 1971.

Because *Les Rendezvous* is a seminal work in the Ashton canon a detailed description is here attempted, based on the version currently being performed (1974): After a brief fanfare the curtain rises on a setting consisting of a pair of tall gates, flanked by railings, painted white, and standing open before a summery sky with a suggestion of green hills below – the entrance to a park or public garden. The dancers begin to enter: first the women of the corps de ballet in high *jetés* from the four corners of the stage. Each pair pauses in the centre for quick greetings, some effusive, some merely polite. Then the men enter and similarly greet each other – one pair bump into one another and then dodge from side to side in an effort to pass. As they all join their partners a female soloist arrives, the one who will dance the *pas de trois*. Some of the basic motifs of the ballet have by now been established, such as the traversal of the diagonals of the stage and (by the solo figure) the *port de bras en couronne* with extreme *croisé épaulement*.

The members of the corps line up on each side of the gates as the two principals come in, separate, and go down the lines to greet their friends. They meet again stage centre and he displays her in supported *jetés en tournant* and *posés en arabesque*, while the others applaud. The corps dancers exeunt, and the two Lovers have a passage by themselves in which he lifts her in an enlarged version of *pas ballotté*. The corps re-enter in *grand jeté* lifts from one corner to the centre and away to the next corner, followed by the principals alternating in fast *soutenu* turns with the arms *en couronne*, and as the first number ends the four 'little girls' run on.

To a polka-like tune they perform a sprightly dance, which introduces new motifs that will recur in the course of the ballet, in addition to repeating those already established: little flicks of the wrists and a throwing gesture from the shoulder. In a very Petipa-esque figure, they form a square and exchange places with one another. As the dance ends, four men enter at the back, the girls run to them and are lifted. The male soloist comes in through the gates and begins his variation as the others leave. He jumps with his legs opening wide in *pas ciseaux* three times, then does a *pirouette*, repeats this combination and follows it with a series of *assemblés voyagés*. He runs back to the centre and does *entrechats six* finishing in a kneeling position as he makes the girls' throwing gesture, then back up to *soussus* – this combination also interspersed with *pirouettes*. Kneeling, he sweeps his arms from side to side. The end of the variation finds him at the front of the stage in a deep lunge; he turns upstage as his inamorata enters through the gates for the Adagio.

This is in pure classic style, with supported *arabesques*, *promenades* and *pirouettes*. The corps de ballet also take part – when the principals leave the stage for a few moments the men, in pairs, lift the women and rock them back and forth as though on a swing, echoing the berceuse feeling of the music. The principals re-enter attended by the four little girls, the man carrying the woman along a diagonal path made by the corps in two lines. He supports her in a series of low lifts in which she jumps with a little Russian-style *pas de chat*, landing each time in a kneeling position – foreshadowing the kind of floating lift that was to become an Ashton trademark. She has a brief solo passage, turning in *pas de bourrée*, that is a little reminiscent of Aurora's in the Rose Adagio; at the end she is lifted high by four of the men and carried to the centre, the women make a circle of *arabesques* round them, and her partner kneels in homage.

The music changes back to a livelier tempo as the *pas de trois* dancers enter, circling the stage with a little syncopated prancing step, one arm up, one down, changing every few steps. Arriving stage centre, they do little hops in *arabesque*, turning, then backwards and forwards. The girl twists and turns between her two consorts, goes first to one, then the other and does little supported hops in *attitude en avant*, while the 'odd man out' does *cabrioles* alone. They repeat both sections, then move backwards in small *entrechats quatre*, and finally criss-cross the stage in big leaps, backwards and forwards, before coming to a halt, down on one knee.

Next comes the female soloist's variation, a swift, lilting number. She enters with *chassé coupé jeté* finishing with a characteristic gesture in which she crosses one wrist over the other, then opens her arms to the side with another twist and fillip of the wrists. She *pirouettes*, finishing in fourth position *croisée*, and immediately rotates another turn; she seems almost to lose her balance, but rights herself in a movement that ripples through her whole body (this came from one of those rehearsal accidents that the choreographer 'leaves in'). Young men appear at the four corners of the stage and bow to her, one after the other – she acknowledges each with a brief curtsy as she passes by. A last dazzling diagonal of *pirouettes en dedans* into *arabesque*; she pauses, rises on her toes and comes down again, feet parallel, jumps the same way, then, well pleased with her own virtuosity, goes off into the wings.

Now the orchestra plays a bolero, heralded by the sound of hands clapping offstage, and the six corps men enter, pantomiming the playing of mandolines, and go into a rather solemn dance in which they drop to one knee, then quickly turn and switch to the other. As the four little girls did, they exchange places in their formation, but with big *assemblés* instead of little runs. They end in two straight parallel lines across the stage, sitting on the floor with the right leg extended behind.

The women run in and pose in *arabesque*, each supported by her reclining partner. The men rise and all move off into the wings, stage left, in a series of *sissonnes* forwards and backwards. This is the finale, and each of the various groups dances again: the *pas de trois* dancers repeat their little prances at the head of groups from the corps, the woman leading four men and the two men leading four women. The two principals also reprise their own movements in individual entrées: the man is interrupted by the four little girls who try to engage him in a game of blind man's buff, but he flings off the blindfold and waves goodbye to them. As the music gets faster the ballerina hops backwards in *arabesque* in a diagonal, pausing every so often in a *relevé* held on balance; her partner circles the stage in a series of *sauts de basque*, which she echoes in *grands jetés en tournant*. A last traversal in big lifts by all the couples, then they leave through the gates – one woman swoons in her partner's arms and is dragged off, another couple exit with the man giving the woman a good ticking-off, the *pas de trois* dancers leave together, repeating the twisting motif of the torso with arms *en couronne*, and finally the leading couple walk out arm in arm, leaving the little girls by themselves, shrugging their shoulders as the curtain falls.

2 A V Coton's Comments on *Les Patineurs*

As has been noted, *Les Patineurs* is a kind of companion-piece to *Les Rendezvous*. The best description of the later ballet is in A V Coton's *A Prejudice for Ballet*; he gives such a vivid picture of the ballet and of the excitement that it can generate in a good performance that it is here quoted at length:

The setting is of an ice rink and, so far as any locale is indicated, it may be in the Vienna or other equally modish city of gaiety of the period. The dress notation suggests also the Teutonic; hefty young gallants and rosy-cheeked maidens will be the executants of the skating patterns. A few trellis arches form the background and wings, and deeper still, a cloth of a few wind-swept and bare trees against a night-blue sky completes the suggestion of a midwinter carnival occasion; small paper lanterns hang from the trellis. To the simple measures of the tuneful yet undistracting music, the skaters make their entry: the two blue-clad Ice Maidens trip pertly across in bunched skirts and ribboned hats, decorated with frills and ruchings; they carry little muffs; and as they set the pattern in a note of gaiety, confidently and archly glowing to the audience, they complete their track and exit: they are instantly followed by the eight-part mixed chorus, clad in russet and blue, which glides in to etch its patterns on the smooth ice. The whole of the dancing is conditioned by the temporary convention that every one is moving on ice, and every step and stance is rigidly controlled in the peculiarly stiff-thighed and straight-backed walk of the ice-skater. After the series of neat traverses and diagonal figurings, the chorus links in pairs, circles once more the round of the stage, then glides off in the slowly accelerating, rippling rhythm of the skater building up speed; the variation is danced by a tight and wiry figure in navy and sky blue, trimmed with white fur . . . Here a superb and dashing skater is demonstrating his skill, defying all laws of equilibrium in every movement and pose, accenting his skill by a succession of jumps culminating in flat falls to earth, skilfully ending in three-point contacts with the stage; the flooring cracks audibly at each hard blow, as, simultaneously, thigh, hand and knee meet stage together. A *pas de deux* for a pair of lyric figures follows this brilliant character exercise; a deliberately romantic incursion into the unsophisticate fun, danced by a male in tight-fitting satin and fur, with a female in gauzy satin and muslin, fur-trimmed . . . At the next change of rhythm, the chorus returns with the blue-clad pair, and two new females are introduced, decked in maroon and white. The lyric figure is broken and the full assembly sketches a spirited jig and galop, broken to allow swift demonstrations by the duos of soubrettes, the heroic variation figure, and the white-clad pair, who have been drawn into the general grouping. So the pattern is woven with a growing succession of neater and more daring spins, *pirouettes*, moving arabesque figures and series of elaborately furious turns; the variation figure leads in the blue-clad twins and each vies with the other in a breathless and extensive fury of single and double *fouettés*, close turns, and widely flung *jetés*. The variation figure links all the subsequent demonstration pieces with a succession of brief interludes of transverse flight, each time creating a fresh variation in his idiom of moving arabesques and seemingly limitless *pirouettes*. The pace of the dancing rises with the music's tempo as the gaily shrill melodies draw the dancers across, down, and up-stage in solo, in duo, and in supported groupings making more and more daring experiments with equilibrium as the hot pace rises . . . Every figure, male and female, drives the last possible phase of ingenuity and speed into the whirling maze. Two by two the pairs create their final designs on the glittering surface . . . , and, as the lights dim and the soft snowflakes eddy in mid-stage, the blue-clad leader of the rout leaps in, spins high, and crashes into the centre-stage; in a series of jumps as though testing the surface for strain he bounces, then, as the music gaily rattles into the coda, with brass thundering and choking in full clamour, he sets a series of spins on one foot: with free leg extended horizontally stiff and arms driving the helical patterning remorselessly into a higher and madder speed. We count ten, twelve, sixteen turns as the acceleration grows and the strings rocket the peroration up-scale: the brass roars shudderingly as the exciting finale tears towards the last bars: the curtain is slowly closing and the eddying flakes whirl around the thrilling speedy device as the figure is hidden. As the last brazen glory is wound out, the curtain swiftly rushes up, the lights dim even lower and we see the effortless, endless series of turns winding on . . . and on . . . and on . . . The curtain snaps shut at the final bar, leaving the dancer in mid-flight spinning until the last ounce of momentum that he can create finally breaks the figure. The effectiveness of this daring and simple curtain is superb Ballet, superb stagecraft, and dramatic, of its own intensity, in a way that balletic sequences rarely achieve; it is the very utmost note of éclat needed to dress this demonstration of the transition of one code of athletic movement into the rarefying and noble patterns of dancing.

CHRONOLOGY

Notes

Abbreviations: M Music by   D Danced by

  s Scenery by   NP New production

  c Costumes by   R Reproduced by

All theatres named are in London unless otherwise stated.

Dancers are identified by the names under which they were usually known: for example, Andrée Howard sometimes appears in Ballet Club programmes as Louise Barton, but is always listed here as Andrée Howard.

Titles enclosed in square brackets are of productions – ballets by other choreographers, revues, musical comedies, operas, plays and films – in which Ashton choreographed individual numbers or ballets, the titles of which are then given in bold type.

New productions are listed as follows: first those by the company responsible for the original production (in the case of *Façade* all the Wells/Royal productions are listed together following those by the Camargo Society and Ballet Club), then those by other companies.

1926

[Riverside Nights]
An Entertainment in three parts, written and arranged by A P Herbert and Nigel Playfair
Produced by Nigel Playfair
Dances arranged by Penelope Spencer
M   Frederic Austin and Alfred Reynolds; additional music by Lord Berners, Dennis Arundell, Richard Leveridge, Harold Scott and others
SC   Philippe Forbes-Robertson, John Armstrong, James Whale and The Cottars' Market
Players: Nigel Playfair, Elsa Lanchester, Richard Goolden, James Whale, George Baker, Harold Scott, Cavan O'Connor, Penelope Spencer and others
Presented by Nigel Playfair, Lyric Theatre,

Hammersmith, *10 April 1926*. During the General Strike of that year the revue transferred to the Ambassadors Theatre, then reopened at the Lyric with the addition of Frederick Ashton's first ballet:

A Tragedy of Fashion; or, The Scarlet Scissors
A Ballet by Ashley Dukes
M   Eugene Goossens, arranged by Ernest Irving (*Kaleidoscope*, for piano, opus 18)
SC   F.E.D. (Sophie Fedorovitch)
D   Monsieur Duchic (a costumier): Frederick Ashton; Orchidée (his partner): Marie Rambert; Model 'Rose d'Ispahan': Frances James; Model 'Désir du Cygne': Elizabeth Vincent; The Viscountess Viscosa: Esme Biddle; The Viscount Viscosa OBE: W Earle Grey
Lyric Theatre, Hammersmith, *15 June 1926*

NP Mayfair Company of English Dancers;
solo for M. Duchic only, under the title
Youth – 'The Swaggerer':
D Frederick Ashton
Royal Academy of Music, *29 November 1926*

NP Pupils of Marie Rambert; solo for Rose
d'Ispahan only, under the title *Mannequin
Dance*:
D Diana Gould
Arts Theatre Club, *9 March 1928*

(At a performance by Diana Gould and Harold
Turner at the Maddermarket Theatre, Norwich, *8 October 1928*, the programme included
a short suite called *Mannequin and her Beau*, in
three parts – She, He and *Pas de deux* – of
which the first was the *Mannequin Dance*.
Later, they sometimes danced the *Pas de deux*
as a pendant to her solo, but according to
Marie Rambert she herself arranged this. The
Mannequin Dance was included in the divertissements at the first performance by the
Marie Rambert Dancers at the Lyric Theatre,
Hammersmith, *25 February 1930*, and thereafter)

Pas de deux
M Frédéric Chopin (*Prelude* in A flat major,
opus 28 no. 17)
C Flora Fairbairn
D Phyllis Stickland, Frederick Ashton
Mayfair Dancers, probably summer of 1926
(date and place of first performance unknown)

See 1939, **Pas de deux**

1927

[The Fairy Queen]
Opera by Henry Purcell (1692), based on *A
Midsummer Night's Dream* by William Shakes-
peare, adapted by Elkanah Settle
Produced by Dennis Arundell
Dances by Marie Rambert and Frederick
Ashton
C Tom Heslewood Ltd, Ronald Nicholson
and Mrs Cockerell, under the direction of
Lucia Young
D **Dance of Fairies**: Andrée Howard,
Eirene Garratt, Kathleen O'Connor, Pru-
dence Hyman, Pearl Argyle, Joyce Peters

Echo Dance: Diana Gould, Maude
Lloyd
Dance of the Followers of Night:
Winifred Baker, Kathleen O'Connor,
Eirene Garratt, Pearl Argyle
Three Swans: Doola Baker, Maude
Lloyd, Violet Reynolds
Dance of Haymakers: Norah Green-
field, Ursula Humphrey, Muriel Horsey,
Marjorie Kempe, A F Adkins, G G
Beamish, J A W Gibson, W B R Mum-
ford
Attendants on Spring: Diana Gould,
Maude Lloyd
Attendants on Summer: Pearl Argyle,
Andrée Howard
Attendants on Autumn: Doola Baker,
Eirene Garratt
Attendants on Winter: G G Beamish,
Frederick Kempe
Dance of Chinese: (cast not listed in
programme)
Dance of Monkeys: William Chappell,
Kathleen O'Connor, Joyce Peters
Chaconne: Doola Baker, Maude Lloyd,
Andrée Howard, Pearl Argyle
Purcell Opera Society and Cambridge Ama-
teur Dramatic Society, Rudolf Steiner Hall,
23 June 1927; Natural Amphitheatre, Hyde
Park, *25 June 1927*

NP Pupils of Marie Rambert; two dances
only – *Flight of Swans*:
D Diana Gould, Pearl Argyle, Andrée
Howard;
and,
Followers of Night:
D Diana Gould, Andrée Howard, Eliza-
beth Millar, Pearl Argyle
Arts Theatre Club, *9 March 1928*

(**Flight of Swans** was also included in the
divertissements by the Marie Rambert Dancers at the Lyric Theatre, Hammersmith, *25
February 1930*)

See 1946, **The Fairy Queen**

Pas de deux
M Fritz Kreisler (*Caprice viennois*)
C Sophie Fedorovitch
D Eleanora Marra, Frederick Ashton
Presented by Marie Rambert, Imperial Society
of Teachers of Dancing Annual Dance Festi-
val, New Scala Theatre, *23 July 1927*

Suite de danses (Galanteries)
M   Wolfgang Amadeus Mozart (from Ballet for the pantomime *Les Petits riens,* 1778)
D   *Entrée*: Marie Rambert, Frederick Ashton
Pas seul: Frederick Ashton
Danse sentimentale: Marie Rambert, Frederick Ashton
Presented by Marie Rambert, Imperial Society of Teachers of Dancing Annual Dance Festival, New Scala Theatre, *23 July 1927*

See 1928, **Nymphs and Shepherds**

Argentine Dance
M   Artello
C   Sophie Fedorovitch
D   Eleanora Marra, Frederick Ashton
Presented by Marie Rambert, Imperial Society of Teachers of Dancing Annual Dance Festival, New Scala Theatre, *23 July 1927*

(This dance and the Kreisler **Pas de deux** were also performed in cabaret at Murray's Club in Beak Street at about this date)

1928

Nymphs and Shepherds
M   Wolfgang Amadeus Mozart (from *Les Petits riens*)
D   *Passepied*: Pearl Argyle, William Chappell
Entrée de Cupidon: Andrée Howard, Harold Turner
Gavotte joyeuse: Pearl Argyle, Andrée Howard, Harold Turner
Courante: Pearl Argyle, Andrée Howard, Harold Turner, William Chappell
Ballet-Divertissement by Pupils of Marie Rambert, Arts Theatre Club, *9 March 1928* (repeated the following day at a reception in her studio in Ladbroke Road)

(I have been unable to discover whether the first **Suite de danses** from *Les Petits riens* and **Nymphs and Shepherds** had any choreography in common. According to Lionel Bradley's *Sixteen Years of Ballet Rambert*, 'The complete ballet was performed, privately, in practice costume' – presumably in Rambert's studio – in June 1928. He identifies *Nymphs and Shepherds* as 'excerpts' from this. I have not found any account of the June

1928 performance from which it would be possible to deduce what the 'complete ballet' consisted of and how, if at all, it differed from the versions listed here)

Four 'Dances from *Les Petits riens*' were included in the programme at the Lyric Theatre, Hammersmith, on *25 February 1930*, and these would seem to have been drawn from both previous versions, as follows:
D   *Entrée de Cupidon*: Pearl Argyle, William Chappell
Gavotte sentimentale: Marie Rambert, Frederick Ashton
L'Indifférent: Frederick Ashton

(The *Gavotte sentimentale* had been danced by Rambert and Ashton with the Nemchinova-Dolin Ballet at the London Coliseum, *12 December 1927*, and survived into early programmes at the Ballet Club)

Leda
Choreography by Frederick Ashton and Marie Rambert
M   Christoph Willibald Gluck (ballet music from *Orfeo ed Euridice*)
C   William Chappell
D   Leda: Diana Gould; Zeus: Frederick Ashton; Hermes: Harold Turner; Ganymede: William Chappell; Naiades: Pearl Argyle, Andrée Howard, Kathleen O'Connor, Irene Kinsey, Joyce Peters, Prudence Hyman
Marie Rambert's studio, *June 1928*; Sunshine Matinée, Apollo Theatre, *10 July 1928*

NP   Marie Rambert Dancers; revised choreography by Ashton alone, under the title **Leda and the Swan**; C William Chappell and (for Ashton) Bruce Winston: D Leda: Diana Gould; The Swan: Frederick Ashton; Zephyrs: Harold Turner, William Chappell; Nymphs: Pearl Argyle, Andrée Howard, Prudence Hyman, Irene Kinsey, Elisabeth Schooling, Kathleen Suthers
Lyric Theatre, Hammersmith, *25 February 1930*

1929

[Jew Süss]
A Tragi-comedy in five scenes by Ashley

Dukes, based upon passages from the Historical Romance of Lion Feuchtwanger.
The Play produced by Matheson Lang and Reginald Denham
Incidental music arranged by Constant Lambert
s Aubrey Hammond
c Herbert Norris
Players: Matheson Lang, Peggy Ashcroft, Veronica Turleigh, Felix Aylmer, A Bromley Davenport and others

The Ballet of Mars and Venus
Ballet by Marie Rambert
m Domenico Scarlatti, orchestrated by Constant Lambert (*Sonatas*)
s Aubrey Hammond
c Herbert Norris
d Venus: Pearl Argyle; Her Nymphs: Andrée Howard, Anna Brunton; Mars: Harold Turner
Opera House, Blackpool, *29 July 1929*; Duke of York's Theatre, *19 September 1929*

np Marie Rambert Dancers; revised version under the title **Mars and Venus**:
Lyric Theatre, Hammersmith, *25 February 1930*; Ballet Club, *20 April 1931*
    Camargo Society; the same revised version but with music orchestrated 'for full 18th-century orchestra' by Constant Lambert:
Cambridge Theatre, *26 April 1931*
    d (for all these performances) as above, Nymphs listed as 'Attendants'

1930

Capriol Suite
m Peter Warlock, on themes from Thoinot Arbeau's *Orchésographie*
c William Chappell
d *Basse danse*: Pearl Argyle, Prudence Hyman, William Chappell, Robert Stuart
    Pavane: Diana Gould, Frederick Ashton, Harold Turner
    Tordion: Andrée Howard, Harold Turner
    Mattachins: Frederick Ashton, William Chappell, Harold Turner, Robert Stuart
    Pieds en l'air: Pearl Argyle, Diana Gould, Frederick Ashton, William Chappell
    Bransles: Ensemble
Marie Rambert Dancers, Lyric Theatre,

Hammersmith, *25 February 1930*; Camargo Society, Apollo Theatre, *25 January 1931*

np Sadler's Wells Theatre Ballet; choreography rearranged for six couples; sc William Chappell:
    d *Basse danse*: Maureen Bruce, Stella Farrance, Michael Boulton, Pirmin Trecu
    Pavane: Jane Shore, David Poole, Hans Zullig
    Tordion: Patricia Miller, Michael Boulton
    Pieds en l'air: Jane Shore, Stella Claire, David Poole, Hans Zullig
    Mattachins: Michael Boulton, David Blair, David Gill, Pirmin Trecu
    Bransles: Ensemble
Sadler's Wells, *5 October 1948*

np Royal Ballet, Tribute to Sir Frederick Ashton ch cbe; *Mattachins* only:
    d Frank Freeman, Wayne Sleep, Gary Sinclaire, Graham Fletcher
Royal Opera House, *24 July 1970*

np Ballet for All, in Birth of the Royal Ballet; *Mattachins* only:
    d Derek Deane, Colin Dye, Kim Reeder, Oliver Symons
Spa Pavilion, Felixstowe, *13 October 1972*

Saudade do Brésil
m Darius Milhaud (from *Saudade do Brasil*, for piano, 1920–1921)
c William Chappell
d Frederick Ashton
Marie Rambert Dancers, Lyric Theatre, Hammersmith, *23 June 1930*

Mazurka des Hussars
m Alexander Borodin (? from *Petite suite*, for piano, 1878–1885)
c 'Scarlet Scissors' (Dolly Watkins)
d Marie Rambert, Frederick Ashton
Marie Rambert Dancers, Lyric Theatre, Hammersmith, *3 July 1930*

[Marriage à la Mode]
A Comedy, in Three Acts, by John Dryden, Poet Laureate
Produced by Nigel Playfair
Dances arranged by Frederick Ashton
m Alfred Reynolds
sc J Gower Parks

Players: Angela Baddeley, Athene Seyler, Adele Dixon, Glen Byam Shaw, Anthony Ireland, Richard Caldicot
D Alicia Markova, Frederick Ashton, Marie Nielson, Anna Brunton, Hedley Briggs, Walter Gore
Presented by Nigel Playfair, Lyric Theatre, Hammersmith, *9 October 1930*; transferred to Royalty Theatre, *10 November 1930*

Pomona
Ballet in one act by Thomas McGreevy
M Constant Lambert (ballet, 1926)
SC John Banting
D Pomona:Anna Ludmila; Vertumnus: Anton Dolin; Attendants on Vertumnus: Walter Gore, Jack Spurgeon; Principal Nymphs:Doris Sonne, Marie Nielson; Nymphs:Wendy Toye, Joy Newton, Beatrice Appleyard, Iris James, Anna Brunton, Elisabeth Schooling; Flamen Pomonalis (High Priest):Philip McNair
Camargo Society, Cambridge Theatre, *19 October 1930*; Annual Festival of International Society of Contemporary Music, Oxford, *24 July 1931*

(Announced for presentation by both the Ballet Club and the Vic-Wells Ballet in 1931, but not given)

NP Vic-Wells Ballet; SC Vanessa Bell: D Pomona:Beatrice Appleyard; Vertumnus:Anton Dolin
Sadler's Wells, *17 January 1933*

NP Vic-Wells Ballet; SC John Banting: D Pomona:Margot Fonteyn; Vertumnus:Robert Helpmann
Arts Theatre, Cambridge, *3 June 1937*; Sadler's Wells, *28 September 1937*

(*Pas de deux* danced by Margot Fonteyn and Robert Helpmann at Nijinsky Gala Matinée, His Majesty's Theatre, *28 May 1937*; *Pastorale* danced as solo by Margot Fonteyn on BBC Television, *10 June 1937*)

[A Masque of Poetry and Music: 'Beauty, Truth and Rarity']
Produced by George Rylands
Musical Director: Constant Lambert
Players: Lydia Lopokova, Peter Hannen, Geoffrey Toone, George Rylands, Don-

ald Beves, Michael Redgrave, Robert Eddison, Wynyard Brown
'Follow Your Saint': The Passionate Pavan
M John Dowland, arranged by Constant Lambert (from *Lacrymae, or Seven Teares, figured in seven passionate Pavans, with divers other Pavans, Galiards and Almands,* 1605)
C William Chappell
D The Lady:Lydia Lopokova; The Suitors: Frederick Ashton, Harold Turner
Excerpts from *Comus,* a Masque by John Milton
The action concludes with a dance to music by Henry Purcell
Players: Comus, an Enchanter:George Rylands; The Lady:Lydia Lopokova; Elder Brother:Robert Eddison; Second Brother:Michael Redgrave
Dances on a Scotch Theme
M William Boyce, arranged by Constant Lambert (from *Eight Symphonies*)
C William Chappell
D The Lassie:Lydia Lopokova; Her Lads: Harold Turner, Frederick Ashton
The Masque presented by Arnold L Haskell, Arts Theatre Club, *10 December 1930*

NP of **'Follow Your Saint'**; Camargo Society:
      D Lydia Lopokova, Frederick Ashton, William Chappell
Cambridge Theatre, *26 April 1931*

NP of **'Follow Your Saint'** under the title **The Passionate Pavan**, a dance-scena; Camargo Society:
      D Pearl Argyle, Walter Gore, William Chappell
Adelphi Theatre, *4 December 1932*

NP of **'Follow Your Saint'** under the title **Passionate Pavane**, suite of dances; Ballet Rambert:
      D Maude Lloyd, Walter Gore, Frank Staff
Mercury Theatre, *11 October 1936*
      (Sometimes included in Divertissements as **Trio (Lacrymae)** – this may have been an abbreviated version.)
Performed at Nijinsky Gala Matinée:
      D Maude Lloyd, Frank Staff, Frederic Franklin
His Majesty's Theatre, *28 May 1937*

NP of **Dances on a Scotch Theme** called variously **Dances on a Scottish Theme** or **The Tartans**; Ballet Club:
D The Lassie: Alicia Markova; Her Lads: Harold Turner, Frederick Ashton
31 December 1931

A Florentine Picture
Groupings by Frederick Ashton
M Arcangelo Corelli (*Violin Sonata* in D minor, '*La Follia*', opus 5 no. 12)
C 'Scarlet Scissors' (Dolly Watkins), after Sandro Botticelli
D The Madonna: Marie Rambert; Angels: Diana Gould, Pearl Argyle, Andrée Howard, Prudence Hyman, Elisabeth Schooling, Maude Lloyd
Marie Rambert Dancers, Lyric Theatre, Hammersmith, *20 December 1930*

1931

La Péri
The Flower of Immortality†
M Paul Dukas (*Poème dansé*, 1912)
SC William Chappell
D The Péri: Alicia Markova; Iskender: Frederick Ashton; Companions: Pearl Argyle, Andrée Howard, Maude Lloyd, Elisabeth Schooling, Suzette Morfield, Betty Cuff
Ballet Club, *16 February 1931*
† Subtitle added later

See 1956, **La Péri**

The Dance of the Hours
Choreography credited to Anne Fleming but that for Markova and Chappell at least was by Ashton
M Amilcare Ponchielli (ballet music from *La Gioconda*, 1876)
C William Chappell
D Alicia Markova, William Chappell and The Regal Ballet
Regal, Marble Arch, *14 March 1931*

[Cabaret français]
Foxhunting Ballet
M ?

D The Fox: Alicia Markova, with chorus
Regal, Marble Arch, *4 April 1931*

[Excerpts from *Faust*]
Opera by Jules Barbier and Michel Carré
M Charles Gounod (1859–1869)
Choreography again credited to Anne Fleming but that for Markova by Ashton
Singers: Faust: Henry Wendon; Marguerite: Paulyne Bindley; Mephisto: Hubert Dunkerley
D Principal danseuse: Alicia Markova, with the Regal Ballet Corps
Regal, Marble Arch, *18 April 1931*

Façade
A ballet in one act freely adapted to music originally written as a setting to poems by Edith Sitwell†
M William Walton
SC John Armstrong
D *Scotch Rhapsody*: Prudence Hyman, Maude Lloyd, Antony Tudor
Jodelling Song:
Milkmaid: Lydia Lopokova; Mountaineers: Frederick Ashton, William Chappell, Walter Gore
Polka: Alicia Markova
Valse: Pearl Argyle, Diana Gould, Maude Lloyd, Prudence Hyman
Popular Song: William Chappell, Walter Gore
Tango Pasodoble: Lydia Lopokova, Frederick Ashton
Finale – Tarantella Sevillana: Lydia Lopokova, Frederick Ashton and ensemble
Camargo Society, Cambridge Theatre, *26 April 1931*

NP Ballet Club:
D as above except Milkmaid: Andrée Howard; *Tango* and *Finale*: Alicia Markova
4 May 1931

NP Vic-Wells Ballet:
† Subtitle added at this time; choreography and costumes somewhat revised
D *Scotch Rhapsody*: Mary Honer, Elizabeth Miller, Robert Helpmann
Swiss Yodelling Song: The Milkmaid: Gwyneth Mathews; Mountaineers: Harold Turner, Frederick Ashton, William Chappell

Polka: Margot Fonteyn
Waltz: Pamela May, June Brae, Beatrice Appleyard, Peggy Melliss
Popular Song: Harold Turner, William Chappell
Country Dance (new item): A Maiden: Pearl Argyle; A Yokel: Richard Ellis; The Squire: Robert Helpmann
Tango Pasodoble: A Débutante: Molly Brown; A Dago: Frederick Ashton
Tarantella Finale: Pearl Argyle, Frederick Ashton and company
Sadler's Wells, *8 October 1935*

NP Vic-Wells Ballet; new SC John Armstrong:
D *Scotch Rhapsody* (later called *Ecossaise*): Guinevere Parry, Molly Brown, Claude Newman
Noche Espagnola (*Nocturne péruvienne*) (new item): Frederick Ashton
Yodelling Song (*Tyrolienne*): The Milkmaid: Julia Farron; Mountaineers: John Hart, Michael Somes, Richard Ellis
Polka: Margot Fonteyn
Foxtrot (new item): June Brae, Pamela May, Robert Helpmann, Frederick Ashton
Waltz (*Valse*): Ann Spicer, Julia Farron, Palma Nye, Moyra Fraser
Popular Song: Richard Ellis, John Hart
Country Dance: A Maiden: Mary Honer; A Yokel: Michael Somes; The Squire: Robert Helpmann
Tango Pasodoble: A Débutante: Margot Fonteyn; A Dago: Frederick Ashton
Tarantella Finale: Margot Fonteyn, Frederick Ashton and ensemble
Sadler's Wells, *23 July 1940*

NP Sadler's Wells Opera (later Theatre) Ballet; new items omitted; SC as 1940:
D The Milkmaid: Sheila Nelson; *Polka*: Anne Heaton; *Popular Song*: Donald Britton, Alexander Grant; A Débutante: June Brae; A Dago: Frederick Ashton
Sadler's Wells, *29 April 1946*

(On 2 June 1949 the scenery and costumes were destroyed by fire at the Theatre Royal, Hanley; for a brief period following this the ballet was performed in the original décor, borrowed from Ballet Rambert, but with new costumes made from the 1940 designs.)

NP Sadler's Wells Ballet; new items omitted; SC as 1940:

D The Milkmaid: Anne Heaton; *Polka*: Moira Shearer; *Popular Song*: Michael Boulton, Donald Britton; A Débutante: Moira Shearer; A Dago: Frederick Ashton
Foxtrot and *Country Dance* (with Julia Farron as the Country Girl) added *20 June 1950*, with new costumes for these numbers and minor revisions in the *Finale*
Country Dance dropped again as from *7 April 1951*. At two performances on *5* and *7 May 1956* the *Nocturne péruvienne* was restored, and again during the company's tour of Australia, *1958–1959* (D Robert Helpmann)
Royal Opera House, *1 August 1949*

NP Royal Ballet New Group; music performed in its original form, with narration by Peter Pears; original choreographic version plus *Foxtrot*, with abbreviated *Finale*; SC as 1940:
D The Milkmaid: Meryl Chappell; *Polka*: Carole Hill; *Popular Song*: Nicholas Johnson, David Morse; A Débutante: Margaret Barbieri; A Dago: Hendrik Davel
The Maltings, Snape, Aldeburgh, Suffolk, *28 July 1972*; Sadler's Wells, *9 October 1972*
At later performances the music was again performed in the orchestral version

NP Ballet for All, in Birth of the Royal Ballet; *Yodelling Song* only:
D The Milkmaid: Jennifer Jackson
Spa Pavilion, Felixstowe, *13 October 1972*

By other companies:

NP Borovansky Ballet, R Laurel Martyn; SC William Constable (after John Armstrong, 1931 version)
Australia, *c. 1946*

NP Repertory Ballet Theatre of New Zealand; excerpts only: R Yvonne Cartier and Jill Beachen, after Laurel Martyn's Borovansky version
Auckland, *July 1946*

NP Illinois Ballet; R Richard Ellis; SC Dom Orejudos:
D The Milkmaid: Anna Marie Longtin; *Polka*: Bonnie Black; *Popular Song*: Eric

Braun, Richard Ellis; *Tango Pasodoble*: Carol Fleming, Dom Orejudos
St Alphonsus Theatre, Chicago, *25 September 1959*

NP New Zealand Ballet; R Walter Trevor; SC Raymond Boyce (?):
D A Débutante:Gloria Young; A Dago: Poul Gnatt
South Island, *1960*

NP Norwegian National Ballet; R Harold Turner; SC after John Armstrong:
D The Milkmaid:Edith Roger; *Polka*: Henny Mürer; *Popular Song*: Rolf Daleng, Egil Åsman; A Débutante: Mette Møller; A Dago:Harold Turner
Opera House, Oslo, *4 October 1960*

NP City Center Joffrey Ballet; R John Hart and Richard Ellis; SC John Armstrong (1940):
D The Milkmaid:Rebecca Wright; *Polka*: Pamela Johnson; *Popular Song*: Frank Bays, Haynes Owens; A Débutante: Barbara Remington; A Gigolo (sic): Luis Fuente
Auditorium Theatre, Chicago, *28 January 1969*

NP Répétition générale for the Greatest Show on Earth; *Popular Song* only:
D Doreen Wells, John Gilpin
Coliseum, *22 June 1971*

NP Minnesota Dance Theatre; R Brian Shaw; S Jack Barkla; C Judy Cooper and Peter Hauschild:
D The Milkmaid:Roberta Stiehm; *Polka*: Marianne Greven; *Popular Song*: Bobby Crabb, Dana Luebke; A Débutante:Lise Houlton; A Dago:Andrew Thompson
Jacob's Pillow, Lee, Massachusetts, *25 July 1972*

NP The Australian Ballet; R Peggy van Praagh; SC John Armstrong (1940):
D *Nocturne péruvienne*: Robert Helpmann; The Milkmaid:Patricia Cox; *Polka*: Lucette Aldous; *Popular Song*: Alan Alder, David Burch; A Débutante: Carolyn Rappel; A Dago:Robert Helpmann
Princess Theatre, Melbourne, *8 September 1972*

NP Chicago Ballet; R Richard Ellis and

Christine Du Boulay; SC Dom Orejudos:
D The Milkmaid:Cynthia Ann Roses; *Polka*: Deidre Grohgan; *Popular Song*: Dorio Pérez, William Sterner; A Gigolo: Ben Stevenson; A Débutante:Rosemary Miles
Ruth Page Foundation Theatre, Chicago, *2 October 1975*

NP Ballet van Vlaanderen; R Joy Newton; SC John Armstrong (1940):
D The Milkmaid:Roselinde De Craecker; *Polka*: Teresa Del Cerro; *Popular Song*: Tom Van Cauwenbergh, Gilbert Serres; A Débutante:Winni Jacobs; A Dago:Aimé de Lignière
Royal Opera House, Antwerp, Belgium, *10 January 1976*

Mercury
Ballet by Frederick Ashton
M Erik Satie (*Mercure*, ballet, 1924)
SC William Chappell
D Venus:Tamara Karsavina; Apollo:William Chappell; Three Graces:Maude Lloyd, Prudence Hyman, Elisabeth Schooling; Mercury:Frederick Ashton; His Attendants:Betty Cuff, Suzette Morfield, Elizabeth Ruxton
Marie Rambert Dancers, Lyric Theatre, Hammersmith, *22 June 1931*

NP Camargo Society
D Mercury:Walter Gore: Terpsichore (formerly Venus):Alicia Markova; (rest of cast as above, except that Andrée Howard replaced Elizabeth Ruxton)
Savoy Theatre, *27 June 1932*

[Dance Pretty Lady]
A British International Picture
Produced by Bruce Woolfe
Directed by Anthony Asquith
Screenplay by Anthony Asquith, from the novel *Carnival* by Compton Mackenzie
Photographed by Jack Parker
Choreographer and technical adviser for ballet sequences: Frederick Ashton
M John Reynolds (ballet music by Peter Ilyich Tchaikovsky, from *Swan Lake* and *The Nutcracker*)
Players: Ann Casson, Carl Harbord, Flora Robson, Michael Hogan, Moore Marriott, Sunday Wilshin, Rene Ray, Hermione Gingold

D   The Marie Rambert Corps de Ballet
Filmed during the summer of 1931, released
25 June 1932

Regatta
Ballet in one act by Frederick Ashton
M   Gavin Gordon
SC   William Chappell
D   Cabin Boy: Stanley Judson; Three Yachting Girls: Freda Bamford, Sheila McCarthy, Joy Newton; Two Young Men: Walter Gore, William Chappell; A Foreign Visitor: Ninette de Valois
Vic-Wells Ballet, Old Vic, *22 September 1931*

NP   Camargo Society:
D   as above except Cabin Boy: Hedley Briggs
Savoy Theatre, *13 June 1932*

The Lady of Shalott
Ballet by Frederick Ashton, after the poem by Alfred, Lord Tennyson
M   Jean Sibelius (piano pieces from op. 75, 76 and 85)
SC   William Chappell
D   The Lady of Shalott: Pearl Argyle; Her Reflection: Maude Lloyd; The Reapers: Prudence Hyman, Elisabeth Schooling, Betty Cuff, Suzette Morfield, William Chappell; The Lovers: Andrée Howard, Walter Gore; Sir Lancelot: Frederick Ashton
Ballet Club, *12 November 1931*

A Day in a Southern Port†
M   Constant Lambert (*The Rio Grande*, 1927)
Poem by Sacheverell Sitwell
Curtain SC Edward Burra
D   The Queen of the Port: Lydia Lopokova; Her Sailor: Walter Gore; A Creole Girl: Alicia Markova; A Creole Boy: William Chappell; Women of the Port, Stevedores, Stokers, Loiterers, Natives, etc: corps de ballet
Camargo Society, Savoy Theatre, *29 November 1931*

†The programme read as follows: *Rio Grande*/Music by Constant Lambert/A setting of a Poem by Sacheverell Sitwell for Chorus, Orchestra and Solo Pianoforte/Produced as a Ballet entitled/*A Day in a Southern Port*/By

Frederick Ashton. The title was given as *Rio Grande* in the list of repertory.

NP   Vic-Wells Ballet; under the title *Rio Grande*:
D   The Queen of the Port: Beatrice Appleyard; The Creole Girl: Margot Fonteyn; The Stevedore: Walter Gore; The Creole Boy: William Chappell
Sadler's Wells, *26 March 1935*

NP   Royal Ballet, Tribute to Sir Frederick Ashton; Sailor's Dance only:
D   Alexander Grant
Royal Opera House, *24 July 1970*

The Lord of Burleigh
Scenario by Edwin Evans
M   Felix Mendelssohn-Bartholdy, arranged by Edwin Evans, orchestrated by Gordon Jacob (Overture: *Capriccio in A minor*, opus 33 no. 1; *Song Without Words in E major*, op 67 no. 36; *Characteristic Piece*, op 7 no. 4; *Song Without Words in A minor*, op 19 no. 2; *in F sharp minor*, op 19 no. 5; *Scherzo a capriccioso in F sharp minor*, op 28 no. 6; *Song Without Words in A major (Kinderstück)*, op 102 no. 47; *Scherzo*, from *Octet in E flat*, op 20; *Song Without Words in B minor*, op 30 no. 10; *in E flat major*, op 53 no. 20; *in F sharp minor*, op 67 no. 32; *Andante cantabile e presto agitato in B minor*, 1839; ?*Canzonetta*, from *String quartet in E flat major*, op 12; *Finale*, from *Violin concerto in E minor*, op 64)
SC   George Sheringham
D   Lady Clara Vere de Vere: Diana Gould; Katie Willows: Alicia Markova; Lilian: Andrée Howard; Mariana: Maude Lloyd; Madeline: Prudence Hyman; Adeline: Pearl Argyle; Isabel: Phyllis Stanley; Rosalind: Betty Cuff; Margaret: Elisabeth Schooling; Eleänore: Natalia Gregorova; Lord of Burleigh: William Chappell; Eustace: Walter Gore; Edwin Morris: Frederick Ashton; Edward Gray: Antony Tudor
Camargo Society, Carlton Theatre, *15 December 1931* (in a slightly abridged version)

Complete ballet, somewhat revised:
D   as above, except Edwin Morris: Rollo Gamble
Savoy Theatre, *28 February 1932*

NP Vic-Wells Ballet:
 D Lady Clara Vere de Vere: Ursula Moreton; Katie Willows: Alicia Markova; Lilian: Sheila McCarthy; Mariana: Beatrice Appleyard; Madeline: Nadina Newhouse; Adeline: Marie Nielson; Isabel: Joy Newton; Rosalind: Ailne Phillips; Margaret: Freda Bamford; Eleänore: Gwyneth Mathews; Lord of Burleigh: Anton Dolin; Eustace: Claude Newman; Edwin Morris: Antony Tudor; Edward Gray: Travis Kemp
Old Vic, *17 October 1932*

NP Vic-Wells Ballet; SC Derek Hill:
 D Lady Clara Vere de Vere: Pearl Argyle; Katie Willows: Elizabeth Miller; Lilian: Julia Farron; Mariana: Ursula Moreton; Madeline: June Brae; Adeline: Gwyneth Mathews; Isabel: Pamela May; Rosalind: Wenda Horsburgh; Margaret: Margot Fonteyn; Eleänore: Joy Newton; Lord of Burleigh: Robert Helpmann; Eustace: Richard Ellis; Edwin Morris: Leslie Edwards; Edward Gray: William Chappell
Sadler's Wells, *7 December 1937*

NP Royal Ballet, Tribute to Sir Frederick Ashton; solo *The Lady with the Fan* only: D Deanne Bergsma
Royal Opera House, *24 July 1970*

1932

Pompette
M arranged by Hugh Bradford
C Andrée Howard
D Andrée Howard
Ballet Club, *4 February 1932*

[The Cat and the Fiddle]
A musical love story by Otto Harbach
M Jerome Kern
Staged by William Mollison
Dances arranged by Buddy Bradley; the action of *The Passionate Pilgrim* designed by Frederick Ashton
S Henry Dreyfuss
C The Marchioness of Queensberry (Cathleen Mann); Delysia's Pierrot costume by Norman Hartnell

Players: Peggy Wood, Alice Delysia, Gina Malo, Francis Lederer, Muriel Barron, Austin Trevor
Act I Scene 6 Le Pélerin passionné
 Pierrette: Muriel Barron; Harlequin: Eric Marshall; Béchamelle: Rita Cooper; Pierrot: Alice Delysia
Presented by Charles B Cochran, Opera House, Manchester, *20 February 1932*; Palace Theatre, *4 March 1932*

[Magic Nights]
Dances and ensembles arranged by Buddy Bradley and Frederick Ashton
SC Ada Peacock and William Chappell
Radio Waves
M ?
D *Rumba*: Eve
 The Spirit of Radio/Tango des Fratellini: Pearl Argyle
The Bell Boys Stampede
M W C Handy (*St Louis Blues*)
C William Chappell
D Eve, Frederick Ashton
An 1805 Impression
Ballet by Frederick Ashton
M Franz Schubert (*Waltzes*)
SC William Chappell (after Jacques-Louis David)
D Récamier: Pearl Argyle; Her Suitor: Frederick Ashton; Her Friends: Rita Elsie, Kathleen Gibson, Mary Barlow, Joan Laidlaw, Pamela Gray, Maisie Greene; *Pas de quatre*: Dorothy Jackson, Esmé Oxley, Walter Gore, William Chappell
Presented by Charles B Cochran, Trocadero Grill Room, *4(?) April 1932*

NP of **An 1805 Impression,** under the title **Récamier** (sometimes called **La Valse chez Madame Récamier, suite de danses**):
 D Mme Récamier: Pearl Argyle; Her Suitor: Antony Tudor; *Pas de quatre*: Andrée Howard, Elisabeth Schooling, William Chappell, Frank Staff; Friends: Tamara Svetlova, Nan Hopkins, Yvonne Madden, Daphne Gow, Ann Gee, Aase Nissen
Ballet Club, *3 December 1933*

High Yellow
Choreography by Buddy Bradley, with the assistance of Frederick Ashton

M Spike Hughes (1 Foreword 2 Sirocco 3 Six Bells Stampede 4 Elegy 5 Weary Traveller 6 Finale, from *A Harlem Symphony*)
S Vanessa Bell
C William Chappell
D Mammy: Ursula Moreton; Pappy: Hedley Briggs; Bambu (their son): Frederick Ashton; Mabel, Edna, Pansy and Ninon (His Sisters): Sheila McCarthy, Freda Bamford, Betty Cuff, Nadina Newhouse; Violetta and Cleo (His Sweethearts): Alicia Markova, Doris Sonne; Violetta's languishing friends: Beatrice Appleyard, Maude Lloyd, Elisabeth Schooling, Joy Newton, Felicity Andreae, Mary Skeaping, Joan Day; Cleo's gay friends: Ailne Phillips, Sylvia Willins, Laura Wilson, Kathleen Crofton, Andrée Howard, Dot Rickinson, Prudence Hyman; Joey and Eddy (Two Strangers): William Chappell, Walter Gore
Camargo Ballet, Savoy Theatre, *6 June 1932*

Foyer de danse (after Degas)
Ballet by Frederick Ashton
M Lord Berners (*Luna Park; or, the Freaks*, ballet, 1930)
C William Chappell
D L'Etoile: Alicia Markova; Le Maître de ballet: Frederick Ashton; Les Coryphées: Andrée Howard, Prudence Hyman, Betty Cuff, Elisabeth Schooling, Suzette Morfield, Elizabeth Ruxton; Un Abonné: Walter Gore
Ballet Club, *9 October 1932*

[A Kiss in Spring]
A Romantic Comedy with Music by Julius Brammer and Alfred Grünwald (an adaptation of their operetta *Das Veilchen vom Montmartre*, 1930)
M Emmerich Kálmán and Herbert Griffiths; additional orchestrations by Constant Lambert, Arthur Wood, Alfred Reynolds and Walford Hyden
English Book and Lyrics by L du Garde Peach
The Play Produced by Norman Marshall
SC Hedley Briggs
Players: Billy Milton, Sylvia Welling, Eric Bertner, Eileen Moody, Kenneth Kove, Nancy Neale
In Act II **Carrambolina**
D Prudence Hyman, Walter Gore and corps de ballet

Act III Scene 3 **The Ballet of Spring**
D Alicia Markova, Harold Turner, Prudence Hyman, Walter Gore, Doris Sonne, Anna Brunton, Yvonne Le Sueur and corps de ballet
Presented by Sir Oswald Stoll, Alhambra Theatre, *28 November 1932*

[Ballyhoo]
A Revue, devised and staged by William Walker and Robert Nesbitt
Dances and ensembles by Buddy Bradley; ballets by Frederick Ashton
M William Walker
Lyrics by Robert Nesbitt
S Coombe
C Norman Edwards and William Chappell
Players: Hermione Baddeley, George Sanders, Henry Mollison, Richard Murdoch, Phyllis Clare, Walter Crisham
Act I Scene 4 **Black Magic**
The Salesman: John Byron; 1st Customer: Peggy Cochrane; 2nd Customer: Norman Hackforth; 3rd Customer: George Sanders; The Singer: Zaidee Jackson; The Dancers: Walter Crisham and The Girls
Act I Scene 10 **By Candlelight**
D Pearl Argyle, Walter Crisham, John Byron and The Girls
Act I Scene 12 **Mediterranean Madness**
D The Matelot: Walter Gore; The Dancers: Pearl Argyle, Walter Crisham and The Company
Act II Scene 3 **Far Beyond the Crowd**
D Pearl Argyle, Walter Crisham, Nancy Burne, Richard Murdoch, Aimee Gillespie, Hugh French
Act II Scene 8 **Ballet for Four Pianos and Orchestra**
M arranged by Peggy Cochrane
D Pearl Argyle, Walter Gore, John Byron and The Girls
Presented by Lionel Barton, Comedy Theatre, *22 December 1932*

1933

Pas de deux
M Jean Philippe Rameau
C Phyllis Dolton
D Alicia Markova, Anton Dolin
Coliseum, *27 February 1933*

461

Les Masques; ou, Changement de dames
Ballet by Frederick Ashton
M Francis Poulenc (*Trio* for oboe, bassoon and piano, 1926)
SC Sophie Fedorovitch
D A Personage: Frederick Ashton; His Lady Friend: Alicia Markova; His Wife: Pearl Argyle; Her Lover: Walter Gore; Two Young Girls: Elisabeth Schooling, Betty Cuff; Three Ladies with Fans: Anna Brunton, Elizabeth Ruxton, Tamara Svetlova
Ballet Club, *5 March 1933*

[How D'You Do?]
Revue with book and lyrics by Arthur Macrae, Douglas Byng, Herbert Farjeon, *et al*
Ballets by Frederick Ashton; mime-ballet, *On the Quay*, by Suzanne Stone; dances and ensembles by Tony Smythe
M Ord Hamilton
S Alick Johnstone
Players: Frances Day, Douglas Byng, Edward Chapman, Queenie Leonard, Iris March
The Legend of Berenice
A Mediaeval Ballet by Frederick Ashton
C Michael Weight
D Berenice: Frances Day; Roland: Walter Gore; Attendants on Berenice: corps de ballet
Rumba
A Dancing Scena by Frederick Ashton
C Betty Cooke
D Anna Roth, Walter Gore and The Chorus
Comedy Theatre, *25 April 1933*

Pavane pour une infante défunte
M Maurice Ravel
SC Hugh Stevenson
D Diana Gould, William Chappell
Ballet Club, Mercury Theatre, *7 May 1933*

NP Ballet Club; revised choreography
     D Diana Gould, William Chappell
Mercury Theatre, *29 October 1933*

[After Dark]
Revue by Ronald Jeans
Devised and produced by Kenneth Duffield
Ballets by Frederick Ashton; dances and ensembles by Buddy Bradley

M Kenneth Duffield and Kenneth Leslie-Smith
S Aubrey Hammond
Players: Nelson Keys, Louise Browne, Roy Royston, Charles Heslop, Melville Cooper, Betty Davies, Betty Frankiss
The Orchid and the Cactus (Fahrenheit)
A Ballet by Robert Nesbitt
M Peggy Cochrane
D The Orchid: Louise Browne; The Cactus: Harold Turner
Wall Street
A Ballet by Robert Nesbitt
M Kenneth Leslie-Smith
D Harold Turner, Audrey Acland, Claude Newman, Douglas Phillips, John Gatrell, and Girls
Presented by John Merryman Ltd, Vaudeville Theatre, *6 July 1933*

[Gay Hussar]
A musical play in a prologue, two acts and an epilogue by Holt Marvell
M George Posford
Produced by Julian Wylie
Choreography by Frederick Ashton; comedy dances arranged by Charles Brooks
Players: Gene Gerrard, Viola Compton, Betty French, George Courtney, Bruce Anderson, Bernard Clifton, Mamie Soutter
D Ballerina: Mary Honer, with corps de ballet
Palace Theatre, Manchester, *30 September 1933*

[Nursery Murmurs]
Ballets by Frederick Ashton; tap numbers by Graham Graham
Cavalcoward
M Noel Coward
D Frederick Ashton and the Murmur Young Ladies
Valse de concert
M Alexander Glazunov
Triptych
M Arcangelo Corelli
Perpetuum mobile
M Johann Strauss Jr (*Perpetuum mobile, musikalischen scherz, opus 257*)
See 1937, **Perpetuum mobile**
Also by Ashton: **My Tram, Mary Mary** and **Police Theme** (details unknown)
Empire Theatre, Liverpool, *6 November 1933*

Les Rendezvous
Ballet-Divertissement
M Daniel François Auber, arranged by Constant Lambert (ballet music from *L'Enfant prodigue*)
SC William Chappell
D 1 *Entrance of Walkers Out*: Ensemble
   2 *Pas de six*: Beatrice Appleyard, Sheila McCarthy, Freda Bamford, Hermione Darnborough, Nadina Newhouse, Gwyneth Mathews
   3 *Variation*: Stanislas Idzikowski
   4 *Adagio of Lovers*: Alicia Markova, Stanislas Idzikowski
   5 *Pas de trois*: Ninette de Valois, Stanley Judson, Robert Helpmann
   6 *Variation*: Alicia Markova
   7 *Pas de six*: Robert Helpmann, Travis Kemp, Antony Tudor, Claude Newman, Maurice Brooke, Toni Repetto
   8 *Exit of Walkers Out*: Ensemble
Vic-Wells Ballet, Sadler's Wells, *5 December 1933*

NP Vic-Wells Ballet:
   D 1 *Entrance*: Ailne Phillips, William Chappell, and ensemble
   2 *Pas de quatre* (new number): Molly Brown, Joy Robson, Jill Gregory, Margot Fonteyn
   4 *Adagio of Lovers*: Alicia Markova, Stanley Judson
   5 *Pas de trois*: Ailne Phillips, Claude Newman, Robert Helpmann
Sadler's Wells, *2 October 1934*

NP Vic-Wells Ballet; new SC William Chappell:
   D *Lovers*: Margot Fonteyn, Harold Turner
   Pas de trois: Jill Gregory, Frederick Ashton, Claude Newman
Sadler's Wells, *16 November 1937*

NP Sadler's Wells Theatre Ballet; new SC William Chappell:
   D *Adage des amoureux*: Elaine Fifield, Michael Boulton
   Pas de trois: Sheilah O'Reilly, Donald Britton, Pirmin Trecu
Sadler's Wells, *26 December 1947*
(The décor and costumes for this production were destroyed by fire at the Theatre Royal, Hanley, 2 June 1949; thereafter the ballet was given in Hugh Stevenson's set for *Promenade*, with new gates and new costumes)

NP Royal Ballet; choreography revised for enlarged corps de ballet; S Sophie Fedorovitch (Act I of *La Traviata*, 1948)†; new C William Chappell:
   D *Amoureux*: Nadia Nerina, Brian Shaw
   Pas de trois: Merle Park, Graham Usher, Petrus Bosman
   †Reverted to William Chappell's 1937 décor, 10 October 1962
Royal Opera House, *7 May 1959*

NP Royal Ballet touring section; new C William Chappell (new S added at Pavilion, Bournemouth, 28 September 1961):
   D *Amoureux*: Doreen Wells, Donald Britton
Temple of Bacchus, Baalbek, Lebanon, *29 August 1961*

NP Royal Ballet School:
   D *Amoureux*: Sally Inkin, Christopher Carr
   Pas de trois: Judith Beams, Wayne Eagling, Michael Ho
Royal Opera House, *15 July 1967*

NP Royal Ballet, Tribute to Sir Frederick Ashton:
   D *Amoureux*: Merle Park, Rudolf Nureyev
   Pas de trois: Ann Jenner, Gary Sherwood, Petrus Bosman
Royal Opera House, *24 July 1970*

NP Ballet for All; *pas de trois* only:
   D Jacqueline Tallis, Paul Benson, Douglas Vardon
Village College, Melbourne, Derbyshire, *6 October 1971*

NP Royal Ballet touring section; SC William Chappell (1937):
   D *Amoureux*: Merle Park, Desmond Kelly
   Pas de trois: Brenda Last, Nicholas Johnson, Donald Kirkpatrick
Wimbledon Theatre, *12 October 1971*

NP Ballet for All; *pas de deux* and variations only:
   D Maxine Dennis, Kim Reeder
Spa Pavilion, Felixstowe, *13 October 1972*

463

By other companies:

NP Alicia Markova and Anton Dolin and company; woman's variation only; R Frederick Ashton; C William Chappell (1933):
D Alicia Markova
Empress Hall, *3(?) January 1949*

NP Fonteyn-Helpmann Concert Group; woman's variation only:
D Margot Fonteyn
Tunbridge Wells, *2 June 1950*

NP University of Cape Town Ballet Company; R David Poole; SC Gill Parker (redesigned by Stephen de Villiers, 1965):
D *Amoureux*: Mavis Maastricht, David Poole
Cape Town, *5 December 1952*

NP National Ballet of Canada; R Peggy van Praagh; SC Kay Ambrose, after William Chappell (1937):
D *Amoureux*: Lois Smith, David Adams
Palace Theatre, Hamilton, Ontario, *5 November 1956*

NP The Australian Ballet; R Peggy van Praagh; SC William Chappell (1937):
D *Amoureux*: Marilyn Jones, Garth Welch
Her Majesty's Theatre, Sydney, *30 November 1962*

NP State Ballet of Turkey; R Joy Newton and Dudley Tomlinson:
D *Amoureux*: Ayla Ünal, Hüsnü Sunal
National Theatre, Ankara, *22 October 1964*

NP The New Zealand Ballet; R Peggy van Praagh; SC William Chappell (1937) (redesigned by Raymond Boyce, Palmerston North, *24 February 1968*):
D *Amoureux*: Gillian Francis, Bernard Hourseau
Auckland Festival, *5 May 1967*

NP PACT Ballet; R John Hart; SC William Chappell (1937):
D *Amoureux*: Dawn Weller, Edgardo Hartley
Civic Theatre, Johannesburg, *3 September 1971*

NP Ballet of the Bayerische Staatsoper; R Elizabeth Cunliffe (choreologist), Annette Page and Ronald Hynd; SC William Chappell (1937):

D *Amoureux*: Konstanze Vernon, Heinz Bosl
Bayerische Staatsoper, Munich, *30 November 1972*

1934

Four Saints in Three Acts
An Opera to be Sung
Words by Gertrude Stein
M Virgil Thomson
Scenario by Maurice Grosser
Production by John Houseman
Choreography by Frederick Ashton
SC Created by Florine Stettheimer, designed by Kate Drain Lawson
Singers: Commère: Altonell Hines; Compère: Abner Dorsey; St Ignatius: Edward Matthews; St Theresa I: Beatrice Robinson Wayne; St Theresa II: Bruce Howard; St Chavez: Embry Bowner; St Settlement: Bertha Fitzhugh Baker
D Caro Lynn Baker, Elizabeth Dickerson, Mable Hart, Floyd Miller, Maxwell Baird, Billie Smith
Presented by The Friends and Enemies of Modern Music, Wadsworth Atheneum, Hartford, Connecticut, *7 February 1934*; by Harry Moses, 44th Street Theatre, New York, *20 February 1934*. Transferred to the Empire Theatre, New York, *2 April 1934*. Revived at the Auditorium Theatre, Chicago, *7 November 1934*

Mephisto Valse
Ballet by Frederick Ashton on a theme from Lenau's *Faust*
M Franz Liszt (*Mephisto Waltz* no. 1, The Dance at the Inn from Lenau's *Faust*)
SC Sophie Fedorovitch
D Marguerite: Alicia Markova; Mephisto: Frederick Ashton; Faust: Walter Gore; Young Girls: Elisabeth Schooling, Doris Sonne, Peggy van Praagh; Young Men: Hugh Laing, Rollo Gamble, Frank Staff
Ballet Club, Mercury Theatre, *13 June 1934*

NP Ballet Workshop:
D Marguerite: Paula Hinton; Mephisto: Michael Holmes; Faust: Robert Harrold
Mercury Theatre, *15 March 1953*

See 1952, **Vision of Marguerite**

Pas de deux classique
M Alexander Glazunov (from *The Seasons*, ballet, opus 67)
C Phyllis Dolton
D Alicia Markova, Anton Dolin
Hippodrome, Golder's Green, *16 July 1934*

[Jill Darling!]
A New Musical Comedy by Marriott Edgar, with additional scenes and lyrics by Desmond Carter
M Vivian Ellis
The Play Produced by William Mollison
Dances and ensembles by Fred Lord; 'I'm Dancing with a Ghost' by Frederick Ashton
S Leon Davey
Players: Frances Day, Louise Browne, Arthur Riscoe, John Mills, Viola Tree, Sebastian Smith, Teddie St Denis
I'm Dancing with a Ghost
D Frances Day, Frederick Ashton
Presented by Jack Eggar Ltd, Saville Theatre, *19 December 1934*

[Escape Me Never]
A British and Dominion Picture
Produced by Herbert Wilcox
Directed by Paul Czinner
Screenplay by Carl Zuckmayer and Margaret Kennedy, from her play
Photographed by Sepp Allgeier and Georges Périnal
Edited by David Lean
M William Walton
Choreography by Frederick Ashton
Players: Elisabeth Bergner, Hugh Sinclair, Penelope Dudley-Ward, Lyn Harding, Griffith Jones, Rosalind Fuller, Leon Quartermaine, Irene Vanbrugh
D Margot Fonteyn, Beatrice Appleyard, and the Vic-Wells Ballet
Filmed December 1934, released *1935*

1935

Valentine's Eve
Ballet by Frederick Ashton
M Maurice Ravel (*Valses nobles et sentimentales*)
SC Sophie Fedorovitch
D Constant: Frederick Ashton; Phryné:

Pearl Argyle; Solange: Maude Lloyd; Sylvestre: William Chappell; Bette: Elisabeth Schooling; Robert: Walter Gore; Ninon: Peggy van Praagh; Octave: Hugh Laing; François: Frank Staff
Ballet Rambert, Duke of York's Theatre, *4 February 1935*

See 1947, **Valses nobles et sentimentales**

In a Venetian Theatre
M Vivian Ellis (originally composed for a number choreographed by George Balanchine in Charles B Cochran's *1930 Revue*)
D Louise Browne
Anna Pavlova Memorial Matinée, Palace Theatre, *21 February 1935*

[The Flying Trapeze]
English libretto by Douglas Furber from the libretto by Hans Müller (*Zirkus Aimé*, 1928)
M Ralph Benatzky and Mabel Wayne
Lyrics by Douglas Furber, Desmond Carter and Frank Eyton
The Play Produced under the personal direction of Erik Charell
Dances arranged by Frederick Ashton; Jack Buchanan's dances by Buddy Bradley; 'Angel on Horseback' by Tony Smythe
SC Ernest Stern
Players: Jack Buchanan, June Clyde, Ivy St Helier, Fred Emney, Bruce Carfax, Richard Hearne
D Paulette (a dancer): Pearl Argyle; A Dancer: Hugh Laing; and corps de ballet
Life in a Circus
Marie Louise
Operatic Burlesque (including **Speciality Dance** by Argyle and Laing)
The Wedding in the Stars
Alhambra Theatre, *4 May 1935*

[Round About Regent Street]
Created, devised, and produced by George Black, assisted by Charles Henry
Dances and ensembles arranged by Frederick Ashton and J Sherman Fisher
Orchestrations and arrangements by Billy Ternent and Jock Prentice
S G McConnell Wood, Alec Shanks, Max Weldy and Harry Delvin
Players: Flanagan and Allen, Nervo and Knox, Naughton and Gold (The Crazy Gang)

2 **A Flower Market**
c   Max Weldy, from designs by Freddy Wittop
d   Jeanne Devereaux

6 **The Very Merry Widow**
m   Franz Lehár
c   Max Weldy, from designs by Freddy Wittop

The Ambassador:Chesney Allen; The Secretary of State:Bud Flanagan; The Ambassador's Wife:Hannah Watt; Prince Danilo: Teddy Knox; The Widow:Jimmy Nervo; and ensemble

8 **Olde London Towne: Buy My Cherries**
m   Roger McDougall
d   The Cherry Maid:Jeanne Devereaux

12 **Vauxhall Gardens, 1750**
Vocalist:Bea Hutten; Prince Frederick:Syd Railton; Milady – Friend of the Prince: Hannah Watt; Maître d'hôtel:Del Foss
'Poor Bride – Poor Groom' sung by the Crazy Gang and Company
'Love's Telegraph' sung by Adrian Burgess and Company

16 **The Moth and the Flame**
d   The Moth:Jeanne Devereaux
Replaced in London by
The Lady in Red
m   Mort Dixon and Allie Wrubel (from the Warner Brothers' film *In Caliente*, 1935)
d   Jeanne Devereaux
Presented by George Black, Hippodrome, Brighton, *12 August 1935*; London Palladium, *27 August 1935*

Le Baiser de la fée
Allegorical Ballet in four tableaux by Igor Stravinsky, after Hans Andersen's *The Ice Maiden*
m   Igor Stravinsky, inspired by the muse of Tchaikovsky
sc   Sophie Fedorovitch
d   A Mother:Ursula Moreton; The Fairy: Pearl Argyle; The Young Man:Harold Turner; His Fiancée:Margot Fonteyn; Spirits, The Villagers, The Bridesmaids: corps de ballet
Vic-Wells Ballet, Sadler's Wells, *26 November 1935*

np   Royal Ballet, Tribute to Sir Frederick Ashton; excerpt from Scene 3 only:
d   The Bride:Jennifer Penney, with corps de ballet
Royal Opera House, *24 July 1970*

[Follow the Sun]
Revue with dialogue by Ronald Jeans and John Hastings Turner
The Entire Revue Produced under the Direction of Charles B Cochran
Staged by Frank Collins
Dances and ensembles by Buddy Bradley and Frederick Ashton
m   Arthur Schwartz
Lyrics by Howard Dietz and Desmond Carter
s   Ernest Stern
c   Ernest Stern, Ada Peacock and Xenia
Players: Claire Luce, Irene Eisinger, Ada Reeve, Jeni LeGon, Eve, Iris March, Frank Pettingell, Eliot Makeham, Vic Oliver, Nick Long Jr (not in cast at opening performances in Manchester)

8 **Love is a Dancing Thing**
d   Eileen O'Connor and Mr Cochran's Young Ladies

10 **Cuba**
d   *Nicotina*: Claire Luce, Robert Linden (later Nick Long Jr, Frederick Ashton)

11 **Polonaise**
d   Mr Cochran's Young Ladies

19 **The First Shoot:** A Tragedy
A Ballet by Osbert Sitwell
m   William Walton
sc   Cecil Beaton
d   Lady de Fontenoy (formerly Connie Winsome of the Gaiety, or Daly's): Claire Luce; Lord Fontenoy:Robert Linden (later omitted from cast list); Lord Charles Canterbury:Frederick Ashton (later Nick Long Jr); The Pheasants, The Ladies, The Gentlemen, The Footmen: ensemble

22 **Dangerous You**
d   The Girl:Claire Luce; The Poet:Robert Linden (later Frederick Ashton); The Man About Town:Philip Morgan; The Tough:Stanley Haig-Brown; The Soldier:W Lawson McLaren

24 **Sleigh Bells**
d   Eileen O'Connor
Presented by Charles B Cochran, Opera House, Manchester, *23 December 1935*; Adelphi Theatre, *4 February 1936*

1936

Siesta
m   William Walton
c   for Pearl Argyle by Matilda Etches

D   Pearl Argyle, Robert Helpmann
Vic-Wells Ballet, Sadler's Wells, *24 January 1936*

See 1972, **Siesta**

Apparitions
A ballet on romantic themes arranged by Constant Lambert
M   Franz Liszt, arranged by Constant Lambert, orchestrated by Gordon Jacob
(Prologue: *Consolation* no 3 in D flat major
        Valse oubliée no. 1
        Nocturne: Schlaflos, Frage und Antwort
Interlude: *Ungarisch*, from *Weihnachtsbaum*, no. 11
Tableau I: *Polnisch*, from *Weihnachtsbaum*, no. 12
        Jadis, from *Weihnachtsbaum*, no. 10
        Galop in A minor
        Elegy no. 2
Tableau II: *Evening Bells*, from *Weihnachtsbaum*, no. 9
        Scherzoso, from *Weihnachtsbaum*, no. 5
        Carillon, from *Weihnachtsbaum* no. 6
        Unstern (Sinistre, Disastro)
Tableau III: *Mephisto Waltz*, no. 3
Epilogue: *R[ichard] W[agner] – Venezia Consolation* no. 1, reprise)
SC   Cecil Beaton
D   The Poet:Robert Helpmann; The Woman in Ball Dress:Margot Fonteyn; The Hussar:Harold Turner; The Monk: Maurice Brooke; Ladies of Fashion, Dandies, Belfry Spirits, etc:corps de ballet
Vic-Wells Ballet, Sadler's Wells, *11 February 1936*

NP   Sadler's Wells Ballet; new SC Cecil Beaton (further revised 17 November 1952):
     D The Poet:Robert Helpmann; The Woman in Ball Dress:Margot Fonteyn
Royal Opera House, *24 March 1949*

NP   Sadler's Wells Theatre Ballet; SC Cecil Beaton (1949 version, with scenery cut down):
     D The Poet:John Field; The Woman in Ball Dress:Anne Heaton

Shakespeare Memorial Theatre, Stratford-upon-Avon, *28 January 1957*; Sadler's Wells, *4 July 1957*

NP   Royal Ballet, Tribute to Sir Frederick Ashton; Ballroom Scene (Tableau I) only:
     D The Poet:Rudolf Nureyev; The Woman in Ball Dress:Margot Fonteyn
Royal Opera House, *24 July 1970*

NP   Ballet for All; excerpt from Tableau I only:
     D The Poet:Colin Dye; Woman with Fan (sic):June Highwood
Spa Pavilion, Felixstowe, *13 October 1972*

See 1956, **The Beloved**

[The Town Talks]
Revue by Vivian Ellis and Arthur Macrae
Staged by Robert Nesbitt
Dances and ensembles by Freddie Carpenter; *The Hat* by Frederick Ashton
M   Vivian Ellis
S   Harry Clifford
C   Felix Harbord, Kit Yorke, Nick Zuber, Adrian, Violet Norton, Charles Judd, *et al*
Players: June, Arthur Riscoe, Phyllis Stanley, George Benson
The Hat
Devised by Vivian Ellis
M   Vivian Ellis, orchestrated by Ken Warner
D   The Vendeuse:June; The Customer:Gertrude Musgrove
Presented by André Charlot, Palace Theatre, Manchester, *26 February 1936*; Vaudeville Theatre, *11 March 1936*

[Die Fledermaus]
Operetta in three acts by Carl Haffner and Richard Genée, after *Le Réveillon* by Henri Meilhac and Ludovic Halévy
M   Johann Strauss Jr
Produced by Clive Carey
Dance arranged by Frederick Ashton
SC   O F Smyth
Cast: Dorothy Kingston, Winifred Kennard, Morgan Jones, Tudor Davies, Valetta Iacopi, John Greenwood
D   Pamela May, Robert Helpmann, Joy Newton, Gwyneth Mathews, June Brae,

467

Anne Spicer, Wenda Horsburgh, Richard Ellis, Michael Somes
Vic-Wells Opera, Sadler's Wells, *28 October 1936*

Nocturne
Ballet in one scene by Edward Sackville-West
M   Frederick Delius (*Paris, Ein Nachtstück: The Song of a Great City*)
SC   Sophie Fedorovitch
D   A Spectator:Frederick Ashton; A Young Man:Robert Helpmann; A Rich Girl (later called A Young Girl):June Brae; A Poor Girl (later called A Flower Girl): Margot Fonteyn; Maskers, Revellers: corps de ballet
Vic-Wells Ballet, Sadler's Wells, *10 November 1936*

NP   Sadler's Wells Ballet:
     D as above, except A Young Girl: Pamela May
Royal Opera House, *18 March 1946*

NP   Royal Ballet, Tribute to Sir Frederick Ashton; excerpt only:
     D A Poor Girl:Margot Fonteyn; The Spectator:Michael Somes
Royal Opera House, *24 July 1970*

[Home and Beauty]
Charles B Cochran's Coronation Revue, by A P Herbert
Devised and staged by John Murray Anderson
Libretto directed by Frank Collins
M   Nicholas Brodszky and Henry Sullivan
S   Raoul Pène du Bois
C   Raoul Pène du Bois, Norman Hartnell *et al*
Players: Binnie Hale, Nelson Keys, Gitta Alpar, Norah Howard, Sepha Treble, Iris March, Greta Gynt, Betty Driver, Leslie French, Rawicz and Landauer, (in chorus, Michael Wilding, Rosamund John)
Act I Scene 3 **Dressing for Dinner**
       Scene 10 **The Tapestry Room**
Act II Scene 1 **Seeing the Estate**
       Scene 6 **At the Music-Room Window: Twilight Sonata**
              D The Statues: Greta Gynt, Frank Staff
Presented by Charles B Cochran, Opera

House, Manchester, *23 December 1936*; Adelphi Theatre, *2 February 1937*

1937

Perpetuum mobile
M   Johann Strauss Jr (*Perpetuum mobile, musikalischer scherz*, opus 257)
C   for Joy Newton by William Chappell
D   Joy Newton, Robert Helpmann
Vic-Wells Ballet, Sadler's Wells, *11 January 1937*

(Another dance to this music choreographed and danced by Frederick Ashton and Tilly Losch, date and place unknown)

Harlequin in the Street
A New Ballet by André Derain
M   François Couperin, arranged by Constant Lambert
SC   André Derain
D   A Pedestrian:Lionel Dixon; A Knife-Grinder:Ivor Harries; A Bread Man: Hedley Briggs; Three Gossips:Peggy van Praagh, Susan Reeves, Mary Skeaping; Harlequin:Stanley Judson; A Bourgeois Gentilhomme:Michael Martin-Harvey; A Marquise:Chrysagon Vaughan; Two Porters:George Welford, Donald Hewett
Given as a curtain-raiser to *Le Misanthrope* by Jean-Baptiste Molière, Arts Theatre, Cambridge, *8 February 1937*; Ambassadors Theatre, *23 February 1937*, with Alan Carter as Harlequin

See 1938, **Harlequin in the Street**

Les Patineurs
Ballet-Divertissement in one act
M   Giacomo Meyerbeer, arranged by Constant Lambert (ballet music and one aria from *Le Prophète*, and Waltz from Act II, Prelude to Act III and Ismailov's aria 'Bel Cavalier' from *L'Etoile du nord*)
SC   William Chappell
D   1 *Entrée*: Mary Honer, Elizabeth Miller
     Pas de huit: Gwyneth Mathews, Joy Newton, Peggy Melliss, Wenda Horsburgh, Richard Ellis, Leslie Edwards, Michael Somes, Paul Reymond

2 *Variation*: Harold Turner

3 *Pas de deux*: Margot Fonteyn, Robert Helpmann

4 *Ensemble*

5 *Pas de trois*: Mary Honer, Elizabeth Miller, Harold Turner

6 *Pas des patineuses*: June Brae, Pamela May

7 *Ensemble*

8 *Galop Finale*

Vic-Wells Ballet, Sadler's Wells, *16 February 1937*

NP Sadler's Wells Ballet; new S William Chappell:
D *Entrée*: Margaret Dale, Avril Navarre; *Variation*: Harold Turner; *Pas de deux*: Moira Shearer, David Paltenghi; *Pas des patineuses*: Beryl Grey, Gillian Lynne

Royal Opera House, *20 March 1946*

NP Sadler's Wells Theatre Ballet:
D *Entrée*: Sara Neil, Doreen Tempest; *Variation*: Donald Britton; *Pas de deux*: Annette Page, David Poole; *Pas des patineuses*: Shirley Bishop, Yvonne English

Sadler's Wells, *23 April 1955*

(This production remained in the repertory of the Royal Ballet touring section, later called New Group, and Sadler's Wells Royal Ballet)

NP Royal Ballet; enlarged version with corps de ballet and *Pas des patineuses* duplicated behind the arches:
D *Entrée*: Annette Page, Shirley Grahame; *Variation*: Brian Shaw; *Pas de deux*: Anya Linden, Desmond Doyle; *Pas de quatre* (formerly *Pas des patineuses*): Brenda Taylor, Valerie Taylor, Meriel Evans, Mary Drage

Royal Opera House, *12 March 1957*

(This so-called 'mirror' version, prepared for the tour of Soviet Russia planned for the autumn of 1956 and cancelled after the invasion of Hungary, was not performed on tour in Britain by the main company, though it was given in the United States; it was dropped altogether from 10 February 1966, though the corps de ballet was then augmented to six couples)

NP Royal Ballet School:
D *Entrée*: Hilary Debden, Ann Jenner; *Variation*: Dudley Tomlinson; *Pas de deux*: Susan Turnham, Derek Rencher;

Pas des patineuses: Patricia Kilner, Ann Wade

Royal Opera House, *13 May 1961*

NP Ballet for All; *Variation* only:
D Kim Reeder

Spa Pavilion, Felixstowe, *13 October 1972*

By other companies:

NP Ballet Theatre (later American Ballet Theatre); SC Cecil Beaton:
D *Entrée*: Barbara Fallis, Cynthia Riseley; *Variation*: John Kriza; *Pas de deux*: Nora Kaye, Hugh Laing; *Pas des patineuses*: Diana Adams, Anna Cheselka

Broadway Theater, New York, *2 October 1946*

NP University of Cape Town Ballet: R David Poole; S Stephen de Villiers; C after William Chappell:
D *Variation*: David Poole; *Pas de deux*: Patricia Miller, Dudley Davies

Cape Town, *6 December 1957*

NP The United Ballet Company; R Philip Chatfield; SC after William Chappell:
D *Entrée*: Rowena Jackson, ?; *Variation*: Walter Trevor; *Pas de deux*: Rowena Jackson, Philip Chatfield

Her Majesty's Theatre, Auckland, New Zealand, *28 November 1959*

NP State Ballet of Turkey; R Ninette de Valois and Ann Parsons:
D *Entrée*: Geyvan McMillen, Shirley Subaşi; *Variation*: Ferit Akin; *Pas de deux*: Ayla Ünal, Engin Akaoğlu; *Pas des patineuses*: Rezzan Ürey, Ümran Ürey

National Theatre, Ankara, *15 January 1962*

NP The New Zealand Ballet; R Walter Trevor; SC Raymond Boyce:
D *Variation*: Walter Trevor; *Pas de deux*: Kirsten Ralov, Arthur Turnbull

Napier, *7 July 1962*

NP Transvaal Ballet; R Alexander Bennett:
D *Variation*: Juan Sanchez

?, *1965*

NP Royal Winnipeg Ballet; R Miro Zolan; SC William Chappell:
D *Entrée*: Anna Marie de Gorriz, Donna Frances; *Variation*: Leo Ahonen; *Pas de*

469

deux: Sheila Mackinnon, Heinz Spoerli; *Pas des patineuses*: Jennifer Sholl, Shirley New
Playhouse Theatre, Winnipeg, Manitoba, *29 December 1966*

NP The Australian Ballet; R Peggy van Praagh; SC William Chappell:
D *Entrée*: Patricia Box, Barbara Chambers; *Variation*: Alan Alder; *Pas de deux*: Elaine Fifield, Kelvin Coe
Her Majesty's Theatre, Adelaide, *23 March 1970*

NP Minnesota Dance Theatre; R Brian Shaw; S Jack Barkla; C Gene Buck:
D *Entrée*: Lise Houlton, Marianne Greven; *Variation*: Andrew Thompson; *Pas de deux*: Sylvia Bolton, Jon Benson
Minneapolis, Minnesota, *2 May 1971*

NP Noverre-Ballett; R Robert Mead; SC Sylvia Strahammer:
D Carl Morrow, Miguel Sanchez, Joyce Cuoco, Catherine Prescott, Jean MacCabe, Brigitte Erdweg, Ludmilla Bogart (distribution of roles unavailable)
Württembergisches Staatstheater Stuttgart, Kleines Haus, *6 May 1973*

First Arabesque
M Claude Debussy (from *Deux arabesques* for piano)
D Margot Fonteyn
BBC Television, Alexandra Palace, *20 March 1937*

A Wedding Bouquet
M Lord Berners
Words by Gertrude Stein (mostly from *They Must. Be Wedded. To Their Wife*)
Curtain SC Lord Berners
D Webster:Ninette de Valois; Two Peasant Girls:Linda Sheridan, Joan Leaman; Two Peasant Boys:Paul Reymond, Alan Carter; Josephine:June Brae; Paul: Harold Turner; John:William Chappell; Violet:Pamela May; Ernest:Claude Newman; Thérèse:Elizabeth Miller; Julia:Margot Fonteyn; Bridegroom: Robert Helpmann; Pépé (Julia's dog): Julia Farron; Arthur:Leslie Edwards; Guy:Michael Somes; Four Guests: Gwyneth Mathews, Wenda Horsburgh, Joy Newton, Anne Spicer; Two Gendarmes:Paul Reymond, Alan Carter;

Bride:Mary Honer; Bridesmaids:Molly Brown, Jill Gregory
Vic-Wells Ballet, Sadler's Wells, *27 April 1937*

NP Sadler's Wells Ballet:
D Josephine:June Brae; Julia:Moira Shearer; Bridegroom:Robert Helpmann; Bride:Margaret Dale
Royal Opera House, *17 February 1949*

NP Royal Ballet, Tribute to Sir Frederick Ashton; excerpt only:
D Jill Gregory, Gerd Larsen, John Hart, Michael Somes, Leslie Edwards, Ann Jenner, Rosalind Eyre (no distribution of roles given)
Royal Opera House, *24 July 1970*

NP Ballet for All; excerpts only:
D Josephine:June Highwood; Julia:Maxine Dennis; Bridegroom:Oliver Symons; Bride:Christine Aitken
Spa Pavilion, Felixstowe, *13 October 1972*

NP Royal Ballet touring section:
D Josephine:Vyvyan Lorrayne; Julia: Margaret Barbieri; Bridegroom:Alain Dubreuil; Bride:Marion Tait
Sadler's Wells, *14 May 1974*

[Floodlight]
A New Revue written and composed by Beverley Nichols
Produced by C Denis Freeman
Dances arranged by Buddy Bradley; ballets by Frederick Ashton
Additional M Vivian Ellis and Benjamin Frankel
SC René Hubert
Players: Frances Day, John Mills, Hermione Baddeley
13 **Waltz** in *Prelude to Battle* (Scene: The Waterloo Ball, Brussels, 1815)
16 **Dancing with the Daffodils**
D Frances Day and The Girls
24 **Sir Thomas Beeton in the Kitchen**
M Benjamin Frankel
D The Cook:Hermione Baddeley; The Chef:Cyril Wells; Conductor:Lyle Evans; Kitchenmaids:Maisie Green, Eily Wilson, Sylvia Taperell, Valerie Stanton; Footmen:Tom Gillis, Edward Britten, Kenneth Carter, Peter Du Calion
Presented by Richard D Rose and A J Shaughnessy, Saville Theatre, *23 June 1937*

1938

Horoscope

Ballet in one act by Constant Lambert

M   Constant Lambert

Curtain sc Sophie Fedorovitch

D   The Young Man (Sun in Leo, Moon in Gemini): Michael Somes; The Young Woman (Sun in Virgo, Moon in Gemini): Margot Fonteyn; The Gemini: Richard Ellis, Alan Carter; The Moon: Pamela May; Followers of Leo, Followers of Virgo, Attendants on the Moon: corps de ballet

Vic-Wells Ballet, Sadler's Wells, *27 January 1938*

NP   Royal Ballet, Tribute to Sir Frederick Ashton; solo for the Moon only:
   D Vyvyan Lorrayne

Royal Opera House, *24 July 1970*

NP   Ballet for All; Young Man's solo only:
   D Colin Dye

Spa Pavilion, Felixstowe, *13 October 1972*

The Judgment of Paris

M   Lennox Berkeley

sc   William Chappell

D   Paris: Robert Helpmann; Venus: Pearl Argyle; Juno: Elizabeth Miller; Minerva: Mary Honer; Mercury: William Chappell

Vic-Wells Ballet, Sadler's Wells, *10 May 1938*

[Running Riot]

A New Musical Show in Two Acts by Douglas Furber, from a plot by Guy Bolton and Firth Shephard

M   and lyrics Vivian Ellis

The Play Produced by Leslie Henson and Herbert Bryan

Dances and ensembles by Jack Donohue; ballet produced by Frederick Ashton

s   The Harkers and René Hubert

c   René Hubert

Players: Leslie Henson and the Gaiety Theatre Company: Louise Browne, Fred Emney, Richard Hearne, Rosalind Atkinson, Gavin Gordon, Roy Royston

The Chinese Ballet

D   The Dancer (Betty): Louise Browne; The Lover: Ann Coventry; The God Ambition: Arthur Ives; and corps de ballet

Gaiety Theatre, *31 August 1938*

[Tannhäuser]

Opera by Richard Wagner (Paris version, 1861)

Produced by Clive Carey

Ballet arranged by Frederick Ashton

sc   Charles Reading

Cast: Arthur Carson, Molly de Gunst, Joan Cross, Arnold Matters

Venusberg Scene

D†   The Three Graces: Pamela May, June Brae, Joy Newton; Eros: Richard Ellis; and corps de ballet

†The opening night programme simply listed the dancers' names; the names of the characters were first given in the programme for 22 November 1938

Vic-Wells Opera, Sadler's Wells, *2 November 1938*

Harlequin in the Street

Ballet after Jean-François Regnard (1656–1710)

M   François Couperin, arranged by Constant Lambert, orchestrated by Gordon Jacob

(1 Prologue – Overture: 22me Ordre no. 1, *Le Trophée*

2 (a) Street Scene: 11me Ordre no. 5, *Les Fastes de la grande et ancienne M∗n∗str∗nds∗, Deuxieme Acte: 1er Air de Vieille – Les Vieilleux et les Gueux*

(b) Knifegrinder†: 1er Ordre no. 14, *La Manon*

(c) Commères: ?6me Ordre no. 7, *Les Commères*

(d) Bread-boy: 2me Ordre no. 12, *La Diane*

3 Messenger: 23me Ordre no. 2, *Les Tricoteuses*

4 Man's Solo: 24me Ordre no. 1, *Les Fastes de la grande et ancienne M∗n∗str∗nd∗s∗, Les vieux Seigneurs*

5 Porters: 24me Ordre no. 2, *Les jeunes Seigneurs, cy-disant Les Petits Maîtres*, 2me Partie

6 Disguising Scene: 10me Ordre no. 1, *La Triomphante*

7 L'Arlequin: ?23me Ordre no. 3, *L'Arlequine*

8 La Superbe: 9me Ordre no. 3, *Les Charmes*

9 Disguised Lovers: 6me Ordre no. 1, *Les Moissonneurs*

10 Dénouement: 18me Ordre no. 6, *Le Tic-Toc-Choc, ou, Les Maillotins*

11 Epilogue: 1st solo, reprise)

SC   André Derain

D   La Superbe:June Brae; Monseigneur: Michael Somes; Harlequin:Alan Carter; Porters:Stanley Hall, John Hart; Commères:Palma Nye, Jill Gregory, Patricia Garnett; Bird-Catcher:Richard Ellis; Bread Boy:Frank Staff; Letter Bearer: John Nicholson

† It will be noted that this is a character from the earlier (1937) version of the ballet; presumably the second version, though revised and extended to the point of being an entirely new work, included music from the earlier version – the list given here is from the two-piano score arranged by Constant Lambert during World War II, now in the Music Library of the Royal Opera House, to which I am indebted for allowing me to examine it.
Vic-Wells Ballet, Sadler's Wells, *10 November 1938*

NP   Royal Ballet, Tribute to Sir Frederick Ashton; excerpt only:
D   Julie Wood, Betty Kavanagh, Rosalind Bury, Christopher Newton, Douglas Steuart, Ronald Plaisted (no distribution given in programme)
Royal Opera House, *24 July 1970*

NP   Ballet for All; solo for Harlequin only;
R   Alan Carter:
D   Kenneth Saunders
Spa Pavilion, Felixstowe, *11 October 1973*

1939

Pas de deux

M   Frédéric Chopin (*Prelude* in A flat major, opus 28 no. 17)
D   Margot Fonteyn, Robert Helpmann
Liverpool Ballet Club, Crane Theatre, Liverpool, *21 April 1939*

Cupid and Psyche

Ballet in one act and three scenes after Apuleius
M   Lord Berners
SC   Francis Rose
D   Pan:Michael Somes; Nymphs:Palma Nye, Joan Leaman; Psyche:Julia Farron; Cupid:Frank Staff; Venus:June Brae; Psyche's Sisters:Mary Honer, Elizabeth Miller; Ceres:Margot Fonteyn†; Minerva:Mary Honer; Diana:Elizabeth Mil-

ler; Apollo:Richard Ellis; Juno:Ursula Moreton;Jupiter:David Grey;Narrators: Kathleen Hilditch, Margaret Tepler; Tanagra Women, Townspeople, Attendants on Venus, Zephyrs, Attendants on Ceres, Attendants on Minerva, Attendants on Diana, Attendants on Juno and Jupiter:corps de ballet

† This role was to have been danced by Pamela May, but when she became ill, Fonteyn replaced her at the last moment.
Vic-Wells Ballet, Sadler's Wells, *27 April 1939*

NP   Royal Ballet, Tribute to Sir Frederick Ashton; solo for Psyche only:
D   Psyche: Marilyn Trounson
Royal Opera House, *24 July 1970*

Devil's Holiday (Le Diable s'amuse)

Ballet in a prologue and three scenes by Vincenzo Tommasini
M   Vincenzo Tommasini, on themes by Niccolò Paganini
Curtain SC   Eugene Berman
D   The Old Lord:Simon Semenoff; His Daughter:Alexandra Danilova; The Young Lover:Frederic Franklin; The Fiancé:George Zoritch; The Devil:Marc Platoff; The Gypsy Girl:Nathalie Krassovska; The Old Woman:Tatiana Chamié; The Beggar:Robert Irwin; The Hat-Seller:Alexander Goudovitch; *Variations*: 1 Alexandra Danilova; 2 Rosella Hightower, Marina Novikova, Tatiana Grantzeva, Anna Scarpova, Roy Milton, Boris Belsky; 3 Nathalie Krassovska, George Zoritch, Chris Volkoff; 4 Tatiana Flotat, Tatiana Grantzeva, Rosella Hightower, Milada Mladova, Marina Novikova, Anna Scarpova; 5 Leila Lelanova, Jean Vallon, Charles Dickson, Ian Gibson; 6 George Zoritch, Chris Volkoff, Roy Milton, Robert Steele; 7 Alexandra Danilova; 8 Frederic Franklin; Bailiffs, Hunters, Guests:corps de ballet
Ballet Russe de Monte Carlo, Metropolitan Opera House, New York, *26 October 1939*

1940

Dante Sonata

(D'après une lecture de Dante)
M   Franz Liszt, orchestrated by Constant

Lambert (*Fantaisie, quasi Sonate: d'après une lecture de Dante*, from *Années de pélérinage: Seconde année – Italie*)

SC Sophie Fedorovitch, after John Flaxman (1755–1826)

D Children of Light†: Margot Fonteyn, Pamela May, Julia Farron, Michael Somes; Children of Darkness†: June Brae, Joy Newton, Robert Helpmann; and corps de ballet

†These designations did not appear on the opening night programme but were added later.

Vic-Wells Ballet, Sadler's Wells, *23 January 1940*

NP Sadler's Wells Ballet:
  D Children of Light: Margot Fonteyn, Pamela May, David Paltenghi; Children of Darkness: Beryl Grey, Robert Helpmann

Royal Opera House, *20 March 1946*

NP Royal Ballet, Tribute to Sir Frederick Ashton; solo for a Child of Light only (Pamela May's solo):
  D Monica Mason

Royal Opera House, *24 July 1970*

NP Ballet for All; excerpt only:
  D Children of Light: Maxine Dennis, Jennifer Jackson, Derek Deane; Child of Darkness: Kim Reeder

Spa Pavilion, Felixstowe, *13 October 1972*

The Wise Virgins

M Johann Sebastian Bach, arranged by Constant Lambert, orchestrated by William Walton

  (1 Cantata 140: *Wachet auf* (final chorale)
  2 Cantata 142: *Dein Geburtstag ist erschienen* (bass aria)
  3 Cantata 99: *Was Gott tut* (opening chorus)
  4 Organ Chorale BWU 727: *Herzlich tut mir verlangen*
  5 Cantata 85: *Ich bin ein guter Hirt* (tenor aria), *Seht, was die Liebe tut*
  6 Cantata 26: *Ach wie flüchtig* (opening chorus)
  7 Cantata 208: *Was mir behagt* (soprano aria), *Schafe, können sicher weiden*
  8 As 3, with different scoring, orchestrated to two ritornelli without chorale

  9 Cantata 129: *Gelobet sei der Herr* (concluding chorale setting))

Curtain SC Rex Whistler

D The Bridegroom: Michael Somes; The Bride: Margot Fonteyn; The Father: Claude Newman; The Mother: Annabel Farjeon; Wise Virgins: Julia Farron, Olive Deacon, Joan Leaman, Joan Sheldon, Palma Nye; Foolish Virgins: Mary Honer, Elizabeth Kennedy, Joy Newton, Patricia Garnett, Jean Bedells; Angels: Richard Ellis, John Hart, Leslie Edwards, Leo Young, Stanley Hall; Cherubs: Deryk Mendel, Margaret Dale, Guinevere Parry, Mavis Jackson

Vic-Wells Ballet, Sadler's Wells, *24 April 1940*

NP Royal Ballet, Tribute to Sir Frederick Ashton; solo for the Bride only:
  D The Bride: Margot Fonteyn

Royal Opera House, *24 July 1970*

NP Ballet for All; solo for the Bride only:
  D The Bride: June Highwood

Spa Pavilion, Felixstowe, *13 October 1972*

1941

The Wanderer

Choreographic Fantasy by Frederick Ashton

M Franz Schubert (*Fantasia* in C major, opus 15; arrangement for piano and orchestra by Franz Liszt used from 5 January 1942)

SC Graham Sutherland

D Robert Helpmann
  Alan Carter, John Hart, Leslie Edwards, John Field
  Julia Farron
  Pamela May, Michael Somes
  Margot Fonteyn
  Mary Honer, Patricia Garnett
  Joy Newton, Palma Nye, Wenda Horsburgh, Guinevere Parry, Joan Sheldon, Elizabeth Kennedy
  Margaret Dale, Deryk Mendel

Sadler's Wells Ballet, New Theatre, *27 January 1941*

NP Royal Ballet, Tribute to Sir Frederick Ashton; duet for the Lovers (Pamela May, Michael Somes) only:
  D Vergie Derman, Donald MacLeary

Royal Opera House, *24 July 1970*

NP Ballet for All; duet for Lovers only:
    D Jennifer Jackson, Kim Reeder
Spa Pavilion, Felixstowe, *13 October 1972*

1943

The Quest
An adaptation by Doris Langley Moore of a theme from Edmund Spenser's *The Fairie Queene*
M   William Walton
SC John Piper
D   Archimago (a Magician personifying Hypocrisy):Leslie Edwards; Female Servant (transformed into Una):Celia Franca; Male Servant:Anthony Burke; Bats (Evil Spirits):Pauline Clayden, Lorna Mossford; St George (the Red Cross Knight, personifying Holiness):Robert Helpmann; Una (personifying Truth): Margot Fonteyn; *Saracen Knights*:Sansjoy:David Paltenghi, Sansloy:Alexis Rassine, Sansfoy:Franklin White; Duessa (personifying Falsehood):Beryl Grey; *The Seven Deadly Sins*:Pride (as Queen): Moira Shearer, Sloth:Nigel Desmond, Gluttony:Ray Powell, Wrath:Celia Franca, Lechery:Anthony Burke, Avarice:Gordon Hamilton, Envy:Palma Nye; Faith:Julia Farron; Hope:Moyra Fraser; Charity:Jean Bedells; Courtiers and Attendant Virtues:corps de ballet
Sadler's Wells Ballet, New Theatre, *6 April 1943*

1945

[A Midsummer Night's Dream]
A comedy by William Shakespeare
Directed by Nevill Coghill
Dances arranged by Frederick Ashton
M   composed and arranged by Leslie Bridgewater
S   Hal Burton
Players: John Gielgud, Peggy Ashcroft, Max Adrian, Leslie Banks
Theatre Royal, Haymarket, *25 January 1945*

1946

[The Sleeping Beauty]
Ballet in a prologue and three acts by Marius Petipa and Ivan Vsevolozhsky, after Charles Perrault
Produced by Nicholas Sergeyev after the choreography of Marius Petipa, with additions by Frederick Ashton and Ninette de Valois
M   Peter Ilyich Tchaikovsky (*La Belle au bois dormant*, ballet, opus 66)
SC Oliver Messel
D   Princess Aurora:Margot Fonteyn; Prince Florimund:Robert Helpmann; The Lilac Fairy:Beryl Grey; Carabosse:Robert Helpmann
Act I **Garland Dance**
D   Corps de ballet
Act III **Florestan and his Two Sisters**
D   Moira Shearer, Gerd Larsen, Michael Somes
(first woman's variation by Petipa, from 'Jewel' *pas de quatre*; from 20 January 1950 the programme credit for this *pas de trois* read 'by Frederick Ashton after Petipa')
Sadler's Wells Ballet, Royal Opera House, *20 February 1946*
Act II **Aurora's Variation** ('after Marius Petipa')
D   Aurora:Beryl Grey
Sadler's Wells Ballet, Royal Opera House, *9 January 1952*
Act III **Florimund's Variation** ('after Marius Petipa')
D   Florimund:Michael Somes
Sadler's Wells Ballet, Royal Opera House, *23 February 1955*

NP Royal Ballet touring section:
    D Aurora:Anya Linden; Florimund: Bryan Ashbridge; Florestan and his Two Sisters:Simon Mottram, Joan Blakeney, Elaine Thomas
Grand Theatre, Leeds, *14 September 1959*

Act I **The Rose Adagio**
D   Aurora:Nadia Nerina
Specially produced by Frederick Ashton for the Royal Performance, Prince of Wales Theatre, *4 November 1963*

Act II **Awakening Scene**
D   Aurora:Violette Verdy; Florimund: David Blair

474

Royal Ballet, Royal Opera House, *29 February 1964.*

NP Royal Ballet; production devised and staged by Peter Wright, with new and additional choreography by Frederick Ashton; s Henry Bardon; c Lila de Nobili and Rostislav Doboujinsky:
Prologue: **The Fairy of Joy**
D Georgina Parkinson
Act I **Garland Dance** (new version)
D Corps de ballet
Act II **Prince Florimund's Variation**
D Anthony Dowell
Act II **Pas de deux (Awakening Scene)**
D Aurora: Antoinette Sibley; Florimund: Anthony Dowell
Act III **Gold and Silver pas de trois**
D Jennifer Penney, Brian Shaw, Keith Martin
(Original *Florestan pas de trois* restored 15 March 1972, under the title *Gold and Silver pas de trois*:
D Jennifer Penney, Ann Jenner, David Ashmole)
Royal Opera House, *17 December 1968*

NP Royal Ballet; produced and with new and additional choreography by Kenneth MacMillan; sc Peter Farmer
This production retained Ashton's choreography for Prince Florimund's variation in Act II (D Anthony Dowell) and for the variation of the Fairy of Joy, which was incorporated into a new 'Jewels' *pas de six* in Act III (D Georgina Parkinson)
Royal Opera House, *15 March 1973*

Symphonic Variations
M César Franck
SC Sophie Fedorovitch
D Margot Fonteyn, Pamela May, Moira Shearer, Michael Somes, Henry Danton, Brian Shaw
Sadler's Wells Ballet, Royal Opera House, *24 April 1946*

NP Royal Ballet touring section:
D Antoinette Sibley, Jennifer Penney, Laura Connor, Anthony Dowell, Robert Mead, Michael Coleman
Theatre Royal, Nottingham, *9 November 1970*

By other companies:

NP Fonteyn World Tour, 1963:
D Margot Fonteyn, Annette Page, Shirley Grahame, Royes Fernandez, Ronald Hynd, Alexander Grant
Athens Festival, Herod Atticus Theatre, Athens, *9 August 1963*

Les Sirènes
Ballet by Frederick Ashton
M Lord Berners
SC Cecil Beaton
D Mermaids: Palma Nye, Gillian Lynne; Seagulls: Margaret Dale, Alexis Rassine; Children: Pauline Clayden, Alexander Grant, Guinevere Parry, Mavis Spence; Nannies: Anne Gieves, Fiorella Keane; Gendarmes: Paul Reymond, Alec Martin; Flowerwoman: Betty Cooper; Countess Kitty: Beryl Grey; Captain Bay Vavasour: Michael Somes; La Bolero: Margot Fonteyn; Her Chauffeur: Leslie Edwards; King Hihat of Agpar: Frederick Ashton; Adelino Canberra (of the Adelaide Opera): Robert Helpmann; The Smart Set, King Hihat's Suite: corps de ballet
Sadler's Wells Ballet, Royal Opera House, *12 November 1946*

The Fairy Queen
Masque in three acts, after William Shakespeare's *A Midsummer Night's Dream*
M Henry Purcell, adapted by Constant Lambert (in association with Edward J Dent)
Production by Frederick Ashton and Malcolm Baker-Smith
Curtain SC Michael Ayrton
Players: Margaret Rawlings, Robert Helpmann, James Kenney, Tony Tarver, Edgar Evans, Audrey Bowman, Constance Shacklock, Harcourt Williams, Michael Hordern
D Titania's train: Julia Farron, Gerd Larsen, Palma Nye, Lorna Mossford, Rosemary Lindsay, Joan Grantham, Christine du Boulay, Margaret Sear; *Ballet of the Birds*: Anne Negus, Pauline Clayden, Avril Navarre, Jill Gregory; Echo Dancers: Beryl Grey, Gillian Lynne, Margaret Dale; The Followers of Night: corps de ballet; Four Fairies: Anne Negus,

Pauline Clayden, Jill Gregory, Avril Navarre; A Nymph: Moira Shearer; Savages: Franklin White, Kenneth Melville, Paddy Stone, Alexander Grant; Spirits of the Air: Margot Fonteyn, Michael Somes; Phoebus: David Davenport; Attendants on Spring: Moira Shearer and corps de ballet; Attendants on Summer: Beryl Grey and corps de ballet; Attendants on Autumn: Michael Somes and corps de ballet; Attendants on Winter: David Paltenghi and corps de ballet; Four Chinese Dancers: Alexis Rassine, John Hart, Pauline Clayden, Margaret Dale; Two Chinese Children: Veronica Vail, Peter Clegg; Hymen: Richard Ellis

Covent Garden Opera and Sadler's Wells Ballet, Royal Opera House, *12 December 1946*

NP Ny Norsk Ballett; Spirits of the Air *pas de deux* only:
D Margot Fonteyn, Robert Helpmann
Norske Theatre, Oslo, *30 January 1950*

1947

Manon
Opera in five acts by Henri Meilhac and Philippe Gille, from the novel by Abbé Prévost; English version by Norman Feasey:
M Jules Massenet
Production by Frederick Ashton
SC James Bailey
Cast: Manon Lescaut: Virginia McWatters; The Count des Grieux: Jess Walters; Lescaut: Dennis Noble
Covent Garden Opera, Royal Opera House, *30 January 1947*

Albert Herring
A Comic Opera in three acts by Eric Crozier, freely adapted from *Le Rosier de Madame Husson* by Guy de Maupassant
M Benjamin Britten (opus 39)
Production by Frederick Ashton
SC John Piper
Cast: Lady Billows: Joan Cross; Florence: Gladys Parr; Miss Wordsworth: Margaret Ritchie; Mr Gedge: William Parsons; Mr Upfold: Roy Ashton; Super-

intendent Budd: Norman Lumsden; Sid: Frederick Sharp; Albert Herring: Peter Pears; Nancy: Nancy Evans; Mrs Herring: Betsy de la Porte; Emmie: Leslie Duff; Cis: Anne Sharp; Harry: David Spenser
English Opera Group, Glyndebourne Opera House, *20 June 1947*

Valses nobles et sentimentales
M Maurice Ravel
SC Sophie Fedorovitch
D Anne Heaton, Donald Britton, Michael Boulton, Elaine Fifield, Maryon Lane, Jane Shore, Yvonne Barnes, Kenneth MacMillan, Michael Hogan, Peter Darrell
Sadler's Wells Theatre Ballet, Sadler's Wells, *1 October 1947*

1948

Scènes de ballet
M Igor Stravinsky
SC André Beaurepaire
D Margot Fonteyn, Michael Somes, Alexander Grant, Donald Britton, John Field, Philip Chatfield, and corps de ballet
Sadler's Wells Ballet, Royal Opera House, *11 February 1948*

NP Ballett der Deutschen Oper; R Monica Parker and Ray Barra; performed in practice dress, without scenery
D Silvia Kesselheim, Klaus Beelitz
Deutsche Oper, Berlin, *11 March 1968*

[La Traviata]
Opera in four acts by Francesco Piave, from the play *La Dame aux camélias* by Alexandre Dumas fils; English version by Edward J Dent
M Giuseppe Verdi
Production by Tyrone Guthrie, with the assistance of Frederick Ashton
SC Sophie Fedorovitch
Cast: Marguerite (sic): Elisabeth Schwarzkopf; Armand Duval (sic): Kenneth Neate
Covent Garden Opera, Royal Opera House, *6 April 1948*

Don Juan

A Choreographic Impression in one act by Frederick Ashton†

M   Richard Strauss (Symphonic Poem, opus 20)

SC   Edward Burra

D   Don Juan:Robert Helpmann; 'La Morte Amoureuse':Margot Fonteyn; Her Attendants:Alfred Rodrigues, Bryan Ashbridge; A Young Wife:Moira Shearer; Her Husband:Richard Ellis; Amours: Anne Heaton, Gerd Larsen, Julia Farron, Rosemary Lindsay, Nadia Nerina, Gillian Lynne; Rivals:John Field, Kenneth Melville, Philip Chatfield; Carnaval: corps de ballet

Sadler's Wells Ballet, Royal Opera House, *25 November 1948*

†Subtitle added 13 September 1952

Cinderella

Ballet in three acts

Devised and produced by Frederick Ashton

M   Serge Prokofiev (ballet, opus 87)

SC   Jean-Denis Malclès

D   Cinderella:Moira Shearer; Cinderella's Stepsisters:Frederick Ashton, Robert Helpmann; Cinderella's Father:Franklin White; The Ragged Fairy Godmother: Pamela May; A Tailor:Donald Britton; The Dressmakers:Anne Negus, Margaret Dale; The Shoemaker:Paul Reymond; The Hairdresser:Leslie Edwards; A Jeweller:Henry Legerton; The Dancing Master:Harold Turner; The Coachman: Robert Lunnon; The Fairy Spring:Nadia Nerina; The Fairy Summer:Violetta Elvin; The Fairy Autumn:Pauline Clayden; The Fairy Winter:Beryl Grey; The Prince:Michael Somes; The Jester:Alexander Grant; Suitors:Alfred Rodrigues, Donald Britton; The Prince's Friends: Bryan Ashbridge, Philip Chatfield, Kenneth Melville, Kenneth MacMillan; A Negro:Ronald Kaye; Violinists, Pages, Lackeys, Stars, Courtiers, Guests, Townswomen, Footmen:corps de ballet

Sadler's Wells Ballet, Royal Opera House, *23 December 1948*

NP   Royal Ballet touring section:

D   Cinderella:Margot Fonteyn; The Prince:Michael Somes; Stepsisters:Rosemary Lindsay, Meriel Evans; The Ragged Fairy Godmother:Barbara Remington;

The Jester:Donald Britton; The Fairy Spring:Doreen Wells; The Fairy Summer:Elizabeth Anderton; The Fairy Autumn:Audrey Farriss; The Fairy Winter:Carole Needham

Royal Opera House, *14 December 1960*

NP   Royal Ballet; some revisions including new variation for the Fairy Godmother to music from Prokofiev's *Visions fugitives*, opus 22 no. 7, orchestrated by John Lanchbery; curtain SC Henry Bardon and David Walker:

D   Cinderella:Margot Fonteyn; The Prince:David Blair; Stepsisters:Frederick Ashton, Robert Helpmann; Fairy Godmother:Annette Page; The Jester:Alexander Grant; The Fairy Spring:Antoinette Sibley; The Fairy Summer:Vyvyan Lorrayne: The Fairy Autumn:Merle Park; The Fairy Winter:Deanne Bergsma

Royal Opera House, *23 December 1965*

NP   Royal Ballet, Tribute to Sir Frederick Ashton; *pas de deux* from Act II only:

D   Cinderella:Merle Park; The Prince: Donald MacLeary

Royal Opera House, *24 July 1970*

NP   Ballet for All; solo for Cinderella, Act I, only:

D   Cinderella:Belinda Corken

Spa Pavilion, Felixstowe, *11 October 1973*

By other companies:

NP   Ballet of La Scala, Milan; *pas de deux* from Act II only; SC Emanuele Luzzati:

D   Cinderella:Margot Fonteyn; The Prince:Michael Somes

Teatro alla Scala, Milan, *11 February 1960*

NP   The Australian Ballet; R Robert Mead; SC Kristian Fredrikson:

D   Cinderella:Lucette Aldous; The Prince:Kelvin Coe; Stepsisters:Frederick Ashton, Robert Helpmann; Fairy Godmother:Kathleen Geldard; The Fairy Spring:Patricia Cox; The Fairy Summer: Carolyn Rappel; The Fairy Autumn: Gailene Stock; The Fairy Winter:Marilyn Rowe; The Jester:Alan Alder

Elizabethan Theatre, Newtown, Sydney, *17 March 1972*

NP PACT Ballet; R John Hart; SC Reinhard Heinrich:

D Cinderella: Dawn Weller; The Prince: Keith Rosson; Stepsisters: James Riveros, Wilhelm Schoeman; Fairy Godmother: Ethne Klein; The Fairy Spring: Margaret Sim; The Fairy Summer: Sianne Strasberg; The Fairy Autumn: Myrna Stasin; The Fairy Winter: Kay Ashton; The Jester: Edgardo Hartley

Civic Theatre, Johannesburg, *25 August 1972*

1949

Le Rêve de Léonor
Ballet in one act by Léonor Fini

M Benjamin Britten, orchestrated by Arthur Oldham (*Variations on a Theme by Frank Bridge*, opus 10)

SC Léonor Fini

D Girl without Hair: Renée Jeanmaire; Girl with Hair: Joan Sheldon; Two Hirsute Men: Oleg Briansky, Stanley Hall; Sphinx: Ursula Kubler; King of Nougat: John Gilpin; Four Whipped Creams: Joan Sheldon, Kathleen Gorham, Mireille Lefebvre, Ruth Helfgot; Proserpine: Renée Jeanmaire; Sombre Seducer: Milorad Miskovitch; Owl: Renée Jeanmaire; Three Ephebes: Oleg Briansky, John Gilpin, Stanley Hall; Two Bouquets: Joan Sheldon, Kathleen Gorham

Les Ballets de Paris, Princes Theatre, *26 April 1949*

1950

Illuminations
Ballet in one act

M Benjamin Britten (*Les Illuminations*, opus 18)

Poems by Arthur Rimbaud (from *Les Illuminations*, 1871–2)

SC Cecil Beaton

D I *Fanfare*: Nicholas Magallanes
II *Dreamtown*: Barbara Bocher, Arlouine Case, Dorothy Dushock, Jillana, Barbara Milberg, Francesca Mosarra, Pat McBride, Margaret Walker, Tomi Wortham, Robert Barnett, Brooks Jackson, Shaun O'Brien, Roy Tobias

III *Phrase*: Nicholas Magallanes
IV *Antiquity*: Sacred Love: Tanaquil LeClercq; Profane Love: Melissa Hayden
V *Royalty*: ensemble
VI *Anarchy*: Tanaquil LeClercq, Dick Beard, Audrey Allen, Doris Breckenridge, Ninette D'Amboise, Peggy Karlson, Robert Barnett, Walter Georgov, Karel Shook
VII *Being Beauteous*: Tanaquil LeClercq, Dick Beard, Arthur Bell, Jacques D'Amboise, Roy Tobias
VIII *Sideshow*: ensemble
IX *Farewell*: ensemble

New York City Ballet, City Center, New York, *2 March 1950*

1951

Daphnis and Chloe

M Maurice Ravel

Curtain SC John Craxton

D Chloe, a shepherdess: Margot Fonteyn; Daphnis, a goat-herd: Michael Somes; Lykanion, a young married girl from the town: Violetta Elvin; Dorkon, a herdsman: John Field; Bryaxis, a pirate chief: Alexander Grant; Pan: Alfred Rodrigues; Nymphs of Pan: Rosemary Lindsay, Gillian Lynne, Julia Farron; Shepherdesses, Shepherds, Pirates, Pirate Women, Dryads, Fauns†: corps de ballet

†Dryads and Fauns omitted from 4 July 1951

Sadler's Wells Ballet, Royal Opera House, *5 April 1951*

[The Tales of Hoffmann]
A London Films production
A Fantastic Opera
Produced and directed by Michael Powell and Emeric Pressburger
Screenplay by Michael Powell and Emeric Pressburger, adapted from Dennis Arundell's English libretto based on the French text by Jules Barbier

M Jacques Offenbach

Photographed by Christopher Challis

SC Hein Heckroth

Players: Robert Rounseville, Robert Helpmann, Pamela Brown, Moira Shearer, Frederick Ashton, Léonide Massine,

Ludmilla Tcherina, Ann Ayars, Mogens Wieth, Monica Sinclair, Bruce Dargavel, Murray Dickie

Prologue: **The Enchanted Dragonfly**

M   arranged by Sir Thomas Beecham

D   Moira Shearer, Edmond Audran

The Ballad of Kleinzack

D   Kleinzack: Frederick Ashton; His Lady-Love: Moira Shearer

The Tale of Olympia

D   Olympia: Moira Shearer; Dr Coppélius: Robert Helpmann; Spalanzani: Léonide Massine†; Cochenille: Frederick Ashton; Marionettes: corps de ballet

†Léonide Massine choreographed his own solos

The Tale of Giulietta

D   Giulietta: Ludmilla Tcherina; Hoffmann: Robert Helpmann

Epilogue: **Pas de deux** (Barcarolle)

D   Moira Shearer, Edmond Audran

Release date, *18 April 1951*

Tiresias

A Ballet in three scenes by Constant Lambert

M   Constant Lambert, partly orchestrated by Robert Irving, Christian Darnton, Humphrey Searle, Denis ApIvor, Gordon Jacob, Alan Rawsthorne and Elisabeth Lutyens

Curtain SC Isabel Lambert

D   Tiresias (male): Michael Somes; Neophyte: Margaret Dale; Snakes: Pauline Clayden, Brian Shaw; Tiresias (female): Margot Fonteyn; Her Lover: John Field; Zeus: Alfred Rodrigues; Hera: Gerd Larsen; Athletes, Warriors, Priestesses, Shepherdesses, Shepherds: corps de ballet

Sadler's Wells Ballet, Royal Opera House, *9 July 1951*; revised version, *26 February 1952*

Casse Noisette

Two scenes from a ballet in two acts and three scenes by Lev Ivanov, after Alexandre Dumas's version of E T A Hoffmann's *Histoire d'un casse-noisette*

Choreography by Lev Ivanov, revised by Frederick Ashton

M   Peter Ilyich Tchaikovsky (ballet, opus 71)

SC Cecil Beaton

Scene 1 *The Kingdom of Snow*

D   The Queen: Svetlana Beriosova; The King: Robert Lunnon; Snowflakes: corps de ballet

Scene 2 *The Kingdom of Sweets*

D   The Sugar Plum Fairy: Elaine Fifield; The Nutcracker Prince: David Blair; Sugar Sticks: Patricia Miller, Carlu Carter, Stella Farrance, Annette Page, Veronica Vail; Chocolate from Spain: Sheilah O'Reilly, Margaret Sear, Pirmin Trecu; Coffee from Arabia: Stella Claire, Arnott Mader, Graham McCormack, Peter Wright; Tea from China: David Gill, Maurice Metliss; Nougat from Russia: Donald Britton, Stanley Holden, Donald McAlpine, Walter Trevor; Crystallised Flowers: Maryon Lane and corps de ballet

Sadler's Wells Theatre Ballet, Sadler's Wells, *11 September 1951*

See 1954, **Trepak**

1952

[The Story of Three Loves]

An MGM Picture

Produced by Sidney Franklin

The Jealous Lover directed by Gottfried Reinhardt

Screenplay by John Collier

Photographed by Charles Rosher and Harold Rosson

M   Serge Rachmaninov (from *Rhapsody on a theme by Paganini*)

Players: James Mason, Moira Shearer, Agnes Moorehead

D   Moira Shearer and corps de ballet

Release date *5 March 1953* (filmed January–February 1952)

Picnic at Tintagel

Ballet in three scenes

M   Arnold Bax (Symphonic Poem, *The Garden of Fand*, 1916)

SC Cecil Beaton

D   The Husband (King Mark): Francisco Moncion; The Wife (Iseult): Diana Adams; Her Maid (Brangaene): Yvonne Mounsey; Her Lover (Tristram): Jacques D'Amboise; His rivals (The False Knights): Stanley Zompakos, Brooks Jackson; Her chauffeur and footman (Heralds): Alan Baker, John Mandia; The Caretaker (Merlin): Robert Barnett

New York City Ballet, City Center, New York, *28 February 1952*

Vision of Marguerite
M Franz Liszt (*Mephisto Waltz* no. 1)
SC James Bailey
D Marguerite:Belinda Wright; Her Maid: Wendy West; Faust:John Gilpin; Mephisto:Oleg Briansky
London Festival Ballet, Stoll Theatre, *3 April 1952*

Sylvia
Ballet in three acts by Jules Barbier and Baron de Reinach, based on *Aminta* by Torquato Tasso
M Léo Delibes (ballet, 1876, with additional numbers from *La Source*, 1866)
SC Robin and Christopher Ironside
D Sylvia:Margot Fonteyn; Aminta: Michael Somes; Orion:John Hart; Eros: Alexander Grant; Naiads:Dorothea Zaymes, Anne Heaton, Angela Walton; Dryads:Gerd Larsen, April Olrich, Avril Navarre; Slaves:Brian Shaw, Peter Clegg; Orion's Concubines:Dorothea Zaymes, Shirley Bateman; Diana:Julia Farron; Goats:Pauline Clayden, Brian Shaw; Apollo: Kenneth Melville; Ceres:Anne Heaton; Jaseion:Philip Chatfield; Persephone: April Olrich; Pluto:Ray Powell; Sylvans, Attendant Nymphs, Cortège rustique, Trumpeters, the Muses, Spring Attendants, Summer Attendants, Sylvia's Attendant Nymphs, Diana's Attendant Nymphs, [A Vision of Diana and Endymion—later addition]: corps de ballet
Sadler's Wells Ballet, Royal Opera House, *3 September 1952*

NP Granada Festival; *pas de deux* from Act III only, with new coda:
D Margot Fonteyn, Michael Somes
Jardines del Generalife, Granada, Spain, *30 June 1953*
(This arrangement of the *pas de deux* was often danced by Fonteyn and Somes as a divertissement, e g with London Festival Ballet, Théâtre de Monte Carlo, *15 January 1956*, and later by other dancers)

NP Royal Ballet touring section:
D Sylvia:Doreen Wells; Aminta:Christopher Gable; Orion:Bryan Ashbridge; Eros:Gary Sherwood
Royal Opera House, *6 May 1963*

NP Royal Ballet touring section; with abbreviated third act and new variation for Aminta:
D Sylvia:Margot Fonteyn; Aminta:Attilio Labis; Orion:Bryan Ashbridge; Eros:Richard Farley
Royal Opera House, *9 June 1965*

NP Royal Ballet; abridged (one act) version with some new choreography:
D Sylvia:Nadia Nerina; Aminta:Gary Sherwood; Eros:Alexander Grant; Goats:Ann Howard, Keith Martin; Sylvia's attendants, Friends of Aminta: corps de ballet
Royal Opera House, *18 December 1967*

NP Royal Ballet, Tribute to Sir Frederick Ashton; excerpt only:
D Sylvia:Deanne Bergsma, with corps de ballet
Royal Opera House, *24 July 1970*

[Le Lac des cygnes]
Ballet in four acts by Vladimir Petrovitch Begichev and Vassily Fedorovitch Geltzer
Choreography by Marius Petipa and Lev Ivanov, produced by Nicholas Sergeyev, revised by Ninette de Valois, with additions by Frederick Ashton
M Peter Ilyich Tchaikovsky (ballet, opus 20)
SC Leslie Hurry
D Odette/Odile:Beryl Grey; Prince Siegfried:John Field
Act I **Valse** (**Pas de six**)
D Rosemary Lindsay, Mary Drage, Svetlana Beriosova, Alexander Grant, Kenneth Melville, Philip Chatfield
Act III **Neapolitan Dance†**
D Julia Farron, Alexander Grant
†Sometimes given separately as a divertissement
Sadler's Wells Ballet, Royal Opera House, *18 December 1952*

NP Royal Ballet touring section:
D Odette/Odile:Rowena Jackson; Siegfried:Philip Chatfield
Pas de six: Margaret Lee, Susan Alexander, Lynn Seymour, Simon Mottram, Donald MacLeary, Christopher Gable
Neapolitan Dance: Audrey Farriss, Donald Britton
Royal Opera House, *27 June 1958*

NP Royal Ballet; under the title *Swan Lake*; production devised and staged by Robert Helpmann, with additional choreography by Frederick Ashton, Rudolf Nureyev (*Polonaise*, Act I, and *Mazurka*, Act II) and Maria Fay (*Czárdás*, Act II); M re-edited by John Lanchbery; SC Carl Toms

Prologue (dropped from 4 March 1967)

D Odette:Margot Fonteyn; Rothbart: Keith Rosson; Princess Odette's Attendants:corps de ballet

Act I Scene 1 **Waltz**

D Deanne Bergsma, Vyvyan Lorrayne, Monica Mason, Rosalind Eyre, Carole Needham, Vergie Derman, Robert Mead, Anthony Dowell, Bryan Lawrence, David Drew, Austin Bennett, Kenneth Mason

Act I Scene 1 **Pas de quatre**

D Antoinette Sibley, Merle Park, Brian Shaw, Graham Usher

Act I Scene 2 (formerly Act II) **Dance of the Four Swans**

D Deanne Bergsma, Monica Mason, Vergie Derman, Carole Needham

Act II (formerly Act III) **Dance of the Guests**

D Corps de ballet

Act II **Spanish Dance**

D Georgina Parkinson, Monica Mason, Desmond Doyle, Christopher Gable

Act II **Neapolitan Dance**

D Merle Park, Alexander Grant

Act III (formerly Act IV)

D Odette:Margot Fonteyn; Siegfried: David Blair; Rothbart:Keith Rosson; Swans, Cygnets:corps de ballet

Royal Opera House, *12 December 1963*

NP Royal Ballet touring section; choreography revised by Frederick Ashton and John Field, with additions by Ashton as in 1952/1958: SC Leslie Hurry:

D Odette/Odile:Nadia Nerina; Siegfried: Attilio Labis

Waltz (Pas de six): Anya Linden, Christine Beckley, Deirdre O'Conaire, David Wall, Piers Beaumont, Jelko Yuresha

Neapolitan Dance: Shirley Grahame, Michael Coleman

Spanish Dance: Jennifer Layland, Christine Beckley, Jelko Yuresha, Richard Farley

Royal Opera House, *18 May 1965*

NP Royal Ballet; the touring section 1965 production but with Ashton's 1963 *Waltz, Pas de quatre, Neapolitan and Spanish Dances*, and *Act IV* (formerly called Act III); from 25 October 1972 Ashton's *Act IV* was dropped and Ivanov's restored, Petipa's *pas de trois* was restored to Act I and Ashton's *pas de quatre* moved to Act III; SC Leslie Hurry:

D Odette/Odile:Antoinette Sibley; Siegfried:Anthony Dowell; Rothbart:Derek Rencher

Pas de quatre: Lesley Collier, Laura Connor, Michael Coleman, Robert Mead

Neapolitan Dance: Leslie Collier, Alexander Grant

Spanish Dance: Rosalind Eyre, Monica Mason, Robert Mead, Carl Myers

Royal Opera House, *17 February 1971*

By other companies:

NP Fonteyn World Tour; *Neapolitan Dance* only:

D Pamela Moncur, Alexander Grant

Herod Atticus Theatre, Athens, *9 August 1963*

NP State Ballet of Turkey; R Dudley Tomlinson:

D Odette/Odile:Meriç Sümen; Siegfried:Tanju Tüzer

Neapolitan Dance: Binay Okurer, Selçuk Sayiner

National Theatre, Ankara, *29 October 1965*

NP Pennsylvania Ballet; *Neapolitan Dance* only in *Divertissements from 'Swan Lake'*; R Christopher Newton; S John Conklin; C Derek Rencher:

D Karen Brown, Alexander Belin

Academy of Music, Philadelphia *20 September 1972*

1953

Orpheus

Opera in two acts by Raniero de' Calzabigi; English text after the Reverend J Troutbeck M Christoph Willibald Gluck

Production and choreography by Frederick Ashton

481

sc   Sophie Fedorovitch
Cast: Orpheus: Kathleen Ferrier; Amor: Adele
      Leigh; Eurydice: Veronica Dunne
D   *Dance of the Furies*: Alexander Grant and
      corps de ballet
      Dance of the Blessed Spirits: Svetlana
      Beriosova and corps de ballet
Royal Opera and Sadler's Wells Ballet, Royal
Opera House, *3 February 1953*

See 1958, **Orfeo ed Euridice**

Homage to the Queen
The Coronation Ballet
M   Malcolm Arnold
SC   Oliver Messel
D   *Entrée*: ensemble
     Procession of the Four Elements:
     The Queen of the Earth: Nadia Nerina;
     Her Consort: Alexis Rassine; Her atten-
     dants: Pauline Clayden, Margaret Dale,
     Anne Heaton, Michael Boulton, Peter
     Clegg, Ray Powell; *Pas de six*: Joan
     Benesh, June Lesley, Avril Navarre, April
     Olrich, Angela Walton, Dorothea
     Zaymes; The Queen of the Waters:
     Violetta Elvin; Her Consort: John Hart;
     Her Attendants: corps de ballet; *Pas de
     trois*: Brian Shaw, Julia Farron, Rowena
     Jackson; The Queen of Fire: Beryl Grey;
     Her Consort: John Field; Spirit of Fire:
     Alexander Grant; *Pas de quatre*: Svetlana
     Beriosova, Rosemary Lindsay, Bryan
     Ashbridge, Philip Chatfield; The Queen
     of the Air: Margot Fonteyn; Her Con-
     sort: Michael Somes; Her Attendants:
     corps de ballet
Sadler's Wells Ballet, Royal Opera House,
2 June 1953

NP   Royal Ballet, Tribute to Sir Frederick
     Ashton; *pas de deux* for the Queen of the
     Air and her Consort only:
     D   Georgina Parkinson, Keith Rosson
Royal Opera House, *24 July 1970*

1954

**Entrada de Madame Butterfly (Entry of
Madame Butterfly)**
M   Arthur Sullivan, arranged by Robert
     Irving (Yum-Yum's aria from *The
     Mikado*)

C   Christian Dior
D   Margot Fonteyn
Granada Festival, Jardines del Generalife,
Granada, *29 June 1954*

NP   Sadler's Wells Ballet; under the title
     Entrée japonaise:
     D   Margot Fonteyn
Royal Opera House, *22 March 1956*

Trepak
from *Casse Noisette*, Act II
M   Peter Ilyich Tchaikovsky
D   April Olrich, Alexander Grant, Michael
     Boulton
Granada Festival, Jardines del Generalife,
Granada, *29 June 1954*

[A Midsummer Night's Dream]
Comedy by William Shakespeare
Produced by Michael Benthall
Choreography by Robert Helpmann; *Noc-
turne* by Frederick Ashton
M   Felix Mendelssohn-Bartholdy, arranged
     by Gordon Jacob
SC   Robin and Christopher Ironside
Nocturne
D   Titania: Moira Shearer; Oberon: Robert
     Helpmann
Old Vic Company, Edinburgh Festival,
Empire Theatre, Edinburgh, *31 August 1954*

See 1964, **The Dream**

1955

Rinaldo and Armida
A Dance-Drama in one scene† (after an
episode in *Ierusalemme liberata* by Torquato
Tasso)
M   Malcolm Arnold
Curtain SC Peter Rice
D   Rinaldo, a warrior: Michael Somes;
     Armida, an enchantress: Svetlana Berios-
     ova; Sibilla, a sorceress: Julia Farron;
     Gandolfo, Rinaldo's companion: Ronald
     Hynd
Sadler's Wells Ballet, Royal Opera House,
6 January 1955
† Subtitle added 24 January 1956

Variations on a Theme by Purcell

M Benjamin Britten (*Variations and fugue on a theme by Purcell, The Young Person's Guide to the Orchestra,* opus 34)

SC Peter Snow

D Elaine Fifield, Nadia Nerina, Rowena Jackson, Alexander Grant, David Blair, Michael Boulton, Philip Chatfield, Ronald Hynd, Gary Burne, Ronald Plaisted and corps de ballet

Sadler's Wells Ballet, Royal Opera House, *6 January 1955*

Madame Chrysanthème

Ballet in one act and five scenes by Frederick Ashton and Vera Bowen, adapted from the book by Pierre Loti

M Alan Rawsthorne

SC Isabel Lambert

D Pierre, a French sailor: Alexander Grant; Yves, his brother: Desmond Doyle; Mme Chrysanthème: Elaine Fifield; Mme Renoncule, her mother: Elizabeth Kennedy; M. Très-Propre, her father: Franklin White; M. Kangarou, a marriage broker: Ray Powell; Mlle Wistéria, a courtesan: Anne Heaton; Mlle Pluie d'Avril, a courtesan: Pauline Clayden; Mlle Pureté, Mlle Prune, cousins of Chrysanthème: Merle Park, Angela Walton; A Dignitary: Leslie Edwards; Bambou, a boatman and rickshaw boy: Roy Taylor; Government Officials, Mousmés and Mouskos – Chrysanthème's Friends, Djinns: corps de ballet

Sadler's Wells Ballet, Royal Opera House, *1 April 1955*

Romeo og Julie (Romeo and Juliet)

Ballet in three acts, ten scenes and epilogue after William Shakespeare
Production by Frederick Ashton

M Serge Prokofiev (ballet, opus 64)

SC Peter Rice

D Romeo: Henning Kronstam; Juliet: Mona Vangsaa; Mercutio: Frank Schaufuss; Tybalt: Niels Bjørn Larsen; Benvolio: Flemming Flindt; Paris: Kjeld Noack; Nurse: Britta Cornelius-Knudsen; Peter, a page: Jørn Madsen; Brother Lorenzo: Jan Holme; Lady Capulet: Lillian Jensen; Lord Capulet: Svend Erik Jensen; The Duke of Verona: Poul Vessel; Rosaline: Kirsten Ralov; Friends of

Juliet: Aase Bonde, Ruth Andersen, Elin Bauer, Elisabeth Enevoldsen, Mette Mollerup, Kirsten Simone; Troubadours: Anker Ørskov, Verner Andersen, Tage Wendt; Servants, Guests at the Ball, Citizens: corps de ballet

Royal Danish Ballet, Kongelige Teater, Copenhagen, *19 May 1955*

NP London Festival Ballet; *Pas de deux* (Balcony Scene) only: R Niels Bjørn Larsen and Frederick Ashton; SC Peter Rice; D Romeo: Peter Schaufuss; Juliet: Gaye Fulton

Coliseum, *9 April 1973*

1956

La Péri

Poème dansé

M Paul Dukas

S Ivon Hitchens

C André Levasseur

D La Péri: Margot Fonteyn; Iskender: Michael Somes

Sadler's Wells Ballet, Royal Opera House, *15 February 1956*

NP Royal Ballet; S André Levasseur: D La Péri: Margot Fonteyn; Iskender: Michael Somes

Royal Opera House, *24 August 1957*

By other companies:

NP Ballet 1958 de Paris; SC André Levasseur: D La Péri: Margot Fonteyn; Iskender: Michael Somes

Théâtre de Monte Carlo, *5 April 1958*

NP La Scala, Milan; SC André Levasseur: D La Péri: Margot Fonteyn; Iskender: Michael Somes

Teatro alla Scala, Milan, *11 February 1960*

Birthday Offering

Pièce d'occasion in one scene

M Alexander Glazunov, arranged by Robert Irving
   (1 Overture, *L'Eté* from *The Seasons,* ballet, opus 67

2 *Valse de concert* no. 1, opus 47

3 *Grand adagio* from *Scènes de ballet*, opus 52, and *Coda* from *Ruses d'amour*, ballet, opus 61

4 1st variation, *Marionettes* from *Scènes de ballet*

5 2nd variation, *La Givre* from *The Seasons*

6 3rd variation, *La Glace* from *The Seasons*

7 4th variation, *La Grêle* from *The Seasons*

8 5th variation, *La Neige* from *The Seasons*

9 6th variation, *L'Eté* from *The Seasons*

10 7th variation, from *Ruses d'Amour*

11 *Mazurka*, opus 25 no. 2, orchestrated by Robert Irving

12 *Pas de deux*, *Grand pas des fiancées* from *Ruses d'amour*

13 Finale, *Valse de concert* no. 1, reprise)

C André Levasseur

D Margot Fonteyn, Beryl Grey, Violetta Elvin, Nadia Nerina, Rowena Jackson, Svetlana Beriosova, Elaine Fifield, Michael Somes, Alexander Grant, Brian Shaw, Philip Chatfield, David Blair, Desmond Doyle, Brian Ashbridge

Sadler's Wells Ballet, Royal Opera House, *5 May 1956*

NP Royal Ballet; new solo for David Blair (M *Variation III* from *Grand pas d'action*, *Raymonda* Act II, ballet, opus 57):
D Margot Fonteyn, Svetlana Beriosova, Georgina Parkinson, Antoinette Sibley, Merle Park, Lynn Seymour, Maryon Lane, David Blair

Royal Opera House, *24 March 1965*

NP Royal Ballet; new solo for Rudolf Nureyev (M *Entrée des jongleurs* from *Raymonda* Act II):
D Margot Fonteyn, Antoinette Sibley, Georgina Parkinson, Monica Mason, Merle Park, Ria Peri, Jennifer Penney, Rudolf Nureyev

Royal Opera House, *29 March 1968*

NP Ballet for All; *Entrée*, *Variations* and *Finale* only:
D Maxine Dennis, June Highwood, Jennifer Jackson, Derek Deane, Colin Dye, Kim Reeder

Spa Pavilion, Felixstowe, *13 October 1972*

484

By other companies

NP Margot Fonteyn World Tour; abridged version:
D Margot Fonteyn, Annette Page, Shirley Grahame, Pamela Moncur, Royes Fernandez, Ronald Hynd, Alexander Grant, Laurence Ruffell

Herod Atticus Theatre, Athens, *10 August 1963*

The Beloved
(Based on material from *Apparitions*, 1936, qv)
M Franz Liszt
C Olivia Cranmer
D The Beloved: Nadia Nerina; The Poet: Alexis Rassine

Ballet Highlights, New Theatre, Oxford, *4 July 1956*

1958

La Valse
Poème chorégraphique
M Maurice Ravel
Curtain SC André Levasseur
D Vera Colombo, Mario Pistoni, Carmen Puthod, Giulio Perugini, Elettra Morini, Walter Vendetti and corps de ballet

Teatro alla Scala, Milan, *31 January 1958*

NP Royal Ballet:
D Principal Waltzers: Deirdre Dixon, Christine Beckley, Jacqueline Daryl, Gary Burne, Richard Farley, Keith Rosson; Waltzing Couples, Footmen: corps de ballet

Royal Opera House, *10 March 1959*

[Orfeo ed Euridice]
Opera in two acts by Raniero de' Calzabigi
M Christoph Willibald Gluck
Production by Gustav Gründgens
SC Hein Heckroth
Cast: Orfeo: Fedora Barbieri; Amore: Françoise Orgeas; Euridice: Sena Jurinac
D Vera Colombo, Roberto Fascilla, Carla Fracci, Gilda Majocchi, Mario Pistoni, Bruno Tellosi

Teatro alla Scala, Milan, *18 February 1958*

Ondine
Ballet in three acts, freely adapted by Frederick Ashton from the story by Friedrich de la Motte Fouqué
M   Hans Werner Henze
SC Lila de Nobili
D   Ondine: Margot Fonteyn; Palemon: Michael Somes; Berta: Julia Farron; Tirrenio, Lord of the Mediterranean Sea: Alexander Grant; A Hermit: Leslie Edwards; *Grand pas classique*: Rosemary Lindsay, Annette Page, Ronald Hynd, Desmond Doyle and corps de ballet; *Divertissement*: Maryon Lane, Brian Shaw, Merle Park, Doreen Wells, Peter Clegg, Pirmin Trecu and corps de ballet; Ondines, Hunt, Wood Sprites, People from the Port, Sailors, Wedding Guests, Lackeys, Footmen, Acolytes, Page: corps de ballet
Royal Ballet, Royal Opera House, *27 October 1958*

NP Royal Ballet; revised choreography:
    D (principals) as above
Royal Opera House, *2 June 1959*

NP Royal Ballet; with further revisions:
    D Ondine: Margot Fonteyn; Palemon: Donald MacLeary; Berta: Deanne Bergsma; Tirrenio: Alexander Grant
Royal Opera House, *14 February 1964*

NP Royal Ballet, Tribute to Sir Frederick Ashton; 'The Vision of Ondine' only:
    D Ondine: Christine Aitken, with Derek Rencher, David Drew, Christopher Newton, Paul Brown
Royal Opera House, *24 July 1970*

By other companies:

NP Ballets de Noël; *pas de deux* from Act I Scene 2 only; S André Levasseur; C Lila de Nobili:
    D Ondine: Margot Fonteyn; Palemon: Michael Somes
Théâtre de Monte Carlo, *3 January 1959*

1959

Scène d'amour from **Raymonda**
M   Alexander Glazunov (*Grand adagio* from *Raymonda* Act I Scene 2, ballet, opus 57)

C   Leslie Hurry
D   Raymonda: Margot Fonteyn; Jean de Brienne: Michael Somes
Royal Ballet, Royal Academy of Dancing Gala, Theatre Royal, Drury Lane, *26 November 1959*

NP Royal Ballet touring section:
    D Raymonda: Vyvyan Lorrayne; Jean de Brienne: Barry McGrath
Theatre Royal, Norwich, *5 March 1973*

By other companies:

NP Ballets de Noël:
    D Raymonda: Margot Fonteyn; Jean de Brienne: Michael Somes
Théâtre de Monte Carlo, *31 December 1959*

NP Margot Fonteyn World Tour:
    D Raymonda: Margot Fonteyn; Jean de Brienne: Ronald Hynd
Herod Atticus Theatre, Athens, *11 August 1963*

1960

La Fille mal gardée
Ballet in two acts and three scenes after Jean Dauberval
M   Ferdinand Hérold, freely adapted and arranged by John Lanchbery from the 1828 version
Curtain SC Osbert Lancaster
D   Widow Simone, a rich farmer: Stanley Holden; Lise, her daughter: Nadia Nerina; Colas, a young farmer in love with Lise: David Blair; Thomas, a prosperous vineyard owner: Leslie Edwards; Alain, his son: Alexander Grant; Village Notary: Franklin White; His Secretary: Maurice Metliss; Cockerel: Laurence Ruffell; Hens: Margaret Lyons, Robin Haig, Maureen Maitland, Gloria Bluemel; Villagers, Harvesters, Grooms, etc: corps de ballet
Royal Ballet, Royal Opera House, *28 January 1960*

NP Royal Ballet touring section:
    D (principals) as above
Hippodrome, Bristol, *9 November 1962*

NP Ballet for All; abridged version devised by Peter Brinson and arranged by John Field as a ballet-play entitled 'Ashton and *La Fille mal gardée*'; s Peter Courtier, after Osbert Lancaster; c Osbert Lancaster:
D Lise:Brenda Last; Colas:John Sale
Manor Court Modern School, Portsmouth, *15 September 1964*

NP Royal Ballet School; r Faith Worth, Lynn Wallis and David Gayle:
D Widow Simone:Ronald Emblen; Lise: Jennifer Jackson; Colas:Robert Huguenin; Alain:Denis Bonner
Royal Opera House, *24 June 1972*

By other companies:

NP Margot Fonteyn World Tour; *pas de deux* only:
D Lise:Annette Page; Colas:Royes Fernandez
Herod Atticus Theatre, Athens, *9 August 1963*

NP Royal Danish Ballet; under the title *Den Slet Bevogtede Datter*; r Frederick Ashton:
D Widow Simone:Niels Bjørn Larsen; Lise:Solveig Østergaard; Colas: Niels Kehlet; Alain:Fredbjørn Bjørnsson
Kongelige Teater, Copenhagen, *16 January 1964*

NP The Australian Ballet; r Elphine Allen:
D Widow Simone:Ray Powell; Lise: Marilyn Jones; Colas:Bryan Lawrence; Alain:Alan Alder
Tivoli Theatre, Sydney, *12 October 1967*

NP PACT Ballet; r John Hart:
D Widow Simone:Petrus Bosman; Lise: Merle Park; Colas:Anthony Dowell; Alain:Ken Yeatman
Civic Theatre, Johannesburg, *4 September 1969*

NP Hungarian State Ballet Company; s Gábor Forray; c Tivadar Márk:
D Widow Simone:Viktor Fülöp; Lise: Zsuzsa Kun; Colas: Viktor Róna; Alain: Levente Sipeki
Opera House, Budapest, *28 March 1971*

NP Ballet of the Bayerische Staatsoper; r Annette Page and Ronald Hynd, with Cherry Trevarkis, choreologist:
D Widow Simone:Michel de Lutry; Lise:Gislinde Skroblin; Colas:Heinz Bosl; Alain:Ferenc Barbay
Bayerische Staatsoper, Munich, *18 May 1971*

NP Royal Swedish Ballet:
D Widow Simone:Istvan Kirsch; Lise: Kerstin Lidström; Colas:Imre Dózsa; Alain:Markko Heinonen
Opera House, Stockholm, *1 April 1972*

NP State Ballet of Turkey; r Faith Worth:
D Lise:Meriç Sümen; Oytun Turfanda, Üstün Oztürk, Taner Akakçe (distribution of other roles unavailable)
National Theatre, Ankara, *24 November 1973*

NP Ballet of the Opernhaus, Zurich; r Faith Worth:
D Widow Simone:Max Natiez; Lise: Angelica Bornhausen; Colas:Marinel Stefanescu; Alain:Rudolf Budaváry
Opernhaus, Zurich, *12 October 1974*

[Giselle]
Ballet in two acts by Théophile Gautier and Vernoy de Saint-Georges, based on a theme by Heinrich Heine
Choreography by Jean Coralli and Jules Perrot revised by Marius Petipa, reproduced by Nicholas Sergeyev; production supervised and with additional choreography by Frederick Ashton, in collaboration with Tamara Karsavina

M Adolphe Adam and Friedrich Burgmüller, partly orchestrated by Robert Irving, Gordon Jacob, John Lanchbery and Richard Temple Savage
SC James Bailey
D Giselle:Margot Fonteyn; Count Albrecht:Michael Somes; Berthe, Giselle's mother:Gerd Larsen; Hilarion:Leslie Edwards; Duke of Courland:Derek Rencher; Bathilde:Julia Farron; Wilfred: Richard Farley; *Peasant pas de deux* (new woman's variation by Ashton):Maryon Lane, Brian Shaw; Myrtha, Queen of the Wilis:Anya Linden; Two Wilis: Georgina Parkinson, Christine Beckley; Villagers, Courtiers, Wilis, etc:corps de ballet
Royal Ballet, Metropolitan Opera House, New York, *30 September 1960*; Royal Opera House, *4 April 1961*

NP Royal Ballet touring section:
D Giselle:Margot Fonteyn; Albrecht: Michael Somes; *Peasant pas de deux*:Lynn Seymour, Brian Shaw; Myrtha:Anya Linden
Festival Hall, Tokyo, *17 April 1961*

NP Royal Ballet touring section; production by Peter Wright; with further additions by Frederick Ashton (but omitting some from the 1960 production, including the new variation in the *Peasant pas de deux*);
sc Peter Farmer:
D Giselle:Doreen Wells; Albrecht:David Wall; Hilarion:Adrian Grater; Myrtha: Shirley Grahame
Royal Opera House, *16 May 1968*

NP Royal Ballet, Tribute to Sir Frederick Ashton; variation from the *Peasant pas de deux* only:
D Ann Jenner
Royal Opera House, *24 July 1970*

By other companies:

NP State Ballet of Turkey; R Joy Newton and Dudley Tomlinson:
D Giselle:Meriç Sümen; Albrecht:Sait Sökmen; *Peasant pas de deux:* Binay Okurer, Selçuk Sayiner
National Theatre, Ankara, *22 October 1964*

1961

Les Deux pigeons (The Two Pigeons†)
An Allegory in two acts and three scenes, based on the fable by La Fontaine
M André Messager, arranged and partly orchestrated by John Lanchbery (ballet, 1886, with one number from *Véronique*, opéra-comique, 1898)
sc Jacques Dupont
D The Young Man:Christopher Gable; The Young Girl:Lynn Seymour; His Mother (re-named A Neighbour, 1974): Shirley Bishop; A Gypsy Girl:Elizabeth Anderton; Her Lover:Robert Mead; A Gypsy Boy:Johaar Mosaval; Two Old Gypsy Crones:Lorna Mossford, Valerie Deakin; Friends of the Young Girl, Gypsies, Sightseers:corps de ballet
Royal Ballet touring section, Royal Opera House, *14 February 1961*

NP Royal Ballet:
D The Young Man:Alexander Grant;

† Title given in English from 16 October 1962

The Young Girl:Lynn Seymour; A Gypsy Girl:Georgina Parkinson; Her Lover:Robert Mead; A Gypsy Boy: Laurence Ruffell
Royal Opera House, *16 October 1962*

NP Royal Ballet School:
D The Young Man:Graham Powell; The Young Girl:Lesley Collier; A Gypsy Girl:Margaret Barbieri; Her Lover: Nicholas Johnson; A Gypsy Boy:Wayne Sleep
Royal Opera House, *17 July 1965*

NP Ballet for All; *pas de deux* from Act II only:
D The Young Man:Michael Batchelor; The Young Girl:Susan Burton
Playhouse, Walton-on-Thames, *18 January 1975*

By other companies:

NP CAPAB Ballet Company; R Faith Worth; sc Peter Rice:
D The Boy:Gary Burne; The Girl: Phyllis Spira; Gypsy Girl:Janice Worth; Her Lover:John Simons
Civic Theatre, Bellville, South Africa, *19 October 1968*

NP The Australian Ballet; R Robert Mead; sc Jacques Dupont:
D The Boy:Kelvin Coe; The Girl: Lucette Aldous; Gypsy Girl:Marilyn Rowe; Her Lover:Jonathan Kelly; Gypsy Boy:Paul Saliba
Opera House, Sydney, *30 April 1975*

Poème tragique
M Alexander Scriabin (opus 34)
c William Chappell
D Rudolf Nureyev
Royal Academy of Dancing Gala Matinée, Theatre Royal, Drury Lane, *2 November 1961*

Persephone
Melodrama in three scenes by André Gide
M Igor Stravinsky
sc Nico Ghika
D Persephone:Svetlana Beriosova; Mercury:Alexander Grant; Pluto, King of the Underworld:Keith Rosson; Demeter, Mother of Persephone:Gerd Larsen;

Demaphoön, Persephone's earthly husband:Derek Rencher; Eumolpus, the High Priest (tenor):André Turp; Friends of Persephone:Georgina Parkinson, Christine Beckley, Monica Mason, Audrey Farriss, Pamela Moncur; Oceanides: Deanne Bergsma, Vyvyan Lorrayne, Betty Kavanagh, Rosalind Eyre, Louanne Richards, Heather Clipperton; Hours: same as Oceanides; Nymphs, Shades, Attendants, Adolescents:corps de ballet
Royal Ballet, Royal Opera House, *12 December 1961*

NP Royal Ballet, Tribute to Sir Frederick Ashton; excerpt only:
D Persephone:Svetlana Beriosova; Mercury:Alexander Grant; Demeter:Gerd Larsen; Demaphoön:Derek Rencher; and corps de ballet
Royal Opera House, *24 July 1970*

1962

Pas de deux, Variations and Coda from **Raymonda**
M Alexander Glazunov
C André Levasseur
D Svetlana Beriosova, Donald MacLeary
Royal Ballet, Royal Opera House, *3 May 1962*

1963

Marguerite and Armand
Ballet in one act: Prologue and four scenes, after *The Lady of the Camellias* by Alexandre Dumas fils
M Franz Liszt, orchestrated by Humphrey Searle (new orchestration by Gordon Jacob, 15 March 1968) (*La lugubre gondola*, no. 1, and *Sonata* in B minor)
SC Cecil Beaton
D Marguerite:Margot Fonteyn (in prologue, Ann Jenner); Armand:Rudolf Nureyev; His Father:Michael Somes; A Duke:Leslie Edwards; Maid:Barbara Remington; Admirers of Marguerite: corps de ballet
Royal Ballet, Royal Opera House, *12 March 1963*

NP Royal Ballet touring section:
D Marguerite:Margot Fonteyn; Armand:Rudolf Nureyev; His Father: Adrian Grater
Hessisches Staatstheater, Wiesbaden, *28 May 1968*

By other companies:

NP La Scala, Milan; under the title *Margherita e Armando*:
D Margherita:Margot Fonteyn; Armando Duval:Rudolf Nureyev; Il padre: Leslie Edwards
Teatro alla Scala, Milan, *16 September 1966*

NP Opéra, Paris:
D Marguerite:Margot Fonteyn; Armand:Rudolf Nureyev; His Father: Leslie Edwards
Opéra, Paris, *17 November 1966*

NP Teatro Colón, Buenos Aires; under the title *Margarita y Armando*:
D Margarita:Margot Fonteyn; Armando:Rudolf Nureyev; El padre de Armando:Leslie Edwards
Teatro Colón, Buenos Aires, *14 April 1967*

NP Associação de Ballet do Rio de Janeiro:
D Marguerite:Margot Fonteyn; Armand:Rudolf Nureyev; His Father: Arthur Ferreira
Teatro Municipal, Rio de Janeiro, *25 April 1967*

NP An Evening with Fonteyn and Nureyev; SC Cecil Beaton (new C William Chappell, Uris Theatre, New York, 18 November 1975):
D Marguerite:Margot Fonteyn; Armand:Rudolf Nureyev; His Father: Leslie Edwards
John F Kennedy Center, Washington, DC, *8 July 1975*

1964

The Dream
Ballet in one act adapted from *A Midsummer Night's Dream* by William Shakespeare
M Felix Mendelssohn-Bartholdy, arranged by John Lanchbery (incidental music to

Shakespeare's comedy, opus 21 and opus 61)
s Henry Bardon
c David Walker
d Titania:Antoinette Sibley; Oberon: Anthony Dowell; Changeling Indian Boy:Alan Bauch; Puck:Keith Martin; Bottom: Alexander Grant; Rustics:Lambert Cox, David Jones, Keith Milland, Ronald Plaisted, Douglas Steuart; Helena:Carole Needham; Hermia:Vergie Derman; Demetrius:David Drew; Lysander:Derek Rencher; Peaseblossom: Ann Howard; Cobweb:Mavis Osborn; Moth:Ann Jenner; Mustardseed:Jacqueline Haslam; Fairies:corps de ballet
Royal Ballet, Royal Opera House, *2 April 1964*

NP Royal Ballet touring section; sc Peter Farmer†:
d Titania:Doreen Wells; Oberon:David Wall; Puck:David Morse; Bottom: Ronald Emblen
New Theatre, Oxford, *2 December 1966*
† This production was used by the main company from 2 December 1971 until 8 February 1974 when the Bardon/Walker production was restored to the repertory

NP Royal Ballet School; s Peter Farmer; c Peter Farmer and David Walker:
d Titania:Lorna Murray; Oberon:Mark Silver; Puck:Jonathan Ellingham; Bottom:Denis Bonner
Royal Opera House, *7 July 1973*

By other companies:

NP The Australian Ballet: r Elphine Allen; sc Peter Farmer:
d Titania:Elaine Fifield; Oberon:Kelvin Coe; Puck:Paul Saliba; Bottom:Alan Alder
Her Majesty's Theatre, Sydney, *11 July 1969*

NP PACT Ballet; r John Hart; sc Peter Farmer:
d Titania:Maxine Denys; Oberon: Christian Danhoff; Puck:Petrus Nel; Bottom:Wilhelm Schoeman
Civic Theatre, Johannesburg, *3 September 1971*

NP City Center Joffrey Ballet; r John Hart; sc David Walker:
d Titania:Rebecca Wright; Oberon:

Burton Taylor; Puck:Russell Sultzbach; Bottom:Larry Grenier
Wolftrap Farm, Vienna, Virginia, *9 August 1973*

NP Shakespeare and the Performing Arts; *pas de deux* (*Nocturne*) only:
d Titania:Natalia Makarova; Oberon: Michael Coleman
John F Kennedy Center, Washington DC, *26 September 1973*

NP Royal Swedish Ballet; sc David Walker:
d Titania:Kerstin Lidström; Oberon: Jens Graff; Puck:Klas Rickman; Bottom: Nisse Winqvist
Opera House, Stockholm, *14 October 1975*

1965

Monotones
Pas de trois
M Erik Satie, orchestrated by Claude Debussy and Roland-Manuel (*Trois Gymnopédies*)
c Frederick Ashton
d Vyvyan Lorrayne, Anthony Dowell, Robert Mead
Royal Ballet, Royal Opera House, *24 March 1965*

See 1966, **Monotones**

1966

Monotones
Pas de trois
M Erik Satie, orchestrated by John Lanchbery (*Prélude d'Eginhard* and *Trois Gnossiennes*)
c Frederick Ashton
d Antoinette Sibley, Georgina Parkinson, Brian Shaw
Royal Ballet, Royal Opera House, *25 April 1965* (followed by the first **Monotones**, see above)
New c 13 March 1969 (later reverted to the originals)

NP Royal Ballet touring section:
d *Gnossiennes*:Doreen Wells, Lucette

Aldous, David Wall; *Gymnopédies*: Shirley Grahame, Hendrik Davel, Paul Clarke

Hessisches Staatstheater, Wiesbaden, *28 May 1968*

By other companies:

NP Ballett der Deutschen Oper Berlin; R Robert Mead:
D *Gnossiennes*: Monika Radamm, Marion Cito, Robert Blankshine; *Gymnopédies*: Eva Evdokimova, Klaus Beelitz, Rudolf Holz

Deutsche Oper Berlin, *20 June 1971*

NP Chicago Ballet: R Robert Mead; performed to original piano version of the music:
D *Gnossiennes*: Anna Baker, Jeannine Granger, Orrin Kayan; *Gymnopédies*: Dolores Lipinski, Stephen Jenkins, Robert Sullivan

Hemmens Auditorium, Elgin, Illinois, *9 February 1974*

NP City Center Joffrey Ballet: R Faith Worth:
D *Gnossiennes*: Starr Danias, Rebecca Wright, Burton Taylor; *Gymnopédies*: Pamela Nearhoof, Kevin McKenzie, Robert Thomas

City Center, New York, *11 October 1974*

NP The Australian Ballet: R Robert Mead:
D *Gnossiennes*: Maria Lang, Jan Blanch, Kelvin Coe; *Gymnopédies*: Marilyn Jones, John Meehan, Jonathan Kelly

Her Majesty's Theatre, Brisbane, *18 July 1975*

1967

Sinfonietta

M Malcolm Williamson
S Optical effects by Hornsey College of Art Light/Sound Workshop (Clive Latimer, Michael Leonard, Peter Kuttner, Dick Woods)
C Peter Rice
D *Toccata*: Elizabeth Anderton, Brenda Last, Richard Farley, Kerrison Cooke
Elegy: Doreen Wells, David Wall,

Michael Beare, Hendrik Davel, Paul Clarke, Graham Powell
Tarantella: David Wall, Elizabeth Anderton, Brenda Last, Richard Farley, Kerrison Cooke, and six couples

Royal Ballet touring section, Royal Shakespeare Theatre, Stratford upon Avon, *10 February 1967*

1968

Jazz Calendar

M Richard Rodney Bennett
Curtain SC Derek Jarman
D *Monday*: Vergie Derman
Tuesday: Merle Park, Anthony Dowell, Robert Mead
Wednesday: Vyvyan Lorrayne, Paul Brown, David Drew, Ian Hamilton, Derek Rencher
Thursday: Alexander Grant, Diana Vere, Lesley Collier, Carole Hill, Patricia Linton, Geraldine Morris, Suzanna Raymond
Friday: Antoinette Sibley, Rudolf Nureyev
Saturday: Desmond Doyle, Michael Coleman, Lambert Cox, Frank Freeman, Jonathan Kelly, Keith Martin, Kenneth Mason, Peter O'Brien, Wayne Sleep
Sunday: Marilyn Trounson and ensemble

Royal Ballet, Royal Opera House, *9 January 1968*

NP Royal Ballet School:
D *Monday*: Lucinda Harper; *Tuesday*: Lorna Murray, Stephen Beagley, Nigel Jones; *Wednesday*: Amanda Wilkinson; *Thursday*: Stephen Speed; *Friday*: Denise Nunn, Michael Batchelor: *Saturday*: Desmond Doyle; *Sunday*: Claire Farnsworth

Royal Opera House, *29 June 1974*

Enigma Variations (My Friends Pictured Within)

M Edward Elgar (*Variations on an Original Theme, 'Enigma'*, opus 36)
SC Julia Trevelyan Oman
D Edward Elgar (E D U): Derek Rencher; The Lady—Elgar's wife (C A E): Svetlana Beriosova: Hew David Steuart-Powell (H D S-P): Stanley Holden; Richard Baxter Townshend (R B T):

Brian Shaw; William Meath Baker (W M B): Alexander Grant; Richard P Arnold (R P A): Robert Mead; Isabel Fitton (Ysobel): Vyvyan Lorrayne; Arthur Troyte Griffith (Troyte): Anthony Dowell; Winifred Norbury (W N): Georgina Parkinson; A J Jaeger (Nimrod): Desmond Doyle; Dora Penny (Dorabella): Antoinette Sibley; George Robertson Sinclair (G R S); Wayne Sleep; Basil G Nevinson (B G N): Leslie Edwards; Lady Mary Lygon (✳✳✳): Deanne Bergsma; Schoolgirl: Patricia Linton; Country Boy and Girl: Lesley Collier, Donald Kirkpatrick; Sailor Boy and Girl: Christine Aitken, Frank Freeman; Housekeeper: Julie Wood; Gardener: Ronald Plaisted; The Carrier: Gary Sinclair; Country Woman: Lois Strike; Telegraph Boy: John Haynes

Royal Ballet, Royal Opera House, *25 October 1968*

1970

Lament of the Waves

Devised by Frederick Ashton

M   Gérard Masson (*Dans le deuil des vagues* II)
S   Bill Culbert, adapted from his multiple work 'Cubic Projections'
C   Derek Rencher

Curtain (from *Pelléas et Mélisande*) Jacques Dupont

D   Marilyn Trounson, Carl Myers

Royal Ballet, Royal Opera House, *9 February 1970*

Die Geschöpfe des Prometheus (The Creatures of Prometheus)

An allegorical ballet in prologue and one act

M   Ludwig van Beethoven, edited by John Lanchbery (ballet, opus 43)
SC   Ottowerner Meyer
D   Prometheus: Hendrik Davel; Creatures: Doreen Wells, Kerrison Cooke; Apollo: Paul Clarke; Eros: Paul Benson; Thalia, Muse of Comedy: Alfreda Thorogood; Mars: Adrian Grater; Melpomene, Muse of Tragedy: Sandra Conley; Bacchus: David Morse; Terpsichore, Muse of Dancing: Brenda Last; Warriors, Pastorale: corps de ballet

Royal Ballet touring section, Theater der Stadt Bonn, *6 June 1970*

NP   Royal Ballet:
      D as above except Male Creature: David Wall; Eros: Frank Freeman
Royal Opera House, *31 October 1970*

Tales of Beatrix Potter

An EMI Films picture
Produced by Richard Goodwin
Directed by Reginald Mills
Screenplay by Richard Goodwin and Christine Edzard, from *The Tale of Mrs Tiggy-Winkle, The Tale of Peter Rabbit, The Tale of Mrs Tittlemouse, The Tale of Johnny Town-Mouse, The Tale of Jemima Puddle-Duck, The Tale of Pigling Bland, The Tale of Jeremy Fisher, The Tale of Two Bad Mice* and *The Tale of Squirrel Nutkin* by Beatrix Potter
Photographed by Austin Dempster

M   John Lanchbery, based on themes by M W Balfe, George Jacobi, Ludwig Minkus, Jacques Offenbach, Arthur Sullivan *et al*
SC   Christine Edzard

Masks by Rostislav Doboujinsky

Players: Beatrix Potter: Erin Geraghty; The Nurse: Joan Benham; The Butler: Wilfred Babbage

D   Mrs Tiggy-Winkle: Frederick Ashton; Peter Rabbit: Alexander Grant; Mrs Tittlemouse: Julie Wood; Johnny Town-Mouse: Keith Martin; Jemima Puddle-Duck: Ann Howard; Fox: Robert Mead; Pigling Bland: Alexander Grant; Mrs Pettitoes: Sally Ashby; Black Berkshire Pig: Brenda Last; Jeremy Fisher: Michael Coleman; Tom Thumb: Wayne Sleep; Hunca Munca: Lesley Collier; Squirrel Nutkin: Wayne Sleep; Owl: Leslie Edwards; Tabitha Twitchit: Sally Ashby; Town Mice, Pigs, Squirrels, Country Mice: Carole Ainsworth, Avril Bergen, Jill Cooke, Graham Fletcher, Bridget Goodricke, Garry Grant, Suzanna Raymond, Rosemary Taylor, Anita Young

Release date *1 April 1971* (filmed autumn 1970)

1971

Meditation from Thaïs

M   Jules Massenet
C   Anthony Dowell
D   Antoinette Sibley, Anthony Dowell
Gala performance, Adelphi Theatre, *21 March 1971*

NP   Pacific Ballet:
Nourse Auditorium, San Francisco, *3 June 1971*

NP   Royal Ballet:
Royal Opera House, *14 December 1971*

NP   Festival of Two Worlds; as part of *Celebration: The Art of the Pas de deux*, arranged by Jerome Robbins; s Rouben Ter-Arutunian:
Teatro Nuovo, Spoleto, *29 July 1973*

[c. 1830]
Ballet by Richard Buckle
Choreography of the 5th Song by Frederick Ashton; of the first four by Geoffrey Cauley
Songs by Victor Hugo
M   Franz Liszt and Hector Berlioz
s   Jean Hugo after Victor Hugo, in a frame by Marie Hugo
c   Jean and Marie Hugo
Oh, quand je dors
M   Franz Liszt
D   The Poet: Desmond Kelly; His Muse: Margot Fonteyn
Presented by Richard Buckle, *Répétition générale* for *The Greatest Show on Earth*, Coliseum, *22 June 1971*

1972

Siesta
M   William Walton
D   Vyvyan Lorrayne, Barry McGrath
Royal Ballet New Group, The Maltings, Snape, Aldeburgh, *28 July 1972*

The Walk to the Paradise Garden
M   Frederick Delius (from his opera, *A Village Romeo and Juliet*)
sc   William Chappell
D   Merle Park, David Wall, Derek Rencher
Royal Ballet, Royal Opera House, *15 November 1972*

1973

[Death in Venice]
An opera in two acts by Myfanwy Piper, after the story by Thomas Mann

M   Benjamin Britten (opus 88)
Produced by Colin Graham
s   John Piper
c   Charles Knode
Cast: Gustav van Aschenbach, a novelist: Peter Pears; The Traveller: John Shirley-Quirk
D   The Polish Mother: Deanne Bergsma; Tadzio, her son: Robert Huguenin; Her two Daughters: Elizabeth Griffiths, Melanie Phillips; Their Governess: Sheila Humphreys; Jaschiu, Tadzio's friend: Nicholas Kirby; Street dancer: Sheila Humphreys; Polish, Russian and German children, Beggars: Angela Cox, Mark Sewell, Matthew Hawkins, Andris Plucis, Mark Welford, Ashley Wheater
English Opera Group, Aldeburgh Festival, The Maltings, Snape, *16 June 1973*

NP   Metropolitan Opera; R Faith Worth (choreography revised by Frederick Ashton):
D The Polish Mother: Vicki Fisera; Tadzio: Bryan Pitts; Her two Daughters: Alison Woodard, Claudia Shell; Their Governess: Diana Levy; Jaschiu: Anthony Ferro
Metropolitan Opera House, New York, *18 October 1974*

[World of Harlequin]
A ballet-play by Peter Brinson
Produced by Alexander Grant
Part Two: **Harlequinade: The Wedding of Harlequin** or **Harlequin's Revenge**
Devised and produced by Alexander Grant
Choreography by Ninette de Valois and Frederick Ashton
Prologue and epilogue written by Peter Brinson
M   selected by Stephen Lade and Alexander Grant; arranged by Stephen Lade
sc   Peter Courtier and the Production Wardrobe of the Royal Opera House, freely adapted from Pollock's Toy Theatre
D   Grimaldi, servant of Pantalon: Thane Bettany; Pantalon, Master of the House: Oliver Symons; Columbine, Pantalon's Daughter: Belinda Corken; Pierrot, betrothed to Columbine: William Perrie; Harlequin, Columbine's True Love: Graham Fletcher; Skeleton of Grimaldi: Beverley Parker; Shadow of Skeleton: Kenneth Saunders: Policeman: Ken Binge

Ballet for All, Spa Pavilion, Felixstowe, *11 October 1973*

[Tonight at 8.30]
The Friends of Covent Garden Christmas Party
Directed by Leslie Edwards
Grand Finale
M   Franz Lehár, arranged by Peter Greenwell (waltz from *Die lustige Witwe*)
C   for Margot Fonteyn by Christian Dior
D   Margot Fonteyn, Frederick Ashton and entire company
Friends of Covent Garden, Royal Opera House, *16 December 1973*

1974

Fashion Show
Produced by Roger Hutchins
M   popular songs
C   Janet Lyle, Leslie Poole, Angus Stewart, Michael Fish
D   *Scene 1*: Wendy Woodbridge, Barbara MacGreggor, Joyce Desiderio, Jane Armitage, Kerry-Anne Anderson, Julie Towers, Patricia Stewart, Rosalind Richards, Joseph Deaderick, Nicholas Millington, Shane Colquhoun, Ashley Laverty
Principal dancers: Angalika MacArthur, Kerry Cracknell, Wendy Morsberger, Lucinda Harper, Patricia Dove, Caitlan Maggs, Jayne Plaisted, Amanda Wenban, Jemima Guffog, Julie Smith, Katherine Pianoff, Stella Greenwood, Sarah Miles, Ann Makinodan, Ian Knowles, Robert Loveridge, Michael Pink, Nicholas Kirby, Timothy Storey, Shane Spooner, Paul Tyers, John Whillans, Vincent Hantam, Gerard Charles, Nicholas Dixon
Juniors: James Black, Andrew McComish, Richard Wilde, Carolyn James, Finola Demmar, Sara Throssell
Royal Ballet School, Royal Society of Arts, *1 April 1974*

1975

Scène dansante
Entrée, pas de deux, variations and coda

M   Jacques Offenbach (from *Le Papillon*, ballet-pantomime, 1860)
D   Merle Park, David Wall
Artists of the Royal Ballet, The Maltings, Snape, Aldeburgh, *16 March 1975*

Brahms-Waltz
Choreography by Frederick Ashton after Isadora Duncan
M   Johannes Brahms (*Waltz*, opus 39 no. 15)
C   David Dean
D   Lynn Seymour
Nijinsky Gala, Ballett des Hamburgischen Staatsoper, Hamburg, *22 June 1975*

NP   American Ballet Theatre; under the title *Homage to Isadora*:
Dorothy Chandler Pavilion, Los Angeles, *6 March 1976*

See 1976, **Five Brahms Waltzes in the Manner of Isadora Duncan**

[Floresta Amazŏnica]
Choreography by Dalal Achkar and Frederick Ashton
M   Heitor Villa-Lobos (Suite from the film *Green Mansions*, 1958)
SC   Jose Varona
Pas de deux
D   'Ela': Margot Fonteyn; O Homen Blanco: David Wall
Ballet do Rio de Janeiro, Teatro Municipal, Rio de Janeiro, *6 August 1975*; *pas de deux* given separately, Curitiba, Brazil, *20 August 1975*

NP   New London Ballet: *pas de deux* only:
D   Margot Fonteyn, Ivan Nagy
Teatro Nacional, Madrid, *1 October 1975*

NP   Margot Fonteyn and Rudolf Nureyev; under the title *Final Pas de deux from Amazon Forest*:
D   Margot Fonteyn, Rudolf Nureyev
Uris Theater, New York, *18 November 1975*

1976

A Month in the Country
Ballet in one act freely adapted from Ivan Turgenev's play

493

M Frédéric Chopin, arranged by John Lanchbery (*Variations on 'Là ci darem' from Mozart's Don Giovanni*, opus 2; *Fantasy on Polish airs*, opus 13; *Andante spianato and Grande polonaise* in E flat major, opus 22)

Curtain sc Julia Trevelyan Oman

D Natalia Petrovna:Lynn Seymour; Yslaev, her husband:Alexander Grant; Kolia, their son:Wayne Sleep; Vera, Natalia's ward:Denise Nunn; Rakitin, Natalia's admirer:Derek Rencher; Katia, a maid: Marguerite Porter; Matvei, a footman: Anthony Conway; Beliaev, Kolia's Tutor:Anthony Dowell

Royal Ballet, Royal Opera House, *12 February 1976*

Five Brahms Waltzes in the Manner of Isadora Duncan†

M Johannes Brahms (*Waltzes*, opus 39 nos. 1, 2, 8, 10, 13, 15—the first played as a prelude)

C David Dean

D Lynn Seymour

Ballet Rambert, 50th Birthday Performance, Sadler's Wells, *15 June 1976*

† The title was incorrectly given in the programme as *Four Brahms Waltzes in the Manner of Isadora Duncan*

NP American Ballet Theatre:
State Theater, New York, *12 July 1976*

[The Turning Point]
A 20th Century-Fox picture
Directed by Herbert Ross
Screenplay by Arthur Laurents
Photographed by Robert Surtees
Players: Anne Bancroft, Shirley MacLaine, *et al*

Étude

M Frédéric Chopin (*Étude* in A flat major, opus 25 no. 1)

C Albert Wolsky

Choreographed for Gelsey Kirkland, who subsequently withdrew from the film; to be danced in the final version of the film by Leslie Browne

For release *1977*

NOTES

Abbreviations

BR   Ballet Review
BT   Ballet Today
D & D   Dance and Dancers
DP   Dance Perspectives
DT   Dancing Times
NYPL   New York Public Library: Museum of the Performing Arts, Dance Collection, Lincoln Center

Walter Terry interview: Interview with Walter Terry in Dance Laboratory series, at the YM & YWHA, New York, 18 October 1953 (tape in NYPL)

John Selwyn Gilbert interview: Frederick Ashton in conversation, from Zoë Dominic and John Selwyn Gilbert: *Frederick Ashton: A Choreographer and his Ballets*, Harrap, London 1971

Beryl de Zoete: Frederick Ashton, from Beryl de Zoete: *The Thunder and the Freshness – Collected Essays*, Neville Spearman, London 1963

Don McDonagh interview: *Au Revoir?* – an interview with Frederick Ashton, by Don McDonagh in BR Volume 3 No 4, 1970

Don McDonagh interview (tape): the unedited tape of the above

Foreword (pages xvii–xx)

1 Walter Terry interview
2 Graham Fletcher conversation
3 David Howard conversation
4 Graham Fletcher conversation
5 E M Forster: *Aspects of the Novel*, Edward Arnold, London 1927

1904–1926 (pages 1–12)

1 John Selwyn Gilbert interview
2 *ibid*
3 *ibid*
4 Beryl de Zoete
5 *ibid*
6 *ibid*
7 John Selwyn Gilbert interview
8 Beryl de Zoete
9 John Selwyn Gilbert interview
10 *ibid*
11 *ibid*
12 Beryl de Zoete
13 John Selwyn Gilbert interview
14 Tape in NYPL, recorded 8 May 1969
15 John Selwyn Gilbert interview
16 Penelope Spencer (Mrs H L Barman) conversation
17 John Selwyn Gilbert interview
18 Elizabeth Frank conversation
19 Marie Rambert conversation

495

1926–1930 (pages 13–43)

1 Ailne Phillips and Margaret Craske conversations
2 Marie Rambert: *How They Began – II Ballet Rambert*, DT August 1950
3 Punch 2 July 1930
4 Don McDonagh interview
5 Beryl de Zoete
6 Punch 24 June 1931
7 C W Beaumont: *Dancers Under My Lens*, C W Beaumont, London 1949
8 DT January 1945
9 Anton Dolin: *Alicia Markova, her Life and Art*, Hermitage House, New York 1953

1930–1931 (pages 44–61)

1 DT November 1930
2 DT December 1930
3 The Times 13 October 1936
4 The Times 22 December 1930
5 Punch 7 January 1931
6 The Nation (London) 10 January 1931
7 Mary Clarke: *Dancers of Mercury*, Black, London 1962
8 C W Beaumont: *Dancers Under My Lens*, C W Beaumont, London 1949
9 Lincoln Kirstein, in DP No 54 Summer 1973
10 The Observer 22 February 1931
11 DT June 1931
12 Programme of Gala Performance at Sadler's Wells, 15 May 1950
13 Anton Dolin: *Alicia Markova, her Life and Art*, Hermitage House, New York 1953
14 Anton Dolin: *Ballet Go Round*, Michael Joseph, London 1938
15 Don McDonagh interview
16 C W Beaumont: *op cit*
17 A note by Sir Frederick Ashton, in *Tamara Karsavina*, privately printed, London 1971
18 *ibid*
19 C W Beaumont: *op cit*
20 Agnes de Mille: *Speak to Me, Dance with Me*, Atlantic/Little, Brown, Boston 1973
21 DT September 1931
22 DT November 1931
23 D & D October 1955
24 *Footnotes to the Ballet*, edited by Caryl Brahms, Lovat Dickson, London 1936

1931–1933 (pages 62–95)

1 Richard Findlater: *Lilian Baylis*, Allen Lane, London 1975
2 The Times 23 September 1931
3 Horace Horsnell, The Observer 27 September 1931
4 DT December 1931
5 C W Beaumont: *Dancers Under My Lens*, C W Beaumont, London 1949
6 *Theatre and Stage*, edited by Harold Downs, Pitman, London 1934
7 The Daily Telegraph 19 February 1934
8 Philip Dyer conversation
9 C W Beaumont: *op cit*
10 The Observer 12 December 1937
11 DT February 1932
12 C W Beaumont: *op cit*
13 *ibid*
14 The Times 5 March 1932
15 Star 5 March 1932
16 Evening News 5 April 1932
17 John Riordan, letter in New English Weekly 11 August 1932
18 Spike Hughes: *Second Movement*, Museum Press, London 1951
19 *ibid*
20 C W Beaumont: *op cit*
21 DT July 1932
22 New English Weekly 9 June 1932
23 Sunday Referee 12 June 1932
24 Yorkshire Post 7 June 1932
25 New English Weekly 9 June 1932
26 D & D October 1955
27 Elisabeth Schooling conversation
28 The Times 11 October 1932
29 The Observer 16 October 1932
30 The Times 29 November 1932
31 Evening News 18 January 1933
32 The Observer 12 March 1933
33 Marie Rambert: *Quicksilver*, Macmillan, London 1972
34 BT Volume I No 5, April–May 1947
35 The Observer 12 March 1933
36 The Times 26 April 1933
37 DT May 1933
38 *ibid*
39 Time and Tide 13 May 1933
40 The Observer 14 May 1933
41 DT June 1933
42 DT December 1933
43 The Tatler 5 July 1933
44 Lincoln Kirstein, in DP No 54
45 *Who's Who in the Theatre*, 9th edition, Pitman, London 1939
46 The Times 2 November 1933
47 Sketch 19 July 1933
48 Lincoln Kirstein: *op cit*
49 Stage 5 October 1933
50 DT December 1933

51 Frederick Ashton: *Ballet and The Choreographer*, in The Old Vic and Sadler's Wells Magazine, London, December 1933

1934 (pages 96–105)

1 Gertrude Stein: *The Autobiography of Alice B Toklas*, Harcourt, Brace, New York 1933
2 Maurice Grosser: Preface to the Vocal score of *Four Saints in Three Acts*, Music Press and Arrow Press, New York 1948
3 *ibid*
4 Hartford Courant 9 February 1934
5 Virgil Thomson: *Virgil Thomson*, Knopf, New York 1966
6 Maurice Grosser: *op cit*
7 Beryl de Zoete
8 Virgil Thomson: *op cit*
9 John Houseman: *Run-through*, Simon and Schuster, New York 1972
10 *ibid*
11 *ibid*
12 Virgil Thomson: *op cit*
13 New York Times 9 February 1934
14 New York Sun 24 February 1934
15 Letter to New York Times 18 February 1934: Van Vechten's preface to the Souvenir Programme and the published libretto was substantially the same
16 New Republic 7 March 1934
17 New Republic 11 April 1934
18 Stark Young: *Reading Lesson*, in Theatre Arts, May 1934
19 New York Times 25 February 1934
20 New York Herald Tribune 11 February 1934
21 Hartford Courant 9 February 1934

1934–1935 (pages 106–119)

1 Alicia Markova conversation
2 For these details of the choreography, I am indebted to Elisabeth Schooling
3 Reproduced in C W Beaumont: *Ballet Design, Past and Present*, Studio, London 1946
4 Marie Rambert: *Quicksilver*, Macmillan, London 1972
5 Richard Buckle: *Nijinsky*, Weidenfeld and Nicolson, London 1971
6 Lincoln Kirstein, in DP No 54
7 Correspondence with Norbert Haas
8 Vivian Ellis: *I'm on a See-Saw*, Michael Joseph, London 1953

9 *ibid*
10 Lionel Bradley: *Journals* – ms in the Victoria and Albert Museum, Gabrielle Enthoven Collection
11 Mary Clarke: *Dancers of Mercury*, Black, London 1962
12 The Times 5 February 1935
13 The Daily Telegraph 5 February 1935
14 Mary Clarke: *The Sadler's Wells Ballet*, Black, London 1955
15 The Tatler 11 September 1935

1935–1939 (pages 120–177)

1 Mary Clarke: *The Sadler's Wells Ballet*, Black, London 1955
2 Frederick Ashton: *Baiser de la Fée*, in The Old Vic and Sadler's Wells Magazine, London, November 1935
3 DT January 1936
4 G E Goodman: *Notes on Décor*, in DT January 1936
5 Keith Money: *The Art of Margot Fonteyn*, Michael Joseph, London 1965
6 Unidentified clipping, 1 December 1935
7 The Manchester Guardian 24 December 1935
8 Cecil Beaton: *Ballet*, Allan Wingate, London and New York 1951
9 The Sunday Times 26 January 1936
10 The Times 25 January 1936
11 Letter to Constant Lambert, 18 September 1935
12 Interview in Lilian Baylis Centenary Festival Souvenir Programme 1974
13 Letter to J M Keynes, 9 December 1935
14 Letter to J M Keynes, 13 December 1935
15 Letter to Lilian Baylis, 20 December 1935
16 Letter to J M Keynes, 9 January 1936
17 Letter to Samuel Courtauld, 12 December 1935
18 Letter to J M Keynes, 18 December 1935
19 Letter to Lilian Baylis, 10 January 1936
20 Letter to J M Keynes, 11 January 1936
21 Letter to J M Keynes, 29 January 1936
22 J M Keynes: Letter to Lilian Baylis, 19 February 1936
23 Constant Lambert: Letter to Miss Harvey at the Old Vic, 5 February 1936
24 DT October 1952
25 Cecil Beaton: *op cit*
26 Arnold Haskell, in DT June 1936
27 Frederick Ashton conversation
28 DT June 1936
29 Cecil Beaton: *op cit*
30 D & D April 1957

31 BT Volume 2 No 17 May–June 1949
32 Bystander 25 March 1936
33 The Times 12 March 1936
34 The Daily Telegraph 3 April 1937
35 The Times 28 December 1936
36 The Sunday Times 7 February 1937
37 Alan Carter, in a letter to the author
38 Frederick Ashton: *Les Patineurs*, in Sadler's Wells Theatre Ballet, No 1, Sadler's Wells Foundation 1956
39 *ibid*
40 The Times 17 February 1937
41 Frederick Ashton: *op cit*
42 Clive Barnes, in D & D April 1959
43 Gertrude Stein: *Everybody's Autobiography*, Random House, New York 1937
44 *ibid*
45 *ibid*
46 Radio Times 28 May 1937
47 Alan Bolt, in The Tatler 21 July 1937
48 Richard Shead: *Constant Lambert*, Simon Publications, London 1973
49 The Times 28 January 1938
50 P W Manchester conversation
51 Bystander 9 February 1938
52 DT June 1938
53 E M Forster: The Raison d'Etre of Criticism in the Arts, in *Two Cheers for Democracy*, Edward Arnold, London 1951
54 The Observer 15 May 1938
55 The Times 11 May 1938
56 Vivian Ellis: *I'm on a See-Saw*, Michael Joseph, London 1953
57 The Times 2 September 1938
58 The Daily Telegraph 3 November 1938
59 The Observer 30 April 1939
60 *ibid*
61 Bystander 17 May 1939
62 Allison Delarue: *The Stage and Ballet Designs of Eugene Berman*, in Dance Index Volume V No 2, February 1946
63 *ibid*
64 Alicia Markova conversation
65 Frederic Franklin conversation
66 *ibid*
67 NYPL, Collection of Léonide Massine, to whom I am indebted for permission to view the film
68 Alicia Markova and Frederic Franklin conversations
69 John Martin, in New York Times 27 October 1939
70 New York Times 5 November 1939
71 The American Dancer December 1939
72 Edwin Denby: *Looking at the Dance*, Pellegrini and Cudahy, New York 1949

1939–1945 (pages 178–201)

1 Reprinted in DT January 1949, under the title *Music for Ballet*
2 Sacheverell Sitwell: *Liszt*, Constable, London 1955; with a new Preface, Dover Publications, New York 1967
3 The Manchester Guardian 26 January 1940
4 DT March 1940
5 The Times 24 January 1940
6 Beryl de Zoete
7 Richard Shead: *Constant Lambert*, Simon Publications, London 1973
8 The Observer 24 April 1940
9 The Times 25 April 1940
10 The Times 5 June 1940
11 Alan Carter, in a letter to the author
12 Peter Alexander: *The Ballets of Frederick Ashton*, in Dance Chronicle No 9, July 1941
13 The Times 28 January 1941
14 The Observer 3 February 1941
15 New Statesman 1 February 1941
16 Edwin Evans, in DT June 1943
17 DT May 1943
18 Beryl de Zoete
19 John Harris, Stephen Orgel and Roy Strong: *The King's Arcadia – Inigo Jones and the Stuart Court*. Catalogue of an exhibition held at the Banqueting House, Whitehall. Arts Council of Great Britain 1973. See Entry No 113
20 Mary Clarke: *The Sadler's Wells Ballet*, Black, London 1955
21 The Observer 28 January 1945

1946–1949 (pages 202–237)

1 Ballet Volume IV No 5, November 1947
2 Julia Farron conversation
3 Ballet Volume IV No 5, November 1947
4 BT Volume I No 7, September–October 1947
5 Margaret Dale conversation
6 Quoted by Richard Buckle, obituary notice of Sophie Fedorovitch, The Observer 1 February 1955
7 *Sophie Fedorovitch: Tributes and Attributes*, edited by Simon Fleet, privately printed, London 1955
8 Birmingham News 18 September 1948
9 Mary Clarke: *The Sadler's Wells Ballet*, Black, London 1955
10 Cecil Beaton: *Ballet*, Allan Wingate, London and New York 1951
11 *ibid*

12 *ibid*
13 From *Gertrude Stein and the Ballet* in The Times 23 November 1964
14 Constant Lambert, in Edward Mandinian: *Purcell's The Fairy Queen*, John Lehmann, London 1948
15 *ibid*
16 DT November 1946
17 DT January 1947
18 *ibid*
19 Alan Storey, in BT Volume 1 No 4, January–February 1947
20 Ballet Volume IV No 5, November 1947
21 Richard Buckle: *The Adventures of a Ballet Critic*, Cresset Press, London 1953
22 New Statesman 5 June 1954
23 Richard Buckle: *op cit*
24 *ibid*
25 Clive Barnes, in D & D July 1960
26 Suzanna Raymond conversation
27 BT Volume 1 No 10, March–April 1948
28 New Statesman 21 February 1948
29 The Times 12 February 1948
30 Punch 18 February 1948
31 The Financial Times 28 October 1974
32 Letter to Edwin Evans, in NYPL
33 DT January 1948
34 The Times 26 November 1948
35 Mary Clarke: *op cit*
36 P W Manchester conversation
37 D & D January 1959
38 Reprinted in a symposium on the composer published by the Foreign Languages Publishing House, Moscow 1960
39 BR Volume IV No 6, 1974
40 Nigel Gosling conversation
41 John Selwyn Gilbert interview
42 For an account of the composition of this dance, see also *Ballerina*, edited by Clement Crisp, Weidenfeld and Nicolson, London 1975
43 John Percival, in D & D February 1966
44 Mary Clarke: *op cit*
45 Baroness von Bülop: *My Royal Past*, as told to Cecil Beaton, Batsford, London 1939
46 Edwin Denby: *Dancers Buildings and People in the Streets*, Horizon, New York 1965
47 D & D February 1966
48 John Percival, in D & D February 1967
49 D & D February 1961
50 Peter Williams, in D & D February 1966
51 Edwin Denby: *op cit*
52 P W Manchester, in BT Volume 2 No 17, May–June 1949
53 *ibid*

1949–1951 (pages 238–251)

1 Frederick Ashton: *One Man's Week*, in Leader Magazine 15 April 1950
2 Vogue (London) August 1948
3 Cecil Beaton: *Ballet*, Allan Wingate, London and New York, 1951
4 *ibid*
5 Nicholas Magallanes conversation
6 New York Times 26 March 1950
7 Lillian Moore, in DT April 1950
8 New York Times 26 March 1950
9 DT August 1950
10 Monthly Film Bulletin June 1951
11 Walter Terry interview
12 Clive Barnes, in D & D August 1958
13 Walter Terry interview
14 Dance Index Volume II No 8, August 1943
15 Walter Terry interview
16 Clive Barnes: *op cit*
17 Walter Terry interview
18 P W Manchester, in Dance News November 1953
19 Clive Barnes: *op cit*
20 Walter Terry interview

1951–1956 (pages 252–287)

1 Richard Shead: *Constant Lambert*, Simon Publications, London 1973
2 DT August 1951
3 New York Times 17 and 25 September 1953
4 D & D December 1957
5 David Blair conversation
6 DT October 1951
7 The Times 12 September 1951
8 DT June 1952
9 Monthly Film Bulletin April 1953
10 Robert Irving conversation
11 Anon (Anne E Moberly and Eleanor F Jourdain): *An Adventure*, first published in 1911; 4th edition, Faber, London 1931
12 Newsweek 10 March 1952
13 DT April 1952
14 Walter Terry, in New York Herald Tribune 9 March 1952
15 Edwin Denby: *Dancers Buildings and People in the Streets*, Horizon, New York 1965
16 DT May 1952
17 The Observer 13 April 1952
18 Julian Braunsweg: *Braunsweg's Ballet Scandals*, Allen and Unwin, London 1973
19 Richard Buckle: *The Adventures of a Ballet Critic*, Cresset Press, London 1953

20 Walter Terry interview
21 *ibid*
22 Robert Irving conversation
23 Walter Terry interview
24 Dance News November 1953
25 Mary Clarke: *The Sadler's Wells Ballet*, Black, London 1955
26 In the Catalogue of the Sophie Fedorovitch Memorial Exhibition, Victoria and Albert Museum 1955
27 Simon Fleet: *Biographical Sketch of Sophie Fedorovitch*, privately printed, London 1955
28 The Observer 8 February 1953
29 DT March 1952
30 The Observer 8 February 1953
31 Walter Terry interview
32 *ibid*
33 DT July 1953
34 D & D May 1956
35 D & D February 1953
36 D & D November 1959
37 Frederick Ashton conversation
38 Robert Irving conversation
39 Richard Buckle, in The Observer (review unpublished owing to a newspaper strike)
40 New York Times 16 October 1955
41 Mary Clarke: *op cit*
42 Punch 9 April 1955
43 New York Times 27 September 1956
44 Frederick Ashton conversation
45 Unidentified clipping
46 Peter Williams, in D & D July 1955
47 *ibid*
48 D & D March 1956
49 D & D June 1958
50 D & D April 1956
51 Clive Barnes, in D & D November 1957
52 Clive Barnes, in D & D July 1956

1956–1963 (pages 288–335)

1 D & D April 1958
2 D & D May 1959
3 Peter Brinson, interview with Margot Fonteyn, The Sunday Times 8 March 1959
4 *ibid*
5 Clive Barnes, in D & D January 1960
6 The Sunday Times 26 October 1958
7 Time 3 October 1960
8 D & D December 1953
9 Peter Brinson, *op cit*
10 Clive Barnes, in D & D December 1958
11 D & D January 1959
12 The Observer 2 November 1958

13 *La Fille mal gardée*, Famous Ballets No 1, edited by Ivor Guest, Dancing Times Ltd, London 1960
14 John Lanchbery and Ivor Guest: *The scores of La Fille mal gardée*, Theatre Research Volume III Nos 1, 2 and 3, International Federation for Theatre Research, London 1961
15 John Lanchbery conversation
16 D & D March 1960
17 David Blair conversation
18 *ibid*
19 *ibid*
20 Ivor Guest: *The Romantic Ballet in Paris*, Pitman, London 1966
21 Alexandre Benois: *Reminiscences of the Russian Ballet*, translated by Mary Britnieva, Putnam, London 1941
22 David Blair conversation
23 Natalia Roslavleva: The Royal Ballet in the USSR, in *Ballet Annual 1962*, Black, London 1961
24 Osbert Lancaster: Designing *La Fille mal gardée*, in *La Fille mal gardée*, edited by Ivor Guest, *op cit*
25 Edwin Denby: *Dancers Buildings and People in the Streets*, Horizon, New York 1965
26 The Nation (New York) 15 June 1974
27 John Lanchbery conversation
28 D & D April 1961
29 The Observer 19 February 1961
30 Margot Fonteyn: *Autobiography*, W H Allen, London 1975
31 *Ballet Annual 1963*, Black, London 1962
32 The Sunday Times 5 November 1961
33 DP No 54
34 Robert Craft: *Conversations with Igor Stravinsky*, Faber, London 1959
35 D & D January 1962
36 *ibid*
37 Ninette de Valois conversation
38 Pat Stone: *Diaries* – in manuscript (some excerpts published in Petit Tour, the journal of the London Ballet Circle)
39 Clive Barnes, in D & D January 1962
40 D & D January 1962
41 Peter Williams, in D & D June 1962
42 Pat Stone: *op cit*
43 D & D November 1962
44 Alexander Bland: *Birth of a Ballet*, in The Observer 10 March 1963
45 *ibid*
46 *ibid*
47 *ibid*
48 *ibid*

49 D & D April 1963
50 *ibid*
51 BR Volume IV No 6, 1974
52 Spectator 22 March 1963

1963–1970 (pages 336–373)

1 Don McDonagh interview (tape)
2 D & D November 1963
3 Antoinette Sibley conversation
4 John Lanchbery conversation
5 Antoinette Sibley and Anthony Dowell conversations
6 D & D May 1964
7 Dale Harris, in Dance News September 1969
8 *ibid*
9 *ibid*
10 Rollo H Myers: *Erik Satie*, Dobson, London 1948
11 The New Yorker 11 November 1974
12 *ibid*
13 D & D June 1966
14 Frederick Ashton: The Subject Matter of Ballet, in *Ballet Annual 1959*, Black, London 1958
15 Pat Stone: *Diaries* – in manuscript (some excerpts published in Petit Tour, the journal of the London Ballet Circle)
16 Clement Crisp: programme note
17 Peter Williams, in D & D April 1967
18 Pat Stone: *op cit*
19 Derek Jarman conversation
20 *ibid*
21 BBC broadcast, 17 January 1968
22 *ibid*
23 D & D February 1968
24 Julia Trevelyan Oman: lecture on *Enigma Variations* at the Victoria and Albert Museum, 22 November 1973
25 *ibid*
26 Anthony Dowell conversation
27 Reprinted in About the House Volume 2 No 12, November 1968; in a slightly different form in the programme notes for the ballet
28 Anthony Dowell conversation
29 Don McDonagh interview (tape)
30 Interview with Oleg Kerensky, BBC broadcast, 20 November 1968
31 D & D January 1970
32 *The Fairy Tales of Charles Perrault*, translated by Geoffrey Brereton, Penguin Books 1957
33 BR Volume III No 4, 1970
34 Peter Williams, in D & D March 1970

35 The Times 10 February 1970
36 S S Prawer: *The Penguin Book of Lieder*, Penguin Books 1964
37 The Times 2 November 1970
38 D & D September 1970

1970–1975 (pages 374–392)

1 Rumer Godden: *The Tale of the Tales*, Warne, London and New York, 1971
2 John Lanchbery conversation
3 Margaret Lane: *The Tale of Beatrix Potter*, Warne, London 1968
4 Anthony Dowell conversation
5 The Daily Telegraph 22 March 1971
6 Guardian 22 March 1971
7 The Dickybuckle Star, Series 2, London, May 1971
8 The Times 16 November 1972
9 The Sunday Times 24 June 1973
10 BBC broadcast, 3 March 1965
11 Quoted in Lydia Joel: *Finding Isadora*, in Dance Magazine, New York, June 1969
12 *ibid*
13 Klaus Geitel, in *Die Welt* 24 June 1975
14 *Stuttgarter Zeitung* 27 June 1975

1976 (pages 393–406)

1 Editorial note to Ivan Turgenev: *A Sportsman's Notebook*, translated by Charles and Natasha Hepburn, Cresset Press, London 1950
2 Letter from A F Koni to M G Savina, quoted in *Letters to an Actress/The Story of Ivan Turgenev and Marya Gavrilovna Savina*, edited and translated by Nora Gottlieb and Raymond Chapman, Allison and Busby, London 1973
3 A V Coton: *Writings on Dance, 1938–68*, Dance Books, London 1975
4 New Statesman 20 February 1976
5 The Observer 15 February 1976
6 Jane Austen: *Letters 1796–1817*, selected and edited by R W Chapman, Oxford University Press, London 1955
7 W H Auden: *Making, Knowing and Judging*, Clarendon Press, Oxford 1956
8 The Times 26 September 1975
9 Letter to the author, 16 July 1956
10 Frederick Ashton: Notes on Choreography, in *The Dance Has Many Faces*, edited by Walter Sorell, World, New York 1951
11 Letter to Mary Clarke, undated but c. August 1974
12 BBC broadcast, 12 February 1970

BIBLIOGRAPHY

Writings by Frederick Ashton

(chronologically listed)

A word about choregraphy in Dancing Times, London, May 1930

Ballet and The Choreographer in The Old Vic and Sadler's Wells Magazine, London, December 1933

'Baiser de la Fée' in The Old Vic and Sadler's Wells Magazine, London, November 1935

And now – the secrets of the ballet in an interview in Liverpool Evening Express, 23 February 1940

Marie Rambert: a tribute in Dancing Times, London, January 1945

Pearl Argyle – a tribute in Ballet Today, London, April–May 1947

'Abstract' Ballet (a dialogue with Richard Buckle) in Ballet, London, November 1947

One Man's Week/Dance of the Dollars in Leader Magazine, London, 15 April 1950

Hole in the Linoleum in the Souvenir Programme of a Gala Performance at Sadler's Wells Theatre, London, 15 May 1950

'Notes on Choreography' in *The Dance Has Many Faces* edited by Walter Sorell, World Publishing, New York 1951; second edition, Columbia University Press, New York 1966

'Three Tributes': 1 by Frederick Ashton, in the Catalogue of a Memorial Exhibition of Designs for Ballet, Opera and Stage by Sophie Fedorovitch, edited by Carol Hogben, Victoria and Albert Museum, London 1955; also in *Sophie Fedorovitch/Tributes and Attributes* edited by Simon Fleet, privately printed, London 1955

I once had a dream – it came true in Dance and Dancers, London, April 1955

Why we applaud her (Marie Rambert) in Dance and Dancers, London, October 1955

Les Patineurs in the Sadler's Wells Theatre Ballet No 1, edited by Russell Brown, Sadler's Wells Foundation, London 1956

The Progress of a Poet, excerpts from the conversation at a luncheon to celebrate the seventieth birthday of Dame Edith Sitwell, with Frederick Ashton, John Lehmann, Raymond Mortimer, William Plomer and Edith Sitwell, in The Sunday Times, London, 8 September 1957

'The Subject Matter of Ballet', contribution to a symposium in *Ballet Annual 1959* edited by Arnold L Haskell, Black, London 1958

Miss Rubinstein (a tribute to Ida Rubinstein) in The Times, London, 25 October 1958

'My Conception of "La Fille mal gardée"' in *Famous Ballets I/La Fille mal gardée* edited by Ivor Guest, Dancing Times Ltd, London 1960

Dance Magazine Awards 1962. *Speech by Frederick Ashton* when presenting award to Margot Fonteyn (with her reply) in Dance Magazine, New York, June 1963

Magical Touch of 'Mr B.', review of *Balanchine* by Bernard Taper in The Sunday Telegraph, London, 11 October 1964

A Conversation (with Clement Crisp) in *Covent Garden Book No 15*, Black, London 1964

Ballet's pond, letter to the Editor of The Sunday Times, in reply to *Nureyev throws a stone into the placid waters of Covent Garden* by Derek Prouse (The Sunday Times, 27 December 1964), in The Sunday Times, London, 3 January 1965

Anna Pavlova in the Catalogue to Pavlova/An Exhibition on Her Life and Work, presented by the Globe Playhouse, London, 26 January to 5 February 1965

'Margot Fonteyn' in *The Art of Margot Fonteyn*, photographed by Keith Money, Michael Joseph, London 1965

Unforgettable Isadora Duncan in Reader's Digest, New York, September 1968

Au Revoir? – a talk with Frederick Ashton by Don McDonagh, in Ballet Review, Volume 3 No 4, Brooklyn 1970

Dance Magazine Awards 1969, *Reply by Frederick Ashton* to speech by Agnes de Mille when presenting award to him, in Dance Magazine, New York, August 1970

A 'Note' by Sir Frederick Ashton in *Tamara Karsavina*, privately printed, London 1971 (copyright: Francis Francis and Nesta Macdonald)

'Frederick Ashton in Conversation: Family and Early Life/The Thirties and the War' in *Frederick Ashton/A Choreographer and his Ballets* by Zoë Dominic and John Selwyn Gilbert, Harrap, London 1971

'Façade' in *Façade: an Entertainment by Sir William Walton OM; poems by Dame Edith Sitwell; essays and commentary by Sacheverell Sitwell and Frederick Ashton*, Oxford University Press, Oxford 1972

'Introduction' in *Anna Pavlova* by Oleg Kerensky, Hamish Hamilton, London 1973

'Baylis and Ballet' (interview) in Lilian Baylis Festival Souvenir Programme, edited by Peter Roberts, Sadler's Wells Foundation, London 1974

'From Sir Frederick Ashton' in *50 years of Ballet Rambert/1926-1976*, edited by Clement Crisp, Anya Sainsbury and Peter Williams, Scolar Press, London 1976

Books by other authors

Anthony, Gordon: *The Vic-Wells Ballet – Camera Studies* with an introduction by Ninette de Valois, George Routledge & Sons, London 1938

— *A Camera at the Ballet – Pioneer Dancers of the Royal Ballet*, David and Charles, London 1975

Balanchine, George: *Balanchine's New Complete Stories of the Great Ballets*, edited by Francis Mason, Doubleday, New York 1968

Beaton, Cecil: *Ballet*, Allan Wingate, London and New York 1951

Beaumont, Cyril W: *The Vic-Wells Ballet*, C W Beaumont, London 1935

— *Complete Book of Ballets*, Putnam, London 1937

— *Supplement to Complete Book of Ballets*, C W Beaumont, London 1942

— *Ballet Design Past and Present*, Studio, London 1946

— *The Sadler's Wells Ballet*, C W Beaumont, London 1946; revised and enlarged 1947

— *Dancers Under My Lens*, C W Beaumont, London 1949

— *Ballets of Today* (2nd Supplement to *Complete Book of Ballets*), Putnam, London 1954

— *Ballets Past and Present* (3rd Supplement to *Complete Book of Ballets*), Putnam, London 1955

Bradley, Lionel: *Sixteen Years of Ballet Rambert*, Hinrichsen Edition, London 1946

— *Journals*, ms in Gabrielle Enthoven Collection, Victoria and Albert Museum, London

Brahms, Caryl (editor): *Footnotes to the Ballet*, Lovat Dickson, London 1936

Braunsweg, Julian: *Braunsweg's Ballet Scandals*, as told to James Kelsey, Allen & Unwin, London 1973

Brinson, Peter, and Crisp, Clement: *Ballet for All. A Guide to One Hundred Ballets*, with contributions by Don McDonagh and John Percival, Pan Books, London 1970 (paperback)

Buckle, Richard: *The Adventures of a Ballet Critic*, Cresset Press, London 1953

Chujoy, Anatole: *The New York City Ballet*, Knopf, New York 1953

— and Manchester, P W (editors): *The Dance Encyclopedia*, revised and enlarged edition, Simon & Schuster, New York 1967

Clarke, Mary: *The Sadler's Wells Ballet*, Black, London 1955

— *Dancers of Mercury/The Story of Ballet Rambert*, Black, London 1962

— and Crisp, Clement: *Making a Ballet*, Studio Vista, London 1974

Cohen, Selma Jeanne (editor): *Dance as a Theatre Art. Source Readings in Dance History from 1581 to the Present*, Dodd, Mead, New York 1974

Coton, A V: *A Prejudice for Ballet*, Methuen, London 1938

— *Writings on Dance, 1938–68*, selected and edited by Kathrine Sorley Walker and Lilian Haddakin; foreword by Martin Cooper; Dance Books, London 1975

Covent Garden/25 Years of Opera and Ballet/ Royal Opera House, catalogue of an exhibition organised by the Royal Opera House and the Victoria and Albert Museum; Victoria and Albert Museum, London 1971

Crisp, Clement (editor): *Ballerina/Portraits and Impressions of Nadia Nerina*, Weidenfeld and Nicolson, London 1975

— , Sainsbury, Anya, and Williams, Peter (editors), *50 years of Ballet Rambert/1926–1976*, Scolar Press, London 1976

de Mille, Agnes: *Speak to Me, Dance with Me*, Little, Brown, Boston and Toronto 1973

Denby, Edwin: *Looking at the Dance*, Pellegrini and Cudahy, New York 1949

— *Dancers Buildings and People in the Streets*, Horizon Press, New York 1965

de Valois, Ninette: *Come Dance with Me, A Memoir 1898–1956*, Hamish Hamilton, London 1957

de Zoete, Beryl: *The Thunder and the Freshness*, Collected Essays with a Preface by Arthur Waley, Neville Spearman, London 1963

Dolin, Anton: *Ballet Go Round*, Michael Joseph, London 1938

— *Alicia Markova, Her Life and Art*, Hermitage House, New York 1953

Dominic, Zoë, and Gilbert, John Selwyn: *Frederick Ashton/A Choreographer and His Ballets*, Harrap, London 1971

Ellis, Vivian: *I'm On a See-Saw*, Michael Joseph, London 1953

Emmanuel, Maurice: *The Antique Greek Dance after sculptured and painted figures*; drawings by A Colombar and Maurice Emmanuel; translated by Harriet Jean Beauley; John Lane, the Bodley Head, London 1916

Findlater, Richard: *Lilian Baylis/The Lady of the Old Vic*, Allen Lane, London 1975

Fisher, Hugh: *The Sadler's Wells Theatre Ballet*, Black, London 1956

Fleet, Simon: *Sophie Fedorovitch, a biographical sketch*, privately printed, London 1955

— (editor): *Sophie Fedorovitch/Tributes and Attributes/Aspects of her art and personality by some of her fellow artists and friends*, privately printed, London 1955

Fonteyn, Margot: *Autobiography*, W H Allen, London 1975

Gibbon, Monk: *The Tales of Hoffmann, a study of the film*; Saturn Press, London 1951

Godden, Rumer: *The Tale of the Tales/The Beatrix Potter Ballet*, Warne, London and New York 1971

Guest, Ivor (editor): *Famous Ballets I/La Fille mal gardée*, with contributions by Frederick Ashton, Winifred Edwards, Marina Grut, Tamara Karsavina, Osbert Lancaster, John Lanchbery, Lillian Moore and Nadia Nerina; Dancing Times Ltd, London 1960

Haskell, Arnold L: *The Marie Rambert Ballet*, with a foreword by Tamara Karsavina; British-Continental Press, London 1930

— *Balletomania/The Story of an Obsession*, Gollancz, London 1934

— *Dancing Round the World/Memoirs of an Attempted Escape from Ballet*, Gollancz, London 1937

— *Ballet/A Complete Guide to Appreciation*, Penguin, Harmondsworth 1938 (paperback)

— (editor): *Ballet Annual*, volumes 1–18, Black, London, 1946–1963

Henze, Hans Werner: *Undine/Tagebuch eines Balletts*, R Piper & Co Verlag, Munich 1959

Heppenstall, Rayner: *Apology for Dancing*, Faber, London 1935

Hogben, Carol (editor): *Sophie Fedorovitch 1893–1953*, Catalogue of a Memorial Exhibition of Designs for Ballet, Opera and Stage, Victoria and Albert Museum, London 1955

Houseman, John: *Run-through*, a memoir, Simon and Schuster, New York 1972

Howlett, Jasper: *Talking of Ballet*, Philip Alan, London (no date)

Hughes, Spike: *Second Movement*, Museum Press, London 1951

Kersley, Leo, and Sinclair, Janet: *A Dictionary of Ballet Terms*, 3rd edition, Black, London 1973

Kirstein, Lincoln: *Movement and Metaphor/four centuries of ballet*, Praeger, New York and Washington 1970

Manchester, P W: *Vic-Wells: A Ballet Progress*, Gollancz, London 1942

Mandinian, Edward: *Purcell's 'The Fairy Queen' as presented by The Sadler's Wells Ballet and the Covent Garden Opera*, a photographic record by Edward Mandinian, with the Preface to the Original Text, a Preface by Professor E J Dent and articles by Constant Lambert and Michael Ayrton; John Lehmann, London 1948

Massine, Léonide: *My Life in Ballet*, edited by Phyllis Hartnoll and Robert Rubens, Macmillan, London 1968

Melvin, Duncan (editor): *Souvenirs de Ballet*, Mayfair Publications, London 1949

Money, Keith: *The Art of Margot Fonteyn*, a photographic record with a commentary contributed by Ninette de Valois, Frederick Ashton, Keith Money and Margot Fonteyn; Michael Joseph, London 1965

— *Fonteyn/the making of a legend*, Collins, London 1973

Myers, Rollo H: *Erik Satie*, Denis Dobson, London 1948

Piper, Myfanwy: *Death in Venice*, an opera in two acts based on the short story by Thomas Mann; Faber Music, London 1973

Rambert, Marie: *Quicksilver/The Autobiography of Marie Rambert*, Macmillan, London 1972

Reynolds, Nancy: *Repertory in Review: Forty Years of the New York City Ballet*, Dial Press, New York 1977

Robert, Grace: *The Borzoi Book of Ballets*, Knopf, New York 1945

Rothenstein, John: *Edward Burra*, Tate Gallery, London 1973

Sandon, Joseph: *Façade and Other Early Ballets by Frederick Ashton*, Black, London 1954

Shead, Richard: *Constant Lambert*, with a Memoir by Anthony Powell, Simon Publications, London 1973

Sitwell, Sacheverell: *Liszt*, Constable, London 1955

Stein, Gertrude: *The Autobiography of Alice B Toklas*, Harcourt, Brace, New York 1933

— *Four Saints in Three Acts*, libretto, Random House, New York 1934

— *Everybody's Autobiography*, Random House, New York 1937

— and Thomson, Virgil: *Four Saints in Three Acts*, an opera with scenario by Maurice Grosser; complete vocal score, Music Press and Arrow Press, New York 1948

Stone, Pat: *Diaries*, ms (excerpts published in Petit Tour, the journal of the London Ballet Circle)

Stravinsky, Igor, and Craft, Robert: *Expositions and Developments*, Doubleday, New York 1962

Thomson, Virgil: *Virgil Thomson*, Knopf, New York 1966

van Praagh, Peggy, and Brinson, Peter: *The Choreographic Art*, with a foreword by Cyril Beaumont; Black, London 1963

Vaughan, David: *The Royal Ballet at Covent Garden*, photographs by Leslie E Spatt and Jennie Walton, with Edward Griffiths, Mike Humphrey and Rosemary Winckley; Dance Books, London 1975

Wilson, G B L: *A Dictionary of Ballet*, 3rd edition, Black, London 1974

Articles by other authors

(except in a few instances this does not include reviews of ballets; when quoted in the text, the date and name of the publication in which a review appeared is given in the Notes)

Acton, William: *Two Letters*, with a Memorial Notice by Beryl de Zoete, in Ballet, Volume 2 No 3, London, August 1946

Alexander, Peter: *Ballets of Frederick Ashton*, in Dancing Times, London, May 1939

— *The Ballets of Frederick Ashton – A Reconsideration*, in Dance Chronicle No 9, London, July 1941

Anderson, Jack: *Party Manners and Frederick Ashton*, in Ballet Review, Volume 3 No 4, Brooklyn 1970

Anon: *Big Ballets and Big Names*, Fourth Leader in The Times, London, 25 October 1958

Anon: *Frederick Ashton* (the Observer Profile), in The Observer, London, 26 October 1958

Anon: *Choreographer with a Mind of his Own*, in The Times, London, 27 May 1961

Anon: *How Sir Frederick Ashton Sees the Future of the Royal Ballet*, in The Times, London, 14 October 1963

Anon: *Gertrude Stein and the Ballet*, in The Times, London 23 November 1964

Anthony, Gordon: *In Homage to Frederick Ashton*, in Dance Magazine, New York, June 1970

— *Pioneers of the Royal Ballet: Frederick Ashton*, in Dancing Times, London, March 1970

Asquith, Anthony: 'Ballet and the Film' in *Footnotes to the Ballet*, edited by Caryl Brahms, Lovat Dickson, London 1936

Barnes, Clive: *Ondine*, Ballet Perspectives No 15, in Dance and Dancers, London, part 1 December 1959, part 2 January 1960

— *Scènes de ballet*, Ballet Perspectives No 18, in Dance and Dancers, London, July 1960

— *Cinderella*, Ballet Perspectives No 21, in Dance and Dancers, London, January 1961

— *Frederick Ashton and his Ballets*, in Dance Perspectives No 9, New York, Winter 1961

— *La Fille mal gardée*, Ballet Perspectives No 28, in Dance and Dancers, London, January 1963

— *A new phase*, in The Times, London, 25 July 1970

Beaumont, Cyril W: *Ashton's Cinderella*, in Ballet, Volume 7 No 2, London, February 1949

— 'Frederick Ashton - English Choreographer' in *Souvenirs de Ballet*, edited by Duncan Melvin, Mayfair Publications, London 1949

Bland, Alexander: *Birth of a Ballet*, in The Observer, London, 10 March 1963

— *Ashton's month in the country*, in The Observer Magazine, London, 8 February 1976

Buckle, Richard: *'Abstract' ballet: a dialogue between Richard Buckle and Frederick Ashton*, in Ballet, Volume 4 No 5, London, November 1947

Chappell, William: 'Early Days 1931–1939. A Sadler's Wells Scrapbook' in *Gala Performance*, edited by Arnold L Haskell, Mark Bonham-Carter and Michael Wood, Collins, London 1955

Corathiel, Elisabeth: *How a ballet is born*, in Ballet Today, London, April 1956

Coton, A V: *Three Classics of Ballet*, in Ballet Today, London, September–October 1947

Crisp, Clement: 'A conversation with Sir Frederick Ashton' in *Covent Garden Book No 15*, Black, London, 1964

— *Ashton*, in Les Saisons de la danse, No 58, Paris, November 1973

Croce, Arlene: *New York Newsletter* in Dancing Times, London, July 1970

— *The Royal Ballet in New York*, in Ballet Review, Volume 3 No 4, Brooklyn 1970

— *Waltzing Mice*, in Ballet Review, Volume 3 No 6, Brooklyn 1971

— *How to Be Very, Very Popular*, in The New Yorker, New York, 11 November 1974

— *Isadora Alive*, in The New Yorker, New York, 26 July 1976

Delarue, Allison: *The Stage and Ballet Designs of Eugene Berman*, in Dance Index, Volume 5 No 2, New York, February 1946

de Valois, Ninette: *Frederick Ashton*, in Dancing Times, London, September 1941

de Zoete, Beryl: *Frederick Ashton*, in Horizon, London, July 1942

Fonteyn, Margot: *Creating Ondine*, Ballerinas on their roles – 1, interview with Peter Brinson, in The Sunday Times, London, 8 March 1959

— 'A choreographer of genius' in *Ballet Annual 1961*, edited by Arnold L Haskell, Black, London 1960

Franks, Arthur H: *Ashton, Stravinsky, Gide*, in Dancing Times, London, December 1961

Gilbert, John: *All feet to the pumps*, in Guardian, London, 10 October 1973

Goldner, Nancy: *Ashton's lasting artistic touch*, in Christian Science Monitor, Boston, 9 May 1970

— *Dance*, in The Nation, New York, 15 June 1974

Guest, Ivor: 'Sylvia: from Mérante to Ashton' in *Ballet Annual 1954*, edited by Arnold L Haskell, Black, London 1953

Harris, Dale: *Frederick Ashton's 'Dream' is a statement about life*, in Dance News, New York, September 1969

— *The Royal Ballet: London and New York*, in Ballet Review, Volume 4 No 3, Brooklyn 1972

— *Snowflake to Superstar*, in Ballet Review, Volume 4 No 6, Brooklyn 1974

— *At last we can see more of Ashton*, in New York Times, New York, 15 December 1974

Haskell, Arnold L: *A note on the choregraphy of Frederick Ashton*, in Dancing Times, London, January 1931

— 'The Quality of Ashton' in *Ballet Annual 1961*, Black, London 1960

Hughes, Allen: *Really Royal Ballet* in New York Times, New York, 16 May 1965

Karsavina, Tamara: *Dancing with an English company*, in Dancing Times, London, January 1968

Kennedy, James: *The lord of the dance*, in Guardian, London, 20 September 1974

Kirstein, Lincoln: *Entries from an Early Diary*, in Dance Perspectives No 54, New York, Summer 1973

Kisselgoff, Anna: *Company's U.S. debut in 1949: a joyful beginning*, in New York Times, New York, 23 April 1969

— *Ashton, leaving the Royal Ballet, eyes fresh fields*, in New York Times, New York, 25 May 1970

Kragh-Jacobsen, Svend: 'International choreography takes the lead in Copenhagen' in *Ballet Annual 1956*, edited by Arnold L Haskell, Black, London 1955

Lambert, Constant: *Music for ballet*, transcript of a BBC broadcast, in Dancing Times, London, January 1949

Lanchbery, John and Guest, Ivor: 'The scores of La Fille mal gardée: 1 The original music; 2 Hérold's score; 3 The Royal Ballet's score', in Theatre Research, journal of the International Federation for Theatre Research, Volume III Nos 1, 2, 3, 1961

Lawson, Joan: *Frederick Ashton: 25 years of choreography*, in Dancing Times, London, September 1951

Manchester, P W: *Frederick Ashton after 25 fertile years*, in Dance News, New York, December 1951

Martin, John: *Ashton/Bold work on Rimbaud by English choreographer*, in New York Times, New York, 26 March 1950

McDonagh, Don: *Au Revoir?* – a talk with Frederick Ashton, in Ballet Review, Volume 3 No 4, Brooklyn 1970

Percival, John: *Master of British Ballet*, in The Times, London, 30 September 1967

— *Looking at Ashton's Enigma*, in The Times, London, 2 November 1968

— *Ballet Ashton always wanted to do*, in The Times, London, 6 February 1976

Porter, Andrew: *Frederick Ashton 1960–1970*, in About the House, Volume 3 No. 6, London, Summer 1970

Rambert, Marie: *How they began: Ballet Rambert*, in Dancing Times, London, August 1950

— 'Ashton's early days' in *Ballet Annual 1961*, edited by Arnold L Haskell, Black, London 1960

Read, T J: *Death in Venice*, in About the House, Volume 4 No 3, London, Summer 1973

Roslavleva, Natalia: 'The Royal Ballet in the USSR' in *Ballet Annual 1962*, edited by Arnold L Haskell and Mary Clarke, Black, London 1961

Sinclair, Janet: *Ashton and the choreographer's problem*, in Ballet Today, London, September–October 1947

— *Frederick Ashton*, in Ballet Today, London, May 1960

Somes, Michael: 'Working with Frederick Ashton' in *Ballet Annual 1961*, edited by Arnold L Haskell, Black, London 1960

Storey, Alan: *A ballet-goer's causerie: 2 The stag at bay – a background with figures*, in Ballet Today, London, July–August 1949

— *A ballet-goer's causerie: 3*, in Ballet Today, London, September–October 1949

— *A ballet-goer's causerie: 4*, in Ballet Today, London, March 1950

Thomson, Virgil, and Toklas, Alice B: *Two slants on 'Four Saints in Three Acts'*, in New York Herald Tribune, 27 April 1952

Vaughan, David: *'The Quest': first impressions*, in Arabesque, Oxford, Trinity Term 1943

— *The Royal Ballet: Family Circle*, in Ballet Review, Volume 1 No 2, Brooklyn 1965

— *Reading about Ashton*, in Ballet Review, Volume 4 No 2, Brooklyn 1972

— *Frederick Ashton*, in Dance Magazine, New York, May 1974

— *A Peruvian in Paris*, in Dancing Times, London, October 1974

— *Ashton under limelight*, in Guardian, London, 6 February 1976

Volkova, Vera: 'Frederick Ashton in Denmark' in *Ballet Annual 1961*, edited by Arnold L Haskell, Black, London 1960

Weatherby, W J: *Call it acquiescence*, in Guardian, London, 25 March 1960

Williams, Peter; *Sir Fred*, in About the House, Volume 1 No 6, London, March 1964

Woodward, Ian: '*Fred, you have a great future*', in Christian Science Monitor, Boston, 25 September 1969

Young, Stark: *One moment alit*, in New Republic, New York, 7 March 1934

— *Might it be mountains?*, in New Republic, New York, 11 April 1934

— *Reading lesson*, in Theatre Arts, New York, May 1934

Newspapers and periodicals consulted

Britain:

About the House, Arabesque, Ballet, Ballet Today, Birmingham News, Bystander, Daily Mirror, The Daily Telegraph, Dance and Dancers, Dance Chronicle, Dancing Times, Evening News, Evening Standard, The Financial Times, Guardian, Horizon, Illustrated London News, Leader Magazine, Liverpool Evening Express, Monthly Film Bulletin, New English Weekly, New Statesman, The Observer, Petit Tour, Punch, Radio Times, Sketch, Spectator, Sphere, Stage, Star, Sunday Graphic, The Sunday Telegraph, The Sunday Times, The Tatler, Theatre Research, The Times, Vogue, The Yorkshire Post

USA:

The American Dancer, Ballet Review, Brooklyn Eagle, Christian Science Monitor, The Commonweal, Daily News, Dance Index, Dance Magazine, Dance News, Dance Perspectives, Hartford Courant, The Nation, New Republic, Newsweek, The New Yorker, New York Herald Tribune, New York Mirror, New York Sun, New York Times, Saturday Review, Theatre Arts

INDEX

513